June 07

John, & the King Juan Carlos Center

In appreciation of your interest in this work and your good efforts in related areas — & a million other efforts.

Yasu, Dan

D1713920

To Export Progress

Philanthropic and Nonprofit Studies

Dwight F. Burlingame and David C. Hammack, general editors

Thomas Adam, editor. *Philanthropy, Patronage, and Civil Society*

Albert Anderson. *Ethics for Fundraisers*

Karen J. Blair. *The Torchbearers: Women and Their Amateur Arts Associations in America*

Eleanor Brilliant. *Private Charity and Public Inquiry: A History of the Filer and Peterson Commissions*

Dwight F. Burlingame, editor. *The Responsibilities of Wealth*

Dwight F. Burlingame and Dennis Young, editors. *Corporate Philanthropy at the Crossroads*

Charles T. Clotfelter and Thomas Ehrlich, editors. *Philanthropy and the Nonprofit Sector in a Changing America*

Marcos Cueto, editor. *Missionaries of Science: The Rockefeller Foundation and Latin America*

Gregory Eiselein. *Literature and Humanitarian Reform in the Civil War Era*

David C. Hammack, editor. *Making the Nonprofit Sector in the United States: A Reader*

Jerome L. Himmelstein. *Looking Good and Doing Good: Corporate Philanthropy and Corporate Power*

Warren E Ilchman, Stanley N. Katz, and Edward L. Queen II, editors. *Philanthropy in the World's Traditions*

Warren F. Ilchman, Alice Stone Ilchman, and Mary Hale Tolar, editors. *The Lucky Few and the Worthy Many: Scholarship Competitions and the World's Future Leaders*

Thomas H. Jeavons. *When the Bottom Line Is Faithfulness: Management of Christian Service Organizations*

Amy A. Kass, editor. *The Perfect Gift*

Ellen Condliffe Lagemann, editor. *Philanthropic Foundations: New Scholarship, New Possibilities*

Mike W. Martin. *Virtuous Giving: Philanthropy, Voluntary Service, and Caring*

Kathleen D. McCarthy. *Women, Philanthropy, and Civil Society*

Mary J. Oates. *The Catholic Philanthropic Tradition in America*

Robert S. Ogilvie. *Voluntarism, Community Life, and the American Ethic*

J. B. Schneewind, editor. *Giving: Western Ideas of Philanthropy*

William H. Schneider, editor. *Rockefeller Philanthropy and Modern Biomedicine*

Bradford Smith, Sylvia Shue, Jennifer Lisa Vest, and Joseph Villarreal. *Philanthropy in Communities of Color*

David H. Smith. Entrusted: *The Moral Responsibilities of Trusteeship*

Jon Van Til. *Growing Civil Society: From Nonprofit Sector to Third Space*

Andrea Walton. *Women and Philanthropy in Education*

To April, exporter of progress to our children and others'

Contents

Preface and Acknowledgments

I wish I could thank someone for helping me finish this book expeditiously, but I do not regret the long haul. Research began over twenty years ago, in recognition of a crucial dimension hitherto missing from my work, the international dimension. My research on Latin American higher education had been mostly comparative as it dealt with government-university relations and with private versus public higher education. During fieldwork on those topics, I was repeatedly struck by either the legacy or the seeming lack of legacy of prior efforts to export progress through international assistance to universities.

Preliminary exploration then gave me the exciting sense that the university was a key focal point of an unprecedented peacetime crusade to export progress through resources, ideas, and expertise. This was international assistance for large-scale institutional and national development. It was a period of high hope for Third World domestic reforms, dependent on importing progress on a grand scale. My challenge would be to catalog and understand the efforts and to assess what impact they have had.

The difficulty of meeting that challenge is the main reason for the long period between the start and finish of this project. A related reason developed as accumulating evidence showed the significance of research centers, often shaped by international assistance. Because these centers, many of them private think tanks, play contemporary but sometimes fleeting roles of significance, studying them assumed chronological priority. Two other book projects of immediate policy relevance also intervened between then and now. Revision of this more historical study could be continually postponed, especially since the bulk of fieldwork had been completed, including interviews with retirees and others whose memories were fresh with knowledge and perspectives that needed to be tapped and preserved. The postponements have exacted a price, but they have also allowed time for me to rethink and to gather further perspectives. A nonhistorian has learned much about the difficulties and rewards of historical research.

Although nobody could help much with efficient production of the book, many have helped with its content. The book depends heavily on information and perspectives from interviewees. Appendix B lists the formal interviews, and there were countless additional conversations for which I am grateful. I am especially indebted to those who read and commented on much or all of the manuscript: Eduardo Aldana, Jorge Balán, Jozef Bastiaens, Andrés Bernasconi, John Harrison, Iván Jaksić, José Landi, Lewis Tyler, and Gilbert Valverde. Others who commented on particular chapters, sections, related papers, or grant proposals are Philip Altbach, Robert Arnove, John Brademas, José Joaquín Brunner, Burton Clark, Regina Cortina, Marcos Cueto, Paul DiMaggio, Thomas Eisemon, Philip Foster, Roger Geiger, Manuel Gil, William Gormley, David Jones, Carlos Pedro Krotsch, Kathleen McCarthy, Tim McDaniel, Gil Merkx, Keiko Miwa, Marcela Mollis, Robert Myers, Carlos Ornelas, Beryl Radin, Luis Ratinoff, Jamil Salmi, Simon Schwartzman, Martin Trow, Douglas Windham, and Alfred Wolf. Two doctoral assistants—Jorge Arenas Basurto and Jozef Bastiaens—contributed greatly. With affection, I thank them for their dedication and care. Additional doctoral student help came from Yingxia Cao, Xiaoying Chen, Carlos Colley, Keiko Miwa, and Yan Zheng. Carm Colfer and Barbara Grubalski provided able secretarial assistance.

Ideas for the book began while I was at the Higher Education Research Group, and early research took place while I was a member and then an affiliate of the Program on Non-Profit Organizations; both these research groups were part of the Institution for Social and Policy Studies, Yale University. But most of the research and all the writing has come during my time as faculty member of the Department of Education Administration and Policy Studies (and the Department of Latin American and Caribbean Studies) at the University at Albany, SUNY.

The three institutions that hosted me for extended periods of fieldwork are the Academia de Humanismo Cristiano (CERC) in Chile, El Colegio de México (in its centers for sociological and international studies), and the Center for Economic Teaching and Research (CIDE, in its centers for political and public administration studies). Other host institutions included the University of Costa Rica, FLACSO–Costa Rica, and IBAFIN in Mexico. Valuable feedback was obtained from talks given at these sites, at academic association meetings, and at the American Council on Education, Bildner Center for Western Hemisphere Studies at the City University of New York, Colombian Institute for Higher Education Promotion, Harvard University, Inter-American Development Bank, International Institute of Education, Latin American Scholarship Program of American Universities, National Autonomous University of Mexico, Technological Institute of Santo Domingo, University of Buenos Aires, University of Caldas, University of California–Berkeley, UCLA, University of New Mexico, University of Salvador, World Bank, and Yale University.

I am grateful for the access granted to archives and help from archivists at the Ford Foundation and the U.S. Agency for International Development. At these sites and at the Inter-American Development Bank, other concerned individuals were also vital for the accumulation of material.

For financial support, I thank the Fulbright-Council for the International Exchange of Scholars and the Fulbright-Hays program for making possible my principal Latin American fieldwork. Also important for fieldwork, U.S. archival work at donor organizations, and subsequent writing were four grants from the University at Albany as well as grants from the Social Science Research Council, Yale's Program on Non-Profit Organizations, and the Aspen Nonprofit Sector Research Fund. The Center for the Study of Philanthropy of the City University of New York and the Spencer Foundation indirectly helped through their funding of a related project of mine.

Aaron, April, Joshua, and Morris Levy all helped with particular aspects of the research or writing. They also contributed in their own wonderful ways to delaying the finishing of the book.

To Export Progress

*The Golden Age of
University Assistance
in the Americas*

Daniel C. Levy

Indiana University Press
Bloomington and Indianapolis

This book is a publication of

Indiana University Press
601 North Morton Street
Bloomington, IN 47404-3797 USA

http://iupress.indiana.edu

Telephone orders	800-842-6796
Fax orders	812-855-7931
Orders by e-mail	iuporder@indiana.edu

© 2005 by Daniel C. Levy

All rights reserved

No part of this book may be reproduced or utilized in any form or by
any means, electronic or mechanical, including photocopying and
recording, or by any information storage and retrieval system, without
permission in writing from the publisher. The Association of American
University Presses' Resolution on Permissions constitutes the only
exception to this prohibition.

The paper used in this publication meets the minimum requirements of
American National Standard for Information Sciences—Permanence of
Paper for Printed Library Materials, ANSI Z39.48-1984.

Manufactured in the United States of America

Library of Congress Cataloging-in-Publication Data
Levy, Daniel C.
  To export progress : the golden age of university assistance in the
Americas / Daniel C. Levy.
      p. cm.—(Philanthropic and nonprofit studies)
  Includes bibliographical references and index.
  ISBN 0-253-34577-4 (cloth : alk. paper)
1. Educational assistance, American—Latin America—History—20th
century. 2. Economic assistance, American—Latin America—
History—20th century. 3. Education, Higher—Latin America.
4. Educational change—Latin America. I. Title. II. Series.
  LB2285.L3L48 2005
  379.1'29—dc22
                                                        2004019602

1 2 3 4 5 10 09 08 07 06 05

Acronyms

Note: Asterisks indicate the principal site for institutions that are not national, though sometimes the line between national and international is ambiguous.

ACLS	American Council of Learned Societies (United States)
AID	Agency for International Development (United States)
CEDES	Center for the Study of the State and Society (Argentina)
CHEAR	Seminar of Higher Education in the Americas (United States)*
CIAT	International Center on Tropical Agriculture (Colombia)*
CIDA	Canadian International Development Agency
CIMMYT	International Center for Improvement of Maize and Wheat (Mexico)*
CLACSO	Latin America Social Science Council (Argentina)*
CONARE	National Council of Rectors (Costa Rica)
CPU	Corporation for University Promotion (Chile)
CRESALC	Regional Center for Higher Education in Latin America and the Caribbean (Venezuela)
CSUCA	Central American University Confederation (Costa Rica)*
DAC	Development Assistance Committee of the OECD (France)*
EAFIT	Medellín School of Business Administration and Finance (Colombia)
ESPOL	National Polytechnic School (Ecuador)
FF	Ford Foundation (United States)*
FLACSO	Latin America Faculty of Social Science (Costa Rica)*
FOMEC	Fund for Enhancement of Educational Quality (Argentina)
FUPAC	Federation of Private Universities of Central America and Panama (Guatemala)*
GDP	Gross Domestic Product
ICA	International Cooperation Administration (United States)
ICETEX	Colombian Overseas Technical Specialization Institute
IDB	Inter-American Development Bank (United States)*
IESA	Institute of Advanced Administrative Studies (Venezuela)
IMF	International Monetary Fund (United States)*
INTEC	Technological Institute of Santo Domingo (Dominican Republic)
LASPAU	Academic and Professional Programs for the Americas (United States)
NGOs	Nongovernment organizations
NSF	National Science Foundation (United States)

OAS	Organization of American States (United States)*
OECD	Organization for Economic Cooperation and Development (France)*
SAREC	Swedish Agency for Research Cooperation with Developing Countries
SSRC	Social Science Research Council (United States)
SUNY	State University of New York (United States)
UAM	Autonomous Metropolitan University (Mexico)
UBA	University of Buenos Aires (Argentina)
UCH	University of Chile
UCR	University of Costa Rica
UDUAL	Union of Latin American Universities (Mexico)*
UNAM	National Autonomous University of Mexico
UNDP	United Nations Development Program (United States)
UNESCO	UN Educational, Scientific, and Cultural Organization (France)*
USIA	United States Information Agency

To Export Progress

Introduction: To Export Progress

The middle of the twentieth century brought an unprecedented peacetime crusade by industrialized nations to transform the Third World. This was probably modern history's most ambitious, organized, nonmilitary effort to export progress—to provide less developed countries with resources, ideas, and expertise to enable them to leap forward.[1] The leap was simultaneously and interactively to encompass political, economic, social, and cultural dimensions of progress. This was to be the peak era of international assistance for large-scale institutional and national development. It was also a period of high hope for Third World domestic reforms. These reforms often depended on grandiose importing of progress. Domestic policy reformers wanted to import much of what the First World was eager to share, including through partnership projects designed for export-import linkage.[2] And both the exporters and importers of assistance anointed no social institution more than the university to lead the great transformation to modernity.

Ours is thus a study of change: what change was pursued, and what change was achieved. Change is a broad concept, helping us place our study within far-reaching subject matter. But to guard against excess dispersion of meaning we focus further. We look for transformation—change fundamental enough to bring about new forms; even if lofty development goals make the grade, the aptness of the term *transformation* for actual efforts and results must be explored. We also explore how much change meets Clark Kerr's (1986: xvi) definition of reform—change achieved through voluntary choices made in conscious pursuit of values, amounting to development by design.[3]

Themes and Significance

We focus on a major set of importers and exporters in the Americas. The importers are mainly Latin American universities, upon which so much development hope was placed, although alternative higher education institutions also receive attention, and a broad view of importing must include governments and other actors. The exporters studied are mainly U.S. agencies, leading donors for both the university and the overall development effort worldwide and easily the largest donors for Latin America. Specifically, the donors are private foundations, bilateral agencies, and multilateral organizations with a decisive U.S. presence, headed respectively by the Ford Foundation (FF), Agency for International Development (AID), and the Inter-American Development Bank (IDB). We examine the efforts by the exporters along with their domestic partners and the impacts on the importers. Detailed identification of the givers, along with their national targets, appears in chapter 2.

The time frame is discussed toward the end of the present chapter, but the core, seen by both importers and exporters of that time as a "golden age" for universities, assistance, and development, refers to a period from 1960 until 1975.[4] Coincident with the launching of the Alliance for Progress, the golden age arrived with extraordinary hope and excitement. Sometimes under conditions of expanding political democracy, sometimes not, the reformist zeal and expectations inspired many in ways that now often seem quaint, naive, or noble.

Our principal aim is knowledge and understanding of an extraordinary chapter in modern history. We gather and analyze evidence on what transpired and with what consequences. This endeavor sheds light on wider dynamics of social reform, particularly where it involves exporting and importing. The study is not pitched toward a single bottom-line assessment of whether assistance worked. We evaluate undertakings as well as results, often reaching a much clearer picture about the former. Or we uncover major patterns of results, but these do not add up to simple objective summaries of what is success or failure. All in all, the findings on results allow reasonable variation in how different readers interpret mixed evidence.

This delineation of our endeavor helps explain why our findings appear surprisingly positive. In the absence of significant prior study, the dominant view of the crusade to export progress is that it failed to build the desired outcome. That view is accurate, but it is also very limited. And many beliefs accompanying that impression prove dubious or wrong. In contrast, our picture appears positive in that it is more mixed than negative regarding impacts and usually complimentary regarding undertakings. A substantive theme is that the change in question was impressive. It was large, reformist, pursued often with vigor tempered by prudence, sometimes transforming, and mostly beneficial.

This portrayal, notwithstanding vital qualifying statements, challenges much belief in policy and academic circles about university assistance as dismal or wrongheaded failure. Conventional wisdom might be too grand a term. A feeling that the experience was fundamentally flawed helps explain a lack of interest in investigating what transpired once upon a time; or, for whatever reason, a vague, downbeat interpretation goes mostly unchallenged by more positive interpretations. Where the experience is remembered or even studied, acknowledgment of major effort is more common than views that they were well guided or even moderately successful. Notwithstanding different assumptions about where the blame for failure lies, the dominant view is that university assistance has produced little significant progress, neither sparing Third World universities their rampant crises nor alleviating "the bad shape" in which they are mired.[5] Where impact is not dismissed as minimal, negative is more common than positive portrayal. Today's perceived reality mocks golden age visions of the university leading nations forward.

This does not mean that our substantive theme runs totally counter to conventional belief. Beliefs are far from uniformly negative, and ours is far from uniformly positive, especially regarding ultimate impacts. At stake, however, is a difference between a net positive and a net negative account of assistance to universities. In any event, assessments must be based on more evidence than has hitherto been considered.

Beyond the subject matter of university assistance alone, a contrast between grand hope and subsequent negative portrayal is prominent in fields related to our case, including the role of the university in society, comparative higher education, national development, and Latin American affairs. The contrast is pursued in the next chapter regarding three broad fields keenly concerned with change: international assistance, development (or "dependency"), and domestic policy reform. Each has hatched a major view that any golden age has proved to be much more fiction than fact.[6] Our case study of university assistance has implications for how we retrospectively view crusades for change.

The study's main substantive findings about impressive change sustain the book's main conceptual theme: the change in question corresponds notably to a broad and meaningful ideal type about the nature of change. This I will call a philanthropic ideal type of change. Like the substantive theme regarding change, the conceptual theme holds more for goals and means than results.

The Philanthropic Ideal Type of Change

First, we must state the purpose of the philanthropic ideal type. As with ideal types generally, exaggerated or pure ("ideal") constellations of phenomena serve heuristic ends, aiding empirical and conceptual analysis.[7] The purpose is not, therefore, to represent reality perfectly or invariably, but to help understand reality. Systematic comparison with the ideal type aids the search, organization, and interpretation of raw information. A core task of the book is to explore how reality does and does not correspond to the ideal type. Even where the ideal type does not match reality, it serves well if it helps guide our understanding of reality. On the other hand, the ideal type may fail to so guide. Also, certain evidence can lead us to question the internal consistency of the ideal type. For example, particular goals or means or results may contradict one another, or contradictions may emerge between the ideal type's goals and means, means and results, or goals and results. We will explore how much the ideal type's components truly form a "web."

As we use the "ideal" in ideal type to depict something pure, we do not necessarily depict a desirable ideal. At the same time, the philanthropic ideal type does encompass positive claims made by philanthropists and their partners. Our analysis of the ideal type thus helps us explore how much they actually follow their reform model, and any contradictions within their model demand scrutiny.[8]

Chart 1 outlines our philanthropic ideal type of change. It becomes clear that such change would qualify as reform, by design, and as transformation.

The ideal type derives from assertions about philanthropy, especially its distinctiveness. It is crafted from literature mainly on philanthropy itself, both self-congratulatory and scholarly accounts. The former accounts depict the ideal type as both desirable and substantially fulfilled. Scholarly accounts also depict the claims, but may not endorse the desirability and often deny that they conform to reality. Most writings are specifically about foundations.[9] Also pertinent is literature on the nonprofit sector, that *third* sector which is neither public nor private for-profit (Powell 1987).

Chart 1. The Philanthropic Ideal Type of Change

	Integral Aspect	*Associated Aspect*
Goals	• Altruism, helping others and/or the public good • Attacking root problems • Major changes; reform; transformation	• Progressive, nonrevolutionary modernization and sustainable development • Integrated altruism and enlightened self-interest • Pragmatic goals
Means	• Voluntary giving • Something extra • Specific undertakings	• Consistency with goals identified above • Undertaken with purpose, knowledge, and professionalism • Innovative, experimental, risk taking, flexible • Careful selection of few direct targets • Distinctive, reform-oriented, trusted partners as targets • Giving distinctive from basic public mainstream allocations • Mainstream bypassed or encompassed indirectly (donor to target to mainstream) • Careful concentration on front end (project formulation and target selection), although influence is ongoing
Results	• Achievement of goals identified above (alternatively, achievement is associated aspect, and the integral aspects are limited to goals and means)	• Direct transformation of targets • Leveraged impact on mainstream • More imaginative failures than dull successes

Goals, means, and results identify the ideal type.[10] The delineation among these, while not rigid, is usually clear. For each of the three, Chart 1 labels both integral and associated aspects. Though this distinction is a matter of degree, it seems implausible to define the philanthropic ideal type without the features labeled integral.[11] In contrast, the more numerous associated aspects could vary depending upon how one reads and understands the pertinent literature and claims. "The ideal type" thus refers to the one developed here, not to some singularly necessary one in all its particulars.

Starting with goals, philanthropy is giving with intent to help others, from the Greek word meaning "love for humankind." In the modern sense of philanthropy, that giving must go beyond not only family but also beyond charity alone, which has long historical roots. It must aim to promote the public good, as it attacks root causes and not just emergencies or symptoms of problems. Modern philanthropy is thus development-oriented giving, often by institutions, building up "civil society."[12] And it aims at major change, even transformation in at least some respects. Obviously, the anticipated change must be for the better. This fits a sense of humanitarianism wherein a concern for human welfare is expressed through social reform. Nevertheless, even where grand visions of reform are found, it may be difficult to develop a firm list of goals because much of what donors and their partners envision is not spelled out in their concrete projects. Accordingly, we find it useful to distinguish repeatedly between explicit and implicit goals, the latter generally being more grandiose.[13]

Beyond integral goals, the philanthropic ideal type may be extended to several associated goals. Altruism is neither a mere cloak for self-interest nor a basic contradiction to it. Intelligently pursued, it is concerned and enlightened self-interest. In this sense, philanthropy is not simply charity, and ambiguity arises as to whether philanthropy requires altruism. Development change pursued would thus be nonthreatening to key interests of the givers—progressive but nonrevolutionary. Transformation, then, has its limitations even in the ideal type. Self-interest is not a contradiction to ideal typical behavior by donors, any more than it would be in the case of corporate philanthropy, as long as it is coupled with the aim of helping recipients.[14] Finally, the ideal type suggests that the noble and wise aims are clearly set and understood and formulated into sound programmatic goals.

Moving from philanthropy's goals to its means, a key integral characteristic is *voluntary* giving. Philanthropy is discretionary. There is donor choice about how to reform, whether to give and why, where, when, how much, and to what and whom (Payton 1989; Van Til 1990). Philanthropy is something added, something extra. It contrasts with basic public funding disbursed in response to legal obligations or political demands from constituencies to whom the givers are accountable, and it contrasts with ongoing, regular, mandatory subsidization. Voluntary giving comes from beyond the local core of public responsibility, though "voluntary" allows for giving based on one's belief in religious or other ethical imperatives.[15] Like development assistance, philanthropy comes in many forms, among which we concentrate on funds, ideas, expertise, and other enabling resources shared with or turned over to recipients or contracted intermediaries.

The idea of transferred resources leads to another integral aspect of philanthropic means, if perhaps an obvious one: transfers occur through concrete efforts such as specific projects. We will not identify philanthropy where there is simply exhortation (or simply copying). This point also holds for assistance; for example, it was only when the desire to export democracy switched from mostly exhortation or setting examples to direct, tangible projects that we would mark assistance. Similarly, on the importing side, "borrowing," "transfers of policy innovation," and "lesson drawing" carried out by independent actors rather than recipients lie beyond a study of philanthropy or assistance.[16]

Depiction of philanthropy often focuses on associated means. To match the goals, undertakings are purposive, guided by knowledge, realism, expertise, and professionalism rather than by routine, pressure, or sloppiness. Philanthropy is ideally "scientific giving" (Arnove 1980b: 4). But it is not stodgy, because it accentuates innovation, experimentation, flexibility, and risk taking. Another crucial aspect of development-oriented philanthropic change, as opposed to charitable relief, is that targets are not scattered or selected randomly. Nor are they representative of the mainstream. They are, instead, carefully selected. They are distinctive and reform oriented, rather than status quo oriented. And since they are all these things, they are suitable partners-in-change. These recipients may be enticed, but they are not coerced. Trust is crucial. Donor control is thus concentrated on the front end, especially in target selection, and then perhaps at a back end linked to a possible termination or renewal, whereas mainstream public programs are often seen as either government controlled or very difficult to terminate (Nakamura and Smallwood 1980: 82). Regarding ongoing matters, the ideal type can allow for variation between give-and-take partnerships on the one hand and donors' goal-oriented leadership and influence on the other. The partnership associated with ideal typical philanthropy can be asymmetrical in power and can assume various forms.

Philanthropic selection, with its core notions of distinctive and selective voluntary giving, stands apart from a model of responsive democratic public allocation postulated in political-economic theory, where funds go reactively to the "democratic mean" or, to relax the democratic-egalitarian assumptions, to those who make powerful demands (Downs 1957). It also stands apart from social welfare or statist models featuring annual subsidization on a fairly standardized, equal basis across the board, with general accountability to all parts and often with only incremental changes from year to year. This contrast between basic public allocation and philanthropy fits with classic explanations of nonprofit, voluntary activity as an alternative to that sort of public allocation (Douglas 1987; Weisbrod 1988). Policy transactions take place in the nonprofit private sector to give or get something not manageable through the for-profit sector yet beyond or distinctive from what the public norm provides.

Common usage proceeds to associate philanthropy with private sources. Many works refer to private money for public ends or equate voluntary with nongovernment action (Lagemann 1989). Yet by the criterion of voluntary, targeted giving (as well as goals), philanthropy can also come from public funds. We neither use the potentially jarring term *public philanthropy* nor insist on the superiority of a generic use of *philanthropy* for public as well as private funds that meet the criteria on goals and voluntary targeted giving.[17] Crucially, however, we do not assume that public giving is distinctive from philanthropy, let alone its automatic opposite. *Donor* is thus a term that can be considered for public and multilateral as well as private agencies, and public giving allows for a range of possibilities that can sometimes at least approximate philanthropy. Any findings that even the public or multilateral donors approximate the philanthropic ideal type in giving would be particularly striking. And the more these donors claim to fit elements of the ideal type, the more reason to evaluate them by it, an important point for donors' university assistance.[18] At the same time, we hypothesize that private international giving corresponds more closely than public international assistance to the philanthropic ideal type of voluntary giving. In any case, this book about assistance is also about philanthropy in that (a) the subject matter includes private giving and (b) some public giving may conform to defined elements of philanthropy.

Turning to results, fulfillment of significant goals for change is the simplest representation of what is integral to the philanthropic ideal type. Associated aspects of results depend on the magic of idealized philanthropic means. Only through such means can philanthropy achieve its lofty goals with its comparatively limited resources concentrated on chosen targets. Philanthropic efforts and results are therefore associated with "leveraging" as a key to bridging that gulf. This often means leveraging onto the mainstream of the field the impact first achieved in the selected recipients within the field. Change must radiate out beyond direct targets to the larger population. Big impacts flow from the "generic role and autonomy of philanthropy: its ability to choose, concentrate, and leverage" (Ylvisaker 1987: 372). Success in leveraging suggests promotion of equity through widespread gains more than exacerbation of stratification between targets and nontargets. Results should, of course, be reasonably sustainable and not "snap back" toward the status quo ante.

A different kind of result might also be accepted as falling within the ideal type. In this view philanthropy should produce more "imaginative failures" than "dull successes."[19]

As suggested above, scholarship does not simply equate the ideal type with common behavior by foundations or other donors, whatever enthusiastic views are propagated by those organizations or by individuals within them. On the contrary, most scholarship casts a skeptical eye on the claims. Nonetheless, where it identifies a minority of philanthropic leaders, it often points to the largest foundations, precisely those that dominate in international work.[20] That still leaves a chorus of critics who deny that even the ostensible leaders resemble the ideal type. Severe critics tend to see the giving in question as fundamentally at odds with the ideal type, whereas self-reformers and their sympathizers often propose bringing behavior closer to the ideal type.

Much of the stinging critique has concentrated on the selfish status quo motivations for voluntary giving of ill-gotten wealth, with means and results logical to those ends.[21] But almost every aspect of the ideal type comes under attack from critics. Even something that might appear to some to be an obvious component of philanthropy is not immune. Regarding voluntary giving, for example, a common critique is that it is not very distinctive from public funding. Other critics insist that donor giving is not very distinctive from self-interested corporate funding. And where critics accept a philanthropic claim, they may turn it on its head. Arnove (1977: 100, 105) observes that the Ford Foundation attempted to use higher education to " 'modernize' the world," by relying on "the best minds," leadership cadres, professionalism, managerialism, and the concentration of resources in favored areas, but he regards all these as elitist, technocratic, status quo approaches.

Both critics and proponents of voluntary donors identify higher education as a vehicle par excellence for those donors. They have elaborated on the logic and dynamics of how higher education, naturally linked to selectivity and of course knowledge and expertise, offers great opportunities for donors' goals and means. Several accounts document foundations' extraordinary priority on higher education in both their domestic and international activities.[22] University development was the largest activity in the Third World for foundations like Ford and Carnegie and was very large for others such as Rockefeller (Sutton 1984: 142). This emphasis, along with the accompanying claims and critiques, helps make higher education an attractive field for a study of philanthropy and related reform efforts.

The University Case

The University Travels

The university's role within international development assistance is a modern manifestation of a long-standing phenomenon of international higher education transfer. The university has always traveled.[23]

Spectacularly international is the flow of knowledge, processes, and people across borders among leading nations and from them to less developed ones. Often called "universal," the heavy international sense is commonly traced for Western civilization to the Middle Ages, as students and faculty sojourned and Latin provided a common language.[24] But important biblical and classical precursors come from the Middle East, North Africa, and Asia, in the movement of sages and their schools of study. Later, as nation-states created their own universities, the idea of transfers across national systems took hold. The first massive colonial transfer then involved Spain and its Latin American empire. Great Britain and France led subsequent colonial transports, including to the English colonies of North America. Germany then showed that nations with attractive models could export without empires. Japan and certain other Asian nations showed that noncolonized nations could vigorously import, including by enthusiastic, conscious decision. Zealous importer Peter the Great transplanted the Academy onto alien Russian soil notwithstanding a lack of domestic "demand" to do so.[25]

Latin American importing continued after colonial rule ended in the early nineteenth century. And, paralleling our distinction between traditional charity and development-oriented philanthropy, it was only in the nineteenth century that a true concept of education development through international transfer moved in alongside traditional international educational movement and borrowing (Phillips 1993). U.S. influence was greater at the school than university level, especially where reformers such as Argentina's Domingo Sarmiento lauded ideas like local public education or, later, Deweyian pragmatism.[26] But until well into the twentieth century, foreign influence remained mostly European, predominantly French or "Napoleonic" by late in the colonial era. Clearly, influence did not stem solely from a persistence of colonial forms, however much some see continued importing as evidence of hapless dependency despite formal political independence. The main nineteenth-century importing was far from imposed, unthinking, or indiscriminate, and university building was quite purposively linked to nation building in countries like Chile.[27]

On the other hand, consistent with change hypotheses developed in the next chapter, imports rarely took root as anticipated. Thus the university in place when U.S. assistance programs stormed onto the scene was often only dubiously linked to national development and was neither a simple European transplant nor purely indigenous but rather the product of various international transfers blended with domestic choices, traditions, and obstacles.[28]

However venerable the tradition of international influences on university change, the golden age of the mid-twentieth century would be unprecedented. Historically, most transfer had occurred outside the confines of particular projects or grand planned efforts. The new projects were formulated to be the university counterpart or manifestation of modern philanthropy and development assistance: multiple and functionally interrelated efforts at transformation pushed heavily by external, voluntary funders. Whereas earlier international contact, at least outside colonial imposition, had been generally sporadic and diffuse, the new university assistance was more coherently formulated.[29] It aimed at larger change in a shorter time. It envisioned university change but also, through it, broader-based national development—political, economic, social, and cultural. Reciprocally, it looked to incorporate positive action from beyond the university itself, crafting projects requiring major support for universities from governments and other external actors.

To distinguish among varied university transfers, analysts have considered certain defining dimensions: *weight* of the import relative to the receiving form, degree of *competition* among possible imports, *form* of transfer item (people, funds, ideas, etc.), and *imposition versus voluntary* importing.[30]

We may relate these dimensions to our philanthropic ideal type. The philanthropic emphasis would usually be on forms involving ideas and *selected* people and funds. Above all, that ideal type requires that the importing be voluntary. Competition among imports or models is not a requisite for the ideal type as long as there is not monopolistic coercion. Consistent with the ideal type's leverage principle, the weight of the import should be sufficient to have a major impact but not so large as to engulf the mainstream or undermine selectivity. In contrast, a dependency alternative to the ideal type would look to great weight and imposition of the import as well as injuriously limited competition among models. Selectivity may also be denied—but more likely is emphasized—as elitist. These factors all can make for dependent international transfer, substantially negative, or for failure to transfer. Much of the literature on modern university transfers to the Third World has adopted a dependency perspective.[31]

Exporting the U.S. University Model Southward

One aspect of university transfer that is clear at the outset of our case concerns weight. Reformers on both the exporting and importing ends intended to increase the weight of the U.S. university export, diminishing the weight of indigenous forms and practices.[32] We therefore sketch the reformers' depiction of the indigenous model versus this preeminent export model (see chart 2).

In fact, reformers sometimes identified the Latin American university largely by its contrast with the U.S. model. In assistance circles the leading depiction was Rudolph Atcon's. His 1966 work for President Kennedy's Alliance for Progress and for multilateral agencies became a bible for donors and achieved wide distribution and influence within Latin America as well.[33] Leaving aside for now its vitriolic and most paternalistic assertions, Atcon's basic description of an unhealthy Napoleonic university was routinely echoed. Too dominant were semiautonomous schools and faculties, ducal deans, a few "chaired" professors, national and student politics, state funding, socioeconomic elitism, and instruction by practicing professionals instead of full-time academics. Too dominant also were outdated and rigidly professionalist curricula, pedagogy, and academic and administrative structure, all

Chart 2. U.S. University Export Model versus the Latin American
University Tradition

	United States	*Latin America*
System configuration		
Centralization/ decentralization	Institutional autonomy No sole systemwide form Multifaceted interinstitutional differentiation	Nationally set policies Standardization National university at core
Size	Large Facilitated access Incorporation of more socioeconomic groups	Small Restricted access Elite dominance
Institutional centralization/decentralization		
Administrative	Strong executive institutionwide managerial power with authoritative governing boards and limited student political participation Students as clients Substantial self-financing by institution Unified campus	Power wielded by separate professional faculties with chaired professors and ample student political participation Students as professional trainees and citizens Dependent on government funds Scattered faculty buildings
Academic	Integrated departmental structures General studies or liberal arts Flexible universitywide credit systems Unified library, laboratory, and other facilities	Isolated faculty structures Professional career preparation Lock-step professional program Faculties have own facilities
Academic work		
Quality	Academic professionalization Includes major graduate level and research	Part-time instructors who are practicing professionals Focus on first-degree professional training
Relevance	Importance of applied research ties to productive sector, social service, and lay representation in governance	Priority on setting own course with autonomy or service to professions and state bureaucracy

Note: Circa 1960 and based on key depictions and normative roots of the U.S. export model
and the existing Latin American model—not the complex reality in either case.

linked to low academic quality and detachment from society's broad needs. So, Latin American universities were simultaneously not elite enough in academics and too elite in socioeconomic isolation. Each of these points was largely accurate; alas, they remain part of leading reformist critiques today. Even back then, however, the points were exaggerated and too encompassing and negative to provide an accurate diagnosis (Davis 1965; Castro and Levy 2000). But they highlight what donors had in their cannon sites.

Atcon's prescription was a heavy dose of the U.S. model. The key features may be categorized under three overlapping headings that outline the core of chapters 3–5. Of course, as these features correspond to a model, they do not always represent the complex reality of U.S. higher education. The U.S. university model is an ideal type.[34]

The first feature of the U.S. export model concerned the system's structural configuration (chapter 3). This meant increased system size and diversity. Systems would grow upon a middle-class base well beyond an elite. (See appendix G on low but fast-growing enrollments starting 1955.) There would be more institutions. And the concept of institutional autonomy would be refashioned. It should refer less to standing apart—from government, economy, and society—and more to innovative institutions pursuing distinctive routes.

The second feature of the U.S. export model concerned "institution building" (chapter 4). Institution building largely meant intrainstitutional centralization. This centralization would bolster institutions' ability to chart their own courses autonomously, pursue them vigorously, and compete with other institutions. Institutional centralization was thus essential for successful interinstitutional decentralization, and the two together were crucial to the idea of a vibrant pluralist system. Centralizing measures ranged from enhanced executive power to creation of unified campuses, facilities, and departments rather than traditional professional faculties.

The third feature of the U.S. export model dealt more directly with academic work, its quality and relevance (chapter 5). Quality was linked to academic professionalization, competitive examinations, evaluations, scientific study, and greatly expanded graduate enrollments and research. Relevance meant that all this would happen especially in development-oriented and applied fields, and it meant ties to the productive sector.

However much one must explore and qualify their correspondence to U.S. reality and to real assistance projects, these were the main orienting features of the U.S.–export model as it contrasted with the Latin American reality at the time. One is struck by the focus on a U.S. research university model. The ideal type was thus poorly constructed in some senses, especially those related to academic work. In reality, the research university was atypical of U.S. higher education with its abundant four-year nonresearch colleges, community colleges, research centers not integrated with teaching, professional schools, part-time faculty, noncompetitive access, commuter students, academically low-quality institutions, and both huge and tiny institutions. It is common in higher education international transfer that importers focus on a desired form not characteristic of the exporting country's quantitative mainstream. The focus is usually on the perceived "top" of the model's hierarchy. For example, in the nineteenth century, foreigners who had studied in Germany imported the German research institute form. The U.S. research university model was strongly invoked in the key policy and academic conferences and the preaching of the time we explore. The Latin American university needed a U.S.–oriented "overhauling."[35] The import model was endorsed by key development agencies not just from the North but also from the South, such as the Economic Commission for Latin America in Chile (Urzúa 1973). Even domestic reformers leftist and wary enough of Yankee imperialism to avoid public endorsement often articulated overlapping positions.[36] For the most part, then, the U.S. research university model was the transformation model. Expressing the exaggerated but not uncommon view of the time, one of the foremost U.S. consultants declared: "Perhaps 20 years from now the universities of North and South America will be quite similar" (Waggoner 1973: 147).

An important issue in the development literature is whether proposed modernization has been broad Westernization or more specific Americanization. Among various transfer fields, the university was notable for Americanization, as were public administration and the military. The U.S. model came to surpass any competitive higher education model for Latin American import during the golden age. Thus the weight of the U.S. model was impressive in contrast to both the diminishing weight of the domestic model and to the influence of foreign models. The U.S. weight is especially striking given the European roots of Latin American universities. By the 1960s, Europe found itself in the throes of great self-criticism and reform. And much of that reform followed U.S. examples, a tendency which accelerated later.[37] The U.S. model gained strength in much of the Third World after World War II—sometimes as counterforce to prior colonial imprints—but for Latin America it would be the supreme foreign model. If importing was to be a major Third World path to university development, Latin America's path had the clearest Made in USA stamp. Competitive alternative forms were limited.

Explanations of the U.S. university influence must acknowledge general U.S. military, political, economic, social, and cultural influence, especially in the superpower's backyard, Latin America, as well as the eagerness of U.S. donors. But a further factor was the perception by Latin America's leading reformers that the U.S. university offered the best blueprint for change. As is still the case today, so back then, even many Latin Americans wary of much about U.S. policy and politics saw the U.S. university as the shining model.

Building Scholarship on University Assistance

Inadequacies of scholarship on university assistance are part of broader inadequacies in development assistance literature. Reviewers note a lack of work on educational assistance regardless of region as well as on assistance to Latin America regardless of policy field. They note our scanty knowledge of actual efforts, impacts, and national variation. Within higher education more work deals with individual study abroad than with institutional development or other broad projects, though overlap exists, and some fine studies exist on scientific development or its sluggishness.[38]

Donors have done their own evaluations or commissioned analysts to sift through available numbers, documents, or scattered evaluations. Many reports are unpublished or have limited circulation, but some of them provide valuable cataloguing of donor efforts.[39] The main purpose of donor reports is evaluation, whether for true assessment and policy revision or for self-praise and legitimacy. The 1970s saw an upsurge in donor-mandated evaluations. Still, these only sometimes take us beyond audits to impacts, let alone to long-term or "tertiary" implications, and education has been a notorious laggard.[40] The World Bank (1994: 92), today's clear giant in both funding and research capacity, concludes that little evaluation has been done of its own higher education efforts. Besides, donor evaluations concentrate on recent projects, rarely looking back more than peripherally at the golden age.[41] Evaluative efforts by recipients, often pushed by donors, are limited by similar considerations and individually tend to focus on one place. In sum, donor and recipient reports build the literature by sometimes providing the best of what we have or by contributing data that can be used by scholars, but the reports leave scholarship with responsibility to go further.

Unfortunately, scholars' work on assistance, especially educational assistance, often rests on essaylike or polemical assertions over sustained empirical analysis (Hellinger, Hellinger, and O'Regan 1988). The tendency is marked in education, where simplistic dependency notions dominate over sophisticated ones. Meanwhile, many studies of assistance include little on education.[42]

This leaves us short in both empirical and systematic knowledge about university assistance efforts and, as with the broader literature on development assistance, study of impacts is sparser still. Especially the polemical literature usually attacks goals, motivations, and elitist processes while assuming or dismissing impacts. Also, there has been less attention to recipients than to donors. Typically, scattered references to the recipient side are based on very general observations rather than extended field research. Specifically on university assistance to Latin America we are faced with "key outcomes very little understood."[43]

The most compelling scholarly work to date on university assistance is usually a case study of one institution and donor (Bullock 1980) or one donor and several recipient institutions. Among the latter, Coleman and Court's (1993) book on the Rockefeller Foundation is especially important.[44] No book on Latin American impacts comes close to Ashby's (1964) study of British influence on African universities, and that study was less about assistance projects than colonial relationships. In fact, no work on inter-American university projects has surpassed the scope of a 1960 sketch of thirteen AID-sponsored linkage projects, but that was a hurried account that lacked a conceptual base and could not follow matters beyond incipient undertakings (Adams and Cumberland 1960). A more recent work with regional coverage deals mostly with the period after the golden age and with alternatives—research centers—to university development in Latin America.[45]

Significance of the University Case

To round out this introductory chapter, it remains to set more of the context concerning the university as a significant case in the golden age of development. Already noted is that the golden age looked to the university to spearhead an unprecedented effort to export and import progress. In an era of institutional development efforts in many fields, the university loomed large.[46]

Raw data, elaborated in chapter 2, can make total investments look very large or more modest. Our study's focus on the university and some related higher education matters is not always neatly separable from other aspects of technological and human research development, which together comprise the bulk of development aid (Tisch and Wallace 1994: 40). Whether figures look large or small also depends on the comparisons invoked. A main one here is that the university was probably the social institution in Latin America that received the most foreign assistance (Lavados 1978). Also notable is the rapid explosion of university assistance to all Third World regions, including a proportional rise within total assistance and its easy leadership within overall private assistance.[47] However general, these emphases may be seen as consistent with the philanthropic ideal type's notions of grand aims and undertakings.

Belief in the university's pivotal national development role reigned in both the developed and developing worlds. This role would be crucial to the historic effort to move "cultural diplomacy" beyond the realm of private action alone to become part of foreign policy and development efforts overall (Haines 1989). But to be fit to lead a societal transformation, the university itself would require transformation. Clark Kerr has referred to a golden age of the greatest higher education reforms attempted in the West in the last six hundred years (1986: xv). Yet the envisioned transformation was markedly greater for the less developed countries. And their transformation required importing as well as domestic reform. Especially with the shift to development assistance over charitable relief (or pure military assistance), education was assigned a key role, and the university was assigned the leadership role within education. It provided the "ideological and professional socialization of the presumptive decision makers of the future."[48] This held for those who saw the existing university enmeshed in society (Cepeda 1979: 194) and those who decried its isolation from society: "Higher education is the real crux to the development of Latin America," the best tool for social change and "controlled mutations" much more likely and rapid than those attainable through other educational levels (Atcon 1966: 18–19). According to probably the most prominent book on Latin American universities in the 1960s by an outsider other than Atcon: Whereas the university's failure would plunge the region into "a dark age," its success would bring "the most resplendent [age] in the world's history" (Benjamin 1965: 212).

All this speaks to the university's perceived policy importance in the golden age. The study also has contemporary policy significance, although its primary purpose is to understand the historical experience, and contemporary policy will not be fundamentally driven by any study of the past. The policy significance is perhaps greatest where the study challenges negative views of the golden age undertaking. We characterize those widespread views as usually vague, not scrutinized, and lacking a solid base in study and conceptualization to withstand an assault of mixed to contrary evidence. Moreover, some perceptive participants in the golden age effort have remained skeptical of the negative cast, even as they have acknowledged its grip. They have confessed to holding only inchoate alternative impressions and thus have urged substantial analyses that might uncover patterns that are not obvious (Carmichael i; Black i–2). And those concerned since soon after the golden age with the "regrettable decline" in attention to Third World universities (Sutton 1984: 142) have reason for hope as major agencies now increase activities. No golden age of assistance will return in the sense of the faith, goals, and efforts of the mid-twentieth century. But chapters 2 and 6 show a renewal of interest and undertakings by the 1990s. A detailed study of the earlier period can become a modest part of a continual learning and adjustment process.[49] As Kerr observes for international higher education reform, lessons may seem unimportant as long as a climate persists that "everything fails" but, come the renaissance, the lessons have policy importance (1986: xv–xvi).

Moreover, a renaissance for Latin American higher education is possible even apart from massive assistance projects. The final section of the book suggests how political and economic change, from democratization to neoliberalism, has brought renewed interest in higher education reform, based on strong U.S. orientations. Things *gringo* are in style as never before in Latin American history. As Latin America's old domestic higher education reforms are dusted off and revised, they show some remarkable overlap with the golden age's assistance projects. Many earlier reforms frustrated in relation to their grand aims lay dormant or in potentially influential pockets, the ideas resonating still and providing jumping-off points for modern reform. Contemporary domestic reformers throughout Latin America can join with their international assistance supporters to benefit from an appraisal of prior efforts.

The study's policy significance also stems from the basic importance of the university in Latin America, even without invoking the golden age claim of unique leadership for rapid development. At the turn of the century, the region's enrollments moved to roughly 10 million students, and the public budget on higher education may have doubled from its $33 billion of 1994 (IDB n.d.). And predictions were for another doubling of enrollment within a decade or so. The Latin American university has long occupied a central, visible position in national politics, including political thought, socialization, recruitment, and legitimacy. If the traditional university has lost some of that role in recent years, other higher education institutions have assumed enhanced importance (Castro and Levy 2000: 7–11).

Again, however, our study directs itself much more at understanding than policy impact. We try to gain insights, develop reasonable gauges and assessments, sharpen questions and dilemmas—in short, improve over the prejudices and ad hoc beliefs that often substitute for knowledge in this area. We build a unique historical record of the efforts to export and import progress. For the three major donors this means a categorized database on how much was given, to whom and for what, when, and, to a greater degree than before, why. This allows comparisons across donors and time periods and informed assessment of how much the endeavor to export progress fits the philanthropic ideal type. Such a database, along with evaluative criteria developed in the next chapter, also helps guide the exploration of results.

Analysis of the recipient side produces important information about Latin American universities themselves. Assistance sometimes brings us to the university mainstream. It often brings us to targeted sites where international efforts and domestic reform overlap. Assistance is well understood only with knowledge of the domestic context, and Latin American universities are well understood only with knowledge of assistance. If all this makes evaluation of pure assistance impacts difficult, it also enlarges our view of the domestic development picture beyond higher education alone.

Several literatures, concepts, and debates should benefit from analysis of the golden age of university transfer. As the next chapter uses change-oriented literatures on international assistance, development, and domestic policy to guide and contextualize our case, so it suggests how our case offers an information base and conceptual insights on change for these literatures. A similar point holds for the philanthropic literature underpinning our ideal type.[50]

The Approach

On the recipient side, the study includes the twenty nations traditionally defined as Latin America, leaving aside the English-speaking Caribbean. Similarities in Latin American universities across nations at the inception of the golden age facilitate regional inclusion. But claims that the more than two hundred universities "fit into the same basic structural framework" (Ribeiro 1968: 85) are exaggerated, and our vast geographical scope presents challenges and dangers. To minimize these and to build a contextual understanding of the impact side, the study concentrates on Chile, Colombia, Costa Rica, Mexico, and Argentina, followed by a few other countries, tapering off to Haiti at the other extreme. Chapter 2 discusses the choices.

Our focus on universities bypasses targets that were sometimes intermediary institutions in funneling assistance toward the Latin American university. This means grants for U.S. university area studies, research, conferences, and other activities. It also means scholarships outside university assistance projects.[51] Also bypassed are institutions not concentrating on first-degree or undergraduate studies, which means little space for the private and public centers that play a major role in graduate education and especially research (Levy 1996). The undergraduate focus remains on universities, the region's predominant higher education institutions still and even more so back when massive assistance arrived on the scene.[52]

On the donor side, the focus is on U.S. giving. This choice follows from two points. One is identification of the U.S. research university as Latin America's key import model. The other is the predominance of U.S. giving in aid for Latin America overall and for its universities in particular. Yet the U.S. focus allows inclusion of international agencies operating with heavy U.S. funding.

Our broad time frame is from the 1950s on, but the highlighted period is shorter. The database mostly covers 1960 to 1984. The end point provides a cutoff for systematic data accumulation. It also roughly coincides with the emergence of new, neoliberal domestic reforms in higher education. But the golden assistance age of expectation and effort to transform the Latin American university is best defined as the decade and a half beginning with Ford's entry, formally in 1959, followed quickly by the IDB's arrival. Thus 1960 to 1975 is the period receiving the greatest scrutiny of efforts. The time period for impacts is more open-ended; any significant impact is worth considering, but it becomes increasingly difficult over time to identify impacts and to link effort and impact, cause and effect.[53]

To cover so much ground, diverse data sources are necessary. A challenge is to gather information that is scattered and heterogeneous in form. One major source is archival data, mostly from the donor end. Ford's archives are the best ordered, with grant files for each project. AID's archives lie at the other extreme, improved only just after the golden age as part of an overall upgrading of the agency's evaluation efforts.[54] Like Ford but more so, the IDB restricts access to its archives, but in both cases it was possible to secure almost all documents of interest, though with limitations on citation.[55] IDB project documents are sometimes more than one hundred pages in length, with detailed appendixes, though much of the information is background on the recipient and the rationale for a project. Together, the Ford and IDB files provide a wealth of raw material. Nevertheless, according to Francis Sutton (1984: 138), "Anyone who has ever groped through the reports or files of foundations knows that it is hazardous to try to say either what they were trying to do or what they in fact have done."

Interviews provide a second major source of information. Interviewees include ex-field officers and policymakers from the donor side as well as participants, experts, and critics from the recipient side. Citations in the text, in parentheses, show the interviewee's last name followed by an *i* for interview (e.g., Aldana i). Along with the formal though open-ended, in-depth interviews (see appendix B), I draw on a greater number of less formal conversations on particular points. Research on higher education particularly benefits from such conversations with experts who are also colleagues. Together, a range of discussions and documents provided the core material in site visits. Less directly but fundamentally, assessment of the recipient side draws on the author's years of fieldwork on Latin American higher education.

Different approaches would provide an alternative set of advantages and disadvantages. One such approach would be large-scale quantitative study, perhaps including surveys or systematic tabulation of a particular type of impact. To date, however, the most viable and common alternative to our approach (leaving aside studies that have attracted interest by savaging donor motivation or making polemical attacks) has been the single case study or collection of a few cases involving one major donor. These allow a closer look at a project's undertakings and impacts than we could attempt, but with a price in breadth, generalization, and comparative analysis across donors and recipients.[56] Nor would such a study provide the regional and national contexts and breadth to attract the audience we seek.

Looking beyond this introductory chapter, chapter 1 explores how different literatures fundamentally concerned with analyzing change guide what we look for in our raw material on university assistance and how we interpret it. Readers with limited interest in theory and broad contexts of change could skim that chapter. Chapter 2 identifies the main donors and receivers in broad strokes. It provides basic data on assistance levels over time and analyzes the distribution by nation. Chapters 3–5 then concentrate on both efforts and results. They consider three major components of the export model: system decentralization, intra-organizational centralization, and academic work. Chapter 6 summarizes the findings and evaluates this historic experience of exporting and importing progress.

1

Perspectives on Change

This chapter looks to broad literatures on change to help us explore and interpret information on the golden age of university assistance. In return, our findings should contribute fresh material for the study of change.

The philanthropic ideal type of change can be adapted to three literatures that help orient us in studying reform goals, efforts, and results. These are literatures on international assistance, national development, and domestic policy reform. Our subject matter lies squarely within the first and largely within the second, whereas the third usually treats different subject matter, usually based in the United States. The first two must have a central place in our study of the exporting and importing of progress. Incorporation of the literature on domestic policy reform requires a rationale, provided below, about how it illuminates our subject matter.[1] A potential fourth literature, on international philanthropy, is included within our consideration of international assistance, especially when we focus on private donors, mainly foundations.

Impressive symmetry appears among the three literatures. Each features debate over whether major, worthwhile change is pursued and achieved; if yes, how and why, and if no, how and why not? Laudatory work on all shares much positive ground, all challenged by critical work within the same fields. Positive claims about change through international assistance, national development, and domestic policy reform show important parallels to our philanthropic ideal type while negative claims run counter to it.[2]

The three literatures also show symmetry in sequence. Each undergoes a partial shift from a first stage of golden age optimism, based mostly on faith or broad reasoning, to a second stage of bitter pessimism. A third stage, which the present work promotes, seeks a more balanced and detailed understanding and evaluation. There is, of course, no rigid sequence, and promoters and critics are always present, having at each other, some prudently using evidence, others not. We draw on the three literatures and especially a remarkable work by Fred Riggs (1964) to develop our criteria for evaluating change.

International Assistance

Critics seldom deny that the international assistance we study incorporates means defined in the philanthropic ideal type. First, abundant specific efforts appear, as seen in the sudden surge of projects. Second, both the private and public resource transfers are essentially voluntary. As with philanthropy, a kind of responsibility to give international assistance may spring from a moral basis but rarely from a legal basis.[3] Beyond this, however, the issue of how well the philanthropic ideal type guides analysis of assistance takes us to the heart of the assistance debate. Supporters of assistance make claims that largely parallel the philanthropic ideal type.

Goals and motivations are common points of contention, especially since assistance is voluntary. Supporters insist that donors seek to promote development for reasons that blend altruism with long-range self-interest. Aid should be seen as a transaction that the donor would not make on grounds of economic self-interest alone (Pinchus 1967: 308). "Loans" are assistance according to the portion that has "grant content," meaning gift content. By the same token, donors acting for cold war national interest reasons could nonetheless believe they act to promote development (Packenham 1973). Also fitting the philanthropic ideal type would be assistance aimed at bringing the less developed world to the more developed world (universalism) or at least aimed at spurring sustainable development, donors exiting. Beyond earlier diplomacy or emergency relief, international assistance would mostly mean development aid,[4] a parallel to the contrast between traditional charity and modern philanthropy.

Moving from goals to associated aspects of ideal typical means, a positive view is that flexibility makes even public assistance agencies something between private agencies and the typical civil service (Tendler 1975: 20–22). Innovation flows from the distinctive, nonmandatory nature of funds that exert "marginal influence selectively"; accordingly, aid is the key "marginal increment" or "missing catalyst" for change, especially as it targets domestic reform partners and becomes cooperation rather than passively received assistance.[5] "Partners in Development" captures this sense.[6]

Further on the pro-assistance side lie views that efforts translate into positive results. But these views were still based on faith or reason much more than study at the time that a blistering critique erupted.

Since the 1970s, defenders of assistance have been mostly under siege. Critiques largely like those made domestically about U.S. foundations have challenged assistance on nearly all fronts dealing with goals, efforts, and impacts. Critics have savaged donor motivation. They either deny altruistic motivation or find it subordinate to status quo and selfish interests. They sometimes denounce imperialism in both source and purpose. Some paint official assistance as impossible to reform, since efforts and results stem from selfish and unethical motivation.[7] Even nonradical academic authorities write that assistance "reflects primarily the interests and goals of the donor and not the recipient" (Roett 1972: 169). And for educational assistance, including higher educational assistance, the criticism of motivation is acidic (Berman 1983; Arnove 1980b), widely echoed in journal articles, conferences, and curriculum.

Critics' depiction of donor efforts forms a sharp contrast to the philanthropic ideal type.[8] It often denies, downplays, or disregards the claim that assistance is significantly distinctive from domestic public funding, as well as claims that private assistance is significantly distinctive from public assistance. A related harsh claim is that donors largely push a "monolithic" development model, insensitive to cultural and other variations among their targets (Leach 1999: 392). A moderate branch of the nondistinctiveness criticism is that assistance is basically too lax. For example, multilateral development banks are not enough like real banks in holding out for good proposals and financing for the credible long term rather than indiscriminately spreading money across the board to many countries (Ranis 1996: 14). Even where donors try to give for distinctive purposes, recipients can make funds "fungible." A more caustic branch of the criticism is that donors are too tough. Findings of donor control (Phillips 1976b: 24–25) typically run counter to claims about partnership.

In the negative critique of results, the harsh branch is that impacts are major and deleterious. Impacts include imposition of alien values and power (Weissman 1975; Mundy 1998: 451–52), a weakened civil society (Goodell 1986) whether the state grows weaker or stronger, hierarchy, increased stratification (Ahmad and Wilke 1986), technocratic (Trías 1978) or (more recently) neoliberal policies (Colclough 1991), and a strengthened status quo.[9] All those impacts involve change, but for the worse.

Usually less vehement is the critique that international assistance has produced little change. This is the more common critique held within donor agencies themselves. Paradoxically, then, where harsh critics may see aid effectively fulfilling its (undesirable) goals (Arnove 1980b), donors often bemoan their relative impotency. A two-volume compilation shows that U.S. efforts to export democracy to Latin America have been "usually negligible, often counterproductive, and only occasionally positive."[10] Domestic authorities may use donors' fungible funds in ways that allow them to use their own money for priorities not on the donor agenda. Another finding is growth without change or overall improvement: if growth does not strengthen the status quo, neither does it undercut the status quo.[11] Specifically in education, one common view is that donor efforts "have largely failed" (Leach 1999: 376).

The unpopularity of foreign assistance helps explain AID's defensiveness in making its public case. Views of international development assistance "in considerable disarray" and failing have helped fuel the rise of NGO alternatives and efforts at sustainable development.[12]

Countering the negativism is "third-stage" study that mixes in positive findings, in whatever proportion, however cautiously. Special finance and expertise directed at selected activities spur growth, especially when delivered wisely. Those resources then often help attract further resources. Much of the positive empirical assessment of impact comes from studies focused on the direct recipients of assistance, at least if the contextual conditions are relatively favorable. Some works have suggested how to develop reasonable evaluative criteria against which to weigh data. They find assistance achieving ends that would not otherwise be achieved, while suffering failure rates not higher than in other major systems, such as market systems.[13]

Development: Modernization versus Dependency

The contrasting views of assistance are also crucial in basic modernization versus dependency debates about Third World change and development. In this book the word *development* refers often to national development but also often to institutional development. Moreover, much that is about national development is relevant to institutional development and thus to much of the specific case material in chapters 3 and 4.

Sharp modernization-dependency contrasts have yielded ground to moderate, overlapping formulations, including third-stage reassessment of policy impacts. Without rehashing the evolution of detailed positions, we highlight the tenets that have distinguished modernization from dependency as regards the relationship between assistance and development.[14] At least four reasons explain why the modernization-dependency contrast warrants inclusion here alongside the assistance debate.

One reason is the overlap between the assistance and development literatures. As ours is a study of international development assistance, it is simultaneously a study of development. More particularly, the modernization-dependency conflict significantly concerns the ties between domestic affairs and foreign influence.[15] The greatest parallels between this chapter's sections on assistance and development come as modernization takes a positive view of assistance while dependency takes a negative one. Naturally, the shift in focus from the assistance to the development literature means a shift in emphasis from exporters to domestic actors—importers—but both literatures deal with both actors.

A second reason to consider the modernization-dependency literature is that, as thoughtful critics of both perspectives have granted, and as is part of any third-stage view, each school has pointed to certain questions and factors meriting consideration. Yet, for all the writings on these perspectives, very little empirical work has treated the extraordinary efforts made in higher education assistance and the effects they have had.

A third reason is that the development literature was so connected to the historical experience under consideration: modernization concepts to goals and efforts in the golden age of assistance, and the rise of dependency to disaffection with that assistance. Since the modernization view dominated during the golden age, it is more critical to our study, but we can analyze findings in terms of modernization versus dependency tenets.

A fourth reason for including these contrasting development perspectives is that they are not dead. Survival is passively manifested where perspectives have never been surrendered or replaced. Sometimes, however, survival is vibrant, though usually in less grandiose proclamation than in yesteryear. Despite disappointment with prior assistance efforts, certain modernization ideas drive the work of today's leading donor agencies and their domestic partners, whether we consider higher education, Latin America, or wider settings. At the same time, stiff domestic opposition to today's powerful international agenda echoes dependency perspectives about external imposition, distortion of domestic development, and so forth. We may talk of modernization and dependency in the past tense when referring to the golden age, but that past echoes today.[16]

The correspondence between the modernization perspective and the philanthropic ideal type of change starts with goals. Like the philanthropic ideal type, the modernization perspective expresses a dominant, optimistic, modern liberal faith. The main goal is to achieve desirable change by attacking the root causes of backwardness or traditionalism (values and policies alike) and establishing liberal, nonrevolutionary democracy, which happily marks enlightened self-interest for donor nations. A developing world assisted by donors would also enhance its ability to further its interests in the world community. "Modernization" could be used interchangeably with "Westernization" by golden age donors and could be equated with their universalistic or homogenizing aspirations. Optimistically, the resulting major change would simultaneously bring "all good things" in mutually reinforcing and eventually self-sustaining ways. The multifaceted good things would include political, economic, social, cultural, and psychological development, efficiency and equity, strengthened civil society and pluralism alongside a state weakened as a repressive agent while strengthened as an agent of progressive change.[17]

Parallels between key modernization and philanthropy tenets are also powerful regarding means. First, like the philanthropic ideal type, modernization assigned key roles to education, rational development management, expertise, and ideas. Social science provided orientation, meaning, reinforcement, and legitimacy, if not always specific policy prescription (Packenham 1973: 284). That helps explain why reigning views about development in booming social science literature were so important. Second, partnership was assigned a key role. Those exporting progress would work with ready importers—rational, enlightened, progressive, reform-oriented domestic leaders. Shared interests would minimize imposition, though donors would add incentives to stimulate recipient participation and change.

On two points, however, the modernization perspective does *not* basically fit the philanthropic ideal typical means. First, it at least sometimes suggests an ease of diffusion (Meek 1996: 1–3) or recipient copying that defies the ideal type's emphasis on careful means and strategies. Second, and related, the modernization perspective suggests large-scale resources and is ambiguous about the need for selective targeting of distinctive recipients. It often has been associated with a massive effort smack at the mainstream of recipient systems, boosting resources for basic, government-led systemic transformation. Tied to this second point, whole societies have been the main object of concern more often in studies of modernization than philanthropy.

Dependency perspectives run overwhelmingly against the philanthropic ideal type of change.[18] They therefore offer a pertinent contrast for our study. Dependency literature often emphasized unflattering goals and motivations. Donors wanted to increase political, economic, or cultural (including educational) hegemony, to maintain a fundamental status quo in recipient nations, or to effect a controlled change serving donor self-interest (Foley 1984).

Regarding means, "assistance" would then not be philanthropy or would be bad philanthropy, based on the illegitimate or ill-advised use of external power. Dependency emphasized donors' ongoing control, with considerable coercion or at least inequality in participation. Over time, more sophisticated studies identified alliances with some autonomy and bargaining power on the recipient side but only for elite actors. "World systems" is another conceptualization of an internationalism wherein the weak copy the strong in fundamental historical processes, including educational ones.[19]

As external influence produces negative impact, domestic development requires less rather than more contact with the developed world. Or at least the external is an obstacle that can be overcome only partly and with care.[20] Often, the Third World winds up a "subsidiary" of First World institutions.[21] The result is world systems sameness, as applied by Ilchman and Ilchman to universities (1987; Ilchman i). What is imported slows, blocks, or distorts desirable development. The portrayal of feeble receivers is at odds with ideal typical partnership (Clayton 1998: 488–94). "Assistance" is therefore largely dependency funding. If it strengthens any recipients, they are government and private elites. It weakens civil society and pluralism.[22] Importing also weakens traditional values and institutions. Yet traditionalism does not yield to progressive alternatives. In short, dependency perspectives have featured international dimensions in their core propositions of aggravated stratification between more and less developed nations and within the latter.

U.S. Domestic Policy Reform

The conceptual base for our study of change strengthens by incorporating perspectives from works on domestic policy reform. Two interrelated literatures, mostly from U.S. political science, are especially enriching. The literature on federalism provides suggestive parallels to international assistance, and the literature on policy implementation provides insights into the relationship between goals, efforts, and results.[23] Both literatures identify key dynamics to explore. Together they also sober us about the likelihood of major change that meets original goals. They alert us to fundamental trade-offs. And they push us to identify realistic evaluative criteria.

Federalism and international assistance share the crucial notion that positive change will come as largely external actors step in with targeted material resources and guidance to help local partners develop. Pressman and Wildavsky (1984: 135–39) note this fundamental similarity between foreign aid and federal aid to cities. Derthick emphasizes that the federal government has "no formal right to make decisions," and "no legitimate role within," or its role is "peripheral" rather than "integral," working through those who have prime responsibility.[24] As an external funder the federal government can select recipients and try to "pick winners" (Gilbert and Specht 1984: 171). The federal government's partners include not only local and state governments but also private agencies, underscoring a sense of "privatization" (Church and Nakamura 1993: 109) and "third party government" (Salamon 1987). Indeed, two layers of selection often exist, as in philanthropy, where the donor gives to an agency, which then gives to recipients targeted for development.

To the extent it is an outsider, the federal government does not have to give, so its giving is voluntary. By the same token, its right to terminate its role fits the voluntary ideal, too, marking the ultimate federal power (Derthick 1970: 207). The historical smallness of aid, followed by the doubling of grants-in-aid from the early 1960s to 1967 (Derthick 1970: 3), parallels the "late" rise of major philanthropy as opposed to earlier charity—to build a more coherent, scientific, businesslike national social policy missing in a decentralized public system (Karl and Katz 1981). Like contemporaneous foreign aid, large federal aid represented unprecedented liberal choice. Federal aid was to be for the Great Society at home what international assistance was to be for the golden age abroad.

The significant parallel between federalist principle and the philanthropic ideal type regarding means must not be exaggerated. Compared with a foreign agency, the federal government is less of an outsider. It shares an overlapping tax and constituency base with its recipients, and there is some legal and political responsibility. Federalism involves intertwined rather than separate governments—thus the common depiction of marble cake rather than layer cake federalism.

On the other hand, the basic parallel in means has its counterpart in goals insofar as there is a common rationale for the outside party to step inside. A core rationale in federalism is that the "feds," quite like donors in international assistance, weigh in to provide enabling resources. Justification for federal entrance into fields like education, where the federal government lacks a direct constitutional responsibility, lies with some broad goal perceived as unachievable by the locality. The goal may be either something distinctive or more of something already pursued. The "local failure" stems from a lack of finance, commitment, expertise, or favorable power configurations. There is then a broad parallel to the public failure theory that seeks to explain the rise of private nonprofit action.[25]

As literature on federalism considers practice as well as principle, it helps us identify key questions in determining the fit between our philanthropic ideal type and assistance reality. Both philanthropy and assistance are in fact a range of things, and they evolve over time (Wright and White 1984). Identification of the parallel range is more important for our purposes than the debated conclusions on federalism in actual practice. (Appendix D sketches the correspondence versus noncorrespondence between federal principle and practice regarding goals, means, and results.) The ensuing text concentrates on anticipated results. The federalism studies that deal with results are part of the implementation studies boom initiated in the 1970s. For us these literatures' findings on results signal the difficulty of policy reform but also the possibility that results that first appear negative then appear more mixed to positive when evaluative criteria are made more reasonable.

Most literature on federalism in action has painted a picture defying our philanthropic ideal type of change. Striking is the paucity of very positive reports on results—even where there were consensual goals and ample funds.[26] A frequent conclusion is that federalism's major attempts at reform yield very limited results. Another is that results are perverse: "goal displacement" brings "unintended consequences" (Derthick 1970: 156), state and local governments lose strength (Reagan and Sanzone 1981), and actors on the scene have reason to regard the feds as naive and remote (Pressman and Wildavsky 1984). Symptoms of failure include excessive costs, delays, group conflict, goal conflict, and of course lack of goal attainment (Church and Nakamura 1993). Similarly, policy implementation studies beyond federalism have found a yawning gap between expectations and results.[27]

The results are not clearly negative to all observers, however. For one thing, as with the international assistance literature, more is written about goals and means than about results (Kettl 1983). But precisely on results, there is a third-stage response to studies showing the large gap between claims and realities of federalist reform or between policy declaration and policy implementation. Peterson et al. denounce ridiculous critiques of federalism-as-failure that form conventional wisdom in policy and academic circles as evaluations emerge too quickly and simplistically (1986: 217). Competent, energetic, and continual efforts and adjustments produce variable results, and projects that do not aim at major resource redistribution work well while others should be judged realistically against their ambitious goals. Federal aid pushes change reasonably, with impacts extremely difficult to gauge.[28] Such a view proves a pertinent parallel and guide to much that we will discover about the golden age assistance we analyze.

Most explanations for federalist failure to attain goals can be related to deviation from the ideal type's loop among goals, means, and results. Optimistic assumptions that good things go together for grand change come up short. An initial problem is that many reform plans call for comprehensive change in the mainstream, rather than through distinctive, carefully selected partners. The weightiest study of higher education implementation concentrates on Western Europe's plans for changes that were both systemwide and fundamental in depth regarding values and practices, engendering great opposition.[29] Federal efforts are often doomed because local support is inadequate. Or, as with international assistance, federal money is spread widely, carelessly, or through a politically inclusive formula, rather than in selective ways conducive to impacts. In a sense, too many benefit too little. This watering-down defeats the purpose of targeting special resources on those who most need it or could most benefit from it; response to political pressure may even mean that the neediest get less than others do. When federalism turns to "block grants," giving recipient governments freedom to spread and spend as they see fit, the ideal typical notion of targeting to selected partners crumbles.[30]

On the other hand, greater selectivity often brings its own problems. Reformers rely on the "experiment" to "join a paucity of actual resources with a maximum amount of imagination," but soon exhilaration yields to perceptions of failure, which lead in turn to diminished legitimacy and then real failure (Pressman and Wildavsky 1984: 136). So even selectivity may not escape the negative loop many implementation studies depict wherein problems result in disappointment, thus abrupt concession of failure, thus injury to reform. We will repeatedly see how the problems with selectivity, alongside the problems of indiscriminate funding, pose fundamental philanthropic dilemmas, and how problems with producing ideal typical results through ideal typical selectivity suggest possible inconsistencies in the ideal type itself.

Rather than the philanthropic ideal type's clear goals pursued through sure-handed means and partnership, implementation studies find confusion on goals and means, with much more conflicting interests among actors than initially realized. To attract launching support, policies are framed boldly, which invites opposition, or ambiguously, which only temporarily masks the conflicts (Majone and Wildavsky 1977; Van Horn 1979: 11, 162). Higher education is especially prone to ambiguity, and its "bottom-heaviness"—the strength of units and actors far from the top rungs of institutions or government—affords many participants diverse resistance points.[31]

But all these constraints can prompt revised notions of what constitutes reasonable change. Something short of meeting grandiose goals but different from what had existed may be worthwhile. Especially as mixed results differ from projected ones, they are often very difficult to assess. And results seldom appear conveniently at a given moment such as the end of a project. Instead, street level administrators or implementation entrepreneurs continually discover constraints, learn, and readjust to evolving circumstances, so that implementation involves backward mapping, incrementalism, rejuvenation, negotiation, and experimentation in the trenches.[32]

The policy implementation literature has drawn implications for evaluation that lead into the perspectives and criteria outlined below for our evaluation of university assistance. Evaluators glued to a project's guidelines, formal design, and hierarchical authority miss much of what transpires. Impacts may come in unanticipated yet noteworthy bits and pieces. Change often reflects clashes between designs and local reality at the target site. Policies are continuously transformed by implementation.[33] Most results do not flow neatly from efforts tied to clear goals, but neither do they totally frustrate goals and efforts.

Prismatic Change

The prior sections have all dealt with change literatures on goals, efforts, and results. The last sections of the chapter now concentrate on results that lie in between the ideal typical and simple failure. A range of possibilities proves vital to how we evaluate the golden age of university assistance.

To meet the challenge of identifying real change, a perceptive and too much forgotten work by Fred Riggs will be employed in chapters 3–6. Riggs is prescient on the nature of partial change produced by efforts at transformation. His work also fits the change literatures just discussed.[34] Riggs is a prolific composer of specialized terms, but we can distill these to a few. A *prismatic* model, presented as an ideal type, depicts common results (Riggs 1964). These represent neither the status quo ante nor a pure copy of the export, because the external influence gets diffracted as it enters the system. New mixes destroy boundaries that delineated the traditional domestic and exported models. Our study works with two chief prismatic manifestations, both hybrids between the traditional form and the export. *Displacement,* or *overlap,* involves the two forms functioning simultaneously alongside one another, with some mutual influence. *Formalism* is a mix that amounts to a partly distinctive third form.

Displacement occurs as enclaves emerge in which the new inserts itself while much of the old remains, crowded alongside it. Latin Americanists will recognize similarities to the classic depiction of a "living museum" of Latin American politics, where traditional actors and practices remain on the scene as new ones enter (Anderson 1967: 104). This displacement or superimposition is opposed to modernization and other ideal typical reform notions of *re*placement. Organizational sociologists will recognize "institutional contradiction" as institutions "nest" inside other institutions and "institutional models are unlikely to be imported whole cloth into systems that are very different from the ones in which they originate."[35]

Formalism arises where new laws, statutes, or structures do not produce correspondingly new functions or behavior but are influenced by the older order into which they are enmeshed. The emergent form does not correspond to the export model, and formal structure is often a poor guide to reality. Instead, common prismatic reality is form or function that blends the import and the traditional into something different. Contrary to hypotheses of either modernizing replication or insignificant results, Riggs thus postulates systems with their own "equilibrating mechanisms" and logic (1964: 34). While this, like Anderson's "living museum," allows for continuing change or transition, it contradicts the philanthropic ideal typical notion of inexorable evolution toward the imported model. In fact, the import model may be illogical within systems that lack the beliefs, personnel, surrounding structure, and finances assumed in the exporting society. So the import may be rationally bypassed in practice. Riggs helps us understand that failure to import models fully need not represent errors or irrationalities. Observers are still free to deprecate results but must try to identify and understand them.

There are striking parallels to guidance provided by Albert Hirschman's work on Latin American policy reform. Both Riggs and Hirschman help us to look for results where they are, rather than just under the prescribed proverbial lamppost. Both spur us to understand results in their own terms, including hidden rationality, rather than just as perversity and policy failure. Both instruct us to look for patterns of change that may appear feeble or otherwise distorted in contrast to lofty goals, yet are large in contrast to much conventional wisdom about reform failure. These Riggs-Hirschman parallels are all the more striking because Hirschman is much more buoyant and points to more positive results. Whereas Riggs underscores how mixes of old and new frustrate reform designs, Hirschman writes much more about learning, adaptation, and progress.[36] But Riggs also rejects simple views of static failure. For our purposes the key similarity is that both authors alert us to policy and results that deviate from our philanthropic ideal type and yet amount to significant change, sometimes positive.

Evaluating Change

Riggs contributes to where we look, in a third stage of evaluation of the assistance under consideration, to identify intermediate possibilities between simple success and failure, between an ideal type and its opposite. The possibilities include results different from a replacement of the preexisting by an imported model, yet also different from what preceded assistance or what would have occurred in the absence of assistance. Our review of the literature on domestic policy change also suggested the need for such a third stage of evaluation. But most of the literature reviewed on policy, development, and international assistance showed the prevalence of two stages. The first was characterized by a heady optimism, projecting massive, rapid, and positive transformation through social engineering. Great disappointment and a critical reaction depicting much more limited or negative consequences then characterized the second stage.[37] A similar pattern emerges in organizational sociology where views of organizational change based on technically rational and efficient competition came to be challenged by studies emphasizing *isomorphism*—institutions copying other institutions.[38] If both stages exaggerate, a crucial challenge is to achieve a more accurate and balanced understanding. Among the change literatures surveyed, that challenge probably remains least fulfilled in the international assistance field, and university assistance certainly requires a fresh look.[39]

One implication for our examination of results is that evaluation is difficult and properly complex. For example, the World Bank (1990: 128) could not conclude whether assistance had diminished poverty or not. A Brookings study (Finegold, McFarland, and Richardson 1993) of educational transfer between much more similar exporters and importers than ours concludes that assessment is extremely difficult and suffers from a lack of provable measurements. There is no appropriate, singular, prescribed approach. Evaluators of international development projects have noted the need for evaluation flexible enough to encompass unpredicted results whereas the more rigid hypothesis testing of economics biases its users to find development failure.[40] With realistic criteria we can understand the real world better and also have more chance to say something useful to policy reformers, for as Hirschman has repeatedly pointed out, broad, unrelenting charges of failure are not much help.[41]

A constant for our different evaluative criteria is that they are *comparative*. Change produced through assistance efforts should meet a reasonably selected standard or object of comparison. We also thematically compare results to goals and very much, in that connection, to our ideal type of philanthropic change. Even this allows for degrees of change, since the goals and ideal typical stipulations rarely restrict us to a dichotomy of total success or failure.

Comparison to goals is not nearly as straightforward as it might appear. For one thing, as critics point out regarding federalism, international assistance, and development, correspondence is problematic between stated and true goals. Moreover, as implementation literature has found, goals are often vague and thus difficult to identify in relationship to particular programs (Nakamura and Smallwood 1980: 67–83). We will repeatedly see how a firm list of goals is elusive, as specific projects often do not spell out much of what donors and recipients ultimately envision. Accordingly, as noted in the introductory chapter, we find it useful to distinguish between explicit and implicit goals, the latter generally much more grandiose. This allows for project fulfillment in the most concrete terms, such as hiring full-time professors, while failing to secure what could be called ultimate, implicit aims, such as building a high-quality academic staff or institution. Battles are won more easily than wars. Excessive evaluative attention to the lofty though vague implicit goals too easily confirms conventional wisdom of failure. Excessive evaluative attention to precise explicit goals too easily yields high success ratios without exploring why these do not convert into the better future that reformers envision. We need instead to look at both explicit and implicit goals and the relationship between the two.[42]

To add alternative comparative criteria less demanding than achievement of grand goals is to risk excessively lowering the threshold at which change is labeled significant or positive. Therefore, we do not abandon our first, most challenging standards; our other comparisons qualify but do not replace the comparison with grand goals. The range of comparisons allows flexible, nuanced assessment. Such is the case in our treatment of prismatic change: where ideal typical transformation does not result, we need to look at how significant or positive the prismatic forms are.

Where results do not match grand goals we must often try to determine if they "beat" or otherwise differ from other standards. With Riggs in mind, we will watch for whether inserted change progresses, morphs into something prismatic, or "snaps back" or "recoils," perhaps once the assistance project terminates. Following Cassen's idea of comparing the success/failure rate of assistance programs to other programs (1986), we also can compare university assistance programs to programs without assistance. Additionally, where targeted places reform but do not become levers that transform the entire system, do they stand in some sense above it, above the nonrecipients? Above where they themselves were before assistance arrived, doing something worthwhile better than they had done before? And then there are the counterfactual questions: are targeted places notably different from what they would have been in the absence of assistance? Of course, as in policy innovation generally, it is difficult to say what would have happened in the absence of a program or model. Policy implementation literature likewise notes that usually we can neither convincingly answer "hypothetical unknowns" nor evaluate meaningfully if we ignore them.[43]

While one counterfactual approach considers what might have happened without the reform effort or with a different effort, another considers what might have happened to the same effort had pertinent surrounding conditions been different. We must therefore look at conditions within the higher education realm that lies beyond a project's particular coverage. Projected progress may be hampered by the lack of supporting structures, practices, and norms. And we have to consider the crippling or facilitating effects of economic or political realms beyond higher education itself. "Webs" of mutually reinforcing consistency must be explored not only within models (including both the imported university model and the philanthropic ideal type of change) but also in relation to their fit to their environment. An extensive study of U.S. efforts to promote Latin American democracy concluded that no assistance for democracy has long succeeded "unless local conditions were propitious" (Lowenthal 1991: 260). Accordingly, we ask if university assistance programs have yielded significant change when conditions surrounding the program allowed.

Finally, context relates to time. There is no one time at which to evaluate the impact of efforts as extended and open-ended in objectives as those of golden age university assistance. Political and bureaucratic considerations lead to premature evaluation. Further out in time, however, reality is increasingly shaped by factors unrelated to the projects we wish to evaluate. Results identified at one time may dissipate.[44] Impact need not be immediate or permanent to be significant, but significance must be established by one of the comparative criteria just identified. And any time-related disappointment, whether delay or dissipation, must be explored in relation to how the responsibility falls on reformers' efforts or on factors beyond their control.

Golden age faith tends to be inimical to serious evaluation.[45] As doubt then arises about impact, evaluation often emerges and tends to be harsh, showing that grand goals have not been achieved as anticipated. After implementation is more or less assumed, studies of implementation then provide quite negative evaluations. A sense that reform efforts require serious but realistic evaluation must therefore drive a third stage beyond both faith and a reaction to it that can each be unrealistic and harmful.

❦❦

We are ready to analyze the substantive information on the golden age of university assistance. Reform crusades generally produce goals, efforts, and results far too numerous, scattered, and complex to identify fully, let alone to understand fully or surely. Yet our core task of advancing the documentation, understanding, and evaluation of reality is aided by the lines of inquiry consulted in the different literatures on change.

2

Givers and Receivers

This chapter looks at the chief exporters and importers. It identifies and analyzes the major actors, at a macro level, on both the giving and receiving ends during the crusade to transform the Latin American university and, through it, to promote national development. On the giving side, that means analysis of the principal foundation, bilateral donors, and multilateral donors. On the receiving side, it means a comparison of Latin American nations.

The chapter's macro emphasis on who gave to whom includes attention to why the unprecedented undertaking was made and to the broad picture of how much was given and how it was given (questions pursued at more institutional or micro levels in subsequent chapters). The chapter presents its material in three main parts. The first introduces the main donors and their assistance profile over time. Providing more aggregate data, the second part explores broad dimensions of relationships involving matters such as golden age goals, selectivity, partnership, and control. The third part of the chapter turns to how much different nations received, and why. All three parts are vital to mapping the historic and captivating undertaking.

Unlike the subsequent three chapters, this chapter does not analyze results but, like them, looks at goals and especially efforts, though it examines efforts at the most general level. Thematically, the chapter considers the relative consistency of these efforts with elements of the philanthropic ideal type established in the book's introduction and with related views of change from chapter 1. Thus the chapter's conceptual thrust complements its descriptive overview.

The Givers

Among the multiple and often zealously hopeful donors, it is easy to select the main ones for study. Within each major category—private foundation, bilateral agency, and multilateral agency—a single actor towers over others in its giving to Latin American universities. Moreover, the Ford Foundation, AID, and the IDB are by far the three most important donors regardless of category; no number two from any category would lead the number one in any other. And all three choices fit our emphasis on U.S. assistance. This is unambiguous for Ford and AID, and the United States accounts for a greater share of IDB than of World Bank or UN agency funds. Additional foundations, bilateral agencies, and multilateral agencies are briefly sketched following consideration of the big three.[1]

Ford Foundation

Created in 1936 and limited until 1950 to its native Michigan, the Ford Foundation then rocketed to the premier position among the world's foundations. It would soon command four times the resources of the Rockefeller Foundation, twelve times those of Carnegie, and one-sixth the wealth of all twenty-five thousand U.S. foundations combined. This surge contributed to charges that the "prodigal young giant" was too large and careless—at odds with philanthropic selectivity. On the other hand, Ford has usually ranked near the top when authors list the most important foundations that are innovative and progressive.[2]

Ford's overall primacy holds for philanthropy directed at the Third World (Arnove 1980a: 307). Although Latin America was the last developing region it entered, in 1959, Ford immediately became the clear leader there, too. From that point through the mid-1970s (i.e., during the golden age of assistance), Latin America was the priority region for Ford's International Division and the leading region in the share of Ford funds directed to education. Table 2.1 shows Latin America's leadership in Ford's university assistance as well: the region held first place from 1959 through the 1970s despite the delayed start and the fall below Asia in the late 1970s.

Indeed, the most striking emphasis in Ford's overall giving was its favoring of higher education. This fits philanthropic ideal typical means including an emphasis on operating where knowledge, expertise, and professionalism are available. It also fits regarding selectivity in that higher education was obviously much more limited in size than were primary and secondary education. Following the pattern it had traced at home, Ford decided higher education was the natural foundation route. Even the giant of foundations

Table 2.1 Ford Foundation Grants to Universities in Less Developed Countries by Region

	1952–58	1959–64	1965–69	1970–74	1975–79	Total
Latin America[a]	0 (0)[b] 0.0%	20,871,888 (89) 39.2%	26,492,603 (105) 39.6%	18,435,955 (157)[c] 45.5%	5,446,770 (123) 26.1%	71,247,216 (474) 37.2%
Middle East	5,593,390 (25) 56.4%	4,312,731 (31) 8.1%	7,074,109 (39) 10.6%	4,126,781 (52) 10.2%	1,489,329 (65) 7.1%	22,596,339 (212) 11.8%
Africa	70,000 (1) 0.7%	12,712,033 (80) 23.9%	10,286,727 (60) 15.4%	4,005,277 (51) 9.9%	3,677,913 (92) 17.6%	30,751,950 (284) 16.1%
Asia	4,258,017 (40) 42.9%	15,349,009 (74) 28.8%	22,981,831 (75) 34.4%	13,953,403 (147) 34.4%	10,285,816 (210) 49.2%	66,828,075 (546) 34.9%
Total	9,921,407 (66) 100.0%	53,245,661 (274) 100.0%	66,835,270 (279) 100.0%	40,521,416 (407) 100.0%	20,899,828 (490) 100.0%	191,423,581 (1,516) 100.0%

Source: Moock 1980: appendix 2.
[a]Deletes Jamaica, which had thirty-four grants, totaling $6,479,981.
[b]Figures in ( ) = number of projects.
[c]Two projects in the period of 1974–79 were not counted because they were canceled.

could never account for more than a small fraction of total foreign assistance, but it could make a mark in technical assistance due to the smaller sums involved and the qualitative difference that could result from them. Higher education was the quintessential field where progress could be exported from the top down (or from the center to the periphery). Put another way, impacts at the target site could have secondary impacts elsewhere. Rejecting the bulk of education as too massive and unsusceptible to influence from the outside, Ford pumped more than three-fourths of its Third World human resource development funds into higher education through the 1970s. Almost all its education categories included a considerable higher education portion. These categories involved education research, science and technology, social science, university modernization, teacher training, educational planning, and humanities and arts. Ford's higher education effort goes well beyond the impressive data listed as "university."[3]

The higher education emphasis also characterizes Rockefeller and other foundations more than it does AID and the IDB. At least in this respect, then, there is support for the hypothesis that foundations fit the philanthropic ideal type more than other donors do.

Among the foundations, Ford is the clear choice for our study. For a focus on higher education, U.S. giving, and Latin American receiving, all consulted experts at foundations recommended a focus on Ford, a suggestion also made by Ford's critics. Experts on Latin American universities have in effect agreed, sometimes emphasizing how Ford's role, for better or for worse, has far exceeded its ample financial outlays.[4]

AID

Like Ford, AID is the clear choice in a key assistance category—bilateral assistance. Moreover, although less than Ford, AID shows some broad parallels to the philanthropic ideal type. Its higher education activity, while a smaller share of its overall activity, includes flexible, selective partnership approaches to achieve development aims resembling Ford's.

AID's role in international education had historical roots but was largely unprecedented in its *development* focus. Roots lie in U.S.–Latin American educational exchanges since the nineteenth century, when importers were more conspicuous than exporters. Latin American reformers enthusiastically wanted to emulate U.S. practice. Certain U.S. government agencies engaged in exchanges associated with their main work in diplomacy or defense (Einaudi 1974: 201; Tiller 1973: 79). Only after World War II, however, did the government launch a concerted development effort through new agencies formed primarily for educational and cultural exchange and export. U.S. land grant colleges and universities were among the first to respond to President Truman's Point Four call for assistance to the developing world. The emergence of specific projects aiming at national development after years of more scattered and individually oriented efforts fits the shift in goals we have depicted for philanthropy and for international assistance in general.

In 1961, AID replaced the International Cooperation Administration (ICA), but our database bridges the incarnations. AID was to concentrate fully on the Third World. Constructed geographically, AID was to tie efforts in Latin America to the Alliance for Progress. The Alliance soon aimed at higher education, after initially aiming mostly at illiteracy. Whereas the ICA had pursued an "impact approach" for visible, short-term achievements linked to the cold war, AID added President Kennedy's emphasis on socio-economic aspects of long-term development that required breaking bottle-necks through institution building connected to education and research (Montgomery 1967: 63). The new emphasis fit more with the long-term, expansive goals of development assistance, though with a notable political interest (Ayres i).

Large development goals did not translate into typical big government means, however. AID operated like an autonomous section of the State Department. Additionally, the mode of resource distribution was a conscious alternative to the budgetary public mainstream. The ICA had led the way with Republican Harold Stassen's idea of contracting to U.S. universities rather than relying on direct government administration.[5] For agricultural higher education in developing countries, AID, the leading donor from the mid-1950s, always contracted to pair U.S. land grant institutions with host country institutions (Hansen 1990: v). There is some parallel to U.S. government financing at home through nonprofit organizations entrusted to target funds well and operate flexibly. Beyond that, AID was to fund partnerships. It was not itself to decide which Latin American universities were worthy or how and where they should be engaged. Instead, AID was to fund the mutual matching of U.S. and Latin American universities so that "linkages" would become the primary vehicle of action. However much this contracting-out evokes our ideal type in matters like targeted partnership, critics can decry the close ties between U.S. government and university. Some charge that the U.S. government saw the U.S. university as its administrative agent for Third World change. In any event, where AID higher education funds were at work, the key external actor on the scene was usually one or more U.S. universities. The many examples include North Carolina State at Peru's La Molina agricultural university and Ohio State, the University of Wisconsin, and the University of Arizona at Brazilian institutions.[6]

Whether AID brought formidable funds depends on the reference point. The United States led in total bilateral assistance, and its grants exceeded its loans. But U.S. total assistance as a share of GDP has been notoriously low; for educational assistance, the United States has been near the bottom among Organization for Economic Cooperation and Development (OECD) countries. At 3.8 billion, education accounted for only about 5 or 6 percent of

U.S. bilateral aid in the 1960s and 1970s, and higher education would get only about a fourth of that.[7]

All this still let AID loom large financially in university development worldwide, four-to-one over Ford and more than six-to-one over Rockefeller in the 1960s and 1970s, peaking in 1965 at well over $100 million to seventy-four universities (Coleman 1984: 183). But Latin America captured few of AID's large university development projects and thus only about an eighth of its project money, 1950–69 (Miller 1984: a1–a12), even though this was otherwise the priority region for AID in education, while Europe concentrated on its recent colonies.[8] Unlike Ford, then, AID did not make Latin America its number one region for university assistance. Where AID participated in large Latin American university development projects, it generally left the heavy expense items to the host government or the IDB. Also evoking a philanthropic mode, AID put much of its effort into selected individuals, with well over $100 million for "participant training" from the Latin American bureau. Like Ford, then, AID made an effort that was selective and limited in "weight" compared with the weight of the Latin American university system. Unlike Ford, however, AID's limitation related to the agency's lesser attention to Latin American universities than to other education.

IDB

Though a multilateral organization, the IDB is crucial to the story of U.S. assistance to Latin American universities. The U.S. role is central, as it has been at the Organization of American States (OAS), to which the IDB is formally linked.

The regional bank idea goes back to 1889 and the creation of the OAS's precursor, but the U.S. government opposed the idea for fear of competition with both its own power and private banking. The 1944 Bretton Woods accords, which set postwar international economic policy, perhaps implied an eventual IDB. Meanwhile, Latin Americans found the World Bank and International Monetary Fund (IMF) rigid and conservative, and they thirsted for a multilateral option beyond U.S. bilateral assistance, which had both limited funds and overbearing potential linked to cold war priorities. U.S. opposition waned in the late 1950s. Vice President Richard Nixon's disastrous visit to Latin America led many to believe that the backyard was not safe and that the U.S. role would have to increase, preferably without the political exposure of full reliance on bilateral aid. Creation of the IDB was part of a general shift from bilateral to multilateral aid, promoted by Third World and special commissions on aid.[9]

Each member nation has representation on the IDB board of governors, but most power resides with the board of executive directors and voting is weighted by financial contribution. In 1970, the 43 percent U.S. contribution gave it 42 percent of the votes, followed next by Brazil and Argentina at 12 percent each. Major ties have linked U.S. foreign policy and IDB policy. Moreover, the Social Trust Fund, key to higher education in the early years, drew solely on U.S. funds. In turn, U.S. officials fixed the higher education priority and put higher education advocates in charge (Wolf i-3). By 1965, the Fund for Special Operations absorbed the Social Trust Fund. Within another decade membership expanded beyond the original nineteen Latin American–U.S. core to eight other Western Hemispheric countries and, by 1993, to seventeen developed countries outside the region. But U.S. voting power remained de facto veto power.[10] All this justifies treatment of the IDB in higher education as a largely U.S. actor, which limits the distinction between our bilateral and multilateral categories.

Periodic U.S. pushes to make its formal control more like what it has at the World Bank and IMF have underscored inequality in power within the Americas. Nevertheless, the charge that the IDB is a mere U.S. appendage is excessive. Concerted action has been more common than blatant U.S. imposition. Just as Latin Americans have understood the reality of U.S. might, so U.S. officials have understood the need for Latin Americans to pursue their own aspirations. By convention, the bank's president is Latin American even if the vice president is a U.S. citizen. In higher education, agreement has been frequent and major policy disputes have been rare.[11]

For Latin America, the IDB resources at stake dwarf those of any other contributor. Its billions of dollars provided, secured, or organized for total activity (not just education) put it far in front of the world's other regional development banks.[12] A more modest perspective for our study stems from two factors, however. First, unlike Ford, the IDB has given only a few percent of its total to education. Second, also parting from the philanthropic ideal type, its education giving has been largely for a "bricks and mortar" approach that requires large sums at a time. As at the World Bank, this was marked early on; architects were key professionals for university development projects. The IDB's projects have generally been much larger than those of foundations and bilateral agencies. Indeed, the bank has had trouble running small projects efficiently.[13] Additionally, loans have outstripped grants.

But the IDB has not been the antithesis of the philanthropic ideal type or the Ford Foundation reality in its general giving orientation. First, terms for loans are usually lenient enough to be somewhat like grants. The fund for higher education might allow, for example, decades at 1 percent repayment. Second, the IDB has been the multilateral pioneer beyond pure economic development to social fields. Third, the IDB accounted for most of the golden age giving by regional banks for both higher education and education overall, making the IDB the number two multilateral after the World Bank for these fields.[14]

Fourth, higher education enjoyed special status within IDB education efforts. This was especially noteworthy in earlier years, as table 2.2 shows, but also notable later on as science and technology joined higher education while

Table 2.2 Education Assistance from the IDB, 1962–85 (percentages)

Years[a]	Primary & secondary	Vocational	Higher education[b]	Science & technology	Other	Total
1962–65	0	0	98.9	1.1	0	100.0
1966–70	0	21.9	77.2	1.0	0	100.1
1971–75	2.1	25.2	59.7	13.1	0	100.1
1976–80	16.9	15.4	22.3	44.3	1.1	100.0
1981–85	23.1	19.6	32.6	18.6	6.0	99.9
Total	15.7	18.9	38.5[c]	24.0	3.0	100.1

Source: IDB n.d.: 6.

[a]IDB presents its data here in periods one year removed from the periods we use elsewhere (e.g., 1975–79), and includes 1985, whereas we usually stop at 1984.

[b]The IDB's categories of "higher education" (large) and "student credit" (small).

[c]Inflation and other factors that lead to increased absolute expenditure over time make higher education's overall share appear artificially low, but that is partly offset when higher education with science and technology are combined.

primary education joined vocational education (the secondary level was just 1 percent overall). For the overall period, higher education with science and technology accounts for nearly $1 billion of the $1.5 billion education total. This came in sixty-six higher education and eleven science and technology loans (IDB 1985: 14), even without including the higher education component of another nineteen loans for agricultural research and extension (see appendix E). If the higher education emphasis expressed an informal working agreement wherein AID and the World Bank would focus on Latin America's primary and secondary education, respectively, it also expressed the IDB's own proclivities. Felipe Herrera, energetic president from 1960 to 1970, repeatedly proclaimed the IDB as "the bank of the Latin American university" as well as "the bank of ideas" and "something more than a bank."[15]

Thus the IDB would be easily the weightiest external financier of Latin American higher education. Envisioning the large size of IDB funds, the head of Ford's Latin America division left the foundation for the bank in 1961 and would not be disappointed (Wolf i-1). In the 1960s the IDB gave loans to more than 115 universities, representing each nation and one-third of the region's enrollments—no profile in highly selective giving. In 1997, when the IDB proclaimed its major recommitment to higher education, it pointedly distanced itself from the breadth of its prior role.[16]

Other Foundations

The Rockefeller Foundation is the clear second choice of a foundation active in Latin American universities. With Ford and Carnegie, it long was one of the big three foundations, which were also the big three for international work. As recently as 1986, just six foundations accounted for two-thirds of the $1.8 billion spent internationally by U.S. nonprofits.[17]

In several respects, Rockefeller blazed the philanthropic path that Ford and others would emulate. It has operated internationally since its 1913 creation by John D. Rockefeller to serve worldwide well-being, conceived as compatible with both true development and international capitalism. A post–World War II decrease in international priorities notably spared the university. The cold war era also meant a shift from Europe to the Third World, including Latin America, a region boosted in the 1950s by foundation president Dean Rusk, later U.S. secretary of state. In the 1970s, Ford, Rockefeller, and Carnegie alone accounted for perhaps 90 percent of the funds spent by the leading forty-three U.S. foundations in Latin America. The Rockefeller Foundation had a strong higher education focus. From its inception through 1950 it was the giant in Third World university development. In the last half of the 1950s Rockefeller was spending about $10 million a year on twenty or more Third World universities.[18] Given Ford's late start in Latin America and the IDB's delayed creation, Rockefeller and AID were the two main external actors for Latin American universities in the 1950s.

Rockefeller established the foundation emphasis on a better world through the discovery of knowledge and its professionally administered application to practical problems. This meant special attention to universities, research centers, and libraries both in its declared higher education priority and in its related priorities of public health and medicine, science, agriculture, and eventually social science. The foundation gave over 10,000 leadership development awards in the Third World by 1970. These had a massive impact, not least on ensuing institutional development projects. Both the scholarship and institutional targets, both often operating over extended periods, were designated as "seed" operations, models entrusted to have a big secondary impact.[19]

The Kellogg Foundation, established in 1930, ranks as the third most important foundation. Without making education per se its priority, it stressed the application of knowledge in health fields (including dental) and agronomy, with related interests in tropical biology, forestry, economics, and business. Since 1941, Kellogg has given many scholarships for graduate study abroad, stressing leadership, including for rectors. Latin America accounted for 60 percent of the foundation's international expenditures, which accounted for 17 percent of the foundation's nearly half-billion dollar total by 1980.[20]

The other large and venerable foundation in Third World higher education is Carnegie. Teacher education, university development, and libraries have been priorities. But Carnegie efforts back to the 1920s concentrated on Commonwealth nations and especially on Africa, though some Latin Americans received scholarships to top U.S. universities.[21] Additional foundations have played more limited or recent roles. Guggenheim has given elite scholarships since 1922. Tinker, since 1959, has contributed to national research and U.S.–Latin American conferences. The Lilly Endowment has given to places such as Mexico's University of the Americas. The MacArthur Foundation epitomizes new foundation concentration on Mexico, though not mostly on higher education. Hewlett did initially turn to higher education as it concentrated on Mexico.[22] The Mellon Foundation has given in areas such as library development.

Among corporations, philanthropy was much more limited. Exceptions include the United Fruit Company role in establishing the private Pan American School of Agriculture, El Zamorano, in Honduras. The lack of a corporate role might suggest that self-interest has been inadequate incentive for external giving to Latin American universities (and thus that foundation giving was indeed philanthropic), but critics could argue that an imperialist power structure division of labor leaves foundations to spearhead the private sector end of the university effort.

Foundations have also funded other U.S. nonprofits active in matters related to Latin American universities. For example, Carnegie, Ford, Tinker, Mellon, and Hewlett funded the Joint Committee on Latin American Studies of the SSRC (Social Science Research Council) and ACLS (American Council of Learned Societies), thus sponsoring research and conferences (Coatsworth 1989). Then there are nonprofit associations of U.S. universities, such as the Midwest Universities Consortium for International Activities, Inc., which has managed hundreds of millions of dollars in overseas development contracts. Drawing funds from Ford, other foundations, and government agencies, it has offered technical assistance at leading agricultural centers.[23]

The preceding sketch of U.S. foundations is a far cry from a systematic assessment of their correspondence to a philanthropic change model. Nonetheless, it provides indications of corresponding elements. The foundations have often bet on knowledge and expertise to promote a vision of development through higher education and related fields of research and knowledge application. Measured by tasks and recipients, they have been highly selective in their targeting and have usually operated outside the public university mainstream. Indeed, within higher education most foundations have been more selective than even Ford, though that must be considered against their lesser weight in higher education.

Other U.S. Government Agencies

The most relevant bilateral agency outside AID has been the United States Information Agency (USIA), created in 1952. Its concentration on scholarships and other exchanges makes it resemble some of the secondary foundations. The USIA has handled much of the Fulbright program, including its binational committees.[24] The Council on International Exchanges of Scholars, which helps run the Fulbright scholar program, is a nonprofit under the USIA.

No clear-cut dichotomy separates exchanges and institutional development. Well-trained university people are crucial to institutional development. Moreover, USIA-sponsored linkages (called "affiliations" since the early 1980s) partly resemble prior AID linkage programs explicitly aimed at Third World university development. Some Fulbright officials further acknowledge that, when their program was something of a congressional sacred cow, they took liberties in stretching academic exchanges toward institutional development.[25]

LASPAU (the Latin American Scholarship Program of the American Universities, later renamed LASPAU: Academic and Professional Programs for the Americas) fits into our analysis, though it is not itself a donor. It resembles the Institute for International Education, but is mostly limited to Latin America. A nonprofit affiliated with Harvard University and governed by an independent Inter-American board of trustees, since 1964 LASPAU has administered scholarships for many organizations including the IDB, World Bank, and Latin American agencies. During the golden age, however, it administered overwhelmingly for AID and thereafter for the USIA. LASPAU's funding also was overwhelmingly AID in the golden age, followed by a mix including AID and the USIA and then varied contractors (personal correspondence from LASPAU's Peter Bryant 6/21/87). Although LASPAU scholarships cannot be counted as government's own participant training, they constitute government investment in the region's long-term faculty development. In dealing with LASPAU data, we deal with both AID and the USIA.

Through the mid-1980s LASPAU funds might still be considered about 95 percent for faculty development.[26] Although activities have since diversified, in the golden age LASPAU concentrated on faculty development scholarships and their place in promoting university development. AID wanted that, and LASPAU's organizational culture strongly pushed it. It was a "LASPAU program, AID-funded" as opposed to the subsequent "USIA program, LASPAU-administered" (Tyler i-1). Identified since the 1980s as Fulbright scholars, grantees were earlier identified as LASPAU scholars.

Other U.S. government agencies whose major roles lie elsewhere have played roles for Latin American higher education. The National Science Foundation (NSF) has operated with limited funds but has gained praise for its cooperative scientific research. The Peace Corps worked with Latin American universities starting in 1962, though it soon ran into problems with the region's student movements (Mankiewicz 1965). The Inter-American Foundation (IAF) and the National Endowment for Democracy (NED) are further examples of agencies with indirect roles for higher education. The IAF would, starting in 1972, disburse a budget on a par with Ford's in Latin America; the thrust was grassroots development, but this has allowed for help for junior scholars and research.

Consideration especially of the USIA and LASPAU underscores the importance of another vital actor: the U.S. university.[27] We treat the U.S. university largely as model but additionally as partner. As partner it was a "receiver" of grants for exchanges or contracts for projects abroad; it was a "giver" when it put in its own human or financial resources for technical assistance, collaborative research, scholarships, and tuition waivers.

In sum, most of the additions to AID on the bilateral side intensify the profile of U.S. assistance targeted to partners selected for their potential to use expertise and extra resources. Scholarships, typical of foundation efforts, have been the most significant means. Efforts could thus be simultaneously modest in total funds and yet ambitious regarding individuals reached and the hopes placed upon them.

Other Multilateral Agencies

The largest of all givers of educational assistance since the early 1970s has been the World Bank. Hatched with the IMF from the Bretton Woods conference, the bank came slowly to educational leadership. Until 1963 its limited social undertakings hardly included higher and other education, and then mostly to complement its projects outside education. Subsequently, however, even the roughly 6 percent of its total expenditures going to education has been enough to make it prominent.[28] Like the IDB, it has given low interest education loans and credits through a special agency, providing flexibility and a grant component. Also like the IDB, it has given mostly in large projects lasting years and concentrating initially on equipment and construction, though then also on technical assistance.

The World Bank's educational and regional foci have varied over time. Until 1971, higher education accounted for 23 percent, secondary education 72 percent, but then primary plus especially informal education took the bulk.[29] By 1974, the bank's research unit argued that higher education had too large a share, when judged by equity and rates of return (Psacharopoulos i). But higher education expenditures have remained large, and by the 1990s the "anti–higher education" argument was largely beaten back. Latin America has participated in surges of interest, notably in science and technology, and in recent years in higher education. But in the golden era, notwithstanding programs in Brazil, Peru, and a few other places, the World Bank basically ceded the Latin American higher education terrain to the IDB.[30]

The United Nations Development Program (UNDP), formed from two prior units, is among relevant UN agencies. Education is a small part of its work, and higher education is only a part of that. But if we add science and technology, regional development, and especially agriculture, higher education–related activity is more impressive. Also, the UNDP has joined with governments in higher education institution building and has given many scholarships, emphasizing science and technology.[31] Its activities have been appreciated at places like the Dominican Republic's Catholic university.

UNESCO (United Nations Educational, Scientific, and Cultural Organization) is a UN agency with an education agenda central to its basic human needs agenda. At the same time, its higher education activities have approximated those of an international foundation. UNESCO has dealt with scholarships, graduate education, integration of research and teaching and of research and practice, technical assistance to other agencies as well as to universities such as Chile's Concepción and Católica of Valparaíso, and promotion of "horizontal cooperation" among developing countries (Lavados 1988: 63; Maheu 1965: 130–34). The foundation parallel holds for Organization of American States (OAS) activity as well. Scholarships and horizontal cooperation have figured prominently. Rather than broad university development projects, typical have been specific efforts at curriculum development, pedagogy, distance education, information systems, and the like. OAS officials emphasize how much has been done with little money as the OAS has often entered as catalyst or pivotal facilitator before, after, or alongside the big-money actors, for the study, evaluation, conference, or "people" part of undertakings.[32] Like foundations and the IDB, the OAS has provided a stamp of legitimacy based on its elevation of academic quality and political neutrality over bureaucratic and partisan forces.

Overall Giving: How Much and How

Complementing the preceding identification of donors, the chapter now turns to certain key aspects of overall giving. First, it sketches gross financial outlays to widen the quantitative picture on giving. After that, three sections analyze the efforts associated with the finance. One considers the major retreat in the mid-1970s, tempered by adaptation and some subsequent revival. The two other sections explore the volatile and controversial issue of control. They identify what the overall giving patterns suggest about how much the donors fit the philanthropic ideal typical means of influence via voluntary giving, selectivity, incentives, and cooperative partnership rather than imposition, force, and ongoing supervision.

Gross Figures

Several quantitative indicators on educational assistance help map the effort and relative share of different givers. They also help show trends over time.[33]

Taken together, donors have given ample educational assistance to the Third World.[34] During the main years of our study, bilateral sources accounted for 60 percent or more of educational assistance, while multilaterals rose past 20 to about 25 percent, and private donors slipped from perhaps 20 to 10 percent.[35] As expected, education has represented a much smaller share of multilateral than foundation spending.

The mix of educational assistance by region has also varied by funding source. Latin America trailed Africa especially in the bilateral category. It also trailed Asia in gross amounts, though not in per capita terms. The weight of assistance versus domestic education funds has been moderately lower for Latin America than for the Third World in general and Africa in particular and nothing like the weight that international philanthropy soon would have at Latin America's leading private research centers.[36] Of course, Latin America's share of the education assistance pie rises significantly when the focus is U.S. giving, including its private, public, and multilateral components.

Specifically regarding higher education's share—of both education and total assistance—our examination of individual donors has already noted several key points. First, higher education is prominent. Second, how prominent depends greatly on definition; much expenditure listed under agriculture, health, science and technology, business administration, and so forth could be added to higher education insofar as research, extension, and training appear (see appendix E). Third is sharp variation among individual donors as well as types of donors (foundation, bilateral, multinational). Fourth is foundation leadership in making higher education a priority in giving for development.

Retreat and Revival

The overall downturn in U.S. assistance that ensued was disproportionately large for education, higher education's share within education, and Latin America's share of the total. The Peruvian example illustrates how great the decline could be: the huge and influential university assistance of the 1950s and 1960s diminished to about 1 percent of total public university expenditures in the 1970s, then to 0.1 percent in the 1980s.[37] The golden age of university assistance for Latin America had ended. Analyzing the closing curtain and epilogue helps mark the bounds and context of our study.

Ford cut its total international expenditures by more than a third in the 1970s. By 1978, its international educational expenditures fell to a fifth of their 1965 peak. University modernization, the category quintessentially associated with golden age goals of major institutional and national development, plummeted from its $4.7 million peak in 1965 to 2.0 by 1974 and 0.2 in 1975.[38] For Latin America, Ford's education staff dwindled from ten to two, while university assistance fell by more than two-thirds during the 1970s (see table 2.3). The 1980–84 quinquennium brought university projects for just six nations, totaling only a half million dollars outside Brazil. Moreover, most of the funds were for research projects, policy evaluation, or social causes (e.g., to the Catholic University of Sao Paulo's program on legal services and reform in poor urban communities). Increasingly, funds were not *for* the university as much as *through* the university. Such evolution resembled Ford's growing financing of freestanding research centers more than its prior university development assistance.[39] Ford's archives are replete with documents detailing the phasing out of individual university development projects begun in the golden age.

Table 2.3 The Rise and Fall of Assistance to Latin American Higher Education by Three Donors, 1950–84 (in thousands of dollars)

	FFᵃ	Projects	AID	Projects	IDBᵇ	Projects
1950–54	—	—	$1,731	10		
1955–59	—	—	$10,472	34		
1960–64	$20,872	89	$30,532	44	$29,350	21
1965–69	$26,493	105	$49,227	30	$82,360	27
1970–74	$18,436	157	$68,401	21	$123,822	15
1975–79	$5,447	123	$19,747	6	$320,600	12
1980–84	$2,368	57	$12,341	4	$331,200	10
Total	$73,616	531	$192,451	149	$887,332	85

Sources: See appendixes E, H, I, and J.
Note: Where sources include nations outside our twenty, notably in the English-speaking Caribbean, as well as Puerto Rico, we delete them.
   ᵃOnly university assistance.
   ᵇIncludes three IDB categories: higher education, science and technology, and student credit (loans).

At its 1965 peak, AID engaged in seventy-four Third World university projects. In 1978, it engaged in ten. AID turned away from higher education to informal, media technology, and employment activities. Its inflation-adjusted educational expenditures by 1980 were half what they were in the 1960s, or a fourth by a narrower definition of education. Though some in AID encouraged U.S. universities to lobby against the policy change, AID's prior commitment to university development was severed.[40] Table 2.3 shows the precipitous mid-1970s drop in funding to Latin American higher education by AID and Ford.

IDB deliberations presaged a parallel retreat. Its documents proclaimed that the time for building things like university administrative buildings was over. After the higher education category captured 99 percent of IDB education loans in the early years, it captured a minority of funds by the mid-1970s, as table 2.2 showed, though table 2.3 previewed our explanation below about how that retreat was qualified. The IDB turned more to primary school access and then woefully inadequate secondary school capacity. From 1985 to 1992, the IDB made just three loans in the category it labels higher education.[41]

Why the sudden retreat? Donors' cutbacks stemmed mostly from common factors. Much related to major political developments.

Many factors arose on the receiving end. Host governments sometimes assumed costs once shouldered by assistance; more often, massive enrollment expansion outstripped what donors thought they could appropriately handle.

The first development could fulfill an ideal typical goal whereas the second marked more of a philanthropic insufficiency or failure, as targeted recipients had not led the desired reform of the overall system. At the same time, key Latin American groups politically rejected assistance. Silvert (1976: 8) writes of the virtual expulsion of Ford and other donors from the region's public universities by 1970. Sánchez (1973: 114), exaggerating, describes a general Latin American rejection of U.S. assistance. Where such opposition did not directly push donors out, it raised the risks and costs of their operations.[42] Any notion of international reform partnership, central to our ideal type of voluntary assistance, took a beating.

Obviously, too, from the giving end, donors were dissatisfied. This harks back to the conventional view of failure that arose. Heralded initially as the "second decade of development," the 1970s stalled in despair. Contrary to liberal tenets of exporting progress, donors learned that good aspects of development would not all go together neatly.[43] To some the assistance experience suggested something closer to the opposite, a dangerous and often deadly interrelationship among obstacles to progress.

Just as the golden age showed an affinity for higher education, so the reaction against it was acidic. Once heralded as pivotal to national development, the university was now often dismissed as irrelevant or worse.[44] A salient example concerned equity and finance. Liberal development thinking had generally been favorable to expansion, even ecstatic about it, seeing it as progressive, a notion backed by human capital theory. But higher education was increasingly seen as a budgetary burden on the general public to bring benefits concentrated only on the enrolled minority. The World Bank in particular depicted inequitable effects from expansion, in large part because public universities were free for students from privileged backgrounds. Equity and the reduction of poverty were increasingly taken as a grand failure of early assistance and the priority for future assistance. This helped push all our major donors away from universities as it also tilted Ford and especially AID away from Latin America. Donors' disillusion brought fundamental change in policy, not mere change in "technique."[45]

Among U.S. donors, factors originating at home also contributed to the more skeptical look at international assistance. Recession diminished funds and pressure rose to spend them on problems at home. Such pressure greatly affected Ford and AID, as well as Rockefeller. Compared with politics in other donor nations, U.S. assistance has been especially vulnerable to public opinion because of Congress's role in authorizing expenditures (Rice 1996: 69). The rise of conservatism and its skepticism or hostility regarding much foreign assistance, including educational assistance, played a further role. This reversed much of the golden age logic reviewed in Packenham's (1973) *Liberal America and the Third World*. President Nixon, unlike Kennedy, wanted to lower the U.S. profile in Latin America and turn more to trade than aid.[46]

The simultaneous turn away from historic efforts by all the major donors undercuts a cherished philanthropic claim—that voluntary donors defy conventional practices and move against the grain. Assistance to Latin American higher education is a clear case of the disillusionment and retreat that follow great expectations for change, as found in the literature on international assistance, development, and domestic policy. On the other hand, the downturn underscores assistance's voluntary nature. Donors were not tied to the ongoing commitments that normally limit domestic government's room for maneuver. Furthermore, donors retreated to a scale and form of activity arguably more consistent with careful, selective approaches than those of the golden era.[47]

And in fact, certain impressions notwithstanding, there ensued a retreat rather than a withdrawal. While some other donors showed substantial continuity or even increased activity, each of the three major donors remained active on a revamped, reduced scale. Each of the three pursued a different, partial alternative to prior action.

True to philanthropic tendencies, including perhaps an inclination toward private targets, Ford found mostly a higher education alternative: private research centers, for which it became the single leading funder (Levy 1996). It also provided many scholarships, such as for Central Americans and Mexicans in the social sciences. Its funding of travel, conferences, and research at NGOs (nongovernmental organizations), along with traditional research funding in agriculture, all amounted to partial support for higher education personnel or institutions, though no longer for university development per se.[48]

By contrast, AID is the donor that most turned away from higher education. Yet even AID maintained textbook and other programs, especially in Central America, especially related to the Kissinger Commission and the cold war. It continued myriad other programs that universities wanted, such as equipment for laboratories, computers and techniques for registration, and library development. These generally reflected a profile of cooperation but without the golden age pretense at higher education transformation; training for private sector development (e.g., AID # 5150212 in Costa Rica) was more about economic transformation. Additionally, AID maintained its advanced and participant training linked to its other development goals, especially in fields like management and agriculture. EARTH, College of Agriculture for the Humid Tropical Region, is a rare example of a massive institutional undertaking after the golden age. Launched late in the 1980s as a private institution based on intergovernmental accords, and thus as a private-public venture, EARTH dedicated itself to high-quality undergraduate education. More typical were linkage programs, showing some continuity with the golden age. No longer totally funding LASPAU, AID still provided a share.[49] For its part, LASPAU increased its budget, offsetting the U.S. government cutbacks in part by cultivating relationships with Venezuelan and other contractors interested in human resource development.

Although the IDB stopped giving much to "university development," it greatly increased funding of science and technology programs (as tables 2.2 and 2.3 indicated) that usually passed large sums into the universities, as was also done in agriculture. For example, 46 percent of the IDB's loan to Colombia's science and technology council, 1983–88, went to universities. With science and technology, higher education broadly defined still captured half of IDB education expenditures.[50] Whether in science and technology or in higher education per se, the few loans tended to be large, such as the $63.2 million to Brazil's University of Sao Paulo, 1987, for extensive activities reminiscent of old times. So, amid the general retreat by all major donors, the IDB assumed a more preponderant share of the burden. Also, like AID though less than Ford, the IDB has increased its funding to narrower institutions such as freestanding applied research centers, both private and public, and it has awarded scholarships connected to its science and technology projects in countries such as Colombia and Mexico. In any event, IDB's overall funding of higher education kept increasing through our period of coverage, though in the early 1980s it dropped in real terms (see the GDP price multiplier in appendix A).

The conclusion that the donor retreat from peak university assistance is partial and qualified is reinforced by a subsequent revival. Of course, the revival entails less expectation and activity than in the peak period. Perhaps the pendulum that swung from exaggerated to underestimated importance of higher education in development now swings to an intermediate point. A common argument is that a reinvigorated social agenda, including higher education, is crucial to economic openings, political democratization, and a knowledgeable society.[51] Higher education is neither the golden age leader nor marginal when it comes to overall development.

Bilateral agencies that had soured on higher education assistance because it "did not have the intended impact" showed rekindled interest by the 1990s (Chapman and Claffey 1998). AID collaborates with U.S. higher education associations in linkage programs.[52] Interest also revived at foundations (Coombe 1991) and most powerfully at multilateral agencies. UNESCO sponsors conferences and publishes policy papers that accord a central development role to higher education in a new internationalized context (1995).

By far the most important surge has come at the World Bank, easily preeminent among assistance agencies. This is a reversal on two fronts. First, it has meant greater commitment to social and educational matters in general and higher education in particular, after a period of some frank hostility to higher education. "Tertiary education" is proclaimed vital to a "knowledge society." Education jumped from 4 to nearly 10 percent of World Bank lending from the mid-1980s to the mid-1990s, by which time the bank was investing roughly a half billion dollars a year in Third World higher education. Second, the bank reversed its deference to the IDB regarding Latin American universities. Its fresh action included Argentina, Brazil, Chile, Mexico, and Venezuela. Even a fairly modest effort by the giant bank can be large and influential. For the Third World, some would find cause to denounce an excessive involvement in the sense of pressure for reform in finance and evaluation.[53] Yet the actual projects appear to involve considerable partnership between the bank and domestic agencies.

Among the three principal donors from the golden age, the IDB remains weightiest.[54] It has undertaken to invest billions of higher education dollars within a few years as part of a commitment to spend as much on "social" as "economic" development programs. Accordingly, the IDB has issued its first "strategy paper" for higher education policy (IDB 1997). Although the IDB contemplates no return to widespread assistance for university growth and development, with the nearly exclusive favoring of higher over other education, it disassociates itself from powerful currents that have bashed or marginalized higher education or opposed its growth. It praises key impacts of prior assistance and identifies many efforts that merit resuscitation. A particular point of interest (consistent with golden age interest) is interinstitutional differentiation, now with renewed hope for two-year institutions.

Whatever the future holds, the heart of our investigation lies with the golden age, before the gloomy retreat. It is back to the golden age that we now turn.

Overstepping?

Within the general outlines of how much is given and for what, a major controversy surrounds how funds are given: is imposition or selective partnership the more appropriate characterization? This basic issue for assistance and politics is especially sensitive here because higher education is intensively about molding people, including leaders, and ideas, and because the international dimension raises concerns of dependency and sovereignty. This section considers aspects of the charge that donors abusively overstep their bounds. Like the ensuing section on partnership, it tries to identify patterns found in documentary, site-based, and interview material.

The following three subsections consider arrogant overreach in general, the Rockefeller case, and counterevidence.

Arrogant overreach. With its transforming goals, the philanthropic ideal type naturally moves against the status quo with a reformist agenda. If there were nothing terribly wrong, why embark on major assistance? An interesting tract by a leading foundation analyst was entitled "The University versus National Development in Spanish America" (Harrison n.d.). Moreover, a measure of arrogance is nearly implicit in the assistance notion of making "them" more like "us," as in moving the Latin American closer to the U.S. university. To Oteiza (1993: 73–74), for example, that movement represented a frontal Alliance for Progress assault in the university realm.

The question of whether donors go beyond such almost given aggressiveness to attacks that are inappropriately arrogant and harsh is partly a subjective matter and also depends on how one views the accuracy of those attacks. But disrespect, linked to arrogance and condescension, defies the notion of partnership. Furthermore, it can lead to indiscriminate rejection of what exists and to attempts to impose wholesale substitutes based on external models. That in turn would indicate dependency, coercion, and other charges about assistance and indeed about an overall demeaning, smug, patronizing U.S. attitude and approach to relations with Latin America historically, through the Alliance for Progress, and ever since (Schoultz 1998).

We find disrespectful characterizations by donors to be neither the rule nor the rare exception when it comes to Latin American universities. Foundation documents vary by individual consultant. Unusual are statements like Enarson's (1962: 2) on Central American universities: "These are sick universities struggling to survive in sick societies." The foundations did not usually disparage Latin American universities thoroughly, though they lacked a deep appreciation of their culture (Harrison i-1), just as they historically brought attitudes of superiority along with their good intentions (Cueto 1994). A rather benign characterization might hold for the IDB, aware of its status as a member-based organization. Dismissive postures were more common at AID. AID documents mixed talk of cooperation with harsh language (e.g., AID #540101 on Colombia and #52767 on Peru). Not unusual was a characterization of Brazilian institutions as rife with "administrative incompetence, over-centralized authority, restricted flows of information, archaic methodologies, and untrained and uninspired civil servants" (AID # 5120122, subproject 11). A persistent view was that the Latin American university is its own worst enemy, with mind-boggling inefficiencies (Method i-2) or that it trains people just to be lazy employees rather than enterprising employers (Taylor i-1). As noted in the introductory chapter, best known were the portrayals by Rudolph Atcon. Consultant to Brazil, Chile, and Honduras in the 1950s, Atcon was a U.S. State Department envoy concerned with education's place in the Alliance for Progress. Prone to overgeneralization, he was seen by critics as a pusher of Americanization with "crude frankness" (González 1982: 333; Jaramillo 1963: 170). Atcon (1966: 85) referred to students as the biggest "sinners" and argued that short of a comprehensive overhaul, Latin America's universities would remain perverse institutions either avoiding or squandering technical assistance. Yet consultant George Waggoner (1967: 48) more moderately found it best to "disregard Latin American politics and nationalism in the universities and concentrate all our attention on the educational problem."

Most important is whether harsh judgments, vituperatively and nastily expressed or not, converted into substantive policy. Many observers, including donor officials, believe they did. Some denounce a basic assistance goal of replacing the Latin American university with a U.S. model (Arnove 1980a: 307). Where the external model appears more as imposed alien force than guiding orientation, it defies the ideal type of voluntary action. Even Ford officials reportedly too often said, "This is the pattern. How can you fit?"

without due regard for the dislocations and overload produced by such pushiness (Tierney i; Dye i). Ford trusted the Latin American less than the West Indian or African university to manage itself (Wolf i-3). AID end-of-tour reports sometimes proudly refer to AID involvement in university politics (e.g., helping elect a cooperative official at the University of Guayaquil in the mid-1960s).[55] At least some evidence, then, supports the political critique that donors vilified, patronized, meddled, and pushed in ways inconsistent with the ideal type of philanthropic support.

Clearer and more common excesses concerned expectations. It is difficult or arbitrary to determine exactly when that defies the ideal type, for philanthropy ideally mixes prudence with optimism and boldness. But it is not difficult to see ways in which donors were imprudently zealous. That is part of what characterizes the golden age of exporting progress. As noted in the introductory chapter, exuberance led to underestimation of obstacles. Formidable bottlenecks could supposedly be smashed through applied knowledge (Ward 1974: xv; Kaimowitz 1992: 203–06).

Grand goals sometimes translated into massive programs which, whether ultimately helpful or not, defied assistance claims of carefully managed change. The point, which holds for the zenith of institutional development programs generally, was evident at universities. University development projects replaced traditional foundation targeting of particular individuals or units. The Ford-financed University of Chile project with the University of California has been called unique in the annals of interuniversity cooperation for its grandiose conception and scope.[56] The IDB's project at the neighboring Catholic university stretched from plant enlargement to qualitative changes in curriculum, methods, and ties to socioeconomic and scientific development. Illustrative of AID projects was the 1968 university component of an education sector loan to Paraguay. It highlighted the national university in reforms covering faculty development, central library and other facilities, space utilization, student services, and efforts to bolster liberal arts and social science in the service of the nation's social problems.[57]

Rockefeller's overreaching. The Rockefeller Foundation provides the best case to examine regarding overreach. This is because it is where the switch from traditional, careful philanthropy to a much broader institutional development approach was sharpest. The desire to replace "scatterization" with a more concentrated effort at selected institutions lay within the logic of foundation giving. But the switch was basically motivated by frustration over the failure of earlier undertakings, mostly scholarships, to transform higher education or society as anticipated or as demanded by the foundation's leaders.[58] So when ideal typical means fail to produce their projected ambitious results, they may yield to means that reach beyond the ideal typical.

Rockefeller's three main Latin American sites for its University Development Program were Colombia's del Valle university, the National University of Chile (UCH), and Brazil's Federal University of Bahia. The first two stories are interesting for showing overreach even where institutions were far more attractive than typical public universities, as elaborated for the UCH in the next chapter. The third story is interesting for Rockefeller's overreach right into the public higher education mainstream.

Colombia's del Valle had received ample Rockefeller support in medicine, which helped build praiseworthy results. The foundation then wanted to use that base to drive toward community medicine and overall university development. It therefore selected del Valle despite warnings from perceptive staff about its inferiority to the private Los Andes university in criteria traditionally crucial to foundation decisions: overall quality, the academic level in fields pertinent to the project, support from a progressive, local elite, and freedom from rapid growth and politicization. Rockefeller's multimillion dollar investment would produce little institutional impact at del Valle, especially in the social sciences, while it alienated the bypassed universities and influenced Peru's elite Cayetano Heredia medical university not to follow a conventional Rockefeller public health road. Similarly, Rockefeller reached out to the UCH, citing its own prior work there in several fields, but without a clear-cut case over Chile's Catholic university or the AID-supported University of Concepción. Again cautionary warnings would prove prescient as soon-aborted efforts ran up against both uneven university quality and political imperatives to spread largesse across units.[59]

The Brazilian case shows further how Rockefeller abandoned its hallmark care to settle on a recipient that failed to meet its traditionally rigorous criteria for selection. Led by the University of Sao Paulo and its "Rockefeller school" in medicine, Brazil trailed only China as a Rockefeller Third World recipient since 1917. But the University of Sao Paulo was deemed too advanced. At the same time, it had apparently failed in its seeding mission: the foundation could find no sound alternative for expanded university development efforts. Foundation ambition increased with the 1972 turn from the University Development Program to the Education for Development Program, emphasizing contributions to society. Pressured for greater attention to equity by rising voices including the ministry's and Ford's, Rockefeller rejected more mixed candidates to reach all the way to Bahia in Brazil's impoverished Northeast. It swallowed an overly sanguine image of how much the nation's higher education reform had transformed such institutions. By 1979, it would terminate parts of its $10 million project, producing too little in research and graduate education to offset disastrous political quarrels, failures in community medicine, and possibly a negative impact on Ford's and Kellogg's activities.[60]

Without doubt, the Rockefeller experience shows overreach beyond careful, selective philanthropy during the peak moment of assistance. Yet three fundamental points limit this conclusion and can be generalized beyond the

Rockefeller case: (1) the brevity of the peak overreach period; (2) the mixture of selectivity with breadth even at the peak; and (3) the relative lack of donor control over recipients, a point left for the subsequent section on partners.

Before its university development program, Rockefeller rarely considered projects aimed directly at whole institutions, at least outside a few specialized private ones. Instead, it focused on its chosen disciplines or fields and undertook to find individuals, not universities, with world-class potential. It worked with the university more to accomplish those ends than to develop the university institution per se. And the foundation deviated from that pattern less in Latin America than in Asia and Africa (Harrison i-1; Moock i). Moreover, most foundations, such as Kellogg, never deviated much from their focused course (Aguilar i).

However deviant the overreaching, it did not last long. In fact, many who criticize their foundations for overreaching also criticize them for becoming frustrated too soon, belying foundation claims of long-term commitment. Rockefeller, which had worked in Chile since 1930 and especially 1956 and did not launch its University Development Program until 1964, cut it back in 1968, and closed it within a few years more.[61]

The second limitation on Rockefeller's overreach is that considerable selectivity blended with grand institutional development even during the peak period. For all its new scope and zeal, Rockefeller's development program employed discriminating criteria to reject many more universities, even of the small fraction it considered, than it targeted. Its uncharacteristic looseness was manifested in targeting institutions that normally would have been bypassed, but not in giving to many institutions at once. Nor did Rockefeller undertake to build any new Third World universities after World War II. And whatever the selected universities lacked, they appeared at least partly atypical in their potential as models for others. Furthermore, most projects still aimed in practice at either a particular unit or at several units and only in more limited or nebulous fashion at the whole institution. And insofar as they were institutional projects, they normally embarked from well-honed fields of foundation experience. Then too, when developments failed to follow the foundation script, losses were cut; the fact that much authorized money was unspent is a sign of both failure and limits to the failure.[62]

Counterevidence. Thus the Rockefeller case offers counterevidence as well as evidence regarding overreach. And just as easily as the confirming evidence, the counterevidence could be generalized beyond the Rockefeller case.

For example, regarding the brevity of the peak, even where Ford evaluated its most ambitious programs rather positively, it made clear that it would never do them again. Even IDB president Herrera, university enthusiast, emphasized that peak assistance could not go much beyond the 1960s.[63] Regarding limitations during the peak itself, even the Chile-California convenio, the largest single foundation undertaking at a Latin American university, involved little activity in first-degree education, the heart and bulk of the university. Nor did it undertake much in social science, new administrative policy, or physical construction. Probably no donor truly built a Latin American university.[64]

Even the relatively large efforts sprang from donor views that usually were not all encompassing or wildly arrogant. Expanded donor activities often emerged less as naive pursuit of easy immediate goals than as comprehensible gambles to try to get beyond the positive but limited results of more selective action. In other words, donors confronted the philanthropic dilemma of what to do when limited action produces too little while greater action is too risky. Almost all interviewed ex-officials had soberly identified problems that they hoped to bypass rather than directly attack and fix. Their concrete aim, as translated into specific projects, was typically improvement rather than utopia or a replicated U.S. university.[65] All this should become clearer as subsequent chapters look at particular undertakings.

In fact, some perceptive observers question how much donors truly operated from external models even when the U.S. research university was the vague model. AID worked through U.S. universities and lacked its own strong staff to formulate ideas and plans. Ford exploded on the scene perhaps too quickly to evolve a true philosophy. Kalman Silvert, revered in Latin America for his Ford tenure, would reflect on how the foundation had bent over so far to avoid ethnocentrism that it did not do enough to educate Latin Americans about Europe or the United States. The IDB responded in part to member-state and recipient institution requests and had only a small evaluation unit rather than a major research unit like the World Bank's (D'Etigny i-3). IDB veterans report criticism for the organization's lack of direction over recipients, in contrast with World Bank conditionality (Mehedff i-2). And interviews suggest that even AID, notwithstanding exceptions like those noted above, usually proceeded with respect, modesty, and an experimental approach directly targeted on improving what was in place.[66]

Rather than the absence of an export model, what seems consistent with the evidence is a model used with reserve, sparingly, and sometimes adroitly. A U.S. model might exist as a guiding force operationalized only selectively. Sometimes it operates even when not cited as such, as in Chile's donor-sponsored creation of two-year colleges.[67] All this fits our notion of a mostly *implicit* model. The model could be explicit sporadically, for particular features pursued in particular places, or at the most general level, as a prestigious flag of inspiration. But neither the U.S. university nor any particular manifestation of it was in practice the blueprint for most projects. It was not something to impose in place of the status quo. Instead, it was a reference point to be invoked where feasible and with a rather vague hope or vision that feasible changes would move Latin America toward the model over the long run.

The idea of an implicit model promoted cautiously gains force as the next three chapters identify a range of academic and administrative features of the U.S. model that were *not* actively pursued. Already, however, important limitations are evident in what donors pushed even in the golden age of university assistance.

Partners

Further reason to limit the critique of assistance overreach and political domination comes from convincing evidence that giving was in cooperation with recipients. As this contradicts much work on dependency in education-related assistance, it complements later work that highlighted partnership in such assistance.[68] However grand the transforming goals, they were mostly shared by donors' recipients. Thus the ex-rector of Chile's Austral university found "absolute coincidence" and total respect between the IDB and his administration and even that the IDB did not reject a thing (Thayer i). On the contrary, the IDB realized it lacked pertinent substantive expertise and left matters to Austral and its Western Kentucky University counterpart.

The main partnership patterns fit the ideal type of philanthropy. Donors usually do not take partners in mainstream higher education activity but instead in selected reform-oriented pockets. Admittedly, the mix of recipient choice and donor steering is difficult to discern, even in the few detailed studies of one institution, but it is a mix (Magnusson 1970: 310–11). While we can identify the principal aspects of donor control, those come with evidence of limitation on that control. Moreover, the control itself largely follows the form anticipated in the ideal type, for that type postulates certain types of control (which are limited) rather than an absence of control. The four ensuing subsections analyze front-end control, mutual matching for reform, sequential patterns, and cooperative funding.

Front-end control. The philanthropic norm places donor control mostly at the front end of the process, in donor choice over what to fund. Voluntary contributors determine how much to give, as well as to whom. Although even these amounts are often fixed in negotiation, hopeful recipients lack the legal standing to demand support or, usually, the political standing to force it. Donors have the authority.

AID documents refer to the agency's legitimate "deobligation" when recipients do not fulfill their end of the bargain.[69] Individual IDB project reports show that most loans were much lower than requested: from $10 to $5 million for Argentine national universities, $4.9 to $2.3 million for the University of Chile, $4.8 to $3.3 million for Costa Rica's technical institute, $1.5 to $1 million for the Dominican Republic's Catholic university, and so forth. Ford grant files show much the same. Moreover, donors used renewable grants. This tool, rather than one-shot grants, partly reflects a desire to increase political leverage (Magat 1979: 42).

Our documents also show that cuts often fall in ways that alter recipients' priorities. Here we reach a gray area between philanthropic control, which has much to do with incentives and disincentives, and a forceful imposition that goes beyond the ideal type. The IDB cut the Argentine request in half by tossing out the humanities, law, and philosophy as well as architecture and other professional fields where the IDB judged the job market saturated. The Dominican Republic project at the Catholic university included IDB insistence on student charges and loans. Donors often insisted on tilting toward the hierarchy over the base, as with AID at Colombia's National University.[70] Whether such insistence reflects an inherently pro-hierarchy bias, it surely reflects a natural preference to fund reform that appears to have powerful enough support to succeed.

In turn, donors' manifest readiness to exercise authority over what requests to approve and reject shapes the requests themselves. Donors may influence recipients before formal interactions commence. This sustains dependency charges about recipients pursuing what is fundable, what is "in." Temptations are especially strong where legitimate fear exists that "if we don't take what's available, our competitor will," an attitude found at Colombia's National and Antioquia universities.[71] This then affects the balance of power within the recipient institution or country, favoring those with priorities already aligned or now altered to align more closely with donors. Where givers have what potential recipients want—international legitimacy and especially enabling resources—they have leverage to impose conditions. And, of course, donor influence may increase where donors have an aggressive agenda. Donors' freedom restricts recipients' freedom.

Mutual matching for reform. For the most part, however, the philanthropic norm of selection involves a mutual matching of donor and recipient. Blunt control is more prominent in funding relationships where the actors are more fundamental antagonists.[72] The road is smoother where assistance goes to chosen recipients that share givers' ideas, especially if they also have the internal means to implement the agreed-upon plans.

Where donors become more ambitious or aggressive than usual, they may attempt to work with those who do not match up neatly. This has often meant recipient institutions seriously divided between groups on and off the donors' reform wavelength. The main examples in the golden age in Latin America were national universities in the 1960s, as analyzed in the next chapter. When donors venture beyond comfortable partnership, they usually confront aspects of the philanthropic dilemma in which philanthropic means lead to inadequate results but other means produce great risks: accept the risks of failure that come with lack of control over the substantive agenda or undertake unusually great control in an attempt to prevail. Either way, there may be a serious breach in the ideal typical philanthropic type.

But the circumstances of initial donor-recipient hook-up did not usually presage heavy donor imposition. Reality was sometimes very different, as when locals talked donors into funding. Furthermore, initial donor leverage was weakened where there were plural donors or few attractive recipients.[73]

Furthermore, the most common alternative to donor imposition was not recipients having a clear upper hand. It was where locals had already opted for, or at least inclined toward, a new course. They wanted to use assistance to enable, facilitate, promote, and accelerate. Again to make the point on limited imposition even in the single largest undertaking by any foundation, Ford financed mostly what the University of Chile and University of California decided upon in their convenio (University of Chile/University of California 1979; D'Etigny i-3). The convenio stands out for interuniversity cooperation more than a donor blueprint. In sum, typical is substantial *partnership*.

For both the initial mutual matching and the subsequently limited donor control, the key was domestic reform, a point fleshed out in the coming section on targeted nations and then the next chapter on targeted institutions. Reform leaders were often prestigious academics, including those who had studied abroad. Other reform leaders or at least willing partners were in government posts. Domestic reform attracted international donors interested in that reform, donors who were then mostly supportive. The evidence is wide-ranging and cumulative. At the peak of donor eagerness, the domestic will to reform could alone be enough to attract assistance, as perhaps with Peru under President Fernando Belaúnde in the mid-1960s (Myers 1983a: 506). More often, donor selectivity meant attention to realistic prospects for reform implementation. That explains, for example, LASPAU's heavy involvement in Colombia and Costa Rica rather than Bolivia or the national university in Ecuador (Bloomfield i-1; Tyler i-2). It also helps explain why many participants recall a "lack of controversy" between donor and recipient (Wolf i-1). Where conflict emerged inside university assistance projects, donor-recipient conflict was less common than conflict among domestic groups within the receiver nation or institution, sometimes pitting reformers against nonreformers or recipients against nonrecipients. In fact, as in other assistance fields, Third World leaders have often bought foreign models more zealously than donors have sold them, though a desire for funds sometimes leads merely to feigned enthusiasm and emulation.[74] For university reform, the zeal to import has usually matched if not exceeded the zeal to export. Donors usually understood limitations on how much they could impose or saw little need to impose where there were domestic reformers with whom they could work together.

Sequential patterns. Our view of partnership thus suggests sequential patterns consistent with the ideal type of philanthropy. Donor influence through discretionary "choice" at the inception yields to more limited donor "voice" thereafter. For example, where the IDB insisted on approving the executing agency for a project, it then often turned matters over to a field office that, like Ford's, usually exerted little control, sometimes little enough to invite criticism for the lack.[75]

Another sequential pattern is also consistent with partnership. Higher education assistance often starts with support for individuals. More than internally divided institutions, individuals are partners by choice. Travel and other scholarships open up a world of foreign practices that recipients then champion. This proves crucial to reform even in what we will call targeted nations. For any nation, pivotal exposure comes through such individual contact and a corresponding dissemination of ideas. Thus, the main architect of Argentina's network of alternative public universities designed largely on the U.S. model had, like his scientist father, extensive experience in the United States, and the Atcon and other reports had also influenced him. Many reform plans trace their origins to an assortment of U.S.–Latin American personal contacts.[76]

At the highest administrative level a noteworthy example of the reform sequence from individual partnership to joint projects was CHEAR, the Seminar of Higher Education in the Americas. CHEAR ran from 1960 to 1975, perhaps the U.S. State Department's longest lasting annual seminar. Hundreds participated, mostly Latin Americans picked by U.S. cultural attachés. Other donors supplemented U.S. government funding. Although some participants and observers dismiss CHEAR as a clubby encounter finally spurned by donors, most cite major impacts. Above all, CHEAR forged personal and institutional contacts that would stimulate and facilitate future reform and assistance projects.[77]

Cooperative funding. Another expression of partnership lay in the mix of project funding. Typical projects involved local university money, often augmented by special government or private support, alongside donors' money. The donor-local mix varied. IDB grants often accounted for half a project's costs, up to three-fourths at Colombia's del Valle, 1965, or the University of Chile, 1966, down to one-fourth for Central America's national universities, 1962. Sometimes explicitly to avoid dependency, the domestic chunk would aim to cover basic ongoing expenditures such as salary for the staff expanded from scholarships abroad (IDB/E7: 10; Moock 1980: 14). Also partly to avoid dependency, as well as to ensure sufficient public support back home, AID and other linkage projects encompassed benefits for the partnering U.S. university. This motivational blend is consistent with our ideal typical notion of self-interest blended with altruism. And the combination of local and external funds, like mixes of local and federal money for U.S. urban projects, fits ideal typical notions of a funding partnership between responsible local and voluntary external providers.

While our main concern is cooperation between givers and receivers, a pertinent observation is that cooperation among donors did not constitute the concerted, coherent assault that recipients sometimes fear and critics charge, as in philanthropic "collusion" with government.[78] Most assessments of assistance, education assistance, and higher education assistance to Latin America have found a relative lack of donor coordination. Many reviewers have advocated increased coordination, beyond what was achieved through sporadic conferences. Participants in those conferences recall how ongoing work involved little discussion with counterparts at other agencies even where there was ample activity, as with Ford, AID, and Rockefeller in Colombia in the 1960s.[79]

Explanations for the lack of coordination among donors include donor sloppiness or inability—and donors' quest to maintain their own autonomy (Cassen 1986: 230), autonomy crucial to their role as voluntary givers. Whatever the explanation, however, the lack of coordination suggests that universities were rarely victims of a well-planned assault from a cartel of aggressive external actors. A much more common linkage, compatible with both recipients' and donors' autonomy, occurred when one donor followed another to a target. In fact, such a pattern is consistent with notions of philanthropic sequences and with seed money attracting further funding.[80]

All this leaves one indicator of more formidable donor cooperation than generally reported by participants. As project documents detail, externally sponsored reform commonly involved simultaneous donor funding. Indeed, the funding mix was often negotiated as well as complementary. The IDB and Ford formed the main donor duo because their peak activity in university development overlapped the most and because they concentrated on different aspects of that development. Although each gave some for what the other donor gave most, there is a dominant pattern of Ford for scholarships, visiting professors, and expertise while the IDB spent for capital construction of academic and administrative buildings, libraries, laboratories, cafeterias, and so forth. At Colombia's Los Andes, Ford put in a third of the total and the IDB half, with Ford more than 80 percent toward scholarships while the IDB concentrated on capital activities. Furthermore, multiple donors targeted certain institutions. Brazil's University Rural de Minas Gerais was not unusual among universities in agriculture for having a mix like Ford, Rockefeller, AID, and Purdue University.

To conclude, the giver/receiver relationship in university assistance is mostly characterized by partnership. Though neither uniform nor symmetrical, the partnership is strong. It is also diversely displayed in mutual matching, joint reform, supportive sequential patterns, and cooperative funding. And the main, common example of one-sided control—front-end donor choice—is consistent with ideal typical philanthropic means and is itself conducive to ensuing partnership.

The Receivers: Nations

The balance of the chapter shifts to a focus on recipients, though it continues to look at giver/receiver relationships. It considers the largest target unit, the nation.

The analysis enters the controversial literature on which nations are favored or not by U.S. assistance.[81] But whereas that literature usually treats total bilateral assistance, we add multilateral and private giving in focusing on one policy field. Within that field, we can compare donors according to the scope and orientation of their giving. Mostly, we seek to discover patterns of targeting—and then to explain those patterns.

The philanthropic ideal type suggests a targeting of certain nations rather than a widespread and proportional allocation to all. It may also suggest nations that simultaneously have a great objective need and are important to the donors' self-interest. It surely suggests nations interested in local reform, prepared to break away from traditional Latin American university patterns while not embarked on a wider revolutionary course, and judged able to act in fruitful partnership with donors.

Preliminary data analysis had allowed some identification of national targeting patterns, and the highs and lows had helped determine where to concentrate the archival and field research. Among targeted receivers the choices were Colombia, Costa Rica, and Chile, whereas the low receiver group included Mexico and Argentina. These cases provide considerable variation in size, geography, regime and political context, and key aspects of the higher education system.

Upon more detailed analysis, the recipient side turns out to include (in addition to Colombia, Costa Rica, and Chile) Central America (plus Panama) even beyond Costa Rica, the Dominican Republic, Brazil, and, notwithstanding ambiguous indicators, Ecuador. The fuller list on the lower side includes Cuba, Uruguay, Bolivia, Venezuela, and probably Haiti. While the profiles from Peru and Paraguay contrast with one another, in the aggregate both elude our high and low recipient groups (see table 2.4).[82]

Treating as one case Central America, with Panama but without Costa Rica, gives us seven high recipients, seven low recipients, and two mixed cases. AID gave a third of its funds to another category, Latin America regional; the ensuing text reports national shares of AID's total excluding the regional category.[83] Both AID and Ford have a Central American category (and so our Central American figures add that category to the individual countries in the region). The reason for separating Costa Rica from the rest of Central America where possible is that Costa Rica was so distinct for its extraordinary democracy and civil peace. (Our data for Costa Rica are slightly understated, since they do not include the country's share of funds given to the Central American regional category.)

To facilitate comparisons across time and nation, it helps to concentrate on proportions rather than raw figures.[84] This also allows cautious inclusion of scholarship data, available in recipient numbers rather than funds. In addition to extra Ford data, that brings in LASPAU data (disaggregated in appendix K). Our main benchmark against which to gauge a nation's relative standing is its share of total Latin American higher education enrollment, 1960, supplemented by its share of total population. Use of 1965 as a reasonable alternative to represent where things stood at the point where large

Table 2.4 Country Recipients (% shares)

	Enrollment 1960	FF grants 1959–84	FF scholarships 1960–79[a]	AID[b] 1950–84	IDB 1962–84	LASPAU 1965–84
Argentina	31.8	5.5	8.6	3.1	8.5	0.6
Bolivia	2.3	0	0.9	0.1	0.3	4.7
Brazil	17.7	28.2	21.6	43	34.8	9.9
Chile	4.5	28.1	21.1	0.9	3.4	4
Colombia	4.2	10.3	17	4	10.5	22.3
CR	0.9	2.1	0.8	4.4	4.5	5.8
Cuba	3.6	0	0	0.1	0	0
DR	0.8	0.6	0.3	7.2	1.5	6.4
Ecuador	1.5	0.3	0.8	4.4	4	6.5
ES	0.4	0.6	1.5	0.4	1.3	2.4
Guatemala	1	0.5	0.7	1.7	1.1	2
Haiti	0.2	0	0.2	0	0.1	0.9
Honduras	0.3	0.4	0.8	3.3	2.1	3.7
Mexico	14.4	10.7	10.4	3.5	12.8	9.3
Nicaragua	0.6	0.3	0.9	1.4	1.2	3.3
Panama	0.7	0	0.5	1.3	2.6	3.9
Paraguay	0.6	0	0.1	0.6	2.7	0.9
Peru	7.4	8.7	10.4	4.1	0.9	10.7
Uruguay	2.8	0	0.2	0.1	3.7	0.1
Venezuela	4.2	2.3	3.3	0	3.9	2.5
CA	——	1.3	——	16.3	——	——
Total	99.9	99.9	100.1	99.9	99.9	99.9

Sources: See appendixes E, G, H, I, J, and K and Myers (1983b: table 25).
Note: IDB presents its data here in periods one year removed from the periods we use elsewhere (e.g., 1975–79), and includes 1985, whereas we usually stop at 1984.

[a]7.2% not identified by nation; distributed here by proportions for the other 92.8%: on scholarships included in grants, see appendix E.

[b]A "regional" category accounts for 27.3% of the AID total but is left aside in calculating the country percentages here.

assistance arrived would not much alter comparisons (see appendixes F and G). The data in table 2.4 run through 1984. Special attention might be given to data through the mid-1970s, when the golden age ends. Among the donors, Ford might warrant the most attention because its data are more complete and reliable than AID data and because the IDB choice of nations is mixed with its responsiveness to member nation requests.

Identification of targeted and nontargeted nations facilitates investigation, in the following three chapters, of possible differential impacts made by heavy assistance. At the same time, this can be a tricky matter, since nation is such a large unit and most institutions even in targeted nations do not receive. Nation, then, is just our first recipient unit and helps guide us to the more particular units of institution, field, and project purpose.

Targeted Nations

Several nations are clearly targeted. Colombia is around the top, at least for large nations. In 1960, it held 4.2 percent of Latin America's higher education enrollment as well as 7.6 percent of its population. Yet it would capture 10.3 percent of Ford's funds and 10.5 of the IDB's, along with 22.3 percent of LASPAU's scholarships and 17.0 percent of Ford's. AID is the exception, committing 4.0 percent to Colombia, but through the 1960s giving Colombia more than its enrollment share would predict. Except for AID, Colombia attracts much more than its share and does so across the major donors and time periods, with special weight during the golden age. These data sustain experts' repeated observation about large assistance to Colombian higher education, indeed to Colombia overall.[85]

Chile's priority position is inconsistent yet still impressive. The position is gained through a special relationship with one donor. Chile was Ford's clear number one target in proportional terms, vying with Brazil for the lead in absolute terms. It got 28.1 percent of Ford's grant funds and 21.1 percent of its scholarships, though it had just 4.5 percent of Latin America's 1960 enrollments and 3.7 percent of its population.[86] Much more than Colombia, however, Chile's position waned over time. A strong early recipient of IDB funds, Chile got none after the mid-1970s. The waning helps explain the slightly low LASPAU numbers, given the recent time frame of LASPAU efforts. From AID, Chile's low percentage traces to our database's unexplained omission of certain grants and arguably our own exclusion of others.[87] For the most part, focus on the golden age of university assistance, especially until 1970, shows Chile as a striking target.

Beyond the golden age, Chile's position very much depends on moving beyond universities to private research centers. Chile was Latin America's leader on that assistance front (Puryear 1994; Levy 1996). Even before the golden age, Chile had achieved a unique position for its hosting of major regional research organizations. It had also received pivotal early help from foundations such as Guggenheim and Rockefeller and from U.S. government and European sources, all of which laid a solid base for subsequent assistance consistent with our analysis of sequential giving by donors. Additionally, like its Colombian counterpart, Chilean higher education reflected donors' broader favoring of the nation.[88]

Brazil is also a leader. Although it trails Colombia and Chile in the golden age and in comparisons between assistance and population size, Brazil is high for all donors and across time periods as long as the control measure is enrollment (17.7 percent), which differs significantly from Brazil's national population (34.2 percent). In fact, while LASPAU gives only 9.9 percent to Brazil, the financial donors all come closer to the population proportion, a demanding gauge in Brazil, than to the enrollment proportion. Ford gives Brazil 28.2 percent of its project funds (though only 21.6 of its scholarships) and the IDB gives 34.8 percent. AID's data are shakier, as Brazil's projects are listed inconsistently, but our indication is a hefty 43 percent. In absolute terms, Brazil is also by far the number one recipient from the IDB.[89]

Both Costa Rica and the rest of Central America (with Panama), despite their differences, emerge as spectacular favorites for donors almost across the board. LASPAU is the most striking case. It gave 5.8 percent of its scholarships to Costa Ricans, as against the country's 0.9 percent share of Latin American enrollments, and it gave 15.1 percent for the rest of Central America versus its 3.0 percent of 1960 enrollment. Similarly, AID gave to Costa Rica at quadruple the enrollment percentage. For Costa Rica and the rest of Central America, AID then became proportionally huge after the golden age: from 1975 to 1984, over half its total, nearly 70 percent of the total without the regional category (see appendix I). The IDB's 4.5 percent over time to Costa Rica and its 8.3 percent to the rest of Central America underscore the targeting for the 1962–84 period inclusively. In fact, the IDB made Costa Rica an assistance target overall and especially on the education side (DeWitt 1977: 73–74). Ford funded Costa Rica at twice the enrollment percentage, though its scholarships simply matched it. But Ford's giving to the rest of Central America is the one major exception to the regional favoring; Ford's 3.1 percent, some of which is actually for Costa Rica, merely matches the enrollment share and falls far below the population share.

The Dominican Republic also scores well if the focus is on later years, but it also does well overall except for Ford. Compared to its 0.8 percent enrollment and 1.5 population share, its 0.6 from Ford funds and 0.3 from Ford scholarships stand apart from its 6.4 percent from LASPAU, 7.2 from AID (which would increase were agricultural higher education more amply included), and 1.5 from the IDB.

Nontargeted Nations

Donors' targeting of nations becomes yet more marked as we discover how several nations were marginal to university assistance. There was no standardized or formulaic spreading of resources, even in the golden age.

Argentina is the most telling example. This is startling in relation to its impressive 31.8 percent share of enrollment and even its 9.8 percent share of population. Uruguay follows form on a smaller canvas (2.8 and 1.2 percent, respectively). LASPAU is the most extreme example, allocating 0.6 percent of scholarships to Argentina and 0.1 to Uruguay. A fuller illustration of meager U.S. government assistance is that AID gave just 3.1 percent to Argentina and 0.1 to Uruguay, though the latter would increase with the inclusion of related agricultural projects. Meanwhile, Ford gave no project funds to Uruguay, and its 5.5 percent left Argentina as the most limited per enrollment of all receiving nations. Ford scholarships were similarly low at 0.2 percent to Uruguayans and 8.6 percent to Argentines. Argentina's largest financial share, 8.5 percent from the IDB, still represented a major proportional disfavoring; although the figure would go slightly higher with related agriculture, it would plummet to 1.6 without science and technology (included in our IDB higher education category). For Uruguay, one loan in the 1980s raised it from marginal to slightly favored on the IDB list.

Argentina's standing is linked to the focus of our attention, universities in the golden age. Like Chile, Argentina often worked well early on with external institutions regarding graduate student scholarships, visiting professorships, and collaboration in science. From the mid-1950s lots of international money arrived, but the opening narrowed with the 1966 coup—which itself stimulated the flow of funds to another nonuniversity recipient, the private research center.[90] In fact, even the short-lived opening had been more to ideas and cooperative efforts than to direct assistance for universities. The data show that into the mid-1960s, Ford, the IDB, and AID all gave proportionally more than they would later but still much less than Argentina's enrollment weight might suggest.

Mexico also comes in low. At 14.4 percent, it ranked a close third behind Brazil in enrollments but received little university assistance in the golden age. The IDB's 12.8 percent comes closest to proportionality, but it was only 1.5 percent up to the mid-1970s, when Mexico's Ortiz Mena assumed the bank's presidency. Ford's relatively low 10.7 percent would dip about 2 percent if we attend to an inconsistency in the data.[91] Ford and LASPAU scholarships were also low, at 10.7 and 9.3 percent, respectively, even though LASPAU accounted for the great majority of U.S. government scholarships to Mexican faculty members in the 1980s (Holden 1987: 19). AID directed only 3.5 percent of its university assistance to Mexico.

In Mexico, as in Argentina, low standing in golden age university assistance allows for an international presence. Rockefeller and Kellogg led early foundation efforts from public health to agriculture to the humanities. They were joined by various U.S. government agencies, such as United States Information Service, the NSF, and the Department of Agriculture, along with substantial bilateral convenios, often gaining high grades for quality and relevance.[92] Most of all, since the 1980s Mexico has rejected its previous heavy rejection of U.S. assistance to higher education, but of course that development comes mostly after this study's time period.

Venezuela also appears noteworthy on the low recipient side. There were early convenios, such as the national university's with the University of Wisconsin in the 1950s (Castro 1988: 142–51). Compared to 4.2 percent of enrollments, Venezuela picked up 3.9 of IDB's assistance, 2.3 percent of

Ford's, though near zero after the mid-1960s, and a slightly higher share of Ford but not LASPAU scholarships. It is then AID, uninvolved, that mainly brings down Venezuela's ranking.[93]

Patterns of Selectivity

As our data confirm selectivity across nations and thus a component of ideal typical philanthropic targeting, they contradict an important critique of assistance: that donors spread their aid thinly over nations. The spread is often attributed to sloppiness or criteria for giving that run across diverse historical, strategic, and humanitarian factors.[94]

University assistance indeed shows striking patterns across nations. Fourteen of sixteen nations fall rather clearly into either of two groups—high or low recipients. Beyond that, despite important exceptions, different donors mostly work with similar sets of nations. This pattern is strong for the targeted group and particularly for the nontargeted group. At least in proportional terms, each of our donors is underrepresented in Argentina, Mexico, Cuba, and Venezuela, and the point nearly holds for Bolivia, Haiti, and Uruguay. Most of these seven nations draw not moderately but sharply less than their enrollments would predict.[95] When it comes to national recipients, donors have charted a targeted course that is discernible, indeed well marked, rather than casual or randomly scattered.

Selectivity—crucial to our notion of voluntary assistance—becomes still clearer when we look at individual donors. All the major donors are selective. On the other hand, again consistent with our hypothesis about donor differences, our private foundation is the most selective. Yet, however constrained the IDB is by its multinational, member-nation status, it does not give equally across the board. The view that the IDB is no more than a member bank catering to its clients, without its own agenda, would not prepare us for this finding.[96]

Ford's selectivity is so great that the foundation excludes five nations from its grants: Cuba, Haiti, Paraguay, Uruguay, and Panama except for its part within the Central American category.[97] Chile and Colombia alone account for more than half the total. With Brazil they account for three-fifths of Ford scholarships. Ford initiated its Latin American program by listening to academic experts' assessments of the best targets and chose just Chile, Argentina, Mexico, and Brazil—sometimes for targets other than universities—before broadening to Colombia and Peru (Wolf i-2). The stretch to Peru is comparable to Rockefeller's reach beyond its usual foundation grasp. Ford saw Peru as its roughest country, with shortages of prior assistance experience and other typical requisites for funding (Fraenkel i). Even this overreach probably did not indicate naiveté as much as a foundation gamble—boldness, albeit excessive boldness—in confronting the philanthropic dilemma. Other foundations, even the other large and active ones, concentrated in fewer nations.[98]

At least three points could cut partly against our basic conclusion about selectivity. First, the largely similar giving patterns limit the distinctiveness between private and both bilateral and multilateral government donors.[99] Second, nation does not constitute a tightly selected unit from which donors could count on specific undertakings and accountability. Nations, and even just their higher education systems, range over many disparate structures, policies, and personnel. But for that same reason, evidence establishing a patterned selectivity *even* at the national level is impressive. Exclusion of a nation is a massive exclusion. And targeting a nation is merely the first layer of selectivity. It sets up the next three chapters' deeper investigation into the principal direct targets: institutions and units within them. Most donors by-passed the majority of universities even in targeted nations.

Third, the national patterns weaken if the focus shifts away from university development. They thus weaken both before and after the golden age. For example, Rockefeller's four main nations early on included Mexico and Argentina as well as Brazil and Peru (Cueto i). Strong national patterns regarding universities may dissipate when the spotlight is turned onto research centers, agricultural higher education, or science and technology projects. They weaken regarding scholarships not given as part of university development projects, though LASPAU data, like Ford scholarship data, show only minor weakening.[100] In any case, all this weakening shows that targeted national patterns were strong precisely when international assistance made its most powerful effort to transform the heart of the higher education system, the university.

Why the Patterns?

Striking national patterns beg for explanation. Why do some nations get much more than others? There is no single answer, but there are several persuasive and often interrelated answers. Without presenting all the detailed analysis and evidence, we can nonetheless sketch the main findings. Caring not to jump from correlation to causation, and leaving aside most distinctions among donors, this section identifies key characteristics distinguishing the targeted nations from the other nations. These include regime type, geopolitical relevance, higher education development level, and, above all, receptivity to externally favored reform.

Plugging our data into leading mappings of regime type (Remmer 1985) shows that democracies, defined by standard criteria such as competitive elections, did better than authoritarian regimes on average. Colombia, Costa Rica, and Chile in the 1960s are strong positive examples. Equally strong is the lack of assistance to most South American military regimes. The idea that assistance turns happily to rightist regimes that replace more leftist ones fails here.[101] However, the democratic hypothesis yields only mixed results in the end. Democratic Venezuela and pre-1973 Uruguay are low recipients while undemocratic Brazil and Central America without Costa Rica are high recipients. On balance, the findings mildly support the philanthropic ideal of funding to progressives, but democracies are not always progressive, and donors to fields like education can also take a long-run development approach undeterred by the temporal presence of an unprogressive regime.

Literature on development assistance in general indicates U.S. giving heavily conditioned by cold war considerations (Schraeder, Hook, and Taylor 1998: 310–20). It is difficult to operationalize a geopolitical variable here, however. Reflecting on universities' role in critical thinking and dissident action, donors could be tempted to funnel funds into countries whose governments are not favorably viewed by donors. Or higher education assistance could be separated from immediate geopolitical considerations.[102] Aside from such higher education considerations, identification of which countries are more important than others to donors' self-interest is often debatable. Central America and Brazil could easily qualify for a strategic list in the golden age, but so could democracies like Chile and Venezuela, particularly with the zeal to build showcase alternatives to the Cuban Revolution. And what nations would be excluded? The only clear answers are leftist regimes regarded as threatening and perhaps totalitarian. Cuba was indeed almost completely isolated from assistance. Where leftist executives were more embattled by divided government and society, as in Chile in the early 1970s and Nicaragua a decade later, there was some disfavoring while Ford's continued support helped to sustain foundation claims of independence and distinctiveness from government assistance. U.S. influence blocked much IDB help to Chile, while allowing two grants to private universities (Tussie 1995: 45). Overall, our evidence confirms that assistance from U.S. sources shuns the revolutionary Left, and Central America in the 1970s and 1980s suggests urgency in bilateral assistance to that Left's neighbors. Other than that, donors' strategic interests do not, in the case of higher education, provide the clear guide to their giving patterns that critiques would suggest.

A weightier, tighter fit with giving patterns lies in nations' development level. Operationally, we refer here to a key aspect of the development level of a nation's higher education system, its enrollment. Our indicator is the gap between a nation's share of regional enrollment and of regional population in 1960 (see appendixes F and G). The gap is "large" if the enrollment share is more than 50 percent above or below the population share (e.g., 10 percent of enrollments versus 6 percent of population). Only two nations—Argentina and Uruguay—are "developed" by this measure. In contrast, there are several "least developed" nations, with enrollments greatly trailing population. These include small nations—the Dominican Republic, Haiti, and Central America without Costa Rica. They also include Brazil, Colombia, Ecuador, Mexico, and Paraguay, but these are only moderately low on the development indicator. Moderately high are Costa Rica, Cuba, Venezuela, Chile, and, surprisingly, Peru and Bolivia.

Giving tendencies are clear in the two extreme categories, mixed in the two moderate ones. Argentina and Uruguay thus lead two lists: developed systems and proportionally low recipients. In contrast, three of the four nations in the least developed category are heavy recipients, and only Haiti defies our generalization. Note how our development measure works where the democracy hypothesis proves weakest: Brazil and Central America are preferred targets and Venezuela and pre-1973 Uruguay are low recipients. Ford closed down in Venezuela because it decided that Venezuela had sufficient income on its own, just as governmental donors have "graduated" such nations. The IDB in 1972 set an explicit policy to favor the less developed nations in its Fund for Special Operations, and by 1976 several Latin American nations were net contributors to that fund. Beyond Haiti, exceptions to our basic finding on development level and assistance include some of the moderately developed systems but none of the markedly more or less developed ones.[103]

Overall, university assistance to least-developed recipients shows redistributive tendencies. This finding supports some empirical literature on assistance (Schraeder, Hook, and Taylor 1998: 321), defying the critique that giving flows to "easy," advanced targets. The finding comes closer to what literatures on both foundations and federalism consider idealized than common giving patterns.

The key explanation for the correlation between more assistance and less-developed systems lies in host-country receptivity and reform. Various literatures on change show that the most established large systems are often more set in their ways, less inclined to emulate others, whereas lesser development may allow for more growth via newness, with less need for radical transformation of weighty existing structures.[104] In higher education, at least for the kind of reform that donors wished to export, the less developed systems were readier to change. Donors gave to nations that welcomed them in higher education. Receptivity is decisive in joining domestic reform to international assistance, a point that brings our earlier findings on donor-recipient partnership to bear on the targeting of nations.

The philanthropic ideal type requires such recipient receptivity. And to ensure that targets are attractive to donors, the ideal type also requires recipient reform. This means more than a sporadic disposition to reform. A common assistance variant of our philanthropic dilemma concerns how much to demand favorable conditions beyond disposition alone: demand too little and be doomed to failure, but demand too much and find either too few targets or ones that hardly need external support. This dilemma is pursued in chapter 3 in terms of which *institutions* would be targeted; at the national level, arguably there was no "easy" nation in Latin America, with a relatively unproblematic higher education system, so a key for donors was to find sufficiently facilitating conditions (e.g., government-university cooperation, coherent governance profiles, and flexibility to undertake initiatives without tackling the whole system).[105] Without receptivity and reform, there would be neither partnership nor adequate impact. Insofar as receptivity and reform are indeed associated with less-developed systems, an extra incentive for do-nors is also consistent with the ideal type: relatively small amounts of assis-tance may be pivotal for the recipients.

And so *all* the targeted nations showed substantial interest in and recep-tivity to international assistance that looked to support reform and growth inclining toward features of the U.S. university model. And all the less-funded nations trailed in this receptivity/reform mix. Contrasts emerge powerfully between Colombia, Chile, Costa Rica, and Brazil on the one hand and Ar-gentina, Uruguay, and Mexico on the other. Furthermore, a subsequent turn-around in which the latter group would receive ample higher education as-sistance late in the century largely reflected increased receptivity and domestic reform initiatives.[106] Of course, donors hoped that the targeted nations would provide attractive models for other nations so that assistance would "lever" widespread change, but this was more an implicit hope than a mapped out strategy.

The idea of receptivity and reform is a satisfactory alternative or com-plement wherever the regime variable works. Most democracies have been more receptive than nondemocratic regimes. But receptivity and reform proves a superior variable by working where the regime variable does not: for the large aid to nondemocratic Brazil and Central America and the small aid to democratic Uruguay.[107]

The salience of national receptivity and reform, interacting with the other factors considered here, fits modernization notions of assistance. On the other hand, given dependency's often broad and contradictory claims, the recep-tivity-reform findings are reconcilable with dependency's more moderate and loose claims while negative for its most defining claims. There is valid de-pendency concern insofar as the favoring of one group of nations over an-other suggests that donors have operated with a powerful agenda and that external interests bolster certain domestic internal elites. But, overall, the assistance is neither status quo oriented nor imposed. Second, although do-nors mostly avoid leftist regimes and favor some targets of specific strategic importance, they do not gravitate toward rightist, authoritarian regimes; they emphatically do not gravitate toward regimes content with the higher edu-cation status quo, but instead work with both democracies and dictatorships geared for reform. Third, regarding the targeting of least-developed systems, one could argue that assistance goes where it can dominate, but also that it does not attempt to impose itself where mature alternatives or opposition exist. Moreover, the targeting of least-developed systems runs counter to the idea that assistance contributes to stratification. There is something to the claim of retired IDB officials that they helped least-developed nations "keep up"—or at least they tried.[108]

Conclusion

The overview of giving and receiving in the golden age of university assistance reveals certain limitations, including a few contradictions, to the philanthropic ideal type. First, the U.S. role as Latin America's model and funder was large enough to raise questions about excessive weight from one quarter and consequent lack of choice for recipients. Second, golden age undertakings marked new levels and modes of activity, with decreased selectivity or insistence on carefully reviewed criteria. The tendency was epitomized by Rockefeller's University Development Program, Ford's efforts in Peru, and massive multipurpose projects. Third, political and cultural arrogance also manifested itself at times in expressions about Latin American actors and practices. Such arrogance mocked norms of partnership and mutual respect, just as arrogance in undertakings mocked norms of cautious selectivity and realistic management. Fourth, donors lurched at roughly the same time. Almost like herd animals, they were inspired to act vigorously and then, rather suddenly, to step back. While such behavior underscores the voluntary, unencumbered nature of donor giving, it runs counter to ideal typical claims about innovating against the grain.

Conceptual conclusions obviously depend largely on where one draws lines. Even when agreed on the evidence, different observers may reach conflicting conclusions on whether particular manifestations of donor control, interdonor cooperation, donor-recipient cooperation, or donor boldness are consistent with the philanthropic ideal type.[109] Some facts simultaneously fit both critiques of assistance and ideal typical claims about assistance. For example, there is an asymmetrical relationship between donors and receivers, *and* they are both partners and reformers. Particular facets of projects show overbearing, arrogant approaches by donors *and* also great receptivity by Latin American policymakers.

The abundance, complexity, and ambiguity of the evidence are unfriendly to those inclined to draw simple generalizations from it. The preference here is to put forth the evidence, identify patterns in it, and interpret how well which aspects fit the ideal concepts laid out for the analysis.

Although this approach leads us to qualified and mixed conclusions, where the evidence on the broad giver/receiver relationship allows a judgment, it is mostly consistent with the philanthropic ideal type. Following the chapter's content, this generalization rests on goals and especially efforts, not results.[110] The golden age clearly saw a surge of donor giving, linked to development goals and optimism. Although the age saw instances of overreach, these instances mostly concentrated in just over one decade, albeit an important part of our study, from the early 1960s to the early 1970s. Peak action was short-lived. But even the peak did not see a totally reckless or naive rejection of philanthropic norms about caution. Instead, donors confronted a basic dilemma when carefully circumscribed efforts failed to produce ambitious, desired outcomes: stick with the approach and accept results short of the vision, or modify the approach to pursue the vision. So the record was mixed during the peak itself. Rarely if ever did projects attempt to install the U.S. model in its entirety. Nor did they engage most universities even in targeted nations or most units within their targeted institutions. Not even the IDB undertook any extended responsibility to finance the principal ongoing activity of institutions. This fits with the point that international assistance never assumed the main financial burden. The domestic empirical and conceptual analog for U.S. assistance to Latin American universities almost always remained private philanthropy rather than government funding. The financial assistance was large only if one thinks of voluntary norms, not of government subsidies.[111]

Selective targeting was the key link between how much was given and how it was given. It allowed for avoiding typical as well as particularly hostile places and working instead with those ready or in fact eager to be receivers, even seekers, and who shared donors' goals. Although donors pushed for major change, their means of control involved mostly front-end choice, careful selection and widespread rejection of potential targets, and mutual matching with like-minded and often already familiar reformers. Coercive imposition or ongoing control was less common. Donor-recipient partnership for change was much more central to the giving process than was any interdonor coordination to weaken recipients' bargaining power.

All these patterns played out regarding targeted nations. Donors were selective even during the golden age, concentrating on some countries and more markedly maintaining a distance from others. There was matching up with nations that were receptive and more inclined than others to pursue elements of the reform championed by donors. No macro-political factor was equally important, though several tucked in neatly with the receptivity-reform criteria. The remarkable overlap in nations targeted by donors had more to do with criteria regarding partnership in reform than with any imposing, aggressive, coordinated donor plan. Nations proudly defending their already established university structures and policies were not assaulted. Assistance mostly avoided those who did not welcome it and its concept of progressive change.

Whether or not one accepts the overall picture as mostly fitting the philanthropic ideal type, it is clear that, as hypothesized, the fit is greatest for the private foundation. This finding runs counter to demeaning claims of philanthropic lack of distinctiveness from official assistance (Colwell 1980). What limits our contrast among donors is largely that the bilateral and multilateral donors fit the ideal type more in their higher education than in their other work. Prominent examples included AID's linkage formula and cooperation with U.S. universities and the IDB's special soft-loan fund targeting assistance to particular priorities. Most other bilateral and multilateral organizations might fit even more closely, but their involvement was usually so small compared with AID's and the IDB's that selectivity was almost inevitable.

Among our three principal donors, Ford was far and away the most oriented toward higher education. Other foundations also concentrated on knowledge-based activities. Ford built a clear profile of selectivity, caution, and limited scale. This profile stands out even where Ford collaborated with other donors in particular projects. Misleading as it is to consider any of the major donors laggards when it came to partnership with recipients, Ford went furthest in forging partnership with the fewest, those most able to meet stiffer front-end criteria for donor targeting. That, in turns, figures into why Ford seldom slipped into deprecatory assessment or demands regarding its recipients. It certainly figures into why Ford undertook significant efforts with only certain nations.

Some conclusions from this chapter's broad survey are subject to modification as the next three chapters turn to more specific analysis. The chapters examine how donors selected and worked with or controlled particular actors, structures, and subject matter. What emerges is a more detailed picture of the goals and efforts undertaken. And the picture expands to include the results of those efforts.

3

Modernizing the System: Diversification and Expansion

Selectivity among nations was only the first layer of donor targeting for exporting progress. Assistance directed itself more to the institution than to the nation, though the two were linked and certain nations had more attractive institutions. This chapter looks inside nations to see how, including how successfully, donors promoted the restructuring modernization of university systems through assistance to specific types of institutions. The restructuring was seen as essential if higher education was to fulfill the noble, ambitious roles expected of it for a new Latin America, with rapid political, economic, social, and cultural transformation.

The chapter opens by identifying the twin hefty and hopeful restructuring goals for system modernization—diversification and expansion—and considering how these goals anticipated evolution from a moderately corporatist system toward a decidedly more pluralist system. The chapter then analyzes actual efforts and results. How did donors and their domestic reform partners pursue their goals, and to what effect? One section focuses on assistance to the national universities. A longer section then turns, as donors themselves did, to a wider array of more select institutional targets. The final section explores system expansion, including its scope and how it has both reinforced and undermined the pluralist diversification.

Promoting Pluralist Development

Twin Goals

Consistent with the U.S. export model in higher education, interinstitutional diversification (or differentiation) was a major goal for restructuring.[1] This diversification supposed ample autonomy for institutions to chart and pursue their own course—autonomy for vigorous action rather than traditional autonomy to defend against change. Autonomy with accountability to diverse actors and interests is a reform mantra today but was at least implicit in most reform efforts of the golden age as well. In any event, most projects looked to diversification, some more specifically or fundamentally than others. That much is clear, whatever conclusions one later draws about the trickier matters of why or how the diversification was pursued.

Expansion was the other fundamental goal for a modernized higher education system. The U.S. export model was attractive for its promise of both diversity and scale.[2] As with diversification, there were differences in motivation or particulars regarding expansion. Also as with diversification, donors and their reform partners could associate expansion with multiple objectives. A strong, widespread belief was that expansion would generally promote higher education modernization and national development: more is better. IDB president Felipe Herrera (1985b: 269) and other influential figures repeatedly emphasized the gap between Latin America and the industrialized world in numbers of highly trained citizens. Expansion would also increase opportunity and equity, as more groups would receive a higher education and reap its benefits. Fortuitously, expansion would promote diversification. For one thing, growing systems tend to differentiate institutionally.[3] Most simply, however, growth of selected institutions would itself mean some system growth, as long as this push would not be offset by donor attempts to block growth elsewhere.

It should thus be clear that as most of the chapter concentrates on diversification it is also dealing with growth—growth through the favored promotion of particular institutions. Nonetheless, the overlap between diversification and expansion is obviously not total, and the two goals could have different priorities for different external and domestic reformers at different times.

The gap between the two goals comes through regarding their fit with philanthropically ideal typical goals. Diversification fits beautifully, projecting innovative and progressive change. Alternative institutions would do new things and would be models for change elsewhere in the system. The goal of expansion was more problematic. It fit in its optimistic sense that growth would promote the broad public good, as well as in the considerable degree to which expansion was seen to come through alternative institutions. But expansion could also mean simple enlargement of existing structures and practices. Like federalism that is additive more than redistributive, such expansion fit the generous postulates of modernization theory more than the philanthropic ideal type. Less preoccupied with selectivity or distinctiveness, it was committed to the notion that a good thing (higher education) would be a better thing, with greater impact, when expanded. Such wide rationales for growth were crucial to mainstream development thinking about the value of education, human capital, and increased opportunity. The modernization model outstrips the philanthropic one in assumptions that all good things, including growth, quality, and equity, go together. It looked for reform to come systemwide and simultaneously with growth, or even lagging it, whereas the philanthropic ideal type makes reform the priority, even the prerequisite to appropriate growth.

Of course, the relevance of the philanthropic ideal type to diversification and expansion depends on more than the goals just identified. It depends also on the means employed and on what kind of diversification and growth were pursued and achieved.

From Semicorporatist to Semipluralist

Conceptually, the envisioned system was pluralist. Though this pluralism applies to the growth side, we highlight here the clearer and more striking side—diversification as a pluralist goal. Whereas diversification is a common higher education term, specifically referring to differences among institutions, *pluralism* helps connect our subject matter to broader considerations about assistance and modernization. Pluralist systems with rather innovative, alternative institutions were to replace central systems biased toward standardized structure and policy.

Donors associated pluralist systems with much that brings the public good and sustained reform and development: choice, freedom, autonomy, competitive efficiency, and accountability, as well as growth. These were means to realize goals of progressive change for higher education and, through it, for national development. Donors sometimes explicitly linked their pluralist reasoning to their view of restructured, enlarging higher education systems (Renner 1973b: 3). This fit the general idea that nations could achieve better-balanced regional development by escaping stultifying dominance by the national university, just as they should escape a heritage of political power overcentralized in the capital city. Usually, however, pluralism was implied or could be inferred where project goals featured the growth of diverse institutions. Pluralism thus illustrates our repeated distinction between explicit goals and more common implicit goals.[4]

To assess how transforming the pluralist goals might be, it is necessary to establish what the structure of Latin American higher education systems was in comparison with the import model at the dawn of the golden age of assistance. In broad terms the contrast largely fit the contrast between U.S. pluralism and Latin American corporatism.[5] The U.S. export model was markedly pluralist in its system configuration, stressing an increased variety of forces for an increased variety of institutions growing in their own ways. Seen comparatively, Latin American systems were more corporatist, including a major role for a state shaping and funding a functionally integrated system of mostly noncompeting similar institutions. The U.S. system would become the "paradigm" for dynamism through system differentiation (Tedesco and Blumenthal 1986: 24).

Even in most large Latin American nations, excepting Brazil, a single national university dominated. Though most national universities had lost their earlier monopoly status, in both human and physical resources they loomed large over the rest of the system. They were also the prestigious models. Where other universities existed, they tended to follow the leader, or at least they tried or claimed to follow. They did so for reasons that square with common isomorphic emulation of more established organizations: the nationals' institutional weight and prestige; student, professional, and societal expectations; a lack of alternative conceptions; laws requiring national university recognition of programs or degrees; or even laws mandating adhesion to the forms established at the national university. Thus even uniquely large Brazil, without a national university, developed a strong ideological commitment, reflected in important legal provisions, to the idea that one institutional form should reign (Schwartzman 1984: 210). *Isonomia* in Brazil, *homologación* elsewhere in Latin America, proclaimed the bias for uniformity.

The corporatism of Latin American systems derived largely from European roots. The "Continental" model favored a unified system with tremendous structural similarity throughout and with standardized curriculum, degrees, personnel and admissions policy—and quality, high quality. In short, nations set many rules to apply similarly to all universities. Latin America's national universities, proudly established upon the achievement of national independence, were the state arm in higher education, sometimes in education overall (following the Napoleonic lead). They were seen as society's singular higher education representative, expressing the public interest. Corporatist harmony through concentration on one institution plus standardization across others, joined by some complementing more than conflicting interinstitutional configurations, thus sat at odds with pluralist notions of differentiation and competition.[6]

In contrast, the U.S. system epitomized pluralism. Interinstitutional diversity has been a key to the U.S. export model (see chart 2 in the introductory chapter). Neither a national university nor any overarching institutional pole was ever created. Never did national government policy dominate the system. Notwithstanding increased regulation in the second half of the twentieth century, mostly by individual states, and with consequent diversity nationally, a key characteristic of the U.S. higher education "system" in comparative perspective has always been interinstitutional differentiation, with the accompanying institutional autonomy to make it viable. If there is a U.S. higher education public interest, it is implicitly the product of diverse and conflicting structures and policies variously accommodating themselves to different groups. No country has ever developed comparable interinstitutional diversity. Nor has any developed a comparably large system. Both those statements, true today, were also true when the golden age of assistance began. U.S. donors operated from experience and familiarity when they weighed in to favor the growth of pluralist higher education systems elsewhere.

These realities should not suggest swaggering donors out to convert centralized corporatist systems into decentralized pluralist ones. First, a simple empirical observation is that donors did not fund or otherwise promote the majority of proliferating institutions. Second, in connection with the point about pluralism and implicit goals, donors did not usually push for interinstitutional diversification and certainly not for competition per se when they merely pursued a particular goal or interest represented by a given institution. In fact, there was considerable advocacy for increased system planning and coordination. Although that advocacy came more from domestic actors than donors, and there were few concrete assistance efforts, let alone results, in that direction, assistance projects ranged between aloofness and support more than antagonism for concepts like system planning and coordination. Support for increased central planning echoed a tendency in general development thinking that hotly challenged the applicability of pluralist assumptions to Third World countries, seeing instead the advantages of centralization for rapid reform and progress.[7] It is not surprising that the push toward pluralist reconfiguration in higher education would be qualified.

Fourth, and most broadly, we must avoid a stereotypical dichotomy between U.S. pluralism and Latin American corporatism in higher education, especially in practice. Even the U.S. model included an important state role as well as limits on unbridled institutional proliferation. Latin America was equally far from any corporatist extreme. It came closer to that extreme in normative thought, with a common belief that planning and vigorous coordination of a higher education "system" by a central state were essential to academic as well as national development. In practice the picture was murkier, and central direction and coordination were to prove woefully inadequate to make corporatism work amid incipient rapid growth. Only the small nations entered the golden age with higher education bound up in one university. Cracks included technological and agricultural institutes and, within the university world, some private and public institutions that drifted away from the mainstream in several respects. Key differences from Europe lay in greater uncontrolled institutional proliferation, especially in the private sector, and in the state's lesser control of policymaking for public institutions (Levy 1994).

All in all, then, donors did not attempt to export a pluralist model as a direct replacement of a domestic polar opposite. The imported model was not that pure and would not have that sort of massive "weight." Instead, individual projects aimed at more particular ends that together were expected to shift the mix more toward the pluralist side.

Nonetheless, as golden age assistance began, Latin American higher education was comparatively corporatist, the U.S. export model comparatively pluralist. Latin America's heavy diversification in higher education lay ahead. So did its heavy growth, and donors and their partners could not envision heavy growth without a pluralist institutional reconfiguration. However corporatist or Continental models might fare for elite systems, they were considered inadequate for enlarging systems that would reflect societal diversification. Key questions concerned how much of what reconfiguration was required. Would 10 or 25 percent of the cohort group be enrolled? Would a national university continue to be the clear leader or even supervisor of the system? Could creation of regional units of the national university regulate proliferation? What would be the balance between private and public, elite and nonelite, specialist and generalist institutions? How much diversity would accompany proliferation? To what extent would expansion parallel unfolding West European patterns or U.S. pluralism?[8]

National Universities

The history of assistance to Latin America's national universities tells us much about what donors set out to do and what they did not set out to do, as well as about what they did and did not do. The subsequent retreat from the nationals tells us just as much, especially about the problems that donors ran into where they made major efforts. The following three subsections turn to the donors' arrival, their departure, and one up-close case study.

Donor Arrival

Many Latin Americans, including students, intellectuals, and administrative leaders at the national universities, have regarded the national university as a central point in Latin American culture and identity, justifiably a great symbolic leader. An attack on it could be construed as evidence for major dependency notions. Judging by critiques of intervention, we might expect to see a frontal assault on these central institutions.

In reality, although donors pushed purposefully toward diversification, sometimes infused with an ideological component, there was no frontal assault on the national universities. Donors ignored some national universities. They worked in partnership with other national universities—upon which they pinned much of their early hope. Their big push toward institutional alternatives would come after frustrating experience with national universities. That shift would be at least as pragmatic as ideological. Donors did not start with a plan to harm national universities. They did not even start with a plan to build interinstitutional pluralism by dismissing national universities.

Instead, initial assistance inclined toward national universities. As of 1965, these universities accounted for 41 percent of total Spanish American enrollment (see appendix L), which leaves aside Brazil because it had no national university.[9] Data fleshed out below (including tables 3.1–3.3) in exploring the shift from national to other universities confirm the nationals' early importance as targets. Consistent with the hypothesis about the private foundation most approximating philanthropic norms of selective targeting, Ford is the only one of our main donors that never (at least in any five-year period) gave the majority of its funds to the national universities. But its first decade of giving did include the nationals proportionally to their enrollment share. In its initial years, the early 1960s, the IDB gave more than half of its funds to the nationals. AID in the early 1950s gave mostly to Brazil, which had no national university, but the mid-1950s to the mid-1960s allow a meaningful reading of its Spanish American investment—and national universities received nearly 70 percent of the institutionally identifiable total.

The simplest explanation for the concentration on national universities was the lack of alternatives. This fact restricts any ideal typical notion of voluntary action; although donors could decide whether or not to give, they had limited choice about where to give. In most of the smaller nations, little or nothing existed outside the national university. If AID worked in Paraguay in the 1940s and 1950s in technical training fields and then in the 1950s and 1960s in medical fields, joined by SUNY–Buffalo, the Kellogg Foundation, and others,[10] it perforce worked with the national university. Even in larger nations, other institutions tended to be limited and much less likely than the nationals to be competent in donors' priority areas. The national university held a monopoly in many important fields. Ford's early emphasis on exact science required contact with national universities if there would be any contact within the higher education system. Similarly, AID and foundation efforts to link research and teaching required contact with those few universities that did research; that was a major reason Ford tried to make a Latin American model out of the University of Chile.[11]

But to concentrate only on the lack of alternatives would ignore the fact that in the aggregate our main funders initially gave nationals more than enrollment share would predict, and it would understate the enthusiasm often accompanying the giving. Donors acted voluntarily and with considerable optimism about development: systems could be transformed at the core. Such optimism, like that associated with promoting system growth, fit closer to the modernization than to the more cautious philanthropic ideal type. Various AID documents through the 1960s equated formidable higher education development, and even broader societal development, with the national university. Ford, too, recognized that it was operating mostly right at the urban core (Ford Foundation 1962: 62). Even as assistance slipped off in other directions, consultants emphasized that the heart in Latin American higher education was the national university.[12]

Moreover, contrary to subsequent stereotypes, national universities often appeared as promising recipients. They boasted many traits that donors sought then as well as later. Several embodied domestic reform movements, and radicalism was still mostly in the future. So was massification. The Dominican Republic's Autonomous University of Santo Domingo had but 3,000 students around 1960. Even Mexico's large UNAM (National Autonomous University of Mexico) could be praised in Ford reports as strong and reforming (FF #67281). UNAM's particular strength in science reminds us that as nationals headed into deep political and academic trouble they retained almost unchallenged leadership within higher education in certain fields that did not succumb as much to those troubles. Further national university examples include the University of Buenos Aires in science, Peru's San Marcos in medicine, and Venezuela's Central University in dentistry. Nor did the troubles then make all the nationals unattractive for assistance, as Chile and Costa Rica showed in the late 1960s. Donors could find apparently competent reformist partners in national universities. Assistance to national universities did not always defy principles of our ideal type.

Selectivity characterized even the peak of donor giving to the national universities. Although donors did not launch a frontal assault to undo most of what existed at these universities, they did not make an unselective effort to carry good things to the breadth of the national university world. This was neither an imperial assault nor a reckless, all-out campaign. Donors attempted little "university development" or "institutional development" at the University of Buenos Aires or Uruguay's University of the Republic, where potent faculties and political forces opposed such assistance. They instead often targeted a specific unit, usually an atypical unit, bypassing the university as a whole. Only in the small, undeveloped, and receptive national universities was broad institutional development assistance common. This approach of "broad" undertakings only within small contexts maintained a type of selectivity consistent with notions of what can be reasonably implemented (Cerych and Sabatier 1986). It also parallels for institutions the last chapter's findings on targeting less developed and more reform-oriented nations.

In sum, donors' efforts at national universities reflected a mix of optimism, sometimes excessive, and realism, as seen in various forms of selectivity. Neither grand, harsh critiques of national universities nor grand, transforming goals translated into the actual projects. There was not a politically or culturally arrogant effort to transform the heart and breadth of the national universities or to bypass them by creation of new institutions from scratch. Certainly the evidence does not suggest an antigrowth policy. Donors did not attempt to block growth at national universities, and in certain important cases they promoted it. In those cases they would be guilty not of elitism as much as of disregard of philanthropic guidelines on selectivity. Yet donors were aware, albeit variably and insufficiently, that national universities presented major potential difficulties for assistance reform. They tried to steer clear of some difficulties and to work with certain national universities to overcome other difficulties.

Donor Departure

But the difficulties at national universities soon proved great enough to redirect assistance. Disillusioned retreat followed hard upon enthusiastic arrival. A general preference for decentralizing, pluralist development would become more of a perceived pluralist imperative—and now for negative reasons, avoiding trouble at the core, as much as for positive reasons. For higher education reform to succeed, it would have to escape the tribulations of most national universities. The administrative and academic features of the U.S. university model, elaborated in chapters 4 and 5, would need alternative homes if they were to succeed.

Even then donors did not all become "anti–national university." Their retreat was forced as much as voluntary. Often it was with regret. For example, LASPAU did not want to reject national universities but sadly reacted to the problems they had in reincorporating their ex-scholarship holders to those universities (Tyler i-6; Bloomfield i-4). In almost all cases, however, donors retreated largely because too many of the core conditions of the philanthropic ideal type proved absent or weak. Whether initially or within a very brief time, national universities showed themselves to lack enough of the requisites for partnership with donors.

Most of the following examples indicate how proposed reforms came under attack by unreformed forces at the national universities, testimony to the impact of tradition upon imports and to the difficulties of reform that does not occur all at once. Yet our sketch of difficulties here suggests a changed balance of perceptions about opportunity and obstacles, not a total reversal. Additionally, real and perceived failure was not the only cause of the changing assistance allocations; alternatives to national universities increasingly presented themselves as worthy in their own right. Donors' retreat from national universities was not a retreat from most attitudes, goals, and efforts for higher education development. It was, however, a shift from the modernizing optimism that had driven them to the core toward a more discriminating approach more consistent with philanthropic norms.

Sharp political conflict erupted in national universities. Even when not over assistance per se, such conflict undermined the university's ability to function reliably. Donors seek partners whom they can trust; only this allows limited donor control once projects are launched. Although donors might still find willing and even eager counterparts at national universities, voluntary assistance requires strong and stable counterparts. Getting out when no longer adequately welcome can be as much a sign of donor prudence as of initial failure. In other cases, conflict very much included opposition to assistance, either as a matter of principle or as rejection of a particular project or provision. Compared to other institutions, national universities were especially prone to such conflict due to their heterogeneity and widespread distribution of power. A growing mutual rejection emerged: donors became disenchanted, and their recipient universities no longer welcomed them or at least sent mixed messages. IDB president Herrera lamented the bank's image as a "mere agent of the U.S." controlling Latin America (1985b). Foundations were sometimes rejected on the same basis, sometimes tolerated as less guilty.

Student politics brought the most dramatic rejections, with leftism dominant among activists. Student power expressed itself through institutional representation, as in Bolivia and Central America, where students could hold a third or half of the votes on decision-making bodies and could cast them as a block. More frequently, student power expressed itself through disruptions or the threat of disruptions. Either way, or in combination, students repeatedly pushed donors away in Venezuela (Fuenzalida 1987: 122, 129), Ecuador (Ayala 1974: 205–207), and elsewhere (Franco 1973: 63), even where domestic governments and some leftist professors wanted the assistance. For a nation like Peru, accounts by keen participants on the donor end were harrowing even concerning the sciences.[13] International equipment could not be unpacked; a chemistry professor associated with the Moscow wing of communist activity returned from his scholarship abroad, Ph.D. in hand, only to discover he had lost his job in a faculty now inclined more toward the Beijing wing; graffiti denounced leading U.S. consultant George Waggoner as a Pentagon agent, and so forth. Donors concluded that while similar problems at certain other Peruvian universities remained within tolerable bounds, the national San Marcos had become impossible. Similarly, AID was frustrated and rejected within a few years at the Autonomous University of Santo Domingo, though it could work fruitfully with several private universities in the Dominican Republic (Harding 1968: 14). AID was greatly frustrated even at such a donor-favored national university as Costa Rica's.

Increasingly joined by the activism of professors and blue-collar workers on campus, student politics contributed to a leadership weakness at the national universities that caused donors to retreat. UNAM rector and scholar Pablo González Casanova probably did all he could to keep the door open, but the Ford Foundation concluded that this was insufficient (Tierney i), a judgment apparently vindicated when the rector lost his post over a thorny unionization issue. Guatemala's San Carlos university elected a rector in the late 1960s who renounced his university's IDB loan (Accame i). In an AID project in Ecuador, the University of Pittsburgh team struggled to work with "the few positive elements" (Blaise 1968: 19).

Open political conflict was merely the most visible, dramatic, conclusive way to drive off donors. The evaluation of AID efforts at Ecuador's Central

University found apathy more potent than radicalism (Blaise 1968: 27). Apathy is another opposite of philanthropic partnership based on zeal to import and reform.

Difficulties also hampered efforts at other universities, but their force was greater at the nationals. Donors turned elsewhere, toward alternative institutions, to accomplish their goals. They were not alone. Donor exit was part of a broader exit by those with choice. National universities' deteriorating academic standards and degree value on the job market led privileged students as well as business interests toward alternative institutions (Levy 1986: 36–37, 45–53). Even governments divided their loyalties between their traditional and alternative universities. But the governments retained some fixed responsibility to the nationals; international donors did not. Where governments begrudgingly continued to fund nationals resistant to reform, as in Mexico, or where governments actually reduced budgets, as in Joaquín Balaguer's Dominican Republic, one could hardly expect sustained external assistance.

The departure of donors and privileged domestic groups drove the nationals further down and made at least some alternative institutions more attractive. The gap then widened in the 1970s. Although strands of a national revival could from time to time build upon continued science quality or the selection of impressive rectors at such battered sites as Colombia's National University, the revival was minimal compared to the corporatist dominance of a few years earlier. The substantial donor effort to reform national universities had fallen far short of reasonable expectations, not to mention projected ones. Regarding impact, it was disappointing, a mix of outright failure and qualified successes.

The experience at national universities was mixed regarding the philanthropic ideal type. Donors came voluntarily, with enthusiasm and optimism, and launched specific undertakings. These were usually targeted either at still-small institutions eager for partnership or at reformist units within larger, less reform-oriented universities. Both approaches were efforts at innovation and experimentation. Never was there an attempt to transform the breadth of Latin American national universities, just as there was never an attempt to demolish any of those institutions; rather, there was an effort at partnership with willing counterparts. On the other hand, donors were trying to operate at or near the mainstream, rather than eluding it in favor of distinctive institutional alternatives. As with the Rockefeller Foundation's University Development Program analyzed in the previous chapter, then, for a short period of time donors deviated from the targeting criteria that the philanthropic ideal type requires. Certainly in results the ideal type was not even approximated, overwhelmed by both prismatic results and simpler failures.

The Colombian Case

Colombia is probably the major case where donors launched and then halted a major effort at a national university while proceeding with major efforts at alternative universities. In Chile, the other South American country whose national university was a favored recipient, the effort would continue longer at the national university and then substantially dissolve throughout the system. Colombia's National University is therefore uniquely attractive as a case of donor arrival and departure.

Colombia's National University offered much of what donors wanted to see. Its governance structure was unusual among Latin America's public universities for its hierarchy, topped by a board with extra-university representation and a rector selected by the nation's president. Colombia's national development plan and leading financial agencies gave high priority to the university's development plan. Compared with other national universities, Colombia's had an attractive combination of small size and a readiness to grow. It accepted only about one-fourth of applications (IDB/L20). Its leadership commitment was shown through pledges to provide full-time faculty salaries to those who received assistance for study abroad. The university boasted experience with assistance and got credit for following a Rockefeller study recommending modernization of accounting and financial systems. In 1963 it launched a reform to revamp its faculty structure, a move toward greater intrainstitutional centralization. It then pledged further reorganization aimed at more of a department structure and integration of teaching and research. Given the readiness to assist that characterized the golden age, however, the persistence of faculty structures was also invoked as a reason to fund—to effect change where reformers in authority could try to modernize antiquated structures. Some keen observers at the IDB noted that with major growth on the horizon structural reform assumed urgency. Even by the early 1960s the National University displayed pockets of comparative superiority. Mathematics was one example, and sociology was the main example. In 1964, Ford pledged further support for sociology, noting that its 1962 grant had been accompanied by a promise of additional consideration, now justified for the best program in Latin America's leading social science discipline, under the leadership of the esteemed Orlando Fals Borda.[14]

Accordingly, foreign assistance was impressive. By 1964, the list of donors included Ford, the IDB, AID, Rockefeller, Kellogg, the UN, and European foundations. In Colombia in particular, donors could hope that changes at the National University could fit into wider assisted reforms. Thus training more of the National's mathematics professors, who could then teach mathematics to "nonmajors" elsewhere, could facilitate the push for general studies at other Colombian universities. Two of the relatively prominent alternative public universities had no Ph.D. and just one MS holder each in mathematics.[15]

But the enthusiasm of some for reform and assistance proved inadequate to the opposition of others. The rector greeted World Bank delegates in 1962 already amid the Left's protestations against the substitution of Americanization (e.g., sports) for civic consciousness, and the National Federation of University Students took a revolutionary stance against imperialist U.S. encroachments. Critics equated AID with the Central Intelligence Agency and dismissed Ford for excessive academic professionalism and the IDB for technocratic development (Briones i). Deans split between support and opposition, and consecutive reform rectors lost their posts.[16] Donors found themselves not in smooth concert with chosen partners as much as confronted by actors in conflict. One of Ford's own sponsored academics campaigned for the directorship in sociology on a hostile platform, yet Ford felt compelled to continue financing him lest it appear to take sides. Even before the university's development plan was fully prepared, it was being abandoned.[17] Before the decade was out, the university administration rejected Ford support.

Programs in given units faltered as the units lacked sufficient autonomy from the university bureaucracy. University political conflict also helps explain variation by field; Ford could get along better in mathematics and library development than in sociology. Good training in sociology had its payoffs in faculty for other universities, but few scholarship holders finished their degrees, and the national university turned hostile to perceived international influences. Other disputes arose among partners, as when Fals Borda's desire that graduate sociology become a Latin American center clashed with Ford's preference for basically a national center. The apparent philanthropic advantage of dealing with a strong leader as partner soon looked like the liability of overdependence on one person, dependence referring here to foundation dependence rather than university dependence on the donor (Abraham Lowenthal to the files, 1/27/71 in FF #64293). Many of the assistance-promoted efforts were now regarded as premature, lacking sufficient preparation and care—we might say unphilanthropic.

Ford's grant for sociology was closed in 1971 and called a sad story. Some of Ford's own analysts were already wondering if the foundation could ever return to Colombia's National University (Ralph Harbison to H. Wilhelm, 9/2/70 in FF #64293). The Colombian experience was quickly studied to understand the implications and avoid a repeat at places like Peru's private Catholic university. Similarly, Ford's Kalman Silvert saw the failures in the foundation's economics grant as parallel to those elsewhere in Latin American national universities in crisis.[18] He urged that the foundation should understand its problems as inescapable reflections of that crisis. It should expect further criticism and resentment; without assuming the crisis to be permanent or inflaming resentment by harshly rejecting the nationals, Ford should nonetheless turn attention away from building the national universities, instead concentrating on saving individuals by helping them to jobs with international agencies.

Silvert's caveat about crises passing proved prescient. Once the "Marxist" stage passed, it would be possible to see assistance to Colombia's National University as having produced much long-term good in the social sciences by developing human resources and professionalizing norms in teaching and research (Briones i). Flanked on a more positive side by counterparts in countries such as Costa Rica and Chile but on a more negative side by counterparts in countries like Peru, Colombia showed accomplishments were possible at national universities even amid massive trouble. But there is no escaping the huge gap between results and even the reasonable expectations held when donors launched their major efforts at national universities.

Select Institutions

The Right Stuff

As we know from the previous chapter, no total withdrawal of higher education assistance ensued. Donors' retreat was qualified both by remaining activities at some national universities and especially by the shift to other higher education institutions, not always universities. Donors would enjoy a widening variety from which to choose. The fact that there was choice among institutions, with different commitments, profiles, and abilities, shows the limits of corporatist uniformity. So does the fact that some institutions would seek and engage in partnership, a fact that reflects a degree of institutional autonomy. Moreover, for donors, this was not a static choice among fixed options, since donors had leverage to bring recipients closer to the characteristics they favored.

A more radical donor strategy would have created new institutions. As noted, donors rarely took this route in Latin America, again avoiding an aggressive assault onto foreign territory. Nonetheless, the move from national universities to other institutions was a major move toward selectivity and related philanthropic principles. It also represented a significant higher education parallel to robust reform efforts of the time to spur development by spurning mainstream bureaucracy and instead promoting more autonomous agencies and other "islands of efficiency."[19]

But then which institutions should be selected, on what criteria? Moving away from national universities, donors needed criteria different from and more particular than large size and importance in identifying appropriate recipient institutions. Donors would cling more to ideal typical principles of selectivity, distinctiveness from the mainstream, and recipients' reform trajectory. They looked for more of the "right stuff."[20] This search brought alternative institutions to prominence. Yet our examination of the right stuff includes national universities as well for two reasons. One is that the selective criteria were already partly operative even in the years when the national universities were the overwhelming targets. The other reason is that some national universities, or units within them, qualified for assistance even when the selective criteria became more determinative. In other words, we proceed now to examine the key criteria, citing whatever institutions fit them.

"Low peaks." The critique that assistance supports peaks (Arnove 1980b) finds support. Donors usually turned to places that had some edge over other places. Most recipient institutions were leaders in at least certain respects, and the most esteemed universities were much more targeted than most other institutions. They also tended to have a higher socioeconomic status than other institutions. The critique regarding peaks is thus usually a critique of elitism. Donor efforts had simultaneously pluralist, differentiating, and elite characteristics.

Nonetheless, association of donors with an elite approach is easily exaggerated, as noted by Magat (1979: 58). For one thing, this chapter subsequently explores how donors also favored distinctive nonelite institutions as well as how they promoted system growth overall. Additionally, even as we now examine the support for leading places, qualifications prove interesting (though they should not obscure the simpler fact that the peak institutions were prominent targets).

Conceptually, the critique that assistance favors peaks is far from a polar opposite of the philanthropic ideal type, for both critique and ideal type refer to targeting places that lead, places in some sense at the top.[21] Empirically, we concentrate here on two points. One, generally overlooked by critics of elitism and easy to miss upon first glance, is that the peaks were usually quite modest. This reinforces the argument that assistance to particular institutions was not elitist in the sense of antigrowth but, rather, was basically progrowth. The other point is that the propensity to favor peaks varied by donor. Afterwards, further qualifications emerge as identification of other criteria used by donors shows that peak status was just one among multiple criteria.

First, then, the peaks were not high. No Latin American university matched good First World standards. Myths aside, none came close (Castro and Levy 2000). Research, graduate studies, full-time professors, and ample facilities were lacking almost everywhere. This point holds even including the national universities. Targeting them was not targeting high peaks. But since they usually led in research and so forth, once they were bypassed, the notion of peak becomes still more inflated. To pick just one field, economics, Ford Foundation consultancy reports on leading units (e.g., at the national universities of Costa Rica and Chile and Mexico's University of Nuevo León; 1963) showed them to be not only few but also not so enviable. To pick just one university, Chile's national, the large Chile-California convenio was launched with realization that the university lacked adequate research (at least outside the sciences), library facilities, resources, socioeconomic outreach beyond the campus, academic centralization, administrative and polit-ical centralization, and rational resource distribution policies across units (University of Chile/University of California 1979: 8–9). Where the university had advanced in given fields was usually where prior assistance had been targeted back when the areas had still been weak (e.g., agronomy by the Rockefeller Foundation). The convenio was not to support a great university. It was to help make it great.

In many other cases, donors saw the need for a big push just to make "peaks" viable. Assistance was aimed at helping to make targets become leaders not just in the sense of having an edge over others but also being able to shine a light for them. To a large extent, donors provided assistance aimed at making institutions into the kinds of targets that then would truly fit do-nors' preferred criteria for giving (personal correspondence from John Har-rison 3/4/88, 10/18/88).

Whereas the examples to this point have been public universities, targeted private universities were not formidable peaks either, especially through the 1960s. They were not elite pillars towering over their systems. The Domini-can Republic's Catholic university and Mexico's Las Américas and Autón-oma de Guadalajara were small, rather ramshackle places (Perkins i), assisted in part by having campuses built for them, just as Peru's La Molina had on the public side. Colombia's EAFIT (Medellín School of Business Administra-tion and Finance) was another such institution helped early on by AID, fol-lowed by Panama's Santa María La Antigua (AID #5140101, #5250116). An increasing number of private institutions could lay claim to elite socio-economic status, or be charged with it, but such status never meant broad elite academic status.

For both private and public targeted institutions, then, peaks were rarely very high in any sense and, more importantly, the peak point was atypical of the institution. This echoes the finding about national universities being leaders in certain respects but not in others. The flip side of the observation that most recipient institutions were peaks in some sense is that they were also not peaks in other senses. Our evidence therefore clashes with the com-mon critique that development assistance and philanthropy merely turn to easy, already highly successful, nonproblematic targets. On the contrary, it has been possible for assistance simultaneously to fulfill two ideal typical norms often seen as contradictory in literature on philanthropy, federalism, or other forms of funding change: promoting innovative peaks and giving to those in need.

The second qualification to elite targeting is donor variation. Once again our multilateral bank lies further than our foundation from the philanthropic ideal type. Despite documented consideration of shifting toward more fo-cused efforts, the IDB in the golden age emphasized general institutional de-velopment and then moved from selecting individual institutions toward broader responsiveness to clusters of institutions. The individual institutions that the IDB did target included modest peaks but also places like Costa Rica's new "National University," created in 1973 as a more populist alternative to the University of Costa Rica (the true national university) and still lacking size and basic installations when the IDB came forward in 1978.[22]

Thus, even before we consider IDB-promoted growth later in the chapter, elitist characterizations of assistance are misleading. The famous foundation dictum "to make the peaks higher" was not uniformly apt for all donors, and it hardly had the significance in Latin America that it did when the targets were Johns Hopkins or Harvard. Where donors operated selectively, that rarely meant clear pinnacles of a system and certainly not formidable peaks that could run sure-fire, prestigious activities.

Receptivity to change. Much closer than peak status to a prerequisite for selection was receptivity. This point sustains the last chapter's general claim about partnership greatly outweighing imposition and its specific findings about targeted nations. At the institutional as much as the national level, receptivity to assistance was receptivity to reform. Assistance was heavily change-oriented, to reward and stimulate innovation. Indeed, the basic idea of promoting institutions that develop their own distinctive profiles, away from a corporatist system's rules, was itself promotion of change. At least regarding higher education in the golden age, charges that assistance or foundations favor status quo institutions fail.

In reality, donors often favored universities geared for change over presently superior counterparts. For its economics project in Chile in the 1950s, AID chose the Catholic over the national university, as did the IDB in 1964 for science and mathematics and in 1971 for general institutional development.[23] The Católica was more politically conservative but less academically conservative, an attractive mix by philanthropic notions. Costa Rica had the lead national university target within Central America because it was most advanced in reform prospects, not personnel or productivity (Lungo i). Likewise, the rector of Peru's Catholic university uttered magic words for donor ears: "We must change or die" (Fraenkel i). When IDB president Herrera outlined bank policy for promoting human resource development, he prioritized places "readjusting their traditional academic structure."[24] Such favoring of reform-oriented over other places reinforced the sense of donor selectivity and voluntary choice.

Ability to change. Because their projects to achieve major change were far from sure-fire, donors sought partners who showed ability as well as desire to change. The philanthropic ideal type requires competent as well as willing partners. Recipients should have a governance profile to see the reform fight through. That often meant the perhaps paradoxical combination, just noted for Chile's Catholic university, of a rather conservative political profile to achieve academic reform. Donors liked counterparts who were stable and clearly in charge. At the same time, especially in the years of ambitious aid for institutional development, this preference did not come as close to a prerequisite as did partners' desire for reform. The preference did, however, soon translate into the favoring of public alternative and especially private universities over national ones. The concern for recipients' reform capability proved valid, as strong, stable leadership turned out to be correlated with successful change in places such as the Dominican Republic's Catholic university, Colombia's Javeriana, Costa Rica's new technological university, and only an exceptional national university such as Costa Rica's.[25]

A reassuring indicator of reliability was a track record with assistance. This speaks to the assistance and philanthropy debates on the appropriateness of rewarding performance; our donors, particularly Ford, often returned to places that had worked with them before.[26] Many of the prior partnerships had included other donors as well. Its loan documents in the mid-1960s justified the IDB's role by citing recipients' activities with predecessors: at the University of Chile's public health school, AID, Rockefeller, and Kellogg; at Colombia's National University, all the same plus Ford; at Chile's University of Concepción, the Ford, Rockefeller, Kellogg, and Carnegie foundations plus UNESCO and West European donors; at Chile's private technical university, AID with the University of Pittsburgh and then Ford.[27] Similarly, AID's 1967–73 project documents regarding Ecuador's national university cited Rockefeller assistance from 1959 to 1962. Ford frequently followed both Rockefeller and AID. Foundation grants often were truly seeds leading to other income, but sometimes other agencies sowed the first seeds. Additionally, many targets have received repeatedly from a great variety of donors (e.g., Peru's La Molina from AID, Ford, Rockefeller, and the IDB). Simultaneous commitments have also commonly reassured donors. On the other hand, a lack of initial contacts would handicap institutions such as Chile's public technical university in the scramble for assistance (D'Etigny i-2).

When it results from recipients' pressure, donors' convenience, a search for easy, visible successes, and aversion to risk, the repeated funding of certain places undermines the philanthropic ideal type. When it results from a proven track record of change and underscores the targeting of the few places that can achieve further change, repeated funding upholds the ideal type (as it would uphold the federalist ideal type). Most evidence from documents and interviews is positive. Though short of proving any exact mix of causal factors, it allows the conclusion that at least an important part of what drove the donors to return to prior targets was consistent with the philanthropic ideal type.

Other factors. We can sketchily identify and illustrate five other favored institutional features. The list could be extended, but it conveys the general idea as long as the five are understood rather broadly. Whereas none of the five was required for assistance in all cases, each was required in some and helpful in many.

(1) *Model.* True to the philanthropic ideal type, donors wanted to multiply their impact by having their targets serve as models for other institu-

tions. Costa Rica's national university was to be a model for Central America, Chile's for Latin America. Other institutions were to be models for their countries, as several units were for discrete fields.

(2) *Relevance.* Rarely were projects justified in academic terms alone. Typical were projects to help the University of Chile's public health school in disease protection, food inspection, and sanitation. AID almost always made economic or socioeconomic development its crucial rationale, as with the training component of its huge Brazil project (AID # 5120263, subprojects 05 and 07). Thus, relevance further undermines views that assistance would pick just academic peaks. Relevance also underscores the huge assistance emphasis on change, since Latin American universities were notoriously weak in areas like community service and practical research. And relevance fits both the philanthropic and modernization notions of using higher education as a lever to bring change and sustainable development to the wider society.

(3) *Field.* Often tied to relevance, as in marine science at the Tec of Monterrey, donors favored institutions that offered rare options in critical fields of study. Targeted fields were also often those where there was a general academic lacunae. In engineering doctoral studies, for example, the few options included Chile's private technical university. Field emphases contributed greatly to selectivity as each donor targeted just some fields, as chapter 5 will discuss.

(4) *Importance.* Importance was a factor that in a broad sense pertained to all previous factors. Like them it led to favoring leading institutions (e.g., AID to Peru's National Engineering University), but like relevance and field it sometimes simply made a large public university attractive. Importance in sheer size often led donors to overlook weaknesses on other counts, as at national universities. Beyond that, AID and the IDB often justified their help principally with reference to recipients' needs and deficiencies—criteria that could rationalize their choice of most any recipient (but rarely became a rationalization for carelessly scattering funds). The philanthropic dilemma of insisting on selective criteria and risking limited impact in the mainstream versus reaching toward the mainstream and undermining selective criteria would arise repeatedly.

(5) *U.S. interests.* Efforts to serve U.S. interests were also almost always assumed, though they were not often directly or abundantly evident. Where a U.S. university counterpart was heavily involved, its specific interests were sometimes explicit, as with Ford's University of Chile–University of California convenio. But we see little evidence for a dependency view that donors fundamentally pursued their own interests either in indifference or in opposition to recipients' interests. Instead, as with the role of U.S. interests in favoring certain nations over others, what operated was the optimistic faith of modernization theory and philanthropy that donor and recipient interests are essentially complementary. The notion of philanthropic selectivity gains

force where mutual interest was not considered a given so much as something achievable if projects carefully matched institutions to one another. Where AID or others chose U.S. as well as Latin American institutions for joint projects, there was a double selectivity, as with Chile's Católica and the University of Chicago for economics.[28]

Cases and a summary. The sketched criteria are illustrated and recapped in case studies of two universities that came as close as any of their institutional type to ideal characteristics. With the University of Chile we return briefly to how even some national universities could have much of the right stuff. Then we turn in greater detail to Colombia's University of the Andes as a maximally attractive private university. Both institutions benefited from their nations' favored status; they also contributed to it.

The University of Chile (UCH) boasted academic quality and prospects for excellence probably as high as any Latin American public university. An ex-rector recalls a French counterpart telling him that UCH students surpassed Cornell students in his institution's doctoral program (Barbosa i). The UCH had handled previous aid well, as the IDB noted regarding Rockefeller and agricultural studies. The university boasted regional leadership at places such as its graduate economics school. Leadership included training for foreign students who then built pioneering units at home, as the IDB noted about how its targeted School of Public Health produced spin-offs in places like Venezuela's national university.[29] The UCH naturally enjoyed the advantages of national university status regarding importance and resources, yet, like its Colombian national counterpart, UCH escaped many disadvantageous features of nationals elsewhere as its governance was comparatively effective, helping to maintain both good ties to government and academic integrity. Also like its Colombian counterpart, Chile's national university benefited from Chile's generally attractive features elaborated in the last chapter.[30] Notwithstanding all this, the UCH illustrated risks cited in the prior chapter's discussion of the Rockefeller Foundation reach beyond its typically cautious guidelines. Once again, having enough of the right stuff to attract assistance was far from having all the right stuff. In practice, political considerations of university and national scope repeatedly undermined donors' objectives.[31] Also, the national was selected among other institutions, not to the exclusion of them. The UCH was even helped by the simultaneous attractiveness of Chile's Catholic university. That institution could be targeted for its patterned private advantages regarding possibly greater quality uniformity and effective management alongside lesser political conflict, while still enjoying close, subsidized ties with government.[32] Accordingly, donors sustained their open, pluralistic posture by giving generously to both the Catholic and the national university.

Colombia's University of the Andes appeared almost too good to be true—a donors' pet. It, too, fit a loose private-public package as the National, del Valle, the University of Antioquia, and the Industrial University of Santander comprised the leading group of public universities in any Latin American country. Ford files over the years would contain repeated declarations to the effect that "we" cannot let anything happen to this non-state, non-church pioneer, the best private secular university in Latin America and a model for reform elsewhere in Colombia at least (FF #61188, #64438). Reflecting its status and ability to garner non-state income, Los Andes charged the nation's highest tuition, but, reflecting a progressive socioeconomic position, the tuition was adjusted to family income. Los Andes was both small and eager to grow. Its governance was tight, with great continuity since its founding in 1948, bolstered by strong ties with the oligarchy and government. Its board of trustees included leading industrialists and businessmen. The institution surely fit the philanthropic formula of political conservatism or at least moderation blended with academic radicalism in the sense of breaking from Latin American norms. Ford files pointedly praised the university for being modeled on U.S. rather than European patterns, with engineering as its largest school (FF #65307). They also increasingly included comparisons to the disappointing National University, with its communist student disruptions and scholarships to Eastern bloc countries. Los Andes's founder, a landowner, had studied abroad, including at Columbia University, and Los Andes pointedly followed U.S. administrative and academic norms, such as semester and credit systems, modernized curriculum, and attendance requirements in order to sit for examinations. Many Los Andes students added a stint in U.S. universities. Donors were impressed when a prior Ford Foundation scholarship recipient in engineering, Eduardo Aldana, became rector; furthermore, the university's academic standing was comparatively high at the beginning of the golden age, as suggested by a full-time professorate of 55 percent versus the system's 27 percent, as well as by similar advantages in full-time students.[33]

Foreign assistance arrived early, and its success lengthened the list of attractive features to gain further assistance. In 1957, prominent U.S. citizens convened in New York City to see what they might do for Los Andes. The group's leader was Governor Nelson Rockefeller, ex-president of the university's foundation, succeeded there by ex-secretary of state Adolf Berle, a prominent businessman and donor to the university. The Rockefeller Brothers Foundation invited others and later teamed up with Ford in the arts and sciences. AID played a role in economics. Scholarships came from oil companies as well as foundations. Engineering and economics were major areas for study, while law was omitted. Favorable consultancy reports brought funds that were to prove crucial to the university's triumphs (Aldana i-1).

With the arrival of Ford, the IDB, and the Dutch, assistance accounted for a major share of university funds in critical development years. In 1967, this meant 44 percent of total income, led by Ford. In the following year donations reached their peak, 61 percent, which meant 54 percent foreign funds, led by the IDB. Donors were conspicuous in areas such as engineering, economics, and aspects of academic and administrative centralization and modernization considered in the next chapter. When Ford accounted for roughly 15 percent of operational expenditures at the Faculty of Arts and Sciences, it accounted for more than 80 percent in psychology and sociology (FF #61188, #61188A). The donors' task specialization was typical, with the IDB concentrating on infrastructure and Ford on staff development, scholarships, research, and technical assistance.

Equally striking, however, was the peak period's brevity. Within two years Ford's contribution went from being greater than Los Andes's own to being outpaced more than four to one by it. Similarly, the IDB gave significantly for three years, at one point accounting for over 90 percent of the equipment costs, and then got out. By the early 1970s the only contributions to Los Andes were Colombian. Brief peak periods of assistance obviously characterized not just troubled national universities. At Los Andes the circumstances of donor departure were vastly different, including a sense that assistance had fulfilled much of its seeding role.

Because Los Andes had so much of the right stuff, attracting repeated and significant assistance, it is especially instructive to note that even there donors did not jump in with unreserved abandon. They realized Los Andes did not have all the right stuff. Ford was reluctant to invest where it saw flawed financial structure. It insisted on demanding recommendations including development offices dedicated to fund-raising, endowment building, accounting, management, and planning (FF #64438). Travel to U.S. universities was recommended so that Andes's officials could see the model in action. Los Andes officials were at pains to note that they had already had these ideas themselves, whether or not they had yet been implemented; the role of the rector and vice rector had been strengthened while full-time business experts had been added. University officials pledged to pump in an additional $250,000 to Ford's almost like amount for upgrading financial management.

Nor was Los Andes a paragon in academic quality: a Colombian peak, yes, but no international peak. Files from Ford's first grant (FF #61388) are replete with references indicating that this regional leader needed international assistance just to establish basics such as seminar rooms, proper offices, a work-study center—and the ability to attract further needed assistance. University officials called Ford's help crucial, along with the IDB's, in establishing several departments and the Faculty of Arts and Sciences, with general studies. However much these grants helped, Los Andes would not become a high peak by the time additional grants were contemplated. In 1966, a Ford analyst noted that while university officials claimed the foundation had promised that initial success would produce a big long-term follow-up grant, the Ford office showed no such record and the success was not so large anyway (Hans Simons to the Bogotá office 7/28/66). Late in the decade Ford's staff gave the economics program a "B," even while reaffirming that economics was a university leader and the university was a Colombian leader.

Similarly, AID's evaluation of its joint efforts with the University of Minnesota in Los Andes economics was merely mixed. Much was achieved but remained so fragile that backsliding occurred as soon as the Minnesota team departed; even before then Los Andes did not take sufficient advantage of what Minnesota had to offer and so came up short.[34] Furthermore, some confidential Ford reports continued to criticize Los Andes for its inadequate financial base and ambiguous liberal arts–professional studies mix. Other analysts noted a problem critical to the philanthropic model: how the university's distinctiveness from the rest of the system meant only limited, trickle-down reform from Los Andes to change the system.[35]

To summarize, the criteria used to select institutions were both overlapping and varied. No rigid, static set of characteristics existed. Seen from the other side, no ideal recipient existed. Each project was a compromise from the donor's end. Often donors had to bend criteria or, using them, enjoy only very limited choices as potential targets were so few. The leading works on foundations and other donors operating in Third World universities have left an exaggerated impression of how much givers could insist on their criteria and get what they wanted.[36] Again any image of sweeping, arrogant, frontal imposition fails. Additionally, in the era of heroic giving and philanthropic overreach, the idea was that many would get and succeed despite problems. Thereafter, the IDB rarely attempted to depict its recipient university as the best possible one; it was enough that it had several meritorious traits. Our findings support others' on the difficulty voluntary donors often have encountering suitable targets for change (Pressman and Wildavsky 1984: 51). Such findings also qualify notions of selectivity.

Nonetheless, assistance has not been as haphazard as sometimes suggested (Cambridge Conference Report 1971: 223). Tendencies and patterns emerge. We can explain why certain institutions were greatly favored over others and toward what ends. Donors' criteria for the right stuff, however flexibly managed, resulted in considerable selectivity. Donors targeted only a minority of institutions. These tended to be much more reform-oriented than typical institutions were. Donors' criteria did not lead to a "scatterization" of resources across the breadth of national systems. Donors did not give basically by quota, standardization, corporate right, equalizing formula, or random chance. The philanthropic ideal type has thus guided analysis of the criteria donors used.

The Chosen: Data on Types of Universities

The ideal type also helps us explore what the donors' criteria meant regarding institutional types. Over time, universities that were created or later designated as alternatives to national universities had more of the right stuff than did the nationals. From a negative angle, the alternatives had less of the wrong stuff (e.g., rending internal conflict).

The ensuing data analysis gathers together all private institutions, and it categorizes all public institutions outside the nationals as "public alternatives." Yet the discussion deals mostly with the comparatively elite universities, which are indeed favored recipients; discussion of nonelite public alternatives follows later in the chapter.[37] At play in our analysis are two related phenomena that bring system decentralization in place of central system uniformity. One is privatization. The other is the growth of institutions (like parastatals in fields outside higher education) that remain within the public sector, publicly funded, but lie outside the main state apparatus and are to use their greater autonomy to add distinctiveness, efficiency, and effectiveness.

To save space, and because key conceptual considerations apply to both institutional types, we concentrate on the public more than the private alternative universities.[38] Certainly donor reasons for turning to these two forms as alternatives to the national universities overlapped. Both the public and the private targets offered lots of the right stuff (reform and quality aspirations, stable leadership, serious management, limited political conflict, support for Americanization, and so forth). Both fit the philanthropic ideal type of change-oriented, innovative, newer, and distinctive institutions.

Beliefs that donors have favored privateness per se are both partly true and deceptive. Assistance did go disproportionately to private universities. The tendency was notable if one controls for field of study (donors concentrated in areas where public enrollment was proportionally much higher) and time period (the private sector held only 9 percent of Spanish America's enrollments in 1960, 15 percent by 1965). However important these caveats, the bulk of assistance went to public institutions. This is true for each of our donors for each time period analyzed with the exception of Ford for its already sharply diminished assistance in the late 1970s.

Most private institutions had little claim to modernizing reform and thus little attractiveness for donors. Donors also usually avoided private institutions (e.g., Peru's Lima University) that were very attractive to privileged groups but did not distinguish themselves sufficiently regarding reform. Moreover, even the reform-oriented privates often presented a troubling profile regarding conventional academic criteria. This was a major concern for foundations, with their academic emphasis; thus, though AID went to Mexico's Tec of Monterrey, Rockefeller rejected requests for major assistance in economics, identifying Monterrey as more a business school than a serious social science institution (Harrison i-3). Donors sometimes pointedly favored public alternatives for their lesser susceptibility to charges of isolation, elitism, and antistatism.[39] What a contrast to the Rockefeller Foundation's policy in the United States until the late 1920s of funding only private universities (Bulmer 1999: 41). Also, governmental and multigovernmental donors such as AID and the IDB faced obstacles in working with private institutions; no IDB loan could go to the private sector without government countersigning. Mostly, however, donors were not particularly pro-private or pro-public per se. They either largely ignored the distinction or saw different, valid reasons that favored each type. Some projects gave simultaneously to private and public institutions, as AID did repeatedly.[40] The bottom line is that donors targeted a minority of private institutions as well as a minority of public institutions because both were the only ones that encompassed sufficiently appealing characteristics and furthered a decentralization of the higher education system, a pluralist development based on distinctive, attractive universities.

We assess individual donors' targeting against the background of Spanish America's enrollment distribution. Since the private sector still had only 15 percent private of total enrollment in 1965 (9 percent, 1960), and since our analysis focuses more on the public than private alternatives, the key datum is that the public alternatives and the nationals had about equal enrollment. (Appendix M shows the alternatives had 52 percent of the public total in 1965, dipping a bit by 1970 before moving higher.)

Ford Foundation giving (see table 3.1, country breakdown in appendix O) sustains the theme of philanthropic targeting of change-oriented institutions.[41] Ford's giving often paralleled other donors' regarding institutional types, but where it differed it simultaneously shows how aggregated data could obscure tendencies and how the private foundation best matches the philanthropic norms. Ford never trusted heavily in the nationals overall. We already know that it always gave most of its funds to alternative universities, even when these were few. More striking is how its funds for the nationals concentrated in few places. This explains how national universities' money from Ford could roughly match their share of Spanish American enrollment, suffering no great proportional drop until the mid-1970s. Outside Central America, nationals rarely dominated in Ford grants; Chile's alone accounted for three-fifths of Spanish America's national university total. Without this atypical institution, the national total would always have been very low. Argentina was the only additional South American case where the national university captured even 15 percent of Ford grant money to a country. Thus, one reason that Ford did not lurch away from national universities as sharply as other donors is that it had never targeted them as much. Furthermore, for not just Ford but the other donors, our (Spanish American) calculations have left Brazil aside, since it has had no national university. That very absence, however, coupled with the concentration on those Brazilian publics breaking with the traditional *autarquia* mold, could suggest that Brazilian publics fit closer to the alternative than the national category.[42] In any event, Ford stands out as the major donor that gave the highest percentage to private institutions, higher than the IDB in all five periods examined, markedly higher in four, as seen in comparing tables 3.1 and 3.3.

AID data reach back to the 1950s, as shown in table 3.2 (country breakdown in appendix P). But we cannot include AID funding from 1970 on because little of that is labeled by institutional target.[43] Public alternative

Table 3.1 Ford Foundation Grants to Spanish American Universities, 1959–84

Type[a]	1959–64		1965–69		1970–74		1975–79		1980–84		Total	
Private	$4,411,496 (16)	25.8%	$6,828,594 (29)	34.0%	$4,554,566 (44)	37.2%	$1,785,377 (44)	60.9%	$185,691 (10)	35.4%	$17,765,624 (143)	33.6%
Pub/Alt	$6,133,700 (27)	35.8%	$2,933,729 (15)	14.6%	$1,227,521 (12)	10.0%	$317,153 (16)	10.8%	$193,166 (8)	36.8%	$10,813,269 (78)	20.4%
Pub/Nat'l	$6,085,802 (26)	35.5%	$9,752,639 (30)	48.5%	$5,458,064 (30)	44.6%	$574,392 (13)	19.6%	$145,700[b] (7)	27.8%	$22,016,597 (106)	41.6%
PRC	$491,250 (1)	2.9%	$355,000 (3)	1.8%	$593,000 (4)	4.8%	$253,085 (9)	8.6%	0 (0)	0.0%	$1,692,335 (17)	3.2%
SU	0 (0)	0.0%	$150,000 (2)	0.7%	$79,200 (3)	0.6%	0 (0)	0.0%	0 (0)	0.0%	$229,200 (5)	0.4%
Other	0 (0)	0.0%	$82,000 (1)	0.4%	$315,931 (6)	2.6%	0 (0)	0.0%	0 (0)	0.0%	$397,931 (7)	0.8%
Total	$17,122,248 (70)	100.0%	$20,101,962 (80)	100.0%	$12,228,282 (99)	100.0%	$2,929,907 (82)	100.0%	$524,557 (25)	100.0%	$52,906,956 (356)	100.0%

Sources: Moock (1980: 92–131 for 1959–79); computer printout from Ford archive and appendix E for 1980–84.

Note: See appendixes E and H, and O for further details and breakdown of the data. Figures in ( ) = number of projects.
[a]Pub/Alt = public/alternative universities; Pub/Nat'l = public/national universities; PRC = private research centers included in Moock data (which include none outside Mexico), and fuller higher education data would show much more to PRCs; SU = state umbrella distributions (none outside Peru). [b]CSUCA, included for earlier years, is omitted here because it had become much less a university or interuniversity organization by this time. Three projects accounting for more than four-fifths of the $450,300 total were to help displaced scholars, and the other projects probably also were not university projects. In contrast, earlier CSUCA projects, especially those in 1960–64, were clearly for the region's universities.

Table 3.2 AID Assistance to Spanish American Universities by Institutional Type, 1950–69

	1950–54	%	1955–59	%	1960–64	%	1965–69	%	Unknown	%	Total	%
Private	0 (0)	0.0	$821,000 (1)	11.1	$1,678,012 (3)	10.4	$6,370,333 (6)	43.3	$1,040,000 (2)	18.1	$9,909,345 (12)	20.9
Public-Alternative	$396,536 (1)	9.9	0 (0)	0.0	$3,477,750 (5) a	21.5	$3,900,000 (2)	27.7	0 (0)	0.0	$7,774,286 (8)	16.4
Public-National	0 (0)	0.0	$5,629,500 (13)	75.9	$5,709,992 (10)	35.4	$591,667 (1)	4.2	$1,770,000 (2)	30.8	$13,701,159 (26)	28.9
Unid[b]	$3,611,000 (7)	90.1	$966,000 (9)	13.0	$5,272,700 (14)	32.7	$3,206,000 (7)	22.8	$2,942,300 (10)	51.1	$15,998,000 (47)	33.8
Total[c]	$4,007,536 (8)	100.0	$7,416,500 (23)	100.0	$16,138,454 (32)	100.0	$14,068,000 (16)	100.0	$5,752,300 (14)	100.0	$47,382,790 (93)d	100.0

Sources: Miller (1984: 10–17, 37–46, appendix A); additional sources in our appendix I. Also see appendix E, including to see why sources and figures in appendix I differ from those in the present table. See appendix P for a further breakdown by nation. Figures in () = number of projects.

aOne included Argentine project for $344,750 was for a research institute.

bUnidentified or identified only by field, not institution; much of unidentified would be state umbrella distributions.

cBrazil would add $23,120,481 (25) to the total based on $13,803,604(15) for public universities, $1,130,962 (2) for public research institutes, $88,105,915 (7) unidentified, and one project without funding.

dFigure includes projects listed without funding.

universities were hardly an option until the 1960s but vaulted to a 7:1 advantage over nationals in the late 1960s, by which time private universities were taking the greatest share. Peru is the leading example of AID's turn to public alternatives as vehicles for change.

A complementary look at U.S. government action comes in the distribution of government-sponsored LASPAU scholarships. Not beginning until 1965, the LASPAU data then run much later than the AID data. Whereas the AID data showed an almost 2:1 national over public alternative ratio for the 1950–69 period, LASPAU data show a 2:1 public alternative advantage for the later period.[44] Where public alternatives were slow to appear, private universities were the main alternatives, as in Mexico. Where public alternatives were available, as in Venezuela, Peru, and Colombia, privates were less important. For Spanish America overall, the private option remained strong and steady over time, accounting for 26 percent of LASPAU scholarships. The joint weight of private and public alternatives adds up to a heavy LASPAU targeting of alternative universities.

IDB data also show a marked proportional shift from nationals to public alternatives, as seen in table 3.3 (country breakdown in appendix Q). After trailing nationals almost 2:1 in the early 1960s, the public alternatives caught up later in the decade and then took the majority of IDB money in the early 1970s. Soon thereafter IDB funds favored umbrella organizations, comprising mostly public universities in science and technology; Brazil is the massive case.[45] Regionally, except for a spurt in the early 1970s, when public alternatives also peaked, privates were not favored alternative options. The IDB's government-to-government orientation was a factor, but the main factor concerned fields of study. More than other donors, the bank pushed transformation through fields in which the public sector had a great advantage (agronomy, natural science, engineering, and medicine) as opposed to those with a big private lead (business) or at least major presence (e.g., law). So the targeting of alternatives to the national universities occurred despite the private sector's inherent limitation. In fact, comparing the 1970s to the 1960s, IDB funding directly to national universities fell by over half even without adjusting for inflation. The IDB post-1960s funding to national universities would be even smaller without two small nations: Costa Rica, which had no other university until the mid-1970s and maintained an unusually solid national university, and especially Uruguay, which also lacked a public alternative. Overall, the IDB, like all the donors, worked with those institutions that seemed the best bets for change at the time, in areas of their interest. Its choice of institutions was never clearer than in the period after it tried the most established national universities and before it retreated from individual higher education institutions of any type as the golden age ended. And in that period the IDB concentrated strongly on public alternative institutions along with just a small minority of national universities.

A juxtaposition of institutional type and nation further shows how con-

Table 3.3 IDB Assistance to Latin American Higher Education by Institutional Type, 1962–84

	1962–64		1965–69		1970–74		1975–79		1980–84		Total	
Private	$1,050	3.6%	$7,200		$26,300	28.5%	$12,900	12.1%	$5,400	2.7%	$52,850	10.5%
	(1)		(5)		(5)		(2)		(1)		(14)	
Public	$23,900	82.6%	$46,460		$61,322	66.4%	0(0)	0.0%	$78,400	39.0%	$210,082	
	(18)		(19)		(8)				(4)		(49)	
BA	[$8,200		[$22,000		[$44,300		[0 (0)]	0.0%	[$45,900		[$120,400	41.7%
	(5)]		(10)]		(5)]				(3)]		(23)]	
BN	[$15,700		[$24,460		[$17,022		[0 (0)]	0.0%	[$32,500		[$89,682	
	(13)]		(9)]		(3)]				(1)]		(26)]	
SU	$4,000	13.8%	$25,000	31.8%	(0)	0.0%	$93,900	87.9%	$117,400	58.3%	$240,300	47.8%
	(1)		(1)				(4)		(3)		(9)	
Total	$28,950	100.0%	$78,660	100.0%	$92,422	100.0%	$106,800	100.0%	$201,200	100.0%	$503,232[b]	100.0%
	(20)		(25)		(13)[a]		(6)		(8)		(72)	

Sources: See appendixes E and J. For a further breakdown by nation, see appendix Q.

Note: BA = alternative universities. BN = national universities. BA and BN are both part of the public total. SU = state umbrella distributions, including all the IDB assistance to Brazil. Figures in ( ) = number of projects.

aThe IDB lists under its higher education category one project of $4,800 as "hospital-school," but that project fits none of the categories in table 3.3, which explains why the total here is $503,232 instead of $508,032 for IDB assistance (without student loans or science and technology).

centrated assistance was, when all three major donors moved away from national and toward alternative universities. (See appendixes O–Q.) Again true to hypotheses on foundation behavior, Ford concentrated the most. Only six nations received any Ford grant for public alternatives, only eleven for privates, and only twelve even for nationals.

Governmental donors were less selective. The IDB's cluster funding of umbrella organizations of multiple public institutions (universities or other institutions or both) contrasts with Ford's use of just one umbrella (Peru's Central Bank) for higher education assistance. LASPAU went beyond the most prestigious public alternatives, awarding twenty-one scholarships at Venezuela's University of Zulia versus none at the elite pinnacle Simón Bolívar.[46] AID's selectivity fits between these organizations' and the foundation's, though different time periods skew the comparison. AID had few institutions to choose among in its early years. Only eighteen universities got at least $1 million in the 1950s and 1960s, accounting for half of AID's expenditures and three-quarters of those identifiable by institution; by the 1970s, as funds declined, few projects could be identified by institution, which may suggest increased cluster funding.

But all the donors were selective—and the picture of assistance as a largely targeted, focused, voluntary, additive phenomenon gains force as individual donors did not go their own idiosyncratic ways: As for targeted nations, so for institutions, there are noteworthy similarities in donors' selectivity. These similarities are especially salient within given time periods, leaving aside AID's activities before other donors were involved and the IDB's after others retreated.

As with the analysis of nations, the similarities become still more noteworthy regarding what donors bypassed. It is not so much that all three major donors moved away from national to alternative universities. It is that the targeted alternatives were but a small percentage of the proliferating institutional universe. Among hundreds of universities, and then a greater number of other higher education institutions, donors worked with a small minority. No assistance project directed itself to the demand-absorbing institutions that increasingly constituted the clear majority of privates in Brazil, Colombia, and elsewhere. Any view of assistance as ideologically pro-private must confront the reality that donors steered away from most private institutions.[47] Moreover, the targeting of the few and the bypassing of the many holds for the public sector as well. Even the less selective assistance agencies avoided most proliferating public institutions. The IDB's expenditures on public alternatives concentrated, 85 percent, on institutions in just three countries (Colombia, Ecuador, and Venezuela). These were among the leading countries for LASPAU's public alternatives as well. Yet there, too, donors were selective. They avoided the great majority of Colombia's "departmental" and even Venezuela's newer "experimental" universities as well as its older "autonomous" ones, just as they avoided most of Brazil's *fundaçoes* as well as its older autarquias.[48] In contrast, domestic governments funded all their public universities. Unlike foreign assistance, they scattered their funding much more widely and on much more ad hoc and nonacademic criteria.

A key to the greater targeting of assistance than domestic subsidies was how assistance ignored most nonelite institutions, with exceptions for reform-oriented ones such as Costa Rica's "National" or Venezuela's Oriente. Donors' main public alternative recipients were the leading, more elite universities. These were the ones building most distinctiveness, the ones with greatest programmatic merit and the greatest prospects to serve as models for the system. Venezuela's Simón Bolívar exemplified the profile. Many of its features resembled elite private more than typical public counterparts. It prospered as an alternative to the massifying, degenerating, politicized national university. It followed U.S. models in curriculum, pedagogy, work norms, selective admissions, incentives for publications, and departmental structure. Despite an upheaval in the late 1960s, by the early 1970s it enjoyed high prestige, with average socioeconomic status paralleling the nation's leading private secular university (the Metropolitana) and far outstripping the national university's. It attracted private donations but also vigorously sought international funders (Corso 1988). That search was typical for leading private and public alternatives as limited peaks that needed to grow in size and breadth.

Some nations tried to build viable alternatives universities without anything like the international role exercised in Colombia, Chile, Brazil, or Central America. These initiatives, which started after the assisted ones and represented something of a catch-up effort, provide at least a loose basis of comparison for evaluating impacts; of course, even in the nontargeted countries, U.S. ideas played a part either directly or via diffusion from assisted nations. Critics would find an Americanization to denounce in almost all nations, and we do not have pure U.S.–affected versus unaffected categories. In any event, important examples of basically indigenous efforts to create public alternatives include Mexico's new institutions in the federal district and Argentina's provincial network, both in the early 1970s.

Some of Mexico's "new institutions" would actually be linked to the National University, UNAM, to drain off its excess demand and to provide interdisciplinary education in one set of institutions and general, preuniversity teaching in another. Mexico's major effort at all-new institutions lay with its creation of the Autonomous Metropolitan University. This was in fact a three-institution multiuniversity, each campus located toward the edges of the federal district. Key aims included interinstitutional decentralization, departmentalization, general studies, integration of research to teaching and to service, fresh curriculum and governance, and other alternatives impossible at the National University core. Policymakers took care, however, to avoid *gringo* terminology or reference to the U.S. blueprints they studied (Ornelas i-2). Similarly, the principal architect of Argentina's "Plan Taquini," who drew on extensive firsthand experience as a U.S. National Institute of Health fellowship holder, avoided ideas that appeared too foreign, such as two-year colleges, and publicly downplayed the U.S. inspiration on matters where he privately acknowledged it. These included institutions of moderate size that would be poles of development outside urban centers, campuses, and centers of excellence, as well as departmentalization, a teaching-research link, and innovative fields and pedagogy.[49]

Results at Public Alternative Universities

Results at targeted, alternative universities, such as the Simón Bolívar (IDB/L41; IDB/E7), were important and immediate. Thus, as we look at these universities around the close of the golden age, or even a decade or more later, the philanthropic ideal type finds confirmation beyond just goals and means. We focus on results at public alternative universities partly to parallel our emphasis on efforts there, partly because more is already written about how the private alternatives function (Levy 1986), and partly to take the tougher case. We should not forget, however, that success was more common and less qualified at the private targets; very limited institutions were often converted into superior places with crucial external assistance.[50] Subsequent chapters provide documentation about both public and private targets in matters such as departmentalization, professional development, and research; here we make broad comparative points about the public institutions' successes and limitations.

The main comparative points provide positive responses to the criteria set forth in chapter 1 for evaluating change. The targeted alternative universities got much better than (1) they had been, (2) the great bulk of their domestic systems, and (3) nonassisted alternative universities. Whereas the first two points emerge mostly within systems, the third adds international comparison.

We must remember that the public alternative targets were not initially high peaks. Yet expert opinion and popular opinion would both come over time to place the assisted alternative universities at the top of their systems either alone or alongside only a few less assisted universities.[51] Parallel judgments are evident by those able to choose: the most coveted secondary school graduates, researchers, peers, government evaluators, donors, and employers. U.S. scholars seeking collaborators in their research projects have also often chosen public alternative universities, as shown in Fulbright end-of-tour reports.[52] Furthermore, no heavily assisted alternative university fails to make the lists. Disagreement about rankings concentrates on the margin, with deeper disagreement reserved more for value judgments about appropriate responses to the enormous stratification produced by the success of the targeted alternative universities.

Thus almost any listing of leaders includes the Simón Bolívar in Venezuela, del Valle and Antioquia in Colombia, the University of Sao Paulo and

Campinas in Brazil, and, among more specialized universities, Ecuador's ES-POL (National Polytechnic), Colombia's Santander, and Peru's National Engineering University and La Molina.[53] For example, La Molina has stood supreme among Peru's public universities in attracting private domestic money and foreign professors, containing internal conflict, offering electives, hiring full-time research professors, and influencing students, curriculum, and policymakers in Peru and even in the rest of Latin America. Informed observers are sure that assistance played a decisive role in this broad success.[54] La Molina's prominence would be reflected, for better or worse, by the rise of ex-rector Alberto Fujimori to the presidency in the 1990s.

At the same time, Costa Rica's "National University," not a socially elite institution but a merger of upgraded normal schools, would within a decade of its birth compete with Costa Rica's national university for scholarships and prestige. Professors from the two institutions would interact as peers. Such a result could not have happened without the IDB and LASPAU. The same could be said for the Technological Institute of Costa Rica, opened with an emphasis on middle management, technical skills, two or three years of study, lower costs, a more socially and educationally modest clientele, and a unique curriculum; the IDB's funding allowed for instant viability with distinctiveness.[55] Moreover, because Latin America's peaks were low, even the more elite alternatives found assistance crucial for take-off. Most had been small until assistance allowed growth (e.g., the IDB for physics at Brazil's Campinas). Beyond the national universities lay no large, high-quality universities circa 1960. Early public alternative leaders, such as they were, had already received prior assistance, as with del Valle and Rockefeller. Other public alternative leaders arose only later, as with Venezuela's Simón Bolívar.

The generally unassisted public alternative undertakings in Mexico and Argentina fared less well. Indeed, most became for some time dubious alternatives in practice. The new institutions linked to Mexico's National University were saddled by student/professor ratios over 40:1, a low percentage of staff with graduate degrees, and a passive student role in learning, and failed even on their heralded goals of new interdisciplinary and general education (Galicia and García 1984: 131–49). There would be more formalism than true innovation. At the same time, while the new Autonomous Metropolitan University quickly surpassed the Mexican mode in aspects of teaching and centralized campus administration, it proved a disappointment in research, departmentalization, nonprofessionalist studies, and crippling politicization by workers. Mexico developed no public alternative university into a peak institution, no new influential models. Almost none of the thirty-one state universities, even the newer ones, broke sharply from the National University's model in structure or policies.[56] The National System of Researchers, a 1980s innovation that identifies and rewards the nation's leading researchers, would have scarce representation of universities outside the National University. Not until the 1990s would many Mexican public universities substantially reform (including with tuition, still blocked at the National University).

Argentina likewise achieved few public exceptions and no peaks. Among Latin American nations it would stand out for a relative lack of differentiation (Balán 1992: 29). Of some sixteen public universities created by the Taquini plan, only a handful broke the mold (e.g., Luján, Río Cuarto, Salta, Comahue), none for a convincing period in a convincing way. They provided system decentralization with some attention to local needs, lesser student political activity, and rector flexibility to reward special professors. But they generally failed to establish full-time academic careers, research, departments, alternatives to professional studies, tuition, or other external funding (personal correspondence from Carlos Krotsch 2/24/00). Political forces proved too strong. These included the military government's motivation to buy regional support more than to innovate academically and the persistence of practices that favored traditional degrees and therefore rationally led students and others to push for them even at new places. Argentina was left with little pluralism based on distinct institutional profiles, and in 1993 the government would launch a new reform process to try to change this—belatedly.[57]

In general, nonrecipient nations established little pluralism through quality institutional alternatives, at least outside their technical subsystems. Argentina (like Uruguay) managed no peak until the 1990s. Nor did Mexico peak within the public sector. Thus, the assisted public peaks in Colombia, Peru, Ecuador, and Venezuela stand out by contrast.

That contrast, of course, erodes over time, for reasons that mostly do not constitute assistance failures.[58] But one form of erosion began quickly and did mark an important limitation on assistance's impact: slippage at the public alternative universities. Such slippage undermined success at the targets themselves, and the philanthropic ideal that targeted places should serve as models for wider transformation. Slippage by the most elite and distinctive public universities captures our attention more than the slippage by nonelite public alternatives. It also grabs our attention where private leaders have moved further out front, sometimes benefiting from the losses sustained at the public alternative leaders.[59]

One reason for slippage at the public alternative leaders is the pull of public bureaucracy, strengthened by dependence on government subsidies. This is the pull of mainstream tradition and structure against projected reform, where the two overlap and get enmeshed, as suggested by Riggs. When the Venezuelan government and the National Council of Universities make decisions (e.g., about the distribution of resources) on the basis of numbers of students and professors rather than performance and development plans, they limit Simón Bolívar's chances to soar. National formulae determine salaries, undermining the university's initial flexibility to hire the best (IDB/E7: 73–74). Distinctive, elite public universities usually require extra money, channeled in distinctive ways, but Venezuelan and other national policy often continues to mean the standard rules and policy of *homologación*.[60] Foreign assistance temporarily provided that extra, distinctive funding, but as it declined in the 1970s, domestic governments had trouble filling the void. Naturally, economic crisis in the 1980s and beyond aggravated the political problems.

Put in terms of implementation literature, successful reform at public alternative universities had much to do with focusing radical change within systems on a few targeted places, with strong leadership, thus limiting the number of veto points (Cerych and Sabatier 1986). Yet that very limitation left unreformed places that then exerted pressure curbing and even reversing reforms. Regarding the philanthropic ideal type, one could see how selectivity worked better than overreach but also the dangers when targets do not become strong levers for the system.

Another political pull from the mainstream has been conflict. Into the 1970s student activism was crucial. As it receded in the 1980s, workers' unions became increasingly active. This meant further disruptions within public alternative as well as national universities, extra weight for fracturing elections, and ties to national unions and parties—all diminishing the autonomy and authority of university administration to keep their institutions distinctive. "Hypermobilization" undermined institutionalization (Huntington 1968). In Peru, electoral conflict hurt the engineering university, and La Molina suffered as Ford-backed efforts to infuse the social sciences into agricultural studies introduced forces enveloped in political activism, creating serious intrainstitutional cleavages. What was supposed to be a novel mix at La Molina proved an injection of the institution's problems into a promising field.[61]

Whereas political conflict had initially boosted public alternatives, with elites fleeing the national universities, it came to plague them, too. Still, problems of politicization generally remained worse outside the targeted institutions, while finances deteriorated even more there. Consequently, public alternative universities could maintain an advantage over the mainstream. They have lost some distinctiveness, however, and have yielded ground to private elite universities. Put another way, in its break from more corporatist tradition, Latin America gained enough pluralist steam to create alternative public as well as private universities but not to maintain the projected degree of public distinctiveness. Instead, results have been mixed and prismatic as each reform struggles and evolves in settings that are often more challenging than nurturing.

In several ways, then, the pull of the mainstream meant that public alternative universities lacked sufficient autonomy. They had often enjoyed enough autonomy from their system and national rules to engage in partnership with donors but an insufficient amount to stay the course. This sometimes had to do with insufficient autonomy from government and its national rules or interference, and it sometimes had more to do with insufficient autonomy from other social and political forces.

Targeted public alternatives thus produce results consistent with literature on implementation. They are mostly failures judged against the grand expectations set for them. They neither achieve the degree of distinctive innovation projected, nor become pivotal models through which reformers lever their system's mainstreams. Instead, they slip back partly toward the mainstream. As Riggs would predict, the mainstream's traditions, norms, and claims pull hard and transform the intended reforms (Riggs 1964). This is especially true as the alternative public organizations in question exist in a nontransformed environment and so do not fit into what we would consider a supportive *web* of reform.[62] Prismatically mixed forms emerge. Many represent formalism, as reality is far from what new mission statements and statutes proclaim. There is displacement as enclaves emerge alongside and are affected by preexisting forms. Layers and hybrids develop. On the other hand, these realities allow that public alternative universities have continued to do well judged by more realistic criteria than initial expectations, tower over most institutions, and offer positive alternatives to them. At the most general level, then, evaluation should be mixed as grand goals are mostly unachieved but worthwhile change emerges in various foreseen and unforeseen ways.

The Colombian Case

As we used Colombia for a case study of donor arrival and departure at national universities as well as for our leading case (Los Andes) of institutions having the right stuff, so we return to Colombia for stories of assistance at public alternative universities. This return offers symmetry and takes us back to the country that was unsurpassed in Spanish America for the prominence of multiple, select, public universities in the assistance experience. The shift from the national to other universities was possible in large part because, early in the golden age, Colombia was further advanced with alternative universities than any other Spanish American country except perhaps Chile.[63] Several of Colombia's alternatives surpassed the national in percentage of faculty with graduate degrees, for example (Magnusson 1970: 109). For three public alternative universities in Colombia we look at their right stuff, assistance efforts, and results.

The Industrial University of Santander, founded in 1948, the same year as Los Andes, specialized in engineering. It was a major source of the country's technically trained professionals. It thus met the criteria of both distinctiveness and importance for national development. The governance profile was also attractive. At the top sat a nine-member council chaired by the governor of Santander province, with representation of the national ministry, the church, banking, industry, alumni, and the rector; faculty had only one representative, students none. The rector freely designated his administrative team. Santander was evaluated as efficient, well maintained, and planning further reform. The faculty was mostly full-time in 1961 (IDB/E4: 3–5, 15, 53; IDB/L26). In that year both the UN Special Fund and Ford provided assistance, Ford mostly to broaden professional education through the strengthening of humanities and social science. The IDB followed in 1972 with funds for general improvement and growth. Already prior to that, however, politics and governance had become problematic. The rector who had forged partnerships left, the governor intervened, and student strikes became commonplace. These included direct attacks on U.S. assistance and Americanizing reform; the IDB and others found their efforts hampered by repeated strikes. It became difficult for donors even to get their mail through. Donors faced an institution no longer resolutely in partnership but rent by conflicts between friends and foes of assistance (FF # 61187).

The University of Antioquia held promise in a greater array of fields and particular promise for regional development. Founded in 1803, it suffered an exodus in 1936–37 to private universities in its Medellín region but remained, at least in Ford's eyes, the regional leader, one of the five best of the country's then thirty-six universities (FF #63144, #65118). Although Antioquia was a modest peak, as the staff was mostly part-time, poorly paid, and without access to proper facilities, it promised reform. At least one report compared its potential for innovation favorably to that of Los Andes (Bonner, Gerber, and Morse 1963). It gained autonomous status in 1958 and then chose its first full-time rector, U.S. educated and pro-reform. It committed itself to a general studies plan and a general institutional development plan, and requested external assistance to move forward. This it received. In 1963, Ford accounted for 47 percent of the university's income. AID provided help for a library, the IDB for equipment. With such assistance the university grew from roughly two to eight thousand enrollments between 1963 and 1969, though also suffering problems with retention. It built upon its initially limited base of full-time professors with graduate degrees as it also built a fine plant with central academic and administrative services and data. Nonetheless, at the end of the decade evaluation had a familiar, mixed ring: estimable progress and leadership commitment to further reform but short of clear self-sustaining progress, especially amid persisting and growing problems that led to recommendations against further Ford funding.[64] Chief among the growing problems was politicization. Politically radical students bonded with academic traditionalists, blocking reform. Any student expulsion became motivation for a large strike. When up for reelection, the rector pulled back on reform and appointed more traditional deans, prompting the resignation of the head of the novel general studies program.

Probably the showcase among the public alternative universities was to be del Valle. The Rockefeller Foundation selected it for its University Development Program, and so the last chapter noted the foundation overreach and ultimate disappointment there. Yet we must also appreciate factors that reasonably attracted donors. Del Valle was considered Colombia's best regional public university. As at Antioquia, the governor headed the university's high council. The sense of partnership across sectors was reflected in del Valle's unusual zeal and success in soliciting private funds as well as in its mission of community development. A reformist rector had held office since 1953, and deans were mostly young with some U.S. experience. The university had a strong spirit of self-criticism and zeal to break traditional molds. Del Valle also benefited from its pre–golden age start with an array of consultants and U.S. universities, as well as the Rockefeller Foundation, all linked to its own development of reform plans. But mixed, frustrating results in general studies, institutional management, and other areas eventually gave way to a sense of failure as political confrontations took center stage.[65] A 1971 conflict climaxed with army intervention. Del Valle's governing board dumped its business representation in favor of student representation, and a rector strongly identified with the university's distinctive course resigned. Donors curbed assistance.[66]

With such trajectories at donor-targeted universities, it is not surprising that by 1974 Colombia renounced further AID projects. Comparing the Santander, Antioquia, and del Valle universities to the dreams of a decade earlier yields a mostly negative view.

A more positive though mixed view comes through comparing these three universities to other Colombian public universities or to other Latin American public universities, including those created without direct foreign assistance. For example, the Fulbright end-of-tour reports reveal that U.S. scholars headed to Colombia have frequently chosen the Santander, Antioquia, and del Valle universities and praised them in their written evaluations.[67] In the 1980s, when the IDB's major funding of national umbrella organizations and science and technology represented a turn away from golden age funding of particular universities, the funding was nonetheless expected to be funneled largely to those previous targets (IDB/L27: 13). Further evidence of the sustained achievements at public alternative universities in Colombia and beyond comes when the next two chapters move to particular academic and administrative reforms.

Expansion

Donor strategies considered so far mostly fit a philanthropic model focused on building or lifting up (not just supporting) select, relatively peak institutions, with the hope that they would then affect the bulk of the system. Such strategy defined much university development assistance. Meanwhile, however, as the higher education mainstream was not heavily levered by donors' targeted institutions, it was fundamentally affected by another dynamic related to the U.S. export model: expansion. Expansion was fundamental to modernization beliefs that drove assistance, and it suggested basically nonelite pursuits. Donors usually included access for a widening clientele as reason for assistance.[68] Zealous modernization views that "all-good-things-go-together" held that equity could be nicely blended with more targeted efforts at select institutions. In practice, however, expansionist policies would undermine much of the philanthropic thrust of assistance.

Just as the prior sections of this chapter have shown a pursuit of growth even when the emphasis was on interinstitutional reform distinctiveness, so what follows shows a pursuit of distinctiveness even when the emphasis on growth increases. The dual pursuit is clearest in the subsection on distinctive nonelite options.

Assistance supported domestic growth dynamics. This notably included growth at established places. True to form, Ford and other foundations concentrated the most on distinctive institutions while the IDB spread its giving more, but both, along with AID, mixed their approaches. Ensuing sections consider three routes toward expansion: distinctive nonelite options, cluster giving, and general system growth.

Distinctive Nonelite Options

In contrast to domestic governments, donors did not often succumb to almost indiscriminate expansion. No donor assisted expansion regardless of institutional configuration or financed it mostly in response to political demands. So even when donors turned to nonelite institutions, they still usually insisted on distinctive ones with lots of the right stuff. The difference between the distinctive nonelite options and the more select institutions analyzed above is one of degree; some important criteria for selection are different while others are similar. Then, too, the nonelite recipient institutions varied in just how distinctive they were from system norms.

Whatever the variation and qualifications, however, a key point emerges: donors excluded the great majority of proliferating institutions. They excluded most of those that merely accommodated demand or unreflectively as well as unimaginatively copied entrenched academic and administrative patterns. Herein, rather than in any class bias per se, lies the explanation for why donors disproportionately supported socially privileged institutions: less fortunate counterparts were less likely to have as much of the academic and administrative right stuff. Donors thus steered clear of most provincial public universities and virtually all demand-absorbing private institutions. In short, even when they turned to nonelite institutions, donors' efforts did not slip into any antithesis of the philanthropic ideal type, funding most institutions or the mainstream core of the system.

In at least one respect, assistance to distinctive nonelite options complemented more than contradicted elite pluralist patterns for the system, as funneling expansion into nonelite alternatives helped guard against massification of elite institutions.[69] But donors did not use nonelite institutions just to absorb demand and protect their real targets. On the contrary, they chose institutions receptive to many features of the U.S. export model, such as departments, even where they would not attempt others, such as graduate studies, and the idea of different institutions having different profiles fit the pluralist theory and practice of the U.S. model. Assistance accordingly promoted distinctive nonelite institutions alongside lead universities. It coupled academic reform with equity. And since equity itself was a desired goal and donors rarely insisted that targets have all the right stuff, they compromised on other criteria to support selected nonelite institutions.

Donors worked with several distinctive nonelite institutional forms. Leaving aside technological institutes and agricultural universities,[70] we examine three that have some overlapping characteristics: special public provincial universities, regional branches of public universities, and freestanding two-year colleges.

Provincial universities. The selected public provincial universities illustrate how donor promotion of regional development expressed itself in more than just peak institutions and also how no clear line divided "nonelite" from "public alternative university." One rationale for most of the public alternatives (and indeed for privates such as Colombia's Los Andes and Javeriana, Mexico's Tec of Monterrey, the Dominican Republic's Catholic university, and Chile's Concepción) was increased access for those underrepresented at national universities, located in the capital city. This fit the goal in noneducational as well as educational assistance of promoting regionalization and the development of secondary cities. It fit pluralist logic as well, as these were separate institutions, not regional campuses of the national university.[71]

Donors were active enough to make a notable impact for the provinces. Early examples include AID and Ford and the IDB at Venezuela's provincial Oriente university (Ratinoff i; Escobar i). LASPAU efforts, utilizing U.S. government money, deserve special mention. Although LASPAU's premium on academic development and efficient working relationships often carried it to elite private and public universities, probably the organization's favorite targets were medium-size public provincial universities simultaneously pursuing academic credibility and attracting students from modest backgrounds. Affirmative action operated in that, considering two scholarship candidates of relatively equal merit according to standard indicators, LASPAU favored the one from the less prestigious university (Tyler i-3). A practical measure permitting this nonelite thrust was omission of English skill requirements. In short, LASPAU prided itself on its niche outside foundations' more elite approaches. Accordingly, alongside better-known public alternative targets such as Ecuador's ESPOL and Colombia's Antioquia, were Peru's Altiplano and Amazonia universities. LASPAU found itself able to continue its approach because its targeted institutions—nonelite as well as elite—often made strides in staff development and reform, contributing to academic development as well as system pluralism.

Regional branches. Apart from such freestanding universities, assistance also promoted regional expansion through branches (or "campuses," but rarely in the sense of housing students) tied to larger universities. Regionalization does not here mean established universities opening branches to offer courses and degrees even ostensibly on the same pattern as at the main campus, a development that has become more common in subsequent decades. Information on the golden age points more to attempts to build two-year branches distinctive from the main campus. (Some were three-year branches, but for simplicity's sake we refer to two-year branches.) Geared to local development, the campuses would offer a postsecondary opportunity, either for a terminal degree or for transfer into the university's main campus. Whereas there were many provincial universities and donors targeted few of them, there were few two-year regional campus initiatives and donors targeted most of them. Indeed, donors were crucial partners in creating such branches.

The influence of the U.S. community college model was unmistakable. Attempts to export two-year institutional forms could be interpreted as overreach in that they were alien to Latin America and in some ways particular to the United States. On the other hand, the effort was made in only a few places and with interested domestic counterparts. Moreover, such efforts cut against the more common charge that donors overzealously and rigidly pushed the U.S. research university model.

The regional campus idea, in fact, was from the beginning a compromise or a Riggsian sort of mixed form rather than an alien import ticketed to kick aside or steer fully clear of preexisting forms. New units, after all, would be tied to established ones. Beyond that, they would be smaller than the established ones and in some critical ways subordinated to them. They would emerge only in connection with "parent universities," almost always public, usually national. This assistance strategy thus hedged on distinctiveness and certainly on pluralist proliferation. It was more an accommodation to corporatist centralism than a frontal assault on it, as the national university was neither surrounded nor challenged by autonomous institutions. Like domestic governments, the IDB sold the idea politically as a way to fortify existing universities (Herrera 1985b: 245). The option appeared viable when it predated widespread proliferation, with the expectation of shaping it to the system and its traditional flagship. The two most prominent examples were probably Costa Rica in the 1970s and especially Chile in the 1960s.

The IDB was the major promoter of Costa Rica's regionalization. A small 1972 grant financed a study leading to a formal proposal approved by the bank in 1978. The IDB then contributed $30 million of the total $45 million slated to create regional campuses of the three main public universities: the national (University of Costa Rica), the Technological, and the "National" universities. As was often the case with nonelite initiatives, decentralization was to include attention to regional needs through training of intermediate-level technicians, a strong bank concern.[72]

Important achievements resulted. These included acceleration of higher education's regional presence in places such as Guanacaste and the installation of general studies and short career training. But most evidence suggests that the bank pushed its pet idea when Costa Rican conditions were not ripe. Local student demand for higher education, particularly less prestigious forms, came up short, a problem aggravated by the economic downturn of the 1980s. More than that, the three freestanding public universities created in the 1970s, including two that were now to have their own extra branches, naturally consumed much of the demand on their main campuses. Optimism that new freestanding universities and regional campuses could both flourish proved exaggerated. The image of crossed models sharpens as universities pressured the bank to divert loan money away from branches and toward their central campus facilities (library and laboratories at the "National," modernization of the University of Costa Rica's central administration building, etc.). Then, the more the regional campuses suffered, the more it made sense for good students to shun them and for the main campuses to usurp their equipment. Beautiful, underutilized regional campuses were one paradoxical result.[73] This is a textbook case of how truncated, prismatic reform makes it logical for many actors to choose the preexisting over the new institution. Reform snaps back.

Policymakers modeled the Costa Rican project in part on a pioneering effort at Chile's national university (UCH). This was a little odd, since myriad political factors had already derailed that effort, but it would have been difficult to evaluate Chile's project impacts, given a maze of overlapping events. And at least in its early years, the Chilean experiment attracted great international interest (IDB/L9: 16).

Whereas the Costa Rica effort had one principal foreign donor, Chile's had several. AID contributed $3.4 million in two loans in 1965 and 1966 (AID #513-L-025, #513-L-030), while the IDB provided $2.3 million (cutting the UCH's $4.9 million request) of a total $6.9 million package in 1962, with $900,000 by Ford. The plurality of funders did not hide the weight of one particular model, a U.S. model. More specifically, the Americanization project based itself on the decentralized, multitiered California higher education system. "Junior colleges" were to offer most everything later slated for the University of Costa Rica's campuses: access for provincial students not from the elite; transfer opportunities to the main campus; general studies but also technical training for immediate employment; departmental rather than professional faculty structure; full-time teaching; research geared to local needs; lower unit costs. Yet an essential point distinguished the Chilean experiment from the California model: whereas California had a separate system for two-year institutions and for universities (and another for four-year state colleges), Chile created its two-year institutions as branches of the national university. The sense of alien, frontal imposition dissipates further insofar as donor ideas dovetailed with those of domestic reformers including those committed to preserving the dominance of their national university. Indeed, rector Juan Gómez Millas proposed the plan to his University Council in October 1959.[74]

Success was considerable within the first decade. Chile avoided greater massification at its Santiago facilities, without enduring the proliferation of demand-absorbing private institutions seen in several sister republics. Despite higher education enrollment growth from under 25,000 to over 145,000, Chile added but one university from 1960 until the junta took over in 1973—and the eight universities maintained a level of academic seriousness and achievement unmatched in any Latin American university system.[75] Regionalization did indeed help to curb a shift from corporatist systemic standards to unbridled institutional proliferation. The nine regional campuses came to hold over a fifth of the nation's total enrollments until the military junta turned them into freestanding institutions in the 1980s. Infrastructure at the five IDB-assisted campuses was very good (compared with the four subsequent campuses), and the bank was called "fundamental" to this regionalization (Lavados and Sanfuentes 1986: 44). Access for lower socioeconomic groups, representing 16 percent of the Santiago student body, reached 37 percent in the colleges (1968). Regions took pride in their institutions' contributions in relevant curriculum, research, and trained talent. The campuses excluded law, minimized humanities, and made technical specialties flourish. At least initially, they had more success than Santiago with reforms attempted in both places (a majority full-time faculty, efficient teacher/student ratios, general studies, central libraries and laboratories, student guidance, etc.). Beyond Costa Rica, nations like France and Japan showed interest in the UCH's regionalization.[76]

From the outset, however, obstruction from the central campus hampered regionalization. To speak of outright opposition is to simplify. Even the Communist Party supported many features of the project, particularly the expanded access consistent with the party's "university for all" policy.[77] It was more that different groups had different interests, fears, and notions about how to proceed. The UCH core and periphery campuses naturally fought over control and resources. Some at the core insisted on defining standards, others on denouncing the periphery's inability to meet them. The best-prepared students and professors continued to opt for Santiago; some Santiago students rejected at the main campus headed to the regional colleges, undermining goals of access for provincial candidates. Campuses and full-time staff notwithstanding, the colleges managed little student/teacher interaction. Genuine concern over regional centers' standards coupled with Santiago's adherence to a professional training model stressing early specialization made it reasonable for Santiago to reject transfer students.[78] As Riggs would have it, a new form might be implanted alongside a traditional one, but it might also be stunted by it.

Some reforms just did not fit when shoved into the alien UCH context, and others did not fit the broader professional-social context. "Academic drift" began as secondary school graduates joined the colleges' students and professors and regional political leaders to press for elevated professional status and the financial and other advantages it would bring. Engineering often replaced intermediate technical studies, and curriculum shifted to suit mobility aspirations more than local needs. Nurses blocked innovative two-year programs that promised job competition from technicians accepting lower wages, forcing colleges to drop terminal degrees and face the uncertainties of transfer programs.

Several problems with implementation thus fit warnings from the policy literature. Suffice it to cite three. First, ambiguous, encompassing goals spelled trouble as different actors pushed in different directions. Second, the breadth of the goals engendered widespread opposition. Third, prismatic change arose as existing structures and practices persisted amid change and thereby conditioned actors' rational behavior, including resistance to other aspects of change.

The difficulty of establishing a new regional mix tied to a venerable institution at the center led to repeated restructuring, even renaming of the colleges. Finally, the junta converted them into regional universities and professional institutes (which later became universities), mostly as part of its political assault on the UCH, partly to arrest what it saw as politicized, unplanned regional interests. However pro-market it was in economic policy, the junta in the 1970s was ambivalent about pluralism replacing corporatism in higher education. By that time, foreign assistance had done much to bring higher education to the provinces sooner than it otherwise would have arrived, creating new fields of study and spurring significant though checkered contributions to regional development. Without achieving anticipated forms of change, initiatives still brought some good results, and institutions in many small cities achieved reputable levels (IDB/L14: 27–29; Apablaza i). But the conversion of colleges into freestanding universities mocked the dream of a regionalized national university and illustrated the difficulties of major structural transformations linked to existing institutions.[79]

Freestanding two-year colleges. Our final nonelite institutional form is the two-year college not created as a branch campus. If regionalization of established universities failed to create two-year programs, perhaps freestanding institutions could. This attempt came mostly after the golden age of assistance, part of the retreat from broad university development. It has also in recent years become again a matter of great interest for the IDB.

Formed in 1976, the Consortium of U.S. Community Colleges for International Development has included U.S. and Canadian member institutions. The Community Colleges for International Development has received some U.S. government support for its consultations on curriculum, staff development, physical design, etc., and it has run teacher-training programs with AID. AID support increased as part of the heavy U.S. effort in Central American in the 1980s, with LASPAU involvement. Other donors have included the OAS and the Tinker Foundation (Matthews i). But the impact of the general two-year idea has overshadowed any particular U.S. project or attempt to impose. Sometimes, as seen in earlier experiments in Colombia, Peru, and Brazil, there was crucial advice from places such as the University of California, Columbia University's Teachers College, and Oklahoma State (Jacobsen 1968: 9–13).

Moreover, by the time most Latin American nations got interested enough to seek out two-year models, they could also look to European nations that had diversified their systems (Furth i). Whereas the traditional European higher education model had avoided institutional diversification, the creation of technical sectors, or binary systems (technical and university), was labeled "planned diversity." This meant the structuring was mostly conceived and crafted from above, by government, and that the goal was still a limited number of basic structural forms—a partial contrast to the U.S. model of pluralist proliferation, which encourages individual institutions to map their own path. Venezuela imitated the French university institutes of technology in the late 1960s just before starting "university colleges" based more on their site reviews of U.S. basic cycles, transfers, nontraditional study, and night study (Matthews 1982: 58–60). Neither in its regionalized campuses nor in its freestanding two-year forms did Latin America try to emulate the two-year U.S. model fully. Looking at it from the other side, donors did not arrogantly push the model of their main home country on those whom they assisted.

Results at the freestanding two-year institutions in the 1980s were generally disappointing, though mixed. They parallel several from the Chilean regional campus experience regarding prismatic results short of grand expectations. Much depends on the degree to which the two-year institutions became truly distinctive institutions. Venezuela's attracted a new clientele (first generation in higher education, largely lower middle-class, and older than traditional students) and implemented general studies.[80] But pieces of foreign models again failed to assume prescribed functions in alien contexts. Although some universities welcomed the deflection of excess demand from their doors, they often feared job competition, regarded general studies as a waste, and made transfer from the two-year colleges difficult; any university that would try to be more welcoming would find itself subject to pressure from peers pressing for homogenous university policy (Sada i). Some two-year graduates would find good employment in technical and middle-level management positions anyway, but more would find their lower-status degrees a handicap. Such factors then logically reinforced ingrained norms that push curriculum away from general studies, toward professional training. So did the persistence of free tuition in public universities: Unlike U.S. counterparts, Latin American students have not been lured to two-year institutions as alternatives to costly traditional study.[81] It has been difficult to implant a two-year form inside a system, or web, unsupportive of it. Latin America's two-year institutions and pertinent actors have had to adapt to such considerations rather than to follow a rigid import model. When the IDB at century's end promoted the idea of two-year institutions, it saw few examples in place.

Donors' role in distinctive nonelite institutional options appears weaker than for certain other institutional types. This is partly because efforts fell short of expectations, but mostly because donors focused mostly on more elite options. Latin American nonelite growth did not usually occur in distinctive institutions, and it did not usually attract assistance. Nevertheless, nonelite institutions that were distinctive did attract assistance and added to system pluralism. Overall, distinctive nonelite institutional options contribute to conclusions about the key role of assistance where change occurs alongside a much less reformed system as a whole.

Cluster Giving

Giving to clusters of institutions was another donor option aimed at expansion not tied exclusively to elite institutions. Unlike regional branches of universities, clusters comprised mostly freestanding institutions. But like the regional idea, cluster giving aimed to avoid some of pluralism's negative effects. These included inefficiencies of duplication and heightened difficulties of coordination. Even U.S. higher education systems, statewide, were moving in the 1960s to curb such tendencies. Donors also aimed to maximize their impact by touching a wider base, gambling beyond their typical selectivity. Indeed, donors often gave to cluster associations for their own ease and to avoid tough and alienating political choices. Such an approach, paralleling lax rather than transforming criteria at play in U.S. federalism, fit neither the philanthropic ideal type nor a critique of assistance as alien imposition.

It is imperative, however, to note that cluster giving was uncommon. It was rare except for the IDB and rare outside the largest nations, for their public universities. Additionally, like support for the creation of freestanding two-year institutions, cluster giving came mostly after the golden age.

Only large nations initially earned this deferential treatment, where donors did not exercise their usual latitude to select institutions and touch their internal dynamics. Brazil is the unique example where cluster assistance from both the IDB and AID started in the 1960s and persisted for decades. Argentina, which in the early 1960s had Latin America's largest higher education system, got its first IDB loan for its eight public universities together, but was never a major recipient of cluster aid. By the 1980s, more nations received cluster assistance if we include funds designated for science and technology, as in AID and IDB support for Costa Rica's and Colombia's national science and technology councils. But beyond the rejection of selective assistance to individual institutions, this cluster funding signified a rejection of higher education conventionally defined; the funding went just partly and indirectly to universities.

Foundations' lesser involvement in cluster aid relates to their lesser recent involvement in university assistance, particularly in public universities and science and technology. Moreover, the rather unselective distribution of cluster giving violates foundation norms. Grants to voluntary interuniversity associations, as opposed to government coordinating agencies, suit their norms better, as seen with CHEAR, GULERPE (Latin American Group for the Study, Reform and Improvement of Education), UDUAL (Union of Latin American Universities), and CLACSO (Latin America Social Science Council) (Frodin 1970: 35). On the other hand, the IDB's increased use of cluster funding in later years coincided with a marked decrease in the number of its loans to individual universities. Combined with the growth in the number of Latin American universities, this meant that the IDB itself had gotten more selective. Never again would it fund anything like the percentage of universities it had funded in the 1960s.

One particular cluster effort merits special attention. CSUCA (High Council of the Central American University) was the preeminent cluster effort that—except for the clustering itself—showed many typical characteristics of golden age assistance. This means that the CSUCA effort was atypical among cluster efforts: it involved multiple donors, including foundations, concentrated on small nations, restricted itself to national universities, and took place mostly in the 1960s. CSUCA was also atypical in that it had a cross-national thrust; unlike efforts to build new campuses of national universities across provinces, this effort linked the single-campus national universities of different countries.[82]

CSUCA grew out of meetings financed in part by foundations, and Ford gave the first support (Tunnerman 1965: 87). Ford soon helped lure major assistance from AID, which placed a permanent representative in the field. The IDB followed, as did the OAS, UNESCO, the NSF, and the Kellogg and Carnegie foundations. Though CSUCA traces its beginnings to 1948, the real start came in 1959, fueled by enthusiasm over regional integration including a Central American common market. Some saw a model for Africa, but international integration per se was not the main goal.

The main goal was Americanization. CSUCA was to guide Central American higher education to a departmental structure, general studies, and growth. Sponsored conferences at the University of Kansas and elsewhere reflected the zeal and grand expectations for the reform, heralded as blazing the way for other Latin American universities. CSUCA represented national universities facing still only incipient challenges from alternative institutions but feeling such an urgent need to modernize that each had started a reform program.[83] The selection of CSUCA highlights how targeting less-developed nations often meant targeting Latin America's less-developed institutions. If this defied the philanthropic preference for advanced partners, it fit its preference for reform-oriented institutions. The ambitiousness involved was probably more consistent with modernization approaches than with more cautious philanthropic norms.

Certain accomplishments can be credited. Good training resulted in areas such as sociology and teacher preparation, with graduates carrying programs back to their native nations and universities. A few regional research programs worked well for a time, including both veterinary medicine and sanitation engineering at Guatemala's San Carlos. Costa Rica's national university truly developed. Enrollments and facilities expanded throughout the region (AID #5960012-03; FF #65326).

But CSUCA is not a case where mixed, prismatic change amounted to net results that were significantly positive. Failures dominated. Costa Rica's singular success among the region's national universities translated into stratification across nations much more than emulation. Little standardization (e.g., admissions) or interuniversity coordination resulted. Nor did much Americanization, whether regarding structures, norms, or personnel. By 1968, CSUCA effectively broke with AID, as formally confirmed in 1973. Ford remained prominent, but pessimism grew. Also, Ford's money came to reflect CSUCA's shift toward more of a separate research center (indeed a valuable center, garnering European support) and a promoter of good regional causes and information. But CSUCA hardly pretended to satisfy the universities' needs or coordination.[84] CSUCA did not even possess good basic data about its universities. It failed also in its role as defender of the public university: the public university lost prestige, and private universities arose and increasingly challenged their predecessors. AID's and Ford's new target for Americanization with coordination across Central American nations was FUPAC (Federation of Private Universities of Central America and Panama), an association of Jesuit universities.[85]

Much of CSUCA's failure was in line with our general findings about national universities. On the political side, deans jockeyed, quarreled, and were toppled. As most professors and students stood aside, activists had a major impact. On the macropolitical front, an intense leftward, anti–U.S. trend set in. What had been Central American partnership in policymaking with care to avoid excess dependency turned into a rejection of assistance. The key attraction for donors—domestic reform and receptivity—was reversed. "We punished the *gringos* and paid the price in lost assistance," was one rueful Central American conclusion (Lungo i). CSUCA leadership included exiles from their native countries, future top Nicaraguan Sandinistas, such as Sergio Ramírez as secretary general, and Salvadoran guerrillas. Furthermore, donors' unusual cross-national reach proved quixotic as nations turned out to quarrel more than integrate (Domínguez 1987). Even before the 1969 Honduran-Salvadoran "soccer war," barriers blocked the free flow of students and shared facilities. Yet international disputes merely exacerbated the inability of individual nations to march toward Americanization. Domestic political and economic collapse was the broadest factor. Within higher education, donors' experience at CSUCA paralleled experience with regional campuses of national universities in dramatizing a general failure to coordinate growth in any orderly way, let alone in any semblance of a corporatist system.[86] And like the donor experience at individual national universities elsewhere, failures at CSUCA epitomized the inability to achieve grand modernization expectations of exporting major parts of a model into the core of higher education systems.

General System Growth

In the golden age, back before the era of neoliberalism and "cost recovery," donors were clearly and enthusiastically pro-growth. In promoting both cluster groupings and individual institutions, whether elite or nonelite, assistance nearly always promoted growth. Growth was almost always a goal, usually explicit, and it was usually achieved. Especially as that growth came mostly at institutions other than the oldest, largest ones, it enhanced system pluralism. However, donors and their domestic partners favored growth even apart from its relation to pluralism. Additionally, projects sometimes aimed, though without great success, to limit the pluralism accompanying growth, as with the regional campuses or certain cluster funding. Growth was generally a goal in concert with reform. Reform was the paramount goal for most distinctive institutions, and it was expected at nonelite institutions, where growth was such a visible and crucial goal, tied to development goals of access and equity. Although reform at the nonelite institutions proved largely disappointing, ample growth emerged. Enrollments soared in nonelite institutions and throughout almost all the region's higher education systems.

Of course, assistance was not the only cause of growth. Before the golden age and the IDB's appearance, donors accepted major growth more than they promoted it. Some accused them of a stance against growth. Ribeiro saw Rockefeller's involvement at the Federal University of Rio de Janeiro contributing to restrictive policies that cut numbers there and influenced other Brazilian universities to follow an elitist academic course as a "question of honor" (Ribeiro 1968: 113). Our evidence of support for growth shows that such charges, echoing dependency's broad charge of antigrowth policy, are exaggerated if generalized. They are valid, however, in two comparative senses. One is that donors did not favor the massive expansion that many on the left desired. The other is that the period of donors' overwhelming zeal for growth was short-lived.[87]

The greatest problem with attributing growth to assistance is not that donors were antigrowth but that powerful domestic forces themselves promoted growth. Population growth, expansion at lower educational levels, political demands for access, ideologies of development, and skyrocketing government expenditures played a much bigger role than assistance did.

Abrupt reversals of growth resulted chiefly from repressive military rule or economic crisis, whereas redemocratization could bring enrollment surges (e.g., Argentina 1983). Whatever impact assistance had on growth in the golden age, a great deal of growth has occurred since then, and it would be a stretch to insist on a permanent impact of assistance on aggregate growth in targeted versus other nations. Greater validity lies in a contrast between donors' more philanthropically oriented concept of rational growth (with proper academic preparation, facilities, structures, and funding) and subsequently more unbridled growth.

But several indicators suggest that assistance had major effects on growth, even though these remain inconsistent and hard to prove. First, Latin America's higher education systems had not always been so growth oriented. When donors arrived, many nations had restrictive admissions in their public universities, in addition to appalling retention rates, which also limited enrollments. Against such a background, donors' growth policy often was comparatively liberal. AID launched its $15 million program in Brazil in the late 1950s (AID #5120263), scorning the nation's rigid admissions exams. That a nation as large as Colombia would have fewer than 3,000 students in 1940 and fewer than 10,000 still in 1960 was seen by donors as detrimental to both national development and social mobility.[88]

Second, reality typically involved interwoven, mutually influencing assistance and domestic forces. The norm of partnership was manifest. Most assistance projects were joint projects. Indeed, as a condition for grants and loans, domestic governments and others had to increase their own contributions. Apart from formal agreements, assistance brought into play dynamics that required subsequent domestic financing to maintain new facilities, finance new staff, and so forth. Assistance also stimulated expectations and lobbying for growth and equity by those not themselves targeted by donors.[89]

The third through fifth indicators consider possible impacts of assistance on growth in particular places that donors favored. The third indicator, then, is cross-national. Assistance appears to have had a notable growth impact in certain small nations receiving proportionally high assistance.[90] More general and guarded is a comparison between key assisted nations (Brazil, Chile, Colombia, Costa Rica, and the rest of Central America) and the most striking low recipients other than Cuba (Argentina, Mexico, Uruguay, Venezuela) we have most considered. The first group grows faster, strikingly in the most pertinent period.[91] Given our observations about the weight of the domestic factors and the passage of time, we would not insist on this cross-national comparison involving assistance and causality.

Fourth, donor impacts are clearer when we desegregate to the institutional level. Assistance had an incontrovertible impact on growth at many targeted institutions. It broke bottlenecks at certain national universities (e.g., Colombia and Panama) and brought several young, semidistinctive public institutions to viable size immediately (e.g., Costa Rica's "National"). Even assistance to private institutions was pro-growth, especially given their modest size; IDB help was crucial to making the Dominican Republic's Catholic university grow and offer access to students in the Cibao region (IDB/E5: 18). In general, assistance had a major growth impact at the most distinctive private and public institutions. Notwithstanding AID and IDB evaluations complaining of unfulfilled growth goals at some institutions due to cost overruns, proliferation of competing institutions, underestimation of dropouts, and tough admissions standards, projects usually met growth goals—and they were impressive goals. Probably all major golden age projects increased enrollments at their targeted institutions, usually quite a bit. A solid contrast between mainstream system growth and selective growth is that the latter depended much more on assistance.

Fifth, assistance deserves a greater share of the credit for expansion at the graduate level. Here donors ventured into nearly virgin territory. They sometimes moved beyond facilitating to pushing. In that sense they fit the philanthropic premium on innovation more than its premium on partnership, though this again was partnership in that donors had counterparts wanting to build something fresh. But here the goal may have been more formidable than the result. Compared to the undergraduate level, projects more often fell short of targeted numbers.[92] The more reformers insisted on a high-level focus different from that of first-degree professional education, the harder it was to realize the goal.

Sixth, the tremendous donor effort in the golden age included various measures that directly involved growth. Many projects were directed primarily at building up the human resource base. This meant increased enrollments, scholarships for graduate study, development of full-time faculty, and a great deal of technical assistance. Notable expansion usually resulted even where results fell short of project goals (e.g., AID #5120312 for Brazilian engineering). Building up the physical base with campuses, libraries, and laboratories also fits the growth picture. Academic and administrative reforms ranging from general studies and departmentalization to central registration and student services all brought expanded capacity.[93] Most commonly and simply, assistance provided extra resources for growth.

Finally, seventh, in the golden age *all* major donors prominently promoted growth. Of course, an IDB-foundation contrast held even then. Whereas the bank reflected domestic governments' penchant for responding to social-political demands, foundations concentrated on universities that were not massifying, and they less often called growth "democratization" or identified higher student/professor ratios as improvement. But foundations contributed to system growth even if largely as a by-product of other goals and as a consequence of very concentrated assistance to a few special places. Also, foundation cooperation with governmental donors aided growth at virtually all its targeted institutions.[94]

At a minimum, then, assistance facilitated and accelerated growth, having a fundamental effect for at least some important places and activities. Facilitation and acceleration are consistent with ideal typical notions of philanthropic action.

Without attempting to estimate the proportional role played by assistance, it is therefore pertinent to note the impressive growth of Latin American higher education. As appendix G details, enrollment jumped from roughly 400,000 in 1955 and 550,000 in 1960 to 3.4 million in 1975, and then to over 6 million by 1985 (moving to roughly 10 million by the century's close). Cohort enrollment rates jumped from 3.0 percent in 1960 to 11.8 percent by 1975 and 14.9 percent by 1980. Latin America ascended from half the worldwide average to greater than the worldwide average, 1960–80, even though other regions were also growing fast. Education's share of Latin American GNP grew from 2.3 to 4.5 percent, 1960–84, while its share of the national budget grew from 11.7 to 16.1 percent.[95] Higher education grew even faster.

Whatever the limitations of such data, they place a burden on those who would argue that assistance displaces or depresses growth on the recipient side. Specifically in education, dependency and other critiques of assistance have claimed that assistance retards domestic expenditures and cohort participation. Latin American higher education neither stagnated nor shrank in size during the golden age of assistance and its immediate aftermath. Quite the contrary. Assistance played a part either with the trend or leading it, but certainly not in opposition to it, as Latin America smashed its previously small, restricted higher education system.

Yet growth would not be the manifold blessing anticipated by modernization theory. Here is a broad example of where direct, explicit, programmatic goals were achieved without bringing the results conjured up by donors and their domestic partners. The biggest failure connected with growth lay not in its lack but its realization. Tremendous growth overwhelmed many, sometimes most, other aspects of the university for export model. As with political systems (Dahl 1971: 32–47), academic systems may need to strengthen themselves over time before being challenged by large numbers, and a sound plan of sequences may prove important for policy implementation (Cerych and Sabatier 1986). Instead, alongside institutions and units targeted for development and reform arose or grew more headed for neither. Within some targeted institutions, notably the least select ones, including national universities, enrollment growth usually more than wiped out resource gains. Dropout rates soared. Subsequent chapters will show how growth helped cripple reforms such as general studies and full-time teaching. University degrees lost social and job value. Average academic quality, far from rising through emulation of models, plunged. All good things did not go together. The implicit policy implementation model, here tied to modernization theory, was flawed in this fundamental respect. Growth outpaced reform—and often crippled it. Growth also frequently produced both prismatic formalism and prismatic displacement in which reformed pockets were overwhelmed.

As rapid growth produced a general decline and assistance helped produce positive impacts at targeted institutions, especially those that resisted huge growth, the system became more stratified.[96] Recipient institutions, which were only a minority, surged ahead of others—and did not then become models to lift them up. Donors had generally neither sought nor contemplated this increasingly stratified configuration. Critiques of assistance, including dependency critiques, fare better when they stress stratification than when they charge stunted growth.[97]

The philanthropic ideal type of change proves useful in analyzing the relationship between international assistance and the attempted institutional reconfiguration of Latin American higher education systems. Sometimes the ideal type helps us identify and understand the gap between its stipulations and reality. But it is obviously most guiding where reality approximates the stipulations. And that approximation is impressive.

Conclusion

Donor goals for major system change were ambitious. They included significant movement toward pluralist decentralization through interinstitutional diversification. They also included ample expansion, especially in the worthiest institutions but also in the overall system. To be sure, both the emphasis on expansion and the loose assumption that it was mostly compatible with donors' other goals smacked more of heady modernization theory than careful philanthropic planning. On the other hand, no projects aimed at directly replacing the main institutions or most large system structures and practices. The concrete project goals were much more prudent than were the vague expectations about indirect, multiplier effects. Donors generally aimed at considerable change short of a frontal assault on the system.

Even concrete projects, however, sometimes set ambitious goals that led to means that strained or actually violated philanthropic norms. For a short yet important time, donors placed heavy bets on national universities and thereafter still undertook certain projects at the system's core. They worked with institutions that suffered from much of the wrong stuff: internal division, politicization, apathy, opposition to partnership, and various governance weaknesses. Funding of the largest and most established places, regional colleges, and clusters of institutions cut corners on selectivity. No formula tells us how much such action constituted antiphilanthropic naiveté or philanthropic risk-taking in pursuit of major impact at important places. What is clear is that much effort was made in pursuit of goals that could not be achieved through ideal typical philanthropic means because the goals either were too broad or were in greater conflict with one another than donors and other reformers had figured. This once again suggests inconsistencies or vulnerabilities in the philanthropic ideal type and leads to dilemmas for practical action.

It followed that efforts stretching or straying beyond ideal philanthropic means often led to problems, just as efforts limited to the ideal typical could not have sufficient impact. Assistance did not generally turn national universities or regional campuses or clustered institutions from mixed into much more attractive partners. Instead, a host of unreformed actors, beliefs, structures, and environmental factors blocked innovation or transformed it into something other than what had been intended. Aborted or prismatic reform then conditioned the behavior of rational actors away from projected directions, and even the most favored elite public universities fell victim to backsliding. The inability of new institutions and units to match the export model in practice meant prismatic formalism. Prismatic displacement emerged as elements of reform made inroads alongside traditional practice. "Foreign enclaves" (Scherz-García 1967: 396) failed to become decisive models for most other places, and projected dynamics of a vital pluralist system failed to develop. Meanwhile, system growth came in unanticipated as well as projected forms, producing perverse as well as desired consequences. The juxtaposition of debilitating systemwide growth and the promotion of select institutions brought enormous interinstitutional stratification.

In most important respects, however, the picture has come closer to the philanthropic ideal type of change. The goals of system reconfiguration through interinstitutional differentiation and overall growth were both major and reformist. Regarding efforts, almost all those prominently employed had at least some philanthropic flavor. Even when it was least selective, assistance targeted only a minority of institutions. Usually, the means fit ideal typical hypotheses closely. Impressive is how much those means characterized all the major donors (as well as other donors) and most strongly characterized the foundations (Thompson 1972: 127–32). Only some national universities received major assistance, disproportionately those with more of the right stuff. Or funds to national universities institutions were aimed mostly at their novel or reforming units. When the national university profile deteriorated, donors mostly headed elsewhere and became more selective. They concentrated on those leading and reform-oriented institutions with the greatest prospects of smooth and productive partnership. In that connection, donors did not basically impose themselves, coerce, or either seek or maintain great ongoing control. Where they flexibly chose from among multiple criteria rather than insisting on more rigorous and fixed criteria, they still refrained from standardizing formulas or quotas that would spread largess across the board. Recipients did not have to boast all the right stuff, but the threshold was high enough to exclude the great majority of institutions. Only a small minority of nonelite institutions was attractively distinctive enough to receive. And even the most favored elite targets received assistance sporadically, in contrast to domestic government funds spread much more steadily and thinly across the public system. Assistance to institutions within less-favored nations reinforces the point: after the initial efforts with national universities, it went to but a few atypical institutions. A still more impressive juxtaposition of nation and institution is that donors bypassed most institutions even in favored nations.

Results do not come nearly as close as goals or means to the philanthropic ideal type. But to note only the ways in which results fail would be to fall into the stage two overreaction to stage one's optimism and unrealistic expectations. Instead, what we mostly find are mixed results that make sense in terms of the policy literatures' findings. These results appear at least satisfactory according to our operational criteria for success. While not the main factor shaping the system, assistance was often crucial—through ideas and resources—where institutions have distinctively surpassed the system's mainstream. Assistance made targeted places more formidable than they were or could reasonably have otherwise aspired to become. Targeted institutions have achieved many specific project goals. A striking assistance contribution was the elevation of modest peaks. If the public peaks have proven vulnerable to debilitating forces from the mainstream, appreciating the tenacity of those forces also makes the public peaks' mixed success creditable. Donors' private targets more easily tower over others in their chosen endeavors.

In other words, some important and healthy system reconfiguration was achieved, and much of that was promoted by assistance to particular institutions. To identify institutional leaders at the close of the golden age or still today is often to identify yesterday's assistance targets. Nor was the assistance-promoted growth merely elitist. Donors fostered elite growth but also special growth for nonelite institutional alternatives such as regional colleges. They additionally spurred and accelerated systems' growth overall, a growth too large to be elitist, a growth that exceeded quantitative expectations. Donors played an important role in making systems both larger and more pluralistic.

All this defies critiques that assistance thwarts growth or significant change or that it imposes itself upon and marginalizes local elites, though critiques associating assistance with stratification fare better, both inter- and intrainstitutionally. Also undermined is the more specific hypothesis that assistance helped create a universe of Third World universities with a "remarkable worldwide similarity," experimenting and adapting little (Ilchman and Ilchman 1987: 57–62; Ilchman i). There is, of course, copying and much isomorphism. But these come overwhelmingly from forces within the system, both standardizing state commands and voluntary copying as the easy path to acceptance. Assistance stands out for promoting *breaks* from system standardization. Donors contributed energetically to the growing diversity within the systems. Their diversity and reform intentions were clearest in their support for places already distinctive or committed to change away from system norms.[98]

In sum, the relationship between assistance and system reconfiguration is largely consistent with our thematic hypotheses about transformation. The assistance was change oriented, aimed at breaking away from corporatist, standardizing, system norms that donors took to be stultifying and inappropriate, especially for enlarging systems. Donors found reformist partners for institutional reform, and they targeted only a select group of institutions, a very select group usually and still a minority when nonelite institutions were included and when the goal of growth was highlighted. Compared with these goals and efforts, results would not closely fit the philanthropic ideal type of change, instead better tracking hypotheses generated from policy literatures about mixed change. This has allowed, however, for a measure of success according to reasonable evaluative criteria. Donors operated ambitiously and energetically, leading to both disappointments and successes in pursuit of systems' structural modernization.

4

Institution Building: Centralizing the University

The pluralist U.S. export model was to guide institutions as well as systems. Reform required institutions capable of charting their own effective course. Higher education development would depend more on choices made and executed by individual institutions than on corporatist-standardized policy for all. Autonomous institutions should be strong institutions. They carry responsibility which, when well managed, provides accountability and builds the performance record that ensures the institution's standing. To meet the test of autonomous strength, institutions were thought to need a reasonable degree of solidity through centralization. As it commonly does, the pluralist model wedded system decentralization to institutional centralization. It wedded interinstitutional differentiation to intrainstitutional cohesion.

This centralizing requirement of the pluralist agenda fit a major tenet of modernization theory: *institution building.* For higher education, like public administration, agriculture, and other arenas, development was to rest on strong, well-oriented institutions capable of leading the break away from tradition.[1] Institution building was an exciting and galvanizing concept at the core of the exporting and importing crusade for reform.

Naturally, well-built institutions could be international donors' favored recipients, a targeting consistent with the goal of differentiation within systems. Strengthened institutions were also expected to foster expansion; by centralizing their resources, avoiding internal duplication, and operating more efficiently through appropriate structures and policies, institutions could properly accommodate more students and tasks. Institution building fit other goals of university assistance as well. Examples included those related to academic work, as elaborated in the next chapter, and to assistance's broadest goals—national development through the expanded production and dissemination of knowledge. Once again modernization's faith was that many good goals would go together, from effectiveness and equity to institutional, system, and national development.

Donor Goals

Also again, assistance goals suggested a transformation from traditional Latin American policy. The U.S. model featured strong executive management of policy and diverse finance, with academic as well as administrative integration campuswide. Latin American reality was different. Where corporatism was most prevalent, national policies for the system obviated autonomous management by individual institutions. Where corporatism was weaker, individual institutions still were not usually strong. What was formally left to the "university" was often left mostly to its individual units, especially its professional faculties, not to a unifying entity. Formidable autonomy over academic and administrative matters then resided with the faculties more than the universities. A combination of national power "above" the university and faculty power "below" the university level was a feature of the classic Continental model of a "strong top and bottom" with a "weak middle"—the opposite of the U.S. model. Beyond that, much policy in Latin American universities was the ad hoc result of forces, traditions, and interest group politics, including student groups. Institutions per se usually had limited power. Or they might develop political power and autonomy to protect themselves from outside forces or to pressure them, but this was not usually power and autonomy to make strong institutional policy. Latin America's universities were not coherent academic and administrative organizations.[2]

Donors and domestic reformers alike argued that these institutions, perhaps adequate for traditional professional training, could not handle the demands of changing societies or growing higher education systems. They denounced the duplication of facilities that squandered resources and blocked construction of the larger facilities feasible only at an institutionwide level. And they bemoaned the inability of the university to build a unified academic community or, administratively, to pursue effective reform.

There is a sense, then, in which goals of university centralization envisioned a wholesale change from extant reality. Reformers could claim that their agenda for institution building qualified them as academic revolutionaries, indeed as both academic and administrative revolutionaries. In another sense, however, goals were much more modest: actual assistance projects set more limited goals or limited the revolutionary goals to targeted institutions. As usual, the huge goals were mostly implicit while the more prudent goals in concrete projects were mostly explicit. What connected the two levels was a vague faith that imported Americanization would prove its worth and ultimately win approval through much of the higher education system. If this faith undermines ideal typical philanthropic notions of clear, careful, programmatic goal setting, it is consistent with beliefs in achieving profound change by leveraging systems through key models.

This chapter explores how donors pushed university centralization and what results were achieved. The chapter's two main parts deal with administrative and academic centralization, though overlap emerges as donors see each reinforcing the other. Consideration of administrative centralization concentrates first on management and then on physical facilities. Consideration of academic centralization concentrates on two interrelated reforms—general studies and department structures—aimed at making education much more of a university concern than just a faculty concern.

As it considers the different substantive matters, the chapter explores common sets of issues relevant to the philanthropic ideal type of change. Regarding efforts, the contrast between centralizing reforms and prior reality is one indicator of the magnitude of change proposed. Another is the degree to which donors operate widely or focus selectively on targeted partners. How much do they pursue the U.S. model of centralization wholesale or confine efforts to more modest, circumscribed measures? Regarding results, how severe is opposition, with what consequences? How do targeted places measure up compared with others? Where they lead in the sense of being advanced, do they also lead in the sense of becoming models for university centralization, or do they loom as isolated pockets? Where results are mixed within institutions, what are the degree, shape, and logic of prismatic patterns?

Administrative Centralization: Management

Administrative centralization was largely about management, including both governance and finance. Finance refers here to income source, while the efficient management of resources is a key element of governance. The U.S. model called for a university with the decision making as well as material resources necessary to initiate and implement coherent, self-defining policies. This meant centralizing functions—both new functions and functions previously handled elsewhere—in the hands of university managers. Effective management required a relatively hierarchical system, with stability. Widely dispersed power, whether to deans or to students, undermined the university's ability to speak or act with one authoritative and reliable voice. So did excessive dependence on the state for resources and policymaking.

Strong management would be a big change from Latin American reality at the dawn of the golden age. Atcon's depiction of that reality, however overgeneralized, highlighted the contrast. Universities lacked their own resource base, instead relying almost fully on state subsidies. The main university authority was a council that was merely a forum for bargaining among faculties. Rectors were weak, dependent on faculty deans. Each faculty had its own methods, files, forms, and so forth, so that university policy or management remained a figment, incapable of the vigorous leadership that academic reform required. "Nowhere in Latin America can we encounter a true *University Administration*" (Atcon 1966: 50, his italics; also 45–52). Compared to the U.S. model, university officials depended (both for their own fate and for institutional performance) too much on students and faculties below or on the state above.

Nonetheless, the ensuing analysis of donor efforts shows that actual assistance projects did not undertake to jump from lamented reality all the way to the U.S. model of management. Donors tempered zeal with prudence. Their efforts fell far from either a meek or an aggressive extreme.

Efforts: Governance

Probably no project made a redistribution of power its major thrust. Given donors' views on student politics, it is noteworthy that projects did not take direct aim at that inflammatory matter. Nor did they usually take direct aim at faculties' power. Donors did not confront by directly attacking existing practice. Neither did they often try to install U.S. decision-making bodies such as boards of trustees in place of traditional bodies.

Redistribution of power was more often an implicit or indirect pursuit. For one thing, donors chose partners that had more attractive governance profiles than those at bypassed institutions, partners who would have the authority to carry out shared visions of reform. Soliciting institutions realized they could increase their chances of funding by showing such ability. Besides, even to compose a solid proposal often required a degree of centralization of information, procedure, and authority. To manage a grant well required further centralization. In effect, the grant process itself could have an impact at recipient universities, a professionalization and expansion of the central managerial capacity.[3]

One step more toward the aggressive side, donors proceeded to build up existing central actors. This still was less confrontational than a direct attack on other actors or creation of new actors, but it could change the local balance of power. It could therefore provoke either criticism for interventionism right down to the intrainstitutional level or praise for philanthropic risk-taking even at internally divided places. A common foundation activity was technical assistance to rectors and their staffs. A common IDB activity for the central authorities was construction of formidable buildings and office facilities, along with modern equipment. AID did a fair amount of both. All this allowed central authorities to assume increased functions otherwise handled by faculties or by nobody. Donors sometimes helped changes such as substituting vice rectors, chosen by rectors, for secretaries general, chosen independently by election from below. In short, assistance followed the philanthropic approach of influencing through partnership and incentives rather than direct assaults.

Building up management included support for administrative training, as in the massive AID project #5120263 for Brazil. Critics denounced reprehensible efforts to impose a separate class of administrative personnel lacking even the academic-administrative mix common at good U.S. universities (Scherz-García i). But given the logic of administrative centralization, donors arguably did too little to push training and scholarships in the field of university administration, for example (Lavados i-4). Yet such training gained popularity, with places like Colombia's Los Andes and Venezuela's IESA (Institute of Advanced Administrative Studies) as launching pads. Similar points might be made about efforts to build institutional planning, a pivotal feature of the U.S. export model. This was an alternative mostly to a lack of planning. It was also an alternative to onerous central planning and rules for the whole system, yet donors also undertook some measures aimed at improved system capacity, defying a stereotypical view of hostile antisystem action.[4]

Where targeted private universities resembled targeted public ones, donors' efforts were similar. Challenges were different, however, where the private institutions were much more hierarchical and narrow in governance. Efforts at public institutions focused on building central over faculty power; efforts at private institution focused on building professionalism and rational bureaucracy over extant personalism and clientelism. Whereas donors favored a narrowing of internal political participation within many public universities, they favored a cautious broadening within certain private institutions. Of course, the great majority of privates, which were hierarchical and narrow, never became assistance targets. This fact mostly reflects donors' selective efforts. It also shows that donors did not set out to support Latin America's politically most hierarchical and conservative institutions. An absence of student politics, for example, was hardly grounds for receiving assistance.

Efforts: Finance

By comparison with donors' mix of important and limited effort in governance, their efforts were very limited in finance. What a contrast with what efforts would be in the last decades of the twentieth century. The point is strong regarding tuition and holds also for other nongovernment income (Sandberg 1965: 61).

No major project aimed at imposing tuition, despite donors' beliefs, the U.S. model, numerous references in memos concerning tuition's desirability, and Atcon's (1966: 123–25) view that tuition was necessary for revenue, equity, and instilling responsibility in students. In contrast to the World Bank's later harangue for tuition and other cost recovery mechanisms, the IDB did not so challenge its member nations in the golden age. It sporadically pointed to the desirability (IDB/E1: 20–27, 40–43). Or, like other donors, it supported reforms regarding student payments that were rather marginal to the mainstream financial profile. Like AID it sometimes pressed for educational loans for particular activities on the numerical periphery: study abroad, graduate work, and living costs. For private institutions, which were already tuition-dependent, donors sometimes pushed for loans, compensatory options for needy students, and differential tuition by fields. Overall, however, all the major donors, as well as their government partners, accepted the political unfeasibility of what they saw as economically and socially warranted reform in student payments at public institutions (Vera M. i-1).

More often promoted were basically nonconfrontational reforms involving increased funding from other nongovernment sources. As there was no effort to diminish state support, this was part of a broad pro-growth policy and part of the broad favoring of private-public partnerships and indeed of greater linking of the university with certain external constituencies, notably including business. Also included were innovations wherein the university would sell services or engage in other revenue-raising activity.

Favorable financial policies, in place or as proposed reforms, earned points in universities' solicitation, but few public universities were clear winners in this respect. Accordingly, less in finance than in centralized governance were donors able to find very attractive partners or incentives. Leading private universities could obviously present a more attractive financial profile in some respects, especially nongovernment revenue and certain measures of efficiency, just as they had some advantages in governance. A few public alternative universities followed far behind as the next most attractive partners with respect to finance and governance. Nonetheless, and paralleling findings from the preceding chapter, donors generally refrained from a pointedly pro-private course. First, only a few private institutions managed to achieve cost sharing between private and public sources rather than total tuition dependence, and many had financial profiles decried as elitist. Donors sought those few private universities who could be true partners in progressive change. Second, donors were not out to reject the public sector but rather to work with it where they could.

In sum, donors were not very confrontational in their efforts on either the financial or the governance front. They did not attempt to sweep away mainstream practice. They operated where they found something more attractive than the mainstream offered. They operated with domestic reformers as partners. Positive disposition and efforts toward improved management were often enough to become recipients. On the governance side, this included national universities in the early years. The rector at Peru's San Marcos, holder of a U.S. Ph.D., solicited AID to build his office's capabilities in purchasing, accounting, and the like. The rector portrayed such measures as matters of structural efficiency more than philosophy (Fraenkel i), but of course they would strengthen central authority within the university. Soon such reforms would be associated much more with alternative than national universities, as they always were on the financial side. But even the alternative universities were often attractive to donors for their *promise* more than their performance to date.

Results

No administrative centralization can be credited fully to assistance, for assistance projects to centralize relied on partnership. Additionally, especially beyond the golden age of assistance, centralization sometimes sprang forth as domestic reform whose U.S.-oriented ideas developed outside any particular project. Conversely, because donors did not push anything like a totally new management model, the absence of particular features of that model does not indicate a direct assistance failure. It does, however, indicate the overoptimism of any expectation that directly pursued change would be a springboard for thoroughgoing change.

Another implication of our analysis of donors' efforts for our evaluation of results concerns success rates. Donors stuck mostly to those financial and governance aspects of administrative centralization likely to engender minimal opposition. Visible opposition rarely approached what it would for academic centralization. Donors could see what happened where domestic governments even tentatively promoted tuition: critics decried imperialist influences and vulnerability to multinational corporations and staged powerful protests. Donors rarely gave critics a direct target. A related point is that most administrative reform did not affect students' interests as directly as academic reform did. Sometimes it even promised to ease their lives, offering better services. Consequently, opposition to donors' administrative initiatives usually expressed itself in bureaucratic foot-dragging, or in general ideological criticism of U.S. interference, more than in strong, visible protest against specific administrative projects.

Finance. Finance shows a revealing juxtaposition. Rather limited change resulted in the mainstream of Latin American higher education. But where impressive change occurred, it involved a prominent assistance role.

Until the 1990s, no significant share of funds for public universities came from private sources. Tuition, loans, and donations remained spotty beyond some private universities, and most "foundations" were receiving more than they were giving to organizations (Levy 1996: 108–11). The only major exception was Chile. Key there was the power of a repressive regime to make unpopular reform along lines of neoliberal thinking championed by the "Chicago boys" (Valdés 1995). The role of AID, U.S. consultants, and scholarships in that episode was notable and in some respects a harbinger for the region. But neither during nor soon after the golden age did the domestic source of finance for most of the region's public higher education change much, except of course that volume greatly increased.

On the other hand, specific measures undertaken in assistance projects were often implemented where it is hard to imagine their rise without the international agencies. Loan programs are an example. Donors played a pivotal role in establishing the loan agencies in Central America, Brazil, Ecuador, the Dominican Republic, Peru, and other nations. Early assistance to Colombia paid off in ICETEX's (Colombian Overseas Technical Specialization Institute) success at home and its arguably significant influence in the region. Most nations established loan agencies, and prominent observers have sometimes been impressed or hopeful in this regard (Psacharopoulos and Woodhall 1985: 155). Loan agencies in systems where most students do not pay tuition represent prismatic displacement where new structures assume a position alongside mainstream structures.

In other cases, financial reforms introduced in assistance projects took hold within the targeted domestic institution but did not quickly spread far. The IDB helped Colombia's Santander university move from nominal to low tuition (IDB/E4: 32). Ford reports declaring that the country's Antioquia should have learned fund-raising from Los Andes and especially del Valle speak to the mixed record in one heavily targeted nation. Colombian industry continued to believe that it had little need for university research, thus little reason to contribute funds. The university remained underfunded. Unhappily too, Antioquia was thus much more typical than del Valle of the inertia that gripped public universities within Colombia and beyond regarding financial sources. Colombia's private Los Andes, however, won Ford praise for its timely, balanced, and tuition-enhanced budgets, as well as its data keeping and data circulation among units.[5] Several other targeted private universities in Latin America also beefed up their income profile, including with enhanced public funding, through assistance projects. Indeed, funding that allowed expansion of what had been very small peaks was itself a major contribution.

Governance. Because donors undertook more initiatives on the governance side, and more change occurred there, assessment is more complex than for finance. Certain tendencies nonetheless emerge. A positive assessment revolves around the changes at targeted places whereas prismatic patterns then reveal a more sobering picture.

Some impacts are immediately evident. As noted, institutions had reason to shore up their administrative profile if they solicited assistance, and donors then gave resources that bolstered central administration. Recipients frequently benefited from resources directed to rather noncontroversial expansion. Many knowledgeable observers have found that places where the IDB invested developed greater institutional coherence than otherwise comparable places (Miguel i; Lavados i-2). A favorite IDB pursuit was efficient use of space, money, and other resources-per-student through better planning and central services. Computerized student registration at Honduras's national university illustrates the kind of impact AID managed during and since the golden age where it concentrated on modernization measures that faced little ideological opposition or entrenched bureaucracy.

Differences between recipients and nonrecipients are perhaps spottiest among national universities, where partnership proved shakiest and opposition greatest. Some examples suggest positive impact. Colombia's National University used IDB assistance to create divisions of finance and personnel as well as an admissions office that unified processes previously handled by each faculty using its own criteria (IDB/L24). But the Ecuadorian case shows how it was often difficult to sustain impacts. AID to Ecuador's Central University had a big initial effect on financial management and other matters of central administration, despite a tougher time in academic reforms, but then instability undermined the effects and succeeding university leadership lacked interest in the projects (Blaise 1968: 24).

Given the spotty record at assisted national universities, the lack of U.S. governance features at less-assisted national universities is not a simple consequence of disfavored status. Besides, less-assisted universities sometimes implemented governance reforms. Mexico's UNAM attained a mixed record. Often criticized by the left, UNAM's governing board was copied from the United States in 1945 without a formal assistance project and indeed without public acknowledgment of the model. The board marked the end of elections for rector and helped select competent rectors and improve institutional stability. The UNAM rectorate came to handle personnel, budget, registration, and other tasks universitywide. But UNAM has often proved remarkably unable, in the face of student and other interest groups, to make coherent policy or to reform as it wanted on finance and other aspects of management.[6] The same is true for Argentina's UBA (University of Buenos Aires). And UBA has suffered from a striking lack of centralized data, basic institutional research, and other features (Cano 1985: 99).

Assistance made a clearer impact at targeted alternative universities. These institutions are what mainly separated the overall standing of higher from lower recipient nations. Going beyond the impact that there was assistance-spurred growth at leading alternative universities, increasing their weight within the system, we now identify the strengthened governance at the recipient institutions.

AID helped Colombia's Antioquia to modernize cost accounting, finance, and general management. Earlier on, Rockefeller assisted Colombia's del Valle to institute organized accounting records, centralized supply and storage facilities, and, with Price Waterhouse (a favorite for such tasks), a restructuring of financial and accounting systems. This administrative head start helped the university attract subsequent assistance that affected the management of income, including links to a local private foundation and income from tuition.[7] Venezuela's Simón Bolívar typifies the mixed public alternative success. Party politics, worker participation, and voting for most positions short of rector and dean presented problems that were sometimes severe but generally left intact the university's managerial capacity (Navarro i-3).

Assisted private universities usually came closer than assisted public alternatives to securing the desired governance. Peru and Chile show the general contrasts between the assisted privates and other institutions within the same nations. Informants (Himes i; Fraenkel i) point to the Catholic university as the Peruvian recipient that made the best use of assistance for modern administration. By contrast, the public National University of Engineering tripped into politicization, and San Marcos (national) never got beyond initial attempts before donors came to expect just lip service and pointless luncheons or rectors' use of funds for irrelevant political purposes—or deans' sabotage. In Chile, the Catholic and national universities were twin donor favorites, but administrative centralization went much further at the former (whether viewed in 1973 or decades later). The IDB played a major role in its transformation into a major institution largely because the Católica was receptive to more projects dealing with the university as a managerial whole. It functioned as a more consolidated entity, better able to seek and use opportunities, its dynamism setting it apart from its faculty-oriented, bureaucratically contorted public counterpart.[8]

Because private universities were on more secure ground in that they were naturally less subject to internal conflict, we cannot assume that donors' impact on management was greatest there.[9] But assistance made a big difference, even apart from the general historical influence exerted by the U.S. idea and model of private higher education. A pivotal point is that projects to privates often went for broad institutional development whereas many projects at public places targeted individual units. Many private recipients, including the rather large Catholic ones, had emulated national universities in administrative structure, though they had more stable and hierarchical leadership. Most private universities were weak institutionally when they started receiving assistance, fitting our overall labeling of them as "modest peaks." In the 1980s, senior officials at Peru and Chile's Catholic universities vividly remembered when rectors had paid professors almost literally from their pockets. The Dominican Republic's Catholic University had done poorly in recovering loans until the IDB professionalized operations in the mid-1970s, which in turn allowed institutional growth. Ford's assistance to Mexico's Autonomous University of Guadalajara allowed the institution to have a full-time rector (FF #63220). Targeted private universities were not accomplished modern, centralized partners as much as partners of administrative promise. Results there were not automatic but feasible enough for sound investment. Assisted private universities often became Latin America's leaders in administrative centralization among universities of some size and significance.

Even at private places and especially at public ones, however, results typically followed projected form less than prismatic form. The prismatic configurations help us identify patterns that mark change but change short of the export model. What follows are examples related to the comparative strength of high authorities in governance.

Donors did much to strengthen rectors, but the actual role rectors played depended on domestic political configurations. Funding to national university rectors often inadvertently strengthened actors with more partisan ties to government than the U.S. model would envisage. Or, in a classic prismatic example where prior structures gain power over new activities formally handled by others, faculties determined how rectors would distribute fresh university funds. At Colombia's National University, assistance helped build the rector's tools of universitywide communication—but faculties failed to provide required information (Magnusson 1970: 258–87). At Chile's national, the Ford-backed convenio with the University of California wound up increasing administrative and planning skills but mostly at the faculty level (University of Chile/University of California 1979: 59). For targeted private universities, in contrast, the local context of business influence without offsetting academic traditions sometimes meant excessively increased power for central authorities. Donors would lament the private lay boards' hyperactivity even at good places such as Colombia's Los Andes.

Beyond the results at the targeted institutions, at the region's public universities overall the idea of strong administration often translated into top-heavy, bureaucratic labyrinths (Vessuri 1986: 2). As one observer put it, "We have achieved the size and sometimes even the power, but not the efficiency" (Lavados i-3). A typical result was bloated bureaucracy, as public universities' administrations become political arenas offering the employment demanded and protected by unions. Rectors remained academics stepping "up" into administrative roles because they could play this system, not because they had demonstrated managerial ability to lead institutions academically (Navarro i-3). Such outcomes support Riggs's (1964) view that development theory in general and assistance in particular build heavy, lumbering bureaucratic structures.[10] This was not the happy institutional building that could transform universities and their societies.

Also in line with Riggs rather than with the philanthropic ideal type, prismatic forms were not transitional pauses en route to emulation of foreign models. Neither did targeted institutions become influential levers for financial and governance reform in the public mainstream. Coupled with the pointedly limited scope of donors' direct efforts via projects, the result is that mainstream institutions lack effective central management. Both soon and long after the end of the golden age, reports circulating in donor agencies generally have ranked the region's public universities low on such management indicators as efficiency, information, registration, budgeting, accounting, personnel, and coordination (Seymour 1985: 15; Winkler 1990). Reform of the income base was hardly even pursued until the 1990s.

Administrative Centralization: Facilities

Along with revamped management, administrative centralization requires a range of centralized facilities. We look at both the efforts and results regarding facilities generally, followed by case studies of libraries and campuses.

One major rationale for centralized facilities was their indispensability to handling new governance functions and finance. Another was their indispensability to academic centralization and a sense of university community. Growth was also an explicit rationale for expanded central facilities. More subtle were rationales based, paradoxically, on the lack of other central facilities. For example, reformers hoped that a central library could provide a unifying institutional force where the university lacked a central campus. Such reasoning acknowledged the lack of a supportive centralizing "web," but hoped to overcome it.

The goals were ambitious given the status quo. Latin America's pre-assistance university had only limited facilities. And these operated more at the faculty than the university level. Libraries commonly amounted to ad hoc donations of personal holdings or served particular professional training needs. Spatially, the university often comprised faculty buildings dispersed around the city.

Buildings and Equipment

For all the hope that new physical construction would facilitate multiple aspects of university reform, and for all the impressive scope of construction, undertakings were cautious in certain respects. A key example is that facilities were rarely built as part of ideological assaults on social norms. Such assaults were sure to provoke heated resistance. Projects steered clear of efforts to install common U.S. activities, notwithstanding Atcon's call for sports, dances, and other social pursuits to turn students away from politics.[11] In contrast, nonconfrontational ideas often figured into assistance projects and often took hold. Examples included central cafeterias and student centers— but not the U.S. idea of faculty restaurants or clubs, which would have been denounced as elitist. The new facilities did not challenge any sacred practices or major interests. They found takers easily and indeed were incorporated into decent new unassisted institutions. Thus, Mexico's Autonomous Metropolitan University built a main cafeteria at each of its campuses, whereas the older National University has relied more on numerous eateries spotting its expanse.

For most buildings and equipment, in fact, efforts fit the philanthropic ideal type in that they were specific undertakings involving major change undertaken with willing partners, not attempts to impose controversial, alien modes. Recipients saw this assistance as extra resources. It fit their aspirations to grow. It allowed institutions to gain strength and political support at no painful cost. Finding such high receptivity, the IDB arguably violated norms of "non-scatterization." It led all donors in pursuing such physical development. Both AID and especially the foundations were more selective, targeting fewer institutions and more often concentrating on particular laboratories or other units within those institutions.

Results concerning buildings and equipment have turned out to disappoint in some important respects. Problems have included utilization and upkeep after projects end. Endemic to assistance (Phillips 1976a: 159) these problems support certain dependency critiques. A Hirschmanesque optimism that advanced facilities such as modern laboratories would attract talent to the university yields to frustration where the lack of a surrounding web of academic infrastructure leads to brain drain from the university and even the country. Economic crises like those of the 1980s, with worsening exchange rates, aggravate the upkeep problem, while political crises bring extra reasons that the best personnel often cannot use the best equipment. But even without surrounding political and economic disaster, utilization and upkeep have been problems. According to its own evaluations, the IDB turned in a poor performance at provincial Brazilian universities that quickly showed poor design and underutilization; years later, assessments of Brazilian federal universities still bemoaned very inefficient use of space.[12] Even successful projects such as the bank's with the Dominican Republic Catholic university suffered from underutilization and designs inappropriate to the climate (IDB/E5: 3–4). Pressured by zealous domestic partners, the IDB sometimes pulled standard designs "off the shelf" regardless of real suitability to local conditions (Gheen i), as with libraries for Brazilian universities. Critics charge that the IDB tended to overbuild in quantity or quality.

Other points counter these problems, however. For example, the IDB increasingly stressed simple, low maintenance design, and many of its facilities have been well maintained.[13] Additionally, where problems surfaced, initial or additional donors sometimes came to the rescue, as the UN Development Program did in Chile in the late 1980s with engineering equipment (Singh i).

But the key points that suggest worthwhile results highlight comparative evaluation. First, the realistic alternative to assistance was often the absence of physical infrastructure. If, instead of asking whether infrastructure attracted sufficient new talent, we contemplate how unlikely niches of academic excellence would have been without assistance-supported facilities, evaluation could well be positive. Second, another alternative was inferior construction by domestic governments. In Costa Rica and elsewhere, universities preferred the IDB to the government hand. Venezuelan students likewise reported on the superiority of IDB buildings over those constructed on the same campus without assistance. A 1965 site visit to Paraguay's National University found that its only good and integrated facilities were those provided by AID, UNESCO, and Kellogg.[14] Many evaluations concluded that assistance-expanded facilities improved utilization as well, partly because of the availability and quality of the centralized facilities. Third, institutions targeted for major assistance in building and equipment often did quite well, establishing or expanding their lead over other institutions. Colombia's Los Andes used its new buildings to increase its centralized efficiency, allowing it to accommodate more (paying) students, as it simultaneously abolished practices wherein each unit had to grapple with its own bank accounts, salary scales, and so forth (Vic Johnson to William Cotter, final evaluation, 7/7/69 in FF #64438).

Fourth, evaluations typically find greater success with building and equipment than with academic reforms launched in the same project. Discriminating critics of assistance have sometimes acknowledged the contrast.[15] The contrast is consistent with our conclusions about the positive impact of assistance on growth more than on changed norms.

Libraries

Libraries illustrate how assistance enhanced facilities. They also show how physical aspects of administrative centralization related to academic centralization.

Efforts were ample given the prior dearth of central libraries. But they were much less ambitious than wholesale installation of the U.S. model. Though donors built central libraries where none had existed, they did not try to install them in place of existing faculty-based libraries. This was crucial to partnership at those established universities that were recipients. Chile's national university, for example, sought development mostly of its existing libraries (Fuenzalida 1984). In less-developed nations, recipients saw central libraries primarily as assistance to build up some library. A good example was the SUNY-Buffalo and University of Pittsburgh role with AID for Central American universities (Donnelly i). So efforts for libraries usually took the form of something added—to nothing or to existing structures. Where it was added alongside existing structures, prismatic overlap was in the cards from the outset.

Accomplishments are notable where donors acted. They are clearest regarding physical expansion and technical development. AID helped Paraguay's and Ecuador's national universities increase their volumes, cataloguing, and services.[16] Characteristically concentrating on the human resource and qualitative side, foundations helped in library training. Library professionals thus replaced holders of law degrees. But the major donor was the IDB. Its role was decisive. Most of the large central university libraries in Latin America depended heavily on it. Within Central America, the existence of central libraries (and student centers) paralleled IDB activity—Honduras and Costa Rica benefiting in contrast to Guatemala and El Salvador (Lungo i). Then too, beyond the physical impacts, we must not overlook the impact of the assistance idea, as it persuaded Latin Americans to take libraries more seriously. In the best cases, the idea led universities to devote greater shares of their budgets to libraries and to put a dent in the traditional dominance of learning through lectures and note taking (Molina i).

The gains at targeted alternative institutions also reflect a positive impact from assistance. Consistent with our depiction of modest peaks, these institutions did not provide for automatic success through already terrific facilities but required the building up of eager yet weak recipients. This building up worked particularly well where donors helped construct true campuses. In the 1960s, a few tiny libraries yielded to a centralized library at Chile's University of Concepción (FF #60213). Other private university successes included Peru's Catholic University, in contrast to little centralization at the country's national San Marcos university. Central libraries rarely managed enviable size at unassisted private universities. Successes at assisted public alternative universities included Ecuador's ESPOL with typical IDB help and the library school at Colombia's Antioquia with Rockefeller's participation. But the success was usually prismatic, relative.[17] Colombia's Los Andes would boast a general university library built with foreign loans, operating alongside four specialized libraries, two in research centers, one in the mathematics department, and one in the law faculty.

Low-receiver nations lagged. Mexico's UNAM built two semicentral libraries, but most holdings remained with the libraries of individual faculties unwilling to surrender their possessions and budgets. No common coding system developed. People in one faculty would not know what was owned elsewhere, a crippling situation for interdisciplinary research. A count in the 1990s showed Argentina's national university with eighteen libraries.[18]

But for national universities that already had library facilities in place, even recipients achieved only qualified change. Opposition first limited projects' initiatives, as we have seen, and then limited impacts where initiatives were undertaken. As usual (paralleling the federalism literature) attempts to redistribute resources presented difficulties not encountered when working from scratch. Individual faculties as well as the institution's general political and economic travails blocked library development in the Ford-sponsored convenio at Chile's national university. Faculties like pedagogy presented leftist opposition, while law exemplified the greater number that defended self-interest.[19] On the other hand, the results were positive where opportunities were given to existing units within the university. Financial resources doubled and holdings greatly expanded in the first five years. The library profession advanced and, along with it, services such as rapid copy and interlibrary loan.

The collision of assistance and tradition brought prismatic patterns for libraries. Riggs himself had referred to the prismatic library as one where advances such as improved cataloguing are marginalized and become formalistic as audiences remain passive (Riggs 1964: 358).

There are many examples of facilities outstripping use. Operating budgets slip after donors leave (IDB/E4: 48). Professors do not assign readings, instead continuing to teach by lecture alone. Or they assign readings but students shun the assignments. University acquisition need not lead to student reading. Prismatic patterns appear where faculties control the book ordering and other decision making at the central library. In Ecuador, the risk that borrowers would not return books led librarians to restrict access to books. Under such circumstances it remains rational for individual units and actors to accrue what they can control, especially when they cannot count on identification of, or access to, holdings in others' hands.[20]

For libraries, juxtaposing the mixed picture at targeted places to the general system, one notes what emerges for many other reform initiatives. On the positive side, the targets represent the system's leaders and perhaps a beacon for further reform. On the negative side, impacts at targeted places have not become decisive models for other places and, instead, huge growth in the system has led to a proliferation of institutions where libraries are woefully inadequate to meet the needs of an expanded student body or of new subject matter.[21]

Campuses

The most encompassing facility contemplated was the campus. Campuses could epitomize physical centralization, tying the university together. They could allow for the central construction and use of buildings, equipment, and other facilities and for the establishment and implementation of central management. They could promote the sense of community, identity, and the sharing of resources implicit in academic centralization.

As usual, however, donors' exact goals were unclear. Powerful links between the campus idea and the overall model of university centralization were often left unarticulated. Once more we see the utility of distinguishing between donors' implicit goals, which were vague and ambitious, and explicit project goals, which were concrete and more modest. But even the explicit project goals marked a big contrast to Latin American tradition. They therefore again marked a vision of change that qualifies for the philanthropic ideal type in scope, imagination, and optimism, however much matters fell short in careful conception of the relationship between goals and means. Whether actual efforts matched the goals of projects is a question we proceed to consider.

Efforts. Eager recipients emerged. The added resources were predictably welcome but, beyond that, several universities were truly attracted to the idea of a campus. Heads of all five Central American national universities pushed central campuses in the early 1960s (Enarson 1962). In Chile, where President Carlos Ibáñez had favored a single national university campus back in the 1950s, most of Chile's eight universities jumped at a chance to bring in the IDB in the 1960s; only the Catholic University of Valparaíso rejected free resources.[22] In fact, receptivity was so widespread that direct opposition hardly blocked implementation of undertakings. Some critics warned about the social effects of isolating campuses from "the people," concentrated in capital cities. Others favored the European mode of integrating new institutions within the ongoing life of small cities. Student protesters sometimes opposed campuses as Americanization but sometimes, as at Mexico's UNAM in the late 1980s, demanded campus facilities.

Faced with a pool of willing partners, donors remained fairly selective in those universities they chose. Although their criteria were not very exacting, they bypassed most places.

Further on selectivity, eagerness and partnership did not involve entire campus packages. Efforts were circumscribed. Recipients, donors, and for that matter domestic governments adapted reform initiatives to reality. Here is our clearest case yet of where the incompleteness of the U.S. model refers not just to results but also to efforts themselves. Reformers at least implicitly recognized that full campuses are part of an Americanized administrative and academic web that did not exist in Latin America. Mindless or arrogant imposition of a foreign model is a charge against assistance that lacks credibility here.

An example of a priori accommodation was the common omission of student dormitories, a feature of the classic U.S. (and British) college with a full-time community. This was a prudent acknowledgment of tradition, economics, and the urban roots of Latin American university and cultural life. Even the IDB, champion of construction, realized the high cost of dorms and also students' need to live near where they could find work; it would place universities in secondary cities but not in rural areas that would spawn isolated campuses.[23]

Policymakers also realized that physical construction would not ensure behavior typical of U.S. campuses. Instead, they feared that campuses would mix with political traditions to produce powerful centers of protest. Brazil makes for a national example of restraint, given how extensively Americanization was pursued in other respects (Schwartzman 1988: 106). Policymakers likewise feared placing a favored faculty in with more problematic faculties and student bodies. Agronomy was the main case, with attractive, isolated campuses built away from the rest of the university. Donors were quite ready to bend the U.S. model.

Another example of planned modification of the U.S. campus model was the creation of multiple campuses. This would be something in between a centralized single campus and the tradition of scattered faculties. It recognized the weight of existing structure. Thus the IDB worked to build up centralizing facilities at each of four campuses of Chile's Catholic University. No donor tried to close three campuses while building the other into a superstructure. In contrast, the nation's less developed Austral and Concepción universities were more attractive targets for single campuses. In the aftermath of an earthquake that had hit existing buildings, the Austral got AID's help in 1961 for construction of buildings, a cafeteria, and even some student dormitories and faculty housing (AID #5130096). This is another instance in which donors could more easily find reform partners at sites with less infrastructure and tradition. For reasons ranging from the purely physical to matters of political norms and interests, it is one thing to build a cohesive road system in a new location and another to have to accommodate fresh construction to a complex configuration of existing roads.

Results. The reality of modified efforts is basic to interpreting results. It would be misleading to call the lack of full U.S.-style campuses a failure of assistance. Judged against actual efforts, results are impressive by our evaluative gauge of targets versus nontargets, but with prismatic patterns.

Some universities built campuses without assistance or with just minor or indirect assistance. This could count against the view that assistance makes a difference, or it could suggest the impact of ideas promoted either by strategic donor initiatives or by prior diffusion of ideas. Venezuela and Mexico created national university cities before the golden era. Of course, such construction alone was not true institution building when the academic and administrative web did not surround it. Atcon (1966: 68) blasted university cities as unjustified "pyramids" and "perpetual public works projects," lacking the academic reforms to make them work. Later Mexico created the Autonomous Metropolitan University with three central campuses, tracking U.S. thinking to the point of obeying conventional wisdom about maximum campus size for efficiency, though publicly denying the *gringo* influence. And Venezuela proceeded to create campuses for other institutions.

But the experience of Uruguay and Argentina suggests that the lack of assistance could take a toll in nontargeted countries where domestic funds were not ample early on or where entrenched structures were already strong. These may be the two nations that least accepted the idea of the university as a physical concentration (Vera M. i-1; Accame i). Uruguay built no campus. Over time, the Argentine situation became more complex. The main facility at Argentina's UBA was opened to the entire university, including alumni and a paying public, offering green space, eateries, a pool, and so forth. But this was to be a social more than an administrative or academic facility. Also, it is located with the faculty of science, an IDB-assisted faculty, while the university remains conspicuously scattered around the large capital city.[24] The UBA's massive faculty buildings of medicine, engineering, and law increasingly look dated as well as imposing.

Chile, such a favored nation for assistance, shows intranational contrasts about the role of assistance. Valparaíso's unique rejection of the IDB left it alone in lacking a campus. For most of the nation the campus idea had a huge impact. Policymakers, like their Argentine and Uruguayan colleagues, had previously been more in tune with the Sorbonne idea of universities as urban buildings (Molina i). Probably the greatest assisted reform came at the private Austral University in Valdivia. The IDB helped establish a true, operational campus. All eight faculties were grouped, integrated physically and in decision making. Students would knock on professors' doors, gather informally, frequent the cafeteria and student center, and generally live a campus life. Short of the Austral cohesion, Chile's Catholic university outdistanced the national university in access to central facilities. Indeed, the national university trailed the rest of the system except for Valparaíso.

Further examples at alternative universities tempt one toward the exaggerated but suggestive generalization for the golden era: "no IDB, no campus" (Lavados i-3). We can often identify the most developed campuses as "IDB universities" (e.g., Technological Institute of Santo Domingo, INTEC). True, there are university cities in less-targeted nations, and new universities usually have less scattered configurations than predecessors within their own country. But the closest approximations to formidable, centralized campuses, integrating different knowledge areas, have depended on heavy assistance at a critical, early development moment, often allowing a small unenviable entity to move into an ample new facility. The IDB built the Catholic university's campus in the Dominican Republic, just as it successfully pumped $6.6 million into a new campus for Colombia's del Valle university (IDB/E5; IDB/L25). AID played a key role in replanting Colombia's Antioquia university and Mexico's private Autonomous University of Guadalajara and University of the Americas. The identifying IDB construction showcases itself in many smaller or poorer nations including Costa Rica, Peru, and Panama.

Nor was donors' impact confined to one historical moment. Especially where alternative universities continued to prosper or expand, and because the IDB maintained a significant financial role beyond the golden era, certain major projects postdated the era. One example was a $30.4 million loan for a $38 million campus-building project at ESPOL outside Guayaquil, Ecuador.[25]

If successful physical construction was one of the easier facets of assistance for campuses, two big factors undercut the success. One was extraordinary growth. This strained the capacity of many campuses, though campuses also allowed much of the growth. At some campuses, growth plus the increased percentage of working students led to shifts of students coming and going, depending on the time of day. Mostly, however, growth led to a proliferation of institutions lacking campuses. Many were degree factories, whereas others were decent but specialized or otherwise limited institutions. A new university often crowded its way into one or a few buildings. The powerful role of assistance in building Latin America's significantly increased campus facilities did not translate into a significantly increased percentage of higher education functioning through campuses.

The second factor undermining campuses is how the physical entity functions when partly transplanted onto alien terrain, without a supportive web of other centralization. Some prismatic overlap of traditional and exported forms was inevitable where reformist partners soberly resisted pushing a full campus model. Residency is one example from our list of partial efforts. Del Valle in Cali, Colombia, was among places where the IDB and domestic reformers built dorms just for students coming from outside the city, while Cali's own students would live off campus (IDB/L25). In addition to such programmed overlap, there are situations in which reformers push the campus more but most students continue to live at home or find boarding houses (*pensiones,* or *republicas* in Brazil).

Prismatic patterns that went beyond anticipated overlap usually involved a formalism in which officially prescribed activities failed to take hold. Later in the chapter we will see the disappointing results in academic centralization where the trappings of campuses emerged. Here we look at how campuses have promoted undesired political activity, isolation, and the persistent power of faculty structures.

The reformist rector at Colombia's National University found few takers for a student campus life filled with social activities, "university week," beauty queens, athletic contests, and talks (Magnusson 1970: 121, 133). Those who looked to university cities to separate Latin American students from national disruptions turned out to be less accurate than those who feared the concentration of students. Linked with traditional notions of sanctuary from police authority, the new campuses often became centers of disruption. Moreover, urban sprawl sometimes encompassed a once separate national campus, as in Bogota and Mexico City. San Marcos also became a political trap, leading authorities at some of Peru's large private universities to disperse their faculties. Ecuador's national university showed the special vulnerability to rapid politicization at campuses built with dorms (Blaise 1968). Dorms then became even less common than before as authorities saw fit to close them at national universities such as Venezuela's and Colombia's, as the military would do with Brazil's campuses.[26]

In other ways, however, prescribed campus behavior suffered from physical isolation. Underutilization spelled an inefficiency that donors routinely lamented. AID's work in Brazil left many campuses far from where students lived and worked. And because the campus web rarely extended to full-time teaching with adequate compensation, instructors still needed to live close to their principal job. Only exceptional institutions built enough of the web for the physical campus to make sense. The bulk of experience indicates that reformers showed foresight in not building more campuses away from population centers. This left room for less grandiose yet significant success where campuses truly promoted desired behavior, as at Venezuela's Simón Bolívar, and the IDB infrastructure that encouraged students to spend long hours once they arrived on campus (IDB/E7).

Finally, persisting domination by faculties marks another perversion of the campus model. One kind of prismatic overlap developed immediately where powerful professional faculties refused to relocate while the sciences flocked to the new facilities. The example of Argentina's UBA was largely replicated in this respect in Brazil, despite Brazil's greater push and strides with campuses. Most of Brazil's traditional faculties "kept their old buildings downtown, never moving to the new campuses," and thereafter would implement their own protective faculty adaptations of national academic reforms that aimed at centralizing universities (Schwartzman 1992a: 86). We have also seen initial compromises involving separate campuses for different *groups* of faculties; this practice later leaked over into even fairly small provincial universities (e.g., Chile's La Frontera).

Where faculties did physically assemble together on campus, integration still usually lagged—a classic formalistic configuration where traditional behavior adapted itself only moderately to new structure. Fundamental transformation was rare. Social facilities such as restaurants often developed around individual faculties. Echoing findings on libraries, the faculties retained their power by extending it to control over "central" campus activities. They also protected their academic separateness. That was perhaps inevitable where the web did not encompass academic reforms such as departmentalization, and there could be no realistic prospect that the building of campuses would itself lead to such academic reform at places like Colombia's National University.[27]

Because the campus model revolves around an interwoven web of academic characteristics, our analysis leads directly to consideration next of academic centralization. But it is already clear that working students have little use for a campus when they are taking courses in their professional field from instructors working predominantly away from the university, taught from lecture notes, isolated from the students, professors, and curriculum of other faculties. And the more such realities remain, the more it is rational for actors to put their resources and efforts into traditional structures instead of reform structures.

Academic Centralization

Goals

Reformers undertook centralization of management and facilities largely to allow academic centralization. Students and professors should become more a part of the institution as a whole, less a part of their single unit. This would be crucial as well to the academic work discussed in the ensuing chapter in regard to full-time staff, disciplinary and interdisciplinary foci, and related pursuits.

Our analysis here considers two key reforms in academic centralization: general studies and departmentalization. We concentrate more on general studies when it comes to efforts and results, but the two reforms were interrelated and goals were based on overlapping rationales. General studies (or basic studies, or variants) meant that new students would postpone professional specialization while they explored a range of knowledge areas. De-partmentalization meant organizing teaching and the advancement of knowl-edge around disciplines more than professions. Both reforms promised much more in the way of centralized, common offerings to students across the university in place of compartmentalization by faculties. They thus promised expanded choice and efficiency, the latter from economies of scale, increased information and orientation for informed student "consumers" operating in a marketplace, and decreased duplication of offerings and personnel. Espe-cially where combined with the idea of accommodating a surge of secondary-school graduates not yet ready for professional studies, general studies had a distinctly nonelite, pro-growth tone. On the other hand, another invoked rationale was that university graduates form a country's elite and, as such, should have a broad, cultured education to prepare them for leadership.

General studies and departmentalization are good representatives for the entire interrelated academic centralization package that would include elec-tives, flexible curriculum, common credit systems, and student advisement (Atcon 1966: 113–18; also see Regel 1992). Indeed general studies and de-partmentalization themselves would foster the other elements of the package. Instead of following a prescribed lockstep curriculum within a given faculty, students would earn credits for courses they would choose, with proper guid-ance, in a wider array of interrelated university units.

General studies were regarded as pivotal to Americanization in Central American higher education. Even into the 1970s, it was identified as the "salient" and "vanguard" in grants to the regional association of national universities (CSUCA) and to individual nations.[28] The idea was that general studies would require centralization in admissions, exams, advising, libraries, and laboratories, as well as full-time professors and departmentalization. Re-formers made similar proclamations regarding Colombia, Chile, and other large recipients of assistance.[29]

Reformers thus had some appreciation of the grand academic-adminis-trative web of the U.S. model. But their modernization optimism usually led them to foresee mutually reinforcing reforms rather than a crippling of iso-lated departments and general studies programs.

The goals were ambitious. Common to general studies and departmen-talization was a reversal of Latin American tradition. This meant rejection of the preeminence of the chaired professor and the faculty structure as the decisive academic units. A similar rejection was under way in Western Europe (Van de Graaff 1982). Charges against chairs and faculties included their incapacity in flexibility, participation, institutional growth, research, disci-plines, interdisciplinary work, and other matters related to their lack of in-stitutionwide scope. Chaired professors decided the content of subject areas, without need to consider student choice or the views and actions of other professors, especially those outside their faculty. Departmentalization was a democratizing reform, opening a role for junior faculty, thus undercutting the dependency view that the U.S. model would bring greater hierarchy in the university.

Because Latin American chairs rarely assumed the stature found in Europe, where research was much more prominent, and because they were untenable amid huge enrollment growth, the main traditional structure to consider is the faculty. Quite unlike the U.S. admissions process, entry was basically to individual faculties rather than to the university. Faculties meant immediate specialization, denied electives or transfer with credit, and concentrated on a fixed program of professional preparation taught by their own people to their own people. Secondary school graduates with little informed idea of their future had to make fateful entry decisions that locked them into rigid tracks.[30] Subsequent recognition of error, or simply a change in preference, usually left the student plodding along misplaced or having to start over in another faculty.

In short, the goal of academic centralization fit the philanthropic ideal type in representing a transformation from the status quo. Critiques and initiatives by domestic reformers, often inspired by foreign experiences and ideas, had failed to alter matters much before the golden age. In Argentina, for example, despite interesting national debates in the nineteenth century, Bahía Blanca remained in 1960 a fragile exception to the rule of professional over general education. Throughout Latin America, only a few other alternative universities influenced by U.S. models had joined the list of exceptions.

Efforts

With the arrival of the golden age, the exceptional institutions suddenly saw assistance as an opportunity to expand their innovations, while reformers at other universities saw an opportunity to join. As with administrative centralization, then, assistance for academic centralization did not impose reform but promoted it with domestic partners. Of our two academic initiatives, general studies depended more on assistance projects, whereas departmentalization was more widely pursued by domestic reformers, and this is one reason our analysis of efforts tilts toward general studies.

Selected partners. Donors found some encouraging initial interest in academic centralization at national universities. They could thus weigh in on the reformist side there, but against stiff opposition. This effort represents either innovative philanthropic daring, or careless unphilanthropic meddling, or a combination. Among South America's national universities, Colombia's was probably unsurpassed for vigorous efforts at academic centralization against opposition. After small inroads pushed by Rockefeller for premedical courses, the reform was domestically led, though facilitated by assistance. Paraguay's national university, assisted by a Dartmouth College adviser, approved a school of general studies in 1961 and looked for the money to make it happen. The IDB approved the request after AID denied it. Where AID did fund general studies it reportedly found overwhelming support mixed with fear (Anderson 1965). Similarly in Peru, San Marcos's U.S.-trained rector consulted with advisor George Waggoner and obtained financial assistance. Partnership was paramount as donors voluntarily undertook specific projects and provided something extra, and crucial, for domestic reformers attempting to bring about distinctive and important change. In all these senses, the efforts at academic centralization were consistent with the philanthropic ideal type.

Central America was the focus of general studies efforts at national universities. Donors were active. Both Waggoner and Atcon played major consulting roles, along with OAS and UNESCO support. A 1962 U.S. mission encouraged Costa Rica's university to move away from a European "cultured professional" route and beyond its one-year general studies program, to more inclusive general studies (Karpinsky 1982: 99). But the key was the eagerness of the recipients. Perhaps to make the eagerness more politically acceptable at home, Costa Rican rector Rodrigo Facio could claim to look to Europe for ideas and professors, while others emphasized that influential Spanish philosopher Ortega y Gasset himself had praised the cultured person over the trained professional. But it certainly was the U.S. model that supplied the basic idea of more general studies. Earlier we saw how donors sometimes depicted general studies as pivotal to broader reform. They were not alone. A 1961 CSUCA resolution called general studies the best route to reform and endorsed cultural and sports complements to boot. Its constituent universities had already launched general studies plans. As put by a consultant and academic vice president of the University of New Mexico: "In the eyes of many of the leading educators, general studies is the Holy Grail, and CSUCA leads the Crusade" (Enarson 1963: 202). Again assistance did not mean imposition. Ford flooded Central America with three of its initial nine general studies grants and the IDB pumped in almost $3 million in 1962, while AID was active as well.[31]

Central America was unusual, however, for the heavy effort with national universities. Although some South American national universities were also early partners for donors, it became harder to find partners that were still small and lacked powerful and resistant faculties. Donors concentrated their major general studies efforts on only a few eager South American institutions, decreasingly including national universities. This meant bypassing the great majority of enrollments as well as institutions. It meant giving especially to those alternative universities that had both launched their own reform and solicited assistance to increase its scope and prospects. At Concepción, Chile, reforms included extending the period of preprofessional exposure and extending the concept of institutes (the euphemism for the U.S. word *departments*) from the sciences to the social sciences and humanities, both changes entailing curriculum reform.[32]

The selectivity was predictably clearest for the Ford Foundation, though it launched multiple related efforts aimed at modernizing curriculum and building alternatives to faculties, as at Brazil's University of Sao Paulo and University of Brasilia (Ford Foundation 1962: 62). Ford's initial general studies grants went to only three nations outside Central America, including just one national university (Peru's San Marcos). Private universities received 43 percent of the overall money, and that involved just one major recipient—Colombia's Los Andes—and one minor one (Hans Simons to John Netherton 3/4/68 FF #61188). Other chosen privates with general studies did not require an expensive transformation.

Colombia was probably the lead country for general studies efforts at alternative universities. Los Andes, private, and del Valle, public, led the way. Both universities show how institutional targets of assistance were far from typical higher education institutions. Both already had experimented with general studies. Both called upon donors to help them reinvigorate (perhaps save) their initiatives and to make them much more ample. These "peaks" within their system were modest peaks in need of a major boost.

General studies had been one of the key rationales for creation of Los Andes in 1948. There was a vision of "education for the whole man," rather than just training for a particular job. Not all students and professors shared this vision, and so even in the 1950s hybrid forms arose, with considerable faculty structure control alongside more general courses. Over some opposition the university administration sought and greeted Ford assistance in 1961 for a School of Arts and Sciences, with a basic studies obligation for all students (FF #61188, including NYC office file as well as Bogota field file). In 1962, the nation's del Valle tried to follow. The rector took care to make the changes during vacations and to remind the wary that the Soviet Union and Western Europe were also generalizing and centralizing their academic offerings. Once again the key partners for donors were administrative leaders who could at least undertake action in the name of their institution, notwithstanding internal opposition. Such opposition, as well as indifference, did however mark an element of risk, so donors were hardly jaunting along for easy success. But del Valle too had its own precedent, premedical studies started in 1952, with Rockefeller Foundation support. It had also developed joint activity with Los Andes. In 1962, however, del Valle looked mostly to the Ford Foundation to make general studies integral to its academic development. It sought technical assistance from both Ford and Rockefeller, including Harvard consultant Richard King. At the same time, the public Antioquia also sought assistance to make general studies key to its overall reform.[33]

With the notable exceptions of Colombia, Brazil, and Chile, the Central America–South America contrast was about the greater receptivity of less established structures, a general point established in chapter 2. Donors did not try academic centralization where support was absent or weak, as was common in South America. In El Salvador, by contrast, even anti-American groups pushed general studies in the early 1960s.[34]

Donors respected the level of secondary education in advanced nations. Or at least they honored the argument there that secondary schools handled general education, often at a level unmatched by U.S. high schools and therefore required at U.S. colleges.[35] In Argentina, Uruguay, and beyond donors did not push general studies. Even in its most vigorous period, assistance rarely assaulted a tradition that appeared to have reasonable justification or basic acceptance.

Massification modified the picture in the advanced nations, however. As the student population became much more diverse academically as well as socioeconomically, calls arose within systems for general studies as a remedial and screening device. Even good institutions such as Chile's Concepción university suffered from high dropout rates. The sudden explosion of secondary school graduates and university admissions suggested an unflattering Americanization in which many would graduate from secondary school with poor preparation yet easy access to higher education. Like interinstitutional stratification, general studies would be an Americanizing way to couple inclusiveness into the system with subsequent separation by competence (Atcon 1966: 123, 138). But donors rarely got deeply involved with the idea of remedial general studies as a coping mechanism. They were much more energized by optimistic visions of general studies as a healthy reform for broadening education and strengthening institutions.

Diluted attempts. Choosing a limited number of major institutional targets was not the only prudence donors showed. They also pushed measures that were already compromises between the U.S. model and Latin American tradition. They set a course of addition, overlap, and displacement, not radical replacement. Prismatic results were not simply unanticipated blends from the clash of radical goals and tradition; they were also part and parcel of the efforts themselves.

Indeed the very concept of general studies was a compromise. It lay between U.S. liberal arts education and specialization through faculties. It aimed more to postpone or modify professional training than to replace it. Moreover, actual initiatives often compromised even the idea of one or two years of broad education taken across the university by all students. One alternative was a general studies component spun throughout the years of study of mostly professional training. More common was insertion of a "common trunk" for all students of just an individual faculty (then headed to their specialization) or a small group of faculties. Yet another involved general studies only for new areas of study rather than for traditional professions. Full-time professors were thus sometimes given appointments split between new general studies units and preexisting faculties. All these examples map out a prismatic overlapping between old and new even before attempted implementation. They reflect adaptation that simultaneously spells disappointment for those seeking to emulate the U.S. model and pragmatic attempts to improve in ways congruent with local conditions.

More confrontational ideas rarely translated into actual projects. If some officers at places like UNESCO really wanted to build four-year liberal arts programs (Ribeiro 1968: 134), they did not make donor policy, let alone policy in the receiving countries. Donor restraint was especially notable in the face of sporadic exuberance by domestic reformers as when the rector of Peru's San Marcos endorsed liberal arts, at least as the foundation for professional training (Sánchez 1962: 17).

Departmentalization also shows a mix between pursuit of major change and prudent avoidance of wholesale replacement. Pure departmentalization represented a much more direct alternative than general studies to chairs and faculties, and some consultants did argue for such departmentalization (Frodin 1965). But donors' actual efforts usually paralleled modifications seen in general studies: departments set up to serve one or a few faculties instead of the whole university, departments for only new disciplines (e.g., IDB loans for basic sciences at San Marcos), or just enhanced resources for departments already functioning along these two lines (e.g., the mathematics department that taught math to the engineering faculty at Chile's national university).

Yet the academic centralization promoted by departmentalization was nonetheless ambitious. Donors did not push much further than their domestic partners could reasonably go, but the partners together undertook to make a considerable break from the status quo. Even a part of such a potentially radical reform as departmentalization was an important effort. Once again we see how full adherence to the philanthropic ideal type was inherently impossible. Actual efforts limited change whereas pursuit of more transforming change would have sacrificed prudence and partnership. With that philanthropic tradeoff or dilemma as a caveat, it is fair to conclude that donors' efforts to increase academic centralization were mostly consistent with the philanthropic ideal type.

Opposition Thwarts Results

The ambitiousness of the efforts was enough to generate an opposition, which, in turn, made results less extensive than attempted. Although donors worked with partners, those partners represented only part of the domestic spectrum. This section considers opposition by students, professors, and the professions.

In so doing, it shows that assistance for academic centralization was not about consensual tasks that simply required external resources. More than in most aspects of administrative centralization, donors went beyond easy partnership to what could be called either philanthropic risk-taking or overreach into poorly understood, contentious terrain. And as literature on policy implementation suggests, while the eager allies are the most visible actors during the policy formulation stage, later on others get active. Like many reformers, donors underestimated the degree of opposition that would unfold.

Students. Students presented a major roadblock to academic centralization. If they were to be the main beneficiaries, they failed to see it. Radicals commonly perceived the U.S. helping hand as an imperialist hand. Projects launched in the early 1960s fell victim to the unique politicization that seized Latin America as well as other regions in the late 1960s. Examples included general studies at Concepción, Chile (FF #60213), and the national universities in Guatemala and El Salvador. From Costa Rica to Peru students denounced departments as structural schemes to get around the political participation they had built up in faculties. Some derided the "cultured man" idea as bourgeois, an inferior alternative to practical service orientations.

Except for this spurt of intense leftism, however, the main student opposition was less ideological. It involved fear of the unknown and of extra hurdles. Students cast a wary eye on deviations from a direct path to professional status and rewards. They did not welcome time devoted to general studies or to broad nonprofessional curriculum in departments. AID encountered prescient fears that general studies would become a remedial insertion—adding to the length of study. Where general studies was so perceived, it was hotly protested. Students at Concepción acted like counterparts in India faced with Ford-promoted general education.[36] Alternatively, where the mass of Latin American students did not oppose change, neither did they compose a strong block in partnership with reformers to thwart the hostile and active student minority.

Professors. Professors also resisted for security and ease more than ideology. This helps explain why professors opposed continual attempts even at politically rather conservative places such as Chile's Catholic university (Godoy i). Chaired professors believed they had the earned right to be guardians of a fixed curriculum. Many professors realized they themselves had neither the skill nor the inclination to teach, say, science to architecture students. Besides, professors were themselves trained in the conservative pedagogy of transmitting facts through lectures, which is at odds with liberal modes suited to general studies and departments. And part-timers, the vast majority, realized that general studies and departmentalization supposed major replacements by full-timers. Then too, some scholars with foreign doctorates did not see themselves as teachers but as researchers working with only advanced, specialized students (Croxatto i).

Professors resisted mostly through both nonparticipation and the power of their faculties. In Central America they joined with students to vote down general studies in the 1970s (Lungo i). Less visibly, faculties killed by delay, often demanding further review and discussion of proposals (formulae resurrected when professors faced attempts to install evaluation in the 1990s). The mix of honest concern and disingenuous obstructionism was naturally difficult to determine. Where different faculties lined up on different sides, the more powerful ones tended to be in opposition.[37] This is the same breakdown seen in administrative centralization, as with the incorporation of only certain faculties onto central campuses.

Predictably, professor (and student) opposition was less common or severe in alternative universities. At an extreme, the medical professors who broke off from Peru's national university immediately established departments at their new, private Cayetano Heredia. But protest was not infrequent, at least concerning general studies. Both Colombia's del Valle and Peru's La Molina were examples. As in national universities, opposition was stiffer in traditional professional fields.

Professions. Opposition from both professors and students must be understood within the professionalist context that characterized Latin American tradition. However archaic the relationship may appear from a U.S. perspective, the tight link between faculty and profession was critical. Discussions of Latin American university autonomy too often pass over the fundamental fact of a lack of autonomy from the professions, including professional alumni.[38]

The majority of professors were full-time professionals in private practice or government posts who devoted but a small part of their time to university teaching. Their preferences for the status quo stemmed partly from self-interest as they valued the opportunity that university teaching offered to enhance their prestige and to identify and recruit young talent (Camp 1985). Their preferences also stemmed from natural conviction that they could best teach others to do what they do. Both factors would explain, for example, why physicians opposed reforms that would have medical students taught along with other students by academic biologists or that would allow teaching only by those few physicians who would revamp their offerings to be more academic and general.

For their part, students liked to identify early on with a profession. When they entered a faculty more than an interdisciplinary university they wanted to feel already connected to a profession. Their identification of their role and rational behavior followed course. They knew that faculties granted the degrees essential in order to practice the profession. The existing "web" connecting faculty, curriculum, degree, and employment made it irrational to defy the prescribed professional curriculum.[39] Nor did private higher education blaze a reform path. While a minority were reform partners, most isomorphically copied professional curriculum without general studies. Public universities interested in general studies had to worry about the competitive attractiveness to students of more "efficient" private pathways to the workplace.

Professions also exert influence through their direct action. Through specific pressure or just through hiring practices, they can determine curriculum in professional training. The phenomenon is hardly limited to Latin America. A report (OECD 1990: 47) on Californian higher education concludes that it is "difficult to convince engineering schools of the need for more general and less early specialization." But a key difference lies in Latin America's emphasis on professional training at the basic first-degree level.[40]

Thus students and faculties had powerful backers when they protested de-professionalizing reforms of curriculum. Professional associations joined the fray, weighing in with their connections and resources. To them as to others, these reforms were dangerous whether foreign-assisted or not. Mexican *gremios* (organized groupings) killed domestically proposed core curricula in the 1970s just as Costa Rican dentists fought Kellogg-sponsored reforms at their national university (Aguilar i). In contrast to their university allies, professional associations sometimes denounced reforms as "leftist," though "irresponsible" was a more common label. A typical complaint was that graduates of reformed law schools knew about everything—except law.[41] Professional associations battled hard against curricula flexibility including electives. They upheld the traditional system of fixed requirements set largely by the profession itself and implemented through faculties.

The prudence and selectivity of undertakings by donors and reformers was insufficient to stave off powerful opposition to general studies and departmentalization from students, professors, and professions. Whereas compromises in the efforts themselves foretold mixed configurations down the road, the mix was pushed further away from the import model by the strength of the opposition.

Mixed Results

Many universities lack any semblance of departments or general studies. This results from opposition and also from mass growth and institutional proliferation as rapid responses to skyrocketing demand not accompanied by a proportionate base of reformers, donors, resources, ideas, or will. Most new institutions simply copied or tried to copy traditional practice, an example of normative isomorphism.

Here, however, we explore the mixed results at recipient institutions, especially the more favorable mix at targeted alternative universities. What then emerges is a comparatively positive picture for assistance within an overall portrait that is otherwise disappointing. Our composite view helps make sense out of divergent depictions of Latin American reality regarding matters like the decreased role of the chair and the increased role of general studies.[42] Identification of prismatic patterns likewise illuminates how it is that observers who look at formal structures and additions portray change, while those looking at actual behavior in mainstream activities portray continuity.[43] Classically reflecting Riggs's formulations, the formal structure is not a reliable guide to reality. Such points assume special importance, since ideas like general studies and departmentalization continue to be so resilient, arising repeatedly in one form or another.

National universities. National universities rarely went far with academic centralization. Some hardly tried. Those that did suffered greatly from the opposition. It was at national universities that students, professors, and the professions had their deepest traditions and greatest power. There too, massification went further than at leading alternative universities. This wreaked havoc as most professors and students lacked the preparation and time for the newly prescribed tasks, and class size ballooned. As feared, general studies often became remedial work (e.g., in Bolivia) or a hurdle interposed between easy access to higher education and tougher access to professional programs.

National universities targeted for initial help were quickly in trouble. In Ecuador, donors saw hopes dashed as threatened faculties ensured that their own students remained identifiably and separately grouped within the new basic science unit (Blaise 1968: 12–14). We look in more detail at the national universities of Costa Rica and Chile, two of those most favored by assistance and most touted as potential leaders in academic centralization.

The University of Costa Rica (UCR) certainly moved ahead of other national universities in academic centralization. Incoming students would pass through one or two years of general studies. Before long, 30 percent of students would reside there. Creation of schools with directors undercut faculties and their deans, and schools were often divided into departments. Some of these departments came truly to serve other schools and faculties. Hence, faculties like engineering would not offer their own biology. The sciences came to do particularly well.[44]

For all that, the UCR's reform proved abortive. A U.S. consulting mission noted "massification" problems as early as 1962.[45] By 1980 roughly half the students carried the burden of outside work, and only a fifth of the general studies teachers were full or three-fourths time. Whereas initially general studies meant interfaces between perhaps thirty students and professors with *místico* (inspirational or mystical commitment), it came to mean lectures from poorly prepared teachers to some hundred students. Saturation of their targeted job market then made students even more concerned to be professionally prepared. UCR's general studies would become a conduit to the inflexibility that still characterizes the main years of study. Schools and departments offer few electives. A *licenciatura* degree in history in the mid-1980s required 188 credits of which just 15 were electives, although 21 were general studies and 24 were taken outside the school.[46] Whereas general studies displaced faculties somewhat, it neither replaced nor fundamentally altered them.

For the most part, the UCR's new academic structures would be weak or formalistic. Schools often come to be like faculties, while their departments fail to serve as major academic units. The medical and pharmaceutical faculties give almost all their own courses. Equal representation for each faculty on the university council blocks change as the reformist faculty of science and letters gets only one vote for its roughly 60 percent of total enrollments. An equally subversive strategy is to quarantine general studies in a separate school—and then to isolate the professors and activities of the school as well as to make the school follow standard rules set by and for other schools and faculties.[47]

The prismatic patterns at the UCR put Costa Rica ahead of its Central American neighbors, however. Since all these national universities got heavy, early aid, the differential results provide evidence that donors' success depends on subsequent domestic factors (such as peace and stability) it cannot control. Advances at the region's other national universities have been sparse. There has been some progress with credit systems and where AID has remained active (e.g., in Honduras). An improved political context may yet turn reform ideas to realities. But even El Salvador, which for years led all but Costa Rica in zestful change, has had little to show; no general studies has taken hold, and each faculty has set its own requirements, though some private institutions allow a few electives. Guatemala's San Carlos also faded rapidly. Whatever Nicaragua retained up to 1980 did not survive the sandinistas' assault on measures associated with U.S. influence: electives, credit systems, and general studies yielded to rigid tracks for career development.[48]

Chile's national university (UCH) also did not go as far as Costa Rica's. The domestic reform of the late 1960s boosted academic centralization, and the convenio with the University of California earned praise for increasing credit systems and disciplinary orientations as well as supportive institutional development planning and coordination.[49] Like most of Central America, however, Chile would suffer from disorder and repression. Heavy politicization discredited reform, and then the 1973 coup savaged gains, especially as they had concentrated in the social sciences, pushing the UCH back to a more professionalist profile. Gains were limited and precarious anyway because the UCH faced most of the opposition and obstacles typical for national universities. Faculties never yielded much ground to general studies and departments. Medicine would epitomize the UCH's professional faculty separateness and rigidity. It would have one central location and four branch campuses around Santiago, each affiliated to a hospital and with its own departments such as pediatrics, making for some fifty departments overall (personal correspondence from Andrés Bernasconi 6/20/00). Multiple departments also dotted related areas such as biochemistry (Turina i). Practically no curriculum flexibility exists, despite a three-year core, and professors rarely teach outside their unit. Although the faculty of science allows a little more leeway, rare requests to take a course outside the faculty require special approval, and core courses reach only within the common trunk for science, not toward the rest of the university.[50]

Alternative universities. Evaluation of targeted alternative universities thus comes against this background of continuity over change at the national universities. The evaluation at targeted alternative universities shows a mixture of success, opposition, disappointment, and prismatic results.

The Chilean case manifests both progress and parallels to the national university's problems. Such mixed results could be seen as disappointing considering that several of Chile's private universities received ample assistance for academic centralization. The Catholic University had ambitious, IDB-backed integration plans, but a faculty system persisted. Compared to the national university, its reforms brought more exceptions in common trunks and credited transfer possibilities within them (e.g., among careers within engineering), general education courses, departmentalization within faculties, and professors offering courses in faculties outside their own. Both institutions eventually consolidated two-year *bachillerato* programs, conduits to three years in the professional faculties. The University of Concepción, pioneer in academic centralization, has seen its reforms peeled away, though it too maintains a general program, albeit a conduit to its professional training. It maintains departments as well as many faculties. The Austral University shows more success for its IDB-supported academic centralization. Both departmentalization and general studies of science and humanities have held up better there, supported by a functioning campus, though the Austral too lost ground under the dictatorship.[51]

Outside Chile, the majority of private institutions did not commonly receive international assistance and rarely accomplished fundamental academic centralization. At almost all the Dominican Republic's many private institutions (and its national university), departments either do not exist or exist prismatically within faculties that allow them authority only over research—a rare activity.[52]

Yet Latin America's major private universities usually boast more academic centralization than their public counterparts. Partnership with donors has been easier as the major private institutions have been much less burdened than the major public ones by the crippling factors cited above. Both massification and opposition have been less widespread, more inhibited by the hierarchy. One major catch is the lack of breadth at most private institutions. Academic centralization then results from the paucity of fields to coordinate more than any crafted integration of diversity.

The region's best Catholic universities fall in between, but usually closer to the secular elite privates than to the national universities. They are older than the secular elite institutions, with more classic ties to the professions; academic centralization thus requires more change against greater obstacles.[53] Sometimes key variation arises inside institutions, where it proves easier to institute reforms on fresh terrain than to transform traditional terrain; Peru's Católica departmentalized more in economics than law (Drysdale i). Many alternative universities, especially secular ones, skipped law or other traditional professions.

But the key contrast is not religious-secular. It lies instead between assisted and unassisted private universities and is usually clear in countries that had both.[54] Unassisted and minimally assisted private and public institutions in Peru and the Dominican Republic would not match the academic centralization reforms achieved at the countries' oldest and largest Catholic universities, which were heavily assisted. At targeted institutions the prismatic co-existence of departments and faculties says as much about implemented restructuring as about its incompleteness.

Results are more sporadic at the heavily assisted public institutions than at the heavily assisted private ones. Having already noted the problems at the assisted national universities, we now consider the assisted alternative public universities. Given the tougher conditions in the public sector than in the private sector, the achievements at the heavily assisted public alternative institutions merit note. For some time, leading public alternative universities even matched private leaders, but deceptive prismatic change became more characteristic. A first indicator, consistent with Riggs, is the loss of ground as new forms succumb to older ones in conditioning behavior.

An example of progress and frustration at targeted public alternatives is Venezuela's Simón Bolívar. The young university made rapid progress. Into the 1970s, it appeared that academic centralization was a leveraging reform, giving professors incentives to remain on campus and fostering greater centralization in the distribution of university resources. University officials gave the IDB significant credit for both general studies and departmentalization. They even spoke of liberal arts for all. Trouble then set in and academic reforms soon lost ground (IDB/E7: 8, 45, 54, 68), but Venezuelan experts single out the university for its true department structure, housing teaching and research (Navarro i-1).

The Simón Bolívar mixed record leaves it far ahead of Venezuela's other public alternatives. The nation's next most assisted public alternative, Los Andes in Mérida, never got as far. Despite donor-promoted success in planning, building, and administrative centralization, the basic cycle quickly got tied to separate professional faculties rather than to the university, and departments achieved importance more within new faculties than elsewhere, where most students sought traditional careers (IDB/L42). Meanwhile, unassisted institutions achieved little reform. Thus, except at the Simón Bolívar and perhaps a few privates, Venezuela's general studies disappeared or became a buffer between easy admissions and professional programs, and the typical department became subservient to its individual faculty. The formally installed credit system failed to provide the intended flexibility as it too got enmeshed within the faculty system.

Overall, results at Latin America's public alternative universities have disappointed, but the sporadic successes there, though prismatic, make some of these institutions leaders in academic centralization. They trail only a few significant private universities and surpass all but a very few national universities in small nations.[55] Where success has been achieved, assistance has been crucial.

Country cases. The mix of results also varies by country. A contrast between Argentina and Mexico on the one hand and Brazil and Colombia on the other is instructive.

Both Argentina's UBA and Mexico's UNAM are national universities of faculties. They lack electives, courses taught by professors from other faculties, university courses as opposed to faculty or even career-specific courses, classroom interaction between students from different faculties, and so forth. Prismatic patterns here show mostly ostensible reforms that are merely formalistic, with little impact on activities. "Departments" are normally fitted to accommodate existing faculty or professors' power, or each department offers its own career.[56] Research is often protected outside the faculties (in centers and institutes) but not usually in departments uniting teaching with research. Partial exceptions are confined to pockets such as the IDB-promoted science faculty of the UBA and some graduate education. Basic cycles repeatedly struggle for just a foothold. The UBA's faculties disarm that reform by creating their own cycles, blocking them off from contact with others; a student switching from engineering to architecture would have to start the new cycle from scratch. Even the military failed in attempts to dent the faculty grip, 1966–69, and then did not even try when it again held power, 1976–83 (Pérez Lindo 1985: 152). Notwithstanding the lack of assistance projects, critics at these universities have continually denounced reforms as U.S. imperialism or U.S.-dominated globalization.

Neither Argentina nor Mexico achieved much academic centralization even outside its national universities. This again suggests the importance of assistance to alternative universities in other countries for academic centralization.

Argentina's public Bahía Blanca university, which introduced departments in 1955, has been mostly an exception, though further headway came with the U.S.-modeled Taquini reforms in the early 1970s. Leading privates such as Salvador are faculty-based, and faculties have fought more than a minimal basic studies (Ortiz i). Throughout Argentina, admissions exams, research, and graduate education are, first, still rare and, second, handled more by faculties or separate institutes than by departments; similarly, the authority of chaired professors has yielded mostly to authorities other than truly collegial departments.[57]

By and large, emulation of UNAM has left Mexico's public universities with much less academic centralization than administrative centralization. Initiatives for the public sector inclusively, as for a credit system in the 1970s, were not implemented. Probably Aguascalientes stood alone among Mexico's thirty-one state universities for its departments by disciplines, and many of the universities had no departments at all. Instead, the main attempt at academic centralization came at the Federal District's Autonomous Metropolitan University (UAM), created in 1973. Not facing the power of entrenched faculties, UAM went further than the UNAM. Its professors affiliated by departments, with multiple departments joined in divisions and operated on a quarter system. But UAM's environment largely reproduced habits and interests, showing how little progress could be made even in a new university.

Divisions soon looked suspiciously like faculties. Professors had not under-stood the reform idea. Also, most were unprepared for research; no unit can link research and teaching if there is no research. Students did not enter faculties, but entered careers instead of departments. In any case, units al-lowed little freedom for students to take courses in other units, despite official rules; electives were not implemented. As at the UNAM, formal student ap-plications to the university did not overturn the practice of faculty decision making in admissions.[58]

The mixed results in Brazil and Colombia surpass those in our two main cases of less-targeted nations.[59] The contrast between high and low receiving nations is strongest regarding alternative universities, reflecting the scarcity of targeted institutions in the low receiving nations.

In Brazil the public sector took the lead in unusually broad-based reform. Brazil lacked a national university, and its public sector was academically superior to its mostly demand-driven private sector. Most of all, Brazil was unusual among large countries for its eagerness to join with international assistance. Brazil marks the extreme where heavily assisted reform set its sights on academic centralization across the breadth of an institutionally di-verse public sector—and achieved some notable if prismatic results there. It makes for a telling comparison to broad-based academic centralization launched by Peru without assistance in 1969.[60]

Brazil was easily AID's number one target in the 1950s, part of a huge push to reform the nation's public administration (Figueiredo 1987: 176). AID project #5120263 boldly included a host of measures aimed at admin-istration centralization, flexible curriculum, a credit system, and other alter-natives to faculty-centered higher education. When the University of Brasilia launched the nation's most formidable reform in 1962, it simultaneously trumpeted nationalist or European roots and pushed an astonishing agenda of Americanized academic centralization along with even a campus to pro-mote university community. After Brazil's military coup (1964) undermined Brasilia's experiment, the University of Minas Gerais teamed up with AID and the education ministry to assume a leadership that culminated in a mas-sive 1968 reform. The reform mandated departments, basic studies, credit systems, and electives. Amazingly, the mandates covered the entire system. Indeed AID found itself hampered by the Brazilian university policy of serving all its members and responding to their various requests for assistance so that "project resources could not be focused."[61] This constituted a triumph of bold modernizing optimism and "scatterization" over philanthropic caution, reflecting recipient more than donor overzealousness.

Judged against expectations, the AID-Brazil effort was a terrible failure. At the most established universities, the powerful professional faculties did not yield. Among the colorful images of faculty resistance to centralization were lawsuits by deans against rectors and the transfer of facilities from fac-ulties to central control under the cloak of darkness. Sensitive to its standing with the middle class, as represented by the professors and students, the military government retreated. Innovations often froze immediately into formalistic nuisances. "Unanticipated results" became common as actors found new and complex ways to do old things, the credit system had to reconcile itself to rigid curricula, and students regarded basic courses as a waste of time given persisting vocational realities (Schwartzman 1988: 103).

But compared to other nations, change was ample. Like the Costa Rican case, the Brazilian adds to the argument (chapter 2) about the powerful partnership between donors and domestic reformers in eager and relatively undeveloped higher education systems. Departments became the main unit in many Brazilian universities, grouping teaching and research—especially where there was prior international exposure (Schwartzman 1991: 221). Less than in other Latin American nations would research within universities have to be housed in special centers where teaching is not a function. Brazilian students take courses in a variety of departments, so the credit system has meaning. Moreover, success is probably greatest where AID and other donors maintained partnership. Examples are agriculturally oriented universities such as the Rio Grande do Sul, which enjoyed a helpful relationship with the University of Wisconsin. Agronomy students take their science and technology in general studies and in departments such as chemistry and physics.[62]

In contrast to Brazil's more widespread effort, Colombia's came closer to the ideal type in concentrating on selected institutional targets and the strides proved greatest at those targets. This tends to support Cerych and Sabatier's (1986) cross-national finding that deep change is possible where reform efforts concentrate on a part of a system. Even there, however, results were mixed. On the public side we look at Antioquia and del Valle.[63]

Antioquia funneled all new students into its Arts and Sciences unit, general studies moved past the introductory level, and there was a reasonably adequate body of professors for the new undertakings at least through the first decade. But central leadership crumbled in the face of a severe clash between new forms and traditional ones, breeding troublesome prismatic overlap that included considerable undermining of the new forms. Deans of traditional faculties learned how to spin general studies or fight it with the support of students more concerned with risks to professional preparation than with the superior teaching they themselves reported for the general studies courses.[64] At del Valle too, positive results were twisted. A Cornell University mission helped legitimize early assistance from Ford and speed up general studies. Del Valle came to lead Colombian higher education in departmentalization, as well as central planning and library development. Leaders declared structural reform a great success, and other universities sought advice from them. But as a relatively old public alternative, del Valle confronted entrenched opposition from professional associations and others from the outset. Faculties then gained control over general studies and departments, which they housed. They thereby protected their turf and relieved their fears of lost enrollments to those units or to electives.[65] Most professors and especially students either opposed or misunderstood general studies, or both. The university could not get enough professors qualified to teach general offerings, though the return of scholarship holders from graduate studies abroad helped. Students did not receive the increases in individual attention or career orientation that were supposed to be part and parcel of the reforms (FF #61189).

In the private sector, the Javeriana achieved perhaps the smoothest results of any Colombian university in the 1960s, encountering the least opposition. Ford judged departmentalization and general studies to be part of the overall "structural modernization" achieved through a well-run grant at a well-run university, with the foundation probably playing a critical role in Antioquia's long-term institutional development (K. N. Rao to William Carmichael 12/6/74 in FF # 65-050). Los Andes also achieved considerable success, expanding the size and force of arts and sciences. General studies became a two-year undertaking, with further options outside one's professional faculty even in the subsequent two years. There was considerable variability by faculty, however, including in whether general studies flowed neatly into professional studies. Students and faculties both continued—with reason—to have doubts about the acceptance of a more general degree on the job market.

By the late 1960s, Ford awarded Los Andes a two-year termination grant, lauding it for the most advanced general studies program in Colombia, but also noting that the foundation had no intention of further funding general studies in Latin America. For all the mixed successes of a Los Andes, there were the clear failures of a San Marcos.[66] And since only a handful of places were ever targeted, more troubling than the few outright failures was the inability of the academic centralization achieved at most targets to influence much beyond those targets, even within a country like Colombia.

As it did for system decentralization, the philanthropic ideal type of change has guided our understanding of the trajectory of university centralization. Again donors' efforts have matched the ideal type well whereas results have turned out to be a mixed bag of match, failure, and prismatic alternatives.

Conclusion

Efforts were impressive in magnitude. Institution building involved major reforms. As in attempts aimed at interinstitutional differentiation, the U.S. model was the weighty, nearly uncontested foreign model, and it pushed away from the predominant reality of faculty-based, decentralized universities. Yet for such large-scale undertakings, efforts were reasonably compatible with notions of philanthropic selectivity. Dependency claims that assistance tries to impose foreign models wholesale wind up as far off the mark as claims that assistance is pro status quo.[67] The implicit hope so characteristic of assistance for modernization was that careful successes would spur institutionally centralizing forces, set examples, and thus ultimately produce more thorough change.

Donors looked to universities already centralizing, or at least inclined to centralize. This was targeted voluntary giving based on merit and promise. Donors repeatedly distinguished themselves from domestic governments by not scattering their efforts widely or randomly throughout the system. They certainly did not try to impose a standard U.S. model. Where donors stretched criteria most, at national universities, they still attempted to fortify centralizing allies, and they soon pulled back. These findings on targeting apply to all the donors, especially the private foundations. The closest to a systemwide effort spanning many institutions was in Brazil, and while that effort received ample U.S. backing, the greatest zeal for such broad transformation came from Brazil's policymakers. Major systems were not broadly assaulted from the outside. Partnership was paramount. The U.S. model was essentially a voluntary model, which reformers found attractive.

Even at Latin America's targeted institutions the direct reform agenda was remarkably selective. Donors did not try to impose pure U.S. forms, just as recipients usually did not blindly copy them. Thoughtful, flexible adaptation of centralized forms was more the norm. However inflated the implicit goals, pragmatism usually reigned in practice. Almost nowhere did projects reach for tuition, campuses with dormitories for most students, or liberal arts colleges. Moreover, the elements of the U.S. model that were on the agenda were pursued alongside traditional forms. The effort was to bypass or displace much more than to assault and replace directly, as shown by almost every aspect of centralization examined.

Results disappointed. This generalization may be harsh regarding administrative centralization, but even there projects that did fairly well at their target points failed to produce levers powerful enough to achieve the desired transformation in other parts of the targeted institutions. Particularly for academic centralization, assistance only partially achieved stated project goals, leaving it far from its wider, more implicit goals. Development-by-design proved elusive.

One reason was opposition. The philanthropic hope is that careful selectivity with partners minimizes opposition. Donors underestimated how much they deviated from selectivity when their optimistic zeal for rapid modernization initially tempted them into operating with conflicted national universities. In addition, compared to system decentralization, university centralization brought assistance *inside* institutions, a more invasive approach that triggered fierce opposition. Opposition was stronger regarding academic centralization, which threatened self-interest on sensitive issues more than administrative centralization did. For all the caution, efforts at general studies and departmentalization were "anti-faculty." In between, opposition developed where the administrative centralization was most interrelated with controversial academic centralization (e.g., central libraries tied to new pedagogy) as opposed to just increased buildings and equipment. The more we understand the opposition that made results lag far behind expectations, the more we appreciate that some of the main efforts were indeed ambitious.

Perhaps the stickiest if least obvious resistance comes less from outright, articulated disagreement with reforms than from the persistence of behavior patterns inside a still formidable "web" that is not reformed. Without the nutrition from other centralized practices, an inserted reform aimed at centralization often winds up illogical, isolated, and then deformed. The lack of a campus or centralized library, for example, renders U.S.-styled departments inappropriate, perhaps infeasible—just as the lack of academic centralization could make construction of U.S.-styled central facilities irrational. Nor could projected general studies make sense as long as students rely on getting all the needed facts from class, without integrating outside study. Similarly, electives cannot be easily imported if professors are unprepared to be advisors, let alone if they are unprepared to teach broadly. Departments and general studies programs must compromise with the reality of professionalist environments and expectations. And it is difficult to make these and other academic reforms where the administrative structure continues to turn heavily on elections, making it unlikely for reformers to get to the institutional top or to have independent power there.

Prismatic patterns become salient. Significant overlap is inevitable where donors and their partners, aware of stiffer opposition if they press further, limit their efforts to displacement rather than replacement. Here again is the philanthropic dilemma of prudent selectivity that limits transformation versus bolder and riskier efforts. Additional overlap develops where efforts at change produce gains in some but not other targeted places. Overlap between targets and nontargets or between more and less successful targets means living museums with powerful student associations alongside a new governing board, faculty libraries alongside a new central library, scattered professional buildings alongside a new campus for fresh fields of study, faculties alongside new departments or general studies, and so forth.

Often too, the new forms represent less change than appears on the surface. Formalism emerges where real power remains where it had been, preventing new forms from charting centralizing policies. Faculties lock departments and general studies inside their jurisdiction, faculties and chairs govern curriculum through their collective hold on the more centralized structures that technically lie above them, and traditional actors turn enlarged university bureaucracies into bloated dispensers of goodies for them. New units emulate old ones or serve them as much as they challenge them, as with departments that teach just within their own faculty rather than for broad integration of curriculum. Overlap involves not only the old sitting alongside the new but also the old influencing the new, enmeshing it, sometimes encircling and strangling it. The philanthropic ideal type posits that progressive niches inserted into traditional webs will be influential models and spread. Often, however, the clashing forms have led to cease-fires and compromises unhealthy for academic and administrative development, and sometimes they have led to unconditional surrender by the reformers.

The prismatic results certainly fail to meet anything like the expectations held by donors and their reform partners for university centralization. This is not the transforming modernization envisaged. Reform and institution-building centralization have hardly gone hand-in-hand.[68] Still today, dominant critiques of the Latin American university find a lack of centralized institutional power geared to healthy output and reform.

Results nonetheless meet other evaluative criteria. Once again, policy reform and implementation turn out to be tougher and more complex than anticipated but more extensive and positive than usually realized. Seeing how inflated expectations contributed to a sense of failure and gloom, it is then important to move to a third stage in which evaluation is more reasonable and complex. Our analysis has concentrated on differences between targeted and other institutions, but other major considerations include how even partial achievement of ambitious goals is noteworthy, especially in circumstances in which reforms were hammered by national political repression or economic crisis.

Evidence repeatedly shows that Latin America's major recipients of assistance would be leaders in university centralization, both administrative and academic. Allowing that recipients had often been ahead of the field anyway, assistance enabled them to vault above their limited centralization. For much administrative change that did not engender major opposition, the key assistance role was provision of extra, enabling resources to selected partners. Beyond the leaders, other recipients also centralized with assistance, and they far outdistanced nonrecipients on the average. These achievements fit our philanthropic ideal type of challenging, innovative change (along with rather imaginative failures) more than dull, easy change. Although restricted by the difficulties that opposition generated, the achievements in academic centralization stand out because so few nonrecipients went far on that front.[69]

Targeted institutions, mostly led by favored private and public alternative universities, often achieved at least a meaningful prismatic change where most of the system got mired in bland continuity or a formalism that brought little real change. Prismatic change involving coexistence and mixes between centralized and decentralized structures beat the system norm. Recipients of assistance built more central administrative and academic units that, while not integrating the whole university, provided something beyond the dominance of specialized professional faculties. Assistance produced positive change.

Assistance also helped build what would be the leading springboards for renewed efforts at centralized institution-building reforms, which gained strength toward the end of the century. To identify the major mixtures of attempted academic centralization and traditional faculty dispersion is to realize that they are not fixed but evolving. The reform models are still influencing configurations. Going further, we see that the reform ideas have considerable support and remarkable resilience, outdistancing structural impacts to date. National re-democratization and socioeconomic reform have often widened the debate over matters such as basic studies and general or bachelor degrees. Chilean professors and other reformers rekindled ideas such as basic cycles instead of premature specialization. The private Central American University in Nicaragua would in the 1990s undertake to convert from a faculty to department structure. Differences between yesterday's targeted and other countries remain but are diluted not only by slippage where progress was attained but also by reforms in the lagging countries.[70] Internationalization is a multifaceted force, increasing ties with a U.S. model that has gained force in Europe and elsewhere.[71] Institutional strength, managerial capacity, enhanced central facilities and authority, departmentalization, general studies and its variants, electives, flexibility, credit systems—such concepts and terms live. That they are the subjects of repeated reform efforts shows both the frustration of prior efforts and the persistence of reformist will.

5

Academic Work

Academic work was the core concern for university assistance. Structural reforms of systems and individual institutions—the concerns of the previous two chapters—were largely to serve the cause of good academic work. Improved academic work was the central direct goal for foundations and other donors, whatever visions they entertained about thereby also promoting wider development.

The first part of this chapter focuses on the academic profession. The second part turns to research, graduate education, and fields of study.[1] The first thus deals mostly with "who," the second more with "what." But the four subjects are highly interrelated, and the analysis traces a parallel pattern for each: ambitious goals, vigorous but selective efforts, and major successes mixed with disappointing results, often including prismatic results.

Professionalizing the Professoriate

Goals: A New Breed

Donors and their domestic partners in reform considered modernization of the professorate crucial to academic work and indeed their entire university model: For the new university, a new professorate. This professorate was to be academically well trained and dedicated to the university. A central aspect of the professionalization, the norm of full-time status, is our focus. Full-time status was pivotal to a mini-web for the projected professorate, for full-timers were assumed to be highly trained academically, properly geared for research and teaching. They would be committed to their special discipline, the academic profession overall, their university, and to universal scientific and cultural horizons.

The goal of full-time status was nothing short of transforming. A rejection of common Latin American practice, it epitomized the orientation of assistance toward big change and the philanthropic ideal type. The majority of professors across Latin America worked mostly outside the university. They were professionals, but not academic professionals. They were lawyers who would teach law courses, or architects, physicians, engineers, and bureaucrats. An apt term was "taxi-professors"—professionals riding in, teaching, and riding out in short order. They spent most of their time and energy where they earned their livelihood, not at the university.

No nation escaped the rule. At an extreme, the University of Buenos Aires, then the region's largest and probably most important university, reportedly had but one full-time professor in 1952 (Pérez Lindo 1985: 136).

Aggravating matters was the status of "chaired" professors among the few full-timers. Reformers denounced these poor alternatives to departments for their stultifying, lifelong control over curriculum and junior associates; however adequate they once might have been, chairs could not handle massive growth in fields of study, enrollments, and the professorate. The chair was an aristocratic or autocratic institution, ill suited to the growth and social mobility championed by the U.S. model (Ben-David 1971). In fact, chaired professors were the exception. This was true even where they had great weight, e.g., Brazil, and especially where they did not, e.g., Colombia.[2] Both the full-time chaired professor and the part-time professor were lamented alternatives to the professorate envisioned by donors, but the part-time professor was the much more common alternative.

Donors and their partners saw the preponderance of part-timers as a root problem of the Latin American university—incompatible with almost all the goals discussed in the previous two chapters. Reliance on part-timers worked against establishment of strong institutions with their own identities. Part-timers identified mainly with their private practice or government job. Loyalties, values, orientations, and priorities all developed outside the university. Ties to professions shielded faculties from university-centered reforms such as strengthened administration, departmentalization, and general studies. Obviously too, part-time status contradicted the ideals of interactive campus life. Nor could a part-time staff accommodate the expanded teaching load that would accompany large enrollment growth.

Part-time status also clashed with other goals for academic work. Certainly research normally required full-time positions, but donors clearly preferred a full-time academic commitment even for teaching.[3] Full-time students should count on professors for more than just a few weekly hours in the classroom. The relationship between full-time professors and graduate students must be tighter still, at least if graduate studies carries the U.S. meaning of degree programs in academic fields tied to research or the ability to enter the academic profession and teach the next generation. Part-time professors cannot keep abreast of the latest academic developments, conduct research with graduate students, and assume the responsibilities of supervising theses or laboratory work. Additionally, at whatever degree level, part-timers more often rely on formal lectures to impart the facts needed for professional practice whereas full-timers would introduce more interactive pedagogy aimed at developing critical thinking and the academic disciplines.

Donors also believed that full-timers were essential to the proper social organization of the professorate. Only full-timers could assert sufficient power as well as academic norms. Otherwise student activists filled the vacuum, substituting politics for academics. That was particularly troublesome since this form of politics often worked against appropriate reform and upgrading of academic work. Similarly, only full-timers could crush control by chaired professors, or counteract excessive control by government or the professions. Only they could form associations to promote disciplinary and other academic concerns, as they did to promote assistance efforts in Colombia, thereby elevating ideal typical goals of universalism over narrow national foci. Additionally, proper evaluation of performance depended on organization of the professorate as full-timers, so that there would be an ample academic performance to judge and peers to do the judging. There could be no academic profession without the professional norm of internal rule setting and policing. Furthermore, when evaluation is coupled with mobility, there are incentives for higher performance. Thus, foreign advisors repeatedly pushed breaking away from uniform pay, which had some logic for part-time service.[4]

In short, the broad goal of elevating academic quality to international standards required an academic profession dedicated and equipped for the task. A full-time professorate was essential to the academic web that donors and their reform partners hoped to spin. It was essential to achieve sustainable academic development.

And the goal of full-time commitment was aggressive not only in its rejection of Latin American tradition but also in its close tie to the U.S. model. "Un profesor full-time" would become common terminology even in countries not as penetrated as others by U.S. words. The "weight" of the U.S. professorial model is plain. Mediterranean nations including Spain relied on part-timers. The most advanced European nations relied on "academic estates" tied to state service more than separate professions associated with autonomous universities (Neave and Rhoades 1987: 213, 223–25; Metzger 1987). Moreover, whereas the U.S. export model envisioned a unity of teaching and research, full-timers in countries like France generally worked in either teaching *or* research institutions. For academic professionalization, modernization meant Americanization.[5]

Major Efforts

Consistent with their ambitious goals, donors pressed ahead energetically. Projects generally included provisions for a full-time academic profession, even where they omitted other elements of the U.S. model (campuses, tuition, etc.). Emboldened by their successful building of the academic profession at home (Lagemann 1989), U.S. foundations were ready to export. And on what projects more than building an academic profession would U.S. universities urge action on AID and other donors?

Commitment to expand full-time faculty was a big selling point, often required, for universities seeking external assistance. What attracted donors were not established peaks—they did not exist—but partner institutions with high aspirations. By the early 1960s several favored universities already had beachheads, largely due to earlier programs with foundations such as Rockefeller, yet these beachheads invariably amounted to a minority of the faculty, usually a small minority. Proposals promised to multiply the seeds. For example, the 1964 IDB loan to Chile's Catholic university called for the hiring of 160 new full-time professors, after assistance from the Doherty and Ford Foundations had helped the number increase from just two to thirty-seven, 1960–64 (IDB/L19: 14, 48–49). Among many contemporary parallels, the IDB loan to the same nation's public technical university called for the transforming addition of seventy full-timers over four years (IDB/L15: 20). Most institutions targeted for major assistance overall were expected to become influential leaders regarding full-time staff.

Where traditional professions reigned and part-time teaching would surely remain common, donors concentrated on installing an important full-time contingent—evidence of philanthropic innovation as well as caution. Rockefeller's initiatives in medical education led the way. As in other developing regions, this deviation from the professionalist model was controversial (Coleman and Court 1993: 49–50). Initiatives encompassed not just classroom teaching but both research and physicians' control of hospitals. A launching pad was the Sao Paulo medical school, known as a "Rockefeller school."[6]

Most efforts concentrated on alternatives *outside* the traditional professional faculties, however. We proceed to analyze those efforts in ideal typical terms of selectivity outside the mainstream, bearing in mind that they were also initiatives for innovative change.

Selective Efforts

Most projects for academic development included provisions on full-time work, but only minorities of institutions or units within institutions were project recipients. The full-time push concentrated on rather carefully selected targets. Donors rarely made a direct assault against the part-time teaching in the mainstream faculties, which constituted the university's numerical and functional core.[7]

Donors restricted their efforts partly because they recognized the case against their push. One point was that the main role of the Latin American university was the training of professionals, not liberal arts and not research. For this training, the best teachers might well be leading practitioners. They could impart required information and also recruit students directly to employment. Besides, they came cheap, serving for the sake of their own practice, profession, alma mater, or society. Furthermore, part-time status made sense in nations with a notable scarcity in human resources and limited differentiation among societal institutions (Silvert 1970). Of course, donors also moved simultaneously to expand the resources and the differentiation; still, part-time teaching allowed time for contributions from beyond the university.

In any event, many realized that a full-time professorate ran up against an alien context: just as zealots could insist that a powerful push would be crucial to many related reforms, so skeptics could point out how the lack of those reforms would undermine the push toward full-time work. Here again, some critics and donors alike realized that certain reforms could be unworkable or irrational outside a web of change. Donors often adapted and tried to move ahead with a deft philanthropic combination of caution and innovation.

Donors went only where partners wanted them. But although the full-time concept ran against common practice and certain arguments, it was popular. Donors easily found domestic reformers. Or eager reformers found donors, or both. Domestic reformers frequently endorsed suggestions made by consultants, visiting professors, or their own scholars returning from foreign universities. The full-time idea gained such currency that it got on the agenda even in the absence of major assistance projects, though usually not as much, and almost always with the help of the actors just cited. Pelczar called the idea perhaps the least controversial part of the academic reform package in Colombia.[8] Opponents of "academic imperialism" in general did not usually reject the full-time concept itself and could speak well of foundations' efforts to professionalize disciplines even while perhaps criticizing AID (Briones i). The relatively high level of acceptance made the full-time concept more like reforms aimed at administrative than academic centralization. Like other reforms of academic work considered in this chapter, it shows how U.S. features could comprise the bulk of the foreign "weight" in the imported model and still not represent imposition of alien practice on hapless or reluctant victims.

Projects rarely tried to install full-time work across the board. Brazilian reform was again an intriguing deviation, possible as zealous domestic reformers teamed up with domestic political power.[9] Donors usually adapted their model to Latin American reality and concentrated their projects where the receptivity and prospects for success appeared propitious. So philanthropic selectivity meant more than limitation; it meant limitation to meritorious islands of experimentation. And that meant built-in prismatic overlap between innovating targets and continued traditional practices where donors did not tread.

The selected targets were usually alternative universities, relatively new fields of study, or special research or other units. Efforts to create niches within traditional professions did not aim at the profession's heart but at exceptional, innovative people and places. In medicine, for example, donors pushed research and public health programs while they left most professors to their private practice and part-time teaching. Rather than trying to abolish part-time status, donors set out to reduce greatly its share of the teaching load by building a formidable full-time core.

As with efforts to decentralize the system or to centralize the university, a contradiction thereby arose between only targeted efforts on the one hand and expectations for widespread change on the other, a contradiction reflecting the ambiguity and faith that characterized donors' attitudes and often characterizes philanthropic undertakings. Statements of either grandiose or limited intention can be cited. But the sometimes articulated and usually implicit hope was that great success at targeted spots would serve as models and seeds for wider efforts. Accordingly, while few were naive enough to claim a specific timetable for a specified final outcome, donors and their domestic partners believed that their actions would have impacts beyond their particular projects. Yet thought and effort concentrated on the project in question much more than on how the overall system would then be transformed. Such lack of clarity in efforts, of course, reflected a lack of clarity in goals that arguably contradicts philanthropic ideals.

Intentions, expectations, and efforts themselves varied by donor (as well as by time period, particular project, and individuals within agencies). Promotion of an academic profession was most notable for foundations. This fit their historical domestic experience and their emphasis on human resource development more than bricks and mortar. Major projects undertaken jointly by donors usually concentrated foundations' efforts on promotion of the academic profession through scholarships abroad, direct funding for new full-time positions over a fixed number of years, or related undertakings.

Roles assumed by other donors also related to the full-time effort, as with IDB and AID funding to build campuses, laboratories, and libraries for these full-timers as well as for students. Moreover, the IDB usually would fund only those places committed to enhancing their full-time staffs, and it often directly funded those efforts. Even when the IDB turned away from university development per se, its science and technology projects, such as those starting in the 1970s with Mexico's science and technology council and one in 1982 with Colombia's, aimed at greatly increasing the number of full-time academics. AID was initially more circumspect and did not attempt to make full-time status the standard operating procedure.[10] From the mid-1960s, however, the AID-funded and then USIA-funded LASPAU became a powerful exponent of faculty development aimed at full-time status. Although LAS-PAU realized that the concept could not be imposed on reluctant places, it concentrated its efforts on many institutions that could not possibly make substantial progress without external assistance (Strong i).

Assisted Results by Nation

Major progress came in establishing an academic profession based on full-time commitment, and assistance was inextricably tied to that progress. As usual, assistance played a big role where a big change occurred. It was crucial both to increasing greatly the number of full-time professors overall and, especially, to building those pockets of academic superiority where the full-time profession is strongest. By our evaluative criteria, all this means considerable success.

For what they are worth, regional data accumulated relatively early and late within the period of peak assistance show gains. In 1962, the respective figures for exclusive, full-time, half-time, and by-hours professors were 3, 11, 12, and 67 percent, with 8 percent other. By 1971, the comparable figures were 9, 14, 11, and 52 percent, with 14 percent other. The improved percentages are noteworthy for a period in which the number of professors doubled (to over 130,000), and the increased number of surveyed universities (from 48 to 76) probably increased the proportion of weak institutions.[11]

Aggregate data obscure the notable gains in favored nations. Foreign assistance there played a major role (Sánchez 1973: 118) through ideas (both introducing and insisting on them), opportunities, and money, adding power to domestic actors already interested in or at least receptive to the full-time concept. Chile became an early regional leader largely because foundations like Rockefeller introduced the full-time concept.[12] By 1966, Chile had achieved a 38 percent full-time staff versus 6 percent for Mexico and similarly unimpressive figures for nations such as Uruguay, Bolivia, and Ecuador (Pelczar 1977: 238). Many Chilean scientists believe that the impact endured, even after political and economic dislocation, helping to explain their positions and their nation's elevated standing within Latin America in both universities and scientific instruction and publication (Croxatto i). Today, notwithstanding concerns with cost, the full-time ideal is strong and pursued by many universities.

Like Chile, Brazil received an early boost from assistance preceding the golden age, but it did not reach relatively high national percentages of full-timers until it combined substantial IDB and national funds. It jumped from perhaps 17 to 35 percent between 1972 and 1982 and doubled its absolute number in the 1980s.[13]

Lacking equal pre–golden age foundation boosts or post–golden age national resources, Central America better shows the concentrated impact of assistance projects. In a fifteen-year period starting from the mid-1960s, the number of professors who taught just by hours at Nicaragua's National Autonomous University held steady at around 200 while the full-time number multiplied tenfold to over 300 and the half-time number multiplied fivefold to over 100.[14] Although the political and economic crises of the 1980s hurt Central American numbers overall, many full-timers continued in the natural and social sciences; at least the numbers were much higher than they had been before assistance or would have been without assistance (Lungo i).

Less-favored nations did not generally get as far and they weigh down regional figures. Allowing for varied definitions and methods of counting full-time across nations, it still appears that favored nations produced more success. The fate of other nations obviously suggests a failure of favored nations as models for the region, but also some general difficulties that confronted all nations and thus make the achievements in favored nations impressive.

Argentina and Mexico are our main two cases of less-favored nations.[15] Argentina remained very low in full-time staff at the end of the golden age. Roughly 75 percent of the teachers worked for few hours for pay that was minimal, almost honorary. Full-timers rose to over 10 percent of the staff in some areas of science but much less in the humanities. Public provincial universities set up with full-time aspirations did better than the University of Buenos Aires, but that says little, and private universities employed virtually no full-timers.[16] To address this poor overall situation, the science and technology council began to give supplementary income, which has helped some university professors to work full-time at decent pay.

Mexico's averages would be better, but short of regional leaders. From 1966 to 1976, the full-time percentage rose only from 7 to 10 percent, as 82 percent still were hired by hours, the rest half-time. Joint IDB-CONACYT (National Science and Technology Council) projects, which sent unprecedented numbers for advanced study, helped boost the full-time figure to 21 percent by 1985. Incredibly, Mexico's figure was only slightly higher for those teaching at the graduate level, 25 percent.[17]

Mexico's national university, UNAM, showed little advance in percentages. Some 90 percent of its professors continued to teach by hours. Only about 10 percent of those teaching UNAM's first-degree students merited the label academic professionals, and fewer than 20 percent of those teaching graduates were career professors, some of whom held half-time appointments. Only the research centers boasted high full-time percentages within UNAM, contributing to mammoth intrauniversity stratification in academic status.[18] For example, the engineering institute would be virtually all full-time while the engineering faculty was roughly 10 percent full-time (Resendiz i; Esteva i). Particularly painful was that over 90 percent of professors taught by hours in the special units for the bachillerato level created by the university in the 1970s to establish full-time status as the norm and as a model for institutionwide reform. Also, the reality regarding full-time status reflected the overall reality regarding academic professionalism—no better in these units than in the mainstream faculties.[19]

Assisted Results within Nations

Differences between assisted and unassisted places are clearer within nations. Targeted alternative universities are the main reason nations such as Chile and Colombia gained comparatively high national averages. Outside its national university, roughly two-thirds of Chilean professors in the mid-1980s would be full-time.[20]

Targeted alternative universities also show the quick impact projects had. Dramatic change concentrated within just a few years is strong evidence, albeit not airtight, of projects' impact. Colombia supplies multiple examples. Del Valle in the 1960s is one. EAFIT blazed a similar path with AID's help. With Ford's help the Javeriana quickly increased its full-time basic science staff to forty, exceeding the goal of twenty-five.[21]

At Chile's Catholic university, after early assistance helped lead the rise from 3 to 13 percent between 1953 and 1967, Rockefeller scholarships in the 1960s, a 1965 Ford grant, and a 1964 IDB loan fueled the leap to roughly 50 percent by 1970.[22] The university has given the foundations major credit for establishing its full-time concept. The 50 percent figure is especially impressive when we realize that Ford had decided that fields like engineering enjoyed good job links and therefore could continue well without major change and that full-timers had studied at places like Stanford and Berkeley; though such success did not fulfill the university's goal of matching the leading U.S. and European universities in science and engineering, it represented significant progress (Peter Hakim to Peter Bell, 1/31/72, final report, FF #62515). Nonelite targets also showed results. Chile's regional colleges would have 58 percent full-timers, handling 86 percent of the teaching (Lemaitre 1985: 10).

Targeted universities within less-favored nations likewise made rapid progress. Venezuela's Simón Bolívar moved from paltry to leading numbers, 75 percent full-time by 1983, under the impact of large IDB loans along with philanthropic grants (IDB/E7). It quickly outdistanced Venezuela's national university in those fields where both operated by 46 to 30 percent in exclusive time commitments while having just 25 versus 49 percent in the "hours" category.[23] Around Latin America, striking impacts came at institutions— nonelite as well as elite—that worked extensively with LASPAU in that organization's crusade for faculty development.

Grants targeted to units or fields within institutions also produced summits above the surrounding landscape. Ford's grant to Mexico's UNAM for science and engineering allowed a doubling of full-timers in those fields within just a few years and contributed to the fact that sciences like chemistry would have the institution's lowest proportion of professors by hours (FF

#67281). Ford's grant providing for doctorates abroad was largely responsible for transforming the sociology institute of Chile's Catholic university: between 1967 and 1973 full-time numbers grew from 4 to 34 while those employed by hours fell from 23 to 2. At Chile's Concepción university, a 1960 Ford grant made it possible, building from scratch, for all professors in the four institutes (departments) to be full-time.[24]

Similarly, an IDB loan to the University of Costa Rica produced big percentages of full-timers in the newer faculties and 25 of 31 instructors in general studies were full-time (IDB/L29: 24, 51). In contrast, the unassisted basic cycle at Argentina's UBA would sometimes use students as teachers. Central America's full-time numbers rose in assisted social and natural science fields while remaining very low in law and other professional fields; but where traditional professions added full-time university people it was usually with crucial foreign assistance. Probably the majority of Chile's full-timers in these fields had studied abroad with scholarships.[25]

The success at targeted places goes beyond numbers alone to the broader web of what reformers wanted full-timers to be. The best quantitative indicators of this qualitative dimension are graduate degrees. Full-time professors are much more likely than part-timers to have those degrees. Projects that increased full-time staff also increased staff with advanced degrees. Returning to a couple of cases just cited, when the Simón Bolívar achieved its high percentage of full-timers, it built a staff in which one-fourth of the members held doctorates. When Brazil doubled its full-time percentage, 1972–82, as reported above, it also doubled the percentage of professors with a master's degree or doctorate, from 13 to 27 percent. As del Valle moved ahead of Colombia's overall system by 80 to 34 percent in full-timers, it moved ahead by 39 to 7 percent in professors with graduate degrees (Wickham 1973: 99). Colombia's Santander university shows that, even where a project's numerical goals were not met, doctorates could be doubled and master's degrees greatly increased within a decade (IDB/E4: 6).

More qualitative indicators tell a similar story. Assistance generally funded advanced training at the world's finest universities.[26] Taught better, these full-timers would teach better. And scientists were increasingly trained by scientists rather than by professors in medical or pedagogical faculties, social scientists by social scientists rather than by lawyers. Projects and scholarships produced Colombian professors who outperformed part-timers in subject matter taught, written assignments and reading lists given, and other methods employed both within and beyond the classroom.[27] Similar impacts emerged in many other places as well, such as the Ford-funded economics program at Chile's Catholic university. Peru's main Catholic university made a long-standing tradition of faculty retreats, the practice initiated with Ford sponsorship, and few believe it would otherwise have developed. Assistance-produced international contacts often then persisted as fountains of continuing benefits. The IDB's projects were vehicles for introducing concepts like peer review to regional leader Brazil, as foundation-funded activities would do more through private research centers in much of Latin America.[28]

At targeted places, the general goal of professionalizing the professorate and the operationalized one of building a major full-time staff translated into both considerable effort and considerable impact. Of course, specific project goals might be met without their then generating self-sustaining movement, as to a predominantly full-time staff, but this could still mean advancement far over what had existed and what nonrecipients would achieve.

As we proceed to analyze shortcomings in implementation, we should bear in mind one other resilient success. The idea of academic professionalization, and specifically of a full-time academic profession, gained great currency. Perceptive IDB officials regard this as one of donors' principal achievements.[29] The idea has remained alive through years of austerity, chaos, or repression, ready for renaissance as conditions permit. Targeted places and people are the best jumping-off points from where domestic higher education systems try to build their full-time academic profession.[30]

Prismatic Displacement

The assistance success regarding the academic profession was a relative one. It brought a good deal of prismatic displacement. The initial juxtaposition of forms produced by careful targeting alongside an untouched mainstream was supposed to diminish as targets turned into models, but this dynamic was overwhelmed by the massification of enrollments that inevitably meant massification in the professorate. Most new professors were very poorly trained. They were not brought in through careful assistance projects. What was "new" was mostly old, or traditional, not innovative or superior. All this obviously violates the philanthropic ideal type of change.

Massification limits or proportionally wipes out otherwise impressive increases in numbers of full-time professors.[31] The regional percentages cited earlier showed a jump in exclusive and full-time from 14 to 23 percent while the professorate more than doubled, to around 130,000 by 1971; by the late 1980s the region had nearly 515,000 professors. A case like Mexico, where the professorate grew 954 percent from 1960 to 1992, shows the difficulty of raising the percentage of full-timers.[32] Except at targeted places in Latin America, the number of full-time professors rarely rose enough for the percentage to increase dramatically. At typical places—and therefore in the system overall—the number of full-timers rose very much while the percentage did not.

Consequently, gains in full-time staffing left Latin America far from where designs had projected it and behind many African and Asian nations as regards a full-time norm or overall professional status. No Latin American nation approached India, where the norm was full-time, most university professors had doctorates whereas professors at the colleges had master's, and the academic profession tended to lobby against massification of enrollments

(Altbach 1987a: 89). Moreover, though comparisons with U.S. levels are mostly unwarranted, differences remained greater than expected. In 1980, Brazil would lead Latin America with only 12,000 full-time researchers, roughly 2 percent of the U.S. total (Segal 1986: 144).

As was the case regarding other components of their higher education agenda, donors and domestic reformers anticipated growth but not its full volume and certainly not its full negative impact on realization of their objectives. Even less did they anticipate the injurious political and economic developments outside the university. Instead they hoped the wider political and economic arenas would evolve in ways positive for their reforms, either by actively joining as reform partners or at least by standing aside and allowing new higher education dynamics to prosper unhindered.[33] Besides, realistically, what else could they do?

Military rule and political disorder were especially devastating to reforms in academic work, more so even than to reforms considered in prior chapters. They brought outright purges and other realities that made many abandon academic aspirations. Insofar as the university was "the enemy," full-time members of the academic profession were more at risk than part-timers who worked mostly in professional practice. Indeed, many full-timers were knocked back to part-time plus professional practice. Contributing to this change were military decisions to cut higher education's share of the national budget. Additionally, beyond political choice, resources often declined because the overall national economic situation deteriorated.

Macro political and economic conditions contributed to a brain drain, which further reduced the full-time core. Those who did not abandon their academic aspirations often pursued them abroad in universities or in international organizations. Another type of brain drain involved an internal flow from academia to different jobs. In tough times, a previously marginal but satisfying economic existence often became untenable. Paradoxically, the internal brain drain has also resulted from favorable macro conditions when opportunities have opened in business or to serve reform governments, either way offering more money than universities can offer. Riggs (1964: 156) has referred to the "sucking" attraction of bureaucracy and power away from prismatic universities. Those effects have varied by field. Argentina's UBA and Chile's two major universities could hold onto physicists and mathematicians, who lacked an alternative job market, while economists and engineers headed elsewhere.[34] That said, positive developments beyond the university also sometimes improved chances for full-time university work as budgets improved.

A different sort of internal brain drain has occurred within academic settings. This has the advantage of avoiding complete losses from academia, but it leaves unsettling prismatic mixes. The university fails to approximate the U.S. export model. Instead, academic development occurs largely in research centers. Centers created within the university sit alongside faculties where part-timers remain the norm. Or centers and faculties share personnel, but again the faculty teaching commitment is part-time. A different overlap emerges interinstitutionally, where centers develop outside the university. These include freestanding centers, private or public, and centers within or linked to church, NGO, business, government, or international associations such as those involved in research on food production.[35]

The contrast between full-time status in centers (or institutes) and part-time status in faculties is acute at universities like Mexico's UNAM. It is a logical contrast wherever true research centers gain a place alongside faculties that continue to offer mostly professional training in the traditional Latin American university model. Research requires much more academic training and usually less training in other professions. To be sure, many centers also have many part-timers, and the full-timers usually have a mix of tasks. Research blends not only with teaching (usually graduate) but also with administration of the center, service beyond the center, and consultancy. These tasks are not always academic in nature, but the academic-nonacademic balance suggests more of an academic profession than the reality in most university faculties. The closest approximation to a full-time academic life has often come at those classic research centers that are best known internationally, such as El Colegio de México, Argentina's Center for the Study of the State and Society (CEDES), and Chile's Latin America Faculty of Social Science (FLACSO).

Research centers represent a remarkable achievement for international assistance. For leading centers, the success redounds notably to philanthropy, for foundations were clearly the main donors, especially the main U.S. donors. Foundations directly promoted the centers, and often were crucial in launching them. International philanthropy fully funded many of the private centers. All this obviously goes well beyond donors' share of university finance even during the golden age. International, public, and other centers have been major targets for foundations, AID, the IDB, and other bilateral and multilateral agencies before, during, and after the golden age. Additionally, donors played another crucial role for centers' development, however inadvertently: before and during the golden age, through both projects and individual scholarships, they expanded the supply of well-trained researchers who then established or subsequently worked in centers. The rub—the failure regarding the U.S. export model—was that Latin America's university faculties did not provide more adequate homes for this new supply of trained individuals. Centers often offered more academic freedom, institutional autonomy, research opportunity, international contacts, access to top graduate students, job stability, and financial reward. The great academic, social, and political contributions that research centers have made have thus depended on donors' greater success in building a base of human resources than in transforming mainstream university structures. Donors' intensified turn toward research centers in the mid-1970s was very much connected to its turn away from universities. Indeed, in some ways the centers' success has further hindered efforts to establish an academic profession at the university.[36] Attempts have been made to forge creative links, notably where the centers' researchers teach at the universities' faculties. Donor-promoted centers have influenced and sometimes reshaped university faculties, often in positive ways, but little of this corresponds to the philanthropic ideal type in which promoted targets meet goals for their own development and then make the wider system like themselves.

Certainly the centers themselves do not meet the original goals established for the academic profession. Their most critical void concerns teaching. Researchers usually do little or no teaching at their own centers, however much they may do as part-timers at nearby universities. This leaves the export model frustrated not only regarding numbers of full-time staff but also regarding the many reforms that are feasible within a web featuring full-time staff: pedagogical modernization, departmentalization, general studies, graduate studies, campus life, and so forth.[37] Above all, the teaching-research nexus that was supposed to characterize the full-time academic professional goes largely unrealized. The separation of functions that were to be integrated is a typical prismatic characteristic.

The campaign to professionalize the professorate has resulted in neither clear net failure nor clear net success. It has instead produced a complicated process of prismatic displacement and overlap in which failure and success are intertwined and also evolve into new and unanticipated forms.

Prismatic Formalism

Where full-time university positions exist, they usually represent much less than meets the eye. Data on Latin America's full-time staff overstate functional reality. Formalism is common and multifaceted. What sits alongside or overlaps the traditional professorate is less often the export model's projected professorate than a hollow pretense of it, a disappointing hybrid of traditional and exported forms. Few of the nominally full-time professors work as reformers envisioned. They lack the qualifications, performance, or rewards, and they do not form a centerpiece in an integrated web of academic modernization. Such formalism is a blow to the quest for ideal typical philanthropic results.

To begin with, "full-timers" often do not work at the university full-time. Their classroom hours may resemble those of U.S. counterparts, but their other university activities, including research, are minimal. They may even hold full-time jobs elsewhere, rarely academic jobs. Thus, Central America's high full-time percentages translate into very few academic jobs of total dedication in reality; many hold one-and-a-half full-time posts (Lungo i; Gutiérrez i). Similarly, apparent success fades as professors rarely work full-time at public universities in Brazil's Northeast, title and salary notwithstanding. Policymakers have therefore created an "exclusive time" category, testimony to the bogus nature of full-time contracts. Where respected, the new category eliminates major outside jobs while allowing consultancies and the like, and matches the full-time concept of the U.S. model. But such practice is rare in Latin America. Even a leader like Venezuela's Simón Bolívar would have only about half its full-timers in exclusive posts.[38] Usually, no separate category emerges for exclusive time.

Another sort of formalism concerning what is full-time arises as itinerant professors take on large teaching loads. Nominal full-timers work part-time in other universities, or those with no full-time title accumulate so many courses by hours that they in effect teach full-time. This accumulation is possible within one university but is most common across different institutions, sometimes in different cities. Itinerant Argentine professors roam from Buenos Aires to the provinces as Chileans do among institutions in Valdivia, Temuco, and Santiago (Balán n.d.; Apablaza i). Such practice hardly advances the notion of a campus-based academic profession or university community.

Even where commitments are full-time to one university, the increased number of full-timers has usually been formalistic because professors have lacked the qualitative level supposed in the export model. They rarely comprise an academic profession. Consider advanced education. Shortly after the end of the golden age, two-thirds of those teaching Latin America's first-degree students had just a first-degree education or less, and that figure comes from just the one-third of professors whose highest degree could be identified. Similarly, less than a third of UNAM's academic personnel were reported to have any graduate education at all, and even in heavily assisted Colombia only 15 percent of professors held a master's or doctorate.[39]

As with full-time staff, so for degrees held, massification turned growing numbers into stagnant percentages. In 1975, when the University of Costa Rica launched a program to send professors for graduate education, 16 percent of the staff had some graduate education; in 1988, after hundreds went and returned, the figure was 14 percent (Estrada i). Moreover, that university illustrated how degree requirements were often moot as massification demanded more hiring. The same occurred at Mexico's UAM and UNAM; despite UNAM's statutory requirement of a doctorate for the "titular" category, 40 percent of *titulares* lacked it (UNAM 1984: 430).

These sobering facts allow for superior levels at assisted places. Full-timers there are much more likely to approximate the characteristics associated with the export model. This is particularly true where foundations played a major role. In contrast, where domestic governments acted alone or with the IDB (i.e., less selectively than the foundations), fewer full-timers would have graduate degrees or their degrees would come from weaker programs. Brazil's nominal full-timers often hold just first-degrees or dubious national graduate degrees (Schwartzman 1988: 104). It follows that quantitative measures routinely used by the IDB exaggerated success regarding full-time goals.

To attract well-qualified people, an academic profession requires decent pay. The same holds for retention: low pay leads to the brain drain and to situations where full-time loses meaning. Just as a lack of pay holds down the full-time percentage in the overlapping professorial pool, so it leads to decreased commitment by nominal full-timers, contributing to formalism. Donors concentrated on building exceptions to Latin America's demoralizing tradition of paying professors much less than that earned by other professionals. But pay then sometimes fell when external assistance ended, as dependency notions would have it, and certainly when domestic political-economic circumstances deteriorated. Professors at favored targets such as the Dominican Republic's INTEC were forced to "finance their present with their past" by selling off possessions.[40]

Like pay, other aspects of recruitment and retention deviate sharply from principles of philanthropic selectivity or the U.S. model. Hiring is rarely a rigorous screening into the academic profession. Massification means increased numbers of both part-timers and full-timers who lack qualifications. Serious university documents acknowledge the tendency. Revolution brought an extreme as more than three-fourths of Nicaragua's professors in 1984 had been hired since 1979, and the average age was twenty-eight.[41] But a greatly expanded, ill-prepared professorate became common in almost every nation. Youth increasingly entered the professorate easily and directly from their own studies or by assuming some other employment and then coming back to the university as nominal full-timers (Gil 1994: 90–102).

Perversely, then, as the number of full-timers grew, the average quality of the professorate may have fallen. Many new professors who lack the training associated with academic professionalization also lack the practical professional training and standing of their predecessors.[42] The venerable lawyer, physician, engineer, or architect who brings accumulated expertise to class becomes the exception—and a more worthwhile contributor than the typical full-time professor. Quality drops in the traditional faculties that are still important parts of Latin American universities, while mediocrity characterizes newer "academic" fields, especially in social and administrative studies. Meanwhile, a decreasing percentage of full-timers gets hired according to long-emulated European procedures including public examinations or competitions (*concursos*) and presentation of a thesis (Schwartzman 1985: 104). This is not to denigrate the rigor of the academic hurdles overcome by many individuals aspiring to enter or move up in the professorate. It is not to impugn others who work hard and do their best without having the academic preparation or the available resources to be academic professionals. And it is certainly not to overlook the fine teaching many professors offer at reputable institutions like the national universities in Chile and Argentina from engineering to science to various other faculties.

It does not help, however, that it is as hard to fire as it is easy to hire. The very growth of full-time positions sometimes aggravates the problem as full-timers "own" their spot whereas part-timers depend on rehiring (Mignone i). Debate can surround the desirability of tenure in any circumstance, but here is a typical example of the perverse consequences when new forms burst in without the web that makes them sensible elsewhere. There is security and authority without merit certified through competition. In some countries, professors hired provisionally receive tenure without serious review. Government officials who occasionally or never teach may receive tenure (*definitividad* in Mexico). Rights properly associated with a full-time few pass politically to others.[43] Professors who are poorly prepared academically lobby to extract rights appropriate only for those who are so prepared. They lobby to standardize such rights regardless of the academic level of the individual or institution. This extension of rights to the undeserving means, indirectly, denial of rights to the deserving. That is, the truly qualified ought to have more privileges and power than others do; moreover, they are denied merited rights where authorities cannot afford the cost of giving those rights to all. Of course, the lobbying is rational for individuals who could not fare as well through academic criteria or competition. This is a further example of where prismatic formalism is perverse measured against original goals of transfer yet has its own logic.

Unions strengthen the lobbying. Again the Argentine and Mexican cases show a series of troublesome results distressingly common in Latin America. Unions protect lowered quality. They pressure through disabling strikes, once associated more with students. Some lobbying joins professors and other university workers in a common organization that undermines the notion of an academically elite profession.[44]

Although discernible differences appear between institutions that were more and less targeted, it is difficult to demonstrate consistent differences between nations that received more or less assistance. The professorate has sat more on the union side than on the academic prestige side, however healthy its political involvement may have been for democratic flowering. Brazil suffers from a weak academic ethos. Its National Association of Higher Education Professors, linked to the national workers union, is a combination of "political radicalism and educational conservatism"[45]—the antithesis of the assistance dictum. Like Mexico, Brazil features a corporatist clientelism, culture of resistance, hyper politicization by some alongside apathy by most, and strong political ideology and skepticism; criteria for professional organization and reward are heavily nonacademic, while morale is low. Like Peru and other nations, Brazil has also basically followed a civil service model with standard salaries for professors at its nationally financed universities. The standardization usually cuts across fields as well as institutions; at the heavily assisted University of Costa Rica, salary is uniform by four ranks regardless of whether one is a law or education professor. At the assisted Simón Bolívar, which boasts the most academic professionalization of any Venezuelan university, the IDB's evaluators joined their recipient partners in bemoaning how the nation's "homologación" (standardization in salaries, benefits, etc.) denies the university its earlier flexibility to hire the best (IDB/L41). Homologación remains a major obstacle to academic professionalization throughout Latin America.

Although Latin America's private universities have a governance structure that can escape the standardization, they rarely have the financial or academic structure to hire many full-time professors. Where flexible, competitive practices have most triumphed is outside universities, in private and other research centers. As a leading longtime observer noted for Chile, foundations established at their private centers the practice and norm of differential rewards, which professors would not have accepted at their universities in the golden age of university assistance.[46]

Donors inadvertently contributed to the quite antiphilanthropic formalism of Latin America's full-time professorate. The major example was where their assistance allowed rapid expansion in enrollment. Another example was promotion of university administration. This meant new positions with enhanced responsibility, international contacts, and pay. It meant that some of those who had received the best academic training abroad either abandoned the professorate or formally retained full-time professorships while devoting much of their time to administration.

To identify such unanticipated consequences undermining donors' goals is not to assign the major blame to assistance. Failures resulted mostly from the domestic factors cited. The main effects of assistance on the academic profession were positive. The biggest problem with assistance was its lack of greater impact. Perhaps this reflected too small an assistance effort to achieve goals of academic professionalization, but there were major efforts and the philanthropic ideal type assumes limited, focused effort. It is difficult to imagine an assistance assault grand enough in scale to have overcome the indigenous lack of a wider professionalizing web including much more solid university finance and management, research, graduate studies, departmentalization, and other reformist undertakings.

In sum, efforts to build a strong, full-time academic profession yielded mixed results. The contrast between what Brazilians call the "high clergy" and the "low clergy" (Schwartzman 1988: 105) relates to the considerable successes that donors and domestic reform partners achieved in promoting an academic profession in certain places alongside two disheartening realities: the failure of full-time practice to take hold more widely and the fact that most full-timers do not conform to the expectations associated with the U.S. model.

Other Academic Work

This account does not give the same attention to other aspects of academic work as to the academic profession. In addition to saving space, this is because the major points follow similar form; details change, of course, but not the concepts used to understand them.[47] The second part of the chapter considers three concerns central to the drive to modernize academic work at Latin America's universities: research, graduate education, and fields of study.

Research

Ambitious goals. Donors and their partners had transforming goals for Latin American research. Planning to build research universities, they criticized the region's existing universities, including the best ones, as very backward in research. Much too little was done, and isolated achievements came more in spite of university norms, policies, and structures than because of them. They came from heroic, sacrificing, exceptional individuals. Such uncoordinated efforts were not equal to modern research needs. Nor could they contribute sufficiently on pressing issues of national concern. The research lacked a strong service function. And it did not integrate itself with the university's main traditional task, teaching and professional training (Stitchkin i; Atcon 1966: 104–11). In short, research was marginal.

Donors looked to expanded research to serve many of their other goals. Here again, defying notions of dependency, assistance aimed for major change tied to major growth. At the broadest level research was crucial to what gave higher education centrality within development assistance: the contribution of knowledge to economic, social, and political progress. Research was to be relevant. Meanwhile, there was to be a great contribution to goals involving other academic concerns within the university.[48] Research was vital to general studies and especially departmentalization, with their emphasis on discovery and broad knowledge rather than the professional training paramount in the faculties. Furthermore, the full-time academic profession was to make research rather than extra-university practice the natural counterpart of teaching. Creation of a strong graduate level, improvement of teaching, and elevation of scientific fields were also necessarily tied to the pursuit of new knowledge and the means to pass on research skills to others.

The integration of research and these other academic pursuits epitomizes the weight, indeed the preeminence, of the U.S. model. Such integration was a facet of academic professionalization that set U.S. practice apart from that of most other advanced nations, which separated research and teaching much more.[49]

Selectivity in major efforts. To achieve goals of such magnitude, donors pushed hard in several respects. These mostly parallel their efforts regarding full-time professors: inclusion of such effort in most projects; requirements of commitment as a major criterion in selecting targets; innovative attempts to install a reform component within the professions. Moreover, donors and their partners wielded a rather free hand in research, new terrain compared to teaching. They also found new terrain, even during the golden age, by funding research in extra-university centers as well as inside universities. Agriculture is a mammoth example.[50]

But vigor again blended with selectivity. Donors did not directly confront entrenched practice in teaching so much as they deferred to established practice. They aimed much more to add a task than to replace one with another. The hope was that their successful projects would become beacons for installing research and research-teaching links more widely.

Donors targeted few places. The majority of universities could not meet criteria for assistance in research. Most projects included research, but most institutions and units within them did not get projects, just the juxtaposition seen in the efforts to create a full-time professorate. Despite some excessive rhetoric, actual projects never tried to install research in all universities, let alone all units within them. Efforts inside the professional fields targeted a particularly small minority of places.

The selectivity becomes still more impressive when we appreciate that willing partners were plentiful. Widespread support existed for the idea of expanded research. A minority view was that research was an unwarranted luxury. There was also doubt about whether the university should be the central site for expanded research, since it might indulge in exploration not vital to national development. Nonetheless, most reformers supported the U.S. model for incorporating research mostly inside the university. Even within the professions, where support was spottiest, many were ready for research assistance.

Less selective efforts came from domestic reformers whose zeal to modernize was not tempered by philanthropic reserve and whose political calculus pushed toward inclusiveness. Once more, Brazil is the major example. Most extreme there and elsewhere were attempts to legislate research into existence, mandating it as a major role for all universities, and not distinguishing sharply from other higher education institutions that would not be so charged. The blanket approach to research indicated a distorted view of U.S. reality, where many institutions undertake no research or little research.

Typically, the foundations were most selective and concerned with quality, whereas the IDB worked with domestic governments to reach a wider number of institutions. The foundations usually concentrated on researchers directly, whereas the IDB often worked more to provide the required infrastructure of space, equipment, laboratories, and libraries (IDB/E1: 27).

Assisted results. Efforts produced significant successes. Above all, the amount of research, including high quality research, expanded greatly. This expansion and its ties to other aspects of the modernization model were most evident where assistance concentrated. Places like Venezuela's Simón Bolívar and Chile's Austral universities emerged as examples of institutional success (Kelly i; Fortoul i). Most successes have related more to particular units within institutions.

Assistance was most clearly pivotal where research gained a foothold within professional fields. Examples include AID's and other donors' work to blend in agricultural research with extension and training, as in Brazil, and work by Rockefeller, Kellogg, National Institute of Health, UNESCO, and others to promote novel and public health–related medical research.[51] Such innovations increased the social relevance and importance of the professions and of the university. Although this study does not examine the issue of relevance closely enough to assess sophisticated arguments about it, it finds simplistic at best the charge that assistance promoted esoteric academic over practice knowledge. IDB support would promote Brazilian soybean research, Argentine biological research to fight diarrhea, Costa Rican technological and computer development, and so forth.[52] Further positive suggestions on relevance come from the section below on fields of study.

The impact of assistance is harder to prove on a nation versus nation basis.[53] Too many other factors determine the size and efficiency of a nation's research effort and whether it takes place substantially within the university. Like other aspects of academic work, the expansion of research was a popular goal in much of Latin America and thus was not as dependent on assistance to push the idea as was the case with many of donors' other goals. Furthermore, strides in university research have generally occurred in only some units within institutions, and even some low-receiver nations had targeted units. Although this factor limits nation-to-nation differences, it does not limit the importance of assistance. Where nontargeted nations made significant strides, massive programs for scholarships abroad were vital, as with Venezuela's Ayacucho or Mexico's CONACYT-IDB program. Moreover, the structure of research shows cross-nationally differential impacts. Chile went far beyond Mexico in truly mixing university research and teaching (Molina i; Kent i), though in the 1970s and 1980s Chile's military rule delivered a major setback in the social sciences. Perhaps the greatest cross-national difference is that nontargeted nations developed fewer alternative universities strong in research. This refers mainly to public alternatives, since few privates would do much research, at least until after the golden age. Colombia's public del Valle and Santander universities would stand in contrast to the research failures lamented by domestic architects of public alternative universities in Argentina (Taquini i-2).

Disappointing results. Research remains quite limited beyond the assisted pockets, however. These pockets did not leverage a systemic transformation. Instead, they sit precariously alongside a much larger mainstream. Research is a major example where implementation fell far short of grand expectations and even of more prudent programmatic goals. The ensuing paragraphs focus on paltry production, on how little is produced outside a comparatively few fine places. The picture would grow yet bleaker if we took fuller account of qualitative features—of the common formalism in which "researchers" put much into print that includes very little discovery or true research content.

Where legislation mandates research or other policy rewards it, professors and institutions often simply label their activities accordingly, formalism directly parallel to what occurs with full-time status.

A dismal picture emerges on standard indices of scientific production. With 11 percent of the world's higher education enrollments, 8 percent of its total population, and 6 percent of its GDP, Latin America could claim just 1.4 percent of the publications in science journals with international circulation and 2 percent of its research and development scientists (IDB 1988: 289). This limited presence basically remained unchanged from what it had been, exploding dreams that imported ideas would bring fast-track modernization. In fact, some indicators show increasing distance from leading regions (Cueto 1989: 186–87). A balanced assessment should note that Latin America does much better where research is more subjective, tied to local issues, and inexpensive, often in the social sciences and humanities—though again this often takes place outside university faculties (Levy 1996: 180–91). In any event, the region's universities remain internationally marginal in many important areas of research. Research is not a major activity in most Latin American universities or even in most units within those universities where it does exist.

The common absence, alongside pockets of progress, means enormous stratification. Consider Colombia, unsurpassed as a favored nation. Studies postdating the golden age found that, out of more than one hundred universities, fewer than twenty-five housed research. Five universities—all assistance targets—did more than four-fifths of that research. Moreover, all universities together did just one-fourth of all Columbian research.[54] Stratification based on a poor mass and a few advanced pockets was also the fate of Venezuela, which had not been a favored target. Its key research pockets, usually assisted, modeled on U.S. practice, and staffed with many graduates of foreign study, would be denounced by many in the mainstream as elite, denationalized enclaves (Vessuri 1984: 65). Scherz-García's (1967: 389) apt conclusion that assistance to Latin American universities has helped produce a great "dualism," separating pockets of research, with full-timers, from most of the university, fits our conceptualization of prismatic displacement.

New institutional forms brought some change but greater continuity. The rapid growth of private universities, however novel in other respects, augmented the nonresearch mainstream much more than the research vanguard. As with the academic profession, exceptions were mostly Catholic universities that donors had targeted. It was further outside the traditional university mainstream that research gained substantially, with a big boost from assistance. Prominent examples included UNESCO and the IDB for national councils of science and technology, foundations for private research centers, and various donors for international research centers in agriculture. The success in both university research centers and centers completely outside the university has been more striking than for full-time status, though paralleling it.

Such success is nonetheless a failure to integrate research into university departments, leaving instead prismatic overlap between the nonresearch faculties and research centers within universities and between mostly nonresearch universities and freestanding research centers. Whether the centers primarily have sapped or nourished the mainstream is debatable, but research and teaching is more separated than reformers in the 1960s intended.

In short, research development has been a disappointment in that there is far too little meaningful research and much of what there is has not found the projected structural home. Prismatic patterns, including quite unanticipated productive structures, offset some disappointment. Other disappointment, chiefly the paltry overall output of good research, is stark.

Forces beyond higher education contributed to the disappointing results. Most repressive regimes prohibited certain areas of research, blocked dissidents in others, and purged some researchers from the universities or the country. Their underfunding of universities was often severe in research either because of ideology or simply because research funding was vulnerable and not institutionalized, seen as a luxurious pursuit desired by academics whereas professional training in many fields was an ongoing activity with a stronger political constituency. Elsewhere, disorder often made research unsafe or a low priority, as most of Central America showed. In effect, altered political and economic circumstances robbed domestic reformers of their ability to be effective partners. These circumstances also meant that favorable conditions for donors no longer existed, so their retreat was justifiable and prudent. On the other hand, the decline of assistance just when domestic funding was cut is evidence of donors not moving with philanthropic daring against the grain. The decline thus contributed to making the 1980s too close to a "lost decade" for university research. Thereafter, the rise of neoliberalism, which has arguably reinvigorated other aspects of the U.S. university model, has so far been hard on university-based research. An environment that replaces a denial of freedom with a denial of funds still does not allow "researchers" to do research.

Forces within higher education have also contributed mightily to the disappointing results. They have not built a supportive web for research, sometimes not even maintaining positive features that existed previously. Faculties, tied to professional practice and training rather than research, feared reforms that would undermine their goals, role, and power. Where departmentalization went further than usual, as in Brazil or especially in several targeted universities, research found surer footing and less opposition. Since departments could rarely replace faculties, however, donors and their partners often turned to university research centers as a reasonable, flexible adaptation of their model. The adaptation again presents an instance of prismatic overlap resulting not just from unanticipated consequences but also from prudent adaptations made in the face of realities within a university system that did not permit more direct importing of the U.S. university model.[55]

The adaptation appears vindicated by the failure of rarer, more confrontational efforts to replace traditional faculty form with the research model and by the successes of the university centers in producing research and even influencing other parts of the university. However, the cautious approach often left forces in place that crippled reform, enough to then accelerate the proliferation of the extra-university alternatives. Within the university, the prismatic dynamic was such that the unreformed core pulled down the research centers, often rendering them largely formalistic, or the centers could sustain themselves only through significant isolation. Centers at Costa Rica and Mexico's national universities have presented respective examples.[56] Centers have had trouble getting resources or gaining influence over research-related aspects of first-degree or even graduate education. Ford found anti-center sentiment and other evidence that the Colombia's National University could not sustain a high quality economics center or shield it from the faculties; it thus considered funneling returning scholarship holders into extra-university centers (Guillermo Calvo and Reed Hertford to files, 7/13/70, FF #68759). A fair generalization for Latin American universities is that the special needs of research have too often been denied or converted into standardized across-the-board demands.

Finally, forces from both outside and within higher education brought the growth in enrollments that also subordinated research through overlap and formalism. Assistance itself contributed, though never to the extremes of massification, which, for example, overwhelmed Argentine more than Chilean scientists (Vargas i). Serious full-time professors wonder how to do research when they must teach six courses. New is not reformed when the professorate multiplies by hiring people untrained to do research. Students are likewise unprepared to handle teaching that blends in research and independent study. And in circular fashion, the problems of university research signal even intellectually oriented students not to contemplate university research careers, while most students dismiss university research as a peripheral matter.[57]

Massification thus occupies a major place among factors that partially offset foreign and domestic reformers' otherwise notable success in increasing the number of researchers and the amount of research. There is no big increase in the proportion of researchers among university personnel. And the increase of nominal researchers and research structures far outstrips actual research production, just as, on the teaching side, growth in enrollments outstrips actual learning. However much targeted places achieve project goals, they do not act as levers that transform the system toward much more of a research model.

Graduate Education

Ambitious goals. Conventionally considered alongside research is graduate education. Assistance for the two purposes overlapped and each was necessary for the other as well as for the full-time concept and for reforms such as departmentalization. A formidable graduate level was also considered pivotal to the university's ability to contribute to a national attack on root problems through highly prepared leadership for social, economic, and political development.[58]

Donors and domestic reformers found much to bemoan about Latin American graduate education. Mostly, like research, it was far too limited. It could not sustain other aspects of university modernization. Very little graduate education existed even in the largest higher education systems, headed by Argentina (Morles 1983: 23). Terminology could mislead as many gained the title of "doctor" from a first-degree education in law.

Moreover, most of the graduate education that existed was not connected to degree programs. Instead of master's and doctoral programs, typical graduate education involved "specialization." This meant a continuation of professional training, not an academic or research orientation. And what academic study there was generally followed the European tutorial model, largely unstructured, rather than the U.S. model of a distinctive level of graduate education based on extensive and structured coursework (Clark 1995).

Selective major efforts. To push the U.S. model in graduate education was therefore to push major change. The vigor of the push shows up in the fact that donors included provisions for graduate education in most of their projects, simultaneously encouraging expanded effort and expenditure by domestic governments. There was even some assistance overreach, considered in the analysis below of disappointing results. But certain now-familiar kinds of selectivity tempered the ambitiousness.

For one thing, like research, graduate education allowed donors to target their efforts on building new areas, avoiding the bulk of the entrenched higher education system. A key point about assisted reform in the golden age was simply how much it focused selectively on graduate education. This contrasted with domestic practice and policy, since the great bulk of enrollments and of ongoing domestic expenditures and political constituencies concentrated at the first-degree level. For example, LASPAU scholarships came to be overwhelmingly for graduate study, and Ford's were markedly for advanced study.[59] Donors' major effort in graduate education was simultaneously a very selective effort as regards higher education overall.

Consistent with the philanthropic ideal type, the push for graduate education was innovative and involved risk-taking, but the risk was managed largely by avoiding the mainstream. Of course, donors anticipated some positive top-down influences from the graduate level on the first-degree level. AID's projects in Brazilian agricultural higher education were among those that made explicit the expectation that first-degree education would benefit (Betts printout AID #5120321). Also, success with more invasive efforts at the first-degree level (e.g., departmentalization) could facilitate reform at the graduate level. Usually, however, crossover effects were implicit hopes more than fixed, stated project goals. Beyond that, at least some donors realized early that superimposing a master's degree on top of any rigorous six-year course of professional study would be difficult (FF Peter Hakim to Peter Bell, 1/31/72, final report, FF #62515). They also realized the pointlessness of a master's atop a lax program. Probably insufficiently realized was how lax programs would grow and how many would claim to be serious programs ready to add a graduate layer. The main point here is that donors' efforts in graduate education mostly bypassed basic, first-degree university education. This represents another example of displacement rather than replacement and thus of planned overlap.

Nor would donors try to support the installation of graduate education throughout the system. Specific efforts concentrated on building something extra more than on transforming the core of what existed, again allowing for vague or implicit hopes that the focused project efforts would build influential models. Ford saw no need to establish graduate education at each institution even in its few targeted countries, or to establish it in most fields even in targeted institutions. In Colombia, for example, the idea was to build different graduate programs at different universities (FF #65118). This, of course, fit the idea of a pluralist system with interinstitutional differences and identities rather than a corporatist or uniform system with a fixed commitment to graduate education.

As donors would promote graduate education only at selected places, they would do so only with partners. Action was basically voluntary. Unlike bread and butter first-degree education, graduate education was not necessary for institutional life. And the partners were relatively few. Although the idea of building up graduate education was not a particularly controversial part of the import model, neither did many places have the necessary combination of zeal and resources to launch serious efforts. Brazil's exceptional move away from a limited European orientation to a massive U.S. orientation was promoted by AID's heavy involvement, but it would have been implausible without a powerful domestic drive.[60]

Assisted results. Graduate education is an excellent example of assistance playing a major role where Latin America made great strides. Credit claimed by donors repeatedly finds testimonial corroboration from domestic reformers (e.g., FF #72107; D'Etigny i-2). Successes are quite visible because they occurred at places that had been but very modest peaks. In fact, assistance often provided critical seed money to establish graduate programs where none had existed at a given institution or where none had existed in a given field. AID's contribution for a master's program of business administration at Colombia's EAFIT is an early illustration (James Smith, AID evaluation,

6/18/73). So is AID's work in many graduate programs in agriculture. Rio Grande do Sul in Brazil is one place that then maintained good quality and expanded to the doctoral level (Murdoch i). Few if any universities had had large, high quality graduate programs before significant assistance came, and few if any built them (during the golden age) without such assistance.

As with the development of full-time staff, some of the most convincing institutional examples of the graduate success have come in the public alternative universities. The Simón Bolívar gained a reputation for higher-quality graduate programs than those in other Venezuelan universities.[61] It also shows how donors have often returned to their institutions to help sustain existing graduate programs or establish new ones, as the IDB did in 1984. Projects also produced results at a few targeted national universities. Ford, the OAS, and others made a strong impact in social fields of graduate study in places like the University of Costa Rica, where the structures and standards overwhelmingly drew from the U.S. model (Estrada i; Paniagua i). Projects produced results at national universities mostly where they targeted only certain units. Thus, Ford's grant helped UNAM double its number of graduate students in science and engineering within just a few years in the late 1960s (FF #67281).

As usual, impacts also show themselves less neatly and consistently through nation-to-nation comparisons. Two nontargeted nations greatly increased their numbers of graduate students, but Mexico used huge loans from the IDB while Venezuela used uniquely ample national funds. Both achieved their highest quality levels by sending students abroad, mostly to the United States. Despite noteworthy exceptions, neither succeeded in establishing in the 1970s and 1980s the ample high quality graduate study built in Brazil. A frustrated rector of Mexico's UNAM noted that at least 90 percent of their graduate students failed to finish their programs (Carpizo 1985: 109).

The nation where assistance made its biggest effort in graduate education, Brazil, became the nation with easily the most formidable and successful graduate level. Between 1970 (just after the push began) and 1982, Brazil increased its master's programs from 161 to 766, its doctoral programs from 67 to 285, and its graduate enrollments from under 5,000 to almost 25,000. It became unique for having a master's program in practically all fields. In comparison, Argentina did not develop an academic doctorate or an overall graduate network comparable to that of even some much smaller nations; only from the mid-1980s on did it engage in vigorous expansion, with some quality—using Brazil as a model.[62] Expansion of graduate education allowed much of the Brazilian success in building a full-time professorate with advanced degrees. Brazil's graduate numbers also were weighty because they reflected students in formal coursework, as Brazil went furthest in establishing the U.S. model, whereas other nations mixed in various European features. Along with the coursework and formal degree programs, Brazil copied U.S. policies on credits, minimum requirements, comprehensive examinations, and dissertations. Furthermore, the Brazilian success in graduate education has been sustained. As Latin American nations today reset their sights on development of sound graduate education, competitively run and objectively evaluated, Brazil is accepted as the regional beacon.[63]

Disappointing results. Although universities came to offer more graduate education than they previously did, the absolute numbers remained low throughout and even after the golden age. Such limited growth was a rarity for assistance-promoted reform, contrasting with results for full-time professors, research, and first-degree enrollments.

Some projects failed to meet their quantitative goals in graduate education, even when they met them for the first-degree level. A $50 million IDB loan, partnered with twice as much Brazilian money, produced many successes but only 60 percent of its graduate enrollment projections (IDB/E3: iii). Numerous IDB evaluations would decry inefficiencies resulting in Latin America's scattered graduate programs, with very high professor/student ratios.

Most of Latin America's small nations failed to establish more than a trickle of graduate education. Colombia failed to build doctoral programs or meet quantitative goals for expansion despite large IDB support in the 1980s. Most aggregated data remained dismal: graduate students made up 1 percent of Latin America's total higher education enrollments, versus roughly 13 percent for the United States (Vessuri 1986: 9). Places that benefited from assistance lacked the proportional weight or influence to become models replicated on a grand scale.

Research centers do not augment the graduate numbers nearly as much as they do for research productivity (Levy 1996: 207–20). It is partly that more research than graduate education is possible through individual effort without institutional development. It is mostly that the institutional development that has bolstered research has not encompassed much graduate education. Within the centers themselves, especially those outside the university, the most common graduate offerings are seminars or courses leading to no degree and forming part of no structured program. Many centers have just small programs that form a minor part of their overall activities. Only a subset of centers makes graduate education a major part of its mission. These tend to be among the largest and best academic centers, often providing the nation's top graduate education in the social sciences or management. El Colegio de México and Brazil's Getulio Vargas Foundation, both favored targets of international philanthropy, have been leaders. But even these are small institutions compared with major universities.

If the centers' personnel teach graduate courses, they typically do so part-time in university faculties. This prismatic overlap brings much good to graduate education, as well as to first-degree education, making results more positive than they might appear if one focuses only on university sites targeted for assistance. Yet they do not usually bring the ongoing, on-site contact and guidance for students that shape the U.S. ideal. If the centers' personnel are willing to teach more, protective faculties often deny them the chance, even when the personnel are from the universities' own research centers. Faculties have also exerted pressure to deny centers the right to offer more graduate education. In some cases, as in Guatemala, centers have been housed inside the faculties. Venezuelan universities helped put a stop to the right of other institutions to offer graduate degrees. Even at assistance targets such as the University of Costa Rica, faculties have fought to maintain control over the highest degree offered within the institution (Macaya i). Or there are few proscriptions but also few inducements for researchers to teach more. For all these reasons, the overlap of research centers and university faculties has produced little integration for graduate education.

Where graduate study has grown most, in university faculties, it usually lacks the form associated with the U.S. model and the quality associated with any reasonable model. Mexico's graduate enrollments jumped from under six thousand to over twenty-four thousand in the 1970s, with additional universities in many states joining UNAM. But most of the new graduate education was a haphazard extension of the first-degree, with no more funding per pupil, and graduating only one in ten. Master's programs were mostly tied to professional practice. Doctoral programs comprised only 3 percent of graduate enrollments and usually continued to involve a loose tutorial experience.[64]

In Latin America generally, the growth of graduate education has come mostly not from reformist blueprints but from factors antithetical to the philanthropic ideal type. It has obeyed mostly nonacademic commands. It has followed dynamics of institutional pride or student demand much more than those of program preparedness or extra-university economic demand (Tedesco and Blumenthal 1986: 21). It has smacked of massification and become wastefully expensive (Drysdale 1987: 33) even when the total numbers remain comparatively small. It lacks the substantial public funding that academic graduate education usually requires worldwide; in fact, a curious inversion of the university export model comes in countries such as Colombia and Argentina where tuition makes its public sector entrance at the graduate rather than the first-degree level. And so graduate education usually is a mere add-on to poor first-degree education, is not tied to research, and gains little respect. As one observer sums it up, Latin American graduate education is mostly "just another layer," a "new roof" over a still academically weak institution.[65] The old form of first-degree education prismatically shapes an ostensibly new form. Faculties have thus undermined the graduate export model not only where they have blocked its spread beyond limited pockets but also where they have built their own graduate education along different lines. Paralleling so many other areas, then, stratification is large as assistance-promoted graduate peaks tower over a vastly expanded plateau of mediocre graduate education.[66]

Although problems usually have come from domestic factors altering the exported initiatives, sometimes in the golden age donors themselves violated norms of selectivity. Whereas earlier graduate initiatives by foundations had been highly selective, the zeal associated with rapid university development gave rise to wider programs. This sealed the fate of graduate initiatives in Rockefeller's University Development Program (Coleman and Court 1993: 295). Graduate studies built atop mediocre first-degree programs would be weak. At Colombia's del Valle university, a pioneer in Latin American graduate education, this characterized the social sciences in contrast to the more careful, solid Rockefeller development of medical studies (Seeley i). And if donors earn plaudits when they contribute to salutary domestic growth, then they also should be cited when a partner like the University of Costa Rica opened as many as seventy graduate programs, far above what was reasonable (Estrada i). It was one thing for donors to adapt to domestic context by becoming more selective, as when they assisted graduate education in only some fields within only some institutions, but another when they yielded to domestic pressures or temptations to become rather unselective.

Whereas domestic actors would try to install graduate education at many institutions, assistance overreached itself mostly at national universities. This overreach stemmed partly from donors' zeal at national universities in the 1960s. But, in fairness, they had little choice if they were to be very active and more than marginal. That is because only the national universities often had the beginnings of graduate education, as well as the research, top professors, political clout, and other factors reasonably associated with the development of graduate education. But no national university went on to develop anything remotely resembling the breadth or quality of graduate education envisioned. This disappointment should be tempered by the fact that while some projects yielded little, others produced pockets of the best that joins graduate education at targeted alternative institutions.

In general, assistance did not get the graduate model to take wide root in Latin America. Efforts did not find a supportive web. Political repression, economic weakness, and apathy hurt graduate education overall and crippled many specific undertakings. From within the university, the lack of other reforms took its toll. For example, spotty progress in departmentalization and general studies left U.S.-style graduate education as an odd entity to follow first-degree professional training; in turn, as at Colombia's Antioquia, small graduate programs could not produce the professors needed for envisioned departments and general studies (Vic Johnson evaluation 6/20/69 FF #5118). Instead of fitting comfortably on top of persisting professional education, graduate education had to battle threatened faculties. Results, as with research, were to block, isolate, or weaken development outside the faculties or to twist its meaning when molding it within faculties. Meanwhile, poorly prepared full-time professors were not suited to teach serious graduate students.

In sum, Latin American graduate education failed the philanthropic ideal type by becoming both too large and too small. Its growth mostly deviated from projected form or worthwhile levels of quality, often making graduate education formalistic. It exceeded the pool of trained talent, drained resources from the main university level, contributed to the overall sense of Latin American universities as not academically serious or transforming themselves to modernity, and contributed also to the overall sense of assistance as failure. At the same time, graduate education overall and especially quality graduate education, remained much smaller than required for fulfillment of the assistance model of university development. The good graduate education that was created should be seen as a special triumph for the donors and their reform partners precisely because it was so rare, precious, and hard to achieve without assistance. That success does not change the fact that the prismatic displacement and overlap have featured much more unreformed than reformed terrain surrounding the new hybrid terrain where the graduate education mix simultaneously represents improvement and disappointment.

Fields of Study

Ambitious goals. Donors wanted a new mix in the fields of study that constituted Latin American universities. They found the status quo terribly deficient. They regarded the liberal professions as greatly overrepresented. These included medicine, civil engineering, and architecture, and—most vilified—law. In fact, low-recipient nations such as Argentina, Uruguay, and Venezuela most resembled the description though none matched it. There was apparent overproduction of professionals in certain areas. As of 1963 Argentina led the United States in medical doctors per population (Pérez Lindo 1985: 277).

Mostly, though, the critique was that many other fields were too small. These included fields crucial to the university modernization package. Research, graduate education, general studies, departmentalization, and internationalization all depended on the development of academic fields, "scientific" fields understood in broad terms. For example, departments would be based on disciplines, whereas faculties were based more on professions. In turn, the switch to new fields was seen as a way to introduce new structures and norms into the university. A good example was the pioneering departmentalization (through "institutes") at Chile's University of Concepción (Stitchkin i). Building the new fields was also part and parcel of building the academic quality that a university should have. Like other academic reforms, then, the new fields would place the university's raison d'être less with professions and more within its own institutional perimeter, which would reinforce the university identity and centralization discussed in the previous two chapters.

At the same time, changing fields of study would promote elements of the assistance model transcending the university. This meant fields that contributed to economic growth primarily, as with tying the university to a job market of productivity beyond just professional practice and growing state bureaucracy.[67] It meant fields linked to technological and social change. And it meant more general education for a participatory citizenry. In short, it meant fields geared to accelerated, multifaceted, progressive though unrevolutionary national development.

Selective efforts. Compared with other topics treated in this chapter, field of study covers much more assistance. That is, much money was given for activities that would take place in one or a series of fields. Our focus, however, is on efforts made for the development of particular fields as such. That covers still a good deal of assistance, and so assistance for fields of study is in some sense broad. Nonetheless, selectivity follows familiar patterns.

First, donors worked in cooperation with domestic partners bent on changing the field profile of their universities. Allies included those within and outside the institutions. They were often found among prior recipients of grants for study abroad. A well-documented case concerns the partnership between foreign philanthropy and pioneering Chilean professors in the introduction of scientific sociology.[68] In fields like agriculture the partnership often included government officials. Evidence shows great overlap between assistance and government-proclaimed national field priorities, as in Mexico (Weissberg 1980: 80–90). In fact, donors chose to sustain those national priorities much more than students did (when they chose what fields to enter). A still tighter and more direct link lay between donors and recipient institutions. For example, LASPAU early on gave for science and engineering largely because that is what institutions stated as their need (personal correspondence from Lewis Tyler 11/22/88).

And once donors' priorities became clear, few Latin American requests were rejected outright, as institutions did not request for unfundable fields. In the IDB's first major university grant an Argentine request was cut in half by eliminating medicine and architecture as prone to excess enrollments, and law, philosophy, and humanities as not tied to economic development. As word spread, donors and their logical potential field recipients paired more naturally. This fits the philanthropic notion of front-end influence followed by collaboration.

Second, fields allowed for pretty narrow targeting. That helps explain how donors stayed involved in particular fields even after they abandoned broad institutional development. During the golden age, fields allowed donors to operate within otherwise untargeted institutions within untargeted nations. More often, they allowed extra targeting within favored settings. Furthermore, donors usually focused *within* fields, on special atypical aspects, including research and graduate education.

Third, each donor limited its coverage to certain fields at least for certain periods of time. Most foundations limited themselves mostly to just one or two fields, as with Kellogg in health-related fields. Beyond just Latin America,

Rockefeller pumped about 90 percent of its funding, 1917–70, into health-related fields with all but 1 percent of the rest going into natural science and agriculture, figures that basically are paralleled in Brazil, its major Latin American nation (Coleman and Court 1993: 63). Even the major donors, considered in more depth here, focused on certain fields. Engineering was heavily favored by the IDB along with AID and LASPAU but not Ford. Science initially drew on Ford but then the IDB and LASPAU, as Ford shrank from the high costs and the problems at national universities. Social science became the focus of Ford but not the IDB. Business and management relied heavily on AID but much less on others.

Fourth, while different donors promoted different fields, a remarkable convergence was their common *avoidance* of many fields. Thus, assistance did not spread itself widely over fields that attracted enrollments and domestic funds. Donors dismissed humanities as too European-oriented, philosophically unscientific, elite, and, most important, remote to development. Donors thus were not drawn to the Latin American assertion of *humanidades* as including social science. Some early Rockefeller support and ongoing weight in cultural exchange programs were little compensation for the near absence of AID and the IDB. In contrast, library development was a favorite because it created infrastructure for research and graduate education across fields.

What donors mainly avoided were the traditional professions. They did so despite the foundations' rich history of funding the professions at home, especially in relation to the professions' university roles and despite a similar thrust in their early work in Latin America. One obstacle was the association between the professions and university status quo. Another lay in the difficulty of providing scholarships in these areas for graduate study in the United States, because the two regions' first-degree structures were so different.[69] The most inclusive possible data on AID, IDB, and Ford projects, as well as separate scholarships from Ford and from U.S. government funded LASPAU, show the following: virtually nothing from any of the five for architecture; less than 3 percent for medicine except for the IDB; for law, zero from three of five sources and only a tiny bit from the other two (see table 5.1).

Their avoidance of traditional professions meant that donors did not try to transform, let alone frontally attack, the most powerful fields in place. Voices within the Ford Foundation argued that fields like law were too central to university and societal power to bypass, but they were overruled.[70] If mainstream fields were to be weakened, it would be relatively, through strengthening other fields. At most, this was a strategy of displacement rather than replacement, and it was mostly just a strategy of bypassing or leaving aside the mainstream. In that respect it was less aggressive than initial institutional strategy, which worked with national universities, the power core, and more like subsequent institutional diversification strategy, which tended to bypass the national universities.

Table 5.1 Assistance by Field of Study (in percentages)

	Business	Economics	Other basic social sciences	Law	Humanities	Education	Medical studies	Veterinary studies	Agricultural studies	Natural sciences	Engineering	Architecture	Misc.	Total[a]
AID[b]	28.3	3.1	1.2	0	0	10.0	2.6	0.6	31.7	5.9	16.9	0	0	100.2
IDB	0	0	0	0	0	16.8	23.3	0.5	18.7	17.5	23.3	0	0	100.1
FORD[c]	4.1	18.8	16.9	1.3	3.5	8.3	2.2	0.2	11.2	24.2	6.5	0	2.7	99.9
FORD-S[d]	0.0	23.9	19.3	0	3.9	9.5	0	0	17.2	19.7	6.6	0	0	100.1
LASPAU	9.3	4.3	9.4	0.1	7.0	11.2	1.6	0	12.7	16.8	26.6	0.6	0.5	100.1

Sources: Table covering these years for individual donors: AID 1950–69, Miller (1984: 37–46); our appendix I for sources providing data on countries eluding Miller (five countries but only Mexico and LA regional show data by field); IDB 1962–85, IDB (1985: table 1); FORD 1959–79, Moock (1980: 92–131); FORD-S 1960–80, Myers (1983b: table 25), scholarship ("awards") data on 3,909 Ford scholarships 1960–80 (28 of which cover nations not in the rest of the table). As "science/engineering" was grouped we divide it by a 3:1 ratio, similar to that found in Ford institutional grants. Economics = "economic development" and includes some management (and perhaps business). "Population" was counted as demography, under social science; LASPAU 1965–87: Data printout June 21, 1987 and October 23, 1987 provided by Steven Bloomfield.

[a]Omits funding outside specific fields. A category of "university development" would otherwise account for 84.5% of the IDB total, 29.1% of Ford's, and 12.5% of AID's. See appendix E for further details on data and discrepancies regarding the FF, AID, and the IDB. Field categorization from Levy (1986: 268–69, 345–55) and UNESCO *Statistical Yearbooks*, various years. In some cases, however, donors' categories could not be confidently matched to our categories, and it was more prudent to divide their figures 50/50 into two of our categories. For AID, mining studies was split into exact science and engineering. For FF, this meant rural economics and agricultural studies and other basic social science; both agricultural marketing and agricultural business as agricultural studies and business.

[b]Some figures shown by Miller without a dollar amount were not counted. More consequential is that roughly a fifth of the funding Miller finds is not identified by field.

[c]See also appendix H.

[d]S = Scholarships or awards

Efforts to transform. At the same time, such highly discriminating giving is evidence of a drive to stimulate change. For all the reserve and caution involved in bypassing major professional fields, concentrated efforts on novel terrain were consistent with goals of transformation. Our evidence shows that donors pursued a vigorous agenda quite divergent from typical domestic policy.[71]

Even very aggregated data show a powerful effort to affect the field profile of Latin American universities. A summary will suffice, drawing on a database that could allow separate analyses of each donor cited. We use an extant if simplified dichotomy of "modern" versus "traditional" fields (Labbens 1968: 119). Modern fields include natural science, social science, agronomy, education, and technology. Traditional fields include humanities, architecture, law, and medicine. We find that assistance went to the former over the latter by roughly *seven to one,* as seen in table 5.1.[72] The ratio exaggerates where measures refer to project expenditures, since favored fields were more expensive. But table 5.1 also includes the number of scholarships given outside wider projects by both Ford and LASPAU (funded mostly by the U.S. government), and these numbers fit the basic conclusions drawn regarding project money.[73]

Compare such assistance to the domestic configuration of fields. As of 1955, perhaps 39 percent of Latin American enrollments were in the modern fields versus 61 percent in the traditional ones.[74] In other words, assistance went seven to one in favor of fields that represented a minority in the domestic profile. Here then is further evidence of how voluntary donors could concentrate their efforts away from the system's bulk, which is driven by mass demand and domestic government accommodation to it. A further example would be that major assistance went to the graduate level, which held only a tiny share of total domestic enrollments across fields.

Inside data by fields, the effort to transform sharpens further. One example concerns the quantitatively limited efforts in professional fields. Assistance there focused on quite atypical, change-oriented aspects far from mainstream activity. Not a frontal assault, it was nonetheless an effort to build something new and innovative. Such ideal typical action was Ford's support through the International Law Center for selected law schools in Chile, Peru, and Colombia. It pushed such radical ideas as case-study pedagogy, incorporation of social science, research, and extension or service through clinical training and aid for the poor.[75] The inclusion of law in projects like the University of Chile–California convenio really meant the inclusion of some Chilean law students for activities outside their traditional programs at home. Then, after the golden age, foundation efforts connected to law concentrated more on human rights programs than development within the university.

Rockefeller and IDB activity in medicine was for research, the integration of both natural and social science, and extension, public health, and population control. Money was also given through "medical studies" because that is where the only science often was, but the attempt was to establish science in its own right. Ford otherwise proscribed grants for medical studies. Rare assistance to architecture pushed novel development orientations over traditional humanistic ones; much more common assistance for engineering favored embryonic areas over the traditional enrollment leader, civil engineering.[76] Within agronomy, a favored profession, assistance pushed innovations that incorporated social science, research, and extension. Such integration aimed to tie agriculture more to the university, the new university. The same could be said for medicine. Donors encouraged professions to move beyond training in their own, rather self-contained faculties.

Similarly, assistance went heavily to promote atypical tendencies and tasks within *nonprofessional* fields. Or it went to unestablished, small fields. Donors envisioned business, administration, management, and demography as bona fide academic fields. This meant transforming practical pursuits or creating fields, major expressions of orientations toward change. Public universities were only sometimes receptive. AID helped create business administration in Bolivia at the Catholic university. It vigorously helped establish institutions with field specialization in business, administration, and management. Examples included Peru's Graduate School of Business Management with Stanford, Colombia's EAFIT with the University of Georgia, and Nicaragua's Central American Institute for Business Administration with Harvard. Latin America was perhaps the region to which AID most directly transferred the U.S. business school model with its graduate and undergraduate components.[77] A common and important adaptation, however, was that many such schools were freestanding, not integrated into the university.

Donors and their partners also breathed autonomous academic life into studies that had previously existed within other fields, often in subordinated form. Economics is a crucial example, promoted out from under schools such as accounting.[78] Other social science was promoted out of faculties of law or philosophy.

Much of assistance was a campaign to build academic quality into both emerging and preexisting fields or to otherwise modernize them. Were this movement along a consensual road it would still have represented a major effort for change. Usually, however, it also involved controversial qualitative changes. Like economics, sociology is an excellent example here. Assistance, especially from foundations, promoted empirical work and many norms dominant in U.S. universities, to the displeasure of those who defended a tradition of more philosophical or politically engaged work.

Donors thus engaged in vigorous efforts at change regarding fields of study. They utilized their freedom as voluntary actors to experiment and innovate, to give in specific ways that moved sharply away from traditional patterns. The extra resources and ideas they provided were a weighty contribution to what was new or emerging, even if it was not weighty when gauged against total expenditures for all fields. Such vigorous action was still compatible with selectivity and caution because of the way donors limited themselves to only certain fields at certain institutions and to certain endeavors within those fields—endeavors undertaken with reform partners and often with prudent flexibility. It was also compatible because efforts were directed at adding something new alongside the traditional, more than at directly replacing the traditional. Donors therefore reasonably claimed to contribute to pluralism in form and practice, which our analysis has mostly portrayed as prismatic overlap.

Assisted results. Positive assistance impacts on fields of study follow patterns of success discovered for other assistance pursuits. Assistance has contributed to growth in "modern" fields overall and crucially for such fields at institutions targeted in projects. This also means a major assistance hand where major desired change has in fact occurred. The effect shows in qualitative as well as quantitative dimensions. The field successes come disproportionately at the graduate level and therefore nudge our prior mixed findings on the graduate level more toward the positive side.

Aggregated data show a huge change in the proportions among fields. The balance between the identified modern and traditional fields moved from 39–61 to 69–27 percent, with 4 percent unspecified. Later on, we will see why assistance cannot be credited for what might here seem a huge success.

Nonetheless, enrollments grew rapidly in fields targeted by assistance. Without trying to pinpoint the impact of assistance, certain points can be made. Most obvious is that assistance provided enabling funds. Furthermore, most of these fields were harder to expand, due to lack of student demand, scarce infrastructure of human and physical resources, and the force of inertia and ingrained interests. Without a pointed push, we must suppose, these fields would probably have expanded less. We can discriminate better by noting that these factors about the difficulty of expansion applied much more to the sciences than to several fields of social studies. That likely is one reason for the greater U.S. qualitative imprint on natural than social fields in Latin American universities even though U.S. assistance went to both. In any case, it is hard to imagine without assistance the jump in agriculture from under 8,000 to over 230,000 and in natural science from under 14,000 to over 200,000, 1955–80. It also appears that assistance helped nations increase their expenditures in these fields, though this is difficult to prove; the IDB's impact on Brazilian funding of science and technology is an example (IDB/E3).

The role of assistance in changing fields of study is clear at targeted places, notably at alternative universities. It was crucial to establishing their strong, distinct field profiles. This occurred even at some nonelite institutions, such as Venezuela's Los Andes and Simón Rodríguez universities (Navarro i-2). The impact is most obvious for institutions specialized in one field. Agriculture is a leading case, with places such as Peru's La Molina university, where North Carolina State University played a major role with multiple donors, and the Dominican Republic's Superior Institute of Agriculture.[79] For the special business schools, AID and Ford get credit for building the superior pockets of quality for full-time staff, research, and graduate study, with a range between those few that copy U.S. curriculum and those geared to local development (Anderson 1987: 151, 161). The assistance impact is also hard to deny for leading fields at targeted institutions not restricted to one main field. Examples include engineering at Costa Rica's technological institute and agriculture at its National University, both pivotally assisted by the IDB.

Colombia's Los Andes provides a startling success story in engineering.[80] Ford spearheaded activities that also received British, French, and Dutch aid. It would later award the engineering project superb ratings, crediting it for establishing one of the best two or three programs in the field in any Latin American private university, along with the likewise assisted Tec of Monterrey and Chile's Catholic university. From 1965 to 1973, staff credentials jumped from sixteen masters and no doctorates to thirty-four masters and nine doctorates and the full-timers had obtained high-quality degrees, including doctorates from Stanford, MIT, Notre Dame, Northwestern, Cornell, and Case Western; fifteen of sixteen Ford scholarship holders studied in the United States. Innovative courses were established at different degree levels, enrollments leaped beyond projections, and there was broad impact on Colombian engineering education and practice. Good research was undertaken. Additionally, engineering withstood the student unrest and rapid turnover in the rectorate, which undermined other fields at Los Andes.

Another illustration of donors' big role where positive field transformations occurred lay in exceptional breakthroughs where success was otherwise scarce, as with innovations in the professions. The revamping of law at Peru's Catholic university fits here. So do many earlier efforts when foundations "academized" professions, tying them to university teaching, research, service, and arguably overspecialization (Moros Ghersi 1991: 45–46).

Where success became more common, pioneering donors had often planted crucial seeds, followed by other donors or domestic agencies. Instances include the IDB with its early science loan to Argentina's UBA, Ford with its early grant in geophysics to the University of Chile, and foreign professors for sociology at the University of Sao Paulo. Donors deserve credit for their pivotal help in establishing new fields, such as marine biology, and the building of critical masses for fields that had been tiny, as with chemistry in Brazil. Abundant, repeated, multi-donor efforts at a variety of institutions had major positive impacts, if also disappointing and debated ones, in agricultural studies and research. Particularly striking successes came in a variety of fields where assistance was originally jeered as imperialistic, as in reproductive biology, demography, microeconomics, and business administration. In any case, newer assisted fields often grew alongside older ones less affected by assistance.

Another manifestation of where assistance efforts translated into impacts for ascendant fields came where donors helped fields emerge in their own right, with strong claims to scientific legitimacy, from under more traditional fields. This encompasses natural sciences springing from medicine and social sciences springing from humanities. Disciplines such as sociology in Chile gained a respected university presence (Brunner 1988: 46–134). Ford, AID, and the IDB played major roles in building economics as a serious and important academic field in Latin America. Economics then overtook law as the key to mobility to high government positions in many nations and as a key for policymaking. The most detailed account (Valdés 1995) of the single most decisive case—assistance led by AID, Ford, and the University of Chicago for Chile's Catholic university—documents a big transmission of professional values, content, and methods. This includes transfer to places outside Chile, such as Colombia's del Valle and Argentina's Cuyo universities. Unlike cases where assistance introduces new forms that remain subordinate to traditional ones, here the new triumphed and assistance was surely responsible for decisively changing the balance of power, even before Chile's military took over and proscribed Marxist economics.[81] AID also claimed success for less elite efforts in economics, such as its work with second-tier places in Brazil (Lusk i).

In other fields as well, assistance had a major impact on qualitative matters of what is done, how, and how well. Projects boosted empirical research, academic quality and rigor, and laboratories and libraries within aided fields. They infused social and natural sciences into various other fields of study. Assistance built graduate and research components of fields, often from near scratch. It was crucial in creating peaks of quality for many fields and in making previously very modest peaks more formidable. Multi-donor involvement for natural science at Chile's national and Catholic universities is among dozens of major examples. Ford's largest project, the convenio between the University of Chile and the University of California, earned great credit for building Chile's peaks in agronomy, veterinary medicine, and science (University of Chile/University of California 1979). For agriculture in Brazilian universities, AID-assisted places pulled far ahead of others (Murdoch i).

Furthermore, many of the assisted peaks at least maintained their relative lead in ensuing years. That explains why Fulbright files in the 1980s showed that visiting U.S. scholars continued overwhelmingly to choose places such as the University of Chile in chemistry and to praise them in the end-of-tour reports.[82] Another effect transcending immediate gains at project sites was the frequent impact produced at other places, often through scholarship holders or just demonstration effects, sometimes through subsequent projects. Early work by AID at Argentina's Castelar agricultural graduate school influenced the best Mexican institutions in the field. The Ford-assisted engineering faculty at UNAM, where half the students came from outside Mexico, would come to be called the "patron saint" for key parts of Peru's National Engineering university as well as for Mexico's own Autonomous

Metropolitan University (FF # 67281). In cases like these, results approached the philanthropic ideal type in that they moved from direct transformation of targets to leveraged impact beyond those targets.

In other instances, such as Rockefeller's attempt to carry its advances in medicine at Colombia's del Valle to Brazilian universities, nationalism was a problem in achieving transfer (Black i-1). That particular problem merely added to the usual difficulties of emulating at lesser institutions the success of targeted institutions, even within countries. This point begins to carry us from the positive to the disappointing results.

Disappointing results. Donors did not come close to achieving their goals regarding fields of study. Given all the success just identified, this finding does not justify a simple conclusion of failure, but success was accompanied by disappointment. Some of that disappointment was justified.

One problem lay in the now familiar distinction between absolute and proportional numbers. The huge jump cited above for natural science enrollments, 1955–80, translated into only a 0.4 percent increase in the field's share of total enrollments. Targeted institutions that built novel field profiles did not become sufficient catalysts for transforming the overall field profile of higher education, though without assistance innovative change would have been scarcer.

Instead, the biggest growth in Latin America's enrollments occurred in administrative and commercial fields. Aggregate UNESCO data include such fields under "social science," and social science plus education then comprises four-fifths of the percentage gain cited above for "modern" fields. Much of the administrative and commercial growth was indeed modern in some sense. Some, as seen, was even promoted by assistance. Yet such growth in special assisted institutions was dwarfed by the growth of those fields in unassisted faculties. Little of the administrative and commercial growth had estimable academic content. Growth was much slower in the main social science fields that donors emphasized, headed by sociology and economics. For its part education continued to be a poor quality field and the education data category came to include much that had previously not been categorized as higher education. Just as such expansion contributed more than donors' targeted efforts to the proportional rise of modern fields, so it contributed more heavily to the fall in the traditional professions from over half to roughly one-fifth of total enrollments. Massification again meant that much of what grew was not new in kind, or at least was not the projected form, and led to an overlap in which innovative, projected change was numerically overwhelmed.

A particular disappointment lay in the private sector's performance. After all, this sector was less bound to traditional fields and professions and more generally receptive to U.S. ideas. But it was here that low quality administrative and commercial fields first took off and then grew largest, here that all fields expensive to offer languished in lower proportional enrollments than in the public sector. This included medical studies but also the assistance-favored fields of natural science, engineering, and agriculture (Levy 1986: 266–74). Again donor-targeted private universities would be the major exceptions but without invalidating the general private/public comparison. When it has come to fields of study, most new private universities have mostly copied older public universities or set out on new paths not corresponding to assistance goals.

Again, the success of research centers is only partly offsetting. The success is greater for "hard" disciplines in public centers and for "soft" ones in private centers, but the research often inclines away from the disciplinary core, and the major shortcoming is that the centers do not contribute massively to teaching in their fields. In other words, the centers do not fulfill the expectations held for university fields of study. Their limitations mark a degree of assistance failure. Agriculture shows the problems. The greatest research advances came at internationally sponsored centers, such as the International Center for Improvement of Maize and Wheat (CIMMYT), where training but not formal educational programs were the norm. On the other hand, land grant universities produced many "strange configurations" and only a "partial success," which reinforced donors' inclination to turn away from them and toward more direct practical activities by the 1970s.[83] Failure to produce a more substantial university infrastructure contributed to a brain drain in agriculture in nations such as Ecuador.

Then there are the deficiencies in quality. Assistance was especially important where fields attained high quality, but this attainment was not common. Where AID promoted commercial fields, massive expansion hardly developed the envisioned qualitative dimensions. The highest peaks in most fields have remained below goals or peaks in more developed nations. Latin America still fails to earn coveted international prizes in science, so heavily assisted, faring better in literature, which was mostly excluded from assistance. Perhaps worse than the near absence of international peaks is the limited proportion of enrollments in modest peaks. Also troubling is that the few modest peaks tower above the vast and expanding terrain where fields neither achieve high quality nor play grand development roles. Stratification is ample, and the better portion is the smaller portion.

Neither the hard nor the soft sciences penetrated the traditional professions very deeply. Even at prized targets like Peru's La Molina results were mixed. Instead, the professions often made a deleterious imprint on the newer fields. A sad example of debilitating prismatic overlap came where emerging fields emulated established ones in their emphasis on credentials and entitlements above knowledge. Sociologists demanded that a sociologist be hired within each of several government units, and social workers, pharmacists, and others lobby for their own protected job niches.[84] Whereas assistance had pushed a more science- or discipline-oriented university, such pressures and developments pushed back toward a more professionalist university. In this sense, too, the old often captured the new. The extension of professionalist norms into the pedagogy, curriculum, and employment goals of newer fields would become a major problem in Latin American universities (Castro and Levy 2000).

Once more, we see the difficulties of reforming academic work when an integrated, supportive web was lacking. Part of the problem lay outside the university. The wider society still lacked a scientific culture (Aldana and Orozco 1993: 19). Macroeconomic and political developments took their toll on needed resources, job opportunities, and freedom essential to certain fields and to innovation. New fields in Brazil often failed to match traditional ones in employment—which then reinforced student disinclination to change enrollment choices (Schwartzman 1992b: 8–13).

Professionalist and other retarding forces emanated also from within the university, where the supportive web for assistance's transformation of fields was also lacking. On top of opposition from faculties in unassisted fields, there was opposition from those—the majority—unassisted even within fields that received heavy assistance. These included, for example, "traditional," "humanist," or "revolutionary" social scientists. Again what reformers had hoped to bypass turned out to be powerfully overlapping actors and structures that thwarted much of what the donors attempted. At the same time, failure to implement departmentalization and general studies meant that the anticipated structural homes were not created for promoted academic fields. Additionally, weaknesses in research, graduate education, and full-time staff all inhibited establishment of either the distribution across fields or the tasks and quality within them that donors had intended. In turn, as is logical in thinking about a web, inability to achieve the desired field profile made it that much more difficult to reform other aspects of academic work.

Basic patterns characterize U.S. assistance efforts and impacts regarding crucial components of academic work. Analyzed in detail for the academic profession, the patterns are also strong in research, graduate education, and fields of study.

In their choice and pursuit of goals, donors lived up to the philanthropic ideal type's emphasis on transformation. Animated by a fundamental view that the Latin American university was not up to its potentially grand academic and broader development mission, donors and their reform partners pushed away from the common teaching roles and foci of first-degree education. They promoted major features of the U.S. university model, including full-time status, the research-teaching nexus, the distinctive graduate level, and academic and development-oriented fields of study. Although mainstream domestic forces also promoted expansion, a key to assistance in all four areas of academic work was to shape growth in fresh directions, directions quite different from, even at odds with, what was common. Assistance diverged powerfully from the bulk of ongoing domestic practice and policy.

Compared to internationally promoted reform in the present day, and its trust that changes in finance, governance, and accountability will improve academic performance, golden age efforts concentrated heavily on direct transformation in academic work—academic modernization by design.

Conclusion

The great selectivity of donors' efforts is evidence simultaneously of restraint and vigorous pursuit of academic transformation. Donors bypassed the mainstream and worked to build alternatives elsewhere—innovative alternatives. In contrast to domestic demand and government subsidies, assistance did not scatter across the panoply of offerings at Latin American universities. Donors did not try to transform most powerful university faculties directly, certainly not to assault them. Instead, major recipients were places and activities identified with big change. Donors almost invariably worked as partners with the domestic reformers eager to initiate or expand modern academic work at their institutions. To concentrate where serious graduate education and research could occur was to skip the bulk of higher education, including most professional fields. The same could be said of efforts to build an academic profession. Overall, the effort to displace by creating strong new alternatives rather than to replace by confrontation illustrates the combination of vigor and restraint. The optimistic if vaguely articulated idea was that the new academic work would then bring change more widely to the system through the power of demonstrated performance, competition, follow-up efforts by domestic actors, or other dynamics.

Assistance contributed to great successes in modernizing academic work. Quantitatively, it promoted notable expansion in the full-time professorate and some priority fields of study and research, alongside more moderate expansion in other priority fields and in bona fide graduate education. In results as well as goals and efforts, assistance once again qualifies as pro-growth. It built and enlarged where undertakings were otherwise sparse, and it did so without replacing prior forms or government investment. Instead, it built alongside prior forms and joined with expanding government investment in academic development. Where change involved high academic standards, assistance was decisive. Repeated examples emerged at targeted institutions, public and private alike. Where major change occurred in given units or fields within institutions, it was usually those heavily favored by assistance. Donors and their partners achieved this great victory: they were pivotal where Latin America has gone furthest with the academic profession, research, graduate study, and fields of study.

These were real accomplishments because donors rarely encountered ready-made peaks within the academic profession or the other areas of academic work. Instead, they helped to establish peaks or to raise very modest ones. Additionally, even where there were willing partners, limitations of resources, experience, and know-how had to be overcome. These limitations are natural in truly novel undertakings, but they are often underestimated and were probably underestimated even by those donors and domestic reformers who usually tempered their optimism for academic modernization with prudence and flexibility.

Other results have been mixed. They involve disappointments and prismatic outcomes that do not meet assistance and reformist goals. Some are failures by almost any reasonable evaluation. Others are clear failures only when measured against the inflated expectations associated with grand policy reform in general and the golden age of university modernization in particular. They are complex outcomes that can be evaluated differently depending on the criteria chosen. Repeatedly intriguing examples arise with a variety of research centers. Many add significantly to the quantity and quality of Latin America's academic work. The university research centers enhance their host institution, though even they deviate from basic features of the U.S. export model. Other centers deviate still more. For example, scholars blend research mostly with nonteaching activities, basic disciplinary research is not at the forefront, and, most of all, few students are incorporated. Centers are inadequate substitutes for envisioned universities for each of the major aspects of academic work considered in this chapter, especially graduate education. Yet to call them failures is to capture only part of the story.

Similar assessment is apt for a range of concerns about academic development where the export model highlighted a certain university configuration. To focus on universities, especially typical ones, is to see results largely as failures. Yet to focus on the broader academic goals, treating the university model mostly as the anticipated vehicle for these goals, is to see mixed results. Assistance decisively helped build capacity and production through scholarships, research centers, and novel arrangements, notwithstanding the deficiencies compared with projected university development. Reflection upon such results spurred donors to shift strategy after the golden age more toward human resource development than university development (Olsson 1992).

Another kind of prismatic overlap in academic work emerges as the unassisted university mainstream trails far behind the quantitatively smaller area of targeted impact within and across institutions. Most professors are part-timers, research and graduate education usually remain absent or slim, and fields of study do not approximate the proportions envisaged. Moreover, the true balances deteriorate with the substantial formalism that involves nominal full-timers and researchers who do little more than teach part-time, nominal graduate education that really just extends professional training or lacks a scholarly base, new fields that replicate patterns of traditional ones, and so forth. Assistance successes have thus become pockets and peaks of academic work within a very stratified system. They buttress Cerych and Sabatier's (1986) finding that major change can be implemented if focused on part of a higher education system. On the positive side, the pockets and peaks have provided much of what is best and have sometimes been useful models within the system. On the negative side, they have usually failed to transform the rapidly enlarging mainstream.

Striking on all four of our aspects of academic work is the poor performance of most private universities, notwithstanding the largely unanticipated successes in private research centers. Previous chapters found an edge in private over public universities regarding certain features of the export model associated with the system's pluralism and the institution's coherence in management and other matters. But the private universities have rarely been beacons when it comes to a strong academic profession, research, graduate education, or scientific fields of study. On the contrary, they have often lagged behind the public sector in these regards. Most private institutions have grown through response to student demand and commercial and cost considerations—none fundamentally conducive to meeting assistance dreams about modern academic work. Even elite private universities have been disappointing, sometimes not doing much in these areas. But key exceptions come in the heavily targeted private universities and in some developments since the golden age of assistance.[85]

The identified successes in both public and private sectors are more impressive when we consider the opposition and confounding factors that surface in all four analyzed areas of academic work. They include extra university political and economic factors and intrauniversity dynamics. Whereas private sector massification mostly meant the proliferation of academically weak institutions, in the public sector it also meant suffocating growth within the very universities, headed by the national universities, which otherwise were the leaders in areas like research and graduate education. Massification took its toll on academic work at least as much as it did on other aspects of university reform. Meanwhile, the largely unmet need for a surrounding web of reform showed itself with special force among our highly interrelated aspects of academic work.

As found in other chapters, the absence of the web means that actions and policies lamented by reformers may be rational ones within the importing system. Thus, nominally full-time professors who lack the training or the salary, library, laboratory, or other resources to carry out good research minimize their commitment to campus, graduate education, and so forth. Among those with better training, many rationally choose research centers over university faculties. Elsewhere in the cycle, bright young students rationally decide against scientific fields of study or doctoral study aimed at entry to the academic profession. It is against this tide that islands of academic strength have developed by weaving their own mini-web of full-timers, research, and graduate education in given fields.

Another parallel to findings from other chapters closes this chapter on a hopeful note. Alongside the important successes in academic work to date, assistance provided ideas that retain power, indeed greater power than their degree of implementation would suggest. To be sure, the ideas may prove impotent when cast against realities that reward other behavior or impose costs on implementation. Additionally, support for these ideas remains abstract for many, while programmatic support concentrates among those few most directly exposed to the ideas in practice, including those who did doctoral study abroad. But there is eagerness among leading academics for a strong, full-time academic profession, blending research and both first-degree and formal graduate education, and focused on high-quality, discipline-oriented fields of study. If academic leaders find growing sympathy among counterparts in high political positions—counterparts who have resources available and the vision and power to beat back otherwise crippling forces—academic peaks may yet prove to be beachheads from which to launch further reform of academic work.[86] Positive legacies from the golden age of university assistance live on in academic work and may gain enhanced influence.

6

Promise and Performance
in Exporting Progress

Our view of the crusade to export progress through universities has been reasonably positive. Worthy tasks were undertaken with intelligence, and much good was done. That bottom-line performance fell far short of grand expectation is no surprise. A wide gap between promise and performance is common in policy reform. Similarly, reality rarely matches ideal types exactly; ideal types are to help us understand reality, and such understanding has been our primary undertaking.

This final chapter therefore first assesses the relationship between the facts discovered and the ideal type of philanthropic change. After that, the chapter synthesizes the evaluation of performance. It concludes with a brief look beyond our history.[1]

Ideal Types and Dilemmas in Voluntary Action

The ideal type of philanthropic change has guided us very well when it comes to donor efforts. This conclusion is important, since our study has concentrated so much on documenting and understanding efforts (not just goals or "bottom-line" results). Most efforts fit the ideal type and are illuminated by it, helping to give us a good picture of what was actually done in an extraordinary era of university and development assistance.

The ideal type has also helped when it comes to goals and results. It illuminates in considerable terrain where a match exists between the ideal typical and the real world. There is also ample terrain, however, where the match is not close. The ideal type has been useful in such cases, too, in identifying and drawing contrasts between matches and discrepancies or even contradictions. But in these cases the concrete realities we uncover also lead us to reflect back on the ideal type. Beyond the simple fact that reality trails ideal type, the reflection exposes ambiguities, loose links, and tensions within the philanthropic ideal type itself. Certain ideal typical goals are partly incompatible with other ones, and the same holds for certain means and for certain results. More striking are inconsistencies in the interrelationships among goals, means, and results. An ideal typical flow is less common than inconsistencies. Most ideal typical means are inherently inadequate for the ideal type's transforming goals and results.

Such inconsistencies and contradictions have great practical importance because the ideal type reflects basic beliefs and assumptions of reformers.[2] The soft spots in the ideal type parallel difficulties in the reality of voluntary action. In both, the problems are natural and not fully resolvable. Instead, a choice of one type of goal, for example, casts doubt upon another, and attempts to address the slippage between goals and efforts, or between efforts and results, create other inconsistencies. This leaves a basic dilemma in how to envisage and achieve change: directly pursue fundamental and widespread change but allow efforts to deviate from the ideal type, or stick with ideal typical efforts but then settle for less than the loftiest ideal typical goals and results. Similarly, if the ideal type is revised to come closer to reality, then it surrenders either much of what is distinctive and presumably strongest about voluntary efforts or what is most ambitious about goals and results.

Our evidence has repeatedly shown this to be an assistance dilemma, a dilemma for donors. At the broadest level, it also pertains to reform in general, squaring with important findings from implementation studies.[3] But our findings have particular relevance where key contributors (of fresh models and resources) are largely *voluntary* and aspire to major change. A major debate in U.S. philanthropy has pitted advocates of carefully focused, prudent means where donors can do things distinctly and successfully against critics who say philanthropy must daringly tackle wider, tougher problems, pursuing grander aims (Halpern 1998: 6–7; National Commission on Philanthropy and Civic Renewal 1997). The first group upholds ideal typical means but is vulnerable on whether goals are sufficient. The second group is vulnerable on means. The tensions and tradeoffs presented by each approach are commonly ignored, skirted, or wished aside.[4] Yet subject matter like ours suggests how basic the inconsistency is between the careful efforts and the aim and achievement of fundamental change.

The philanthropic ideal type includes a mechanism for surmounting the dilemma. This mechanism is the lever or recipient model. Grand goals can be pursued through selective, prudent means by targeting ripe partners and structures that then become springboards for widespread, fundamental change. But the evidence from the attempt to export progress through the universities in the Americas proves disappointing for this hope, however much we simultaneously argue that assistance was successful by more modest evaluative criteria.

The following sections contrast the generally close fit between philanthropic ideal type and reality regarding efforts with the difficulties in the linkage between goals and efforts and between efforts and results.

Goals versus Efforts

Assistance goals were in many ways ambitious enough to fit the ideal type of philanthropic change. Assistance was mostly very change-oriented, mocking dependency charges of status quo orientations, especially as change was to include considerable growth. Assistance was rarely anti-growth, and it was markedly pro-growth in targeted countries, institutions (elite and not), and new units and activities. The U.S. university model represented a sharp alternative to the traditional Latin American university model; after chapter 1 made the general contrast, chapters 3–5 identified specific and formidable ways in which assistance aimed to move from one toward the other. Interinstitutional diversity and growth meant a major departure from tighter system parameters, homogeneity, and belief in national rules, standards, and undertakings. Simultaneously, a goal was to build more powerful, cohesive, centralized institutions. On the administrative side this goal had financial and governance components and on the academic side it looked to diminish faculty-centered autonomy with innovations like general studies, departments, and campuswide activities. All this meant aspired movement away from a Continental model of national rules at the "top" joined by faculty-based structures at the "bottom" (with student power) toward a more "middle-centered" idea of strong, autonomous institutions. Equally revolutionary were goals for the introduction or sudden and massive expansion of aspects of academic work such as full-time teaching and research, graduate education, and new disciplines.

But efforts grand enough for those goals would violate fundamental notions about philanthropic means. In fact, then, while efforts were major enough to justify the notion of a golden age of development undertaking, they were limited and partial compared to those goals. Usually, for example, projects targeted particular places or concerns, to add and perhaps displace but not directly to replace existing structures and policies. A campaign directed more at the higher education mainstream and root causes of its problems would have made efforts deviate from ideal typical notions of prudence, partnership, selectivity, and targeting and would have often rendered them failures.[5] This was largely the experience when assistance did become uncharacteristically bold (or imprudent or both), overreaching. It is important to realize that such deviation was not the result of ignorance or crassness nearly so much as it was a reaction to the inadequacies of typical means (which were ideal typical as well) to achieve grand goals. Sometimes it was a conscious reaction, usually with a hope that the deviation would be less negatively consequential than it proved to be.

The other way to cope with the contradiction between grand goals and focused efforts was to adjust on the goals side. Whereas large adjustment (overreach) in efforts characterized only a minority of projects (though more features within projects), a de facto distinction between implicit and explicit goals characterized most projects. It obscured the goals-efforts contradiction, not resolving it. The implicit goals could remain grandiose, yet vague. The explicit goals, however, apart from brash proclamations here and there, would be much more specific and attainable. They were still ambitiously change-oriented but within particular venues, and they were mostly reasonable. It was the explicit goals that dominated in specific projects. Donor efforts with their partners, we have repeatedly argued, were largely consistent with those explicit goals and projects. The stated goals were often already pragmatic compromises between reformers' ultimate visions and existing practice.

Rarely were the grand goals discarded. They remained instead as hopeful, sketchy visions for some uncertain future. Meanwhile, projects were not viewed as disconnected from grand goals or as acceptance of far inferior alternatives. Instead, they were expected to push *toward* the Promised Land. They would build examples, seeds, ideas, and models. How these were to translate into wider transformation was rarely specified. Competition could be a major dynamic but might have appeared too invasive, "U.S.," or challenging for ideal typical notions of partnership and cooperation. Another possibility was simply liberal faith that good ideas and practices would win adherents. There was also hope that project successes would build a virtuous cycle and install more and more elements of positive "webs" so that further reform would become logical and feasible. All such hopeful notions could diminish the contradiction between explicit goals and grander, implicit goals.

A significant gap between explicit and implicit goals applied not only to matters within higher education but also to the relationship between promoting university development and promoting national development. University assistance projects simultaneously carried explicit goals about university development and implicit visions about impact on national, economic, social, and political development. How one would lead to the other was the topic of treatises on the role of education in development and of rousing phrases in some project rationales, but the mechanisms through which one would lead to the other usually had to be left very vague. Linkages were assumed or proposed out of sincere conviction and out of political necessity, to build support for expenditures and other efforts, and even sometimes to build rationales for painful change.[6]

A gap between explicit and implicit goals, however common in policy reform, carries particular importance in the golden age because, reflecting reigning modernization theories, the implicit goals for exporting progress through assistance and partnership were so grand. Only by juxtaposing a set of more specifically operationalized, explicit goals in projects could the goals flow into actual efforts.

Sticking with the less grandiose explicit goals makes assistance goals more reasonable but at the same time less transforming than otherwise. Thus the chief inherent contradiction about ideal typical goals is that they may not simultaneously meet the criteria of transformation and pragmatism. Also, failure to identify these clashing criteria and the difference between explicit and implicit goals meant deviation from ideal typical notions of goal clarity in planning. However, and here is another inherent contradiction in the philanthropic ideal type, greater clarity in planning would likely lead to fewer undertakings, because more modest goals would not sufficiently motivate politically, or would inflate explicit goals and thus contribute to wider inconsistencies between goals and both efforts and results.

The philanthropic ideal type suggests that grand goals of change can be achieved through selective means. We repeatedly find, however, that efforts are too limited, too narrow in scope and weight, to alter or overwhelm common practice. But a major turn to broadened and fortified efforts usually sacrifices key tenets of philanthropic means. On the other hand, to make goals more consistent with efforts (and results) is to rob them of much of the character of fundamental change and innovation with risk that is important to the ideal type.

Efforts

Efforts, mostly tied to the explicit goals, overwhelmingly corresponded to efforts suggested in the philanthropic ideal type. They fit notions of selectivity with targeting, partnership, innovation, risk, and distinctiveness, often undertaken with reasonable knowledge, skill, and flexibility.

Some efforts pursued grand goals in ways that constituted a kind of overreach for the philanthropic ideal type. Although overreach partly reflected the exuberance of an overlapping modernization ideal type and its underestimation of obstacles, we stress that it also reflected a sober sense of the insufficiency of more limited efforts to achieve grand goals. So as not to concede too much ground to the status quo, donors sometimes attempted to engage in less-promising countries, innovate at conflict-ridden national universities, achieve growth at nonelite institutions, and promote academic centralization where opposition to it was formidable. The basic idea of university development, paralleling other assistance efforts at institutional development, often represented a broadly ambitious effort.

Yet we have seen important qualifications to overreach. It was the exception, not the rule. Much of it occurred in just a few years of peak aggressiveness in assistance. Overreach within particular projects tended to be for only very short periods. Moreover, overreach in certain respects was accompanied by selectivity in others. Mainly, even when donors' peak efforts amounted to overreach, they bypassed the great majority of potential receivers and activities. Finally, consistent with our hypothesis about different donors' fit to the ideal type of philanthropic change, it was especially rare for foundations to abandon philanthropic means as the Rockefeller Foundation did with its University Development Program.[7]

The usually great selectivity buttresses the depiction of assistance as largely voluntary. Donors mostly provided something extra, not for most actors in the mainstream. All donors gave to the few, not the many. This generalization holds regarding national, public institutional, private institutional, and intrainstitutional targets. The critique that assistance gets spread out to where it loses focus lacks credibility in these efforts to export progress (and thus does not parallel findings in policy literature on U.S. federalism). Of course, limited resources contribute to narrow efforts, but assistance could have been spread out more.[8] Donors have to find recipients, but they selected on the basis of discriminating criteria and usually refrained from working with the mainstream. "Scatterization" was uncommon.

Targets were not only few but atypical. Omitted were most faculties and the bulk of first-degree, professional training. The targets instead were usually among the most reform-oriented, with a record of willingness to innovate academically and administratively—and a governance and other profile deemed adequate to the reform task. Such characteristics were expected to help targets serve as models, thus converting donors' limited efforts into wider impacts. A contradiction was that the more donors moved to the most distinctive targets, the further they were from the mainstream to be reached through secondary effects. The targets were disproportionately newer institutions or fields or types of work, such as graduate education, and among nations those with less developed, less-entrenched systems received relatively more assistance. Yet donors bypassed even most of what was new on the ground in Latin America, as with proliferating provincial and private universities or fields of study.

Selective targeting meant partnership. Donors did not try to go it alone. Even in the rare instances in which they attempted to build from institutional scratch, they worked with domestic counterparts.

However, here contradictions within the ideal type appear even regarding efforts themselves: clashes among components individually associated with ideal typical partnership. Probably no perfect partners existed. Even if there were partners with near perfect scores on ability, they might not be those for whom assistance could have a needed, distinctive reform impact. In contrast, bold reform efforts at traditional or resistant places would be very risky, as seen at certain national universities. In any event, few potential partners had near perfect abilities. Nations, institutions, and other units were conglomerations of individuals and structures, not all equally willing or ready for partnership. The ideal type does not tell donors whether to target a unit with limited opposition but few able leaders or to target a unit with more opposition but more able leaders. In reality donors worked with countries, institutions, and units internally divided among supporters, opponents, and at least initially rather indifferent actors. If the question is whether donors worked with partners, the answer is a resounding yes. If the question is whether the partners fit the ideal type, the answer is probably a cloudy yes.

Partnership meant limitations on donor control, fitting the philanthropic ideal type much more than dependency arguments. Regarding the type of university transfer model, assistance was largely voluntary. Most of the time, there was no obligation to give or to receive. Although the U.S. model carried the great weight, it came basically without imposition, to only certain parts of Latin American higher education systems, and diluted by initial hybrid accommodations to dilemmas in how to transform existing practice. What donors pushed in practice was flexible and varied. Rarely did they try to impose a pure model's features like liberal arts education or dormitory-based campuses. On the other side, domestic partners generally supported the ideas they imported, whether they were labeled as made in the USA or not. Like donors, they had plural options.[9] There were, of course, instances of donor arrogance, but even most instances of substantive overreach reflected less of that than of mutual efforts to break with tradition.

Moreover, while the ideal type requires extensive voluntary cooperation, it does not exclude all forms of donor control. Again a dose of ambiguity arises in both the ideal type and practice, but this ambiguity is far from outright contradiction: the type of donor control repeatedly found is not only compatible with partnership but also necessary to other ideal typical means. Ideal typical donors are not timid and are not mere sources of funds. They exert influence—otherwise, one must wonder whether their efforts are novel and challenging enough to fit the philanthropic ideal type. Ideal typical partnership includes recipient acceptance of such influence. Recipients in our case often eagerly solicited such influence. They aspired to follow elements of a U.S. university model requiring major changes in norms and power. They accepted partnership as something in between donor imposition and donor nondirection. Assistance, wrote critic Scherz-García (1967: 395–96), "brings about a recognition of certain informal rights of the benefactors." Also crucial to reconciling notions of partnership and donor control was voluntary entering into bargains involving donors' front-end control to choose targets, purposes, and general parameters of projects. Their freedom to choose and promote partners also allowed donors to alter the balance of power between reformists and others, including opponents. Donors thus had the power to stratify, even if they hoped secondary efforts would then diminish stratification by bolstering whole systems. A contradiction for donors to confront (or skirt) arose when the urge to make bold and telling efforts led to some target sites that lacked much of the "right stuff" for smooth partnership. In those cases, donors then had to choose whether to try to control more than partnership generally implies or to accept other inadequacies in project efforts.

A similar contradiction concerned persistence. The ideal type counts on front-end influence to set matters on course, with partnership later yielding to recipients' self-sustaining progress. Donors were often disappointed by how little this worked out in practice at public institutions (Dye i). They then faced the dilemma of accepting the disappointing results or extending the length of their control and support.

Because ambiguities and even contradictions exist among the ideal typical means, no definitive, neat fit could emerge between them and real efforts. Nonetheless, the main generalization that flows from our findings is that actual efforts mostly fit the philanthropic ideal type—and in ways crucial for understanding undertakings in the golden age.

This generalization holds regarding each of our major donors. Sustaining the hypothesis that the fit would be strongest for private foundations, Ford and other foundations were the most voluntary actors. They selected in the most discriminating ways, targeting the fewest units, insisting most on finding able partners, pursuing the most focused activities, and concentrating the most on higher education in their overall assistance efforts. Our scantier evidence on AID points to a surprising degree of parallel, particularly as AID worked through U.S. university partners. Even IDB efforts mostly fit the ideal type, despite much more direct responsiveness to member-state demands, pressures for basic growth, and funding for brick and mortar expansion, including for institutions that are not elite. Even the IDB focused its projects regarding nations, institutions, units, and actors, and bypassed most of the higher education mainstream. There was great similarity in the many places none of the donors went and the many higher education activities they hardly touched. More variation emerged regarding what that did undertake; there they often undertook complementary roles, above all where the IDB built physical infrastructure essential to Ford's human resource targeting.

Furthermore, efforts would fit more tightly with the philanthropic ideal type were we to have included more efforts directed at private research centers, which were generally smaller and more focused and select than universities. Though these efforts increased after the golden age, they were already prominent during it. Still more, the fit would tighten had we concentrated on scholarships. Even the scholarships given within broader assistance projects (as opposed to scholarships given outside projects, individually) make the point. Efforts with scholarships and centers were particularly prominent for the foundations yet not limited to them.

It might generously yet reasonably be concluded that donors often blended Dantian virtues of prudence and courage with hope and faith. Assistance efforts largely followed the philanthropic ideal type. This generalization must allow for a degree of ambiguity and even conflict among different ideal typical means. But the main qualification to the generalization lies in the interface between the efforts and the results they were supposed to achieve in order to meet grand goals.

Efforts versus Results

The adequacy of the philanthropically ideal typical efforts depends largely on whether the test concerns the more modest or most ambitious results anticipated in the ideal type. This range largely parallels the range regarding goals. Efforts were adequate for most goals in most projects. But failure to achieve the grandest results—overcoming root problems, building widespread transformation, and achieving other ends often left implicit or thought to emerge indirectly—led to widespread disappointment among donors, domestic partners, and observers.

Lacking were the key mechanisms, the levers, to set powerful, extensive, virtuous cycles in motion. Targets did not affect the breadth of higher education nearly as much as donors and others had expected. A still greater gap developed between expectation and results regarding how efforts within higher education would contribute to national development. Events dealt harshly with beliefs, like those in overlapping modernization theory, that the force of positive diffusion would generally be powerful enough to overcome obstacles. Instead, events repeatedly showed the great force of the wider higher education and national context not only to restrict but also to dwarf and distort much of the targeted higher education progress.

The asymmetry between efforts and grand results points again to the basic philanthropic dilemma. If selective efforts fail to induce potent leverage effects that lead to widely transforming results, then voluntary action like that in assistance must surrender much of its large claims. If results are recast downward to be more in line with efforts, then they are not so lofty and galvanizing.

Because they were attentive and thoughtful more than sanctimoniously operating from a rigid blueprint, and because the attempt to export progress through universities extended over years, donors developed a sense of the inconsistencies involving their preferred efforts and what they could achieve. They would then lean more heavily than prescribed on some means, cutting corners with others. At times, realizing that typical means carried their own risks of not generating desired results, they overreached into riskier ones. At other times, and ultimately to end the golden era, they retreated into much more modest efforts, further from the higher education mainstream and with little pretense to change it. All these moves and reasons were found, for example, in donors' private-public choices.[10]

Alternatively, donors might have viewed results more benignly. Ideal typical efforts inadequate for the grandest goals and results in the ideal type can be adequate for goals and results that are nonetheless important and worthy. Major pragmatic change met explicit goals and transformed targets much more than it met implicit goals or reformed broader systems.

Evaluating Performance

Our evaluation of performance is very different if we focus on the grandest claims of the ideal type or the more modest yet still significant ones. Other evaluative criteria for assessing reform, introduced in chapter 1 and now summarized here, reinforce the positive side of the picture.

One general qualification is that the factors identified in pertinent literatures on the difficulties of gauging reform results in social policy are borne out in this study. Criteria of success are themselves vague and variable, as our discussion of goals indicated. AID, Ford, and IDB evaluations can usually tell us that targeted places improved things like curriculum and number of degrees, but judging success remains vastly more complicated. There are so many variables. These include context largely beyond partners' ability to influence, different starting points, and fungibility. While assistance impacts on targets are thus hard to gauge, it is yet more difficult to pinpoint how much diffusion there is beyond targets (Robertson and Waltman 1993). The variables include time, too. No magic point exists at which to gauge impact, and contexts themselves change over time. Although donors and critics rushed to give too negative an overall appraisal of assistance, no single, objective, alternative evaluative time frame exists. Counterfactual speculation can be nearly boundless. Where results appear positive, they might have been superior through alternative policies. Where they appear negative, they might have been inferior through alternatives. Apropos the voluntary dilemma, avoidance of choices that brought some problem or limitation often would have brought other ones. No wonder, then, that "lessons" drawn from evaluations are usually vague—and much less certain than merely plausible. For example, donors might undertake longer-term commitments, and they might concentrate on just a few policy objectives (Verspoor 1991: 32), but there have usually been tradeoffs and reasons for doing otherwise. Lessons are often really exhortations or hopes or guesses.

Such difficulties in evaluation leave a study like this one short of definitive proof regarding many points concerning results. The discernible facts are subject to more than one reasonable set of conclusions. Apparent failures may not be failures. Apparent successes may amount to less than meets the eye or may have involved investments or tradeoffs too high to be cost-effective. Within this maze, however, the interpretation here is that results have been mostly positive. One key to that assessment is that the negative side of the picture is best characterized less by massive outright failure than by disappointment.

Disappointing Performance: Opposition and Rationality

Opposition was a major reason for disappointing performance. Like other policymakers, donors knew there would be opposition. They were not totally naive. But neither were they generally geared to deal with it or to think through sufficiently the challenges it would present. Overcoming opposition was presumably more the role of domestic partners. Mostly, the dynamics and impact of opposition, marginal to the ideal type, were largely left aside. A vague hope was that opposition might have only minimal negative impact; this was the flip side of the vague hope that positive levers would convert selective efforts into wider results. Opposition was underestimated. Overestimated was the ability to bypass or overcome it. Although donors might have had more foresight, it is unclear how much more success they could have achieved, since the voluntary dilemma would again arise: insufficient ceding to opposition risked running headlong into conflict whereas more ceding (or bypassing) would minimize the breadth of impact.

Opposing actors included students, professors, associations in the traditional professions, and an array of institutions and units to be transformed or bypassed. Opposition was especially extensive if defined to include uncooperative behavior and not just aggressive combat. In effect, much of the mainstream was at least potential opposition. That opposition was often initially potential more than active contributed to donors' underestimation of problems. Many actors were simply unaware of planned reforms or how they themselves would be affected. Often the reform ideas seemed generally fine and the devil lurked in the details or the unanticipated consequences. As matters moved closer to the implementation stage, more actors saw they could lose out. When donors attempted to move beyond great selectivity in order to achieve greater impact, many interests were directly threatened. When donors found the mainstream too opposed to tackle, they reinforced the sense that the mainstream would lose ground to favored targets and purposes. Either way, opposition was stimulated.

Significantly, opposition had a largely rational basis. The philanthropic ideal type skirts this reality as it emphasizes the unity of donor and recipient self-interest. But reforms that aim at major change generally translate into conflict. Even reforms that are "good for" recipient systems are not seen that way by all. Moreover, what is good for some is not good for others. Many reforms that are rational for a system and the wider interests it should serve are irrational for important actors. And what would be good in the long run injures many in what may appear to reformers as the short run but which is simultaneously the entire run for students and a long run for others.

It is easy to miss the fundamental reality of rational opposition. If ideal typical change is rational, opposition can easily appear to donors as irrational. Even standing on the sidelines represents "tradition" versus reasoned progress. Tradition is associated with habitual continuation of norms and practices that are viewed as undesirable or less desirable than reform.[11] Furthermore, the 1960s and 1970s were times of historically radical and dramatic protest, which many could see as irrational or at least ideological. There was, of course, much ideology at play on all sides, most visibly among radical protesters. But opposition usually came from those who could reasonably view themselves as losing out. Often this meant losing out to targeted individuals and units or to favored practices. Selectivity was very much about choosing some over others. Selectivity was also very much about performance, or at least potential for performance, over guarantees and equality. Those who would not fare well in competition rationally defended *homologación* (equal treatment across the board). This defense was probably clearest in matters of academic work and associated reforms for rigor, merit, and professionalism. In other cases, rational concern was less tied to invidious losses relative to targeted partners than to a more generally inflicted hardship. Thus students saw general studies as an added requirement, a postponement of job entry, and alumni already in the professions joined in the opposition, concerned over the professional preparation of those whom they would hire.

Opposition was logically greatest where actors had the most to lose. This often meant where the most transformation was attempted. Features of the U.S. model clashed with much more infrastructure and related interests at national universities than at public alternative universities and especially private universities. Similar points could be made at a more micro level about units and fields within institutions or at a more macro level about national systems. The counterpoint is that donors were mostly aware of this logic and limited trouble by reliance on partnership and mutual matching. The dilemma lay in how partnership and mutual matching were inadequate to the breadth of envisioned major reform.

Rationality blocking reform was not, however, always a matter of perceived self-interest and pointed opposition. Many reforms that make perfect sense in the abstract or as part of the U.S. model lose their rationale or become infeasible when injected inside a foreign context. Others lose at least some of their rationale or become infeasible in certain respects. This problem was especially marked where there was already considerable infrastructure and extant practice, again making it difficult to move successfully beyond targets that were highly atypical for their systems. The absence of a supportive "web" has continually surfaced as crippling for reform. Graduate programs are problematic without a supportive web of research, ample finance, libraries, laboratories, academic culture, or receptive job markets. Departments lack their anticipated meaning when campuses and central libraries are absent. Central libraries will not play their anticipated role if teaching and learning continue to center around lectures. Competitive, autonomous institutions cannot flourish where reigning law preserves *homologación*.[12] Indeed, the list of examples could be extended to each reform in its interrelationship with many other reforms. Additionally, we have seen the importance of a wider

232 | TO EXPORT PROGRESS

web, linking higher education to broader political, economic, and social contexts. Here our examples have been fewer and more obvious—and often devastating. Economic crises and political purges blow away progress otherwise made in the higher education trenches. Political responsiveness to social demand allows a massification that overwhelms plotted academic reforms.

Like others, donors underestimated how negative the context beyond higher education would often be. Projects usually postulated a rather positive context or avoided the issue. Hope and avoidance were understandable: donors could not and did not expect to control the broader context. Yet great progress especially on donors' ambitious, implicit goals required a much more positive context. Again a supposition of donors and of the philanthropic model of major change turned out to be based on dubious, tenuous linkages that were not spelled out.

Donors naturally spent more time contemplating the relationship between particular reforms and the higher education web pertinent to those reforms. Appreciation of how most reforms would lack a supportive higher education web in most places contributed to the tendency to avoid those places and head instead to those that could construct a more supportive web. The voluntary dilemma thus resurfaces and so does the escape valve critical to the philanthropic ideal type: targeted efforts in projects must achieve successes that through example or competition drive wider changes beyond the projects. This escape valve can work if the implanted reform increases the rationality of practices that did not make sense prior to the reform. Build new disciplines, for example, and departments become more logical; make learning depend more on independent study than on rote note taking, and libraries will have greater purpose and support. Such change is akin to Hirschman's hopeful notions of linkages. These linkages can be strategically planned in specific ways or can be expected to emerge in ways and forms that are not blueprinted. Though more such change emerged than critics have appreciated, our evidence is that implanted reform spurred new and supportive webs less often than existing webs mangled reforms.

Disappointing Performance: Results

As virtuous cycles proved difficult to generate, putting a hole in the ideal typical dynamics of change, results fell far short of expectations. Even in these cases, however, we have not usually found the results of assistance to be damaging, making things worse. Of course, much depends on one's views of good and bad. Critics then and now could regard many of the reforms themselves as undesirable, whether feasible or not. For some, the very idea of exporting or importing models was offensive.

Two sorts of worsening have repeatedly emerged in our analysis. The clearest one is stratification, creating or usually exacerbating inequalities.

Here is our strongest evidence that favors basic dependency theory. Examples abound concerning students, professors, institutions, and smaller units. Stratification seems a natural consequence of an ideal type of change that rests heavily on selectivity. Mitigation is at least implicitly expected to come from how the targets' successes lead to secondary reform in the wider system. Our history shows such effects but also considerable worsening in the massifying mainstream. Though not the fault of assistance, this worsening has often then meant increased gaps between assisted targets and others, even where targets fall short of expectations.

The second sort of worsening is subtle yet arguably more damaging insofar as it involves not just a relative but also absolute deterioration. Interaction between imported aspects of reform and domestic reality often produces a formalism inferior to prior practice. For example, professors with poor training who are hired full-time and forced to publish research are often "worse," including much more costly, than competent professionals who serve as taxi professors. For another example, where rectors continue to be political more than academic figures, it may be a net negative for them to have formidable administrative capacities at their disposal.

Mostly, though, our findings about disappointing results are much less about bad consequences than a relative lack of consequences. Certainly higher education reform failed to become the motor of broad-based national development associated with modernization theory. Within higher education, the combined effects of progress at targets and positive secondary effects elsewhere were quite insufficient to produce major net improvements in systemic indicators. Before, during, and after assistance, most places lacked distinctive institutional profiles, diverse funding bases, dynamic articulation with external communities, efficient central administration, decisive academic centralization, or generally good research and teaching, let alone a departmental fusing of the two. The mainstream resisted and eroded reforms. Insightful observers referred to "successes" that did not have great effect. Huge growth took place outside the reach of assistance and usually along lines fundamentally at odds with the philanthropic ideal type of change.[13] Harking back to the distinction between explicit and implicit goals, project "outputs" could be fine while performance "outcomes" for the system could be abysmal. The operating assumption of donors (implicit in the ideal type) that their targeted spots introduce changes into an otherwise fairly static (if not improving) system, one whose growth is not such as to overwhelm their selective efforts, failed dismally.[14]

But where assistance actually went, assessments of a lack of impact usually base themselves on a comparison of results versus expectations. Some of the shortcomings appear relatively modest. IDB evaluations (IDB/E1: 10) found that projects often took longer, cost more, and advanced less than planned. Other shortcomings are huge but measured against quite unrealistic hopes. The University of Chile did not become like the University of California. The Latin American university did not fulfill dreams of becoming like the U.S. university (Fuenzalida 1984).

Positive Results

Disappointing results must be weighed against evidence of positive results.[15] The clearest such evidence is achievement of explicit project goals. On this score, credible project evaluations at AID, Ford, and IDB fit findings from our interviews, site visits, and varied documents. Additionally, although targeted successes did not convert into basic levers of systemic transformation, in many instances they radiated influences to some other institutions or actors within or beyond the national system, occasionally even beyond the region. Similarly, there were notable if sporadic examples of impacts beyond higher education, as in contributions to democratic government or revamped economic policy. And for all the examples of disappointing and unanticipated consequences, instances of positive ones also arose, such as contributions to the flourishing of fine freestanding research centers.

Beyond clear achievement of explicit project goals, our main evidence of success follows the criteria of comparison developed in chapter 1 (other than comparison with ideal typical results or grand expectations). This is the evidence that most cuts against common views of university assistance failure. When the evidence is framed by these criteria—which is rare—informed observers generally confirm it.

At the broadest level, performance seems reasonable compared with that found in other studies of international assistance, reported in chapter 1. It is generally superior to that depicted in some studies and consistent with the mixed results depicted in other studies. Performance thus seems in step with findings from research on varied policy reforms once literature gets beyond both a first stage of exaggerated hope and a second of devastating disappointment, to arrive at a third stage of mixed assessment. Also at a broad level, performance often is positive, given the difficult contexts beyond the control of donors and their partners. This factor is especially important because contexts were often catastrophic, as with political repression or instability and economic crisis. A related factor was the breadth and strength of political opposition.

Assistance targets do well compared with nontargets. They outperform them. This conclusion emerges at the national but especially institutional and intrainstitutional levels. The gap between the targeted minority and the bypassed majority is striking in qualitative matters and exceeds that accounted for by the "head starts" targets often enjoyed. Many of the targets had been quite modest and yet rose to become relatively impressive peaks. Often, donors and partners started nearly from only a minimal base, with tiny and unimpressive institutions, new disciplines, or novel activities such as graduate education. The gap also remains visible despite complex factors of diffusion and related reforms occurring without assistance. Favored public alternative universities, for example, often rose quickly and have maintained leadership on matters like financial diversification, academic and administrative centralization, and fresh curriculum.[16]

Rarely could assistance wholly create change, but it was usually a vital facilitating partner, and promoted, bolstered, expanded, and accelerated change. Targets often quickly became very good and formidable compared with what they had been. And while it cannot prove the point, evidence strongly suggests they became much better than they otherwise would have been. Targets were often transformed.[17]

Assistance was thus crucial to creating a major portion of what would be best in Latin American higher education. It makes all the difference whether we ask the common question—what is the overall state of Latin American higher education?—or we ask a different question—where are its leading parts and how did they emerge? Both questions are important. The fact that assistance did not do more to allow a positive answer to the first is a profound disappointment. The fact that it was crucial to positive answers to the second question is a profound achievement (which runs basically counter to dependency theory).[18] Not key to the modal patterns of Latin American higher education, assistance has been key to much change and progress within the system.

Prismatic Change

We have found evidence of rather clear-cut change, often in projected positive directions, and evidence of lack of change, as well as negative change. But an important part of the story is not captured adequately by these conventional categories: we have repeatedly discovered prismatic change, where reality results from the clash and mix of preexisting with imported structures and practice. Because it does not match goals and falls far short of expectations, prismatic change (where perceived) is usually taken as negative. It certainly is a disappointment. But compared to most of what was, most of what surrounds it, and most of what would have been without assistance, prismatic change is better seen as bolstering our view of mixed results than negative results.

The results of assistance are therefore mixed not only because there are both positive and negative results but also because many individual results are mixed.[19] Whereas much modernization and dependency (and world systems and institutionalist) theory highlights replication of forms from advanced countries, prismatic reality is distinct.[20] Such reality, Riggs points out, is not merely a brief stage on the way to replication, although our post–golden era evidence shows that prismatic reality is not immutable either but rather evolving. Imported form does indeed weaken traditional form, as many theories of change stress, but traditional form also weakens imported form. Slippage is thus common. Crucial has been our concept of a supportive web, the lack of which makes reform difficult to implement or makes it largely "snap back." As Riggs argues regarding reforms for rational administrative bureaucracy, so we find for universities: U.S. assistance greatly overestimated the autonomy of the activities it proposed to reform.[21] It proved difficult to transform individual structures, practices, and norms that were parts of intricate webs.

One major type of prismatic change has been displacement. This has come where imported form, or a variation, moves in alongside traditional or other unassisted form—nudging it aside without replacing it. In fact, massive growth that is mostly unassisted means that even an otherwise impressive presence of something imported may amount to a small or proportionally diminishing share of the system. Examples include truly alternative institutions alongside proliferating ones that mostly ape traditional ones (or worse), university libraries alongside faculty libraries, incentive structures alongside *homologación*, capable full-time staff alongside traditional or decreasingly qualified staff, and disciplines, departments, academic graduate programs, and research centers alongside traditional or massifying professionalist teaching faculties.

The other major type of prismatic change has been formalism. New nomenclature, structures, or rules lack the function or meaning held in the imported model. The "new" is largely the old or some third form. Innovation is lacking or gets knocked back by *homologación*, opposition, or other aspects related to a missing web. Examples include "alternative" institutions and units that fail to assume distinctive forms, libraries with few holdings and little use, central facilities and governance structures controlled by faculties or nonacademic political processes, departments and general studies programs inside and subordinated to faculties, campuses without full-time students or professors, full-time professors who work part-time and lack either ability or incentives to undertake worthwhile research or teaching, research without discovery, new disciplines that operate like professional programs, and graduate programs without adequate staff, research, or funds.

Prismatic patterns bring us back to the philanthropic dilemma. It is not just where donors and other reformers fail outright that they are left with the choice of striving to get closer to their major goals by undertaking efforts beyond those contemplated in the ideal type of philanthropic change. Efforts would somehow have to expand into the unreformed mass that dwarfs the initially targeted innovative segments and would have to challenge the practices, norms, and interests attached to formalism. In fact, donors' propensity for prudence over boldness in dealing with this tradeoff is shown not only by their retreat in the mid-1970s but also by their earlier action. They in effect accepted that displacement rather than replacement meant major overlap because they operated only selectively, not trying directly to change the bulk of the expanding systems or institutions. Furthermore, the more donors successfully helped certain targets, the more receptive, able, and logical they, and not others, became for subsequent donor efforts. A "living museum" of old forms alongside new was inevitable. Donors also initially compromised on forms. For example, instead of liberal arts, general studies were tucked into the students' beginning years in one way or another, usually as conduits to professional programs. Departments were likewise inserted into faculties. Campuses were built without dormitories. Although donors and reformers did not seek the formalism that ensued, they did already bend considerably from the export model's forms. They did so principally because they recognized that a more ambitious approach would have required much more extensive and intrusive means and still have had less chance to carry the day.[22]

From the beginning, then, donors and reform partners operated with the idea that much of what we call prismatic change would be an improvement. Of course, they neither anticipated nor wanted the overlap balance or shape of formalism that usually ensued, and they hoped that levers and other dynamics would put matters on a positive evolutionary course. In reality, displacement has only sometimes led into driving forces for expanding positive change, progressive Hirschmanesque linkages, and islands with effective bridges to the mainland. It has more often meant enclaves, cease-fires, and even corroding influences on the enclaves from the surrounding elements. The gap between actual performance and ideal type has turned out to be far larger and sustained than donors and partners had imagined or set out to achieve.

Nonetheless, consistent with our overall view of mixed rather than negative results, prismatic change includes positive elements if the evaluative criteria are more modest than the most demanding ones of the philanthropic ideal type. Almost all the comparative criteria summarized above are relevant to prismatic change.[23] Prismatic change often makes matters better than they were, better than they are where such change fails to occur, and better than they would otherwise be. This is clearer for displacement than for formalism. Enclaves that rise high above the overlapping bulk of the system are far better than nothing. In fact, leading institutions and units, like innovative practices, often exercise great importance for the higher education system and beyond. Even regarding formalism, forms that bend to reality often still are superior to static or isomorphically proliferating forms. Or the overlapping and partially formalistic pockets are superior in certain crucial ways. Full-time professors who teach in several institutions need not be preferable for the entire system in order for them to make significant contributions that part-timers cannot. The same goes for campuses, private universities, research centers, departments, and much more that in practice deviate from the export model. Prismatic change may also be seen as reasonably positive, given the difficult contexts and webs that reformers must confront. In fact, given local reality (traditions, norms, structures, rules, interests), much prismatic change is arguably superior to ideal typical change that would be too alien to achieve through partnership or to sustain itself.[24]

238 | TO EXPORT PROGRESS

Prismatic change leaves much to be desired but also represents important progress. Undoubtedly donors and their partners could have achieved a somewhat more favorable balance. But the means available to them under the circumstances placed powerful limitations on what was possible.[25]

Then and Now

Both similarities and differences characterize university assistance during and since the golden age of activity. As chapter 2 noted, retreat from the golden age peak was not total abandonment, and it has been followed by partial revival, including parallels to and modifications of prior patterns. Whereas many of the implicit, ultimate hopes and goals have remained similar, explicit project goals have often differed. Some efforts show mostly continuity, others change; one can identify much from the past in the present and much from the present in the past, but in different degrees and mixes. Regarding results, comparison between then and now obviously is premature because we cannot yet know the effects of contemporary efforts.[26] Even comparisons dealing with goals and efforts must be limited and tentative, since we have studied only the historical experience. We therefore refer often to contemporary policy and trends without knowing the extent to which they are pursued in reality.

The philanthropic ideal type appears relevant to contemporary assistance but is less salient and differently operationalized than before, reflecting a modified approach to dealing with the voluntary dilemma. Identifying movement from "liberal" to "neoliberal" approaches in assistance captures part of the change. Neoliberal approaches involve greater emphasis on market competition, private actors, and economic considerations (as do the increasingly widespread domestic neoliberal higher education policy agendas).

The fit between assistance efforts and philanthropically ideal typical means is not as close today as in the past—mixed rather than tight. To be sure, donors still select targets and bypass many potential recipients and activities. Indeed, they often return to those they targeted in the past. Also, the neoliberal tenet of funding through competitive criteria that are based on performance favors discriminating selection, as does the diminished sense of responsibility to a mainstream now viewed more harshly than in the past. But, working against ideal typical means, this harsher view also translates into more frontal attacks on the mainstream. There is less benign bypassing. Assistance often demands changes in fundamental practices, insisting that domestic policy be righted. The agencies may press directly for the prescribed change or may make the change a condition of their working with selected targets within a system. Either way, they move away from the sharp targeting of the past. They place less faith in the philanthropic proposition that their targets can thrive despite the mainstream and in fact can leverage that mainstream.

"Conditionality" obviously cuts against prior emphases on partnership, bolstering the massive critique of the World Bank and other agencies as interventionist. [27]

These tendencies are not clear-cut, however. On the contrary, debate rages about appropriate assistance modalities. One school favors fewer conditions, greater targeting, and increased "ownership" of projects by recipients (O'Hanlon and Graham 1997: 51). Recent World Bank studies of aid have concluded that large financial undertakings do not work, that conditionality does not bring reform, and that impact comes more through the force of ideas, innovation, programs emphasizing quality over quantity, working together, supporting reformers, finding "a champion," and being "focused" (World Bank 1998: 44, 103–04). Since the 1990s, the bank has thus moved somewhat closer to philanthropically ideal typical means.[28] This move might be contrasted with an IDB move toward greater conditionality than in the golden age, but this move is only one of degree (Castro n.d.). Moreover, the IDB pointedly emphasizes the need to be more foundationlike, citing matters linked to ideal typical means: targeting willing and able reform partners, steering clear of places where its policies are not welcome, and striving for leverage on a problematic mainstream (IDB 1997: 29–30).

A major reason that the balance shifts away from the close fit with the philanthropically ideal typical means is the shift in the weight of the donors for Latin American higher education. In fact, one could say that resources now come much more heavily than before from "lending agencies" rather than "donors." The most important increase comes from the significant entry of the World Bank. AID has decreased, and the most important decrease concerns the Ford Foundation—a decrease precisely where the fit with the philanthropic ideal type was greatest. At the turn of the century, Ford launched the largest grant in its history, roughly $300 million for higher education scholarships, and Latin America was one of the targeted regions. But the undertaking was pointedly not for institutional development, focusing instead on access and equity for deprived groups.

Compared to the situation regarding means, it is less clear whether goals and general orientations are further now from the ideal type. The mix has changed in some respects. Especially right after the golden age, goals were revised downward. Although that trend has since reversed, ambition and optimism remain below what they had been. A gap once again separates explicit project goals and grander implicit goals.

Contemporary goals arguably follow a more pronounced ideology or sharper edge than in the past. There is diminished adherence to the philanthropic ideal that different actors have similar objective interests, that those who are uninvolved will not hurt projects, and that project successes will show the happy road to others. For example, interinstitutional differentiation is now a more explicit goal, portrayed not just as desirable but also as a necessary alternative to rotted, uncompetitive, inefficient systems. By the same token, there is a direct verbal and policy attack on *homologación,* a practice always at least implicitly at odds with the export model but assaulted only in specific reforms of specific projects. Many features of the U.S. model that were previously submerged are now pointedly favored. Privatization is a major example, regarding both proportional expansion of the private higher education sector and increased proportions of nonstate money for public institutions. Such features make today's agenda appear more confrontational than yesterday's, particularly where they link to conditionality regarding the system overall. Critics see an international neoliberal agenda that undermines democratic social welfare, undermining at least potentially progressive growth and equity-oriented state and public action (Mundy 1998: 453).

It is inaccurate to call today's approach simply "anti-state," since it favors strengthened state governance, discretion, and evaluation—increasing the enlightened and voluntary components of state action over the purely political or reactive ones. But policy does aim at curbing the financial role of the state and the grand missions often asked of it, even if seldom fulfilled. The state was to be a partner in the golden age, and it is to be a partner today, but there is now much more antipathy to an oversized state and much more skepticism about trusting in partnership with anything other than a fundamentally reformed state. Although "institutional building" remains a key, today it often carries a greater edge of limiting the state by building institutions in civil society (Quigley and Popson 1999: 239).

Neoliberal policy is more ambivalent about growth than was yesterday's liberal policy (Eisemon and Kourouma 1994). Reflecting modernization theory, the bias was pro-growth, even to the point of contradicting certain ideal typical philanthropic means. We repeatedly found how donors specifically promoted growth in their preferred areas while usually ignoring it elsewhere. Although the critique that contemporary policy is sharply anti-growth is inaccurate, faith in growth has diminished greatly, and the dominant neoliberal idea is that poorly constructed growth can do more harm than good. Poor construction includes excessive public versus private financing and inadequate academic rigor. "Cost recovery" through tuition and other measures, a concept rarely promoted in the golden age (though at least implicitly consistent with other goals), is sometimes prominent in donor policy in a neoliberal age. Donors today may continue just to stand aside from unwise growth, but they sometimes condition their assistance on avoidance of that growth.

Perhaps the most fundamental though inexact shift in assistance is that the university has been pushed off center stage. One meaning of this statement is that the university is no longer so dominant in conceptions of the role of higher education. Whereas assistance was already on the side of diversification that would end the university monopoly or near monopoly, today radically changing the balance is a major explicit assistance goal, and there is an acerbic component to the side of reducing the university presence. Yet the shift is far more basic than that, for diminishing the university is diminishing the claim to something ambitious, transcendent, and in a sense above the mundane. Technical institutes, short-cycle institutions, and the like lack that grand, uplifting claim. So the broadest shift after the golden age was away from the crowning of the university as central to internationally promoted national development. Both modernization theory and the philanthropic ideal type endorsed—heartily—a deeply held view within the university itself: the university has a vital leadership role to play in national development. The golden age of assistance was a golden age for this view.

Dashed hopes produced a strong rejection of the view in the immediate aftermath of the golden age. Then, in the mid-1980s and accelerating since has come a third-stage position between enthusiastic faith and rejection.[29] Compared with the strongest rejection, this middle position reasserts the importance of higher education to development. But even this revival does not approach the assumptions of the golden age. The reassertion is that higher education has *an* important role to play (or important roles), not that it plays a special towering role. And the new role is not primarily leadership. Although it is always a mix, the golden age university was asked in many ways to blaze trails whereas neoliberal assistance implores the university to fit in (Levy 1998). What it basically has to fit into is overall political-economic development policy. Insistence on tight alignment between higher education and economic policy is stronger today than in the past.

Although the goal of university development always was based on the implicit idea that it would foster wider development, now the demand is that higher education be assisted only where there is a plausible, strong, explicit claim of how that assistance translates into the wider development. The university is not the target if other institutions, higher educational or not, can do the job better.

All this ties into the international rage for accountability. The value of higher education depends on how it serves. And this service should be demonstrated through evaluation, not assumed through faith in the university role. Compared to before, assistance now makes autonomy, like interinstitutional differentiation and privatization, a more central and explicit goal, but it conditions the autonomy much more on demonstrated accountability. The new contract (Dill 1998; Neave 1998) in domestic governments' funding of higher education (institutions get increased autonomy but need to perform on government criteria to get rewarded) is applicable to relationships between international agencies and higher education as well. Putting ongoing accountability at center stage cuts against the philanthropic notion of front-end control followed by autonomy and self-sustained development.

Associated with accountability is a great emphasis on matters of financial policy. Again what stands out today had certain counterparts in the golden age; for example, chapter 4 considered finance as an element of management connected with institutional centralization. Now, however, there is much greater emphasis on financial efficiency, especially in achieving higher education's service roles. Moreover, there is greater emphasis on the idea that finance must be reformed for higher education to be worthy of assistance and play its roles. Without proper financial and other management, adequate overall performance is impossible. Here, too, we see a contrast with the earlier philanthropic idea that problems could be bypassed in the hope that assistance would nonetheless work at targets and that the targets would then stimulate further change.

In fact, for some after the golden age, financial policy became the new lever of faith: reform it and higher education will perform well. Rational incentive structures that reward desirable behavior and impose penalties for undesirable behavior should lead to sound decisions about who gets what kind of higher education, where, at what cost, assumed by whom, in what fields of study, with how much of what kind of research, graduate education, full-time staff, and so forth. Strengthened institutions, forced to accountability, will improve performance or lose out; competition for funds will also drive healthy diversification.

A striking point is how much this financial focus of the newer agenda substituted for the academic focus of the golden era. Of course, there was a financial and management concern before and an academic concern now, but with marked shifts in the balance and leadership role. It is unclear whether the neoliberal approach fails to make academics the bottom-line concern or it relies on the financial reform to achieve it. Much less attention is now paid to the content and structure of academic activities (Buchert and King 1995: 36).

An emphasis on differences between the contemporary and the golden age agenda suggests a sense of abandonment, but many changes have been matters of degree and emphasis. Moreover, there is often a striking continuity—or revival—of ideas that donors championed in the golden age. And in many instances these ideas have gained wider acceptance within Latin America than they previously enjoyed.[30] Often they were not beaten as ideas, even though their conversion into practice was thwarted. Support for most ideas about academic work and many about academic and administrative centralization has far surpassed implementation. Examples regarding academic work and structure include more full-time professors, interactive teaching, formal graduate studies, basic and applied research, disciplinary development, work-related studies, unity of advanced teaching and research, curricula flexibility, common credit systems, postponed specialization, departments, campuswide libraries and laboratories, and incentives for outstanding academic performance. Concentrating more than others on ideas, foundations probably had the greatest impact on ideas, but most donors promoted similar and complementary ideas. Sometimes ideas entered through prismatic routes, as when norms of performance-based competition for extra finance took hold in research centers sitting alongside faculties or outside universities altogether.

Matters like performance-based competition show also that ideas that still meet great opposition within universities enjoy increased support there and promotion by government as well as international agencies. Although basic national subsidies usually remain tied to standardized rules, proliferating special agencies are much more discriminating. They combine centrally set priorities with peer review, performance indicators, or the like. Most countries have special agencies and funds to reward outstanding researchers. Some have the equivalent for graduate programs, and a few have similar setups for improvements of first-degree education. More than for central education ministries, though less than for donors, there is a voluntary component to their role. They have had considerable success parallel to that of donors in matters like promoting, facilitating, and accelerating change, altering balances of power between reformers and others, and basically contributing to the system's points of strength. They also have been limited as far as transforming overall systems. Perceptive evaluations of their roles and activities bring us back to the voluntary dilemma of how to use selective, careful means to achieve extensive change (Comité Internacional de Seguimiento 1998).

In many instances ideas previously overwhelmed by negative contexts reemerge or gain ground when the contexts become more favorable.[31] Ideas from the golden age remained alive in the hearts and minds of reformers who lacked the strength to make changes. Changes in contexts showed that the ideas could still be dormant or delayed models. Democratization with more open economies, active private sectors, and private-public collaboration provides a context more hospitable than in the past for major elements of the U.S. university model.[32] The globalization of U.S. norms represents a grand diffusion and large degree of acceptance. Even Europe is heavily influenced. Its "Bologna" process, for example, moves toward a broad undergraduate rather than professional school outlook. The U.S. model becomes more dominant than ever before. In the realm of ideas, it has at least for now largely triumphed.[33]

Of course, our sketchy consideration of the current period is mostly for the purposes of drawing broad contrasts to the grand historical period we have scrutinized much more closely. The impacts of past assistance policy on contemporary higher education remain mostly impossible to prove, but the bulk of the evidence—judged by our evaluative criteria—is rather positive. About donor goals and especially efforts in the golden age, our conclusions are more definitive. Implicit goals were grandiose whereas explicit project goals were much more prudently limited, yet still mostly worthwhile and ambitious. Donors' efforts matched up strikingly well with the means elaborated in the philanthropic ideal type of change. Useful to help us understand and evaluate goals and results, the ideal type has proven most suited for our mapping and analysis of the extraordinary efforts made by donors with their Latin American reform partners in the golden age of university assistance.

Detailed Table of Contents

Appendix A. GDP Price Multiplier

Year	Implicit Price Deflator (2001 = 1.00)	Multiplier	Year	Implicit Price Deflator (2001 = 1.00)	Multiplier
2001	1.00	1.00	1980	0.52	1.92
2000	0.98	1.02	1979	0.48	2.09
1999	0.96	1.05	1978	0.44	2.27
1998	0.94	1.06	1977	0.41	2.43
1997	0.93	1.07	1976	0.39	2.59
1996	0.91	1.09	1975	0.37	2.73
1995	0.90	1.12	1974	0.33	2.99
1994	0.88	1.14	1973	0.31	3.26
1993	0.86	1.16	1972	0.29	3.44
1992	0.84	1.19	1971	0.28	3.59
1991	0.82	1.22	1970	0.27	3.77
1990	0.79	1.26	1969	0.25	3.97
1989	0.76	1.31	1968	0.24	4.16
1988	0.73	1.36	1967	0.23	4.34
1987	0.71	1.41	1966	0.22	4.47
1986	0.69	1.45	1965	0.22	4.60
1985	0.67	1.48	1964	0.21	4.69
1984	0.65	1.53	1963	0.21	4.76
1983	0.63	1.59	1962	0.21	4.81
1982	0.61	1.65	1961	0.21	4.88
1981	0.57	1.75	1960	0.20	4.93

Source: Calculated from the GDP deflator series produced by the U.S. Department of Commerce, Bureau of Economic Analysis, in its National Income and Product Accounts Tables, available from the department's Web site: http://www.bea.doc.gov/.

Note: The price multiplier is provided to give a sense of the magnitude of allocations from different years. For example, a USAID expenditure of $10 million in 1965 would represent the equivalent of about $46 million in 2001 prices. The text (including tables and appendixes) reports actual dollar amounts, unless indicated otherwise. Wherever possible, however, the text uses percentages, as in funds to different fields of study, thus avoiding the problems of comparing dollar amounts over time.

Price indexes compare expenditures for a fixed basket of goods and services in each year. Since the basket of goods and services is fixed, differences in expenditure derive from differences in prices. The index sets these differences relative to a base year. For the base year, the price index is 100. There are a number of price indices and various assumptions underlying their calculations. The price index used to express gross domestic product (GDP) in terms of the base year—called the GDP deflator—is generally regarded as a good measure of general inflation. It is based on the basket of goods and services in the entire economy.

The calculations do not yield exact equivalents of allocations. One reason is that the index relies on comparisons for a basket of goods and services that do not correspond fully with the items covered by donor assistance. Another reason is that the calculations do not take into account the "purchasing power" made available to a receiving country. For such comparisons, adjustments would have to reflect differences in price levels between the United States and that country. See "Purchasing Power Parities and Derived Indices for All OECD Countries," from *Main Economic Indicators,* published monthly by the OECD on its Web site: http://www.oecd.org/EN/document/0,,EN-document-0-nodirectorate-no-1–9066–0,00.html

Appendix B. Interviews

Accame, Ferruccio. 11/2/88, Washington, D.C.

Aguilar, Teresa. 8/25/88, San José.

Albornoz, Orlando. 5/3/91, Caracas, 11/18/94, Washington, D.C.

Aldana, Eduardo. (1) 7/1/91, Kuala Lumpur, (2) 9/19/94, Bogotá, (3) 4/10/2000, Bogotá.

Allard, Raúl. (1) 12/4/86, Santiago, (2) 5/30/89, Santiago.

Allende, Jorge. 5/31/89, Santiago.

Apablaza, Víctor. 4/13/89, Santiago.

Aroni, Fernando. 8/23/88, San José.

Arregui, Patricia. 5/24/89, Lima.

Ayres, Robert. 5/6/87, Washington, D.C.

Balán, Jorge. 5/12/89, Buenos Aires.

Barbosa, Ruy. 6/6/89, Santiago.

Barnés, Dorotea. 2/22/89, Mexico City.

Barquín, Miguel. 6/11/87, Mexico City.

Betts, Ardith. (1) 5/26/87, (2) 3/7/88, (3) 8/10/88, all by telephone.

Black, Joseph. (1) 2/16/88, (2) 7/15/88, both by telephone.

Bloom, Ron. 8/29/88, Albany.

Bloomfield, Steven. (1) 10/27/86, Cambridge, Mass., (2) 8/31/87 Cambridge, (3) 11/18/87 telephone, (4) 11/16/88 Cambridge.

Boyer, Ernest. 8/2/84, Bellagio.

Briones, Guillermo. 4/5/89, Santiago.

Brunner, José Joaquín. (1) 3/10/89, (2) 4/3/89, both in Santiago.

Bryant, Peter. 2/29/88, by telephone.

Cano Valle, Fernando. 2/20/89, Mexico City.

Cano, Daniel. (1) 5/4/89, (2) 5/6/89, both in Buenos Aires.

Carmichael, William. 12/16/87, New York.

Cavarozzi, Marcelo. 5/9/89, Buenos Aires.

Chinchilla, Guillermo. 8/25/88, San José.

Colonia, Nicanor. 5/24/89, Lima.

Correa, Jorge. 3/23/89, Santiago.

Cotler, Julio. 5/23/89, Lima.

Croxatto, Horacio. 3/22/89, Santiago.

Cueto, Marcos. 3/12/91, New York.

Cuneo, Andrés. 4/3/89, Santiago.

Davidson, Ralph. 2/8/88, telephone.

D'Etigny, Enrique. (1) 12/3/86, (2) 3/17/89, (3) 6/15/89, all in Santiago.

Díaz, Heliodoro. 2/25/89, Chapingo, Mexico.

Donnelly, Thomas. 8/18/88, San José.
Drysdale, Robert. 11/23/88, Washington, D.C.
Dye, Richard. 1/26/88, New York.
Echeverría, Luis. 2/13/89, Mexico City.
Escobar, Ismael. 6/10/88, Washington, D.C.
Esteva, Luis. 2/2/89, Mexico City.
Estrada, Luis. 8/23/88, San José.
Fischel, Astrid. 8/17/88, San José.
Fortoul, Freddy. 4/27/88, Santiago.
Fraenkel, Peter. 11/17/88, telephone.
Fritz, Paul. 4/18/89, Santiago.
Frondizi, Arturo. 5/2/89, Buenos Aires.
Fuente, Juan Ramón de la. 2/8/89, Mexico City.
Fuentes, Eduardo. 4/24/89, Santiago.
Furth, Dorotea. 8/2/84, Bellagio.
García, Rolando. 2/17/89, Mexico City.
Gheen, William. 9/14/88, telephone.
Godoy, Oscar. 4/25/89, Santiago.
Gómez Millas, Juan. 12/3/86, Santiago.
González, Ignacio. 4/12/89, Concepción.
Grooms, Sally. 6/24/87, Mexico City.
Gullickson, Gail. 5/14/87, Washington, D.C.
Gutiérrez, Miguel. 8/19/88, Heredia, Costa Rica.
Harrison, John. (1) 3/14/88, telephone, (2) 3/20/88, telephone, (3) 10/17/88,
    telephone, (4) 11/3/88, Washington, D.C., (5) 11/28/88, telephone.
Hellman, Ronald. 4/27/87, New York.
Himes, James. 3/7/88, New York.
Ilchman, Warren. 12/9/87, Albany, N.Y.
Izquierdo, Luis. 6/16/89, Santiago.
Jaksić, Iván. 6/20/89, Santiago.
Kelly de Escobar, Janet. 1/14/92, Caracas.
Kent, Rollin. 6/16/95, Mexico City.
Koth, Marcia. 5/22/89, Lima.
Krasno, Richard. 1/26/88, New York.
Kreimer, Oswaldo. 11/3/88, Washington, D.C.
Krotsch, Carlos. (1) 5/3/89, (2) 11/28/93, (3) 7/7/95, all in Buenos Aires.
Landi, José. (1) 5/2/89, (2) 5/13/89, both in Buenos Aires.
Larraín, Hernán. 3/22/89, Santiago.
Lavados, Iván. (1) 12/4/86, (2) 3/9/89, (3) 4/4/89, (4) 6/8/89, (5) 6/20/89, all
    in Santiago.
Livingston, Duncan. 5/30/89, Santiago.
Lomnitz, Larissa. 2/23/89, Mexico City.
Lungo, Mario. 8/22/88, San José.
Lusk, Howard. 11/21/88, telephone.

Macaya, Gabriel. 8/18/88, San José.
Maier, John. 11/8/88, telephone.
Marrou, Estuardo. 5/23/89, Lima.
Martínez, Carlos. 4/17/89, Santiago.
Masís, José Andrés. 8/18/88, San José.
Mason, Orlando. 11/3/88, Washington, D.C.
Matthews, Donald. 3/7/88, by telephone.
Mayorga, Román. 4/21/87, Washington, D.C.
Mehedff, Nassim. (1) 8/29/86, (2) 6/10/88, both in Washington, D.C.
Meneses, Ernesto. 6/25/87, Mexico City.
Method, Frank. (1) 5/7/87, telephone, (2) 5/15/87, Washington, D.C.
Meyer, Lorenzo. 6/17/87, Mexico City.
Mignone, Emilio. 5/10/89, Buenos Aires.
Miguel, José A. de. 2/12/90, Santo Domingo.
Miguens, José Enrique. 5/9/89, Buenos Aires.
Miller, Alvin. (1) 3/16/1988, (2) 3/22/88, (3) 3/30/88, (4) 6/21/88, (5) 7/5/88,
    all by telephone.
Molina, Fernando. 4/12/89, Santiago.
Mollis, Marcela. (1) 5/7/89, (2) 2/16/93, (3) 7/7/95, all in Buenos Aires.
Montenegro, Sergio. 3/20/89, Santiago.
Moock, Joyce. 4/27/87, New York.
Mundet, Eduardo. 2/15/93, Buenos Aires.
Muñoz, Humberto. 2/18/89, Mexico City.
Murdoch, John. 11/8/88, telephone.
Myers, Robert. (1) 3/24/87, New York, (2) 2/9/89, Mexico City.
Navarro, Juan Carlos. (1) 1/14/92, Caracas, (2) 5/17/93, Caracas, (3)
    11/7/96, Cambridge, Mass.
Nelson, Mary. 3/7/88, Washington, D.C.
Ornelas, Carlos. (1) 12/14/88, Mexico City, (2) 2/2/89, Mexico City, (3)
    2/13/89, Mexico City, (4) 3/6/96, Tampico, Mexico.
Ortiz, Octavio. 5/2/89, Buenos Aires.
Padua, Jorge. 1/14/89, Mexico City.
Paniagua, Carlos. 8/25/88, Santiago.
Perkins, James. 3/24/87, New York.
Piva, Alfio. 8/19/88, San José.
Prawda, Juan. 6/24/87, Mexico City.
Psacharopoulos, George. 5/14/87, Washington, D.C.
Puryear, Jeffrey. 5/22/89, Lima.
Ramírez, Mariano. 8/17/88, San José.
Ratinoff, Luis. 5/15/87, Washington, D.C.
Reséndiz, Daniel. 2/1/89, Mexico City.
Sada, Pablo. 1/14/92, Caracas.
Sánchez M., Julio. (1) 2/17/90, Santo Domingo, (2) 6/10/91, Albany.
Santa Ana, Soledad. 3/25/89, Santiago.

Sarukán, José. 6/16/87, Mexico City.

Scherz-García, Luis. 4/13/89, Santiago.

Schiefelbein, Ernesto. (1) 8/29/86, Washington, D.C., (2) 5/14/87, Washington, D.C., (3) 4/20/89, Santiago.

Schwartzman, Simon. 3/18/88, New Orleans.

Seeley, Clayton. 8/10/88, telephone.

Serrano, Mariana. 8/13/90, Buenos Aires.

Singh, Estela. 3/21/89, Santiago.

Stavenhagen, Rodolfo. 2/14/89, Mexico City.

Stitchkin, David. 5/30/89, Santiago.

Strong, Ned. 12/6/94, Cambridge, Mass.

Sutton, Frank. 1/30/87, New York.

Taquini, Alberto. (1) 5/11/89, Buenos Aires, (2) 4/14/2000, Cambridge, Mass.

Taylor, Samuel. (1) 6/12/87, (2) 2/28/89, both in Mexico City.

Tedesco, Juan Carlos. 3/16/89, Santiago.

Teitelboim, Claudio. 5/17/89, Santiago.

Thayer, William. 5/30/89, Santiago.

Tierney, James. 11/29/88, New York.

Trebat, Tom. 1/30/87, New York.

Turina, Pedro. 11/3/88, Washington, D.C.

Tyler, Lewis. (1) 2/4/88, (2) 12/6/91, (3) 2/22/92, (4) 9/24/93, (5) 2/10/94, (6) 12/6/94, all in Cambridge, Mass.

Urquidi, Víctor. (1) 1/12/89, (2) 1/24/89, both in Mexico City.

Valle, Víctor. 11/3/88, Washington, D.C.

Vargas, Luis. 3/30/89, Santiago.

Vera, Manuel. (1) 11/2/88, Washington, D.C., (2) 11/23/88, by telephone.

Vera Lamperein, Hernán. 5/29/89, Santiago.

Vessuri, Hebe. 5/3/91, Caracas.

Vielle, Jean-Pierre. 2/15/89, Mexico City.

Waissbluth, Mario. 6/20/87, Mexico City.

Wilhelmy, Manfred. 3/7/89, Santiago.

Wolf, Alfred. (1) 9/29/88, (2) 11/3/88, (3) 3/1/92, (4) 6/13/92, all in Washington, D.C.

Yates, Leslie. 4/5/89, Santiago.

Yepes, Ernesto. 5/24/89, Lima.

Zorrilla, Juan Fidel. 2/2/89, Mexico City.

Appendix C. IDB Documents

IDB/E1. "Summary of Evaluations of Secondary Technical-Vocational and University Education Projects." GN-1543. September 1962.

IDB/E3. "Project Performance Review: Program for Expansion and Improvement of Higher Education in Seven Federal Universities (MEC-BID-II)." Loans 305/OC and 459/SF. PPR-13/84. May 1984. Brazil.

IDB/E4. "Evaluación ex-post programa de desarrollo de la Universidad Industrial de Santander." Loan 334/SF-CO. OER-43/85. February 1985. Colombia.

IDB/E5. "Evaluación ex-post Plan de Desarrollo Institucional Universidad Católica Madre y Maestra: Etapas I y II." Loans 300/SF-DR and 478/SF-DR; Technical Cooperation ATP/SF-1115 and ATN/SF-1490. OER-37/84. September 1984. Dominican Republic.

IDB/E7. "Evaluación ex-post del programa de desarrollo académico e institucional de la Universidad Simón Bolívar." Loan 354/SF-VE; Technical Cooperation ATP/SF-1230. OER-35/84. May 1984. Venezuela.

IDB/L1. "Loan to the Government of the Argentine Republic for Re-Equipment of the National Universities." CO-FF/62/P-6. March 14, 1962.

IDB/L8. "Loan to the National Universities of Central America." CO-FF/62/P-26. December 6, 1962.

IDB/L9. "Loan to the University of Chile." (Junior Colleges.) DE-FFD/62/60. November 1, 1962.

IDB/L10. "Loan to the University of Chile." (Public Health.) DE-FFD/64/55. September 21, 1964.

IDB/L11. "Loan to the Universidad Católica." (Physical Sciences and Mathematics.) DE-FFD/64/63. October 9, 1964.

IDB/L12. "Loan to the Universidad de Concepción." (Educational and Social Sciences.) PR-91. October 25, 1965.

IDB/L14. "Préstamo a la Universidad de Chile." (Agronomy.) PR-142. April 15, 1966.

IDB/L15. "Loan to the Universidad Técnica del Estado." (Engineering and Technology.) PR-210. March 15, 1967.

IDB/L16. "Préstamo a la Universidad Austral de Chile: Primera etapa del Programa de Desarrollo de la Universidad para el período 1970–1980." PR-436. August 11, 1970.

IDB/L17. "Préstamo a la Universidad Austral de Chile." Pr-436-A. August 11, 1970.

IDB/L18. "Préstamo a la Universidad Católica de Chile: Primera etapa del

Programa de Desarrollo de la Universidad para el período, 1970–1980." PR-437. August 11, 1970.

IDB/L19. "Préstamo a la Universidad Católica de Chile." PR-437-A. August 11, 1970.

IDB/L20. "Loan to the Universidad Nacional de Colombia." DE-FFD/64/3. January 15, 1964.

IDB/L21. "Loan to the Universidad del Valle." (Colombia.) PR-23-1. June 1, 1965.

IDB/L22. "Loan to the Universidad de Los Andes." (Colombia.) PR-106. December 1, 1965.

IDB/L23. "Loan to the Universidad de Antioquia." Colombia. PR-152. July 5, 1966.

IDB/L24. "Loan to the Universidad Nacional de Colombia." PR-186. November 17, 1966.

IDB/L25. "Loan to the Universidad del Valle." (Colombia.) PR-283. March 22, 1968.

IDB/L26. "Préstamo a la Universidad Industrial de Santander." PR-524-A. July 25, 1972.

IDB/L27. "National Program for Scientific Research and Technological Development." PR-1226-A. October 19, 1982.

IDB/L28. "Higher Level Distance Education Program." PR-1395-A. November 21, 1984.

IDB/L29. "Loan to the University of Costa Rica." PR-213. April 11, 1967.

IDB/L30. "Middle-Management Technical Program: Instituto Tecnológico de Costa Rica." PR-632-A. July 23, 1974.

IDB/L31. "Student Loan Program." PR-754-A. September 3, 1976.

IDB/L32. "Higher Education Program." (Costa Rica.) PR-868-A. March 31, 1978.

IDB/L34. "Loan to Nacional Financiaera, S.A., of Mexico (National Agricultural Center in Chapingo)." DE-FFD/63/56. December 16, 1963.

IDB/L35. "Loan to Enseñanza e Investigación Superior, A.C., for the Instituto Tecnológico y de Estudios Superiores de Monterrey." PR-86. October 5, 1965.

IDB/L41. "Préstamo a la República de Venezuela: Proyecto de Desarrollo Educacional, Universidad Simón Bolivar." PR-545-A. November 14, 1972.

IDB/L42. "Programa de expansión de la Universidad de Los Andes, Mérida, Venezuela." PR-551-A. November 28, 1972.

Appendix D. Federalism's Parallels to Assistance on the Philanthropic Ideal Type

	Tends to Fit the Ideal Type	Tends Not to Fit the Ideal Type
Goals		
To help:	recipient and/or general welfare	giver, to enhance security, popularity, and power
	especially neediest or those most able to do a particular task	those whose favor is curried
To achieve:	big substantive change	limited substantive change
	basic reform; redistribution	noncontroversial development or even just increased satisfaction with status quo
	new policies at local level	
	pluralist innovation	enhanced resources for ongoing local policies
		standardization
Means		
Recipients tend to be:	few compared with potential targets	many or even all potential targets
	distinctive and change-oriented plural laboratories of experimentation	mainstream bureaucracy
		core of the recipient government
	nonprofit or autonomous government bodies that bypass host government core	subordinates, treated disrespectfully
	partners, with professional ties	chosen by political pressures that develop over time for responses to interest groups, entitlements, standardization, objective formulas, or routine refunding
	chosen by federal discretion through merit competition for their capabilities or needs	
	beneficiaries of aid that constitutes a small but pivotal share of local budget	dependent for the bulk of their budget (or marginally involved)

Federal (funder) control through:	indirect means atypical of politically mainstream mechanisms	direct means typical of the political mainstream mechanism
	incentives and strings attached	coercion and regulation
	altered balance of power at recipient site	substantive rule over recipient site
	repeated or sporadic selection of partners and their proposals, with ease of termination	ongoing, detailed supervision
		block grants or general revenue sharing with superior federal authority
	categorical grants, "creative federalism," and clear goals	(or a *lack* of control by funder due to lack of discretionary targeting related to federal laxity, routine refunding, or ambiguous goals)
	(or a *lack* of control by funder due to partnership and mutual agreements)	
Results	achieves ideal type's goals	fails to achieve ideal type's goals, whether or not it achieves its real goals.

Sources: Anton (1989: 157–79), Derthick (1970: 6, 43–70, 93), Kettl (1983: 16–17, 24–42, 180), Peterson, Rabe, and Wong (1986: 5), Pressman and Wildavsky (1984: 60–61, 108–109, 135–39), Reagan and Sanzone (1981: 59–66, 154, 175–76), Salamon (1989: 16), Van Horn (1979).

Appendix E. Data on Three Main Donors: Sources and Coverage

This appendix deals with two interrelated issues in the book's use of data for its three main donors—the Ford Foundation, AID, and the IDB. One issue concerns the *best sources* for our data. The other concerns the data's *coverage,* including uncertainties and particularly the ways in which our data understate total amounts for higher education. Thus, the appendix has six sections, dealing with the best source and then coverage concerns for each of the three donors.

Understatement or underestimation sometimes refers to inability to find reliable data on higher education expenditures. It sometimes refers to circumstances where data are found but judged to deal primarily with something other than higher education or with a combination about which the higher education share cannot be confidently established. Where we choose to exclude such data, the idea is not that the total exclusion is underestimation—or the data would have been included. But there is underestimation because a dichotomy of exclusion-inclusion oversimplifies a reality in which projects may be partly about higher education or lie on an ambiguous gray area yet get left out of our data set as the preference is to understate rather than overstate the numbers in question. If there were a more precise or convincing way to do so, it would be sensible to include a share of the gray area. However much the exclusions lead to underestimation for higher education broadly conceived, they generally do not greatly understate expenditures geared to the development and reform of higher education per se (e.g., university development), the focus of this book.

Additionally, understatement of assistance would come from using figures unadjusted for inflation, but a deflation index is used (see appendix A) and where possible we show expenditures as percentages (e.g., share to private institutions). On the other hand, especially for AID, actual disbursements may be less than the project allocation figures commonly used.

More contexts on the data appear in chapter 2. And considerations about particular points appear wherever they are most pertinent, in chapter text and tables, including tables in other appendixes. This appendix concentrates on general points about data use and coverage that are relevant to much of the book.

Ford Foundation: Use of Sources

The book's main source for Ford Foundation data is Moock (1980), which in turn draws on Ford's computerized printout. This source gives a solid reading on grants to universities through 1979, which covers the main years we study. These data were cross-checked and extended to 1984 by using Ford's annual reports and especially by producing additional, more detailed printouts from the archive's computer. This involved running programs both by inclusive grants to nations, from which the university entries were identified, and by university grants, which could then be disaggregated by nation. The printout shows a plethora of categories beyond "university," though mostly still within at least a broad understanding of higher education, but our main analysis sticks with universities.

A purpose of extending beyond 1979 is to parallel data on other donors. However, as the text in chapter 2 on Ford's retreat notes, few of the 1980–84 grants are really university assistance, even of those given to universities and thus counted here. On the other longitudinal end, Ford's Latin America program began in 1959, but the only university grant awarded that year went to the University of the West Indies, outside the twenty nations we cover. Likewise excluded were later grants to universities in places such as Jamaica and Puerto Rico. It was also necessary to identify projects properly where they were listed ambiguously (e.g., Guatemala's del Valle university on a page labeled Mexico, Jamaica, Puerto Rico, and Costa Rica), to label the recipient institution by its private or public affiliation, and to categorize from the "Purpose" column into our fields of study. CSUCA was placed not under Costa Rica, for its listed location as San José, but under Central America, since it is an organization of the region's national universities; likewise, the Federation of Private Universities of Central America was placed under Central America rather than under Guatemala. The only distinct error found and corrected concerned project FF #740507: Listed by Moock as for Peru's Catholic university, it was in fact for Ecuador's Catholic university as shown by the pertinent annual report (FF 1974: 44, 48), the absence on a separate printout for Peru, and the presence on the printout on Ecuador.

We count projects by the authorization year, which corresponds to the first two digits of the grant number. Since expenditures usually occur over several years, this practice overestimates totals for the starting years and underestimates them for ensuing ones. No feasible alternative exists because grant files do not neatly or consistently break down actual expenditures by year. Moreover, the initial year is a gauge of policymaking intent, since that is when the main decisions were made. Sometimes payments continue even when policy has changed, as in Chile after 1973. But more than for other donors, we can disaggregate Ford data. This is because the data show the years for subprojects. The subprojects reflect the philanthropic tendency to return to its favored targets as well as to retain its own flexible discretion by not committing at one point for too long. The counting of subprojects produces a very high number of undertakings in comparison with cost and in comparison with the other major donors. It thus reinforces the basic philanthropic tendency toward relatively small projects. That tendency would appear still stronger had we not excluded projects under $1,000 in the 1980–84 period (mostly in Brazil).

Ford Foundation: Underestimation

As our data represent Ford's "university" category, they provide a gauge of the foundation's most pertinent efforts for our study but a variable share of Ford's total effort related to higher education. A crosscheck with Ford's annual reports for three years shows that the university category predominates in the golden age, then loses proportional strength, falling from roughly three-fourths to one-fourth of total higher education financial allocations and a much lower percentage of the number of projects (since universities are usually much larger than other recipients of Ford grants). In other words, the Moock data prove consistently good in capturing the university category, but that becomes decreasingly inclusive over time. For 1965, the annual report lists $48.9 million, of which much is payment on earlier grants; new grants appear to reach $12.9 million. The university share is about 64 percent of higher education (including $1.7 million that might reasonably be deleted from the higher education total). For 1974, the university share of $2.2 million compares with a higher education total of around $10 million (or a reasonably lower estimate of about $8 million). For 1979, the university figure falls to about $700,000 of a higher education total of just $3.5 million (or a reasonably lower estimate in the $2 to $3 million range). In addition to the longitudinal variation, data focused on universities cover most of the higher education grants for some nations, not for others.

A truer reading of higher education expenditures would consider at least portions of grants not listed under higher education. Ford has given some funds to Latin American universities through U.S. universities and other entities. The Moock data list these for only three nations. Chile easily leads with over $10 million in four grants including the large University of Chile–California convenio. Mexico and Argentina follow with over $100,000 each in three and two grants, respectively. We do not know how much higher the figures would go beyond these nations, especially in nations where the foundation's ultimate target lies outside the university.

More common were Ford grants to U.S. universities for Latin American studies or grants through the SSRC's Latin American division. Figures show about $120 million, in the peak 1965–67 period, for international studies overall at U.S. universities (Sutton 1984: 140; Frodin 1973: 26). Such funds certainly represented an important share of Ford's Third World assistance to fields like the humanities. Although we want to exclude funds for which Latin America was merely the object of study, much of the money actively supported Latin American higher education. U.S. universities have given tuition waivers and scholarships to Latin American students who were or would be professors, researchers, and administrators back home. They have financed visiting professorships, joint research projects, conferences, and travel, and have donated equipment and books. (Some conferences appear under the university category and thus are included in our count.) Ford has given grants to the main professional scholarly organization of Latin Americanists (Latin American Studies Association) for many purposes that have directly benefited Latin American institutions or their personnel, including travel grants and activities that have supported and protected persecuted scholars. Ford has also given to regional social science associations that have likewise protected and promoted scholarship.

Mostly, inclusive higher education figures would cover direct giving to targets in Latin America other than universities. First, a variety of research, study, training, travel, and other scholarships would come into play. By 1983 and at prices of that year Ford had spent a quarter of a billion dollars for study abroad by 12,000 individuals from the Third World (Myers 1983a: 505) and that excludes several types of scholarships (for undergraduates, within research projects, etc.). The travel and study grant was one type of widespread and influential scholarship listed apart from the university project grants. Ford contracts and consultancies assumed increased significance after the golden age of university development (Levy 1996: 90–133). Indeed, Ford became not just a partner but also the main financial pioneer in the huge university to private research center movement (sometimes paralleled by academically oriented public research centers). Centers were thus a second major category of nonuniversity recipient. Ford was a major funder of centers even in the 1960s, but the centers were fewer and smaller back then. By the 1970s they were far ahead of universities as Ford recipients. Yet the Moock data omit almost all of even those centers that most resemble universities in that they have degree programs (in graduate education, tied to research). El Colegio de México is an exceptional inclusion (totaling $1.6 million, 1959–79), despite the exclusion of parallel places such as Brazil's IUPERJ and Getulio Vargas Foundation. (This juxtaposition means Mexico's share of Ford's assistance is exaggerated.)

Whereas academically oriented private and public research centers could reasonably be considered part of Latin American higher education, the matter is more debatable for a third major nonuniversity recipient that our data also omits: the international research center. In fact, measured by the size of grants, CIMMYT in Mexico and CIAT (International Center on Tropical Agriculture) in Colombia are giant Ford recipients. Yet they are not national organizations. By juridical status and governance, as well as finance, these are international institutions, and their purposes too are regional and international. On the other hand, Ford printout lists them under their host nations, toward which they are especially oriented and from which come much of their staff. The main point here is that our Moock listing excludes such international research centers.

Moreover, fourth, we also omit other regional targets listed in archival printout under the host nation. After the golden age these targets (e.g., CLACSO, organizations of Andean social scientists, etc.) came to receive a major share of Ford's funds. Some, in turn, have passed the funds through to scholars outside the university, but CLACSO includes university as well as nonuniversity units.

Related especially to the institutional omission of international research centers is omission of grants that Ford labels under agriculture rather than under higher education. Ford grants for agriculture in fact often meant agricultural research, including agricultural economics. A good case could be made that a portion ought therefore to be included as higher education. On the other hand, between 1959 and 1978 Ford's Latin America grant money for agriculture totaled only a little more than half that for higher education (Moock 1980: 28). Compared to the agriculture versus higher education figures below on other donors, this suggests that exclusion of agriculture affects our Ford figures less than our AID and IDB figures. Nor, for Ford or the others, does this mean that all agriculture is excluded in our figures; some agriculturally focused grants are categorized by university recipients such as Peru's La Molina university and thus lead to possible underestimation of agriculture. The point is that it depends on how the donor codes the project, and we are left with an underestimation of higher education, certainly in absolute terms.

Although less money is involved, other fields present parallel considerations about underestimation. The "research and education" category generally means research and education plus graduate work in social science. "Population" is mostly research in areas such as reproductive biology. "Development planning and management" is mostly support of research and training centers, some tied to universities. If we placed these categories and "agriculture" under higher education, higher education would account for almost all Ford grants to Latin America until at least the mid-1970s (Ford Foundation 1973: 59–65; Sandberg 1965: 60; Trebat i). Accordingly, one might even justify counting the basic operating costs of the foundation's field offices under higher education.

By the early 1980s, matters become more variegated and ambiguous. For example, research refers decreasingly to basic research and increasingly to applied matters such as employment generation (Ford Foundation 1984: 69–80). Thus, there is less of a higher education sense both by how much less is listed under higher education and by the nature of what is listed elsewhere. Just as data on universities decreasingly encompass a reasonable estimate of the higher education total, so higher education even by a fairly broad understanding decreasingly encompasses Ford grants to Latin America, thus diminishing underestimation of foundation efforts in higher education. But during the golden age Ford was for Latin America largely a higher education foundation, and our data focused on universities understate its higher education support.

AID: Use of Sources

AID data are the least reliable among our three major donors. As AID veterans have lamented, the data come from a variety of sources and often under bewilderingly different labels. Even the number of digits in project numbers varies. (This book cites whatever number is shown on the item consulted.) Appropriation codes are less reliable than project codes. Only since 1974, in response to congressional prompting and rising belief in evaluation and documented accountability, have more orderly data been kept, but of course that date coincides with AID's retreat from higher education. At the extreme, researchers may pursue boxes marked by country into which items have been dropped unsystematically over time. Moreover, AID projects have been internally diversified, certainly more than Ford's, covering several fields, institutions, and purposes, and thus complicating categorization. Our frustrations echo the authors of an intensive retrospective data search on AID for all Third World education, finding "considerable inconsistency" (Method and Shaw 1981: 178) due to different classifications and reporting over time and place, changes in assistance policy and terms, and the very nature of educational assistance, which assumes varied forms and routes.

Two data sets provide most of our AID figures and are the source except where otherwise identified. One is AID's *Completed Projects and Activities,* compiled by AID's Office of Financial Management. The other is the *AID Project History* (PAICHIST), from AID's database, printout by archivist Ardith Betts; this printout includes not only financial data but also task descriptions and evaluations. The two sources basically overlap, at least regarding higher education grants. Since each strives to cover all AID grants, their labeling codes and text were used to identify the relevant projects.

Beyond that, several sources proved helpful for particular points, though not reliable enough to draw on for our composite data. One source was *Congressional Presentations,* starting with more recent years and working back. Especially before 1965, these were erratic, lacking data, showing projects without showing dollar amounts, variously including special volumes on Latin America or wider statistical supplements with requests rather than approved amounts, listing nations in inconsistent order, or changing project names over time. Even for the period covered in the *Congressional Presentations* for 1965–86, the source was not trustworthy enough to add items it showed that are not found in the two main sources. In any case, only six projects were found there that were not otherwise on our composite AID listing; only three of these, two for Paraguay and one regional, showed dollar amounts. Also, even obligated (and certainly "proposed") *Congressional Presentation* dollar amounts might not all be spent and, unlike Ford, AID data would not show us that. The major gain from the *Congressional Presentations* data lies in their sometimes allowing us to disaggregate otherwise more inexact data. The main example is disaggregation by year of large projects listed in the main two sources with just one amount for a long time period; this applied to the country categories of Brazil, Central America, and regional. In a few cases the *Congressional Presentations* allowed inclusion of projects where the financial amount was otherwise missing.

Another source consulted, and ultimately marginalized, was computer printout from AID's Document-Information Service, also provided by archivist Betts (5/26/87), along with a spottier printout of evaluation reports (9/8/87). The service begins in 1974 and provides written summaries of purposes and evaluations. AID archivists ran the search under the higher education code. The result proved informative in many respects but unreliable for compiling a data set, as the archivists cautioned (Betts i-1–3; Nelson i). Even combining the basic printout of projects labeled main purpose higher education but "higher education *very* broadly defined" (archivists' emphasis) with the accompanying supplemental printout of projects ("thrust of project is something else, but some higher education is involved—usually training"), the compilation lacked almost half the projects in our main data set. The compilation is plagued by inconsistencies such as changes over time in project numbers, without identification or explanation. Problems are especially severe because the compilation tries to include all projects in progress in 1974 but lacks so much information on pre-1974. To add projects from this compilation would risk unwitting duplication of projects or parts thereof already included under a different number. Instead, for our main data set, the compilation led to identifying the dollar amount of subsequent parts of long-running Peruvian project AID #5270067, the first subproject of which was already in our set. (As the archivists warned, an additional printout of projects and descriptions for pre-1974 turned out to be very spotty, lacking the majority of grants shown on our main data list, and including many "false drops.") Still, this and AID printout provided by Frank Method and by Matt Seymour show some projects not on our main list, such as AID # 5120122 for Brazil.

A third source that could not be substituted for our main AID database or simply added to it concerns archival printout under the category of "higher agricultural education projects." Several such projects are not on our main AID database. Many of these still showed no financial allocation by 1984. For the period prior to 1970, nine of the twelve entries amounted to under $20,000, which may well mean they did not truly materialize as projects (Miller i-3); one is on our list and another is not a higher education grant. Omissions in agriculture do understate AID's higher education role in El

Salvador, Bolivia, and the Dominican Republic in more recent years, Uruguay in early years, and Peru throughout. But another reason for not including the archival printout for "higher agricultural education projects" is that it differs from the listing of (seventeen) higher agricultural education projects in Morton and Miller (1985: 82–98).

A fourth source we ultimately must use only marginally is an attempt to compile all relevant education projects. A retrospective study attempted "to determine the exact character, magnitude, and distribution" of all AID to Third World education in the 1960s and 1970s, using all available sources and searching project by project (Method and Shaw 1981: 1–3). But one table (169–71) lists only four Latin American higher education projects, all of which were already on our main data list, while another table (207–25) shows an additional five also on that list, plus two (Brazil for training and Uruguay in agriculture) not on that list but found in other auxiliary sources, and just a few more in borderline areas of science and technology (Brazil), public administration (Guatemala), and training (Panama).

Much more consequential for our purposes, since it concentrated on higher education and listed many more pertinent projects, is the study done by veteran AID analyst Alwin Miller (1984: appendix A: 1–12). Miller was the leading authority for identifying AID higher education grants, at least those prior to 1970. However, a major problem for us is that his 1984 compilation ends with 1969. Another problem is that he had to search without benefit of the more centralized data shortly thereafter available to us through printout. If his data were simply to match our other pre-1970 data, there would be no gain. If it would be clear where his data matched other data and where one located assistance that the other missed, then the two lists could profitably and reliably be combined. Unfortunately, uncertainty surrounds grant identity and omissions. The lament may also apply to our main database; for one thing, even AID's attempts at comprehensive listings had to draw on the ad hoc sources available from scattered offices up to that point (Nelson i). Combining our data with Miller's would risk duplication and even further inconsistency. Changes in project numbers over time, even already by the time of Miller's analysis (Miller i-1), and ad hoc filing cause problems for lists compiled years apart. The leading national recipient, Brazil, presents perhaps the greatest problem in this respect. Few of the grants carry the same number on Miller's list and ours. Yet they almost surely cover overlapping ground, as suggested by similarities in the number codes. What appears in one place as one long grant appears in the other as several related grants over time. Miller usually shows fewer and longer inclusive projects. His list and ours show several slightly different starting dates for what may in fact be the same grants. And Miller's list—which thankfully includes a reliability rating of high, medium, and low—places a low reliability rating on the included grants that lack a full project number. Both our list and the Miller list (Miller i-4) might include—each a little differently—some agriculture, public administration, medical, or other projects in which higher education is really a subordinate element or exclude some projects in which it is a substantial element. Where possible we have read project descriptions to aid in these judgments. Then too, Miller's list shows no higher education grant in five countries where our list shows them (Cuba, Dominican Republic, Honduras, Mexico, and "Latin America regional." Additionally, Miller reached for inclusiveness since his purpose was to call attention to targets that could then be evaluated. Our approach was more conservative in deciding what to include. Finally, Miller (i-2) has approved the basic reasoning, decisions, and extensions made for our AID data here.

All that said, Miller's data corroborate our pre-1970 data in most respects. Although his includes only 68 percent of our over $90 million expenditures, the five nations he misses (four plus Latin America regional) show projects equaling just over 70 percent of the difference. Thus, in the nations covered by both Miller and us, the totals are less than 10 percent apart. He shows 110 projects versus our 118, or 98 without the five nations. Although these comparisons could exaggerate the overlap, since each data set lists items not found on the other, some of that discrepancy traces to variability in project numbers and labels. For example, our agricultural economics project of $1.1 million for Argentina, 1963–72, may well subsume Miller's $300,000 for agriculture, 1964–66. Moreover, our data set misses very few large efforts that Miller includes under his high reliability rating (1 rather than 2 or 3); only Brazil and Chile have more than one such project larger than $750,000. And only six Miller projects with the clear 660 higher education code are absent from our list; five of them have Miller's lowest reliability rating, 3.

Moreover, in chapters 3 and 5, we use Miller's data in order to identify AID assistance by institutional type and field of study. His search allowed him to discover these more often than we otherwise could for pre-1970. In fact, cautiously limiting ourselves to projects not on Miller, we add only modestly to his list for that period. And we do not try to extend it beyond 1969. First, too many data uncertainties could arise by crossing that time line. Second, AID came to identify a decreasing percentage of its projects by specific institution or field, and turned to larger, more diffuse assistance to or through institutional consortia.

AID: Uncertainties and Underestimation

Evidently, no source or known combination of sources provides certainty about the number and size of AID higher education projects. Furthermore, additional uncertainties increase the difficulty of estimating totals. Our judgment about what is reliable enough to include leaves many possible projects aside whereas ideally some share would be counted as higher education.

Before tackling the underestimation per se, we should at least note how our data might give a misleadingly low indication about the magnitude of

AID efforts insofar as AID launched several large projects right after our 1984 cut-off year. Many concerned private sector management and development, including a $7 million project in Peru, 1985, another half that large in the following year in Ecuador, and a few in the Dominican Republic. These were potentially dwarfed by scholarship programs for Central Americans, as part of the cold war struggle there. CAPS (Central American Peace Scholarships, AID #5960130) sprang from the Kissinger Commission recommendation with an initial price tag for 1985–93 projected as $148.5 million, soon cut to $97.8 million. In contrast, even with an up tick around the same time, Ford's largest projects generally remained only in the $200,000 range (e.g., El Salvador, Nicaragua, and Peru).

Even for the years under scrutiny, however, an alternative process of estimation of AID's efforts could yield a much higher total. Of an estimated 3.8 billion dollars for Third World education overall in the 1960s and 1970s, over a third comes from programs listed outside education (Method and Shaw 1981: 9). If we elevated our figures by any remotely similar factor, our total for Latin American higher education would rise significantly. It would rise more significantly still were we to use the same Method and Shaw source in a different way. Total AID to Third World education was $2.2 billion for the 1960s and $1.6 billion for the 1970s. Latin America's share was 28 percent for the 1960s and 38 percent for 1971–76, which we might roughly estimate as 35 percent for the decade. That could indicate a Latin American total around $1.176 billion. Since Latin America's higher education to total education ratio is given at 41 percent for 1960–68, one could take 40 percent of the $1.176 billion and get around $470 million, or nearly three times our more conservative listing.

Identification of the components leading to underestimation is no easier to identify than is the magnitude of underestimation. For one thing, some uncertainties may not lead to underestimation. An example concerns grants and loans: they are not distinguished clearly in the sources. AID lists at least one project (Brazil's AID #5120321) alternately as a loan and a grant. However, this problem is not grave because most projects involved grants, and the loans were soft enough to avoid major distortions on that count (Miller i-2; Nelson i).

Another example of ambiguity that does not necessarily mean underestimation concerns the distinction between separate projects and subprojects within the same project. (Subprojects may involve undertakings at different times with different U.S. universities but the same Latin American university as in other subprojects, or it might involve a change in the Latin American university within a project aimed beyond one institution. Subprojects are generally indicated by a number such as 02 or 06 at the end of the basic project number.) Related examples of ambiguity concern separate vs. lumped listings for generally ongoing but renewed, refinanced, or revised undertakings; the same data might appear as one project or several. It is in this vein that we make one major adjustment to the labeling from our two basic data sources. We disaggregate where huge projects would otherwise greatly exaggerate the sums linked to the initial allocation year. Only Brazil, Latin America regional, and Central America had such projects, defined here as greater than ten years in duration and $1.5 million in funds. Otherwise, for example, the data on Brazil would suggest a ridiculous concentration of disbursed funds in the late 1950s. We distribute the data on funds over time either as guided by information provided by AID project documents or evaluation reports, where possible, or just proportionally over the life of the project. (Of course, proportionality could miss the mark, where heavy disbursements come early on or, the other way around, where implementation lags; then too, the common practice of counting projects by their first or approval year obviously exaggerates that year and understates subsequent years). Each entry then counts in our numbering of projects. Thus, AID #5960012, for $4,158,000, 1963–81, counts as three projects of $1,322,000, $1,885,000, and $951,000 for the periods 1960–64, 1965–69, and 1970–74, respectively. Nonetheless, because of reluctance to alter data from our sources except where the need was compelling, we are left with some rather long grants that by themselves would exaggerate the expenditures of early years and underestimate them in the latter years. This is a partial corrective for inflation, which exaggerates the weight of expenditures in recent years over early years.

But if some problems only sometimes produce underestimation, related problems essentially produce underestimation. For example, we exclude potential entries where higher education is a subproject within a larger education or other project, unless the subproject is clearly labeled and accompanied by a financial allocation, which is rare. Archivists' searches yielded useful printout on subprojects (8/10/88) but sometimes with the confounding presentation of dollar amounts alongside each subproject identical to the cost of the total project (e.g., Bolivia #5110082-06, 1973–78, and Colombia #5140165-02). Other subproject listings we could not include were #5200198-02 for Guatemala and #5260018-04 for Paraguay. In the late 1960s, AID started to engage in ample education sector assessments and loans, as in Brazil, Colombia, Panama, and Paraguay (AID 1974), sometimes making it difficult to identify a higher education component to include. Only for two exceptionally large regional projects do we take the luxury of hedging rather than identifying as higher education or not. Thus numbered as projects but included for half their total expenditures were #5980005, Regional Technical Aids Center, 1957–77, for $18,108,000, and #59815995475, Education, Science, and Technology, 1970–76, for $29,473,000.

Further underestimation is likely where we exclude projects that AID archives label as higher education—but without showing a corresponding dollar figure. For example, AID #51015690066 for Human Development in

Argentina aimed mostly at the university, but expenditures cannot be established. The same holds for Bolivian grants #511082 to the Institute of Public Administration and #5110584 for Training.

Consideration of omissions naturally carries us back to our discussion of which AID sources we included, for we therein excluded several potentially auxiliary sources. The post-1974 period could add close to $100 million (and more than that then for 1985 alone) had we included the archivists' category of "higher education very broadly defined." (Another problem with that figure, besides its vague breadth, is that it includes dollar amounts for total projects within which higher education comprises just some unspecified subproject amount.) Reaching further, the archivists' "supplemental" printout for post-1974, labeled "thrust is something other than higher education but higher education included," could add over another $100 million. It would not be difficult with these two sources alone to double the AID totals we show.

Less consequential is the exclusion of projects found ad hoc. Some turned up through scanning of archive shelves, such as #5260095, 1958–72 for $1,215,000, connected to medicine and Paraguay's national university. Those uncovered through reading of outside documents (i.e., not produced by AID or by an analysis of AID) include CSUCA's $325,000 grant. Even the book by Adams and Cumberland (1960) would add little to our total. Some of its entries go to government rather than university, and only thirteen are true projects with contracts and execution. It is unclear which might already be on our list, especially since their entries lack project numbers.

Where we can identify AID expenditure it is often not sufficiently clear that it should be added to our higher education data. The key factor or ambiguity concerns the focus of activity. This factor often relates to an undercounting of nonuniversity institutions not classically considered higher education yet housing related fields and activities that donors targeted. The underestimation parallels some of what was described for Ford.

Only code 660 is sure to designate AID projects as higher education. Yet several other codes in education, public administration, agriculture, and medicine label projects that usually went partly or mostly to higher education, and some funds given to upgrade ministries of education were in effect partly assistance to each level of education. Public administration may be the field that most fits higher education as some projects went to universities and others went to specialized institutes for education and/or research in the field, some of which tried to link up with or emulate universities while others pointedly tried to distance themselves from universities. Project descriptions or evaluations sometimes provided information to help decide but were often not available, and as Miller (i-5) points out, some projects start with a code listing in one field and then shift to another. Because we were conservative about what to include, any overestimation from including projects that are not fully higher education falls short of underestimation from the exclusion of many projects where the higher education component could not be gauged well and of many others where the component was subordinate. Among the consequent exclusions are two in the early 1970s to Peruvian agricultural economics.

Notably omitted from our higher education data count were many projects labeled "training for development" or "leadership"—not to mention all the scholarships given directly to individuals outside the project rubric—that lacked a clear domestic higher education component, though they encompassed study in the United States. (Other AID studies point to the large amounts for "participant training.") An example was a 1984 grant for Costa Rican development training, but the best known and largest examples around that time were the Central American Peace Scholarships. From earlier days another politically controversial training grant was #5130172, 1963–77, providing $1,590,000 to train Chileans for development pursuits via both university and government. That sum alone far surpasses the entire project allocations to Chile included in our data set. So does the $3.4 million listed on loans #513-L-025 and #513-L-030, 1965–66 for regional colleges of Chile's national university. The same source on AID to Chile also lists #5130009, 1955, for $843,000 to economics at the Catholic University of Chile (Fritz 1980). Caution also dictated exclusion of AID grants to for Third World education where the Latin America component was not shown.

Further on the matter of AID for scholarships, data from recipient LASPAU (from Peter Bryant, financial director, 6/21/87) exceed what our AID data show. Our AID data show $5,980,453 for LASPAU, 1966–83. LASPAU income data show $10 million for 1970–74 alone, when virtually all income came from AID. Additionally, AID's contribution for 1975–84 (the data do not cut off in 1983) amounts to roughly a third of LASPAU income, which could mean another $8 million could be involved. Accordingly, AID money for LASPAU could total as much as three times the figure listed by AID.

Grants to individuals account for innumerable expenditures not seen in project form. Thus, while Mexico received no project grants, AID's longtime director (Taylor i-2) there cites frequent small allocations to individuals and places, as conditions seemed to merit. This is another of the general points that relate to underestimation of expenditures by all three major donors.

Among fields of study, science and technology is a major example of what lies on the ambiguous periphery of higher education. Three reasons for this field's importance are (1) it applies to all three major donors—whereas most other fields vary more among the donors; (2) it entails high expenditures; and (3) it applies to both fields and institutions (since it usually involves nonuniversities). It is unclear how much science and technology assistance, which got a push from President Nixon in the early 1970s, finds its way into the AID higher education figures.

But probably the most important example for our study is agriculture.

The reasons are the same three just identified for science and technology, but whereas science and technology surged toward the end of the golden age and afterward, agriculture was prominent during the golden age as well as before and after. As with Ford and the IDB, the omission of international research centers is crucial. Grants to places like CIAT do not make our list. We do include AID projects labeled "agricultural research" and "agricultural education," as long as we can see the higher education component, but we exclude the category of "agriculture" and that of "agricultural research and extension."

A review of AID grants worldwide to agricultural higher education suggests the possible magnitudes in question (Morton and Miller 1985: 8–12, 16–17, 22–23, 82–98). For Latin America, 1971–84, it shows some forty projects totaling about $275 million, of which our list includes only four at $4.5 million (and soon after that several additional large projects ensued, including some $26 million for EARTH in Costa Rica). Just three small nations—El Salvador, Bolivia, and the Dominican Republic—comprise over half the total (and 70 percent with Peru), so omission of all these agricultural grants (as well as most to Peru) leaves us with an arguably very low estimate for these nations. For the pre-1970 period, the review shows perhaps eighteen projects at $24.4 million, of which our data set may not include more than five at $5.2 million. Here again omissions may heavily underestimate a particular nation. Two Uruguayan grants at $3.2 million dwarf all other AID to that nation's higher education over the years. Obviously, to the extent that the Morton and Miller (1985) review covers higher education terrain, our pre-1970 omissions are major, our later omissions more so.

In fact, the weight of these figures for agricultural higher education is one reason to resist adding them in, however troubling the omissions and however useful the Morton and Miller (1985) volume is for its own purposes and as a separate source of information for us. They would overwhelm the data set, obscuring otherwise notable patterns. This could be justified only if they definitely belonged. But most of the objections about the Miller (1984) data and their possible addition to our numbers hold here. Thus, at least pre-1970, our set may have some of the grants listed differently in the Morton and Miller (1985) study. For example, its #512094 of $965,000 to Brazil's University of Sao Paulo for 1964–66 may be part of our #512110094 of $20.2 million for Brazil's Agricultural Education for 1963–78, of which we estimated $8.2 million for the early 1960s. Moreover, only five of the pre-1970 grants carry the authors' high confidence rating. None of their later grants does. Many lack some basic identification, such as project number. And the entries are not entirely consistent in the separate listings within the same volume. As Miller confirms, the authors include grants that go in some part to universities, but many of the grants go elsewhere as well, sometimes predominantly. The large grants listed for Uruguay and Peru, for example, may be only partially higher education and the latter may well involve double counts (Miller i-5, i-2). Thus, Dominican Republic project #5170160, Agricultural Sector Training for 1983–90, is listed in the Morton and Miller study (and the AID archival printout) as a $10 million grant, but a separate study of the higher education institution listed shows much more modest figures and in categories hard to reconcile with basic allocation into a higher education category (Hansen, Antonini, and Strasma 1988: x). In fact, the 1970s Morton and Miller figures are generally suspect regarding higher education, since AID turned toward the "poorest of the poor" and production-oriented efforts outside higher education. Miller (i-5) agrees that the Morton and Miller items not on my data set should be left off, though noted on the side.

Projects like those listed in Morton and Miller (1985) often include a good deal of money that goes to institutions outside Latin American higher education. This prominently includes government, as with #512094 in Brazil. It includes vocational or secondary education. And of course it includes the partner U.S. universities (Purdue, Ohio State, Michigan State, Texas A & M, California Polytechnic Institute, New Mexico State, Montana State College, North Carolina State, Iowa State, Colorado State, and the universities of Nebraska, Kentucky, Tennessee, Arkansas, Pennsylvania, Idaho, and Arizona). Virtually all AID project money for personnel services, as opposed to commodities, passed through U.S. universities (Miller i-2).

IDB: Use of Sources

Consideration of IDB data can be much briefer for two reasons. One is that many factors common to the IDB and other donors have already been discussed in the prior sections (e.g., the link between agriculture and higher education expenditures).

The second reason is that the IDB data are presented in much clearer form than the AID data (slightly clearer than the Ford data). Certainly they are much more reliable. The IDB data source is centralized, so different reports do not contradict one another. We use two of these reports, which mostly duplicate each other. The first is merely a six-page compilation of data (IDB n.d.). It shows by year each loan number, recipient, date approved, amount, and whether it is for primary, secondary, vocational, higher education, student credit (loans), science and technology, or other. The second report comes in multiple tables attached to a more general report (IDB 1985). It also shows the loan number, recipient, date approved, and amount, but adds three items: the category of agricultural research and extension (while omitting student loans), a brief blurb on project purpose (which allows us to identify the project's field), and the local and other contributions besides the IDB's.

The two basic data sources give the same figures where they overlap for both higher education and science and technology. Slight differences in project count stem from different listings on subprojects. Additionally, IDB (1985) lists $7 million for higher education for two regional projects whereas IDB (n.d.) lists only one such project at $5 million; we deleted the amounts in question for the ambiguity they raise and the small amounts involved to the only recipient that is not a single nation. The key issue then is not which of the two sources to use—we work from the first source, using the second for the additional information it offers—but which of their mutually displayed categories to include. Although again no single correct answer exists, analysis of projects as well as data suggested inclusion of most of what the IDB labels higher education, student loans, and science and technology, but not agriculture. Mainly, rather than a preoccupation with producing one total figure, which could never be definitive, the approach here is to delineate what is in and out and how things would change with different inclusions and deletions.

Whereas the statistical data come from the two very overlapping sources, much more detail and description comes from many other IDB documents. These include several evaluation reports and they include many individual project reports all from Brazil, Chile, Colombia, Costa Rica, and Mexico as well as others. See appendix C for a listing of those cited in this book.

IDB: Underestimation

As with Ford and AID, for the IDB, too, on balance we probably underestimate higher education. This is because data again exclude a good deal of training, individual scholarships, contracts, and consultancies. It is also because the case to include the agriculture we omit is stronger than the case to delete the science and technology we include. Student loans definitely belong but constitute only $17,400 million, covering only three small nations led by Honduras. Agriculture, at $382,026,000, in twelve nations, is really "agricultural research and extension." In other words, the category already leaves aside most IDB loans for agricultural production and the like. This delineation allows one to reach a more reliable estimate of a higher education component (whether or not one ultimately chooses to include it under higher education) than for Ford and especially AID on agriculture. The research end could merit incorporation into a higher education listing, while the extension portion would be more debatable. Our basic exclusion of research and extension is consequential for the period starting in 1975, which accounts for nine-tenths of such expenditures for 1962–84 overall. As with AID, the exclusion also affects mostly a few nations. Peru (which gets 20.9 percent of this sum) and Brazil lead the way among the twelve recipient nations, with Argentina, Venezuela, Ecuador, Guatemala, El Salvador, Bolivia, Honduras, Paraguay, and Costa Rica (and Jamaica) following. Argentina and Venezuela show how an inclusive definition of higher education blurs our list of marginalized nations (elaborated in chapter 2); the blurring also occurs because Chile, Colombia, and Costa Rica would become slightly less prominent were agricultural research and extension included in our data. The delineation of targeted versus other countries works best for projects that are most clearly directed to higher education.

Unlike the agricultural research and extension category, the science and technology category is listed by the IDB under education. From there, it seems appropriate to say that the "education" category it shows is higher education. As shown in chapter 3, the pertinent project reports help delineate what parts of these loans include universities. A problem is that some are handled by universities that, however, are not the exclusive ultimate targets while some are handled by other entities that ultimately use them at universities. Beyond that, we would not want to rule that only university money qualifies as higher education money. Although some of the nonuniversity funds are for rather applied research, some are for more basic research, and of course applied research is not alien to higher education.

The science and technology amount in question, $361,900,000, is similar to the agricultural sum just considered. It is moderately lower than the conventional higher education total of $508,032,000, which can be augmented by the $17,400,000 in higher education loans, all together giving our higher education total of $887,332,000, 1962–84. But critical is that the science and technology sum is dwarfed by conventional higher education funds until the mid-1970s and then exceeds them. Even more than the agricultural sum, it is concentrated in a few nations. Four large nations—Brazil, Mexico, Argentina, and Colombia—account for the total, reflecting the view that smaller nations could not do much in this field; the presence of Mexico and Argentina again shows how the marginalized nation profile blurs as one moves toward broad definitions of higher education, but this presence is included in our aggregate data, which nonetheless allow the distinctions between less and more targeted nations. As far as student loans, there are only five projects, to just three nations, and they total a mere $3.5 million, with much going to small Caribbean nations outside our study.

One ambiguity is central to the IDB data, compared with the Ford or AID data: To what extent can loans be considered to reflect allocation policy? This question relates to the bank's status as a multilateral membership organization. (It relates also to the OAS and its higher education projects.) With a mix of pride in IDB's "responsiveness" and frustration over the implications for IDB-directed reform, IDB officials over the years have emphasized the organization's member-state nature. If nations are just borrowing from themselves or according to a quota that allows them a share of bank expenditures, then it becomes difficult to treat as IDB decisions the allocation of loans (e.g., to "selected" targets). Nations are the most obvious targets thus thrown into question, and so the question is most pertinent in the latter part of chapter 2. According to this perspective, Mexico, for example, makes its own decision to borrow for agriculture rather than for higher education, while Chile early on asks for a good deal of higher education funding (Waissbluth i). Of course, a nation borrowing for purposes outside higher education may then have its own funds free for greater expenditure on higher education.

Most interviewees (connected with both the IDB and the OAS) qualify this perspective, however, and maintain that IDB higher education funds can largely be seen as allocations made by the IDB to chosen targets. First, the overwhelming U.S. role in funding belies a picture of members drawing on their own funds. The section on the IDB in chapter 2 shows that the soft money used for higher education comes mostly from a special fund over which the United States has great influence and which has not functioned by quota (Vera M. i-1; a contrary view is held by others, such as in personal correspondence from José Landi 2/23/00). Second, even insofar as member nations set the fund's criteria, these criteria take us well beyond a quota system (Wolf i-1). The bank's staff, while perhaps adding its own perspectives, resists proposals that it could not sell to the board. Third, the pertinent independent variable is perhaps not the nation per se but its higher education system. A nation getting its share of IDB loans overall may have an unattractive higher education system. Fourth, usually it is those systems that meet the IDB criteria that actively seek loans. If this detracts a bit from the notion of IDB as decision-making funder, it fits our thematic notion of donors and recipients as partners in cooperative efforts, as highlighted in chapter 2 and throughout the book. The process is interactive. University actors not interested in IDB-style reforms do not look to the IDB, and the IDB does not look to them. The IDB then differs from other donor agencies only by a matter of degree in this respect. Fifth, there is ample reason for some domestic actors to solicit the IDB rather than passively accept what comes their way. An adequate political model suggests that a university will want to solicit even if that means less IDB money for its nation's roads. It also suggests reasons that the host government or other actors, especially reformist ones, might want IDB higher education funds. Compared to funds from domestic government, they may allow more autonomy, efficiency, honest administration, status, and political power (Gheen i). Government agencies that have administered the loans, such as NAFINSA of Mexico's finance ministry, may undermine these tendencies or may welcome them and the escape from higher education politics as usual. Sixth, allocation patterns that overlap those of Ford and AID suggest that the IDB does more than fill quotas and satisfy demands; the IDB is like other "donors." The common listing of marginalized nations (chapter 2) is a salient example. Seventh, more generally, the strong allocation patterns regarding nations, institutions, fields, and other tar-gets—patterns so far from uniform or proportional or random giving—un-dermine the idea that the IDB just responds to claims made upon it with-out its own set of preferences and criteria.

Appendix F. Population of Latin America, 1955–85 (estimated in millions)

	% of Sp. Am.	1955	% of L. Am.	% of Sp. Am.	1960	% of L. Am.	% of Sp. Am.
Argentina	15.8	18.5	10.4	14.8	19.9	9.8	14.3
Bolivia	2.8	3.3	1.9	2.8	3.8	1.9	2.8
Brazil		60.2	33.9		69.7	34.2	
Chile	5.8	6.8	3.8	5.6	7.6	3.7	5.5
Colombia	11.0	13.0	7.3	11.5	15.4	7.6	11.6
Costa Rica	0.9	1.0	0.6	0.9	1.3	0.6	1.0
Cuba	5.3	6.3	3.5	5.2	7.0	3.4	5.0
Dominican Republic	2.2	2.5	1.4	2.3	3.0	1.5	2.3
Ecuador	3.2	3.8	2.1	3.2	4.4	2.1	3.3
El Salvador	1.8	2.1	1.2	1.8	2.5	1.2	1.9
Guatemala	2.8	3.3	1.9	2.9	3.8	1.9	2.8
Haiti	3.2	3.7	2.1	2.7	3.6	1.8	2.5
Honduras	1.4	1.7	0.9	1.4	1.9	0.9	1.4
Mexico	26.0	30.6	17.2	26.8	36.1	17.7	27.5
Nicaragua	1.0	1.2	0.7	1.0	1.4	0.7	1.0
Panama	0.8	0.9	0.5	0.8	1.1	0.5	0.8
Paraguay	1.3	1.6	0.9	1.3	1.8	0.9	1.3
Peru	7.5	8.8	5.0	7.5	10.0	4.9	7.5
Uruguay	2.0	2.4	1.3	1.9	2.5	1.2	1.7
Venezuela	5.2	6.1	3.4	5.5	7.4	3.6	5.6
Total Latin America		177.8	100.0		204.2	100.1	
Total Spanish America	100.0	117.6		99.9	134.4		99.8

Source: UNESCO, Statistical Yearbook, various years.

1965	% of L. Am.	% of Sp. Am.	1975	% of L. Am.	% of Sp. Am.	1985	% of L. Am.
22.2	9.4	12.9	26.0	8.5	12.0	30.6	7.8
4.3	1.8	2.4	4.9	1.6	2.5	6.4	1.6
81.0	34.3		104.9	34.1		135.6	34.7
8.6	3.6	5.0	10.2	3.3	4.7	12.1	3.1
18.0	7.6	11.7	23.6	7.7	11.2	28.6	7.3
1.5	0.6	1.0	2.0	0.6	1.0	2.5	0.6
7.8	3.3	4.6	9.3	3.0	4.0	10.1	2.6
3.5	1.5	2.3	4.7	1.5	2.4	6.2	1.6
5.1	2.1	3.5	7.1	2.3	3.7	9.4	2.4
2.9	1.2	2.0	4.0	1.3	1.9	4.8	1.2
4.4	1.9	3.1	6.2	2.0	3.1	8.0	2.0
3.9	1.7	2.3	4.6	1.5	2.1	5.3	1.3
2.2	0.9	1.5	3.1	1.0	1.7	4.4	1.1
42.7	18.1	29.7	60.2	19.6	30.5	77.9	19.9
1.6	0.7	1.1	2.2	0.7	1.3	3.3	0.8
1.2	0.5	0.8	1.7	0.5	0.9	2.2	0.6
2.0	0.9	1.3	2.7	0.9	1.4	3.7	0.9
11.7	4.9	7.6	15.5	5.0	7.7	20.0	5.0
2.7	1.1	1.4	2.8	0.9	1.2	3.0	0.8
8.7	3.7	5.9	12.0	3.9	6.8	17.3	4.4
236.0	99.8		307.7	99.9		391.4	99.7
155.0		100.1	202.6		100.1	255.5	

Appendix G. Enrollment in Latin American Higher Education, 1955–85

	% of Sp. Am.	1955	% of L. Am.	% of Sp. Am.	1960	% of L. Am.	% of Sp. Am.
Argentina	45.8	151,127	37.5	38.7	173,935	31.8	35.1
Bolivia	3.1	10,213	2.5	2.8	12,756	2.3	2.4
Brazil	0	73,575	18.2	0	96,732	17.7	
Chile	5.1	16,971	4.2	5.5	24,703	4.5	5.9
Colombia	4	13,284	3.3	5.1	23,013	4.2	6.3
Costa Rica	0.8	2,537	0.6	1	4,703	0.9	1
Cuba	7.4	24,273	6	4.3	19,551	3.6	3.4
Dominican Rep.	0.9	3,016	0.7	0.9	4,241	0.8	0.7
Ecuador	1.8	5,859	1.5	1.9	8,331	1.5	1.8
El Salvador	0.4	1,393	0.3	0.5	2,360	0.4	0.5
Guatemala	1	3,198	0.8	1.2	5,578	1	1.2
Haiti	0.3	887	0.2	0.3	1,220	0.2	0.2
Honduras	0.4	1,459	0.4	0.4	1,674	0.3	0.4
Mexico	14.1	46,605	11.6	17.5	78,599	14.4	19
Nicaragua	0.3	1,048	0.3	0.7	3,182	0.6	0.4
Panama	0.7	2,298	0.6	0.9	4,030	0.7	1
Paraguay	0.7	2,352	0.6	0.8	3,425	0.6	0.8
Peru	6.4	21,029	5.2	8.9	40,263	7.4	11.3
Uruguay	4.4	14,550	3.6	3.4	15,320	2.8	2.6
Venezuela	2.3	7,664	1.9	5.1	23,116	4.2	5.9
Total Latin America		403,338	100.0%		546,732	100.0%	
Total Spanish America (without Brazil)	100.0%	329,763		100.0%	450,000		100.0%

Sources: Levy 1986: 4–5, for 1955–75; for 1985, UNESCO Statistical Yearbook: 1990 (table 3.11), 1991 (table 3.11), 1992 (table 3.12).

[a]1984 figures.

[b]University of San Carlos only.

1965	% of L. Am.	% of Sp. Am.	1975	% of L. Am.	% of Sp. Am.	1985	% of L. Am.
246,680	28.7	25.7	596,736	17.6	18.1	846,145	13.7
16,912	2	1.5	35,364	1	2	95,052	1.5
155,781	18.1		1,072,548	31.6		1,479,397	24
41,801	4.9	6.3	147,049	4.3	4.2	197,437	3.2
44,403	5.2	8.3	192,887	5.7	8.4	391,490	6.4
7,225	0.8	1.4	32,928	1	1.4	63,771	1
23,901	2.8	3	68,882	2	5	235,224	3.8
5,231	0.6	1.8	41,352	1.2	2.6	123,748	2
12,486	1.5	5.9	136,695	4	6	280594[a]	4.6
3,438	0.4	1.2	28,281	0.8	1.5	70,499	1.1
8,593	1	1.2	27,675	0.8	1	48283[b]	0.8
1,705	0.2	0.1	1,607	0	0.1	6,288	0.1
2,542	0.3	0.5	12,096	0.4	0.8	36,620	0.6
133,374	15.5	21.8	506,287	14.9	25.8	1,207,779	19.6
2,729	0.3	0.8	18,282	0.5	0.6	29,001	0.5
7,247	0.8	1	22,581	0.7	1.2	55,303	0.9
5,890	0.7	0.7	17,193	0.5	0.6	30,222	0.5
79,259	9.2	9	210,071	6.2	9.5	443,640	7.2
18,507	2.2	1.4	33,664	1	1.7	78,221	1.3
41,372	4.8	8.4	194,213	5.7	9.5	443,064	7.2
859,076	100.0%		3,396,391	100.0%		6,161,778	100.0%
703,295		100.0%	2,323,843		100.0%	4,682,381	

Appendix H. Ford Foundation Grants to Latin American Universities by Nation, 1959–84[a]

	1959–64	%	1965–69	%	1970–74	%	1975–79	%	1980–84	%	Total	%
Argentina	2,611,765	12.5	935,611	3.5	542,510	2.9	(−35,220[b])	−0.6	0	0	4,054,666	5.5
Bolivia	0	0.0	0	0.0	0	0.0	20,000	0.4	0	0	20,000	0
Brazil	3,749,640	18.0	6,390,641	24.1	6,207,673	33.7	2,516,863	46.2	1,843,801	77.9	20708618	28.1
Chile	4,144,946	19.9	9,721,387	36.7	6,572,658	35.7	224,634	4.1	0	0	20,663,625	28.1
Colombia	3,480,000	16.7	3,044,053	11.5	546,736	3.0	426,371	7.8	80,850	3.4	7,578,010	10.3
Costa Rica	307,200	1.5	591,200	2.2	521,690	2.8	25,973	0.5	90,000	3.8	1,536,063	2.1
Dominican Republic	308,996	1.5	150,760	0.6	(−2,424)	0.0	0	0	0	0	457,332	0.6
Ecuador	0	0.0	0	0.0	75,000	0.4	110,000	2	0	0	185,000	0.3
El Salvador	250,000	1.2	199,740	0.8	0	0.0	5,000	0.1	0	0	454,740	0.6
Guatemala	0	0.0	0	0.0	376,000	2.0	20,000	0.4	0	0	396,000	0.5
Honduras	357,500	1.7	(−41,257)	−0.2	0	0.0	0	0	0	0	316,243	0.4
Mexico	1,920,990	9.2	3,167,848	12.0	1,973,788	10.7	685,756	12.6	99,807	4.2	7,848,189	10.7
Nicaragua	200,000	1.0	0	0.0	0	0.0	0	0	25,000	1.1	225,000	0.3
Peru	1,673,851	8.0	2,098,900	7.9	1,554,324	8.4	892,893	16.4	228,900	9.7	6,448,868	8.8
Venezuela	1,491,000	7.1	233,720	0.9	0	0.0	0	0	0	0	1,724,720	2.3
CA[c]	376,000	1.8	0	0.0	68,000	0.4	554,500	10.2	0	0	998,500	1.4
Total	20,871,888	100.1	26,492,603	100.1	18,435,955	100	5,446,770	100.1	2,368,358	100.1	73,615,574	100

Source: See table 3.1.

a. See appendixes E and O for further details and breakdown for the data.

b. Negative amounts are refunds of previous allocations.

c. Central America and Panama, except for grants to specific nations in Central America as listed in the table; Jamaica, not included in our twenty nations, had thirty-four projects totaling $6,479,981.

Appendix I. AID Assistance by Nation and Year (in thousands of dollars)

Nation	1950–54	1955–59	1960–64	1965–69	1970–74	1975–79	1980–84	Total	% w/o Regional
Argentina	0 0%	380 (1) 3.6%	3786 (8) 12.4%	158 (3) 0.3%	0 0%	0 0%	0 0%	4324 (12) 2.2%	3.1%
Bolivia	0 0%	0 0%	52 (2) 0.2%	70 (1) 0.1%	0 0%	0 0%	0 0%	122 (3) 0.1%	0.1%
Brazil	0 0%	4476 (6) 42.7%	11602 (5) 38.0%	18792 (4) 38.2%	23736 (4) 34.7%	1525 (l) 7.7%	0 0%	60131 (20) 31.2%	43.0%
Chile	0 0%	643 (6) 6.1%	603 (l) 2.0%	16 (l) 0%	0 0%	0 0%	0 0%	1262 (8) 0.7%	0.9%
Colombia	36 (l) 2.1%	476 (1) 4.5%	2025 (2) 6.6%	2731 (1) 5.5%	395 (1) 0.6%	0 0%	0 0%	5663 (6) 2.9%	4.0%
Costa Rica	0 0%	866 (6) 8.3%	352 (2) 1.2%	0 0%	450 (1) 0.7%	4500 (1) 22.8%	0 0%	6168 (10) 3.2%	4.4%
Cuba	0 0%	201 (l) 1.9%	0 0%	0 0%	0 0%	0 0%	0 0%	201 (l) 0.1%	0.1%
Dominican Republic	0 0%	0 0%	0 0%	2233 (2) 4.5%	1750 (1) 2.6%	0 0%	6119 (l) 49.6%	10102 (4) 5.2%	7.2%
Ecuador	924 (2) 53.4%	16 (l) 0.2%	1167 (2) 3.8%	4083 (2) 8.3%	0 0%	0 0%	0 0%	6190 (7) 3.2%	4.4%
El Salvador	0 0%	0 0%	609 (4) 2.0%	0 0%	0 0%	0 0%	0 0%	609 (4) 0.3%	0.4%
Guatemala	1 (2) 0.1%	1002 (2) 9.6%	1354 (2) 4.4%	0 0%	0 0%	0 0%	0 0%	2357 (6) 1.2%	1.7%
Honduras	0 0%	0 0%	0 0%	46 (1) 0.1%	2000 (1) 2.9%	2628 (1) 13.3%	0 0%	4674 (3) 2.4%	3.3%

Appendix I. Continued

Nation	1950–54	1955–59	1960–64	1965–69	1970–74	1975–79	1980–84	Total	% w/o Regional
Mexico	198 (3) 11.4%	144 (1) 1.4%	0 0%	4500 (2) 9.1%	0 0%	0 0%	0 0%	4842 (6) 2.5%	3.5%
Nicaragua	0 0%	35 (2) 0.3%	316 (1) 1.0%	700 (1) 1.4%	0 0%	493 (1) 2.5%	422 (1) 3.4%	1966 (6) 1.0%	1.4%
Panama	0 0%	665 (1) 6.4%	76 (2) 0.2%	1142 (2) 2.3%	0 0%	0 0%	0 0%	1883 (5) 1.0%	1.3%
Paraguay	548 (1) 31.7%	260 (1) 2.5%	0 0%	0 0%	0 0%	0 0%	0 0%	808 (2) 0.4%	0.6%
Peru	24 (1) 1.4%	210 (3) 2.0%	1586 (3) 5.2%	2588 (3) 5.3%	1295 (3) 1.9%	0 0%	0 0%	5703 (13) 3.0%	4.1%
Uruguay	0 0%	0 0%	107 (2) 0.4%	0 0%	0 0%	0 0%	0 0%	107 (2) 0.1%	0.1%
Central America	0 0%	0 0%	2234 (3) 7.3%	3830 (2) 7.8%	7623 (3) 11.1%	3329 (1) 16.9%	5800 (2) 47.0%	22816 (11) 11.9%	16.3%
Regional	0 0%	1098 (2) 10.5%	4663 (5) 15.3%	8338 (4) 16.9%	31152 (5) 45.5%	7272 (1) 36.8%	0 0%	52523 (17) 27.3%	
Total	1731 (10) 100.1%	10472 (34) 100%	30532 (44) 100%	49227 (29) 99.8%	68401 (19) 100%	19747 (6) 100%	12341 (4) 100%	192451b (146) 99.9%	

Sources: AID Office of Financial Management, Completed Project Assistance and Activities, 1985; AID, "AID Project History List," FY 1986, 1987 (printout provided by AID archivist Ardith Betts); Congressional Presentations (various years), used just to ascertain details on dates and amounts not shown in the two main sources. See also appendix E.

[a]Regional = Regional for Latin America.

[b]139,928 without Regional.

Appendix J. IDB Higher Education Allocations, 1962–84 (in thousands of dollars)

	1962–64	%	1965–69	%	1970–74	%	1975–79	%	1980–84	%	Total	%
Argentina	5,000	17	4,800 (2)	5.8			66,000	20.6			75,800 (4)	8.5
Bolivia	325	1.1	2,040 (4)	2.5							2,365 (5)	0.3
Brazil	4,000	13.6	25,000	30.4	32,000	25.8	130,000 (3)	40.5	117,500 (2)	35.5	308,500 (8)	34.8
Chile	4,600 (3)	15.7	13,700 (4)	16.6	1,600 (2)	9.4					29,900 (9)	3.4
Colombia	1,100	3.7	21,100 (5)	25.6	5,900	4.8			65,500 (2)	19.8	93,600	10.5
Costa Rica	765	2.6	1,370	1.7	3,300	2.7	34,800 (2)	10.9			40,235 (5)	4.5
Dominican Republic	900	3.1			3,400	2.7	3,900	1.2	5,400	1.6	13,600 (4)	1.5
Ecuador	1,000 (2)	3.4	1,500	1.8	2,600	2.1			30,400	9.2	35,500 (5)	4.0
El Salvador	675	2.3	2,000	2.4			9,000	2.8			11,675 (3)	1.3
Guatemala	785	2.7			9,300	7.5					10,085 (2)	1.1
Haiti			1,300	1.6							1,300 (1)	0.1

Appendix J. Continued

	1962–64	%	1965–69	%	1970–74	%	1975–79	%	1980–84	%	Total	%
Honduras	350	1.2	2,800	3.4	4,800	3.9	3,000	0.9	7,500	2.3	18,450 (5)	2.1
Mexico	2,500 (2)	8.5	1,000	1.2			60,000 (2)	18.7	50,000	15.1	113,500 (6)	12.8
Nicaragua	350	1.2	250	0.3	10,122 (2)	8.2					10,722 (4)	1.2
Panama			700	0.8	8,300 (2)	6.7	13,900	4.3			22,900 (4)	2.6
Paraguay			1,500	1.8					22,400	6.8	23,900 (2)	2.7
Peru	6,000 (3)	20.4	1,800	2.2							7,800 (4)	0.9
Uruguay									32,500	9.8	32,500 (1)	3.7
Venezuela	1,000	3.4	1,500	1.8	32,500 (2)	26.2					35,000 (4)	3.9
Total	29,350 (21)		82,360 (27)		123,822 (15)		320,600 (12)		331,200 (10)		887,332 (85)	
Percentage	99.9		99.9		100.0		99.9		100.1		99.9	

Source: IDB n.d. See also appendix E.

Note: ( ) = number of projects, where more than one. A few loans counted as single projects had two loan numbers, indicating two parts of one project. This category includes for 1965–69 one loan to Chile, for 1970–74 one to Brazil, for 1975–79 two loans to Brazil, and for 1980–84 two to Brazil and two to Colombia.

Appendix K. LASPAU Scholarships to Latin American Students by Nation and Year

	1965–69	%	1970–74	%	1975–79	%	1980–84	%	Total	%
Argentina	9	1.3	3	0.3	0	0	6	0.8	18	0.6
Bolivia	56	7.9	35	4	44	5.4	13	1.7	148	4.7
Brazil	13	1.8	125	14.3	83	10.1	92	12.3	313	9.9
Chile	17	2.4	44	5	52	6.3	14	1.9	127	4
Colombia	247	35	220	25.1	174	21.2	60	8	701	22.3
Costa Rica	37	5.2	24	2.7	51	6.2	71	9.5	183	5.8
Dominican Republic	21	3	31	3.5	54	6.6	97	13	203	6.4
Ecuador	47	6.7	60	6.8	58	7.1	40	5.4	205	6.5
El Salvador	25	3.5	23	2.6	26	3.2	3	0.4	77	2.4
Guatemala	28	4	9	1	11	1.3	14	1.9	62	2
Haiti	0	0	0	0	5	0.6	24	3.2	29	0.9
Honduras	25	3.5	23	2.6	31	3.8	36	4.8	115	3.7
Mexico	32	4.5	72	8.2	77	9.4	112	15	293	9.3
Nicaragua	26	3.7	16	1.8	35	4.3	26	3.5	103	3.3
Panama	39	5.5	15	1.7	18	2.2	50	6.7	122	3.9
Paraguay	7	1	4	0.5	0	0	18	2.4	29	0.9
Peru	73	10.4	138	15.7	78	9.5	47	6.3	336	10.7
Uruguay	0	0	0	0	0	0	4	0.5	4	0.1
Venezuela	3	0.4	35	4	23	2.8	19	2.5	80	2.5
Total	705	99.8	877	99.8	820	100.0	746	99.8	3148	99.9

Source: Data printout (October 23, 1987) from LASPAU's Steven Bloomfield.

Appendix L. Enrollment in Spanish America: National Universities and Total Systems

	1965			1970			1975		
	National University	Total	%	National University	Total	%	National University	Total	%
Argentina	80,966	246,680	33	89,446	274,634	33	171,897	596,736	29
Bolivia	6,319	16,912	37	9,470	25,595	37	12,969	35,364	37
Chile	23,007	41,801	55	42,058	76,979	55	63,777	147,049	43
Colombia	9,617	44,403	22	13,609	85,560	16	22,724	192,887	12
Costa Rica	5,883	7,225	81	12,347	15,729	78	22,145	32,928	67
Dominican Republic	6,606	5,231	126	13,118	15,377	85	24,464	41,352	59
Ecuador	4,646	12,486	37	10,813	31,824	34	50,502	136,695	37
Guatemala	5,337	8,593	62	12,396	15,284	81	22,821	27,675	82
Honduras	2,217	2,542	87	4,175	4,744	88	10,588	12,086	88
Mexico	74,900	133,374	56	106,038	188,011	56	223,093	506,287	44

Nicaragua	1,317	2,729	48	4,942	9,385	53	6,645	18,282	36
Panama	6,859	7,247	95	7,542	8,159	92	21,338	22,581	94
Peru	14,411	79,259	18	20,669	128,251	16	21,861	210,071	10
Venezuela	22,254	41,372	54	32,466	75,105	43	48,087	194,213	25
Total	264,339	649,854	41	379,089	954,637	40	722,911	2,174,206	33

Sources: Total enrollments from Levy (1986: 4–5). National University figures from Union of Latin American Universities, various years, *Censo Universitario*, Mexico; Higher Education Planning Office, 1980, *Estadística de la educación superior*, San José, Costa Rica, p. 16; Consejo de Rectores, 1978, *Anuario Estadístico*, Santiago, Chile, p. 8; and data from Argentina's Ministry of Education and Culture.

Notes: Some caution is due because national university and total figures sometimes come from different ultimate sources; in one case (Dominican Republic, 1965), the national number exceeds the total. For Bolivia and Guatemala, I estimated the 1970 national figure by using the national/total percentages from 1965 and 1975 along with the total number for 1970. Missing still from the Spanish American data on national/total are Cuba, Uruguay, Haiti, Paraguay, and El Salvador (whereas they appear in our data on assistance). Inclusion of these five small systems would not alter percentages greatly but would increase the national/public and especially the national/private percentages. Finally, the designation "national" applies by convention within the countries; the national has been the largest and, at least into the 1970s, the most important. Our designation is unaffected by the fact that in a few nations many or all public universities are called national in the sense of federal or that in Costa Rica the "National University" was created well after the University of Costa Rica laid irrefutable claim to the crown.

Appendix M. Enrollment in Spanish America: National Universities and Public Sector

	1965			1970			1975		
	National University	Public Sector	%	National University	Public Sector	%	National University	Public Sector	%
Argentina	80,966	226,068	36	89,446	226,871	39	171,897	523,654	33
Bolivia	6,319	16,542	38	9,470	24,841	38	12,969	34,303	38
Chile	23,007	26,355	87	42,058	50,750	83	63,777	96,051	66
Colombia	9,617	25,359	38	13,609	46,618	29	22,724	92,825	24
Costa Rica	5,883	7,225	81	12,347	15,729	78	22,145	32,928	67
Dominican Republic	6,606	4,969	133	13,118	11,846	111	24,464	28,533	86
Ecuador	4,646	12,486	37	10,813	25,141	43	50,502	116,808	43
Guatemala	5,337	7,807	68	12,396	12,532	99	22,821	22,821	100
Honduras	2,217	2,295	97	4,175	4,459	94	10,588	11,361	93
Mexico	74,900	113,540	66	106,038	160,735	66	223,093	430,344	52
Nicaragua	1,317	2,178	60	4,942	5,692	87	6,645	12,066	55
Panama	6,859	7,015	98	7,542	7,553	100	21,338	21,338	100
Peru	14,411	62,746	23	20,669	100,367	21	21,861	141,910	15
Venezuela	22,254	36,296	61	32,466	67,028	48	48,087	175,270	27
Total	264,339	550,881	48	379,089	760,162	50	722,911	1,740,212	42

Sources and Notes: See appendix L.

Appendix N. Enrollment in Latin America: Private Universities and Total Systems

	1965			1970			1975		
	Private	Total	%	Private	Total	%	Private	Total	%
Argentina	20,612	246,680	8.4	47,763	274,634	17.4	73,082	596,736	12.2
Bolivia	370	16,912	2.2	754	25,595	2.9	1,061	35,364	3.0
Brazil	68,194	155,781	43.8	236,760	430,473	55.0	700,571	1,072,548	65.3
Chile	15,446	41,801	37.0	26,229	76,979	34.1	50,996	147,049	34.7
Colombia	19,044	44,403	42.9	38,942	85,560	45.5	100,062	192,887	51.9
Costa Rica	0	7,225	0.0	0	15,729	0.0	0.0	32,928	0.0
Cuba	0	23,901	0.0	0	26,342	0.0	0.0	68,882	0.0
Dominican Republic	262	5,231	5.0	3,531	15,377	23.0	12,819	41,352	31.0
Ecuador	2,243	12,486	18.0	6,683	31,824	21.0	19,887	136,695	14.5
El Salvador	275	3,438	8.0	1,343	5,230	25.7	2,848	28,281	10.1
Guatemala	786	8,593	9.1	2,752	15,284	18.0	4,854	27,675	17.5
Haiti	223	1,705	13.1	150	1,607	9.3	150	1,607	9.3
Honduras	247	2,542	9.7	285	4,744	6.0	725	12,086	6.0
Mexico	19,834	133,374	14.9	27,276	188,011	14.5	75,943	506,287	15.0
Nicaragua	551	2,729	20.2	3,693	9,385	39.4	6,216	18,282	34.0
Panama	232	7,247	3.2	606	8,159	7.4	1,243	22,581	5.5

Appendix N. Continued

	1965			1970			1975		
	Private	Total	%	Private	Total	%	Private	Total	%
Paraguay	11,766	5,890	30.0	2,018	8,150	24.8	5,832	17,153	34.0
Peru	16,513	79,259	20.8	27,884	128,251	21.7	68,161	210,071	32.4
Uruguay	0	18,507	0.0	0	27,157	0.0	0	33,664	0.0
Venezuela	5,076	41,372	12.3	8,077	75,105	10.8	18,943	194,213	9.8
Total	181,674	859,076	20.0	434,746	1,453,596	29.9	1,143,393	3,396,341	33.7
(Spanish America)	113,480	703,295	14.7	197,986	1,023,123	19.4	442,822	2,323,793	19.1

Sources: See appendix L and, for private enrollments, Levy 1986: 4–5.
Note: This table includes data on the small nations not found in appendixes L and M. It also includes Brazil because this table does not require identification of any one national university. Since the Brazil inclusion makes a big difference, totals are shown also for Spanish America.

Appendix O. Ford Foundation Grants to Spanish American Universities by Institutional Type and Nation, 1959–84

	Private	%	Public-Alternative	%	Public-National	%	Total	%
Argentina	1,153,250 (9)	28.4	1,697,770 (11)	41.9	1,203,646 (9)	29.7	4,054,666 (28)	100.0
Bolivia	20,000 (2)	100.0	0 (0)	0.0	0 (0)	0	20,000 (2)	100.0
Chile	7,114,460 (35)	34.4	46,000 (2)	0.2	13,503,165 (30)	65.3	20,663,625 (67)	100.0
Colombia	3,096,545 (25)	40.9	3,445,842 (21)	45.5	1,035,623 (12)	13.7	7,578,010 (58)	100.0
Costa Rica	0 (0)	0.0	0 (0)	0.0	1,536,063 (13)	100	1,536,063 (13)	100.0
Dominican Republic	70,596 (1)	15.4	0 (0)	0.0	386,736 (3)	84.6	457,332 (4)	100.0
Ecuador	185,000 (2)	100.0	0 (0)	0.0	0 (0)	0	185,000 (2)	100.0
El Salvador	5,000 (1)	1.1	0 (0)	0.0	449,740 (2)	98.9	454,740 (3)	100.0
Guatemala	396,000 (6)	100.0	0 (0)	0.0	0 (0)	0	396,000 (6)	100.0
Honduras	0 (0)	0.0	0 (0)	0.0	316,243 (2)	100	316,243 (2)	100.0
Mexico	2,290,584 (20)	38.4	2,258,342 (28)	37.8	1,427,928 (12)	23.9	5,968,854 (60)[a]	100.0
Nicaragua	0 (0)	0.0	25,000 (1)	11.1	200,000 (1)	88.9	225,000 (2)	100.0
Peru	2,809,469 (38)	46.8	2,330,315 (11)	38.8	868,953 (11)	14.5	6,008,737 (60)[a]	100.0
Venezuela	514,720 (2)	29.8	1,010,000 (4)	58.6	200,000 (1)	11.6	1,724,720 (7)	100.0
Central America	110,000 (2)	11.0	0 (0)	0.0	888,500 (10)	89.0	998,500 (12)	100.0
Total	17,765,624 (143)	35.1	10,813,269 (78)	21.4	22,016,597 (106)	43.5	50,587,490 (327)[a]	100.0

Sources and Notes: See table 3.1 and appendixes E and H.

[a]Several Mexican and Peruvian projects had institutional targets outside our three categories, which helps explain why the figure is moderately lower than in table 3.1.

Appendix P. AID to Spanish American Universities by Institutional Type and Nation, 1950–69

	Private	%	Public-Alternative	%	Public-National	%	UNID	%	Total	%
Argentina	999,000 (2)	20.2	2,022,750 (3)	40.9	364,127 (1)	7.4	1,559,000 (8)	31.5	4,944,877 (14)	100
Bolivia	0 (0)	0.0	0 (0)	0.0	709,865 (2)	100.0	0 (0)	0.0	709,865 (2)	100
Chile	1,861,000 (2)	49.3	0 (0)	0.0	1,917,500 (2)	50.7	0 (0)	0.0	3,778,500 (4)	100
Colombia	281,262 (1)	4.1	0 (0)	0.0	581,000 (2)	8.5	5,960,700 (5)	87.4	6,822,962 (8)	100
Costa Rica	0 (0)	0.0	0 (0)	0.0	864,000 (2)	66.0	446,000 (5)	34.1	1,310,000 (7)	100
Cuba	0 (0)	0.0	0 (0)	0.0	201,000 (1)	100.0	0 (0)	0.0	201,000 (1)	100
Dominican Republic	1,641,333 (2)	73.5	0 (0)	0.0	591,667 (0)	26.5	0 (0)	0.0	2,233,000 (2)	100
Ecuador	1,684,750 (2)	27.1	1,165,000 (1)	18.7	2,796,000 (1)	44.9	579,300 (2)	9.3	6,225,050 (6)	100
El Salvador	0 (0)	0.0	0 (0)	0.0	0 (0)	0.0	310,000 (2)	100.0	310,000 (2)	100
Guatemala	0 (0)	0.0	0 (0)	0.0	1,918,000 (3)	77.6	555,000 (3)	22.4	2,473,000 (6)	100
Honduras	0 (0)	0.0	0 (0)	0.0	0 (0)	0.0	46,000 (1)	100.0	46,000 (1)	100
Mexico	2,600,000 (1)	53.7	1,900,000 (1)	39.2	144,000 (1)	3.0	198,000 (3)	4.1	4,842,000 (6)	100
Nicaragua	700,000 (1)	64.3	0 (0)	0.0	0 (0)	0.0	388,000 (3)	35.7	1,088,000 (4)	100
Panama	142,000 (1)	5.2	0 (0)	0.0	1,938,000 (3)	70.3	676,000 (1)	24.5	2,756,000 (5)	100
Paraguay	0 (0)	0.0	0 (0)	0.0	610,000 (3)	34.4	1,163,000 (3)	65.6	1,773,000 (6)	100
Peru	0 (0)	0.0	2,396,536 (2)	46.3	1,000 (1)	0.0	2,780,000 (7)	53.6	5,177,536 (10)	100
Uruguay	0 (0)	0.0	290,000 (1)	21.4	1,065,000 (1)	78.6	0 (0)	0.0	1,355,000 (2)	100
Total	9,909,345 (12)	21.5	7,774,286 (7)	16.9	13,701,159 (23)	29.8	14,661,000 (43)	31.8	46,045,790 (86)[a]	100

Sources and Notes: See table 3.2 and appendix E.

[a]The figure is 1,337,000 less than that shown in table 3.2 because appendix P includes only nations, thus omitting three projects for Central America. Also, unlike table 3.2, appendix P does not count projects listed with no funding.

Appendix Q. IDB Assistance to Latin American Higher Education by Institutional Type and Nation, 1962–84

	Private	Public-Alternative	Public-National	State Umbrella	Total
Argentina	0.0% 0 (0)	0.0% 0 (0)	9.8% 8,800 (2)	0.0% 0(0)	1.7% 8,800 (2)
Bolivia	0.0% 0 (0)	1.1% 1,300 (3)	1.2% 1,065 (2)	0.0% 0(0)	0.5% 2,365 (5)
Brazil	0.0% 0 (0)	0.0% 0 (0)	0.0% 0 (0)	72.4% 174,000 (6)	34.6% 174,000 (6)
Chile	30.9% 16,350 (5)	4.2% 5,000 (2)	9.5% 8,550 (3)	0.0% 0 (0)	5.9% 29,900 (10)
Colombia	1.9% 1,000 (1)	28.1% 33,800 (6)	9.8% 8,800 (2)	0.0% 0 (0)	8.7% 43,600 (9)
Costa Rica	0.0% 0 (0)	2.7% 3,300 (1)	2.4% 2,135 (2)	12.5% 30,000 (1)	7.0% 35,435 (4)
Dominican Republic	24.0% 12,700 (3)	0.0% 0 (0)	1.0% 900 (1)	0.0% 0 (0)	2.7% 13,600 (4)
Ecuador	0.0% 0 (0)	29.2% 35.100 (4)	0.4% 400 (1)	0.0% 0 (0)	7.1% 35,500 (5)
El Salvador	20.8% 11,000 (2)	0.0% 0 (0)	0.8% 675 (1)	0.0% 0 (0)	2.3% 11,675 (3)
Guatemala	17.6% 9,300 (1)	0.0% 0 (0)	0.9% 785 (1)	0.0% 0 (0)	2.0% 10,085 (2)
Haiti	0.0% 0 (0)	0.0% 0 (0)	1.4% 1,300 (1)	0.0% 0 (0)	0.3% 1,300 (1)

Appendix Q. Continued

	Private		Public-Alternative		Public-National		State Umbrella		Total	
Honduras	0 (0)	0.0%	0 (0)	0.0%	3,150 (2)	3.5%	0 (0)	0.0%	3,150 (2)	0.6%
Mexico	1,000 (1)	1.9%	2,100 (1)	1.7%	0 (0)	0.0%	0 (0)	0.0%	3,100 (2)	0.6%
Nicaragua	0 (0)	0.0%	0 (0)	0.0%	10,722 (4)	12.0%	0 (0)	0.0%	10,722 (4)	2.1%
Panama	0 (0)	0.0%	0 (0)	0.0%	6,900 (1)	7.7%	13,900 (1)	5.8%	20,800 (2)	4.1%
Paraguay	0 (0)	0.0%	6,300 (3)	5.2%	1,500 (1)	1.7%	0 (0)	0.0%	7,800 (4)	1.5%
Peru	0 (0)	0.0%	0 (0)	0.0%	1,500 (1)	1.7%	22,400 (1)	9.3%	23,900 (2)	4.7%
Uruguay	0 (0)	0.0%	0 (0)	0.0%	32,500 (1)	36.2%	0 (0)	0.0%	32,500 (1)	6.5%
Venezuela	1,500 (1)	2.8%	33,500 (3)	27.8%	0 (0)	0.0%	0 (0)	0.0%	35,000 (4)	7.0%
Total	52,850 (14)	100.0%	120,400 (23)	100.0%	89,682 (26)	100.0%	240,300 (9)	100.0%	503232 (72)	100%

On sources and notes, see table 3.3 and appendixes E and J.

Appendix R. Assistance by Field of Study in 1960s (in percentages)

	Business	Economics	Other basic social sciences	Law	Humanities	Education	Medical studies	Veterinary studies	Agricultural sciences	Natural sciences	Engineering	Architecture	Misc.	Total[a]
AID	12.0	3.4	2.3	0	0	16.8	0.4	0.6	41.7	3.2	19.6	0	0	100.0
BID	0	0	0	0	0	8.2	9.8	0.7	26.1	24.4	30.9	0	0	100.1
FORD	6.1	17.1	9.7	2.2	3.2	8.5	0	0.4	9.9	30.2	10.0	0	2.8	100.1
FORD-S[b]	0	23.6	8.2	0	4.2	5.8	0	0	18.4	29.9	10.0	0	0	100.3
LASPAU	7.0	7.2	11.9	0	5.4	7.5	0.7	0	5.4	23.3	29.7	1.7	0	99.8

Sources: See table 5.1.

[a]Omits funding outside specific fields. A category of "university development" would otherwise account for 43.8% of IDB's total, 33.9% of Ford's, and 20.4% of AID's.

[b]Includes tiny countries not in our study and omitted from table 5.1 because Myers (1983b: table 27) does not provide a country breakdown by year. But for 1960–80 inclusively those nations received only twenty-eight awards.

Appendix S. Domestic Enrollment by Field of Study, 1955–85

	1955	1960	1965	1970	1975	1980	1985
Natural sciences	4.2%	5.8%	4.7%	5.6%	5.4%	4.6%	6.7%
Agriculture	2.4	3.8	3.8	4.0	3.9	5.0	4.5
Engineering	12.8	15.2	14.4	15.4	16.1	15.7	16.1
Social sciences	13.3	15.8	23.8	22.5	21.5	24.6	26.3
Education	6.5	9.2	11.6	9.4	9.1	19.1	11.7
Humanities	4.2	8.6	8.6	14.0	6.7	3.6	4.7
Fine arts	4.2	5.1	4.6	4.4	2.9	4.0	4.1
Medical studies	26.7	21.1	16.7	13.3	13.5	11.3	10.6
Law	25.5	15.2	9.9	9.2	8.4	8.2	8.9
Not specified	0.2	0.2	1.8	2.1	12.7	3.9	6.4
Total	100.0	100.0	100.0	100.0	100.0	100.0	100.0

Sources: UNESCO *Statistical Yearbook*, various years (Paris: UNESCO); Levy 1986: 268–71, 345–55, for data through 1975 and categorization of fields. The yearbooks include numerous specific notes, such as that a particular country's count in a given field is for one year prior or excludes a particular institution, etc.

Notes

Introduction

1. "Nonmilitary" is qualified by the raging "cold war" and by how the assistance under study can be related, regarding motivation and goals, to simultaneous military assistance.

2. An alternative main title for this book would be *To Export and Import Progress,* and one side cannot be treated well without the other side. The Third World's development would be more externally driven than Western Europe's had been (Riggs 1964: 39), and it would be directed by collaboration between exporters and importers.

3. Our treatment of change sharpens further by concentrating on the international dynamics of development-by-design. "Transfermation" would capture the sense of transformation through transfer.

4. Both *to export progress* and *golden age* evoke the tenor of the time in university and general development assistance in the Americas. As our evidence builds, the words prove reasonable regarding efforts as well as goals, but *golden age* proves exaggerated if extended to results. *Golden age* or *golden era* has been used extensively, including for university development assistance (Eisemon and Kourouma 1994: 276), North-South university linkages (Bastiaens 1997: 10), development of U.S. research universities in the 1960s (Geiger 1993: 198–229), higher education in Europe (Cerych and Sabatier 1986: 224), and the role fields like the economics of education could play in studying and promoting national development (Blaug 1985: 17). The golden age label stands out still more in contrast to an ensuing era of "profound pessimism," far from "the euphoria of the 1960s," as Neave argues for West European higher education (Neave 1995: 387). And the contrast between hope and ensuing disappointment was especially pronounced in the Third World.

5. Phillips (1976b: 123–25). A "synergistic negativism" emerged in attitudes on development, assistance, and higher education (Eisemon and Holm-Nielsen 1995: 6). Donors' disillusionment contributed to abandonment of university development goals (Eisemon and Kourouma 1994). Skepticism likewise grew about how well international university linkage programs worked (Berry 1995: 8). The World Bank's landmark policy paper on higher education cites evaluations highlighting problems in prior giving and inability to obtain institutional and development objectives (World Bank 1994: 93). A bottom-line if indirect and harsh indication of failure, as in the Phillips citation in this endnote, is the sad contemporary status of higher education in developing areas. For Africa, efforts to create "development universities" (1970s) "ultimately had little impact" (Saint 1998: 55–56). For Latin America, too, both agencies and scholars have made mostly negative assessments of the state of higher education (IDB 1997: 5–10). Specifically on assistance, observers interviewed in the late 1980s, a time by which impacts from golden age efforts should have been discernible, assessment was downcast. As one authority put it, "It's the fashion in donor organizations to belittle university assistance," especially that directed through insti-

tutional development projects rather than the narrower efforts, including individual scholarships, that overlapped, preceded, and followed the golden age (Schiefelbein i-2). A veteran AID official reported the agency's general view that its grand efforts in the Latin American university were an overall failure (Taylor i-2). One of the most prominent consultant-scholars of the golden age saw frequent failure in AID projects linked to universities (Waggoner 1972: 186). Indeed, as analyzed in chapter 2, by the mid-1970s all major donors dejectedly and sometimes bitterly turned away from the Third World university, especially in Latin America. A negative tone then lingered, partly through reiteration, partly through lack of challenge. The donor community mostly sees its historic university effort in disillusioned, chastened terms. Also negative is the academic literature (however limited) on assistance to the Latin American university. Probably the most prominent scholar of philanthropic assistance to Latin American universities in the golden age was quite negative; his edited book, *Philanthropy and Cultural Imperialism,* was in the same vein for the Third World overall: "A central thesis is that foundations like Carnegie, Rockefeller, and Ford have a corrosive influence on a democratic society" as powerful yet unregulated actors that strengthen the status quo and the ruling class against "Third World peoples" (Arnove 1980b: 1). Another leading, related critique was Berman (1983). If such views have not been reaffirmed by equally prominent scholarship, neither have they been challenged by it. Finally, a negative view characterizes public opinion regarding foreign assistance, as reflected in polls and media reports. More information on disenchantment appears in chapter 1, on the critique of international assistance generally, and in chapter 2, on donors' retreat in the mid-1970s.

6. It is worth noting two key parallels between our study and an oral history of the Alliance for Progress (Mesmer, Baskind, and Lerdau 1998), and in fact education is one of that study's concerns. First, the lack of study of the Alliance is incredible given that the undertaking was large and filled with optimism. Second, the conventional wisdom is that the effort basically failed whereas the oral history's findings are far more positive than that.

7. See, for example, Hekman (1983: 26–38).

8. On the other hand, we will find examples where critics see elements consistent with the ideal type but denounce them. There the difference between critics and supporters lies in what they emphasize or in conflicting norms of good and bad more than in conflicting empirical information.

9. Useful sources for us on foundations and construction of the ideal type include Ylvisaker (1987), Nielsen (1972), and McCarthy (1984b), as well as Andrews (1956), Bulmer (1999), Cheit and Lobman (1979), Cunningham (1972: 235–56), Fosdick (1952: 279–80), McIlnay (1991: 152–57), O'Connell (1987: 267–79), and Useem (1987). Nonetheless, there is too little literature on private philanthropic foundations, rare creatures internationally (Anheier and Toepler 1999), and on philanthropy generally, which has major international traditions (Ilchman, Katz, and Queen 1998: ix). Concerns from the nonprofit literature that find expression in our ideal type include analyses of private actors on both the donor and recipient side, as well as comparisons between them and public counterparts. And a pivotal link between concerns with philanthropy and nonprofits is our thematic notion of voluntary action. Nonetheless, as a matter of emphasis, this study treats issues of philanthropy more than nonprofits (Levy 1986; 1996).

10. The terms *means* and *efforts* are mostly interchangeable. *Means* refers more

to the ideal type, *efforts* more to actors' actual activities. Additionally, *results* and *impacts* are interchangeable. Both deal with efforts' effects, direct and indirect, intended and unintended.

11. In fact, any definition of philanthropy without these integral goals and means would be quite limited; for example, it might then be any giving, or any giving by an agency legally labeled philanthropic.

12. Ilchman (n.d.); Bremner (1988); O'Neill (1989: 151); McIlnay (1991: 45).

13. In their Alliance for Progress, U.S. policymakers "assumed that somehow economic growth and social reform would facilitate actual promotion of democracy" (Lowenthal 1991: 248); by our reckoning, then, democracy was an implicit goal.

14. Philanthropic altruism often has universalistic aspirations, bringing the world closer together, as by carrying progress to those who lag, though altruism sometimes concentrates on a localized notion of community development. Whereas today a common philanthropic injunction is to "think locally, act globally" (Clark 1991: 204), historical resonance was in a sense to think globally, act locally.

15. See Payton (1988: 47) on religious imperatives slightly weakening an otherwise "comfortable" generalization about philanthropy as voluntary. The idea of voluntary action is so basic to our meaning that we might have substituted an "ideal type of voluntary action" or giving. But that would have left aside much that our ideal type of philanthropic change includes in goals and results that are major, positive, and beyond charity. It would also have left aside associated means such as targeted giving to reform-oriented partners.

16. On democracy: Lowenthal (1991); on importing policy innovation without assistance, Robertson and Waltman (1993); Westney (1987); Rose (1991). Rose indicates how "lesson-drawing" is more than "diffusion," since it involves conscious and voluntary action to substitute concrete programs for a status quo perceived as unsatisfactory; these are useful distinctions, though we will see that they are often difficult to pinpoint in reality. In any event, our disassociation of philanthropy from other forms of transfer is consistent with our notion of reform as something consciously pursued. Where important change emerges as an unanticipated consequence of philanthropy, it is worth noting and can even be positive, as we will find, but does not fit the planning aspect of the philanthropic ideal type.

17. Consider ambiguities concerning government funding. First, the typical government action modeled in nonprofit and other political-economic theories exaggerates policy responsiveness to the "median voter" (Levy 1995: 9). Even democratic governments have decentralized public agencies that lack direct, fixed responsibility to groups that benefit from them, let alone groups that do not. More basically, democracies respond unequally to groups holding unequal power. They also often initiate rather than merely respond. And the more there is a nonaccountable state, the more government is a voluntary actor. Thus, second, a dictatorship may display aspects of a kind of philanthropic state, especially when it benevolently moves beyond charity to development. Attempts to reform "from above" or to "export" progress below share conceptual ground with our subject matter. Examples include autocracies launching modernizing reforms. Autocracies are governments not accountable to the base, competing powers, or fixed law (McDaniel 1991: 6) and thus are rather voluntary actors. Third, as historically many governments were dynastic or patrimonial, they were also rather "private" in their discretion to act (Ilchman, Katz, and Queen 1998: xii). Although Payton (1988: 47–48) inclines to exclude a notion of "state

philanthropy," since the state is giving away other people's money, he notes ambiguities and that his approach would also negate a concept of corporate philanthropy. Additionally, even foundations often give away others' money rather than their personal money. Fourth, exclusion of public sources also seems artificial given the widespread reality of private-public partnership. For example, where private organizations spend money given to them by the government (Smith 1990), the money is often seen as philanthropic; why not the same when governments give through public multilateral agencies?

18. Since multilateral development banks are still banks, and since bilateral assistance agencies must get their funds from their domestic revenues, standards for judging public assistance success can lie outside the philanthropic ideal type. (See appendix E on the IDB as a membership bank.) But we will see overlap in objectives and also the use of "soft" loans. Additionally, the IDB has claimed at least in higher education to be a bank of ideas, while AID's golden age disbursements for higher education usually went through intermediary agencies, mostly universities. And while AID and the IDB sometimes have to "push money out," the same is sometimes true for foundations. Again, our idea is to explore such matters empirically rather than to get locked into rigid definitional distinctions based a priori on assumed funding behavior.

19. Cunningham (1972: 176). As with models in general, a breakdown in one aspect of the ideal type can lead to unraveling elsewhere. If, for example, the impact on targets does not radiate out to the field's mainstream, donors may deviate from tenets such as targeted funding and undertake broader initiatives closer to the mainstream, which could then raise the difficulty and lower the success rate of their projects. We leave such twists and turns for the heart of our analysis.

20. Nielsen (1972: 273–76); Ylvisaker (1987: 370–74); Cheit and Lobman (1979: 8); Commission on Foundations and Private Philanthropy (1970: 117–19); McCarthy (1984a: 85). Renz (1997) documents the persistence of large foundations' tendency to focus on international activities much more than typical foundations do.

21. Among the critics: Lindeman (1988 [1936]); Odendahl (1989); Fisher (1983). See Karl and Katz (1981) on continuity in critiques. Critics often stress donors' imposition, sometimes finding that foundations coordinate their actions in ways that limit options for recipients. Yet other experts on philanthropy have concluded that motivation is so naturally mixed that it is pointless to argue about *the* motivation (Ilchman n.d.: 2). Recent criticism of both philanthropy and assistance has focused less on motivation than on lack of positive impact. For a brief historical overview of debates about the relationship between philanthropy (as well as the nonprofit sector) and the democratic public interest, see Hall (1998).

22. Curti and Nash (1965); McIlnay (1991: 143–46); Cheit and Lobman (1979); Ylvisaker (1987: 371); Levy (1996). Berman (1983: 12) notes that education has been the primary emphasis of organized U.S. philanthropy since its inception.

23. D. Jones (1992). This phenomenon has generally been depicted in positive terms. The university is "perhaps the most successful of all Western concepts in terms of overseas impact" (Altbach 1989: 12). Such positive depiction contrasts with much literature on modern university assistance projects.

24. Orr (1971). Works on education or training that do not concentrate on assistance projects or asymmetrical relationships may nonetheless deal with a broad phenomenon of educational borrowing that overlaps our concerns. Examples include international transfer, reasons for emulation, combinations of direct copying, diffi-

culty, and unintended consequences, and problems of evaluation of hybrid transplants (Finegold, McFarland, and Richardson 1993).

25. On these transfers, see Armytage (1964) and Rabkin (1992: 1049–50).

26. Sánchez (1973: 114); Olivera (1985: 229–32); Fischel (1987: 189).

27. Serrano (1993: 111–15). In the nineteenth and early twentieth centuries, Spanish America's native-born elite—for Brazil did not manage to create a bona fide university until the 1930s—opted for strands of European positivism, intended to invigorate tendencies toward state-led university and national development through the use of scientific knowledge and its objective application, as opposed to tradition, religion, and other nonrational approaches. At least that was the case for what would be the predominant public sector; the Catholic Church had long imported its own institutional models from abroad, although by the early nineteenth century these were generally relegated to a separate private sector (Levy 1986: 28–36; Schwartzman 1992c: 970). Europe also inspired isolated experiments with alternative institutions (such as Argentina's La Plata university, drawing on British ideas) and especially units and practices within institutions (such as German ideas of research institutes).

28. Among the relevant sources are Lanning (1955) and Góngora (1979). Steger (1979: 94–98) calls Latin America's nineteenth-century universities nearly a "province" of France's educational system but proceeds immediately to a section entitled "Latin American Variations on the French model"; he also (p. 88) identifies "heteromorphism" rather than "isomorphous" results.

29. Adiseshiah (1979); Coleman (1965: 362–64); Ribeiro (1968: 22); Stepan (1976); Valdés (1995). U.S. government involvement illustrates the evolution from ad hoc support of cooperative programs; even with stepped up action in 1889 and again in the 1930s, U.S.–Latin American cultural relations remained "almost exclusively" privately inspired until the mid-twentieth century (Espinosa 1976: 29); see also Glick (1957: 3–50).

30. Impact is not necessarily proportional to weight of effort or degree of imposition. Clark (1983: 232) argues that voluntary importing allows for better local adaptation, and Eisemon and Kourouma (1994: 276–77) find that Asia and Africa became more oriented to foreign ideas as dependency declined. On the four dimensions of university transfer see D. Jones (1992); Clark (1983: 227); Rose (1991).

31. Even an outstanding predependency account (Ashby 1964), not unchallenged, stresses Great Britain's dogmatic imposition on Africa of a model alien to local reality and needs. Ashby does, however, include evidence of voluntary elite cooperation and of results resembling what we will later call formalism, where behavior deviates fundamentally from stated policy. French policy went further in contemplating colonial replicas or branches of mother country institutions (Kater 1976: 145).

32. Also notable is how seldom and unsuccessfully Third World countries tried to create any major university model different from that found in the more developed world, a point often taken as evidence of the weight of import over indigenous form (Altbach 1989: 20; Ilchman and Ilchman 1987). Chapter 1 notes the relevance to theories of isomorphism and world systems. Chapters 3–5 show that forms turn out to be more variegated and less cloned than such theories are typically taken to suggest.

33. González (1981: 230). See Huneeus (1973) on Atcon's major impact in Chile. On the other hand, Eduardo Aldana (personal correspondence 8/7/2000) downplays the impact in Colombia (though Atcon was read), emphasizing instead that reform stemmed from Colombians' convictions. A 1961 U.S. congressional report (Giaimo

and Brademas 1961: 1) argued for putting the university into the Alliance for Progress, indeed prioritizing it over other levels of education, because it is "an indispensable key to the economic development and social reform which these nations must have if they are to create democratic societies." The report also characterized the university reality as problem ridden.

34. Again *ideal type* means abstraction or purification of reality, not necessarily a desirable state. One could disfavor the U.S. model or at least its application to Latin America; however, as with the ideal type of philanthropic change, many participants did regard much of the model as desirable for both export and import. Nevertheless, we will find that rarely did reformers seek to export or import the U.S. model fully— and assistance rarely tried to create Latin American universities from scratch.

35. Adams and Cumberland (1960: 95); Atcon (1966: 128); Diégues and Wood (1967: 10); Waggoner (1965: 10).

36. They placed less blame for backwardness on the universities themselves and more on their surrounding domestic and international power structure. Darcy Ribeiro (1968) was such a reformer in Brazil, with influence in sister republics. Others acknowledge how they eschewed U.S. terminology while only slightly altering U.S. forms (Silva and Sonntag 1981: 198–200), a pattern we will see repeatedly in nations that largely rejected direct assistance projects while nonetheless importing ideas and practices (Cano 1985).

37. Daalder and Shils (1982). Indeed, the ascendancy of the United States over European models affected even some former colonies of Europe, though more noticeably Asian nations without colonial pasts. Certain features of the U.S. export model overlapped the British export model (Ashby 1964), as with institutional autonomy, a sort of depoliticization, full-time professors, lay boards, and expanded campuses. But where the British model departed from the U.S. model, it was not the Latin American import model. Examples include an emphasis on pure knowledge over application and relevance and a fairly standardized system quality pursued through selective entrance standards. On the rise of the United States over European models in countries like Brazil, see Castro (1983). An interesting but limited exception, England's Open University, mostly followed the golden age.

38. There is little examination of the shape of assistance within given fields, including education (Valverde 1999: 402). On the lack of work on educational assistance, see Mundy (1998: 448) and Spaulding (1997: 207–13). Also, lack of study on private assistance is particularly harmful in a field like higher education, where special claims and criticisms have been launched about the role of private foundations. On the lack of empirical work on development assistance, see Schraeder, Hook, and Taylor (1998: 296); on private assistance, O'Connell (1987: 282–308); Phillips (1976b: 96); Smith (1990); Thompson et al. (1974). On assistance to Latin America generally, see Lavados and Montenegro (1980: 77); on U.S. philanthropy to Latin America, Cueto (1994); on study abroad, Goodwin and Nacht (1984); on science, Cueto (1991); Schwartzman (1991); Stepan (1976); Vessuri (1984). Related work on technological transfers deals more with multinational corporations than universities (Lavados 1978: 139–40; McIntyre 1986).

39. Method and Shaw (1981); Miller (1984); Myers (1983b); Flora and Flora (1989).

40. Mattocks (1990); Sommer (1977: 81); CIDA (1987: 47); Cassen (1986: 188); Eisemon (1992).

41. Nor can donors' studies usually be expected to have the conceptual or literature framework of scholarly studies or to share all their concerns. This helps explain some scholars' worries about today's dramatic increase in the proportion of donor or donor-funded over independent academic study on assistance and on educational development.

42. Cassen (1986); White (1974); Burnell (1997); Grant and Nijman (1998); Gwin and Nelson (1997); Hook (1996).

43. Lavados i-1. Examples of noneducation studies focused on donors more than recipients include Smith (1990); Lissner (1977); Sommer (1977). On the donor emphasis specifically regarding university assistance, see Bullock (1980: xviii); Berman (1983); Spitzberg (1980); Altbach (1989). Similarly, most literature on cultural reproduction internationally discusses macro-level factors but includes little research on detail and content (Rathberger 1985: 300–301). Ilchman and Ilchman (1987: 49) identify the incredible proliferation of Third World universities in the second half of the twentieth century, and the First World's role therein, as an incredibly understudied chapter in modern world history.

44. On the Rockefeller Foundation in Latin America, Cueto (1994), but on U.S. medical models, not on the university. See also Maxwell on the British University Linkage Program and Coombe on international development programs in higher education (Maxwell 1980; Coombe 1989).

45. Levy (1996). Chapter 4 of that book examines donors' contributions and control, and much of the book analyzes institutions, especially private research centers, that owed much to international philanthropy; however, the book is not mostly about such philanthropy or assistance. On the political role of the centers in Chile, see Puryear (1994). A gripping account of the university rise of Chile's "Chicago boys" concentrates on one institution and only partly on assistance projects (Valdés 1995).

46. U.S. universities like the University of Pittsburgh participated in institutional development programs spanning diverse fields, including higher education (Magnusson 1970:16).

47. Eisemon and Kourouma (1994); Parkinson (1976: 54); Pearson (1969: 180); Phillips (1976b: 94).

48. Coleman (1965: 364); see also Packenham (1973: 196–97).

49. On learning and adapting in assistance policy based on study, see Berg and Gordon (1989); Packenham (1973: 123); Rondinelli (1989). An evaluation loop can help grind down the gap between policy and knowledge, providing lessons or at least insights and leading to improved efforts. Thoughtful donor officials repeatedly lament their agencies' lack of institutional memory. Where agencies conduct studies, these tend to have a short shelf life.

50. Additionally, literatures on university assistance, Latin American studies, and comparative education should be informed by our case. The leading journals in comparative education and especially in Latin American studies have included few studies of university assistance—despite both literatures' successive concern with modernization and dependency and their interest in the interrelationship between developed country influence and Third World domestic change. Latin American studies features, for example, works on the influence of foreign investment on industrialization. Meanwhile, comparative education often generalizes about colonial and postcolonial foreign influences in ways much less relevant to Latin America than Africa and parts of Asia. And the growing literature on comparative higher education still gives scant

attention to development assistance even though such assistance is crucial to key contemporary concerns of that literature, such as reform, finance, autonomy, private-public relationships, institutional diversification, and quality.

51. The original intention was for this book to include a chapter on scholarships and how ex-scholarship holders affect their institutions; space and time precluded that, though some points are interspersed. Indeed, one cannot dichotomously distinguish between separate scholarships and scholarship components within institutional projects (Sutton 1986; i).

52. *University* and *higher education* are much overlapping terms for our study, the former more focused and the latter more inclusive. In many instances there is reason to use one over the other, sometimes pointedly to contrast the terms; in other instances, the terms would be reasonably interchangeable.

53. Most of the field research was done by 1990, and much of the archival and other data used record observations made during and immediately after the golden age. Naturally, impacts can appear before the end of golden age efforts. See the end of the next chapter on the time dimension in evaluating impacts.

54. Kumar (1998). Similarly, the World Bank's evaluation of its higher education work (Eisemon 1992) does not provide much information on the period and geographical subject matter we study. AID evaluations sometimes outdistance development bank evaluations, going beyond the purely technical (Ayres i).

55. IDB rules generally prohibit public access to project evaluations, limited to "official use." The main exception is that recipient nations may grant access. This was a major source for me, rather comprehensively for Brazil, Chile, Colombia, Costa Rica, and Mexico, as well as for particular documents on Argentina, Central America, Paraguay, Uruguay, and Venezuela. Further materials were shared by officials at the Washington headquarters and partners and consultants in the field. Although I avoid certain specific citations and sometimes refer broadly to a group of studies, I also refer to designated numbers on my list of IDB documents, e.g., IDB/L25 (see appendix C). Ford is more permissive, though quotations require authorization. Authorization was also required for access to Ford files closed for fewer than ten years, but when that presented a problem for my archival work, officials usually approved exceptions. I cite Ford Foundation grants only by their overall grant number, e.g., FF #60337; the first two digits specify the initiation year. AID's inferior storage was only partly offset by open access and by the willingness of staff to run requested computer searches for data and to share shelved reports. Where possible, AID reports are cited like Ford's, except that AID's first two digits designate the recipient nation. Ford archivists did repeated computer runs according to the national, institutional, or other specifications I requested.

56. Our eclectic, flexible approach parallels that used in leading works on policy implementation, a parallel topic discussed in chapter 1. See, for example, Williams (1982) on the use of open-ended interviews, ranging from semistructured to spontaneous, conducted with those selected for their knowledge or status, along with site visits built around single or multiple cases, all supported by documentary research. Sources on the methodologies featured in our study include Dexter (1970) on elites and Van Maanen (1983) on qualitative research.

1. Perspectives on Change

1. Our study obviously contributes less directly to literature on domestic policy reform than to the other literatures we use. Regarding international assistance, this chapter's review is conceptual and broad, to help guide the investigation of university assistance case material; in contrast, the introductory chapter reviewed the specific literature on university assistance, establishing what has been done and remains to be done.

2. This generalization allows that critics can acknowledge aspects of assistance, development, or reform that fit the ideal type while supporters can acknowledge aspects that do not. Also, as discussed below in the section on evaluation, some net positive results do not fit the ideal type.

3. Member-state status and accords make for some legal obligations for the IDB to give. But further evidence of a voluntary core in assistance lies in the weak and indirect political basis pressuring donors to give across borders (Tendler 1975: 38–39). Also, like much philanthropy and nonprofit activity, international assistance may be perceived as "needed" where there are inadequate basic public funds. But whether to meet that need remains a matter of donor choice.

4. Curti (1963); Packenham (1973); Smith (1990: 27–44)

5. The first quotation is Montgomery (1967: 62); the others are Geiger (1967: 7). Also see Phillips (1976b: 3); Pinto-Agüero (1978: 123–24).

6. Pearson (1969). Private donors often get especially high marks for their ability and inclination to home in quickly on small, innovative targets and build trust transcending narrow political ends (Friedman 1980; Method and Shaw 1981; Phillips 1976b: 224). Especially since the 1970s, such views of private actors would lead even large bilateral and multilateral agencies to deliver assistance through NGOs (Fisher 1993, 1998).

7. Concentrating on bilateral and multilateral agencies, Hancock (1989) blasts secrecy, lack of accountability to home country as well as host country publics, confusion, blundering, a need to fill lending quotas, and other means quite at odds with our ideal type. The concluding chapter of his book is entitled "Aid Is Not Help."

8. Tendler (1975: 1–2) cites arguments about means (e.g., assistance is too large or heavy) and adds her concern about how organizational environment features lead to practices such as pushing funds and avoiding risk.

9. See, for example, Weiler (1983) and Roett (1972: 170). Of course, not all critics have endorsed each element of the critique.

10. Lowenthal (1991: 243). The conclusion is noteworthy for us as that study had aims parallel to ours in analyzing when and where the United States promoted progress in Latin America, why, how, and with what consequences, and it too addressed an academic and policy audience stricken by "collective amnesia" (Lowenthal 1991: viii). But that study finds *less* impact than is conventionally believed, whereas ours finds more. For development administration assistance, no consensus exists on whether effects are negligible, positive, or negative (Rondinelli 1989). Generalizing about assistance for Third World and Latin American development, Ruttan says the "conventional wisdom" is that it has been a sincere but misguided effort (1996: 49, 240). See also the World Bank Institute's *Development Outreach* 1, no. 2 (1999): 15–24. The classic study of Liberal America's efforts in the Third World, while concentrating on the assumptions and motivations involved in assistance, and acknowl-

edging the lack of empirical evidence on impact, inclines toward the view that most goals were not achieved (Packenham 1973).

11. On fungibility see White (1970: 104–105). On growth see Maglen (1990); Adiseshiah (1979: 226). Growth may be viewed as short-run, technical, and specific rather than structural (Honey 1968; Richardson 1984: 39) as aid is too small or ill-conceived to have a substantial development impact (Gordenker 1976; Riddell 1987: 176; Tilak 1988).

12. Clark (1991: 3); Tisch and Wallace (1994). AID (1998) points out that it accounts for only 0.117 percent of the GDP, is lower than ever, lower than Japan's effort, and amounts to just 17 percent of the world's official development assistance versus 63 percent in 1956.

13. Riddell (1987); Cassen (1986: 11, 21, 146–47, 294–95); O'Hanlon and Graham (1997); World Bank (1998). Also on the positive results see Schwartzman (1991); Pinchus (1967: 301); White (1974: 106); Pearson (1969); Psacharopoulos and Woodhall (1985: 10). Development bank studies claim excellent rates of return on investments (Cassen 1986: 11). See also Murphy (1976).

14. Bath and James (1976); Becker (1983); Valenzuela and Valenzuela (1981).

15. Evans and Stephens (1988); Gereffi (1983: 8). As Almond (1987) notes, dependency charges that modernization ignored international influence are exaggerated at best. Modernization assigned a crucial role to international influence generally and to assistance projects specifically. Whatever evolution the Third World might manage on its own, assistance was essential for a jump-start toward modernity. On the other hand, Valdés (1995: 45–48) is right that modernization theory often assumed rather than studied the transfer of ideas and values; our study is about assistance projects as specific modernization and transfer efforts.

16. In fact, extreme dependency assumptions retained a following in the field of comparative education (Sanyal 1982; Mazrui 1975), including Latin American education (Solórzano nd), even after they lost most of their weight in wider development studies (Packenham 1992).

17. On "all good things," see Packenham (1973). Alternatively, some theorists allowed for sequences of good developments or even for contradictions that require resolution (Huntington 1987: 6). The parallels between modernization and our ideal type are perhaps most keenly expressed where modernization goes to "soft" areas like education, which have strong social, cultural, and values components. One example would be the study of movement from traditional to modern personalities, including dimensions such as readiness for social change, energetic information acquisition, belief in progress and human ability to control events, and flexibility (Inkeles and Smith 1974).

18. Dependency theories have sometimes allowed that goals were ambitious, efforts included donor discretion to select and work with targeted partners with whom they share interests, and results could be important within a nonrevolutionary context. This can include a degree of change, though the dependency emphasis is on constraints.

19. On coercion and inequality, Silva and Sonntag (1981: 142); on greater autonomy Evans (1987); Becker (1983); on world systems, Meyer and Hannan (1979). Assistance projects need not loom large in world systems theory; most emulation occurs outside specific international projects.

20. Bath and James (1976: 7–11). See Sheehan's discussion of the development-

contact relationship (1987: 156–62). For an education example of the negative view, see Kelly (1980). In its emphasis on costs to the Third World, dependency is anti-thetical to the philanthropic ideal of mutual benefit; in between, "interdependence" highlights the costs that fall to both sides in an international relationship (Keohane and Nye 1977: 9). Much dependency literature, notably in education, concentrates on identifying huge inequalities in resources, influence, and power (Raghaven 1983; Altbach 1987b). Even where it focuses less on causes, it usually suggests that external influences contribute to the inequality, as with the international distribution of knowl-edge or textbooks. For example, the "neo-imperialist effect" of Western transfers to the Third World "leaves little doubt" that the transfers reinforce center-periphery inequalities (Mundy 1992: 19).

21. Fuenzalida (1982: 141). See also Hotta (1991); Altbach and Kelly (1984). One view is that the Third World copies too much, whether due to coercion or an unfor-tunate inclination to imitate. As argued in studies of higher education, what they copy is either not laudable anywhere or is inappropriate for the copier as it serves donor nation interests better (Spitzberg 1980: 19–20; Hall 1980: 29; Selvaratnam 1986). Just as we wind up with the automobile industry in Mexico rather than a Mexican automobile industry (Bennett and Sharpe 1985: 55), so we could get the international university in Mexico rather than a Mexican university. Modification is possible: there may be partial copies, which may continually adapt to donor values and structures (Scherz-García 1967: 393), or capitalism on the periphery may involve development even though it fails to replicate development in the center countries (Evans 1985).

22. Berman (1983: 39). Part of the general modernization-dependency debate, on the other hand, turns on whether pluralist manifestations are desirable. As in edu-cation, supporters see diversity, choice, centers of excellence, and competition where critics see stratification, inequity, and persistent or worsened problems in the system's mainstream.

23. Thus this domestic policy literature is introduced to help develop the concep-tual scope and methodology of the study, whereas the study's substantive concern lies with how international assistance affects (Latin American) domestic policy.

24. Derthick (1970: 201). Bossert (1984) also notes how both federal government and international agencies mostly provide finance, technical assistance, and broad guidelines while locals provide most personnel, facilities, and organization.

25. Weisbrod (1988); Douglas (1983: 132–41). An equity rationale for the exter-nal aid—federal or foreign—is reinforced where funds are generated from a more wealthy or progressive base than the recipient base. The similarity between a federal and an international donor role can include the quest to do good, especially to attack difficult problems in the targeted area, and thus to diminish inequalities. Criticisms of the federal role show a much more negative view of federal goals, efforts, and impacts (Piven 1971).

26. Federal aid sometimes exceeded local government budgets. See Anton (1989: 207, 217); Pressman and Wildavsky (1984); Van Horn (1979).

27. The negative tone has run across considerable territory, including U.S. higher education (Levine 1980), comparative education reform (Weiler 1980), and Latin American bureaucracy (Geddes 1994), to cite a few pertinent examples.

28. Derthick (1970: 4). Furthermore, difficulties are inherent in the reform process more than in poor policy formulation or execution per se.

29. Cerych and Sabatier (1986). Unlike those who emphasize the general problems

of major reform in centralized systems (Clark 1986), Cerych and Sabatier insist on the feasibility of big changes in depth when targeted on just part of the system; they add that small reforms can fail for inability to inspire support. Other implementation studies (Mazmanian and Sabatier 1983; Nathan 1993) also parallel development theory's recent emphasis on strategy, sequence, and realistic expectations.

30. Indeed, realization that such flawed means lead to flawed results when it comes to federal grants to states and localities sometimes prompts contracting out to nonprofits (Kettl 1983; Salamon 1987) to get closer to the ideal type. On the watering down see Reagan and Sanzone (1981), and on the local support see Derthick (1970).

31. On higher education see Clark (1983: 187–96). Political science that likewise shows how established groups and organizations have reason and power to resist change includes work on interest groups (Lowi 1979), rational choice in governance (Chubb and Moe 1988), and bureaucracy (Gormley 1989). Many works find or report a view that key actors' self-interest is a huge obstacle to reform and that efforts to clean things up are either ineffectual or tend to make matters worse. For education, however, literature on the sociology of organizations may be the most extensive in this regard. "Population ecology" holds that individual organizations change only minimally, so system changes come more from the birth and death of organizations (Hannan and Freeman 1989).

32. Majone and Wildavsky (1977: 113–15); Elmore and Williams (1976); Mazmanian and Sabatier (1983: 21–24); Williams (1980); Peterson, Rabe, and Wong (1986); Nakamura and Smallwood (1980: 111–43); Gormley (1989).

33. Majone and Wildavsky (1977: 109–11). On bits and pieces, Grindle and Thomas (1991: 121–25); on clashes with local realities, Pressman and Wildavsky (1984: 83).

34. Riggs (1964:) deals with complex implementation issues, and his substantive focus is Third World development, especially the effects on less developed countries and their institutions of efforts to transfer modernization models. Riggs's picture also squares with wide-ranging literatures that deal with change produced by the encounter of two models, institutions, groups, cultures, or civilizations. The targeted entity is less likely to become like the invading entity than to transform into a layering of the two or a new form evolving out of the two. With all the interaction among peoples in the Ancient Near East, for example, Egypt developed an "accumulation of mixed traditions" as new practices were introduced whereas old ones rarely died, and new languages and civilizations kept arising out of a mixing with old ones (Gordon 1963). On educational transfers, Steiner-Khamsi (2000: 163, 171) claims that every transfer leads to a recontextualization process but that neither the process nor educational transfers overall have been much studied.

35. DiMaggio and Powell (1991: 29). Moreover, some traditional values prove compatible with modern values, and others are adaptable to them (Gusfield and Friedland 1968).

36. Riggs (1964: 12–17). Hirschman emphasizes "journeys toward progress" that neither follow clearly anticipated routes nor sustain conventional wisdom that Third World reforms fail (Hirschman 1963). Several of Hirschman's works expose the shortsightedness of focusing on "obvious" obstacles and failures. Even on a matter such as how obstacles are underestimated at the outset, Hirschman emphasizes how a "hiding hand" helps launch efforts which sobriety might have shied away from yet which yield net benefits, albeit inexact ones (Picciotto 1994: 223). More than Riggs,

Hirschman could be translated into our conceptualization as allowing for very positive results without following many of the means or goals-means relationships postulated in the philanthropic or assistance ideal type of change.

37. Whereas the optimism tends to be fundamentally liberal, the reaction often has both a conservative form ("it's a waste or inappropriate use of tax money") and a radical form ("dependency"), along with liberal despair. The reaction against U.S. domestic policy reform has been mostly conservative whereas the dependency reaction to modernization has been mostly radical. Criticism of international assistance came mostly from the left wing, but then a rightist critique also pointed to negative impacts, emphasizing how assistance stifles market forces (Bauer 1976).

38. DiMaggio and Powell (1983). Others then argued that skepticism about organizations was overdone (Hall 1996). The literature on isomorphism highlights motivations and dynamics mostly at odds with ideal typical notions of change. Like dependency, "coercive isomorphism" highlights where forms are imposed and "mimetic isomorphism" highlights where they are unwisely or haplessly imported. "Normative isomorphism," on the other hand, is largely about emulation of professional norms. Although dependency also tends to see this isomorphism negatively, such professional emulation is a key hope in philanthropy, modernization, and university assistance projects. Overall, however, isomorphism runs mostly counter to our philanthropic ideal type of change, which instead finds a more comfortable counterpart in the notion of technically rational and competitive organizations.

39. For organizational sociology, Westney offers an especially relevant third stage assessment because it concerns international transfer (Westney 1987). Like Riggs, Westney does not focus on assistance projects but does treat efforts to import progress. She reaches mixed and complicated findings. Meiji Japan chose selectively from Western models that differed greatly from its traditional models and innovated and adapted them to its environment; dichotomies of emulation versus innovation fail, since successful imitation requires innovation, and only sometimes does the original model remain the blueprint.

40. Tendler (1975); Picciotto (1994: 212). A leading authority on international educational evaluation argues that social projects require flexibility and readjustment; thus the choice is not short, smooth, and efficient evaluation versus long, bumpy, and bad evaluation, but long and bumpy with realistic criteria versus long and bumpy with unrealistic criteria (Castro 1996: 5).

41. Hirschman also argues that rhetoric, evaluation, and policy on reform all depend heavily on the models, concepts, and orientations one brings to the table (1991).

42. Consideration of the difference between explicit and implicit goals is essential for confronting apparent contradictions in results. For example, the World Bank is generally dissatisfied with what assistance has done for Third World education, yet finds that 79 percent of its human resource development projects have been successful, a figure which exceeds that for industry-related projects (Picciotto 1994: 215). Early positive evaluations of AID projects in Latin American higher education clearly fit the mode of quick review of explicit points (Adams and Cumberland 1960: 169–264).

43. Nakamura and Smallwood (1980: 158–59). On policy innovation, Robertson and Waltman (1993).

44. Schwartzman (1996: 93–94) notes that the successes found for technological self-reliance in Brazil's computer industry and Argentina's nuclear energy industry

(Adler 1987) largely dissipated by the 1990s. On premature evaluation, see Ranis (1996: 17).

45. This faith helps explain what scholars have called an amazing lack of evaluation by big foundations attempting to export progress (Arnove 1978; Sutton 1986: 5).

2. Givers and Receivers

1. The three donor categories also make sense elsewhere in the Third World, but leading examples would change: Ford would share the scene more with the Rockefeller and Carnegie foundations, as AID would with other governments, while the World Bank would easily overtake the IDB.

2. Quotation from Nielsen (1972: 78, 98) and further on the charges, Magat (1979: 18). By 1987 Ford had given $6.6 billion (O'Neill 1989: 147), more than $9 billion by 1998, when its assets exceeded $9 billion. Raynor (2000) focuses on the foundation in its early decades.

3. On Ford data, Moock (1980: 3–4, 28, 31). Also see appendix E and note that agriculture and other Ford categories not labeled as education generally included considerable research and advanced training. After the golden age, Ford was preeminent in giving to NGOs with research as at least one major activity (Levy 1996).

4. See, for example, Miceli (1990: 40); among foundation experts, Sutton i and Black i-1; on critics, see Arnove (1978).

5. On the contracting, Adams and Cumberland (1960: 8, 133); Humphrey (1967). Regarding autonomy, AID's chief was appointed by the president, and its development vision often conflicted with the State Department's (Roett 1972: 28; Rondinelli 1989; Parkinson 1976: 52–53; Packenham 1973: 68). Our evidence that AID's approaches resemble the philanthropic ideal type contrasts with critiques of AID as lacking innovation and flexibility (Tendler 1975: 8).

6. AID #5120094, PD-AAA-251-A1. On the charges, González (1981: 238). By the same token one could cast conflict between AID and U.S. universities as evidence that collaboration was strained, or could emphasize complaints that AID's regulations were too controlling (Gardner 1964; Wood 1968: 13). Funding for linkages has come largely from federal agencies that support area studies at U.S. universities, which then helps many Latin American students and institutions (Drake 1989: 5).

7. The U.S. higher education/education ratio appears unremarkable for donor nations: higher education garnered about 14 percent of the DAC's (Development Assistance Committee of the OECD, Organization for Economic Cooperation and Development) $1.1 billion bilateral education assistance in 1973, just over a fourth of the assistance labeled by educational level (Method and Shaw 1981: 83, citing OECD data). But on the disproportionately weak U.S. educational effort overall, Method and Shaw (1981: 9–14, 69–70); Gardner (1964: 2); Hüfner and Naumann (1986: 126); Hurst (1981: 121). Although the U.S. education share rises if we add multilateral and especially private expenditures, it still would not approach the U.S. share in overall assistance (Cassen 1986: 144; Selim 1983: 40; Phillips 1974: 258). On the weak U.S. ranking in total assistance, O'Hanlon and Graham (1997: 23), although the U.S. share is significant in peacekeeping and military operations. Obviously, other studies could devote greater attention to other donor countries. Japan

considered Latin America too developed for bilateral aid, but by the 1980s, in a bid to increase its influence and image, Japan vied to be the world's largest source of funds (Hotta 1991: 476–78, 485; Theberge and Fontaine 1977: 8–14), though with loans much more than grants. France, Germany, Italy, the Netherlands, Sweden, and the United Kingdom have been prominent in bilateral higher education assistance. Specifically regarding Latin American universities, European and Canadian donors have played key roles in certain places, such as German aid for Chile's Austral and Concepción universities (personal correspondence from Luis Scherz 9/30/87). Sweden's SAREC led European agencies that became more important for private research centers whereas its role in universities concentrated on Africa (Olsson 1992). Canada's International Development Research Center shows some similarities and has provided scholarships; Canada's CIDA (1985: 8; Berry 1995) used part of the one-fourth of its budget dedicated to Latin America to support university development. Meanwhile, Communist nations gave little, although an increase in Soviet scholarships in the 1970s, many for four or more years of full-time undergraduate study, made some U.S. conservatives dizzy with fear.

8. Through at least 1970, Latin America got none of AID's largest forty-six grants and none over $4 million. Almost 80 percent of the region's grants were for under $1 million, accounting for the contrast between Latin America's 12 percent of AID's university assistance and about 27 percent of its projects. The Latin American leader, Brazil, got just 4.4 percent of total AID funding, followed by Colombia at 1.3 percent (Miller 1984: 53–54). Claims that AID grants to Latin America were often large and long lasting (Seymour 1985) appear to be valid only for Brazil and region-wide grants. A major explanation is that AID did not build Latin America's universities from scratch. Meanwhile, although Ford's grants to Latin America were on average a little larger than its grants elsewhere, just a few grants exceeded $1 or $2 million. By the end of the 1970s, only four Latin American universities had received over $1 million in their total Ford grants. The average Ford grant to Latin American universities was only about $150,000 (see table 2.1).

9. On the multilateral rise, Pearson (1969: 134). Between 1965 and 1980 the bilateral portion of aid from the DAC fell from 94 to 60 percent (Selim 1983: 31, 5–6; White 1970: 12, 45–50). On the changed U.S. position, DeWitt (1977: 3–6); Herrera (1985a: 167–68); White (1970: 29, 144–46, 210); Dell (1972).

10. The United States retained one-third of the votes while project approval required a two-thirds vote (versus a simple majority for ordinary capital). By 1994, the U.S. share fell to 30 percent, still allowing a key role (Tussie 1995: 18, 27); on the earlier IDB shares, Dell (1972: 37–38). Also on the U.S. role in the IDB, Bujazan et al. (1987) and DeWitt (1977: 48–67), and in the World Bank, Gwin (1994: 1, 65, 84–87), who also notes how this role has favored giving to Latin America.

11. On agreement, Wolf i-1; Vera M. i-2; on mutual understanding, White (1970: 142, 154); on IDB dependence, Bath and James (1976: 21), and on U.S. pushes, Mehedff i-1. Seeing U.S. control as neither suffocating nor marginal, we do not draw here any major conclusion about correspondence with the philanthropic ideal type in this respect.

12. IDB (1993); Ayres (1983: 248); Phillips (1974: 265); White (1970: 138). From 1961 through 1997, the IDB total included $3.5 billion in educational disbursements as well as $1.2 billion in science and technology and lots more in related agriculture. Also see Navarro, Rodríguez Braña, and Pacheco (2004).

13. Dell (1972: 176); IDB (1978: 33); also see Dell (1972: 130) on the IDB percentages to education.

14. Dell (1972: 129–31, 157–59); Ortiz Mena (1975: 9). But until the World Bank altered its mission late in the century, the IDB was the world's leading development institution (Tussie 1995: 1). On the 1 percent repayment, Vera M. i-2. On how much IDB disbursements should be considered giving or not, see appendix E. One general guideline is to consider loans as aid as long as they are at least 25 percent grants (World Bank 1990: 127–37).

15. Herrera (1985b: 14, 169, 233, 241, 285); on the working agreement, IDB (1978; Mayorga i). The IDB's "STAIRS" database shows a lessened higher education share subsequent to 1985; thus out of a total of nearly $4 billion for education lending for 1965–98 primary is greater than higher ($1.3 to $0.9 billion), although higher there does not include science and technology.

16. IDB (1997: 2–3). Any argument about impact pursued through targeted giving must confront the plain fact that the IDB has given widely and amply, much more than our foundation and bilateral agency.

17. Friedman (1980: 62); O'Neill (1989: 123).

18. Coleman and Court (1993: 37–38). On the 90 percent, Moller and Flores (1985: 119–20). By contrast, the independent Rockefeller Brothers Fund, established in 1940 with a Latin America focus linked to the family's financial interests, lacked a higher education focus (Curti 1963: 605).

19. On seeds, Phillips (1976b: 92–100); on awards' impact, Thompson et al. (1974: 195). Many of our interviewees praised Rockefeller and other foundations' decisive role in science, public health, and agriculture in the decades before the golden age, as with Chilean science (Croxatto i). Among the relevant works on the Rockefeller Foundation overseas are Coleman and Court (1993) and Bullock (1980); specifically on Latin America, see Bustamante (1985), but especially Cueto (1994) on using science for public health. Also see Fosdick (1952). Fitting the philanthropic ideal type, Rockefeller was also a model for U.S. government programs; for example, the NSF emulated the emphasis on scholarships, research, and institutional development from its inception in 1950 (Nielsen 1972: 64–65).

20. Bolling (1982: 81). On Kellogg fields, personal correspondence from Aaron Segal 5/8/87; Córdoba (1985: 41–50). Kellogg was also an early financier of Partners of the Americas, a nonprofit that since 1964 has supplied scholarships as well as exchanges and technical assistance, although its main thrust is community linkages. The USIA and other U.S. government agencies, as well as overseas affiliates of U.S. companies, then came aboard to fund Partners. For example, AID was the main financier for Partners' Central American Development Program, including advanced training (Partners of the Americas 1985: 5).

21. Sutton 1984: 142; Phillips 1976b: 100; Curti 1963: 317–22; Espinosa 1976: 45. In its U.S. work, Carnegie promoted standardized testing as pro-meritocracy (Lagemann 1989: 100–129). On Carnegie in Africa, Murphy (1976).

22. Through 1987, Hewlett's $1.1 million for Latin American higher education had gone exclusively to Mexico, mainly to El Colegio de México; in the 1990s Latin American universities were not targeted (personal correspondence from Clint Smith 1/4/88; personal correspondence from David Lorey 2/8/99). Exxon's Latin America funding in the mid-1980s included education but not higher education, and Merrill's slimmer funding included higher education for only a small share of its Latin Amer-

ican philanthropy (Merrill 1986: 410–29). The Rotary Foundation gives scholarships at both the undergraduate and graduate levels. Outside the United States, the pertinent foundation panorama varies. Latin America's foundation world has been weak, but Europe's is noteworthy, including private-government hybrids (Levy 1996: 93–95, 108–11). Germany has a strong tradition of private foundations, usually linked to the country's party and ideological cleavages. The Joseph Seidel, Konrad Adenauer, Friedrich Ebert, and Bertelsmann foundations are among those already active in the golden age. Other foundations include Japan's Sasakawa Peace Foundation.

23. These include CIAT in Colombia, La Molina in Peru, and Superior Institute of Agriculture in the Dominican Republic, although the Consortium focuses mostly outside Latin America (MUCIA n.d.). The International Council for Educational Development represents more freestanding nonprofits that offer analysis and advice worldwide on higher education, including in Latin America.

24. A 1961 reform brought all U.S. federal education exchange programs together. By the early 1980s, over 100,000 foreigners and 67,000 U.S. citizens had received scholarships. Binational commissions exist in almost fifty nations, and the program is run through U.S. embassies in more than another hundred.

25. In later years, this liberty eroded as congressional conservative pressure rose. In the mid-1980s, the USIA annual budget for Latin America and the Caribbean, without its priority Central American component, was about $9 million (Gullickson i).

26. LASPAU's finance came to about $54 million, 1965–87, although data on the early years are incomplete. With this funding, LASPAU worked with over twenty nations and handled thousands of awards, roughly 10 percent of which went to individuals getting more than one, and roughly 75 percent of the awards were for graduate study (Bloomfield i-2; Bryant i; LASPAU 1990 annual report; personal correspondence from Dotti Saroufin 8/13/88). LASPAU also offers a window on the importance of tuition assistance by U.S. universities, amounting to tens of millions of dollars for LASPAU students (Tyler i-4). LASPAU is thus a generator as well as a transmitter of funds.

27. The U.S. university also advocated for assistance programs and scholarships. Thus, a more comprehensive account of golden age efforts could include more research on the U.S. university role. Even public universities are not U.S. agencies, just as private ones are not foundations.

28. By 1998, the World Bank had invested $8.6 billion for 439 education projects in 108 countries (Salmi 1998). Also see Verspoor (1991); Method and Shaw (1981: 69–73, 90); Psacharopoulos and Woodhall (1985: 9); P. Jones (1992: 84–125); World Bank (1994: 92–93). The bank has accounted for about five-sixths of multilateral education assistance to developing countries and, as of 1990, about one-fourth of all external assistance for education as compared to about a tenth a few years earlier and a twentieth up to 1970 (Burnett 1996: 215; Eisemon and Holm-Nielsen 1995: 6).

29. Verspoor (1991: 2–3); Hultin (1984: 168); World Bank (1980). P. Jones (1992: 207) reports higher education around 30 percent of the bank's education total. But the share reportedly moved to 43 percent, 1981–85, in spite of the bank's own proclamations, then slipping to 37 percent for 1986–91 while still rising in absolute amounts (Eisemon 1992: 8). Teacher training was important through the mid-1970s (Eisemon and Holm-Nielsen 1995: 5).

30. Wolf i-2; Phillips (1976b: 177). Only about $180 million of the World Bank's roughly $4 billion higher education, 1963–90, went to Latin America (Verspoor 1993: 59); also see P. Jones (1992: 207); Eisemon and Holm-Nielsen (1995: 10). On education overall, Latin America received less than Asia and more than Africa, but the 1970s shift to poorer regions hurt both Latin America and Asia outside China (Method and Shaw 1981: 126–33).

31. Faure et al. (1972: 242). As with the World Bank and IDB's main agencies for funding higher education, the UNDP fund has relied on voluntary government contributions.

32. Allard i-1; Turina i; Kreimer i; Mason i; Valle i.

33. The mapping and trends are broad, and it is good to accept the gross data figures with a certain reserve given the way agencies have recorded and reported and the vague or variable nature of some of the labeled categories.

34. The World Bank reports high figures for total "external financing of education," even without related training. It suggests almost $3 billion in 1975, nearly double that of a few years earlier, and accounting for about 12 percent of overall assistance (World Bank 1980: 73). The annual figure would double in absolute terms to around $6 billion on average for 1989–96 (World Bank 1999: 23).

35. The declining bilateral share, reflecting both a lower giving/GNP ratio and a rise in multilateral giving, is striking for overall assistance: from 94 to 66 percent, 1965–80 (Selim 1983: 31–34). Nonetheless, for 1980–86 education still accounted for 11 percent on the bilateral side versus 5 percent on the multilateral side and 7 percent of total international assistance (King and Singh 1991). Foundation sums have been more modest, perhaps $20–30 million per year in the early 1960s, however significant due to focus and impact (Method and Shaw 1981: 74; World Bank 1990), a contrast consistent with the philanthropic ideal type. With NGOs, private giving to all purposes was over $1.3 billion in 1973, mostly from U.S. sources, and around $5.5 billion by the late 1980s, slightly exceeding the development banks' $5 billion as well as the UN's nearly $4 billion (Phillips 1976b: 94; World Bank 1990: 129); also see Smith (1990: 3–4). Except for foundations, however, private giving has not often prioritized education.

36. The Third World percentage for 1973 was about 17 percent. On regional shares and the declining weight of assistance starting in the 1970s, see Phillips (1976b: 5–13); Pinto-Agüero (1978: 148); and Muñoz Izquierdo (1989), who cites IDB data on assistance amounting to an average of 13 percent of educational funds for Latin America, 1962–77, down by 1977 to about 10 percent, and largely in loans. On the private centers' funding, King (1981: 248); Levy (1996: 92–94). On foreign assistance to African education over the years, see Ilon (2003).

37. On Peru, Arregui and Melgar (1992: 10); on the general data, Lavados (1978: 19); UNDP (1991: 54). Clear indications of donors' financial retreat in Latin American higher education come where absolute figures fall, but also where proportions fall relative to other giving or to domestic finance. Where raw figures are cited, inflation-adjustment (to offset about a 300 percent rise, 1960–80) would be required to specify the magnitude of the retreat. Greater volatility would come into play were we to work with local currencies.

38. Moock (1980: 15, 25, 31); Ford Foundation (1972: 21–22). Computed in 1983 dollars, Ford funding to the Third World for long-term scholarships for graduate education peaked in 1973 at over $5 million and then fell below $2 million at the decade's end (Myers 1983b: appendix A-table 1).

39. Levy (1996). Method and Shaw (1981: 75) conclude that even where other donors compensated for the dollar decline in foundations' education assistance, no such compensation arose for the foundation emphases on research, social science, long-term scholarships, and related professional activity. Put another way, other donors did not make up for the foundations' distinctive contributions. To extend our point on simultaneous retreat to a European foundation, SAREC (Olsson 1992) moved its African higher education assistance away from broad university development aims.

40. Fritz i. On AID's decreases, Seymour (1985: 3); Coleman and Court (1993: 15); Christiansen-Wagner (1986); Method and Shaw (1981: 98). By 1986, AID assistance to Latin American education included $246 million for basic, vocational, and management levels, versus $34 million for higher education. On the precipitous 1973–78 higher education fall in DAC bilateral educational assistance, see Method and Shaw (1981: 83, citing OECD data).

41. Mayorga (1994); Ratinoff i; IDB (1978: 30); Allard (1983: 452). Note that table 2.3 adds the IDB's large science and technology sums and its small student loans to the loans the IDB specifically labels higher education.

42. The most notorious episode poisoning the atmosphere in Latin America was Project Camelot, 1964, the government's largest social science grant. Close association with U.S. military interests angered many Latin Americans, although the effect may have been greater in increasing the wariness about gringos than in directly curbing assistance, which continued to thrive (Horowitz 1967: 3–22). Portes (1975: 132) writes that Project Camelot made AID more circumspect and moved Ford and other agencies to become more collaborative with their recipients.

43. Robinson (1971: 247); on overturning the tenets, Pearson (1969: 179); Baum and Tolbert (1985: 6), along with Phillips (1976b: 16–25), specifically on education.

44. King (1991: 243); Court (1995: 109); Eisemon and Kourouma (1994: 277–81).

45. Berman (1983: 166). On the World Bank critique, Psacharopoulos and Woodhall (1985: 64, 88); Blaug (1974: 23). The bank increased loans for poverty reduction from 5 to 30 percent from the late 1960s to the early 1980s (Cassen 1986: 50). This is not the place to try to gauge the relative weight of different factors in different situations involving donor retreat. Eisemon and Kourouma (1994: 282, 293, 300) conclude that donors cut money for university development before literature emerged on overinvestment in higher education; they also assert that, contrary to the canard, higher education has received but a modest portion of overall assistance money.

46. On Nixon, Theberge and Fontaine (1977: 123, 52–66). On the rising skepticism regarding educational assistance, Method i-1; Weiler (1983: 24–25); Method and Shaw (1981: 101); Phillips (1976b: 128). Doubts grew over whether recipients, at least in Latin America, had a valid claim on large-scale help. Even if needs remained, perhaps donors had done what they could; sometimes this feeling would contradict conventional wisdom about assistance failure, but sometimes it would be a sad conclusion that an earnest but ill-fated effort had been made.

47. The OAS can make a further claim of matching a philanthropic vision, since its higher education projects emerged mostly after the mid-1970s, independently against the grain of other agencies' cutbacks.

48. When Rockefeller prioritized poverty reduction with its expanded international assistance budget in the 1980s that included the traditional foundation approach of progress through research (*New York Times* 5/4/86).

49. On AID's cold war and other programs, Storrs (1987: 11–12); Donnelly i, Seymour i; on training, see our appendix E; AID (1966); Method and Shaw (1981: 99). On LASPAU's budget, personal correspondence from Peter Bryant 6/21/87. Certainly related to intensified cold war conflict was LASPAU's activity in Central America in the 1980s, as with the CAMPUS project (Tyler i-4). AID also supported the Caribbean and Latin American Scholarship Program as part of the Caribbean Basin Initiative. Moreover, various agencies seized upon the linkage concept, which AID had always championed, as a way to redefine their activities without surrendering completely to growing criticism about higher education assistance (Bastiaens 1997).

50. Of the IDB's $5 billion lent 1970–91 for higher education and science and technology, half came from 1985 on (though the unadjusted figures inflate the weight of the recent sums), and the science and technology part accounts for over $2 billion of the total. Compared with 16 percent for "higher education," 65 percent of the 1962–93 science and technology sum came starting in 1985 (Mayorga 1994; Castro and Alic 1997). Argentina, Brazil, Chile, Colombia, Costa Rica, Mexico, and Uruguay all received science and technology loans in the new era. The World Bank (AID, too) also let the university share of its higher education outlays decline while giving attention to scientific research (Eisemon and Holm-Nielsen 1995: 6–10).

51. On the other hand, communism's demise has meant that Latin America has faced more competition for international assistance. However much the peak period saw action based on simple notions of how easy development could be, subsequent efforts often require a research basis; Samoff (1993: 183–84) points out the operative phrase now is "based on research findings." In a related vein, the decade starting in the late 1980s saw a doubling in the foundation share of giving for foreign and U.S.-based international programs, and Latin America is the number one region (Renz 1997: 3).

52. Attempts to rev up U.S. bilateral efforts in the 1980s produced some results. Senator Paul Simon pushed for a major USIA science and technology effort in the region (Tyler i-1). AID received proposals for renewed projects with universities (Seymour 1986). For the developing world, Hansen (1990: v) could then speak of a "significant number of university development projects" and an apparent "second wave." In July 1997, AID adopted higher education and training as a sixth major goal of AID activity.

53. Buchert and King (1995); Eisemon and Holm-Nielsen (1995). On the World Bank present favorable view of what higher education can do for development, see World Bank (2002). For the 1980–90 data, see Burnett (1996: 215); Salmi (1998).

54. By the 1990s, Ford officials were concerned about whether the foundation had beaten an excessive retreat from the region's main universities or at least about what could be done to improve matters there. However, "revival" would be a stretch regarding actual efforts. Typical of concern much more than major finance was Ford's sponsorship of the Comparative Project on Higher Education Policy, focused on analyzing trends and reforms in five Latin American countries (Brunner 1995; Kent 1996).

55. Donors could differ in how interventionist their goals were in a given arena; AID but not Ford set out to change the balance of power among Chilean economists of the Left and the Right (Valdés 1995: 186). It does not appear that donors often intervened in matters beyond the project's scope. Ford stayed out of Chile's higher education reform debate, although it received information through its ex-scholarship holders (FF #60213 George Sutija to John Netherton 5/15/70).

56. K. N. Rao to William Carmichael, 2/23/82 in FF #650327; also on the project, Sutton i. On the replacement of traditional targeting, Urzúa (1973: 46); Arnove (1980a: 307).

57. AID #52695; Lester Anderson et al. (1965), AID Final Report, #5260095, subproject 02, May–June 1965.

58. Cueto (1991: 6); Maier i. See Thompson et al. (1974: 195) on the desired change.

59. On del Valle and lessons: Coleman and Court (1993); Harrison i-4; on the University of Chile, Fuenzalida (1984); Harrison i-4; D'Etigny i-3. Another manifestation of Rockefeller's overreach was its insistence on outreach programs for which the universities were unsuited (Moock i).

60. Coleman and Court (1993); Krasno i; Maier i; Moock i. The Latin American cases failed alongside other Rockefeller university development efforts, as did several in Africa, but not those in Thailand and a few other countries (Coleman and Court 1993).

61. Coleman and Court (1993). Criticism of premature surrender includes Dye i; Kritz i.

62. On units, Urzúa (1973: 40, 47); Scherz-García (1967: 394); on models, Phillips (1976b: 99); on other reserved action, Thompson et al. (1974: 196–97); Stifel, Davidson, and Coleman (1982: 68–69).

63. Herrera (1985b: 231, 241). On Ford, Peter Hakim to Peter Bell, 1/31/72, FF #62515; Himes i.

64. The line blurs where donors were involved in projects from or near the university's inception, as with the IDB at some of Brazil's federal universities. Donors did establish some specialized institutions in fields such as agriculture and business and would play a key role in the creation of many private research centers. Hayhoe (1986: 536–38) has found a lack of imposition by U.S. and other actors even where they established universities in China. On the Chile-California convenio's limitations, D'Etigny i-3; FF #650327. Finally, regarding the short peak, note that Packenham's classic 1973 account of overly ambitious assistance included little information on 1968–72, by which time some of his generalizations no longer characterized donors' attitudes.

65. For example, Davidson i; Wolf i-2; see also Waggoner (1967: 48).

66. Briones i; Ratinoff i; Montenegro i; Seeley i. The view that multilateral agencies control less than bilateral ones led some, like the Pearson Commission, to suggest shifting the aid mix more to the former (Cassen 1986: 260). Our point about donors' lack of a coherent plan could be related to recipients as well; Scherz-García (1967: 395) concludes that "in the majority of cases" university authorities "do not have plans of their own," responding instead to short-term considerations. However much the evidence defies views of heavily planned imposition or collusion, it also defies the ideal typical notion of undertakings by partners acting from clearly thought-out reform orientations.

67. Pelczar (1974: 58–59); Martínez i; Molina i. In other circumstances, something antithetical to the U.S. model was noted as a reality, but neither denounced nor directly targeted for reform, as with Chilean student politics at the Catholic University or party politics at the University of Concepción (IDB/L12 and IDB/L18; FF #73595). Our view of a model used with reserve again fits philanthropic norms of prudence and partnership while undercutting claims of goals and strategies carefully linked for development by design.

68. Levy (1991); Levy (1996: 112–32); Kohler (1991).

69. For example, J. R. Davison, 2/1/77 in PD-AAA-351-E1 of AID #5120312. Adams and Cumberland (1960: 136) found frequent readjustments in AID's universities projects.

70. On AID, Magnusson (1970: 315) and on the IDB cases, IDB/L1 and IDB/E5. The efforts to redistribute power appear consistent with dependency notions about foreign influences aligning with the more over the less powerful domestic actors, but insofar as the leadership was pro-reform, the notions can mislead.

71. Magnusson (1970: 320). On "in" topics, Cepeda (1979: 497); Sutton (1972); Levy (1996: 199–222).

72. But the mutual matching idea would be more pertinent for donor hookups with private research centers and related NGOs, which overlapped the golden age but gained special prominence just after it; compared with universities, the centers were usually more specialized institutions, with greater hierarchy and fewer simultaneous donors (Levy 1996). In a study of educational assistance to Greece, Pesmazoglou (1989: 32–33) also finds mutual matching of the right people for the modernization effort, although he criticizes "carbon copy replication."

73. Such supply-demand considerations parallel findings on U.S. federal aid to cities (Pressman and Wildavsky 1984: 99). A prominent example of locals persuading funders is the Chile-California convenio, and indeed donor relations with the University of Chile in general (D'Etigny i-1; Barbosa i; Fuenzalida 1987: 118). Adams and Cumberland (1960: 135) find AID-recipient differences variously leading to insistence, withdrawal, or AID's making the project more attractive to the recipient.

74. On Brazil, for example, see Ribeiro (1968: 135). Such feigning obviously undermines donor control. On recipients' true zeal, Hirschman (1986: 8); Phillips (1976b: 265); Selvaratnam (1988: 42). Valdés (1995: 131) finds such enthusiasm at Chile's Catholic University that officials actively protected donors from attack. Valdés appears to see less partner participation than we do, but no less enthusiasm. The IDB, like the World Bank, deals with governments and requires their guarantees of loans. Those who worked at the IDB maintain that it gave as long as a university was reforming (Allard i-2). Our findings align with studies identifying congruence between technical assistance and national priorities (Lavados and Montenegro 1980: 92). Regarding conflict among domestic actors, dependency theory highlights how international activity increases such conflict whereas modernization theory highlights the progressive impact of donor-reformer alliances.

75. IDB (1978: 40–45); IDB/L14; Ratinoff i.

76. Espinosa (1976: 49, 293). On Argentina, (Taquini i-1; Tedesco i). The IDB felt confident funding Chile's Austral university in part because its reformist rector had participated in a State Department conference on higher education in the Americas and the vice rector had been a Rockefeller scholarship holder (IDB/L16–L17).

77. Further CHEAR impacts included an emphasis on national development fields including new social sciences, "horizontal" (e.g., Peru-Colombia) as well as "vertical" or "North-South" (e.g., Peru-U.S.) cooperation, and creation of a crucial "mística" (profound conception and commitment) for academic reform. On ineffectiveness, Urquidi i-1 and Enarson (1962: 80). On effectiveness, personal correspondence from Eduardo Aldana 8/7/2000; Aldana i-1; Tierney i, D'Etigny i-3, Molina i, Vera M. i-2, Wolf i-2, Dye i. The Tinker Foundation helped fund CHEAR.

78. On control through donor coordination, Cassen (1986: 231) and Berman

(1983: 14, 50–55). Ironically, however, a lack of coordination has also been viewed as a threat to recipients' autonomy (Phillips 1976b: 36–40). The participation of several donors in an institution's overall development plan often meant more coexistence than coordination. This seemed to allow latitude for recipients, which helps explain why they may favor such coexistence over structured coordination, and again defies a simple concept of donor control. On the other hand, dependency has depicted a variety of multiple donor approaches (uncoordinated and diverse, complementary, or overlapping) as threats, which is both plausible and nonfalsifiable.

79. Participants similarly recall donors merely stumbling into one another at pet targets like Peru's La Molina university. On the general lack of coordination, Pearson (1969: 22); Glick (1957: 341); Coleman and Court (1993); IDB (1978: 12); Schiefelbein i-3. On peak times, Vera M. i-1; Himes i. For Chile, Hellman (1988) observes tight government-foundation cooperation until the 1970s and then a break.

80. Ideal typical hypotheses about private foundations would have them lead the way for other donors. Rockefeller did often help attract other donors, but so did AID (e.g., AID #51315-4431 for Chile's private technical university and the University of Pittsburgh 1958–59, followed by Ford and the IDB). The issue of whether foundations play a special seeding role is confounded by the simple matter of which donor arrives on the scene early. Regardless, the evidence shows that early donors attract other donors and, crucially, enhanced funding from the main local providers; in other words, international higher education assistance often fulfills the seeding role associated with ideal typical philanthropy.

81. Lowenthal (1991); White (1974: 68–77). Our general preference is for "targeted" over "favored" nation. Several readers, ex-officials at donor agencies, believed that "favored" overstates donor preferences where they confronted nations that were simply unreceptive or otherwise infeasible targets. One could further argue that this reality limited the degree to which donors were truly voluntary actors freely choosing among many options.

82. Peru did poorly with the IDB but well with Ford in both grants and scholarships and well with LASPAU. Although Peru was low in our AID ranking, with related agriculture Peru's AID figure would rise a good deal and its IDB figure would jump from 0.9 to 6.7 percent. Paraguay scores very well with the IDB, relatively well with LASPAU, and only moderately low with AID (a standing that could be changed, since some AID projects eluded the database), but it is virtually absent from Ford. Ecuador is also low in Ford's distributions but not nearly as low as Paraguay, and (like the Dominican Republic) Ecuador fits the high recipient category overall because of its high standing with all other donors. Haiti appears low; if the small figures make it difficult to judge, they also show that the case remains marginal, whereas small countries generally receive proportions that exceed their size.

83. We cannot prudently estimate separate nations' shares of AID's regional category. Our AID printout has details on only one project, a LASPAU project (#5980453), although that one accounts for 41.5 percent of the regional total. Together, just two other projects account for an additional 45.2 percent. The Regional Technical Aids Center translated and distributed almost 10 million technical books throughout the region and helped develop university bookstores there (Seymour 1985: 4); we took this project #5980005 as half higher education. The other major project, also taken as half higher education, was #59815995475, for educational science and technology, but our documentation gives no clue on national targets.

84. Donors' unadjusted dollars exaggerate the share for countries that got more in latter years and understate the share for countries targeted in the golden age, through 1974. But the distortion is limited. First, obviously, the two columns on numbers of assistantships are unaffected. Second, neither Ford nor AID gave much money after 1974. Third, a tracing of donor dollars by quinquennium (see appendixes H, I, J) verifies most patterns highlighted in table 2.4. For the IDB, an inflation index would strengthen our finding about Chile and Central America as high receivers, sustain the finding for Brazil and Colombia, and weaken but not overturn the finding for Costa Rica. Among the low recipients, Venezuela would appear a bit higher, but Uruguay lower and Mexico much lower, while Argentina would remain very low. If anything, our pattern of high and low receivers would strengthen for the golden age. Similarly, for AID, Chile, Colombia, and Brazil would look even more targeted if the golden age were weighted in adjusted dollars, although Central America would lose ground. Whereas Mexico and Argentina would also rise, they would remain low and Uruguay and Venezuela would be unaffected. Finally, for Ford, Colombia and Chile would rise even higher, while Brazil would remain high, though less so. Argentina and Venezuela would rise but remain low.

85. Colombia was the country where LASPAU started. On Colombia's share in general assistance, Sheehan (1987: 280); Cassen (1986: 330); Sandilands (1990); AID (1975). On the common observation of targeting Colombian higher education, Harding (1968: 27); González (1981: 239); Pelczar (1974: 57); Magnusson (1970: 205). A study of 1972–80 expenditures by the three leading foundations, which accounted for about 90 percent of total U.S. foundation spending in Latin America, reports that 28 percent went to Colombia alone, most of that at least loosely related to higher education or research (Moller and Flores 1985: 120; Bustamante 1985: 32: Córdoba, 1985 #398: 46). These three tandem studies all include international organizations under their host country, which inflates those countries and slightly deflates others. The international CIAT thus accounts for 29 percent of both Ford and Kellogg and 67 percent of Rockefeller grant money "to Colombia." But removing CIAT still leaves Colombia with 19, 28, and 17 percent shares from the three respective foundations. The methodological problem is much more serious for Mexico, where CIMMYT gets half the Ford money and three-fourths of the Rockefeller money; deleting CIMMYT leaves Mexico on the proportionally low side for the three foundations. Similarly, half of Ford's grants listed under Argentina go to CLACSO, so that the nation's true share is roughly 3 percent. Another problem with the tandem studies' conclusions on priority nations is that they are not adjusted for national size; Brazil always emerges as the top "priority" nation.

86. Colombia was the only other nation that had two of Ford's top seven Latin American university recipients. A key figure at one of those two, Los Andes, recalls how reformers sought the help of Chileans already prominent at the IDB (Aldana i-1).

87. On our exclusion, see the section on AID in appendix E. Clearer is that the AID database we use omits AID projects for Chile, which, however, appear in Miller (1984). U.S. donors saw Chile as a laboratory for its human capital ideas (Valdés 1995).

88. As of the mid-1960s, Chile attracted three times the bilateral assistance and twenty times the UN assistance given to Brazil (Cerych 1965: 182). In its first five years, beginning in 1966, the UNDP gave more to Chile than to any but three other

nations, and Chile also did well with the OAS, IDB, the U.S. government, and other developed countries (Blakemore 1976: 346–57). Between 1943 and 1980 Chile was number one in per capita and number three in absolute terms for U.S. aid, mostly civilian (Fritz 1980: 14–15).

89. On problems with AID data on Brazil, see appendix E. The IDB figure for Brazil (unlike Mexico) holds up even without science and technology. Other foundations also had a crucial presence early on and since (Schwartzman 1991), and the Kellogg Foundation, 1972–80, gave 38.5 percent of its Latin America funds to Brazil (Córdoba 1985: 46).

90. On Argentina's early and later scientific assistance, see García i; Adler (1987: 106–31). Philanthropy to private research centers would beef up the Argentine figures, but Argentina got only 6 percent of Ford's listed total 1972–80 for Latin America (half of that for the regional CLACSO); the same source shows Venezuela also disfavored and both Chile and Peru favored, though less than Colombia (Moller and Flores 1985: 42). Weinberg (1996) makes a parallel comparison in public health to what we have seen in higher education: Rockefeller bypassed Argentina in favor of Chile due to the contrast between one's turbulence and the other's stability coupled with elite support from distinct political parties. A defense of Argentine reluctance to engage enthusiastically with donors was that, unlike Bolivia, Argentina knew relevance was vital (Frondizi i).

91. El Colegio de México was included in Moock's data whereas Latin America's other research and graduate institutions were not. Mexico's IDB share would fall from 12.3 to 8.7 for the overall period if related agriculture were computed in and to merely 0.6 without science and technology—which, in Mexico, largely meant scholarships. In overall IDB assistance through the 1960s, Mexico took much less than its per capita share, in contrast to Chile and Colombia (Dell 1972: 126).

92. Weissberg (1980: 93, 76); Fuente i; Cano F. i. AID began a gradual reentry into Mexico in 1977 and built the largest nonmission general AID presence in the world but based on ad hoc funding of Mexican programs more than large, formal assistance projects (Taylor i-1). On Mexico's basic reluctance during the golden age, Echeverría i, Grooms i, Meyer i, Prawda i.

93. Our higher education data thus fit the general finding that Venezuela receives little of the assistance given to Latin America (Albornoz i-2).

94. Cambridge Conference Report (1971: 223). Other literature concentrates on one donor, whether emphasizing such scattering, e.g., White (1970: 168–69) on the IDB, or efforts to minimize the scattering, e.g., Thorp (1971: 131). Dependency theories could link concentration on certain nations to pointed or even coordinated donor agendas or to efforts that stratified across countries.

95. AID for wider purposes parallels our higher education targeting patterns in important ways. Mexico, Argentina, and Venezuela—ranked between second and sixth in population—were fifteenth to twentieth in both educational and total assistance (including grants, loans, and military aid) in the postwar decades. Meanwhile, Colombia and especially Central America received well beyond their population shares (AID 1975, 1985).

96. There would be a concentration if only some member nations *chose* to draw on their quota from within an open pool (see appendix E), but then we would still have to reckon with the coincidence of IDB distributions that parallel those of unencumbered donors. This is not to say that the IDB simply decided from on high. As

with other donors, its funds could be triggered when suitable national recipient/partners arrived to buy into the IDB's own general guidelines.

97. Nor did Ford give much outside the universities to this group of countries. Printout on all Ford grants to these countries shows that a single institution is the sole recipient in both Paraguay (Paraguayan Center of Sociological Studies) and Haiti (Center for Research in the Social Sciences), although more research centers receive in Uruguay. Panama gets nothing, and the grants listed under Cuba go mostly to or through a U.S. university. For our entire period (1960–84), Uruguay received only $298,600, Paraguay $270,000, and Haiti $171,800 in U.S. assistance.

98. Of Rockefeller's and Kellogg's total giving to Latin America, 1972–80, 94 percent and 76 percent, respectively, went to just three nations—Brazil, Colombia, and Mexico (Córdoba 1985: 57; Bustamante 1985: 40); if international organizations are deleted, Brazil's share increases more than others' decrease. Regarding Ford's affinity for Chile, figures become even more impressive once we realize that projects like the California-Chile one did not include funding such as scholarships through the Institution of International Education for Chileans to study or do research, 1964–70.

99. Although common targets raise doubt about voluntary choice, different donors may independently make similar choices based on similar criteria. Valverde (1999) finds a marked difference between the World Bank's and AID's national targets, but he deals with Latin America's total educational assistance, 1972–87, and just one of our three donors, plus one we do not include.

100. Drake (1989: 22) reports that Fulbright and USIA awards for U.S. scholars to go to Latin America and vice versa, 1949–85, touched Brazil, Colombia, and Chile a good deal, but also Mexico and Argentina (although application of our development gauge based on enrollments as of 1960 would show, for example, Colombia far outdistancing Argentina). Hardly represented in our LASPAU time frame, Uruguay would increase in the second half of the 1980s. For 1990–98, the World Bank gave more higher education funds to Mexico than to any country in the world, and Argentina ranked ninth (Salmi 1998).

101. Hayter and Watson (1985: 17). A stronger pro-democracy conclusion than ours comes for AID's educational assistance to Latin America, 1972–87 (Valverde 1999).

102. Woods (1993). The Ford Foundation's cold war agenda, though insufficient to forestall attacks from Senator Joseph McCarthy in the 1950s, was vigorous enough to draw attacks from the Left, especially in the 1960s and 1970s. Schoultz (1998: 367–74) contends that U.S. policy toward Latin America has for two centuries been determined by three fundamental concerns: U.S. national security, U.S. domestic political demands, and U.S. economic development. For our material, the second factor is dubious unless one considers U.S. academic lobbying as very powerful, and the other two factors do not appear to explain the variation in targeting across countries. Elsewhere, Schoultz's depiction of paramount U.S. self-interest coupled with a mission to help a weaker civilization overcome its deficits appears consistent with some of our material, but with a different basic view. For example, whereas our evidence highlights partnership and ultimately some successes, Schoultz (1998: 384–85) views the Alliance for Progress as characterized by naive U.S. exporting of alien ideas and practices, Latin American rejection and resistance, and ultimately failure.

103. Further exceptions would arise if one gauged more by nations' overall devel-

opment status rather than their higher education enrollment status, but whereas that macro analysis would be appropriate for other concerns it would be inferior in trying to understand the assistance under analysis here.

104. Some developed systems are readier for change than are less developed counterparts. Also, where relatively few nations solicit, the notion of donor selectivity weakens, just as donor choice and control weaken where there are few supplicants.

105. Our finding for higher education thus at least partly cuts against the finding that assistance has generally failed to target places with sound policy and the best prospects for success, but rather targeted mostly for political reasons (World Bank 1998: 40–47). Ford's rather demanding standards for judging reform viability in connection with extant academic quality helps account for its avoidance of three less developed higher education systems supplied by other donors: Central America outside Costa Rica, the Dominican Republic, and Ecuador. A lack of viability may also account for Haiti's near exclusion by all. The existence of a university system apparently unreceptive to reform (with extraordinary student activism and the lack of truly alternative institutions outside the Catholic university) goes far to explain Bolivia's limited assistance in higher education compared with other policy areas. To give special attention to less developed targets was not to go overboard in redistribution quotas at the expense of concerns for merit selection.

106. In the high-receiving group the timing of the reform was crucial. Domestic reform had already been undertaken in certain instances, e.g., Costa Rica in 1957. As in Colombia, some domestic reform efforts broadened out from prior reform and assistance, and some were initiated at the same time as major assistance (Magnusson 1970: 203; Wickham 1973: 147–66; IDB/L25: appendix I-15). A leading Colombian reformer recalls that what stood out about his country was not its disposition to invent but rather its eagerness and ability to import and emulate (personal correspondence from Eduardo Aldana 8/7/2000). Brazil was so receptive to AID it bordered on treating AID's prescriptions as its higher education bible (Goertzel 1967). Regarding the relatively marginalized nations of the golden age, both Argentina and Mexico later undertook a general international opening, including in higher education. On Mexico's radical shift, Lacy (1992).

107. Venezuela's singular case of oil-produced wealth is then perhaps the only case that defies the receptivity-reform hypothesis, and even there Albornoz (i-1) blames Venezuela's own agencies for being unreceptive, "immune to the international dynamic."

108. Our findings also tend toward the view that development variables outweigh political variables in determining donors' development assistance (Nelson 1968: 121). At least that is so regarding commonly invoked macro-political variables, such as regime type. But as is so often the case, other political variables, possibly quite important, are less identifiable from a distance, require more contextual understanding, and cannot be neatly measured. For university assistance, receptivity and reform lead the way among these variables.

109. Then, too, opposite facts can be taken as deviations from the philanthropic ideal type, as when multidonor targeting of a particular nation is taken as a sign of a controlling external agenda but scattering across nations is taken as a violation of selectivity. We have also seen where certain charges of dependency are plausible in one instance and other charges of dependency are plausible in very different instances.

110. Although this chapter's analysis of nations has focused on goals and especially

efforts rather than results, a few general points are possible, previewing specifics in the next three chapters. Mainly, informants who ventured opinions about national differences in relation to assistance uniformly identified higher recipient nations as the leading achievers in reform and performance. They often referred to the "seriousness" or "solidity" of a set of institutions or to a critical mass of well-trained people in countries such as Colombia, Chile, and Brazil (Brunner i-1; Tedesco i; Lavados i-2; Singh i; Ratinoff i). Regarding Brazil, for example, the IDB and other agencies may be seen as "crucial catalysts" for higher education gains and pioneering programs (Vera M. i-2; Schwartzman i), while Ford made a big positive difference despite skepticism and obstacles connected to Brazil's size (Krasno i). Also see Method and Shaw (1981: 110–12) on national differences produced from AID educational assistance.

111. And the sums were small by standards of U.S. higher education at home. As Tiller (1973: 95) observed, even peak U.S. private and public aid was less than the University of Texas budget.

3. Modernizing the System

1. Some scholars in comparative higher education studies (Meek 1996) favor the term *differentiation* over *diversification,* but both terms refer to the process of a system's interinstitutional configuration becoming more varied. Diversity, in turn, refers less to the process and more to a reality at a given time. Where the meaning is clear, we avoid the cumbersome addition of *interinstitutional* to these terms.

2. The U.S. model stands out more for diversity than scale, however, because the U.S. system was so preeminent in diversity whereas growth was increasingly a feature of European and other higher education as well, albeit not as much as in the United States.

3. Smelser (1974). At the same time, there are echoes in the higher education literature of broader modernization theory regarding institutionally diverse systems as more capable of handling growth (Clark 1978: 254–55). For another thing, innovation is easier through fresh structures and the new resources and actors associated with them than through transformation of preexisting institutions.

4. Some might conclude that donors simply promoted certain institutions because they liked their actual or potential profile and that diversification was but a vaguely considered and desired by-product.

5. Wiarda (1981); Schmitter (1974).

6. On corporatist harmony, Levy (1986: 31–32, 83–87, 323–28); on the Continental model, Van Vught (1993); Clark (1983).

7. Huntington (1968: 93–139); Packenham (1973: 151–60).

8. Examples of interest in developed nations' patterns of diversification could be found in many publications like the *Boletín de la Universidad de Chile* in the 1960s.

9. No earlier figure is available for the region, but we could guess that nationals had a few percent more of the enrollment in 1960 than 1965; the 1970 figure slipped only 1 percent from 1965. See appendix L.

10. Fritz (1989); AID #526-11-660-053.

11. FF #650327. A counterpart to Latin America's national universities arose where there was in effect a national technical university. Thus the IDB noted that the

only way to have an impact on increasing skilled human resources in many of Chile's technical fields was to promote the State Technical University, which in any case was geared for internal reform, with Canadian assistance (IDB/L15: 24). Similarly, AID saw an economic development need to go to the National Engineering University because it had the largest and most important engineering program in Peru (AID #527-L-031).

12. Waggoner (1967: 48).

13. Wolf i-2; Fraenkel i; Carmichael i; Himes i. At Peru's National Engineering University radical students pushed out a rector who opposed co-government with students (1962).

14. FF #64293. Where the IDB found only some faculties up to par for funding, and therefore trimmed the university's requests, it found another unit (the Department of Biology; IDB/L20: 7 and annex 2) fit to add.

15. R. Low-Maus to W. R. Cotter, 7/3/68. On the list of donors, IDB/L20; FF #69-0604.

16. Magnusson (1970: 217); Pelczar (1974: 47).

17. González (1981); Magnusson (1970: 217–19, 331–40); Pelczar (1974: 47).

18. Kalman Silvert to Ralph Harbison 8/20/70 in FF #68759. Many of the problems at the Colombian National University with the economics grant parallel those with the sociology grant (John Farrell to William Carmichael 2/19/73; Reed Hertford to files, 11/27/70, both in FF #68759). Again there was an attempt to build quality in teaching and research, providing funds for study abroad and staff enhancement at home, as well as for visiting professors and pertinent library development. Again, plans failed. Only one in eight of those slated to become part of the full-time core did so. Lots of money intended for faculty salaries did not get there. In classic prismatic fashion, library modernization ran into a bureaucratic maze, e.g., needing fourteen authorizations to requisition an item. Most of all, the project design assumption of administrative continuity and support proved naive. In the short life of the grant there would be two deans of the faculty, four directors of the center, and seven rectors, as well as three army occupations of the campus. If the foundation tried to rely on a more isolated center within the university, it would kill its original purpose in university development, but a center strictly under the university would be stultified. Nonetheless, results were mixed, and Kalman Silvert (to William Carmichael 1/27/73 in FF #68758) excepted economics from his generalization that the National University proved unable to maintain good social science.

19. Hirschman (1963); Daland (1967).

20. "The right stuff" was independently chosen both for our subject matter (Levy 1991: 21) and to depict foundations' search for suitable partners through which to promote science in Europe in the first half of the twentieth century (Kohler 1991: 207). Other parallels with Kohler's work include how institutional targets were selected because of relative position within the system, with attractive and upcoming leadership, and their allegiance to donors' principles so that partnership was natural. Kohler (1991: 201, 401) also finds that donors often targeted particular units within universities and that university administration often frustrated that attempt.

21. A parallel can again be drawn regarding federalism's "picking winners" (Gilbert and Specht 1984). Is the winning recipient merely a safe target already far ahead of the pack or a target with winning characteristics that make federal funds likely to have a major impact?

22. Masís i. More than half the students at the new university had fathers with just primary school education (CONARE 1987a: 82). Regarding selectivity, international comparisons find more selectivity exercised by U.S. than European donors largely because of the major role of private U.S. foundations (Cerych 1965: 173).

23. Adams and Cumberland (1960: 140–41); IDB/L11: 7–24; IDB/L19: 1–2, 17–27, 51.

24. Herrera (1985b: 171, 244). Thus, as with federalism that parallels the philanthropic ideal type, assistance funding went to recipients supportive of reform, innovation, and experimentation at the local level rather than to mainstream actors tied to status quo or uncontroversial development based on standard policy.

25. Paniagua i; Piva i; Lusk i.

26. On the debates, Cambridge Conference Report (1971: 224). There were other reasons for donors to return, including accumulated stakes and commitments and the very characteristics that had first attracted assistance.

27. IDB/E10; IDB/E20; IDB/E12; IDB/E13.

28. Valdés (1995); Adams and Cumberland (1960: 207); AID #5130009, including memos by Paul Fritz.

29. IDB/L14: 16–22; IDB/L10: 2, 8–10.

30. The attractive features included national reform-orientation, democratic but nonleftist and friendly to assistance, as well as a still comparatively small higher education system. Along with Costa Rica, Chile and Colombia suggest that attractive national features were particularly important for the prospects of assistance to national universities, although they also helped other institutions in those countries. The special boost for the nationals reflects their central position in the system whereas, in countries that lacked an attractive general profile, donors would need to turn more or more quickly to alternative institutions escaping their systems' mainstream. Donors briefly broke the rule when they went heavily into national universities like Peru's at the beginning of the golden age.

31. Luis Izquierdo 11/19/81 letter to the foundation, FF #79653; Harrison i-2.

32. IDB/L14: 2; Coleman and Court (1993: 58); Peter Hakim to Peter Bell 1/31/72 FF #62515; Frodin (1965). Among the grants to the University of Chile in the golden age were AID's #51321003 with Stanford University and the smaller #51349032 with Cornell University, both started in 1959, the IDB/L9, IDB/L14, and several by Ford, some with subsequent supplement grants: #610-0341, #610-0372, #620-0023, #630-0422, #640-0032, #640-0156, #650-0112, #650-0327, #670-0569, #690-0703, #710-0468, #720-0378, #735-0764, and #745-0374.

33. On Aldana, K. N. Rao to William Carmichael 7/17/74 in FF #65307; on the advantages, IDB/L22: 7–8.

34. AID #514-660-101, #5140101, PAR PD-AAN-414, 10/7/69. Ford found that the economics program still provided only limited first-degree education and nearly no graduate education, while only one of eighteen full-timers had a Ph.D. and there was little research (FF #68758).

35. Harrison i-1; Aldana i-1; Fraenkel i; Wolf i-4; Carmichael i; Safford (1976: 240); IDB/L22: 7–16.

36. Berman (1983: 73); Arnove (1980b).

37. The chapter does not deal much with isolated historical attempts at institutional distinctiveness, such as La Plata's attempt a century ago to stress research and science in contrast to Argentina's typical professionalist profile. In the 1960s, public

technical institutes were built throughout Latin America. These were promoted heavily by international agencies, notably UNESCO. They were to tie themselves to the productive sector, avoiding university problems (Lavados 1987: 129). Other public technical institutions established as alternatives to public universities kept teaching as their main focus; the Technical Institute of Costa Rica (1973) is a good example of one that received a big IDB push. Nor do we deal here much with public alternatives that lacked first-degree programs, whether they would mix graduate education with research (e.g., Mexico's Agricultural College of Postgraduates at Chapingo) or devote themselves overwhelmingly to research or to research and service (Levy 1996).

38. Additionally, we already have much more analysis of the privates than the publics as alternative institutions responding to the perceived failures of preexisting public universities (Levy 1986), although the international role in that private reaction has not been much explored. A few of the private recipients were not "universities" in name, but the great majority were; coupled with the fact that so many private (and public) "universities" in Latin America dubiously carry that nomenclature, with no consistent criteria used, we refer here to private universities. The huge majority of private institutions not called universities, such as Brazil's "isolated schools," did not receive assistance.

39. At least at the Ford Foundation, the sensitivity to charges of favoring privates shows up in archives on several projects. For example, in response to such charges, one analyst points out that over 75 percent of the foundation's support in Peru was at public universities, including the troubled national San Marcos university (James Himes to Nita Rous Manitzas 10/3/67 in FF #64293). Publics were getting all the money in the especially troubled social sciences. Of eight foundation-sponsored visiting professors, seven were at the publics, and the twenty-eight Peruvians who left in 1967 for study abroad were all sponsored by a public institution. Yes, the analyst concluded, to tip the balance toward the private side would be wrong, but Ford was not doing that. A U.S. House of Representatives report (Giaimo and Brademas 1961: 17) recommended giving to Argentina's public universities, finding its private institutions inadequate; but it also found Chilean private institutions worthy, so the approach was pragmatic rather than ideological.

40. For example, AID's #5200198, subproject 02, for new programs in Guatemala and its #5170068 for higher education in the Dominican Republic each went to the national and two private universities. AID's eight-year project for graduate engineering in Rio de Janeiro, Brazil, went to the federal and Catholic universities (AID #5120263, subproject 02; #5120300, subproject 02).

41. In assessing the data in appendixes O, P, and Q on donors' institutional targeting by country, two points should be kept in mind. First, the institutional breakdown is shown by nation, but the totals are then calculated for the region (since giving each country's percentage equal weight would distort the regional average). Second, some distortion comes from aggregating the 1959–84 period, as lack of a deflator overstates the weight of funds in the latter part of that period. However, as with the data on allocations to nations in chapter 2, the problem is limited by the fact that both Ford and AID give relatively little from the mid-1970s forward. Moreover, tables 3.1–3.3 show each donor's funding by short time periods. In the appendixes with pertinent data, the aggregated private share is inflated for Ford and the aggregated national university share is understated for AID. Mostly, the "state umbrella" share is inflated for the IDB (see appendix A for the price multiplier index).

42. Adding the Brazilian publics could thus drive the Latin American public alternative share of Ford grants to as high as 41 percent, alongside the hefty 27 percent for privates and 20 percent for the University of Chile—leaving just 12 percent of the foundation's grants for all national universities save the Chilean.

43. Our data do, however, include four nations not in the Miller data that otherwise form our 1950–69 database; for a fifth potential addition, "Latin America Regional," the data were not listed by institutional target. Table 3.2 and appendix P are unaffected by the lack of clarity regarding AID funding of Brazil, noted in appendix E, because they deal with only Spanish America.

44. These LASPAU data run through 1987, rather than our usual 1984 cutoff. The extra time period accounts for 531 of our 3,366 total (excluding Brazil); we lack the internal (national vs. alternative) breakdown on the 50 percent public share; the private share is just half the public share—with the ample balance to "other" and "unidentified" institutions. Data printout October 23, 1987, from LASPAU's Steve Bloomfield. LASPAU's high alternative/public ratio in the overall period emerges even though five small nations had no public alternative university. In the heavily assisted Colombian case, the National University received only 19 percent of the awards (11 percent without its regional campuses). And Colombia was the only nation outside Central America to have its national university among LASPAU's top twenty institutional recipients. Ecuador shows LASPAU's greatest emphasis on public alternatives (receiving two-thirds of the nation's total, mostly at ESPOL), even where privates also did well.

45. All IDB higher education funds to Brazil went to umbrella organizations. This allows us to include Brazil in the tables on the IDB's institutional targets (unlike the case for Ford and the AID), but with its 72 percent of IDB higher education umbrella funds, Brazil obscures the general picture; for Spanish America, umbrella organizations were targets of only three projects. Including Brazil, umbrella organizations account for the bulk of IDB higher education funds after 1975. (Additionally, umbrella organizations received IDB funds for science and technology, funds often to be employed at public research institutes.)

46. A nonelite scattering emerges regarding the U.S. institutions to which LASPAU sent its scholarship holders. (Data printout October 23, 1987, from LASPAU's Steve Bloomfield.) LASPAU used over three hundred institutions for its 3,740 students. The greatest numbers were not at the private "Ivys" but at the public University of Illinois, the University of Texas, and SUNY–Buffalo. Of course, going beyond the Ivys still allowed for selectivity rather than random linking.

47. Were we to broaden our data to include private research centers, our view of donors' institutional selectivity would sharpen further. We obviously would see assistance going to more institutions, but these would still represent a small minority, and even among these, foundations worked overwhelmingly with the few best. Especially in the 1960s and 1970s, that work distinguished foundations from other donors and more so from domestic governments, which did not make private centers major targets. Moreover, the private research centers usually had more of the right stuff and much less of the wrong stuff than did private universities, and they were much more marked alternatives to the public mainstream (Levy 1996).

48. Although LASPAU's reach extended to nonelite universities, it omitted them on the private side and operated with only a minority of the public institutions selected for reformist vigor.

49. Taquini i-1; Taquini (1972: 127–31); Pérez Lindo (1985: 156); Cano (1985).

50. For example, a $7 million IDB loan has been seen as the most important event in the history of the Dominican Republic's INTEC, building a modern campus and buildings, the nation's second best private library, laboratories, as well as promoting growth, curriculum reform, faculty development via U.S. study, and the rise of INTEC to national leadership in engineering (Sánchez i-1).

51. Debatable cases could arise mostly over institutions that got assistance but were not leading targets. One might think of Mexico's top private universities, though they arguably received help at key development moments and had advantages of proximity in emulating U.S. practice even without formal assistance projects. Some of Brazil's leaders, such as the University of Sao Paulo, figured prominently within umbrella projects in addition to the help they received through projects targeted directly at the institution.

52. Observations made on the basis of "Final Report Forms" filed by grantees of the Council for the International Exchange of Scholars and sent by the organization's Rosemary Lyon, November 22, 1986.

53. The view of such institutions as leaders is reflected, for example, in various IDB evaluations done after the golden age (e.g., IDB/E7: 77–92). Similarly, the main institutional targets of the IDB's science and technology funding (largely after the golden age for university assistance) improved and are the region's most advanced in those areas (Castro and Alic 1997). This includes the national universities in Chile, Costa Rica, and Uruguay, along with the Simón Bolívar in Venezuela.

54. Yepes i; Arregui i; Koth i; Colonia i; Schiefelbein i-1. Another sign of La Molina's specialization is that it would be deemed a competent partner for the later assistance directed less at university development than at agricultural progress (e.g., AID #5270192, #5270238, both in the 1980s).

55. Ramírez (1986: 48); IDB/L30. AID also helped with buildings and then laboratories.

56. On the UAM failures, Paoli (1990: 270–72); Marquis (1987: 31–34, 93–95, 112); Ornelas i-2; Vielle i. The UAM made strides in the 1990s, lessening student politics and increasing research and the full-time professorate including nationally recognized figures. Decades before, Nuevo León, unusual among the state universities for the assistance it received, became a partial breakthrough. Then Aguascalientes, where Atcon may have consulted, became a pioneer. It became the only state university with administrative professionals named by a board. It led the way in matters such as tuition, central services, evaluation procedures, full-time professors, and a lack of disruptive student politics and student or faculty absenteeism (Ornelas 1996: 25–33). Mexican universities with specialized subject matter have presented a mixed picture. Agricultural universities have suffered from many ills, including heavy politicization. Some of these universities were early recipients of AID and Rockefeller assistance; on the other hand, their problems contrasted sharply with the record at the College of Postgraduates (Díaz i; IDB/L34). Meanwhile, the technical subsystem has usually been regarded as a disappointment, although it is too little studied and has offered some distinctiveness from the university system. The National Pedagogical University, created in the late 1970s, has suffered from struggles between the ministry and the unions (Kovacs 1989).

57. On Argentina's profile and belated attempt, García de Fanelli (1997: 38). Also in the 1990s the Fund for Enhancement of Educational Quality (FOMEC), a public

agency promoted by World Bank, undertook a major task of donors in other countries in the 1960s: giving extra funds to public universities that commit themselves to particular reforms. FOMEC represents a new breed of national funding agencies that adopt major tenets of the philanthropic ideal type. Regarding parallels with foreign donors in the 1960s, FOMEC has found it much easier to promote reform and discern positive impacts at eager universities of modest size than at the huge and much more structurally developed and entrenched national university. On the public provincial successes and failures of the 1970s, Cano (1985: 17–18); Cano D. i-1; Pérez Lindo (1985: 160); Taquini i-1; Mignone i; Mollis i-2; Krotsch i-1. Perhaps Argentina's main public alternative would be the Technological University (Mollis i-2; Mollis 1995) established by Juan Perón, just as Mexico's main technical institution was established by Lázaro Cárdenas, two champions of the masses who were hostile to the national university. Neither new institution, however, was intended to be a model for most universities to emulate, but rather more of an alternative apart. Beyond the technological area, Argentine success came more at the Bahía Blanca university, started in the 1950s on the U.S. model and far from the capital. It established departments and avoided the field of law, but never gained much weight or following (García i; Miguens i). Even the private universities in Argentina lacked the distinctiveness and stature found in most Latin American countries in the 1960s through the 1980s (Levy 1986); some observers found even that sector more affected by French than U.S. norms (Mignone i).

58. The major reasons for the erosion of the contrast include (1) we get further from the golden age of assistance; (2) a variety of other (nonassistance) forces play a role; (3) a new wave of public reform emerges, while privatization spreads; (4) both the reform and the privatization are much less dependent on foreign assistance than they were in the golden age; and (5) to the extent that fresh assistance counts, however, willingness and even eagerness to accept it is more widespread across nations and institutions than it was decades ago.

59. At particular times, examples have included Colombia's Los Andes benefiting from del Valle and Venezuela's Metropolitana benefiting from the Simón Bolívar (Lavados i-4).

60. Castro and Levy (2000). Additionally, laws in Venezuela and elsewhere that make the university degree a license automatically to practice the profession studied limits the ability of a given university to set its own curriculum or other academic rules. Orlando Albornoz concludes that Venezuela's experimental public universities, supposedly innovative, have largely reverted to the traditional professionalist university model; most of these universities were spawned without major foreign assistance and therefore could be added to the results we describe for alternative institutions in Argentina and Mexico (Albornoz i).

61. Venezuela's Simón Bolívar illustrated how workers could gain considerable representation, vote out academically oriented rectors, and get locked into national political parties (Lavados i-4; IDB/L41).

62. Within-nation brain drain is a factor here. An institution's isolated success can make it difficult to retain its personnel. La Molina lost many of its professors to a Peruvian agriculture ministry unable to recruit from a wider institutional base (Yepes i; Fritz i).

63. Chile would be the leader if we consider all universities, since all or almost all

of its eight were reform-oriented and good by Latin American standards, whereas Colombia's similar number of promising institutions was flanked by many more that were much less attractive. Colombia better approximated the Latin American pattern wherein select alternatives had more of the right stuff than did the national. Also, six of Chile's eight universities were private, with only the national and the State Technical University on the public side.

64. Vic Johnson evaluation, 6/20/69, and Johnson memo to W. R. Cotter, 5/28/69, both in FF #65118. Another view, however, was that Ford and others retreated prematurely when things did not go smoothly. A middle position was that the Antioquia experience lent support to those who claimed projects tended to elevate human resources greatly but to come up short in institutional development.

65. On the promise at del Valle, IDB/L21: appendix B, p. 21; IDB/L25: appendix B, pp. 6–7, appendix D; on the promise and frustrations, FF #61189, #64444, #63444; Coleman and Court (1993).

66. Our discussion of results at the public alternative universities as well as the National University leaves aside the two main private targets: Los Andes and the Catholic Javeriana. Analyzed above as a pet target, Los Andes has been a lasting success, particularly in engineering, despite difficulties such as a dispute over the rectorship in 1971 (Pelczar 1974: 60–61). La Javeriana was the country's oldest and second largest university. It had relatively high quality and political tranquility, never having undergone a student strike (FF #65050). In conjunction with foreign consultants and donors, La Javeriana too turned out a long-term development plan featuring reforms such as a departmental structure, consolidation of units, a full-time professorate, enhanced quality, fund-raising, enrollment growth, and inclusion of less privileged students. Donors funded their usual package of activities. Growth exceeded project goals, in both enrollments and full-time staff. A Ford evaluation deemed all goals of its project fulfilled, drawing specific contrasts to the experience at Colombia's National University (Rodolfo Low-Maus, Final Evaluation of the Basic Science Component, June 1970, in FF #65050). The targeted education school grew, diversified its student body, and introduced credit systems, semester cycles, and new courses and curriculum (Robert Arnove, "Final Evaluation of the Teacher Education Component," 6/22/70). It was called one of the nation's best two education schools, along with Antioquia's. An indication of the persisting standing of La Javeriana and other alternative universities was that, in Colombia's 1990 presidential elections, two of the four candidates came from La Javeriana, another from del Valle, and the winner from Los Andes.

67. On AID's troubles in Colombia, Coleman and Court (1993: 55); Thompson and Fogel (1977: 348); Magnusson (1970: 331). For favorable comparisons to other Colombian universities, see Serrano i; Lucio and Serrano (1992); Parra and Jaramillo (1985); IDB/E4. Donors also bolstered competitive dynamics among institutions. In fact, Ford came to see competition as excessive and insisted that none of its aided Colombian universities hire away from another unless there was a compelling danger otherwise. Antioquia and del Valle arrived at a gentlemen's agreement to compete in academic quality without luring the other's professors through increased salary and to inform the rival institution if any offer were made; but Antioquia insisted it had lost respect for the National University and would continue to raid it (FF #69-0604; Vic Johnson to files 8/1/68 in FF #65118). Donor-promoted restrictions on inter-

institutional competition appear rare and conflicted with pluralist norms of the U.S. model. The main restrictions on pluralism and the ability of alternative institutions to shine were the domestic factors that affected the entire system, including national legislation that sometimes intensified *homologación* (Lucio and Serrano 1992).

68. Such notions of reaching out to those left behind as gains occur elsewhere are akin to progressive federalism and likewise difficult to achieve.

69. Foundations such as Carnegie have championed such protective logic elsewhere, and this sort of institutional diversification for system expansion is a hallmark of the U.S. higher education model over the Continental European one (Clark 1978: 254–55; Lagemann 1989: 102–103).

70. Assistance from multiple sources including UN agencies vigorously poured into different forms of technical institutions, some for training and some for research, in the 1960s and 1970s (Levy 1996: 39–42). Although places such as Peru's La Molina exemplified targeted agricultural universities on the comparatively elite side, the ample efforts in this field were mostly to more modest institutions, using the U.S. land grant model to emphasize geographical and social decentralization as well as practical application. AID was a major promoter, in partnership with U.S. land grant universities and Latin American governments (Hansen 1990: 15; Miller 1984). Brazil was the dominant receiver, as abundant AID archival material shows (project printout from AID archivist Ardith Betts, e.g., on AID #5120094 for University of Vicosa with Purdue University). Among other major examples were AID with the University of Wisconsin at the Federal University of Rio Grande do Sul and AID with Purdue, Ford, and Rockefeller for multifaceted development through expansion, curriculum reform, staff development, and so forth at the Rural University of Minas Gerais—a small institution when first targeted (Schuh 1970). In the early 1960s, AID gave major support to make a land grant model out of Argentina's Balcare agricultural college. Another alternative institutional form, pointedly nonelite, was the open university. It received support from the OAS and several European governments but was not nearly as important as the technological and agricultural targets in the golden era.

71. Regional and other domestic political pressures also provoked expansion of these public universities—which helps explain why most were not favored assistance targets, whether in Argentina or Colombia. Whatever their own pluralist, decentralizing proclivities, however, donors generally did not impose the alien and internationally unusual U.S. mode of planting institutions outside population centers. Instead, outside its work in agriculture, donors sometimes seemed to have a consciously urban policy (Ford Foundation 1962).

72. Ortiz Mena (1975: 9); IDB/L32, 1–2.

73. Masís i; Ramírez i; Santa Ana i; IDB/L32. The IDB hoped that scholarships and economic recovery would eventually redeem the regionalization project.

74. Gómez i. Some Chileans skeptical about project feasibility were tempted in by AID's abundant resources (Schiefelbein i-3; D'Etigny i-2). Although such examples undermine charges of external control, they also undermine claims of partnership in pursuit of commonly desired change. On the Gómez announcement and the University of Chile college effort overall, see Río and Alegría (1968).

75. At least through the 1980s, then, U.S. Fulbright scholars eagerly based themselves at various Chilean universities, such as the national and the private technical in chemistry and the private Concepción, Catholic, and Austral in ecology, often reporting on parity with facets of good U.S. universities. Although military repression

pushed out such university options in the social sciences and although regionalization was not the cause of the universities' successes in the 1960s and beyond, it did help to allow and then protect that success.

76. Lemaitre (1985: 9–37) as well as William Carmichael to Howard Dressner 5/23/73, Nina Manitzas to file 10/26/64, Barclay Hudson to Peter Bell 9/3/71 in FF #61341; Galdames (1988: 141); Pizarro (1988: 155–57); Comisión Reforma del Centro Universitario de Temuco (1968); IDB/L14: 27–29; Lavados (1987); Ramírez Necochea (1964: 89–92, 147).

77. Ramírez Necochea (1964: 89–93). But the Communists denounced a U.S. attack with Chilean "accomplices" on "our" Latin American university and were wary of a U.S. orientation to prepare students to work in "dad's store" rather than to be professionals.

78. On the negative assessments, "Autofinanciamiento," *El Mercurio* 7/6/1974 and "Formación regional," *El Mercurio* 11/14/1973, both editorials. On the positive side, Comisión Reforma del Centro Universitario de Temuco (1968).

79. In West Germany short-cycle studies likewise ran into difficulties, greater when the attempt was to integrate them into existing universities than when separate institutions were created (Cerych and Sabatier 1986: 240). Chile would subsequently create a markedly differentiated system with universities, professional institutes, and technical training centers (Brunner, Courard, and Cox 1992).

80. Seymour (1985: 18–19). More generally, see Segal (1985: 198); Matthews (1982).

81. Most two-year institutions are public, but Peru and Venezuela and then Chile also created private ones.

82. The CSUCA experience could arguably fit in the chapter's section on national universities, as the organization comprised the nationals and as some CSUCA funds were directly targeted to certain universities, but the distinctive characteristic of this assistance lay in its cross-national clustering.

83. Lungo i; Bloom i; Piva i; CSUCA (1988b: 63–71); FF #62109 and #73661; IDB/L8; Enarson (1962).

84. On the pessimism, Howard Freeman to John Fulnari, 6/1/73 in FF #73661. In 1987 a Ford grant supported research on curriculum development, only a minor exception to the retreat at CSUCA (William Carmichael to Franklin Thomas, Request #DCP-1028, 6/11/87, mimeo).

85. AID pointedly noted that FUPAC was much more receptive than the national universities to assistance (AID #596-11-660-012.2, 6/1/73; #5960012, subproject 02). Although a private target, FUPAC also was an attempt at coordination to ward off the potential ills of pluralist proliferation. Projects there also soon ran into trouble. Additionally, when AID was disappointed in its agricultural project with CSUCA, it turned to the separate Interamerican Institute of Agricultural Sciences (AID #596001206, PD-AAB-473-G1 and PD-AAB-474-D1). In management, the Central American Institute for Business Administration would become a major private target (AID #5960101).

86. A parallel for CSUCA's fate would unfold at the East Africa university. The Rockefeller Foundation's sound technical rationales made little sense politically. How, for example, would Kenya agree to rely on a medical school in Uganda? Such examples should not imply donor inability to foster coordination. The OAS is among organizations that have stimulated interuniversity dialogue and endeavors. The point

here is that scattered efforts have not basically shaped growth. They have not represented a viable alternative through international assistance, to what reformers saw as
the academically and economically less rational growth through institutional proliferation that dominated in most countries.

87. This finding about growth parallels the last chapter's about the short period
of philanthropic overreach. Early on, donors emphasized selectivity, care, and a sort
of elitism. Modernization zeal then made donors push growth per se and increasingly
see it inextricably and positively linked with other goals, as "all good things" could
go together. But the supreme faith in growth faded by the mid-1970s, although the
IDB, like domestic governments, persevered with sporadic yet substantial support.

88. As late as 1984 the IDB read Colombia's tenfold jump over the previous decade
as inadequate, and provided a large loan supportive of accelerated growth (IDB/L28:
12; Parra and Jaramillo 1985: 36).

89. We find more support for the philanthropic principle that seed money attracts
wider funding than for the critique that it builds things that fail to attract financial
support once donors themselves pull away (though the adequacy of that support
remains open to question, particularly regarding maintenance of quality).

90. Considerations of small size and lack of development may have made certain
nations simultaneously attractive to donors and likely to grow anyway. In any event,
the analysis here fits the last chapter's finding on donors' intention and success in
helping smaller, poorer nations catch up or at least not fall behind as much as they
otherwise would. We see impact not just in "easy" proportional increases from low
numerical bases but also in striking movement on cohort enrollment percentages. We
make the generalization about Spanish America because Brazil's weight can otherwise
overwhelm comparative data and Brazil was simultaneously a huge country with a
small higher education system relative to population. In one sense, comparatively low
cohort enrollments in Brazil, Chile, and Colombia, all still between 11 and 13 percent
in 1983 (Hidalgo 1987: 95–96), suggest limited impact of assistance on growth in
large countries, and lagging enrollments in such large countries greatly affect aggregated figures. But because these countries were relatively low in enrollments when
assistance arrived, their relative standing after the golden age is only a weak indicator
of assistance impact, and the next endnote considers growth rates instead. Additionally, Brazil also illustrates some intranational impact of assistance in poor regions, as
shown by massive IDB projects.

91. Although there is no definitive way to make this comparison, an exploratory
focus starting in 1960 seems warranted, since that is around when Ford and the IDB
entered. Less clear is what end point to choose. Because the golden age terminates in
the mid-1970s and over time nonassistance factors would obviously play an increasing role, we look mostly at 1960–75. We use UNESCO's *Statistical Yearbooks* from
1972, 1975, 1981, and 1988. Major growth occurs in most of the heavily assisted
countries, including Colombia, Costa Rica, and Chile, although Chile fades if we look
out to 1980, due to the junta's restrictive policies. At the same time, Argentina and
Uruguay trail markedly, whereas Mexico turns in an average growth performance
and Venezuela, relying on oil revenue, is the singular clear exception to our pattern.
Other leaders in growth were Ecuador and El Salvador whereas other trailers included
Bolivia and Peru; the first two countries were on the list of more targeted nations,
and Bolivia was on the less targeted list, with Peru ambiguous. More striking patterns
emerge if we look more closely at particular periods. For the 1960s, the heavily as-

sisted countries outgrow the others 58 percent to 34 percent, whereas the difference shrinks to 55 percent to 48 percent for the 1970s and by 1980–85 the second group far outpaces the first, so that if we were to compare the entire 1960–85 period the two groups would be about equal.

92. A huge 1982 IDB project in Brazil achieved only 60 percent of its graduate growth goal, compared with 90 percent for the undergraduate level. Efforts at Venezuela's Simón Bolívar faltered in the face of preferences to study abroad (IDB/L41; IDB/E7). The best graduate fields in the Chile-California Ford convenio also came up short, as had graduate targets in individual projects at the Chilean national university (IDB/E3; IDB/E7 51; John Strasma to Peter Bell 9/10/71 in FF #65096, #650327). Consistent with implementation literature, results in graduate studies suffered from the difficulty of a task that required major changes in norms, although implementation was helped by the targeting of new areas of still limited numerical scope. Although growth goals fared better for the first-degree level, technical institutes at that level overbuilt on the false UNESCO faith that large supply would bring large demand (Lavados 1987: 129).

93. Some actions probably promoted growth even in the rare circumstance where the donor recommended against growth, as with AID at Paraguay's National University (Fritz 1989: 16).

94. This growth included selective institutions such as Colombia's Santander, and often meant support for the order of tripled enrollments within seven or ten years as at Colombia's del Valle from 1968 or Chile's private technical university from 1965 (IDB/E4: 32–33; IDB/L25; IDB/L35: 1).

95. On education's shares, Psacharopoulos and Woodhall (1985: 128); on the cross-regional growth, Levy (1986: 4–5, 40). For figures back to 1850 on enrollment per population, Wilkie (1977: 142).

96. Another type of stratification relates back to the last chapter and the fact that assistance concentrated much more on higher education than on primary education. The point here is that as assistance facilitated growth, it further pushed domestic expenditures toward the higher side, though purely domestic factors, such as demography, were paramount. UNESCO data show that higher education's share of the total education budget in Latin America rose from 16 to 24 percent in the 1970s.

97. Raghaven (1983); this conclusion supports Rondinelli's (1989) on assistance generally. Regarding socioeconomic groups, the favored institutions tended to have a higher level than the bypassed ones. This point should be seen, however, against the progressive thrusts identified regarding geographical and nonelite institutional targets as well as assistance's role in overall expansion. Pluralism can be reconciled with a fair amount of stratification, but the narrow top and lack of competition or emulation of models (Tedesco and Blumenthal 1986: 25) fails the pluralist promise of assistance. So perhaps does the loss of accountability when the largest universities are marginalized (Cepeda 1979: 87–88).

98. Other diversity emerged as a rather natural by-product of growth. Most attempts to limit pluralist proliferation failed, including donor efforts at national universities and at regional campuses. Still other institutional diversity appeared where reforms that aimed at new institutional configurations prismatically mixed with pre-existing or other evolving institutional configurations.

4. Institution Building

1. As donors pushed institutional building, they at least tacitly rejected the argument that universities naturally stand out organizationally as anarchic and decentralized. See March and Olsen (1976).

2. In terms of one of the most influential analyses of the modernization school, strong institutions have coherence, autonomy, adaptability, and complexity (Huntington 1968: 12–24). The reformers' position unequivocally emphasized the Latin American university's lack of coherence. It found autonomy at once too limited to protect the institution in some respects yet so excessive in other respects as to undermine adaptability (and accountability to a changing society), while it denounced a complexity that perversely hindered adaptability more than it facilitated accomplishment of varied tasks.

3. As Molina i observed for Chilean and other universities. On the other hand, projects with particular units often produced intrainstitutionally stratifying effects.

4. An example of a governmental agency donor considered key to the system's better management was Colombia's ICETEX, concerned largely with study abroad. Ford supported a research unit within the agency's planning office as well as staff training, improving files, and the like (FF #71576). AID gave to improve the data and managerial capacity of government as well as public universities in Peru, though its purpose was simultaneously too "vague" and "ambitious" (Louis Macary 3/19/76 in PD-AAB0381-D1 of AID #5270067-03).

5. The Ford reports referred to on Los Andes are Vic Johnson evaluation 6/20/69 in FF #65118; William Cotter to Harry Wilhelm 8/29/69 in FF #64438; Vic Johnson to William Cotter "Final Evaluation" 7/7/69 in FF #64438). The praise came despite reservations about socioeconomic elitism and inefficiencies of scale. By late in the century the "U.S. model" had modified itself, in that financial centralization yielded some ground to decentralization in budgeting and planning to schools, departments, and other units within institutions. Chile was Latin America's early leader in that trend.

6. Levy (1994). Colombia went further with governing boards for public universities. Under military rule, the University of Chile had an authoritarian board, but the board disappeared with the restoration of Chilean democracy.

7. On del Valle, IDB/L25: 12–16, appendix B; on Antioquia, James Smith, AID.

8. Wilhelmy i; Larraín i; Vargas i.

9. Many unassisted privates have achieved elements of the U.S. management model. The fact that almost all privates draw fully or mostly on private sources, headed by tuition, stems from the institutions' origins and nature more than from assistance, although Ford and other advice helped (Frodin 1970). Regarding governance as well, the very nature of private institutions tended to favor hierarchy, stability, and (carefully restricted) external representation. Small size and a lack of faculties with formidable academic prestige or tradition also helped centralization. But donors had a discernible impact at the most advanced private places. Fernando Cepeda, a prominent critic of assistance for weakening university councils and other authorities, credited them for strengthening the size and force of administration at the private Los Andes university (Cepeda 1979: 500–503).

10. Worse yet was military rule that put the rectorship under its control. Chile was the main case, although an ironic twist was that the consequently diminished

legitimacy of central administration contributed to a reassertion of faculty power in the 1980s.

11. An example of pushiness outside projects was promotion of U.S. football in Mexican universities. Results were limited: the U.S. sport gained a foothold while soccer continued to predominate. Often, as in Argentina, sports remain quite weak. Throughout Latin America both intramural sports and competitive sports involving teams bearing the name and intensely loyal following of their institutions remain rare. In some countries, such as Chile, teams bearing the names of universities use unrelated professionals, not students.

12. Paul and Wolff (1992); IDB/E3: 39. Others vigorously disagree, arguing that the IDB made a very positive contribution to Brazilian universities by force of its money and credibility. Improved utilization of space facilitated overall expansion and opportunity for new groups to enter higher education as well as for other groups to remain near home rather than to crowd their way toward Sao Paulo and other urban centers (Gheen i).

13. IDB/E1: 40, 28–29; IDB/E4: 3. An additional point was that campuses, like other facilities, simply would be underutilized.

14. On the IDB, Aroni i; on Venezuela, IDB/E7: 96; on Paraguay, Anderson et al. (1965).

15. Personal correspondence from Luis Scherz-García 9/30/87; examples of the evaluations include IDB/L29 and IDB/L32.

16. Fritz (1989: 17) on Paraguay and Blaise et al. (1968: 30) on Ecuador. After the golden age, the Mellon Foundation has remained prominent in niches of library development.

17. Libraries sometimes seem to work by the recipe. Facilities at institutions such as the Dominican Republic's INTEC fill with students diligently at work. I remember chatting in the corridors with officials at Peru's Catholic University when several students admonished us to "shush."

18. Mollis (1995). UNAM lacked a central bookstore as well as a central library, instead relying on perhaps sixty small operations, some carrying only publications by UNAM's own press. Mexico's Autonomous Metropolitan University did much better by starting with central bookstores and libraries at each of its three campuses, with coordination and interlibrary loans—but also with considerable disruption by unionized workers, forcing students and scholars to borrow and buy elsewhere (Ornelas i-4). U.S. Fulbright scholars have commented negatively in their end-of-tour reports on Mexico's university libraries.

19. Harrison i-1. The University of Chile–University of California convenio (1979: 36, 68–70, 105) reports on library modernization, but on measures more modest than university centralization. Ford's reports had bemoaned the proliferation of University of Chile libraries scattered around Santiago. At the end of the twentieth century, there were sixty-five, of which ten were "central" for a whole faculty; engineering had ten libraries and medicine had fifteen libraries on five campuses (Universidad de Chile 2002).

20. An alternative mix occurs where there is no central library but where central administration, cooperation, or computers facilitate sharing across units. U.S. universities show some of these mixes, but the balance there remains much more in favor of the central library. Intriguing but much less common have been situations where the very lack of the Americanized web comprising centralized institutions aug-

mented the role of central libraries. In federal universities in less-developed regions of Brazil, the isolation of campuses, absence of student centers, and students' inability to buy books all contributed to students spending extended hours at the library (IDB/E3: 24).

21. AID in Central America continued efforts to stimulate campus bookstores, as well as the provision of translated books. The latter has allowed for pushing certain ideologies.

22. On the 1950s, see Turina i. Regarding Valparaíso, a new campus in a proposed nearby place as "touristy" as Viña del Mar would have isolated the university from vibrant multiclass urban life. Instead, leaders opted to build up along eight city streets. With government and French support, they could expand physically within months rather than years, thus accommodating huge pent-up enrollment growth. Leaders recall with pride how they placed such principles ahead of easy IDB funds (Allard i-2; Livingston i).

23. Accame i. Similarly, Argentines who planned for integrated campus life for their new public provincial universities recognized the lack of a dorm tradition and instead pledged to help students find pensiones nearby, an attempt at integrating town and gown (Taquini i-1).

24. Cano (1985: 20); Pérez Lindo (1985: 265). Although some Argentine provincial universities proceeded to build campuses, a national university contrast remained between Argentina and nations like Peru regarding campuses (Cotler i; Colonia i).

25. IDB *Newsletter* July/August 1991: 14.

26. Hennessy (1979: 155); Puryear i.

27. Magnusson (1970: 45). On the restaurants, Hennessy (1979: 155). The lack of a supportive university web could lead to paradoxical but understandable desires by exceptional faculties to have their own campuses. See Valdés (1995) on Chile and efforts to avoid the university's politicization. Such efforts suggest prismatic displacement more than ideal typical centralizing reform.

28. Robert Banks and Dorothy Tanck de Estrada, Final Evaluation 7/15/72, FF #65326; William Gamble to Robert Banks 5/29/68 FF #63519; FF #62109; Lungo i.

29. Wickham (1973: 212); Wolf i-2. Further on CSUCA, Frodin (1970: 20).

30. For example, Argentine surveys showed that only some 10 percent of the secondary school graduates had a clear idea of the career they wanted to pursue (Dolcini 1983: 223).

31. Karpinsky (1982: 15–17, 58, 96); FF #62109; IDB/L8; FF #62109; AID #5960012-05.

32. González i; Stitchkin i; Blakemore (1976: 346–47).

33. On Antioquia and del Valle, FF #61189, including Rodolfo Low-Maus's 12/70 "Evaluation of Grant"; on Los Andes, FF #61188, especially the New York office file.

34. Waggoner (1973: 146); Wolf i-3.

35. Critics decried an assistance overreach, more imperialist than philanthropic, where they saw donors pushing the U.S. concept of general higher education in advanced countries. What made sense to them for Central America and Peru, where secondary preparation was admittedly weak, did not make sense to them for much of the Southern Cone (Ribeiro 1968: 133–34; Scherz-García 1967: 399; Sánchez 1973: 123–25; Ratinoff i; Padua i). The argument that general studies was not a fit import where secondary schools provided classical, broad university preparatory education echoed the argument in countries like West Germany (Clark 1995: 43).

36. On Central America, CSUCA (1988a: 54); Paniagua i; Karpinsky (1982: 190); on Concepción, González i; on India, Rudolph and Rudolph (1972: 235); on Peru, Sánchez (1973: 117). Nor would it much matter whether the reform was part of a foreign aid project. At UNAM, for example, the rector's addition of a year to the preprofessional bachillerato led to disruptions that then prompted most faculties to reduce their professional programs from five to four years.

37. Both sides saw centralization as an opportunity for weaker faculties. Such was the case regarding efforts by Rector Juan Gómez Millas to build new universitywide science units at Chile's national university; leading faculties wanted to maintain their own research activities (Fuenzalida 1984).

38. D'Etigny i-2; Renner (1973a: 4). For an argument that such autonomy must be limited by accountability, see Castro and Levy (2000).

39. In the ensuing decades this professional development web has been broken less through innovative academic reform than through the overproduction of students for the job market in particular professions. In fact, students' tenacious defense of the professional option, amid realities that then condemn the majority to frustration, has worked against needed movement from professionalist to more general higher education forms. See Castro and Levy (2000). One proposal to break the web has been to do away with formal rules that promise an automatic link between degree and employment.

40. U.S. debate over the number of required credits, whether for a common generalized core or for "majors," involves a minority of total credits, with flexibility and student choice paramount. Many Latin Americans regard fixed curriculum as a virtue, flexibility as an abdication of responsibility.

41. Lawyers and others made such complaints even though they themselves sometimes defended not the specialization but the generality of the law degree, claiming it offered education for the "cultured man" (Dolcini 1983: 221). They then look approvingly on the fact that "lawyers" work in various jobs. In contrast, foreign consultants and domestic reformers have often seen such work as proof of irrationally excessive enrollment in an overspecialized field of study.

42. For example, one 1972 report to Ford considered results in general studies dismal while another saw it taking hold widely. Robert Banks and Dorothy Tanck de Estrada, final evaluation report, 7/15/72, FF #65326; Ford Foundation (1972). Similarly, some have depicted chaired professors as dominant in most Latin American universities (Vessuri 1986: 1), whereas others find the chair almost dead, even where faculties predominate, as in Bolivia (Escobar i). Although the chair as formal administrative unit has been killed in places like the University of Costa Rica, some persisting privileges, including control over organization of the curriculum in a given knowledge area and its (lack of) articulation with other parts of the university, stem from tradition and the difficulty of otherwise holding onto top people. Finally, the term *catedrático* is used in some nations (e.g., Mexico) for part-time professors more than for exalted or sovereign academics.

43. Reserve marks other accounts, which do not claim to know the degree of behavioral change. For example, Latapí (1978: 9) merely cites the structural arrangements called departments or related names in certain public universities in Colombia, Venezuela, Brazil, and Central America, along with private ones in Mexico.

44. CONARE (1987b: 20); William Gamble to Robert Banks 5/29/68 FF #63519; Fischel i; Chinchilla i.

45. Vicerectoría de Docencia (1987: 11–29); Karpinsky (1982: 18).

46. Vicerectoría de Docencia (1985: 9–18); Durán (1987: 36–37).

47. Macaya i; Paniagua i; Estrada i; Universidad de Costa Rica (1987: 23). And so reformers have continued to seek alternatives. A bachillerato was to be a general academic degree, with access to graduate education or to nonprofessionalist jobs, but it too was soon seen as another screening device, preprofessional and inferior.

48. On San Carlos, Greenwald (1986: 68, 98, 139); Dorothy Tanck to William Gamble 9/23/69; Donnelly i. On Nicaragua, Arnove (1994: 114–15). While it was not an effective model for the region, the UCR was a model for its nation; in most respects, Costa Rica's "National" and technological universities have followed form—with ample foreign assistance (CONARE 1987b).

49. University of Chile–University of California (1979: 102); K. N. Rao to William Carmichael memo 2/23/82 in FF #650327.

50. Teitelboim i. In economics thirty-four of the forty courses (in 1982) were obligatory, leaving just physical education and five electives, which could be taken in or outside economics.

51. On Concepción, Muga and Brunner (1996: 161) and on Austral, IDB/L16–L17. Interviews on these and other Chilean universities with Yates i; Croxatto i; Vargas i; Allende i; Lavados i-1; Izquierdo i; Thayer i; Fortoul i. Additionally, the last chapter reported successes in academic centralization at some of the donor-assisted regional colleges.

52. Silié (1988: 49–50); Consejo Nacional de Educación Superior (1986: 256–82).

53. For example, professors at Mexico's Jesuit Iberoamericana, themselves previously socialized through professional training programs, were uncomfortable teaching students in diverse careers. Ibero's students were disoriented and not used to exercising choice or seeking academic counseling toward that end. Many "departments" were inclined to focus on one career. Besides, until 1973, the Ibero was affiliated to UNAM and could not easily break from its mold. Nonetheless, Ibero managed some common trunks, electives, and departmentalization. Meneses (1983: 135–36); Meneses i; Vielle i.

54. For example, IDB/E5: 17. The Mexican case illustrates qualifications to our argument in that some private institutions achieved academic centralization without large assistance projects. They created themselves with the new model in mind or, like the elite Autonomous Technological Institute of Mexico, they faced less opposition in moving in that direction. But even Mexico, despite its low national standing in receiving assistance projects, shows important influences from abroad. Leaders at Mexico's privates were conspicuous consumers of the U.S. model, carriers of ideas across the border. Also, the foremost private universities got early boosts for academic centralization from several assistance projects. Or projects that focused on administrative centralization set conditions that then facilitated the academic reforms pushed internally. The Autonomous University of Guadalajara and the Monterrey Tec are two examples. The Tec became perhaps Mexico's leader for departments, multisemester common courses for new students, and de-emphasis on professional career training.

55. A 1972 assessment for Ford placed del Valle, Antioquia, and (Venezuela's) Oriente behind the nationals in Costa Rica and El Salvador, among Ford's public recipients (K. N. Rao memo, 11/10/72, FF #65326). El Salvador was then to fall into horrific decline.

56. Prismatic forms thus emerged even in the absence of assistance projects, as long as imported ideas clashed with traditional practice. That helps explain how Atcon (1966: 37–41) would early on find such formalism as departments that neither handled curriculum policy nor promoted general knowledge and new departments and institutes that were hollow structures within which chaired professors and faculties continued to own courses and set policy.

57. Balán (1992: 22–26); Mundet i. Also, Argentine public university rectors continue to be elected.

58. Spain's efforts at departmentalization in the 1980s produced prismatic results reminiscent of Latin America's. Opportunities grew for junior professors, and progress went furthest in the hard disciplines, which were newer and more internationally oriented, but departments usually reported to faculties, which continued to grant the degrees; departments would be repeatedly reshuffled or renamed (McKenna 1985: 464–65; Bunge 1984: 38). Departmentalization in West Germany in the 1970s was launched to substitute for the largest faculties and to influence but not replace institutes; however, the departments fell short as institutes retained their control of courses and examinations, and departmentalization was also hurt by massification (Clark 1995: 40).

59. Uruguay would present an even more traditional picture than Argentina and Mexico. Its University of the Republic would lack academic centralization through curriculum or credit flexibility, just as it would lack administrative centralization; it represented perhaps the Latin American extreme of faculty dominance (Filgueira 1992: 791; Singh i; Landi i). And Uruguay would have no alternative university for many years. With its greater openness to Americanization, Venezuela went further than any other low-receiver nation, but changes would be limited outside the heavily assisted Simón Bolívar. On Argentina, interviews with Cano D. i-2; García i; Krotsch i-2; Mollis i-3; Tedesco i. On Mexico, interviews with Barnés i; Barquín i; Muñoz i; Ornelas i-4; Resendiz i; Zorrilla i; and see Barquín and Orozco (1988: table 1).

60. Unlike Brazil's military rulers, Peru's were rather leftist and their U.S. relationship was more antagonistic. Yet Peru's 1969 blueprint mandated general studies, departmentalization, and other key facets of the U.S. model. A feature that undercut the U.S. model was the corporatist attempt at imposition by central government of a standardized structure throughout the system. U.S. ideas had been introduced in earlier donor activity, and the new reform leaders had traveled and worked with the likes of consultant George Waggoner. Initial success at San Marcos, including electives, common credits, and four semesters of general studies, soon proved unworkable, and pressures built to reverse much of what had changed. Introduced in 1962, general studies would be largely gone by 1964 (Cisneros 1993: 14). Other large public universities also proved hard to change, as deans led resistance, while top privates implemented more. By 1972 the government retreated. Formal registration in general studies, which had jumped from 6,750 in 1965 to 37,111 in 1970, fell back to 3,243 by 1975 (Asamblea Nacional de Rectores 1988: 33). A more modest reform was initiated in 1983 (Colonia i; Vera M. i-1; Cotler i; Marrou i).

61. William Ellis in PAR-AAA-293-E1, 12/29/72 of AID #5120263. Also on Brazil's broad reforms, Machado Neto (1968: 269–73) and Schwartzman (1988: 102–103).

62. Pontes (1985: 8–9), Vessuri (1986: 1); Vera M. i-1; Murdoch i. The importance of AID coupled with eager Brazilian domestic reform of relatively undeveloped

structures, backed by a stable, authoritarian, political regime bent on higher education development, shows parallels to the Indonesian situation (Method 1976) perhaps more than to any Latin American counterpart.

63. At Colombia's National University, heavy assistance accelerated early progress and faculties were cut from twenty-three to nine, but by 1964 faculties asserted their dominance, and reform was as "resisted in practice" as it was "generally accepted in principle" (Magnusson 1970: 371).

64. Vic Johnson evaluation 6/20/69 in FF #65118; Pelczar (1974: 54).

65. On del Valle, Wickham (1973: 99, 155, 174–76), Thompson and Fogel (1977: 348); Magnusson (1970: 371). Formalism also emerged when Santander's departments, created at the IDB's insistence, wound up merely administering careers, achieving neither authority over them nor autonomy from them (IDB/E4: 39). Meanwhile, the University of Cartagena was one example of a lesser public institution, less assisted, failing more.

66. Hans Simons to John Netherton 3/4/68 in FF #61188.

67. Faring better here are dependency critiques that lament the stratifying impacts of assistance. Many targeted institutions moved ahead or further ahead of other institutions in centralizing reforms. Intrainstitutional effects are trickier to assess, however. In many cases, reform was targeted for or took hold only or mostly in just parts of the institution. We have seen that differences then persist as gaps, as leaders beat others while failing to serve as models to which the others elevate themselves. But our findings also undermine the critique that assistance pulls the Latin American university apart (Revéiz 1977; Scherz-García 1967: 399; Garretón 1987: 6). Internal clashes did sometimes lead to destabilization (Arnove 1977: 109), but in important cases of project success, institutions were strengthened administratively and academically, and most often stratification meant prismatic coexistence. Also, stratification was limited by the problems at targeted units, sometimes emasculated by traditional elements and therefore rendered formalistic. In any case, intrainstitutional heterogeneity must be judged against the reality that, after all, the preassistance university was not a unified institution.

68. Today, some governments in countries such as Mexico seek to accomplish reforms in partnership with intrauniversity units, having concluded that central administration (often still elected) is an obstacle to reform.

69. Our comparisons square with impressions held by some keen observers who have maintained intensive ongoing contact with the region's universities. For example, Lavados (i-2) hypothesized that assistance had been pivotal for departmentalization. He cited the IDB first and foremost but also the influence of Atcon in Chile, Brazil, Colombia, and Haiti, among others.

70. In the 1990s Mexico undertook measures to strengthen institutions and their budgets. Tuition was imposed at public institutions other than UNAM, and other supplements to fixed government subsidies grew (Levy 1998). In Argentina's UBA, the demise of military government in 1983 brought renewed rapid expansion and new struggles over the proper role of general studies. One basic cycle was replaced by a cycle of up to two years, leading to a diploma in general studies. In 1989 eleven new public universities opted for a department structure and rector power, with limited student political representation. Public universities started to charge tuition for graduate study (García de Fanelli 1996, 1997). Meanwhile, reformers in Latin American nations that were major recipients hark back to earlier gains in centralization;

there is a lot of tinkering if not reinventing the wheel, as when reformers grapple with ideas to install general studies.

71. On both the administrative and academic side, the circulation (and circularity) of reforms aimed at institutional centralization are hardly limited to Latin America, as Spain's departmentalization efforts show. The 1968 French reform ideas, which engendered great opposition and produced new departments that really remained faculties, are not dead. Many countries have sought to strengthen rectors and other institutional leaders as well as to achieve greater academic centralization in matters like credit systems; results vary greatly by country (OECD 1998: 78–79). The "Bologna" reforms for the European continent now herald a major move toward much of the academic centralization discussed in this chapter.

5. Academic Work

1. The chapter excludes other aspects of academic work such as full-time status for students and interactive pedagogy, as well as matters treated in the last chapter, such as general studies.

2. On Brazil, Ribeiro (1968); on Colombia, Jaramillo (1963: 171–72). Assistance and certainly massification contributed to diminishing the relative weight of chairs within the system, but we lack study of the mix between diminution and persistence. An unfortunate Latin American hybrid has been the *catedrático* who is part-time and may work far from the university while retaining power to block academic reform (Atcon 1966: 76–78). Still today, *catedráticos* are part-timers in nations such as Mexico; this is a problem of semantic confusion for students of comparative higher education, but these professors are usually not the academic powerbrokers.

3. Lemaitre and Lavados (1986: 100–101) affirm the full-time imperative in research, while maintaining that part-timers can teach undergraduates well. Donors' preference for full-timers sometimes extended even to the professional fields (Mosher 1957: 302); AID reports for places like Guatemala's San Carlos argued that too high a percentage of part-timers presented major problems for long-term training efforts (AID #5960012).

4. Atcon (1966: 75). On assistance in Colombia, see Wickham (1973: 81–86).

5. Distance education, which in some sense undercuts the full-time concept, was inspired and pushed more by Europe than by the United States (Kreimer i) but did not have great force.

6. Cueto (1991: 6); Schwartzman (1991: 128, 193–94).

7. Moreover, the picture would look much more targeted if our study encompassed individual scholarships as much as institutional projects. Much of the effort to bolster teaching came through such scholarships (Lavados i-4).

8. Pelczar (1974: 55). Additionally, where large assistance projects did not emerge, reformers could seek help from friendly international agencies for the full-time idea, as with OAS help for Mexico's programs in its provincial public universities (Turina i).

9. The Brazilian reform of 1968 looked to convert all higher education onto a U.S. research university model with full-time professors (Schwartzman 1988: 110). AID and others participated, but this push to standardization was mostly domestic. The push overstated not only transferability to Latin America but ubiquity in the U.S. system. In fact, full-time professors with research and teaching tasks account for only

a minority of the U.S. total. First, there are many adjunct professors and other part-timers, even in major U.S. research universities. Second, full-timers in community and four-year colleges, like full-timers in Mexico's technical institutes, are often devoted exclusively to teaching, rather than to a teaching-research nexus. Third, many large U.S. universities include professional schools with part-timers, nontenure tracks, emphasis on practical experience, and conflicts with the norms of the arts and sciences departments. In U.S. universities, however, the balance of power is such that the departments' norms of full-time work often penetrate the schools of law, medicine, education, and business. See Altbach (1996); Halpern (1987: 321); Boyer i.

10. On occasion, AID-financed collaborative projects operated on the belief that part-time status was preferable for Latin American universities, at least for the field in question. An example was the early project between Mexico's University of Sonora and the University of Arizona, covering several fields (Adams and Cumberland 1960: 258, 133–34).

11. Castellanos (1976: 213). Before and after figures both understate the full-time contribution insofar as full-timers teach more courses than part-timers, thus accounting for a higher percentage of class contact hours with students than of total personnel. Assistance success is limited where projects buy full-timers who do not remain after the project's termination.

12. Fernando Molina i emphasized two related points on full-time professors. First, philanthropy carried to Chile and eventually to many parts of Latin America, an idea that lacked significant indigenous roots. Second, once the idea was in some domestic reformers' minds, assistance was crucial to making it practical. On Colombia's push forward, Franco (1991: 170).

13. Pontes (1985: 21, 49–50); Gusso, Tramontin, and Braga (1988: 184–86, 252–54).

14. Dettmer (1983: 115). The University of Costa Rica became more than one-third full-time, and the "National" and technological universities, which were more dependent on assistance, achieved higher percentages (CONARE 1987a: 151–55).

15. Venezuela is a countercase as a nontargeted country that implemented many practices associated with academic professionalization. In fact, full-time status with salaries, sabbaticals, and other benefits was ample enough to bring reasonable charges of excess privilege (Vessuri 1986: 16–19; Albornoz 1979: 59–78). Receptivity to U.S. norms and oil money to finance efforts without heavy assistance account for the singular case. Roughly half the public university professorate became "exclusive dedication," others "full-time," with high proportions also in public nonuniversity institutions, though not in any private category (IESA 1991: 13, data for 1988–89). Then, however, the country's poor economic performance and political turmoil in the 1990s undermined prior achievements. More difficult to explain was Peru's relatively high percentage of full-timers. The national San Marcos university claimed to have roughly half of its staff as full time. Possible explanations included a legacy of early, assisted reform, lesser massification than at some other national universities, and the lack of alternative employment. But mostly the figure reflected formalism, as most nominal full-timers were not true full-timers. A full-time academic profession was less a reality at San Marcos than at donors' alternative Peruvian targets such as the Catholic and La Molina universities (Marrou i; Yepes i). More toward the bleak Argentine numerical picture were nations such as the Dominican Republic, where there were

almost no full-time university professors, even at the few elite universities (Consejo Nacional de Educación Superior 1986: 302; Miguel i).

16. On the low numbers, Cano (1985: 81) and Vessuri (1986: 19); on the field and institutional variation, Mollis i-1; Krotsch i-3. Subsequent provincial proliferation produced a few notable successes, headed by Quilmes with exclusive time staff accounting for 72 percent, but most other institutions remained much lower (García de Fanelli 1997: 78–87). Nationally, the full-time figure hovered around only 15 percent, a fact reflecting the sad absence of an academic web as there are very few electives and "academic excellence is to be found almost nowhere" (Balán 1992: 27–29, quotation on 29; Balán i).

17. On the increases, Gil (1999: 36); the figure then rose to 27 percent in 1997; on the graduate figure, Segal (1985: 196). Also see Reyna (1991).

18. Kent (1990: 177) on the label; on the overall university data, UNAM (1984: 14, 209–10, 284); Ornelas (1988: 44–45); on the centers, Jiménez Mier y Terán (1982: 206); Kent (1990: 170).

19. On UNAM's bachillerato, Kent (1990: 32); Ornelas i-1; Stavenhagen i; Zorrilla i. Many analysts have in one way or another pointed to a nonacademic web linking the bachillerato and the licenciatura levels of the UNAM and the lack of standards for students and professors (Contreras and Escobar 1987: 11–22; Ruiz Massieu 1987). However, the main public university alternative, the Autonomous Metropolitan University, has maintained a high full-time percentage, over 80 percent versus roughly 15 percent for the UNAM in the late 1990s. Clear is that many professors teach a full-time load by accumulating part-time course assignments, and that academic professionalism declined with lowered salaries and increased brain drain. Still, as at private universities, pedagogical norms kept the absenteeism and other academic corruption lower than at the UNAM (Ornelas i-1; Zorilla i). The National Pedagogical University established in 1978 with a mostly full-time staff was far from an academic stronghold even by the system's standards. State universities achieved moderately higher percentages often because of limited alternative employment opportunities in the provinces, and the system's percentages rose more from the technical institutes, where full-time positions were twice as common (20 percent) as for universities (Gil 1990: 31) but where academic research is limited.

20. Brunner (1988: 102). Colombia's national average for 1983 was 39 percent full-time, 12 percent part-time, and 49 percent *catedrático* or under ten hours weekly (Parra and Jaramillo 1985: 15).

21. On del Valle, Coleman and Court (1993: 50–51); on EAFIT, James Smith, AID evaluation, 6/18/73; on the Javeriana, Rodolfo Low-Maus "Final Evaluation," 6/70, in FF #65050. Similarly, a 1967 IDB loan to the University of Costa Rica produced a major impact after the bank's previous loan had produced only a 17 percent full-time figure (IDB/L29: 7). In Brazil, in fields like physics the Campinas university was already a national leader, but IDB funding fueled a multiplication of full-timers and a vault to international prominence (Vera M. i-1).

22. IDB/L18; FF #65096 John Strasma to Peter Bell 9/10/71; Larraín (1986: 143).

23. IDB/E7: 77. The two universities had rough parity in other "full-timers" while the national led the Simón Bolívar in the half-time category, 11 to 3 percent.

24. FF #60213; on the sociology institute, Barrios and Brunner (1988: 234).

25. On Chile, D'Etigny i-3; Jaksić (1989; i) on how the discipline of philosophy

was academically professionalized within the Chilean university; foreign influences were crucial, as with visiting professors in the 1950s and 1960s, but not through formal assistance projects. On Central America, Lungo i; and the different numbers by field had much to do with employment opportunities outside the university, which helps explain why donors normally limited investment in the universities' professions.

26. There is an element of elitism in this (Arnove 1977: 112), but if Latin Americans were sent to second-tier places, that would have been decried for cementing the gap between First and Third World systems.

27. Pelczar (1974: 56). Parallels exist for assistance to secondary education. For example, a joint UNESCO and OAS effort greatly improved the number and quality of teachers at that level, raising substantially the percentage of even rural teachers who received a higher education degree, whereas previously some teachers in countries like Colombia could barely read (Vera Lamperein i).

28. On Brazil, Schwartzman i; on Latin America, Levy (1996: 174–91).

29. Pelczar (1977: 239); Vera M. i-1; Accame i.

30. National councils of science and technology are good examples in several countries. The councils have often been fortified by the IDB and provide a break from the ministry's centralized and uniform funding. Pockets of excellence have received council money, which assistance once provided them. But in countries such as the Dominican Republic, such councils did not assume the burden of counteracting an alarming generation gap as the assistance generation aged.

31. A similar but more extreme result characterizes promotion of the full-time student idea. Assistance helped some students, especially graduate students, to be full-timers, but massifying enrollment makes part-time status much more common. In fact, reform tried to make the student body more full-time but for shorter periods. That is, it attacked the "professional student" role wherein the lack of tuition and rigor, including examinations and credit systems, encouraged students to hang around for many years, sometimes engaged in politics. Additionally, reform sometimes aimed at shortening even the prescribed period of study to something in between the six or so years associated with Latin America's European heritage and the four-year U.S. norm. Another proposed time-saver of sorts was to limit the number of courses ("curriculitis"), classroom hours associated with traditional lecturing, note taking, and memorization. In its place was to be more student time in laboratories and libraries, working independently and thinking, results to be gauged through more regular and rigorous testing (Atcon 1966: 117–18, 151; IDB/L29; IDB/L11; Frodin 1973: 21; Waggoner 1973: 144; Jaramillo 1963: 178–79). On the other hand, as with Ford at Colombia's Los Andes, donors were cautious regarding curriculum and other core academic matters, lest they appear too invasive (FF #61188A).

32. On Latin America, CRESALC (1991: 12); on Mexico, Gil (1994: 29).

33. As in many other instances, donors and their reform partners may appear more naive than they were. Expectations of regional economic improvement were held not just by donors but also by most informed observers, and did not usually prove way off base except for the 1980s. Democracies ruled in many nations, and extended rule by militaries that harshly repressed universities was rare until 1973. The Brazilian coup of 1964 led to extended rule that was sometimes harsh for higher education but often positive. In contrast, Chile and Argentina endured more repression and devastation (Levy 1981).

34. Brain drain to political power and lucrative private sector jobs limited the

professorial presence (and research) of Chile's Chicago Boys despite successes in raising academic levels in economics (Valdés 1995: 198). Costa Rica (Rodríguez 1986) explored financial and other reasons for the brain drain and in general for the inability to build a more substantial body of researchers. Donors have sometimes recognized that a certain amount of brain drain is natural, even healthy for a good higher education system. AID saw turnover at the Dominican Republic's Superior Institute of Agriculture as good for the institution's vibrancy and innovation (Hansen, Antonini, and Strasma 1988: 19). An outflow suggests that professors have important skills that are valued and usable elsewhere. Where outflows hurt a university but directly help the broader society, donors should ask themselves whether their ultimate goal was university development per se or societal development through the university (D'Etigny i-2). Recognition of logical outflows was one reason that LASPAU concentrated on fields more associated with academic pursuits than with mobility to nonacademic sectors (Tyler i-3).

35. All the information of this and other paragraphs on research centers is developed in much greater detail in Levy (1996), except where another source is shown.

36. About Ecuador, Urrutia (1994: 83–84) concludes that what research centers gained in economics personnel meant lower quality economics teaching at universities.

37. To take the example of departmentalization, the projected structure was to be collegial, with shared power among full-time academic professionals. Where full-time turned out to be formalistic, departments could not function as anticipated. Another example of the tenacity of the traditional web was that most students continued to see the university as a place for professional training. Given that, practicing professionals who taught part-time often were more logical to hire than were true academic professionals. Practicing engineers might be seen to train future engineers better than could professors of engineering (or sociology or physics).

38. IDB/E7. Professors who do not live up to the full-time ideal are not usually shirkers but rather individuals whose activity results from their lack of preparation or incentives in a real world unlike the anticipated academic web. As often happens in policy, support for goals such as full-time status runs into implementation trouble when the goal must be weighed against other factors, such as the opportunity cost when one could leave the academic profession or hold onto a nominal full-time post while also working elsewhere. Some professors tartly note that they endorsed the idea that they be full-time professors, not impoverished full-time professors.

39. Regional data from CRESALC (1991: 38), Mexican from UNAM (1984: 21); Colombian from Parra and Jaramillo (1985: 15).

40. Sánchez i-2; on donor efforts, Pelczar (1977: 243) and on the postassistance falloff, Wickham (1973: 196).

41. A sample university document is Universidad de Costa Rica (1987); on Nicaragua, Arnove (1994: 112).

42. Tedesco i; Tedesco and Blumenthal (1986: 20).

43. UNAM's professors in lower ranks have an automatic right to a *concurso* after three years and are usually accepted, thus blocking competition; UNAM's research institutes have much tighter evaluation for promotion (Fuentes i; Ornelas i-1) while the Autonomous Metropolitan University is generally more rigorous than UNAM but also influenced by friendship and clientelism.

44. Jiménez Mier y Terán (1982: 218); Ornelas (1996: 23); on strikes, Balán (n.d.).

45. Schwartzman (1988: 17, 92, 101–10, with quotation on 109; 1992b). A 1996 law brought the designation "university center" for institutions with university pretensions but not meeting legal requirements such as having at least one-third of its professors as full-time; a 1998 law introduced some differentiation in teacher salaries. On Mexico, Kent (1990: 181). On Chile, Allard and Muga (1989). On Peru, Colonia i. On Costa Rica, Paniagua i. The most extensive surveying of the academic profession in Latin America came with the Carnegie Foundation's international study in the 1990s, including Brazil, Chile, and Mexico, but focusing on a limited set of institutions. It includes data on professors' attitudes and work conditions (Altbach 1996).

46. Scherz-García i; Levy (1996). Where professors define themselves in relation to the state—to lobby for special privileges or standardized rights or even as a focus of their protests—they negate the liberal professional model proposed by assistance projects. They perhaps follow an "academic estate" model closer to the French (Neave and Rhoades 1987: 213) and a bureaucratic model like those of some other Latin American professions (Cleaves 1987).

47. Furthermore, matters such as research and its precarious relationship with both universities and graduate education receive attention in the author's book on private research centers (Levy 1996).

48. Research could promote universalism by building international ties among scholars and could promote interinstitutional pluralism by marking off research from nonresearch places. More naive were assumptions that research would build intrainstitutional coherence. It does in some ways, but it also often ties individuals to their disciplines in ways that undercut such coherence; and in reality the installation of true research in selected units that sit alongside unselected ones has promoted centrifugal forces.

49. This is not to say that U.S. more than other active agencies promoted the research-teaching nexus. It is to say that as assistance promoted the nexus it promoted a key aspect of the U.S. model.

50. A place like CIAT in Colombia received funding from Ford, Rockefeller, the IDB, AID, Kellogg, and Canadian and Dutch sources. By 1980 it had funding from many governments and from the World Bank.

51. Cueto (1989) and (1994) provide balanced accounts of the successes and shortcomings, including examples of where there were and were not multiplier effects. Cueto (1994: 144) stresses that the ample advances were insufficient to fulfill the fundamental assistance goal of "replication and change carried out by external agents."

52. Similarly, this study has not accumulated the data to provide an informed view of how much assistance has introduced overly sophisticated material (or ideas) for research. Perhaps no study has. Meanwhile, disturbing examples and horror stories often impress. They need to be weighed against examples where advanced equipment is well used. Beyond that, advanced equipment has sometimes been a catalyst, building Hirschmanesque (1958) forward linkages. An early evaluation of AID-sponsored programs at Peru's National Engineering University showed how new equipment positively affected the way professors went about their academic work (Adams and Cumberland 1960: 180). Leading scientists in Chilean universities have argued that "oversophisticated" laboratory materials have provided excellent stimuli to learn as well as valuable rationales for obtaining more scholarships (Croxatto i). On the other

hand, the real problems of older equipment have sometimes led to innovative adaptation, clever backup facilities, and a premium on skilled repair personnel.

53. For example, Venezuela spent much more than Colombia or other Andean nations in the 1980s, and Argentina and Uruguay continued to lead the region outside Cuba on some measures of scientists per capita. On the other hand, Brazil has made great strides and Chile retains a leading position. Some of the data and sources are summarized in Levy (1996: 12–13).

54. Parra and Jaramillo (1985: 28).

55. Two caveats. First, U.S. universities also have centers. Still, the bulk of research has been housed in departments, and this fact was more marked during the golden age than today. Second, from early on, prudent adaptation of the department-oriented research-teaching nexus involved both university and extra-university research centers. Indeed, much support for centers simply carried into the golden age and bolstered earlier philanthropy. Then, as the golden age faded, a great proportional increase of funding to extra university centers was certainly a major adaptation, especially by Ford. But even in the heart of the golden age, inside the universities, donors modified the U.S. model when they turned to centers rather than structures that handled the bulk of teaching.

56. Estrada i. Ford and others played a role in building fine science institutes at Mexico's UNAM, but the institutes' personnel do very little teaching, and institute-faculty relations are often tense (Fuente i; Lomnitz i; Sarukán i). Reflecting the intrainstitutional stratification, special research units held two-thirds of UNAM's researchers versus just 9 percent of its total academic personnel (UNAM 1984: 29). For some experts, the fate of Latin America's university centers suggests that even the adaptive approach to reform was too radical: the U.S. model was inappropriately alien, attempts to blend research with teaching were doomed to be costly and infeasible, and European models of separate institutions for teaching and research institutions made more sense (Schiefelbein i-2).

57. Riggs (1964: 154) writes that prismatic universities tend to add knowledge-gathering capabilities but for purposes tied more to bureaucracy and power than to research.

58. A dependency view could emphasize how this training of elites strengthens something closer to the status quo than to revolutionary transformation. Another emphasis could be on donors' desire to produce more counterparts so as to implement their broad development ideas more efficiently. This emphasis could represent a donor blend of enlightened self-interest and altruism.

59. LASPAU early on gave undergraduate scholarships, but they became a minority and by 1975 virtually disappeared. Between 1964 and 1985, just over 10 percent of 3,685 LASPAU scholarships went for undergraduates, just under 10 percent for doctoral studies, and nearly 80 percent for master's degrees (LASPAU 1986). Meanwhile, between 1960 and 1980, 48 percent of Ford's scholarships to Latin Americans went for doctoral study (Myers 1983b). Graduate scholarships were considered best for faculty development, and LASPAU found that rectors' promises to integrate returnees from first-degree study were often not honored (personal correspondence from Lewis Tyler 2/1/2000). LASPAU would return to some first-degree effort only later on, when it assumed roles within programs run basically by domestic agencies.

60. Pontes (1985: 7). Naturally, partnership did not mean the absence of tension

and conflict. For example, the Ford Foundation noted sensitivity to foreign advisors on the part of officials at Colombia's scholarship agency, ICETEX, with consequent misunderstandings (Robert Drysdale to James Himes and Emily Vargas, 3/8/73, FF #71576).

61. IDB/E7: 103. Ford efforts to build graduate studies in education produced reasonable success at Colombia's private Javeriana: with less innovation, social science, and research than projected, the program nevertheless earned respect as a Latin American leader (D. Bell to M. Bundy 1/11/79 in FF #74560).

62. On Brazil's numbers, Pontes (1985: 44) and on the breadth of fields, Vessuri (1986: 9). On the Argentine backwardness, Balán (n.d.); Cano (1985: 103); Cavarozzi i; and on the belated surge, García de Fanelli (1996).

63. On the comparison to other countries, Morles (1983: 29). On the U.S. orientation in Brazil, personal correspondence from Simon Schwartzman 12/5/88. This orientation did not always mean slavish copying of one model. For example, Brazil drew off French as well as U.S. practice when it developed its funding and evaluation policies for graduate education. Donors also tried to make academic work more rigorous for first-degree students, but these efforts were much more diluted at that massifying level. One Ford Foundation undertaking was support for the expansion and reform of testing through grants to Brazil's Carlos Chagas Foundation, the University of Chile, and del Valle in Guatemala.

64. On the enrollment jump, UNAM (1984: 276); on the haphazard extension, Carpizo (1985: 109–15); on the master's, Malo, Garst, and Garza (1981: 70–73); on the doctorate, ANUIES (1988); Padua i. Efforts to create a stronger graduate alternative at the Autonomous Metropolitan University in the 1970s produced immediate disappointments, with students and money in short supply (Ornelas i-3).

65. Ratinoff i. On the lack of respect, Morles (1983: 23–26).

66. While Ford sent two-thirds of its Latin American scholarship holders to U.S. universities and another 16 percent to Europe (Myers 1983b), most Latin American expansion in graduate studies took place at much less advanced institutions. Additionally, where countries like Brazil achieved comparative success at the graduate level, they wound up with sharp stratification between that level and first-degree education, and a good graduate degree became a prerequisite for top jobs. Much of Brazil's graduate education is mediocre. Additionally, some U.S.–style reforms have been eroded, as seen with the resurgence of European-style tutorial work (personal correspondence from Simon Schwartzman 2/5/90).

67. Thus AID gave major support to build graduate education in economics in Brazil, arguing that this hitherto almost nonexistent field was crucial to development. Results were judged to be good, not great (Fred Levy evaluation PD-AAA-291-A1; AID #5120263).

68. Brunner (1988); Fuenzalida (1983).

69. Tyler i-5. Thus sharp differences characterized assistance and domestic funding by fields. Especially after the golden age, however, some special national programs to build academic quality in universities, such as FOMEC in Argentina, would emulate donors in giving very disproportionately to academic disciplines over traditional professions.

70. Wolf i-1. Donors saw law programs as obstacles blocking change much more than vehicles for change. Besides, it was probably the most domestically based profession, and its civil rather than common law orientation made for a U.S.–Latin Amer-

ican gulf. Agriculture, on the other hand, showed that assistance did not aim to transform fully toward the U.S. model even in a targeted field. The adapted land grant attempt allowed, for example, maintenance of a big government role in Brazil; if AID envisioned a more complete copying of the model, the U.S. university professors it sponsored did not (Murdoch i). Critics can nevertheless argue that the land grants pushed a type and level of research associated more with the U.S. model than with Latin American realities (Myers i-1, i-2). In other words, efforts in agriculture show a combination of donor boldness and adaptation.

71. Whether these transforming efforts are evidence of dependency varies according to which tenet of dependency is considered. Donors' vigorous pursuit of change in the mix of fields of study challenges critiques that assistance is for the status quo. So does the favoring of fields directly relevant to material development. More plausible, though elusively nonspecific, is the charge that donors promoted changes in fields in order to strengthen the broader societal status quo. For example, science and technology could help capitalism operate more efficiently. So could economics, demography, and many other assisted fields. A related charge was that the new social science, "structural-functionalist" and empirical rather than humanistic and normative, moved toward support rather than criticism of the status quo. Scherz-García (1967: 398) accurately identified a "pragmatic" donor mentality that opposed not just traditional professionalist norms but also politically radical ones. On curriculum, the OAS and others generally found that recipients adapted imported curriculum appropriately to their circumstances (Kreimer i), but this is obviously a controversial issue. Either wooden copying of imported content or subordination of imported content could constitute prismatic formalism.

72. Differences in the years in which different donors made their main efforts explain some divergence, but the viability of the conclusions presented in the text is supported by our separate analysis of the 1960s, the main overlap decade; see appendix R.

73. Computer printout provided in 1991 by the UNDP's Hyacinth Morgan showed that a total of $27 million expended since 1974 avoided traditional professions except engineering (at 26 percent): nothing for law, architecture, or medicine (except veterinary medicine). In contrast, agronomy at 14 percent and exact sciences at 11 percent are both well over their share of domestic enrollments, and economics at 9 percent and basic social sciences at 11 percent are also favored.

74. See appendix S. Although the data categories in that table are not exactly the same as those cited for the modern-traditional dichotomy, they are close. Thus, the 61 percent traditional for 1955 comes from adding "fine arts" to the humanities, law, and medicine categories, whereas architecture is not separately listed by UNESCO. There could be fungibility where assistance intended to promote one field freed up institutional capacity to finance another. Such divergence would be more likely when institutions were subject to various internal pressures, less likely when donors worked with partners who had the power to carry out reforms. Also, there is a bit of mixing apples and oranges in analyzing donor expenditures versus domestic enrollments; there are no data on domestic expenditures by university field, mostly because subsidies are given to institutions overall, but that institutional giving has largely followed enrollments.

75. Among the interviews in Chile, Correa i; Cuneo i. The military rule commencing in 1973 naturally undermined impacts, which appear to have been mixed in

Peru and Colombia as well. Dezalay and Garth (2002: 73–109) conduct many interviews about related attempts at reforming legal education, as well as economics. Like the present study, they tend to find ample successes in economics, as in Brazil and Chile, and spottier results in law.

76. Many areas of engineering, after all, were highly identified with economic development in countries like Colombia (ASCUN 1967: 81); on architecture, Scherz-García i; on Ford's avoidance of medicine, Wolf i-3; Harrison i-4.

77. Anderson (1963: 23); Rondinelli (1989).

78. Reflections on Ford's economics assistance to Colombia's National University capture the mix of vigor and adaptability (Guillermo Calvo and Reed Hertford to files, 7/13/70, FF #68759). The fairly standard formula included a direct grant, heavy involvement by U.S. professors, scholarships for U.S. study, and requirements to return to the home university to build a critical disciplinary mass. Yet Ford believed that U.S. academic economics often did not play a major practical or policy role—and was rarely progressive. Thus the project pointedly undertook to highlight an atypical U.S. profile, beginning with work by professors like Carlos Díaz Alejandro, and to dilute the U.S. tradition. Additionally, the idea was to postpone aspects of institution building because first people would need to study abroad and then they would have to be protected in specially funded positions. Like other findings in our study, this casts doubt on a simple view that U.S. assistance looked to impose conservative domination through economics.

79. Although less than anticipated, the great impact of assistance for agriculture at international research centers has included research, extension, and influence on first-degree and graduate education. CIAT in Colombia, with outpost staff in Brazil, Costa Rica, Guatemala, Venezuela, and the Philippines is one of many documented examples (FF #69168); Levy (1996) includes further information on the academic performance of such centers.

80. K. N. Rao to William Carmichael 7/17/74 and James Himes to Carmichael 6/7/74 and Universidad de Los Andes final report to the Ford Foundation, 1973, all in FF #65307; Cepeda (1979: 503). Ford assistance also had major impact in installing pioneering political science as well as excellence in anthropology while major efforts in economics also produced positive results. But in economics ratings were mixed, some observers finding disappointment followed by renewal (Cepeda 1979: 503; Aldana i-3; FF #61188). Kalman Silvert (to William Carmichael 1/27/73, FF #68758) bemoaned problems of reentry and insufficient research as he urged the foundation to pressure the university to increase its commitment to building economics and to maintaining itself as an academically elite institution. Engineering has remained the standout. As of 2000 it enrolled roughly half the students while 46 of its 107 professors "de planta" had the doctorate (versus 2 percent for Colombian higher education overall) and 90 were full-time, the other 17 were half-time or more (personal correspondence from Eduardo Aldana 8/16/2000).

81. In several ways, the approach here was rather aggressive. The Catholic university had originally proposed agriculture, but donors rejected this as too tied to landholders' privileged offspring rather than reform, and they counterproposed economics. Whereas Ford aimed to offer, pluralistically, a counterweight to dominant leftist economics, AID arguably set out to subordinate the Economic Commission for Latin America and to change economics in the university—and in national policy—and to carry the crusade beyond Chile to other nations. In addition to Valdés (1995),

Hellman (1988); Hellman i; Coleman and Court (1993); FF #65096 John Strasma to Peter Bell 9/10/71; Meller (1984). On the other hand, donors led by Ford gave major support to the (non-Chicago) graduate economics school at the University of Chile, which from 1961 to 1966 enrolled mostly Latin Americans from beyond Chile and produced major impacts in their nations (FF #61372; Davidson i). Support like this again undermines charges that assistance subordinated the political system by backing a particular kind of economics. Without question, assistance built a "Chicago School" that wielded power in conjunction with repressive military rule, but donors had actually built up other types of economics as well—and their progeny would then prominently serve subsequent democratic governments. Such patterns have been common in Latin America.

82. Impacts in fields also extended beyond higher education institutions, including when the vehicles were scholarships. Enhancement in university fields contributed to extension (as in agriculture), service to government, and so forth. And where fields most improved they engaged in "horizontal cooperation" with colleagues at universities in different Latin American nations as well as in the First World. Among fields where Ford scholarships had the biggest such impact were economics, other social science, reproductive biology, and agriculture (Myers 1983b: 103). As usual, the U.S. influence increases further if we figure in, beyond formal projects alone, the dissemination of ideas. Thus U.S. sociology had an "enormous influence on Latin America" (González Casanova 1984: 9).

83. Flora and Flora (1989: 25–27); Eastman and Grieshop (1989: 33–52); Mattocks (1990).

84. Briones i; Schwartzman (1988: 114). In Brazil and other countries, psychology, veterinary medicine, nutrition, educational supervision, journalism, social work, statistics, geology, and economics were some of the other emerging fields that donned professional trappings in rigid curriculum, narrow pedagogy, job orientations and rights, more than an academic paradigm of broader, flexible teaching mixed with research.

85. In the best of cases, assistance provided the extra resources to overcome financial constraints that usually block advanced academic work in private institutions internationally unless government provides funds. So one could emphasize the impressive successes of the reform partnership between donors and private universities committed to serious academic work but recognize that the overwhelming surge of private growth during and after the golden age has come in private institutions with fundamentally different pursuits.

86. Most countries have established special funds to sustain and reward their base of true full-time professors. Science and technology or other national councils likewise focus on research along with graduate education, usually for designated priority fields. Nearly all such new agencies and funding mechanisms follow a basic philanthropic tenet commonly pursued by donors in the golden age: targeted support for promising people and institutions rather than across-the-board subsidies unlinked to academic policies and performance.

6. Promise and Performance in Exporting Progress

1. Thus, the first part of the chapter builds mostly on the philanthropy literature, the second mostly on the policy and evaluation literature, and the third on the Latin

American and comparative higher education literature, but all three overlap and build prominently on the assistance literature as well.

2. What is ideal typical is often thus also "ideal" for donors and other reformers acting hopefully.

3. See, for example, Cerych and Sabatier (1986) on prospects for particular changes that can be achieved widely or deep changes that can be achieved in a few places—but the difficulty of achieving change that is both broad and deep.

4. When faith in the philanthropic ideal type of change marginalizes the dilemma, it parallels the modernization school's faith that all good things go together. (The modernization school, however, places less emphasis on selective, distinctive means and targets.)

5. Robertson and Waltman (1993) identify the dilemma in policy diffusion of attacking more or using narrower policy instruments.

6. But this political necessity, common to reform efforts, was less weighty for assistance than it is in the case of domestic policy reform, at least in democratic settings reflected in the implementation literature. This is because assistance money involves a more voluntary base and does not require as much broad selling, which often translates into overselling, and the overselling often means declaring the ultimate hopes and goals and visions as project goals. Thus assistance projects could stick more closely to more attainable explicit goals. Obviously, politicking exists in all these contexts, and in our case the need for responsiveness would be greatest at AID, least at Ford. Like other points about how "voluntary" action is, this one is relative.

7. "Cluster giving" to umbrella organizations was rare, especially for foundations, and occurred in only some countries. Also, insofar as cluster giving was unselective in order to avoid donor control over partners, it suggests some natural conflict among ideal typical means; it is not always clear how donors can promote a pointed agenda without being directive.

8. It is indeed arguably very hard for aid to be selective (Collier and Dollar 1999).

9. In the absence of clear-cut criteria that ruled in one partner for each endeavor and ruled out all others, donors worked with different partners. These partners could develop horizontal ties among themselves as well as their vertical ties to donors.

10. Certain private universities were easier to target with capable partnership, but donors were usually keen not to surrender the public sector, the main sector. When they retreated, after difficulties especially in the public sector and disappointingly little leverage on the public mainstream by private frontrunners, they sometimes directed themselves more narrowly to private research centers.

11. In terms of isomorphism, projects envisioned major elements of "normative," aided emulation of advanced professional practices, and thus of progressive change (though dependency theory would find much "coercive" isomorphism at play). Resistance to change would be associated with "mimetic" replication of less advanced practices dominant in the domestic systems.

12. We have handled the web principally as a matter of policies and structures (and the interests related to them), but our information could also support the argument in organizational theory that embedded beliefs within institutions are strong impediments to change. We could thus talk of webs of policies, structures, and beliefs.

13. Massification thus counts mostly as a nonassistance dynamic that undermined assistance dynamics by either distorting them (negative impact) directly or by over-

whelming them (lack of impact). Exceptionally, where donors (mostly the IDB) fostered massification, they undermined their own other efforts. That the risks of rapid growth must be weighed against more carefully shaped change limited in quantitative reach is a manifestation of the voluntary dilemma.

14. We can return to our analogy to Dahl's (1971: 32–47) notion about sequence in political development, that democracy is especially difficult to achieve where liberal structures and norms do not take hold before inclusion occurs. The philanthropic ideal type itself might have to accommodate such a notion of sequences for effective change in fields like higher education and assistance. Arguably, philanthropy is classically suited to circumstances where numbers are still not large and structures are not deeply embedded, circumstances that decreasingly characterize modern development challenges.

15. Purely positive results would hold the voluntary dilemma at bay, but they are rare.

16. Evidence from studies of related subject matter appears mixed. Eisemon and Kourouma (1994) find that within largely ruined African higher education systems institutions once targeted for long-term assistance continue to offer quality under terribly difficult conditions. Harbison and Hanushek (1992) find that major investment, including from the World Bank, did not produce significant differences between targeted and other schools in Brazil's northeast.

17. Comparing in broad strokes to the experience of foundations promoting science in postwar Europe, our case shows more difficult contextual constraints, but by the same token the successes achieved are thus perhaps especially impressive. Also, where we find transformation, this exceeds the assessment that the European targets were "not transformed so much as assisted to do better what they had always done" (Kohler 1991: 198).

18. The varied nature of our evidence but mainly the varied nature of dependency theory obviates a blanket assertion that such theory is wrong or irrelevant to our case, just as we cannot make a blanket statement about modernization theory. Revised, moderate versions of these theories can fit much of the evidence. Dependency ideas that overlap the philanthropic ideal type often fit (e.g., external actors favor some over others and alter local balances of power). But, except for stratification, much of what is negative and powerful in dependency theory does not square with the bulk of the evidence, which highlights matters like change orientation, growth, innovation, partnership, true assistance, and net positive effects.

19. Notable parallels emerge to findings from a study on efforts to transform Latin American development directions. Dezalay and Garth focus more on impacts on the state, mostly for a later (but overlapping) time period, and deal with just the fields of law and economics. But they also highlight northern exporters and southern importers. Without using the term *prismatic,* they conclude that if exported models take root it is only in altered form that fits the local context, and they note the "logic of half-failed transplants" (Dezalay and Garth 2002: 246). They also find that some leading reform ideas from the past remain or reemerge as leading reform ideas in subsequent years or when contextual conditions are more propitious.

20. Prismatic displacement, however, often involves replication alongside a (usually larger) segment that replicates little. Regarding isomorphism, prismatic reality shows a variety of forms and mixes far in excess of what theories of cloning suggest (Ilchman and Ilchman 1987).

21. Trow (2001: 120) arrives at a similar conclusion regarding European efforts to emulate U.S. higher education in recent years: alongside ample borrowing is "difficulty in reproducing the cluster of structural and cultural features," so that European adaptations serve different functions or function differently.

22. Noting that a major social science question is whether all traditional interests are inconsistent with modernizing change, Cueto (1994: 18) perceptively concludes from the experience of the Rockefeller Foundation in Latin America that what is needed is adaptation and interpretation of local circumstances, not blunt dislocation. Our study tends to support that conclusion but emphasizes that donors and their reform partners often already appreciated the point.

23. Such criteria contribute to a somewhat more positive view of prismatic change than Riggs himself offered up, though his undertaking was more theoretical than evaluative, and the overwhelming sense in his work, echoed in ours, is of mixed, nuanced results that fail to match ideals but have their own rationality.

24. This is not to make an argument for the general superiority of prismatic over other change but rather to indicate how complex, variable, and even uncertain assessments must be.

25. We have repeatedly found that assessment of results depends (or at least should depend) on complex factors that elude pinpointing. These factors include the mix of fair yet demanding evaluative criteria, the effect of context, the degree to which targets lead to change beyond targets, and donors' realistic alternatives in handling the voluntary dilemma.

26. Our study nonetheless strongly suggests two interrelated points. First, conclusions would depend on employment of our panoply of evaluative criteria. Second, a "third way" in evaluation, nuanced, would likely find results far below expectations and yet far above that suggested in critiques based on disappointment over shattered expectations.

27. Eisemon and Kourouma (1994: 275) also observe increased control and decreased partnership as donors came to insist more on shaping recipients' higher education policy, decreasing domestic latitude to respond to social demand. Regarding the voluntary dilemma of risking that matters go awry when recipients have considerable autonomy or undertaking more control than the ideal type contemplates, donors moved toward the latter or minimized risk (but also goals) by not acting. Where donors' conditions are not met, donors' efforts can be minimized, consistent with notions of donor retreat; where conditions are met, the efforts can be broader and more aggressive than they usually were in the past, with more goals made explicit.

28. The World Bank declares that its advice is more important than its funds (1995: 14). Even the Bank's resources are limited and leave the Bank facing the voluntary dilemma. For example, there is a need to get to the mainstream and beyond Pyrrhic victories at "cocoons," since the success rate is unimportant if success is narrowly defined (World Bank 1998: 90–91). Where the domestic environment is troublesome, it is better for international agencies to stimulate a policy dialogue than to press its policies (World Bank 1998: 61).

29. World Bank (1994); IDB (1997); Task Force on Higher Education and Society (2000). By the end of the century, emphasis on a "Knowledge Society" as key to development boosted the role of higher education further. Still, compared to the golden age view, this contemporary view has the university fitting in with other forces more than leading them. Also, the contemporary tendency is to look to higher edu-

cation within a network of needed institutions, in contrast to the golden age's special faith in university leadership for development.

30. Given the validity of the general claim that beliefs embedded in organizations often block reform, a claim we have already endorsed, university assistance in the golden age stands out for playing a comparatively strong role in changing ideas. In fact, in certain ways many of the ideas associated with the golden age are *too* widespread. This is so, for example, where ideas derive from a model of U.S. research universities rather than the much more variegated model of the U.S. higher education system. The ideas often are not apt, or are even deleterious, for most institutions or functions of higher education. See Castro and Levy (2000).

31. Our conclusions in this regard support Sikkink (1991: 247–48) that ideas matter when they respond to policymakers' perceived problems *and* when there are supportive institutional homes.

32. Schwartzman (1992b: 30) is among those observing that ideas that were once rejected now "do not stir up the same indignation or perplexity they did just a few years ago." He refers to matters like academic values, evaluation, and private sector roles.

33. We have repeatedly assessed rather positively even mixed results, achieved within unfavorable surrounding contexts. Today, a countercorrective can also be apt: project goals may be reached in part because of matters operating outside the project. In the golden age and just beyond the context was mostly negative—yielding results inferior to what projects would otherwise have achieved and leading us to respect projects that achieved mixed results. Today the context is sometimes favorable enough that it "artificially boosts" projects, which get "too much credit" for developments that are not truly project impacts.

References

Adams, Richard, and Charles Cumberland. 1960. *United States University Cooperation in Latin America.* East Lansing: Michigan State University.

Adiseshiah, Malcolm S. 1979. From International Aid to International Cooperation: Some Thoughts in Retrospect. *International Review of Education* 25: 213–30.

Adler, Emanuel. 1987. *The Power of Ideology: The Quest for Technological Autonomy in Argentina and Brazil.* Berkeley: University of California Press.

Ahmad, Aqueil, and Arthur S. Wilke. 1986. Technology Transfer in the New International Economic Order: Options, Obstacles, and Dilemmas. In McIntyre and Papp 1986, 77–94.

AID. 1966. *The Transfer and Use of Development Skills.* Washington, D.C.: AID Participant Training Program.

———. 1974. *Development Assistance Programs: FY 1974. Presentation to the Congress: Program and Project Data, Latin America.* Washington, D.C.: Agency for International Development

———. 1975. *Congressional Presentation: Fiscal Year 1976.* Washington, D.C.: Agency for International Development

———. 1985. *Completed Project Assistance and Activities.* Washington, D.C.: AID, Office of Financial Management.

———. 1986–87. *AID Project History (PAICHIST),* AID's database, printout from archivist Ardith Betts.

———. 1998. Why Foreign Aid? [Web site]. United States Agency for International Development (USAID) 1998 [cited November 1998]. Available from http://www.infor.usaid.gov/about/y4naid.html.

Albornoz, Orlando. 1979. *Teoría y praxis de la educación superior venezolana. Ediciones de la Facultad de Humanidades y Educación.* Caracas: Universidad Central de Venezuela.

Aldana, Eduardo, and Luis Enrique Orozco. 1993. Educación para la democracia y la competencia. Paper read at Proyecto del Diálogo Interamericano sobre la Educación en América Latina: La situación y las perspectivas colombianas, July, Bogotá.

Allard, Raúl. 1983. Education, Training, and Human Resources. In *Governance in the Western Hemisphere,* ed. Viron Vaky, 425–66. New York: Praeger.

Allard, Raúl, and Alfonso Muga. 1989. Políticas públicas de los 80 en Chile. *Estudios Sociales* 61 (3): 93–118.

Almond, Gabriel A. 1987. The Development of Political Development. In Weiner and Huntington 1987, 437–90.

Altbach, Philip. 1987a. *Higher Education in the Third World: Themes and Variations.* New Delhi: Sangam Books.

———. 1987b. *The Knowledge Context: Comparative Perspectives on the Distribution of Knowledge.* Albany: State University of New York Press.

———. 1989. Twisted Roots: The Western Impact on Asian Higher Education. *Higher Education* 18 (1): 9–29.

———, ed. 1996. *The International Academic Profession: Portraits of Fourteen Countries.* Princeton: Carnegie Foundation for the Advancement of Teaching.

Altbach, Philip, and Gail P. Kelly, eds. 1984. *Education and the Colonial Experience.* New Brunswick, N.J.: Transaction Books.

Anderson, Charles. 1967. *Politics and Economic Change in Latin America.* New York: Van Nostrand.

Anderson, Dole. 1963. *AID End of Tour Report.* Washington, D.C.: United States Agency for International Development.

———. 1987. *Management Education in Developing Countries: The Brazilian Experience.* Boulder: Westview.

Anderson, Lester, et al. 1965. *Final Report: Visit to the National University.* Washington, D.C.: Agency for International Development

Andrews, Frank. 1956. *Philanthropic Foundations.* New York: Russell Sage.

Anheier, Helmut K., and Stefan Toepler, eds. 1999. *Private Funds, Public Purpose: Philanthropic Foundations in International Perspective.* New York: Kluwer Academic/Plenum.

Anton, Thomas. 1989. *American Federalism and Public Policy: How the System Works.* New York: Random House.

ANUIES. 1988. *Anuario estadístico: Posgrado.* Mexico City: Asociación Nacional de Universidades e Instituciones de Educación Superior.

Armytage, W. H. G. 1964. Foreign Influences in English Universities. *Comparative Education Review* 7: 246–61.

Arnove, Robert F. 1977. The Ford Foundation and "Competence Building" Overseas: Assumptions, Approaches, and Outcomes. *Studies in Comparative International Development* 12 (3): 100–126.

———. 1978. Book review of Kenneth W. Thompson and Barbara R. Fogel (1976). *Higher Education and Social Change,* vols. 1 and 2. New York: Praeger. *Higher Education* 7 (November): 471–74.

———. 1980a. Foundations and the Transfer of Knowledge. In Arnove 1980b, 305–30.

———. 1994. *Education as Contested Terrain: Nicaragua, 1979–1993.* Boulder: Westview Press.

———, ed. 1980b. *Philanthropy and Cultural Imperialism.* Boston: G. K. Hall.

Arregui, Patricia, and Ernesto Melgar. 1992. Financiamiento de las universidades públicas en Perú. *Boletín de Opinión* 4 (April): 7–12.

Asamblea Nacional de Rectores. 1988. *Perú: Estadísticas universitarias 1960–86.* Lima: ANR.

ASCUN. 1967. *Plan básico de la educación superior.* Bogotá: Colombian Association of Universities.

Ashby, Eric. 1964. *African Universities and Western Tradition.* Cambridge: Harvard University Press.

Association for Latin American Studies, ed. 1965. *Viewpoints on Education and Social Change in Latin America:* Lawrence: Center of Latin American Studies, University of Kansas.

Atcon, Rudolph. 1966. *The Latin American University.* Bogotá: ECO Revista de la Cultura de Occidente.

Ayala, Enrique. 1974. Movimientos sociales y movimientos universitarios en el Ecuador. In *Hacia una conceptualización del fenómeno de los movimientos universitarios en América Latina,* ed. Patricio Dooner, 178–226. Santiago: CPU.

Ayres, Robert L. 1983. *Banking and the Poor: The World Bank and World Poverty.* Cambridge: MIT Press.

Balán, Jorge. 1992. Argentina. In Clark and Neave 1992, 1:19–29.

———. n.d. *El impacto de la asistencia externa en la institucionalización de las ciencias sociales: El caso argentino.* New York: SSRC.

Barquín, Manuel, and Jesús Orozco. 1988. Constitución y autonomía universitaria en Iberoamérica. *Cuadernos de Legislación Universitaria* 3 (6): 41–71.

Barrios, Alicia, and José Joaquín Brunner. 1988. *La sociología en Chile.* Santiago: FLACSO.

Bastiaens, Jo. 1997. How Can North-South University Linkages Affect University-State Relations in Developing Countries? Albany: SUNY. (research paper)

Bath, Richard C., and Dilmus D. James. 1976. Dependency Analysis of Latin America: Some Criticisms, Some Suggestions. *Latin American Research Review* 11 (3): 3–54.

Bauer, Péter Tamás. 1976. *Dissent on Development.* Cambridge: Harvard University Press.

Baum, Warren C., and Stokes M. Tolbert. 1985. *Investment in Development: Lessons of World Bank Experience.* Ed. World Bank. New York: Oxford University Press.

Becker, David G., ed. 1983. *The New Bourgeoisie and the Limits of Dependency: Mining, Class, and Power in "Revolutionary" Peru.* Princeton: Princeton University Press.

Ben-David, Joseph. 1971. *The Scientist's Role in Society: A Comparative Study.* Englewood Cliffs, N.J.: Prentice-Hall.

Benjamin, Harold R. W. 1965. *Higher Education in the American Republics.* McGraw-Hill Series in International Development. New York: McGraw-Hill.

Bennett, Douglas C., and Kenneth E. Sharpe. 1985. *Transnational Corporations versus the State: The Political Economy of the Mexican Auto Industry.* Princeton: Princeton University Press.

Berg, Robert J., and David F. Gordon, eds. 1989. *Cooperation for International*

Development: The United States and the Third World in the 1990s. Boulder: Lynne Rienner.

Berman, Edward. 1983. *The Influence of the Carnegie, Ford, and Rockefeller Foundations on American Foreign Policy: The Ideology of Philanthropy.* Albany: SUNY Press.

Berry, John W. 1995. *Cooperation for Capacity Building: Improving the Effectiveness of University Linkage Projects. A Study Prepared for the Canadian International Development Agency.* Ottawa: J. W. Berry & Associates, International Consultants.

Blaise, Hans, et al. 1968. *University of Pittsburgh End of Contract Report to AID.* Pittsburgh: University of Pittsburgh.

Blakemore, Harold. 1976. Chile. In *Educational and National Development: An International Comparison of the Past and Recommendations for the Future,* ed. Nancy Parkinson, 330–68. London: Macmillan.

Blaug, Mark. 1974. Educational Policy and the Economics of Education: Some Practical Lessons for Educational Planners in Developing Countries. In Ward 1974, 23–32.

———. 1985. Where Are We Now in the Economics of Education? *Economics of Education Review* 4 (1): 17–28.

Bolling, Landrum. 1982. *Private Foreign Aid: U.S. Philanthropy for Relief and Development.* Boulder: Westview.

Bonner, Frances, Sidney Gerber, and Richard Morse. 1963. *Report to the Ford Foundation Concerning the Developments and Projects at the University of Antioquia.* New York: Ford Foundation.

Bossert, Thomas B. 1984. Health Policy Innovation and International Assistance in Central America. *Political Science Quarterly* 99 (Fall): 41–55.

Bremner, Robert. 1988. *American Philanthropy.* 2nd ed. Chicago History of American Civilization. Chicago: University of Chicago Press.

Brunner, José Joaquín. 1988. *El caso de la sociología en Chile: Formación de una disciplina.* Santiago: FLACSO.

Brunner, José Joaquín, Hernán Courard, and Cristián D. Cox. 1992. *Estado, mercado y conocimiento: Políticas y resultados en la educación superior chilena, 1960–1990.* 1st ed. Santiago: FLACSO.

Brunner, José Joaquín, et al. 1995. *Educación superior en América Latina: Una agenda.* Bogotá: Universidad Nacional.

Buchert, Lene, and Kenneth King, eds. 1995. *Learning from Experience: Policy and Practice in Aid to Higher Education.* The Hague: Center for the Study of Education in Developing Countries.

Bujazan, M., et al. 1987. International Agency Assistance to Education in Latin America and the Caribbean, 1970–84: Technical and Political Decision Making. *Comparative Education* 23 (2): 161–71.

Bullock, Mary Brown. 1980. *An American Transplant: The Rockefeller Foundation and Peking Union Medical College.* Berkeley: University of California Press.

Bulmer, Martin. 1999. The History of Foundations in the United Kingdom and the United States. In Anheier and Toepler 1999, 27–53.

Bunge, Mario. 1984. Los siete pecados capitales de nuestra universidad y cómo redimirlos. *Interciencia* 9 (1): 37–38.

Burnell, Peter. 1997. *Foreign Aid in a Changing World, Issues in Third World Politics.* Buckingham, UK: Open University Press.

Burnett, Nicholas. 1996. Priorities and Strategies for Education—a World Bank Review: The Process and the Key Messages. *International Journal of Educational Development* 16 (3): 215–20.

Bustamante, Maclovia Eugenia. 1985. Fundaciones norteamericanas en América Latina y el Caribe. Educación superior, prioridades y tendencias (1972–1980): El caso de la Fundación Rockefeller. Licenciado thesis, Universidad Autónoma de Guadalajara.

Cambridge Conference Report. 1971. Criteria for Allocating Aid. In Robinson 1971, 223–27.

Camp, Roderic. 1985. *Intellectuals and the State in Twentieth-Century Mexico.* Austin: University of Texas.

Cano, Daniel. 1985. *La educación superior en la Argentina.* Buenos Aires: Grupo Editor Latinoamericano.

Carpizo, Jorge. 1985. Fortaleza y debilidad de la Universidad Nacional Autónoma de México. *Revista Latinoamericana de Estudios Educativos* 15 (2): 105–18.

Cassen, Robert and Associates. 1986. *Does Aid Work? Report to an Intergovernmental Task Force.* New York: Oxford University Press. (There is also a second edition, 1994.)

Castellanos, Juan, et al. 1976. *Examen de una década: Sociedad y universidad, 1962–1971.* Mexico City: UDUAL.

Castro, Claudio de Moura. 1983. The Impact of European and American Influences on Brazilian Higher Education. *European Journal of Education* 18 (4): 367–81.

———. 1996. A Tale of Two Education Projects. *IDB* (March).

———. n.d. BID e Banco Mundial: Qual e a bula? Unpublished paper, Washington, D.C.

Castro, Claudio de Moura, and John Alic 1997. *Technology, Science, and Development in Latin America and the Caribbean.* Unpublished background paper. Washington, D.C.: Inter-American Development Bank.

Castro, Claudio de Moura, and Daniel C. Levy. 2000. *Myth, Reality, and Reform: Higher Education in Latin America.* Washington, D.C.: Inter-American Development Bank distributed through the Johns Hopkins University Press.

Castro, Gregorio Antonio. 1988. *Sociólogos y sociología en Venezuela.* Paris: UNESCO.

Cepeda, Fernando. 1979. La cooperación internacional y la universidad: Aproximaciones al caso colombiano. In *La Universidad Latinoamericana: Visión de una década,* ed. Patricio Dooner and Iván Lavados. Santiago: CPU.

Cerych, Ladislav. 1965. *Problems of Aid to Education in Developing Countries.* New York: Praeger.

Cerych, Ladislav, and Paul Sabatier. 1986. *Great Expectations and Mixed Performance: The Implementation of Higher Education Reform in Europe.* Trentham, Stoke-on-Trentham: Trentham Books.

Chapman, David, and Joan Claffey. 1998. A New Wealth of Opportunities Overseas. *Chronicle of Higher Education* 44 (September 25): b6.

Cheit, Earl F., and Theodore E. Lobman. 1979. *Foundations and Higher Education. Grant Making from Golden Years through Steady State.* Berkeley: Carnegie Council on Policy Studies in Higher Education.

Christiansen-Wagner, Toni. 1986. Historical Summary of AID's Involvement in Education in the Dominican Republic. Paper read at LASA XIII International Conference, October.

Chubb, John, and Terry Moe. 1988. Politics, Markets, and the Organization of Schools. *American Political Science Review* 82 (4): 1065–87.

Church, Thomas W., and Robert N. Nakamura. 1993. *Cleaning Up the Mess: Implementation Strategies in Superfund.* Washington, D.C.: Brookings Institution.

CIDA. 1985. *A Review of Past Experience in Human Resource Development Assistance.* Ottawa: Canadian International Development Agency.

———. 1987. *Corporate Evaluation of Human Resource Development Programming at CIDA.* (n.c.): Canadian International Development Agency. Program Evaluation Division, Policy Branch, CIDA.

Cisneros, Luis Jaime. 1993. La universidad peruana. *GRADE, Notas para el debate* 10: 14–18.

Clark, Burton R. 1978. Academic Differentiation in National Systems of Higher Education. *Comparative Education Review* 22 (June): 242–58.

———. 1983. *The Higher Education System. Academic Organization in Cross-National Perspective.* Berkeley: University of California Press.

———. 1986. Implementation in the United States: A Comparison with European Higher Education Reforms. In Cerych and Sabatier 1986, 259–67.

———. 1995. *Places of Inquiry: Research and Advanced Education in Modern Universities.* Berkeley: University of California Press.

———, ed. 1987. *The Academic Profession: National, Disciplinary, and Institutional Settings.* Berkeley: University of California Press.

Clark, Burton R., and Guy Neave, eds. 1992. *The Encyclopedia of Higher Education.* 4 vols. Oxford: Pergamon Press.

Clark, John. 1991. *Democratizing Development: The Role of Voluntary Organizations.* West Hartford, Conn.: Kumarian Press.

Clayton, Thomas. 1998. Beyond Mystification: Reconnecting World System Theory for Comparative Education. *Comparative Education Review* 42 (4): 479–96.

Cleaves, Peter. 1987. *Professions and the State: The Mexican Case.* Tucson: University of Arizona Press.

Coatsworth, John. 1989. *International Collaboration in the Social Sciences: The ACLS/SSRC Joint Committee on Latin American Studies*. New York: Social Science Research Council.

Colclough, Christopher. 1991. Who Should Learn to Pay? An Assessment of Neo-liberal Approaches to Education Policy. In *States or Markets? Neo-liberalism and the Development Policy Debate*, ed. Christopher Colclough and James Manor. Oxford: Clarendon Press.

Coleman, James S. 1984. Professorial Training and Institution Building in the Third World. *Comparative Education Review* 28 (2): 180–202.

———, ed. 1965. *Education and Political Development*. Princeton: Princeton University Press.

Coleman, James S., and David Court. 1993. *University Development in the Third World: The Rockefeller Foundation Experience*. Oxford: Pergamon Press.

Collier, Paul, and David Dollar. 1999. Target Aid to Performance Not Promises. *Development Outreach (Journal of World Bank Institute)* 1 (2): 18–21.

Colwell, Mary Anna Culleton. 1980. The Foundation Connection: Links among Foundations and Recipient Organizations. In Arnove 1980b, 413–52.

Comisión Reforma del Centro Universitario de Temuco. 1968. *Los centros universitarios*. Santiago: Anales de la Universidad de Chile.

Comité Internacional de Seguimiento. 1998. Informe de la Tercera Reunión del Comité Internacional de Seguimiento. *Informe FOMEC* 4 (6): 19–21.

Commission on Foundations and Private Philanthropy. 1970. *Foundations, Private Giving, and Public Policy*. Chicago: University of Chicago Press.

Compton, J. Lin, ed. 1989. *The Transformation of International Agricultural Research and Development*. Boulder: Lynne Rienner.

CONARE (Consejo Nacional de Rectores). 1987a. *Estadística de la educación superior 1986*. San José: Oficina de Planificación de la Educación Superior.

———. 1987b. *La educación superior en Costa Rica*. San José: Oficina de Planificación de la Educación Superior.

Consejo Nacional de Educación Superior. 1986. *Diagnóstico de la educación superior dominicana*. Santo Domingo: CONES.

Contreras, Gabriela, and Herón Escobar, eds. 1987. *Empezar de nuevo: Por la transformación democrática de la UNAM*. Mexico City: Equipo Pueblo.

Coombe, Carol. 1989. *International Development Programmes in Higher Education*. London: Commonwealth Secretariat.

Coombe, Trevor. 1991. *A Consultation on Higher Education in Africa: A Report to the Ford Foundation and the Rockefeller Foundation*. New York: Ford Foundation.

Córdoba, Maria Clarisa. 1985. Fundaciones norteamericanas en América Latina y el Caribe, educación superior prioridades y tendencias (1972–1980): El caso de la Fundación Kellogg. Licenciatura thesis, Universidad Autónoma de Guadalajara.

Corso, Irene. 1988. The Emergence and Development of Institutions of Higher Education in Developing Countries: The University Simón Bolívar in Venezuela as a Case Study. Stanford University, Palo Alto.

Court, David. 1995. The Challenge of the Liberal Vision of Universities in Africa. In Buchert and King 1995, 109–21.

CRESALC. 1991. *Visión cuantitativa de la educación superior en América Latina y el Caribe.* Caracas: CRESALC.

CSUCA. 1988a. La integración de la educación superior en Centroamérica. *Estudios Sociales Centroamericanos* (46): 43–58.

———. 1988b. Mecanismos de cooperación e integración entre las universidades centroamericanas. Un esbozo histórico. *Estudios Sociales Centroamericanos* (46): 59–72.

Cueto, Marcos. 1989. *Excelencia científica en la periferia: Actividades científicas e investigación biomédica en el Perú, 1890–1950.* Lima: GRADE-CONCYTEC.

———. 1991. Philanthropy, American Perceptions, and Latin America. *Rockefeller Foundation Newsletter* (Fall): 4–6.

———, ed. 1994. *Missionaries of Science: The Rockefeller Foundation and Latin America.* Bloomington: Indiana University Press.

Cunningham, Merriman. 1972. *Private Money and Public Service: The Role of Foundations in American Society.* New York: McGraw-Hill.

Curti, Merle. 1963. *American Philanthropy Abroad: A History.* New Brunswick: Rutgers University Press.

Curti, Merle, and Roderick Nash. 1965. *Philanthropy in the Shaping of American Higher Education.* New Brunswick: Rutgers University Press.

Daalder, Hans, and Edward Shils, eds. 1982. *Universities, Politicians, and Bureaucrats: Europe and the United States.* New York: Cambridge University Press.

Dahl, Robert A. 1971. *Polyarchy: Participation and Opposition.* New Haven: Yale University Press.

Daland, Robert. 1967. *Brazilian Planning: Development Politics and Administration.* Chapel Hill: University of North Carolina Press.

Davis, Russell. 1965. Prototypes and Stereotypes in Latin American Universities. *Comparative Education Review* 9 (3): 275–81.

Dell, Sidney. 1972. *The Inter-American Development Bank: A Study in Development Financing.* New York: Praeger.

Derthick, Martha. 1970. *The Influence of Federal Grants: Public Assistance in Massachusetts.* Cambridge: Harvard University Press.

Dettmer, Jorge. 1983. Nicaragua: La revolución superior en la educación. *Revista Latinoamericana de Estudios Educativos* 13 (1): 103–30.

DeWitt, Peter R., Jr. 1977. *The Inter-American Development Bank and Political Influence, with Special Reference to Costa Rica.* New York: Praeger.

Dexter, Lewis Anthony. 1970. *Elite and Specialized Interviewing.* Evanston, Ill.: Northwestern University Press.

Dezalay, Yves, and Bryant G. Garth. 2002. *The Internationalization of Palace Wars: Lawyers, Economists, and the Contest to Transform Latin American States.* Chicago: University of Chicago Press.

Diégues, Manuel, Jr., and Bryce Wood, eds. 1967. *Social Science in Latin America.* New York: Columbia University Press.

Dill, David. 1998. Evaluating the "Evaluative State." *European Journal of Education* 33 (3): 361–77.

DiMaggio, Paul J., and Walter W. Powell. 1983. The Iron Cage Revisited: Institutional Isomorphism and Collective Rationality in Organizational Fields. *American Sociological Review* 48: 147–60.

———. 1991. Introduction. In *The New Institutionalism in Organizational Analysis,* ed. Walter W. Powell and Paul J. DiMaggio, 1–38. Chicago: University of Chicago Press.

Dolcini, Horacio A. 1983. Ingreso a las universidades nacionales en la República Argentina. Paper read at Primer Seminario sobre Transferencia o Pase del Ciclo Secundario al Universitario, Buenos Aires.

Domínguez, Jorge I. 1987. Political Change: Central America, South America, and the Caribbean. In Weiner and Huntington 1987, 65–99.

Douglas, James. 1983. *Why Charity? The Case for a Third Sector.* Beverly Hills, Calif.: Sage.

———. 1987. Political Theories of Nonprofit Organizations. In Powell 1987, 43–54.

Downs, Anthony. 1957. *An Economic Theory of Democracy.* New York: Harper.

Drake, Paul. 1989. From Retrogression to Resurgence: International Scholarly Relations with Latin America in U.S. Universities, 1970s–1980s. Report to Joint Committee on Latin American Studies.

Drysdale, Robert. 1987. *Higher Education in Latin America: Problems Policies and Institutional Changes.* Washington, D.C.: World Bank.

Durán, Fernando, et al. 1987. *Paradigma académico de la UCR.* San José: UCR.

Eastman, Clyde, and James Grieshop. 1989. Technology Development and Diffusion: Potatoes in Peru. In Compton 1989, 33–55.

Einaudi, Luigi R. 1974. A Note on U.S. Government Exchange Programs. In *Beyond Cuba: Latin America Takes Charge of Its Future,* ed. Luigi R. Einaudi. New York: Crane, Russak.

Eisemon, Thomas Owen. 1992. *Lending for Higher Education: An Analysis of World Bank Investment, 1963–1991.* Washington, D.C.: World Bank.

Eisemon, Thomas Owen, and Lauritz Holm-Nielsen. 1995. *Developing Capacity for Research and Advanced Scientific Training: Lessons from the World Bank Experience.* Washington, D.C.: World Bank.

Eisemon, Thomas Owen, and Moussa Kourouma. 1994. Foreign Assistance for University Development in Sub-Saharan Africa and Asia. In *Revitalizing Higher Education,* ed. Jamil Salmi and Adriaan Verspoor, 274–304. Oxford: Pergamon.

Elmore, Richard F., and Walter Williams, eds. 1976. *Social Program Implementation.* Quantitative Studies in Social Relations. New York: Academic Press.

Enarson, Harold. 1962. *University Education in Central America.* New York: Ford Foundation.

———. 1963. University Education in Central America. *Journal of Higher Education* 34 (4): 196–204.

Espinosa, J. M. 1976. *Inter-American Beginnings of U.S. Cultural Diplomacy, 1936–1948.* Washington, D.C.: Department of State.

Evans, Peter. 1985. After Dependency. *Latin American Research Review* 20 (2): 149–60.

———. 1987. Foreign Capital and the Third World State. In Weiner and Huntington 1987, 319–52.

Evans, Peter, and John D. Stephens. 1988. Studying Development since the Sixties: The Emergence of a New Comparative Political Economy. *Theory and Society* 17: 713–45.

Faure, Edgard, et al. 1972. *Learning to Be.* Paris: Unesco.

Figueiredo, Maria. 1987. Politics and Higher Education in Brazil, 1964–86. *International Journal of Educational Development* 7 (3): 173–81.

Filgueira, C. 1992. Uruguay. In Clark and Neave 1992, 1:788–91.

Finegold, David, Laurel McFarland, and William Richardson, eds. 1993. *Something Borrowed, Something Learned? The Transatlantic Market in Education and Training Reform.* Washington, D.C.: Brookings Institution.

Fischel, Astrid. 1987. *Consenso y represión: Una interpretación socio-política de la educación costarricense.* San José: Editorial Costa Rica.

Fisher, Donald. 1983. The Role of Philanthropic Foundations in the Reproduction of Hegemony: Rockefeller Foundation and the Social Sciences. *Sociology* 17: 206–33.

Fisher, Julie. 1993. *The Road from Rio: Sustainable Development and the Nongovernmental Movement in the Third World.* Westport, Conn.: Praeger.

———. 1998. *Nongovernments: NGOs and the Political Development of the Third World.* West Hartford, Conn.: Kumarian Press.

Flora, Cornelia Butler, and Jan L. Flora. 1989. An Historical Perspective on Institutional Transfer. In Compton 1989, 7–31.

Foley, Douglas. 1984. Colonialism and Schooling in the Philippines, 1898–1970. In Altbach and Kelly 1984, 69–95.

Ford Foundation. 1962. *Annual Report.* New York: Ford Foundation.

———. 1972. *Assistance to Latin American Education in the Seventies.* New York: Ford Foundation.

———. 1973. *Annual Report.* New York: Ford Foundation.

———. 1984. *Annual Report.* New York: Ford Foundation.

Fosdick, Raymond Blaine. 1952. *The Story of the Rockefeller Foundation.* New York: Harper and Brothers.

Franco, Augusto. 1973. El gobierno de los Estados Unidos y las universidades latinoamericanas. In Renner 1973b.

———. 1991. Financing Higher Education in Colombia. *Higher Education* 21, no. 2 (March): 163–76.

Friedman, Ray. 1980. *The Role of Non-profit Organizations in Foreign Aid: A Literature Review.* New Haven: Yale University Program on Non-Profit Organizations.

Fritz, Paul. 1980. *U.S. Assistance to Chile: AID and Predecessor Agencies, 1943–1980.* Washington, D.C.: Agency for International Development

———. 1989. *AID History (Paraguay).* Washington, D.C.: Agency for International Development

Frodin, Reuben. 1965. *Report on the Catholic University of Chile.* (Report #8516). New York: Rockefeller Foundation.

———. 1970. *"Ford and Latin American Universities,"* #002375 card catalog memo to the Ford Foundation.

———. 1973. U.S. Foundations and Latin American Universities in the Sixties. In Renner 1973b, 8–31.

Fuenzalida, Edmundo. 1982. The Contribution of Higher Education to a New International Order. In Sanyal 1982, 124–45.

———. 1983. The Reception of Scientific Sociology in Chile. *Latin American Research Review* 18 (2): 95–112.

———. 1984. Institutionalization of Research in Chile's Universities: 1953–1967. In *Education and Development,* ed. R. M. Garrett, 55–122. London and New York: Croom Helm and St. Martin's Press.

———. 1987. La reorganización de las instituciones de enseñanza superior e investigación en América Latina entre 1950 y 1980 y sus interpretaciones. *Estudios Sociales* 52 (2): 115–38.

Galdames, Francisco. 1988. Nuevas orientaciones en la extensión universitaria. In Oyarzun 1988, 135–45.

Galicia, Elba, and Amalia García. 1984. Análisis del personal académico. In UNAM 1984, 123–80.

García de Fanelli, Ana. 1996. *Estudios de posgrado en la Argentina.* Buenos Aires: CEDES.

———. 1997. *Las nuevas universidades del conurbano bonaerense.* Buenos Aires: CEDES.

Gardner, Deborah S., ed. 1998. *Vision and Values: Rethinking the Nonprofit Sector in America.* New York: Nathan Cummings Foundation in association with the Program on Non-Profit Organizations.

Gardner, J. W. 1964. *AID and the Universities.* New York: Education and World Affairs.

Garretón, Manuel Antonio. 1987. Notas sobre los orígenes y desarrollo de la Reforma en la Universidad Católica de Chile (1967–1973). *Realidad Universitaria* (3): 4–13.

Geddes, Barbara. 1994. *Politician's Dilemma: Building State Capacity in Latin America.* California Series on Social Choice and Political Economy, 25. Berkeley: University of California Press.

Geiger, Roger L. 1993. *Research and Relevant Knowledge.* New York: Oxford University Press.

Geiger, Theodore. 1967. *The Conflicted Relationship: The West and the Transformation of Asia, Africa, and Latin America.* New York: McGraw-Hill.

Gereffi, Gary. 1983. *The Pharmaceutical Industry and Dependency in the Third World.* Princeton: Princeton University Press.

Giaimo, Robert, and John Brademas. 1961. *The University in Latin America: Argentina and the Alliance for Progress.* Washington, D.C.: Committee on Education and Labor, House of Representatives, 87th Cong., 1st sess., September, U.S. Government Printing Office.

Gil, Manuel. 1990. *La formación del cuerpo académico en México, 1960–1990.*

———. 1994. *Los rasgos de la diversidad: Un estudio sobre los académicos mexicanos.* Mexico City: UAM-A.

———. 1999. El mercado de trabajo académico. *Este País* 103 (October).

Gilbert, Neil, and Harry Specht. 1984. "Picking Winners": Federal Discretion and Local Experience as Bases for Planning Grant Allocation. In Wright and White 1984, 171–86.

Glick, Philip M. 1957. *The Administration of Technical Assistance: Growth in the Americas.* Chicago: University of Chicago Press.

Goertzel, Ted. 1967. Ideología de desenvolvimento americano aplicado. *Revista Brasileira* 3: 123–38.

Góngora, Mario. 1979. Origin and Philosophy of the Spanish American University. In Maier and Weatherhead 1979, 17–64.

González Casanova, Pablo. 1984. Las ciencias sociales en América Latina. *Revista Mexicana de Ciencias Políticas y Sociales* 30 (117–18): 9–24.

González, Gilbert. 1981. Educational Reform and the University of Colombia. *Comparative Education* 17 (2): 229–46.

———. 1982. Imperial Reform in the Neo-Colonies: The University of California's Basic Plan for Higher Education in Colombia. *Journal of Education* 164 (4): 330–50.

Goodell, Grace. 1986. *The Elementary Structures of Political Life: Rural Development in Pahlavi Iran.* New York: Oxford University Press.

Goodwin, Craufurd, and Michael Nacht. 1984. *Decline and Renewal: Causes and Cures of Decay among Foreign-Trained Intellectuals and Professionals in the Third World.* New York: Institute for International Education.

Gordenker, Leon. 1976. *International Aid and National Decisions: Development Programs in Malawi, Tanzania, and Zambia.* Princeton: Princeton University Press.

Gordon, Cyrus. 1963. *Introduction to the Old Testament Times.* Ventnor, N.J.: Ventnor.

Gormley, William T. 1989. *Taming the Bureaucracy: Muscles, Prayers, and Other Strategies.* Princeton: Princeton University Press.

Grant, Richard, and Jan Nijman, eds. 1998. *The Global Crisis in Foreign Aid.* Syracuse: Syracuse University Press.

Greenwald, Rene. 1986. *Regional Education Profile: Central America.* New York: IIE.

Grindle, Merilee S., and W. Thomas. 1991. *Public Choices and Policy Change: The Political Economy of Reform in Developing Countries.* Baltimore: Johns Hopkins University Press.

Gusfield, Joseph, and William Friedland, eds. 1968. *Tradition and Modernity: Conflict and Congruence. The Journal of Social Issues,* vol. 24. Ann Arbor, Mich.: Society for the Psychological Study of Social Issues.

Gusso, Divonzir Arthur, Raulino Tramontin, and Ronald Braga. 1988. *Educação e cultura 1987.* Mimeo. Brasilia.

Gwin, Catherine. 1994. *U.S. Relations with the World Bank, 1945–1992.* Washington, D.C.: Brookings Institution.

Gwin, Catherine, and Joan M. Nelson, eds. 1997. *Perspectives on Aid and Development.* Ed. Overseas Development Council. Policy Essay no. 22. Baltimore: Johns Hopkins University Press.

Haines, Gerald. 1989. *The Americanization of Brazil: A Study of U.S. Cold War Diplomacy in the Third World, 1945–54.* Wilmington, Del.: SR Books.

Hall, Budd L. 1980. Knowledge as a Commodity: The Inequities of Knowledge Creation. In Spitzberg 1980, 25–41.

Hall, Peter D. 1998. Philanthropy, Public Welfare, and the Politics of Knowledge. In Gardner 1998, 11–27.

Hall, Richard H. 1996. *Organizations: Structures, Processes, and Outcomes.* 6th ed. Englewood Cliffs, N.J.: Prentice Hall.

Halpern, Charles R. 1998. Foreword. In Gardner 1998, 5–9.

Halpern, Sydney A. 1987. Professional Schools in the American University. In Clark 1987, 304–30.

Hancock, Graham. 1989. *Lords of Poverty: The Power, Prestige, and Corruption of the International Aid Business.* New York: Atlantic Monthly Press.

Hannan, Michael T., and John H. Freeman. 1989. *Organizational Ecology.* Cambridge: Harvard University Press.

Hansen, David, Gustavo Antonini, and John Strasma. 1988. *Dominican Republic: The Superior Institute of Agriculture.* Washington, D.C.: Agency for International Development.

Hansen, Gar. 1990. *Beyond the Neoclassical University: Agricultural Higher Education in the Developing World.* Washington, D.C.: Agency for International Development.

Harbison, Ralph, and Eric Hanushek. 1992. *Educational Performance of the Poor: Lessons from Rural Northeast Brazil.* New York: Published for the World Bank by Oxford University Press.

Harding, Timothy F. 1968. *The University, Politics, and Development in Contemporary Latin America.* Riverside: University of California, Latin American Research Program.

Harrison, John P. n.d. *The University versus National Development in Spanish America.* Austin: University of Texas, Institute of Latin American Studies.

Hayhoe, Ruth. 1986. Penetration or Mutuality? China's Educational Cooperation with Europe, Japan, and North America. *Comparative Education Review* 30 (November): 532–59.

Hayter, Theresa, and Catharine Watson. 1985. *Aid: Rhetoric and Reality*. London: Pluto Press.

Hekman, Susan J. 1983. *Weber, the Ideal Type, and Contemporary Social Theory*. Notre Dame, Ind.: University of Notre Dame.

Hellinger, Steve, Doug Hellinger, and Fred O'Regan. 1988. *Aid for Just Development: Report on the Future of Foreign Assistance*. Boulder: Lynne Rienner.

Hellman, Ronald. 1988. *The Impact of the Ford Foundation on the Economic Sciences in Chile*. New York: Bildner Center, City University of New York.

Hennessy, Alistair. 1979. Students in the Latin American University. In Maier and Weatherhead 1979, 147–84.

Herrera, Felipe. 1985a. 25 Años del Banco Interamericano de Desarrollo. *Estudios Sociales* 45 (3): 167–77.

———. 1985b. *Experiencias universitarias: Escenarios nacionales e internacionales*. Santiago: Pehuen.

Hidalgo, Jesús. 1987. La universidad latinoamericana en cifras. In *Anuario universidades,* ed. UDUAL, 75–104. Mexico City: La Unión.

Hirschman, Albert O. 1958. *The Strategy of Economic Development*. New Haven: Yale University Press.

———. 1963. *Journeys toward Progress: Studies of Economic Policy-Making in Latin America*. New York: Twentieth Century Fund.

———. 1986. *Rival Views of Market Society*. New York: Viking.

———. 1991. *The Rhetoric of Reaction: Perversity, Futility, Jeopardy*. Cambridge: Belknap Press.

Holden, Robert. 1987. Measuring Mexican Studies in the United States. Report prepared for the MacArthur Foundation. June. Mimeo.

Honey, John C. 1968. *Toward Strategies for Public Administration Development in Latin America*. Syracuse, N.Y.: Syracuse University Press.

Hook, Steven W., ed. 1996. *Foreign Aid toward the Millennium*. Boulder: Lynne Rienner.

Horowitz, Irving Louis, ed. 1967. *The Rise and Fall of Project Camelot: Studies in the Relationship between Social Science and Practical Politics*. Cambridge: MIT Press.

Hotta, Taiji. 1991. Japanese Educational Assistance to Developing Countries. *Comparative Education Review* 35 (3): 476–90.

Hüfner, Klaus, and Jens Naumann. 1986. UNESCO: Only the Crisis of a "Politicized" UN Specialized Agency? *Comparative Education Review* 30 (1): 120–31.

Hultin, Mats. 1984. Researchers and Policy-Makers in Education: The World Bank as Middleman in the Developing Countries. In *Educational Research and Policy: How Do They Relate?* ed. T. Husen and Maurice Kogan, 165–77. Oxford: Pergamon Press.

Humphrey, Richard A., ed. 1967. *Universities and Development Assistance Abroad.* Washington, D.C.: American Council on Education.

Huneeus, Carlos. 1973. *La reforma en la Universidad de Chile.* Santiago: CPU.

Huntington, Samuel P. 1968. *Political Order in Changing Societies.* New Haven: Yale University Press.

———. 1987. The Goals of Development. In Weiner and Huntington 1987, 3–32.

Hurst, Paul. 1981. Aid and Educational Development. *Comparative Education Review* 17 (2): 117–25.

IDB. 1978. *Evaluation Report on IDB Operations in the Education Sector.* Washington, D.C.: Group of Controllers of the Review and Evaluation System, Inter-American Development Bank.

———. 1985. *Enfoque y contribuciones del BID en ciencia y tecnología.* Washington, D.C.: Inter-American Development Bank.

———. 1988. *Economic and Social Progress in Latin America: Science and Technology Section.* Washington, D.C.: Inter-American Development Bank.

———. 1993. *The Bank at a Glance.* Washington, D.C.: Inter-American Development Bank.

———. 1997. *Higher Education in Latin America and the Caribbean. A Strategy Paper.* Washington, D.C.: Inter-American Development Bank.

———. n.d. *Distribution of IDB Education Financing by Areas, 1962–1985.* Washington, D.C.: Inter-American Development Bank.

IESA. 1991. *Soporte estadístico.* Caracas: Centro para el Desarrollo de Recursos Humanos.

Ilchman, Warren F. n.d. *Philanthropy: A Definition.* Bloomington: Indiana University Center on Philanthropy.

Ilchman, Warren F., and A. Ilchman. 1987. Academic Exchange and the Founding of New Universities. *Annals of the American Association of Political and Social Sciences* 491 (May): 48–62.

Ilchman, Warren F., Stanley N. Katz, and Edward L. Queen II, eds. 1998. *Philanthropy in the World's Traditions.* Bloomington: Indiana University Press.

Ilon, Lynn. 2003. Foreign Aid Financing of Higher Education in Africa. In *African Higher Education: An International Reference Handbook,* ed. Damtew Teferra and Philip Altbach, 61–72. Bloomington: Indiana University Press.

Inkeles, Alex, and David H. Smith. 1974. *Becoming Modern: Individual Change in Six Developing Countries.* Cambridge: Harvard University Press.

Jacobsen, J. 1968. The Junior College Idea in South America. *Community and Junior College Journal* 39: 9–13.

Jaksić, Iván. 1989. *Academic Rebels in Chile: The Role of Philosophy in Higher Education and Politics.* Albany: SUNY Press.

Jaramillo, Jaime Uribe. 1963. Observaciones al informe Atcon. *Revista de la Cultura del Occidente* Librería Buchholz: 170–86.

Jiménez Mier y Terán, Fernando. 1982. *El autoritarismo en el gobierno de la UNAM.* Mexico City: Ediciones de Cultura Popular.

Jones, D. R. 1992. National Models of Higher Education: International Transfer. In Clark and Neave 1992, 2:956–69.

Jones, Phillip W. 1992. *World Bank Financing of Education: Lending, Learning, and Development*. London: Routledge.

Kaimowitz, David. 1992. Aid and Development in Latin America. *Latin American Research Review* 27 (2): 202–11.

Karl, Barry, and Stanley Katz. 1981. The American Private Philanthropic Foundation and the Public Sphere, 1890–1930. *Minerva* 19 (2): 236–70.

Karpinsky, Rose Marie. 1982. *Los estudios generales*. San José: Universidad de Costa Rica.

Kater, Adri. 1976. Senegal. In Parkinson 1976, 136–64.

Kelly, Gail P. 1980. The Myth of Educational Planning. In Spitzberg 1980, 93–108.

Kent, Rollin. 1990. *Modernización conservadora y crisis académica en la UNAM*. Mexico City: Nueva Imagen.

———. 1996. *Institutional Reform in Mexican Higher Education: Conflict and Renewal in Three Public Universities*. Washington, D.C.: Inter-American Development Bank.

Keohane, Robert O., and Joseph S. Nye. 1977. *Power and Interdependence: World Politics in Transition*. Boston: Little, Brown.

Kerr, Clark. 1986. Foreword. In Cerych and Sabatier 1986.

Kettl, Donald F. 1983. *The Regulation of American Federalism*. Baton Rouge: Louisiana State University Press.

King, Kenneth. 1981. Dilemmas of Research Aid to Education in Developing Countries. *Comparative Education* 17 (2): 247–54.

———. 1991. *Aid and Education in the Developing World*. Harlow: Longman.

King, Kenneth, and Jasbir Sarjit Singh. 1991. *Quality and Aid*. London: Commonwealth Secretariat.

Kohler, Robert. 1991. *Partners in Science: Foundations and Natural Scientists, 1900–1945*. Chicago: University of Chicago Press.

Kovacs, Karen. 1989. Intervención estatal y transformación del régimen político: El caso de la Universidad Pedagógica Nacional. Ph.D. diss., El Centro de Estudios Sociológicos, El Colegio de México, Mexico City.

Kumar, Krishna, ed. 1998. *Postconflict Elections, Democratization, and International Assistance*. Boulder: Lynne Rienner.

Labbens, Jean. 1968. Las universidades chilenas: Evolución de la matrícula, 1957–1967: situación actual. *Revista Consejo de Rectores* 3 (2): 65–195, (3): 35–58.

Lacy, Elaine. 1992. Autonomy versus Foreign Influence: Mexican Educational Policy and UNESCO. *SECOLAS Annals* 23: 53–59.

Lagemann, Ellen. 1989. *The Politics of Knowledge: The Carnegie Corporation, Philanthropy, and Public Policy*. Middletown, Conn.: Wesleyan University Press.

Lanning, John Tate. 1955. *The University in the Kingdom of Guatemala*. Ithaca: Cornell University Press.

Larraín, Hernán. 1986. Nivel académico en Chile. In Lemaitre and Lavados 1986.

LASPAU. 1986. *Annual Report*. Cambridge: LASPAU.

Latapí, Pablo. 1978. *Trends in Latin American Universities*. Paris: UNESCO International Association of Universities.

Lavados, Hugo, and Andrés Sanfuentes. 1986. Algunos comentarios sobre financiamiento y uso de recursos en las universidades chilenas. *Estudios Sociales* 49: 33–44.

Lavados, Iván. 1987. Financiamiento de actividades académicas. *Estudios Sociales* 51 (1): 119–34.

———. 1988. Tendencias e impactos de la cooperación internacional en América Latina. *Estudios Sociales* 57 (3): 49–70.

———, ed. 1978. *Cooperación Internacional y Desarrollo*. Santiago: CPU.

Lavados, Iván, and Sergio Montenegro. 1980. Evolución de la cooperación técnica internacional en Chile. *Estudios Sociales* 22 (2): 77–134.

Leach, Fiona. 1999. Dilemmas between Economics and Culture in Educational Aid: Lessons for Donors. In *Education, Cultures, and Economics: Dilemmas for Development*, ed. Fiona Leach and Angela Little, 371–94. New York: Falmer Press.

Lemaitre, María José. 1985. *Algunas reflexiones acerca de las universidades regionales*. Santiago: CPU.

Lemaitre, María José, and Iván Lavados. 1986. *La educación superior en Chile. Riesgos y oportunidades en los '80*. 2nd ed. Santiago: CPU.

Levine, Arthur. 1980. *When Dreams and Heroes Died: A Portrait of Today's College Student—A Report for the Carnegie Council on Policy Studies in Higher Education*. San Francisco and New York: Jossey-Bass & Carnegie Foundation for Advancement of Teaching.

Levy, Daniel C. 1981. Comparing Authoritarian Regimes in Latin America: Insights from Higher Education Policy. *Comparative Politics* 141 (1): 31–52.

———. 1986. *Higher Education and the State in Latin America*. Chicago: University of Chicago Press.

———. 1991. *Targeted Philanthropy: How U.S. Donors Selected Latin American Universities*. New Haven: Yale University, Program on Non-Profit Organizations.

———. 1994. Mexico: Towards State Supervision? In *Government and Higher Education Relationships across Three Continents*, ed. Guy Neave and Frans van Vught, 241–63. Oxford: Pergamon.

———. 1995. Latin America's Think Tanks: The Roots of Nonprofit Privatization. *Studies in Comparative International Development* 30 (2): 3–25.

———. 1996. *Building the Third Sector. Latin America's Private Research Centers and Nonprofit Development*. Pittsburgh: University of Pittsburgh Press.

————. 1998. Fitting In? Making Higher Education Part of the New Development Model. *Mexican Studies/Estudios Mexicanos* 14 (2): 407–40.

Lindeman, Eduard C. 1988 (1936). *Wealth and Culture.* Society and Philanthropy series. New Brunswick, N.J.: Transaction Books.

Lissner, Jorgen. 1977. *The Politics of Altruism: A Study of Political Behaviour of Voluntary Development Agencies.* Geneva: Lutheran World Federation.

Lowenthal, Abraham, ed. 1991. *Exporting Democracy. The United States and Latin America: Themes and Issues.* Baltimore: Johns Hopkins University Press.

Lowi, Theodore J. 1979. *The End of Liberalism.* New York: W. W. Norton.

Lucio, Ricardo, and Mónica Serrano. 1992. *La educación superior: Tendencias y políticas estatales.* Bogotá: IEPRI-Universidad Nacional.

Machado Neto, A. L. 1968. El derrumbe de la Universidad de Brasilia. In Ribeiro 1968, 263–80.

Magat, Richard. 1979. *The Ford Foundation at Work: Philanthropic Choices, Methods, and Styles.* New York: Plenum Press.

————, ed. 1989. *Philanthropic Giving: Studies in Varieties and Goals.* New York: Oxford University Press.

Maglen, Leo. 1990. The Impact of Bilateral Aid on Educational Development: The Case of Australia and the South Pacific. *Comparative Education* 28 (1): 83–93.

Magnusson, William L. 1970. Reform at the National University of Colombia: Administrative Strategy in Institute Building. Ph.D. diss., University of California, Berkeley.

Maheu, René. 1965. International Cooperation and the Development of Higher Education in Latin America (the Role of UNESCO). In *Higher Education and Latin American Development Roundtables,* 121–41. Washington, D.C.: Inter-American Development Bank.

Maier, Joseph, and Richard Weatherhead, eds. 1979. *The Latin American University.* Albuquerque: University of New Mexico Press.

Majone, Giandomenico, and Aaron Wildavsky. 1977. Implementation as Evolution. *Policy Studies Annual Review* 2: 103–17.

Malo, Salvador, Jonathan Garst, and Graciela Garza. 1981. *El egresado de posgrado de la UNAM.* México: UNAM, Secretaría ejecutiva del consejo de Estudios de Posgrado.

Mankiewicz, Frank. 1965. The Peace Corps and the Political University. In Association for Latin American Studies 1965, 56–58.

March, James G., and Johan P. Olsen. 1976. *Ambiguity and Choice in Organizations.* Bergen: Universitetsforlaget.

Marquis, Carlos. 1987. *Democracia y burocracia universitaria: El caso de la Universidad Autónoma Metropolitana.* México: División de Ciencias Sociales y Humanidades, Universidad Autónoma Metropolitana-Unidad Azcapotzalco.

Matthews, Donald R. 1982. A Case Study of Developing Short-Cycle Postsecondary Education in Venezuela: Colegios Universitarios. Ph.D. diss., University of Florida.

Mattocks, David. 1990. Beyond Institution Building. Ph.D. diss., University of Wisconsin.

Maxwell, I.C.M. 1980. *Universities in Partnership: The Interuniversity Council and the Growth of Higher Education in Developing Countries*. Edinburgh: Scottish Academic Press.

Mayorga, Román. 1994. IDB data printout. Washington, D.C.: Inter-American Development Bank.

Mazmanian, Daniel A., and Paul A. Sabatier. 1983. *Implementation and Public Policy*. Scott, Foresman Public Policy Analysis and Management series. Glenview, Ill.: Scott, Foresman.

Mazrui, Ali A. 1975. The African University as a Multinational Corporation: Problems of Penetration and Dependency. *Harvard Educational Review* 45 (2): 191–210.

McCarthy, Kathleen. 1984a. Non-U.S. Foundations. In McCarthy 1984b, 85–101.

———, ed. 1984b. *Philanthropy and Culture: The International Foundation Perspective*. Philadelphia: University of Pennsylvania Press.

McDaniel, Tim. 1991. *Autocracy, Modernization, and Revolution in Russia and Iran*. Princeton: Princeton University Press.

McIlnay, Dennis P. 1991. *Foundations and Higher Education: Dollars, Donors, and Scholars*. Baldwin Place, N.Y.: George Kurian Books.

McIntyre, John R. 1986. Introduction: Critical Perspectives on International Technology Transfer. In McIntyre and Papp 1986, 3–24.

McIntyre, John R., and Daniel S. Papp, eds. 1986. *The Political Economy of International Technology Transfers*. New York: Quorum Books.

McKenna, James B. 1985. University Reform in Spain: New Structures for Autonomy and Accountability. *Comparative Education Review* 29 (November 1985): 460–70.

Meek, V. Lynn, ed. 1996. *The Mockers and the Mocked: Comparative Perspectives on Differentiation, Convergence, and Diversity in Higher Education*. Oxford: Pergamon Press.

Meller, Patricio. 1984. *Los Chicago Boys y el modelo económico chileno, 1973–1983*. In *Apuntes Cieplan n° 43*. Santiago.

Meneses, Ernesto. 1983. La Universidad Iberoamericana, un caso de departamentalización en México. *Cuadernos del Centro de Documentación Legislativa Universitaria* 3 (7): 127–58.

Merrill, Charles E. 1986. *The Checkbook: The Politics and Ethics of Foundation Philanthropy*. Boston: Oelgeschlager, Gunn and Hain.

Mesmer, Theodore, Irwin Baskind, and Enrique Lerdau. 1998. Reflecting on an Alliance. *Americas* (October): 52–55.

Method, Francis J. 1976. External Assistance to Education in Indonesia (chapter 11 included in H. M. Phillips). In *Educational Cooperation between Developed and Developing Countries, 206–52.* New York: Praeger.

Method, Frank, and Saundra Kay Shaw. 1981. *AID Assistance to Education: A Retrospective Study.* Washington, D.C.: Creative Associates.

Metzger, Walter P. 1987. The Academic Profession in the United States. In Clark 1987, 123–208.

Meyer, John W., and M. Hannan, eds. 1979. *National Development and the World System: Educational, Economic, and Political Change, 1959–1970.* Chicago: University of Chicago Press.

Miceli, Sergio. 1990. The State of Graduate Social Sciences in Latin America and the Role of Independent Research Centers. Paper read at Ford Foundation Meeting on Higher Education in Latin America, November 16, at New York.

Miller, Alwin. 1984. *United State Assistance to Higher Education in Developing Countries prior to 1970.* Washington, D.C.: Agency for International Development

Moller, Mónica, and Ana Maria Flores. 1985. Fundaciones norteamericanas en América Latina y el Caribe. Educación Superior, prioridades y tendencias (1972–1980): El caso de la Fundación Ford. Licenciado, Universidad Autónoma de Guadalajara.

Mollis, Marcela. 1995. *Estado, universidades y gestión de políticas científico-tecnológicas en Argentina.* Washington, D.C.: Document elaborated for the IDB.

Montgomery, John Dickey. 1967. *Foreign Aid in International Politics.* America's Role in World Affairs Series. Englewood Cliffs, N.J.: Prentice-Hall.

Moock, Joyce. 1980. Ford Foundation Assistance to University Level Education in Developing Countries. Paper read at Rockefeller Foundation Education for Development Program's Review Advisory Committee Meeting, April 6–8, at New York.

Morles, Victor. 1983. Los estudios de postgrado en América Latina. *Interciencia* 8 (1): 23–30.

Moros Ghersi, Carlos A. 1991. El futuro de la enseñanza de la medicina. *Universitas 2000* 15 (4): 43–69.

Morton, Alice, and Alwin Miller. 1985. *Evaluation of AID-Assisted Agricultural Universities.* Washington, D.C.: RONCO Consulting Corporation.

Mosher, Arthur. 1957. *Technical Cooperation in Latin American Agriculture.* Chicago: University of Chicago Press.

MUCIA. n.d. *Quality in International Development, Education, and Programs.* Columbus, Ohio: Midwest Universities Consortium for International Activities.

Muga, Alfonso, and José Joaquín Brunner. 1996. Chile: Políticas de educación superior 1990–1995. *Revista Paraguaya de Sociología* 33 (97): 137–76.

Mundy, Karen. 1992. Human Resources Development Assistance in the Canadian ODA Program. Toronto, Ontario, Institute for Studies in Education. Conference paper.

———. 1998. Educational Multilateralism and World (Dis)Order. *Comparative Education Review* 42 (4): 448–78.

Muñoz Izquierdo, Carlos. 1989. Financiamiento de la educación superior y endeudamiento externo en América Latina. *Revista Latinoamericana de Estudios Educativos* 19 (2): 9–54.

Murphy, E. Jefferson. 1976. *Creative Philanthropy: Carnegie Corporation and Africa, 1953–1973.* New York: Teachers College Press.

Myers, Robert. 1983a. External Financing of Foreign Study: The Ford Foundation in Peru. *Prospects* 13 (4): 503–13.

———. 1983b. *Ford Foundation Support for Education Abroad of Third World Nationals, 1960–1980: A Report to the Ford Foundation.* New York: Ford Foundation.

Nakamura, Robert T., and R. Smallwood. 1980. *The Politics of Policy Implementation.* New York: St. Martin's Press.

Nathan, Richard P. 1993. *Turning Promises into Performance.* New York: Columbia University Press.

National Commission on Philanthropy and Civic Renewal. 1997. *Giving Better/Giving Smarter: Renewing Philanthropy in America.* Washington, D.C.: National Commission on Philanthropy and Civic Renewal.

Navarro, Juan Carlos, Eva Rodríguez Braña, and Valeria Pacheco. 2004. El BID y el desarrollo educativo de América Latina y el Caribe. In *Hacia visiones renovadas del financiamiento educativo en América Latina y el Caribe. El financiamiento de la educación: Una inversión a largo plazo,* ed. Juan Carlos Navarro and Eva Rodríguez Braña, 221–36. Cumbre de las Américas. Monterrey, México: IDB.

Neave, Guy. 1995. On Living in Interesting Times: Higher Education in Western Europe, 1985–1995. *European Journal of Education* 30 (4): 377–93.

———. 1998. On the Cultivation of Quality, Efficiency, and Enterprise. *European Journal of Education* 23 (1–2): 7–23.

Neave, Guy, and Gary Rhoades. 1987. The Academic Estate in Western Europe. In Clark 1987, 211–70.

Nelson, Joan M. 1968. *Aid, Influence, and Foreign Policy.* New York: Macmillan.

Nielsen, Waldemar. 1972. *The Big Foundations.* New York: Columbia University Press.

O'Connell, Brian. 1987. *Philanthropy in Action.* New York: Foundation Center.

Odendahl, Teresa. 1989. Independent Foundations and Wealthy Donors. In Magat 1989, 159–79.

OECD. 1990. *Higher Education in California.* Paris: Organisation for Economic Co-operation and Development.

———. 1998. *Redefining Tertiary Education.* Paris: OECD.

O'Hanlon, Michael E., and Carol Graham. 1997. *A Half Penny on the Federal Dollar. The Future of Development Aid.* Washington, D.C.: Brookings Institution Press.

Olivera, Carlos. 1985. Is Education in Latin America Dependent? *Prospects* 15 (2): 227–38.

Olsson, Berit. 1992. *The Ownership and Cultivation of Knowledge: The Rationale for Swedish Support to Universities in Developing Countries.* Stockholm: SAREC.

O'Neill, Michael. 1989. *The Third America.* San Francisco: Jossey-Bass.

Ornelas, Carlos. 1988. Formación de cuadros profesionales, mercado de trabajo y necesidades sociales. *Reforma y utopía: Reflexiones sobre educación superior* 2 (October/November): 27–63.

———. 1996. Evaluación y conflicto en las universidades públicas mexicanas. *Reforma y Utopía* 15: 5–35.

Orr, James Darby. 1971. The Foreign Scholar Returned Home: A Review of Selected Research. Ph.D. diss., Teachers College, Columbia University, New York.

Ortiz Mena, Antonio. 1975. *Development in Latin America: A View from the IDB.* Washington, D.C.: Inter-American Development Bank.

Oteiza, Enrique. 1993. La universidad argentina en transición. *Sociedad* (November): 45–76.

Oyarzun, Luis, ed. 1988. *Juan Gómez Millas (1900–1987): el legado de un humanista.* Santiago: CPU.

Packenham, Robert. 1973. *Liberal America and the Third World: Political Development Ideas in Foreign Aid and Social Science.* Princeton: Princeton University Press.

Packenham, Robert A. 1992. *The Dependency Movement: Scholarship and Politics in Development Studies.* Cambridge: Harvard University Press.

Paoli, Francisco José, ed. 1990. *Desarrollo y organización de las ciencias sociales en México.* Mexico City: UNAM, Centro de Investigaciones Interdisciplinarias en Humanidades.

Parkinson, Nancy. 1976. *Educational Aid and National Development.* London: Macmillan.

Parra, Rodrigo, and Bernardo Jaramillo. 1985. *La educación superior en Colombia.* Caracas: CRESALC-UNESCO.

Partners of the Americas. 1985. Central American Development Program. *Partners* 17 (4): 5–6.

Paul, Jean-Jacques, and Laurence Wolff. 1992. *The Economics of Higher Education in Brazil.* World Bank (Human Resources Division, Latin America and Caribbean Region) #30, August.

Payton, Robert L. 1988. *Philanthropy: Voluntary Action for the Public Good.* New York and London: American Council on Education/Macmillan; Collier Macmillan.

————. 1989. Philanthropic Values. In Magat 1989, 29–45.

Pearson, Lester B. 1969. *Partners in Development. Report of the Commission on International Development.* New York: Praeger.

Pelczar, Richard. 1974. University Reform in Latin America: The Case of Colombia. In *University Reform,* ed. Philip Altbach, 42–64. Cambridge: Schenkman.

————. 1977. The Latin American Professoriate: Progress and Prospects. *Higher Education* 6, no. 2 (May): 235–54.

Pérez Lindo, Augusto. 1985. *Universidad, política y sociedad.* Buenos Aires: EUDEBA.

Pesmazoglou, Stephanos. 1989. *Technical and Educational Assistance to Greece.* Vol. 5. Minneapolis: University of Minnesota.

Peterson, Paul, Barry G. Rabe, and Kenneth K. Wong. 1986. *When Federalism Works.* Washington, D.C.: Brookings Institute.

Phillips, David. 1993. Borrowing Educational Policy. In Finegold, McFarland, and Richardson 1993, 13–19.

Phillips, Herbert Moore. 1974. The Redeployment of Educational Aid. In Ward 1974, 255–307.

————. 1976a. *Educational Cooperation between Developed and Developing Countries.* New York: Praeger.

————. 1976b. *Higher Education: Cooperation with Developing Countries.* New York: Rockefeller Foundation.

Picciotto, Robert. 1994. Visibility and Disappointment: The New Role of Development Evaluation. In *Rethinking the Development Experience: Essays Provided by the Work of Albert O. Hirschman,* ed. Lloyd Rodwin and Donald A. Schön, 210–30. Washington, D.C., and: Cambridge: Brookings Institution and the Lincoln Institute of Land Policy.

Pinchus, John. 1967. *Trade, Aid, and Development: The Rich and Poor Nations.* New York: McGraw-Hill.

Pinto-Agüero, Carol. 1978. Relaciones entre cooperación técnica y desarrollo de los países. Algunas consideraciones. In Lavados 1978, 119–70.

Piven, Frances Fox. 1971. *Regulating the Poor: The Functions of Public Welfare.* New York: Pantheon Books.

Pizarro, Marino. 1988. La descentralización universitaria: Los colegios regionales. In Oyarzun 1988, 147–60.

Pontes, Helio. 1985. *La educación superior en Brasil.* Caracas: CRESALC-UNESCO.

Portes, Alejandro. 1975. Trends in International Research Cooperation: The Latin American Case. *American Sociologist* 10 (3): 131–40.

Powell, Walter W. 1987. *The Nonprofit Sector: A Research Handbook.* New Haven: Yale University Press.

Pressman, Jeffrey L., and Aaron B. Wildavsky. 1984. *Implementation: How Great Expectations in Washington Are Dashed in Oakland.* 3rd ed. Berkeley: University of California Press.

Psacharopoulos, George, and Maureen Woodhall. 1985. *Education for Development: An Analysis of Investment Choices.* New York: Oxford University Press.

Puryear, Jeffrey M. 1994. *Thinking Politics: Intellectuals and Democracy in Chile, 1973–1988.* Baltimore: Johns Hopkins University Press.

Quigley, Kevin F. F., and Nancy E. Popson. 1999. Rebuilding Civil Society in Eastern and Central Europe: The Role Played by Foundations. In Anheier and Toepler 1999, 235–54.

Rabkin, Y. M. 1992. Academies: Soviet Union. In Clark and Neave 1992, 2: 1049–55.

Raghaven, J. Veera, ed. 1983. *Education and the New International Order.* New Delhi: Concept.

Ramírez, Mariano. 1986. *Recursos humanos para la investigación: El caso de Costa Rica.* San José: Centro Internacional de Investigaciones para el Desarrollo.

Ramírez Necochea, Hernán. 1964. *El partido comunista y la universidad.* Santiago: Ediciones de la Revista Aurora.

Ranis, Gustav. 1996. *Successes and Failures of Development Experience since the 1980s.* Center Discussion Paper #762. New Haven: Yale University Economic Growth Center.

Rathberger, Eva M. 1985. Cultural Production in Kenyan Medical Education. *Comparative Education Review* 29 (3): 299–316.

Raynor, Gregory K. 2000. Engineering Social Reform: The Rise of the Ford Foundation and Cold War Liberalism, 1908–1959. Ph.D. diss., New York University.

Reagan, Michael D., and John G. Sanzone. 1981. *The New Federalism.* 2nd ed. New York: Oxford University Press.

Regel, Omporn. 1992. *The Academic Credit System in Higher Education: Effectiveness and Relevance in Developing Countries.* Washington, D.C.: World Bank.

Remmer, Karen. 1985. Redemocratization and the Impact of Authoritarian Rule in Latin America. *Comparative Politics* 17 (3): 253–75.

Renner, Richard R. 1973a. Introduction. In *Universities in Transition: The U.S. Presence in Latin American Higher Education,* ed. Richard R. Renner, 1–7. Gainesville: Center for Latin American Studies, University of Florida.

———, ed. 1973b. *Universities in Transition: The U.S. Presence in Latin American Higher Education.* Gainesville: University of Florida, Center for Latin American Studies.

Renz, Loren. 1997. International Grantmaking: Examining the Role of U.S. Foundations in the Post–Cold War Era. *Inside ITSR* 5 (3).

Revéiz, Edgar, et al. 1977. *Poder e información: El proceso decisorio en tres casos de política regional y urbana en Colombia.* Bogotá: Centro de Estudios Sobre Desarrollo Económico, Facultad de Economía, Universidad de los Andes.

Reyna, José Luis. 1991. *La educación en México: Tendencias y perspectivas dentro de los marcos institucionales e internacionales existentes.* New York: SSRC.

Ribeiro, Darcy. 1968. *La universidad latinoamericana.* Montevideo: Universidad de la República.

Rice, Andrew. 1996. Building a Constituency for Development Co-operation: Some Reflections on the U.S. Experience. In *Public Support for International Development,* ed. Colm Foy and Henry Helmich, 67–84. Paris and London: Development Centre of the Organisation for Economic Co-operation and Development.

Richardson, Malcolm. 1984. The Humanities and International Understanding. In McCarthy 1984b, 25–41.

Riddell, Roger. 1987. *Foreign Aid Reconsidered.* Baltimore: Johns Hopkins University Press.

Riggs, Fred W. 1964. *Administration in Developing Countries: The Theory of Prismatic Society.* Boston: Houghton Mifflin.

Río, Blanca del, and Ricardo Alegría. 1968. *Centros universitarios de provincia.* Santiago: Universidad de Chile.

Robertson, David Brian, and Jerold L. Waltman. 1993. The Politics of Policy Borrowing. In Finegold, McFarland, and Richardson 1993, 21–44.

Robinson, Ronald, ed. 1971. *Developing the Third World.* Cambridge: Cambridge University Press.

Rodríguez, Mariano. 1986. *Recursos humanos para la investigación: El caso de Costa Rica.* San José: Centro Internacional de Investigaciones para el Desarrollo.

Roett, Riordan. 1972. *The Politics of Foreign Aid in the Brazilian Northeast.* Nashville: Vanderbilt University Press.

Rondinelli, Dennis. 1989. Reforming U.S. Foreign Aid Policy: Constraints on Development Assistance. *Policy Studies Journal* 18 (Fall): 67–85.

Rose, Richard. 1991. What Is Lesson-Drawing? *Journal of Public Policy* 11 (1): 3–30.

Rudolph, Susanne H., and Lloyd I. Rudolph. 1972. *Education and Politics in India.* Cambridge: Harvard University Press.

Ruiz Massieu, Mario. 1987. *El cambio en la universidad.* Mexico City: UNAM.

Ruttan, Vernon W. 1996. *United States Development Assistance Policy. The Domestic Politics of Foreign Economic Aid.* Baltimore: Johns Hopkins University Press.

Safford, Frank. 1976. *The Ideal of the Practical: Colombia's Struggle to Form a Technical Elite.* Austin: University of Texas Press.

Saint, William. 1998. *Implications for Development Assistance: Section Contributed to Michael Gibbons, Higher Education Relevance in the Twenty-first Century.* Paris: UNESCO World Conference on Higher Education.

Salamon, Lester. 1987. Rise of Third-Party Government. *Bureaucrat* 16 (2): 27–31.

Salamon, Lester (assisted by Michael S. Lund), ed. 1989. *Beyond Privatization: The Tools of Government Action.* Washington, D.C.: Urban Institute Press.

Salmi, Jamil. 1998. *World Bank Experience in Support of Tertiary Education.* Paris: UNESCO World Conference on Higher Education.

Samoff, Joel. 1993. The Reconstruction of Schooling in Africa. *Comparative Education Review* 37 (2): 181–222.

Sánchez, Luis Alberto. 1962. The University in Latin America: Part IV. *Américas,* February: 14–17.

———. 1973. Aspectos de las universidades norteamericanas válidos en las latinoamericanas. In Renner 1973a, 114–27.

Sandberg, Donald F. 1965. The Ford Foundation and Latin American Higher Education. In Association for Latin American Studies 1965, 60–65.

Sandilands, Roger J. 1990. *The Life and Political Economy of Lauchtin Currie.* Durham, N.C.: Duke University Press.

Sanyal, Bikas C., ed. 1982. *Higher Education and the New International Order.* Paris: UNESCO.

Scherz-García, Luis. 1967. Some Dysfunctional Aspects of International Assistance and the Role of the University in Social Change in Latin America. *International Social Science Journal* 19 (3): 387–403.

Schmitter, Philippe. 1974. Still the Century of Corporatism? In *The New Corporation,* ed. Frederik Pike and Thomas Stritch, 85–135. Notre Dame, Ind.: University of Notre Dame Press.

Schoultz, Lars. 1998. *Beneath the United States: A History of U.S. Policy toward Latin America.* Cambridge: Harvard University Press.

Schraeder, Peter J., Steven W. Hook, and Bruce Taylor. 1998. Clarifying the Foreign Aid Puzzle. *World Politics* 50 (January): 294–323.

Schuh, Edward. 1970. *The Agricultural Development of Brazil.* New York: Praeger.

Schwartzman, Simon. 1984. The Focus on Scientific Activity. In *Perspectives on Higher Education,* ed. Burton Clark, 199–232. Berkeley: University of California Press.

———. 1985. The Quest for University Research: Policies and Research Organizations in Latin America. In *The University Research System,* ed. Bjorn Wittrock and Aant Elzinga, 101–16. Stockholm: Almqvist and Wiksell International.

———. 1988. Brazil: Opportunity and Crisis in Higher Education. *Higher Education* 17 (1): 99–119.

———. 1991. *A Space for Science.* University Park: Pennsylvania State University Press.

———. 1992a. Brazil. In Clark and Neave 1992, 1:82–92.

———. 1992b. *The Future of Higher Education in Brazil.* Washington, D.C.: Woodrow Wilson International Center for Scholars.

———. 1992c. Non-Western Societies and Higher Education. In Clark and Neave 1992, 2:969–75.

References | 387

—. 1996. *América Latina: Universidades en transición.* Vol. 6, *Colección INTERAMER.* Washington: Organización de los Estados Americanos.

Segal, Aaron. 1985. Higher Education in Latin America and the Caribbean: An Overview. *Interciencia* 10 (4): 196–98.

—. 1986. Science, Technology, and Development. In *Latin America and Caribbean Contemporary Record, 1984–85,* ed. Jack Hopkins. New York: Holmes and Meier.

Selim, Hassan M. 1983. *Development Assistance Policies and the Performance of Aid Agencies.* London: Macmillan.

Selvaratnam, Viswanathan. 1986. Dependency, Change, and Continuity in a Western University Model: The Malaysian Case. *Southeastern Asian Journal of Social Science* 14 (2): 29–51.

—. 1988. Higher Education Co-operation and Western Dominance of Knowledge Creation and Flows in Third World Countries. *Higher Education* 17: 41–68.

Serrano, Sol. 1993. *Universidad y nación: Chile en el siglo XIX.* Santiago: Editora Universitaria.

Seymour, Matthew. 1985. *AID and Higher Education in Latin America for the Eighties.* Washington, D.C.: United States Agency for International Development. Latin America and Caribbean Unit.

—. 1986. *University Linkages Project Proposed.* Washington, D.C.: Agency for International Development, Latin America and Caribbean Unit.

Sheehan, John. 1987. *Patterns of Development in Latin America.* Princeton: Princeton University Press.

Sikkink, Kathryn. 1991. *Ideas and Institutions: Developmentalism in Brazil and Argentina.* Ithaca: Cornell University Press.

Silié, Rubén. 1988. Educación superior dominicana: Situación y perspectiva. Manuscript, Santo Domingo.

Silva, Michelena Héctor, and Heintz Sonntag. 1981. *Universidad, dependencia y revolución.* Mexico City: Siglo XXI.

Silvert, Kalman. 1970. An Essay on Interdisciplinary and International Collaboration in Social Science Research in Latin America. In *Latin America in Transition,* ed. Stanley R. Ross, 105–18. Albany: State University of New York Press.

—. 1976. *The Foundations, the Social Sciences, and Latin America.* Villa de Leyva, Colombia: Ford Foundation (Latin America and Caribbean office).

Smelser, Neil J. 1974. Growth, Structural Change, and Conflict in California Public Higher Education, 1950–1970. In *Public Higher Education in California,* ed. Neil J. Smelser and Gabriel Almond, 9–141. Berkeley: University of California Press.

Smith, Brian H. 1990. *More than Altruism: The Politics of Private Foreign Aid.* Princeton: Princeton University Press.

Solórzano, Armando. n.d. A Conceptual Framework to Analyze Philanthropic Foundations in Developing Societies. Mimeo. Salt Lake City.

Sommer, John G. 1977. *Beyond Charity: U.S. Voluntary Aid for a Changing Third World.* Washington, D.C.: Overseas Development Council.

Spaulding, Seth. 1997. Needed Research on the Impact of International Assistance Organisations on the Development of Education. In *Informed Dialogue,* ed. Fernando Reimers and Noel McGinn, 207–13. Westport, Conn.: Praeger.

Spitzberg, Irving, ed. 1980. *Universities and the International Distribution of Knowledge.* New York: Praeger.

Steger, Hanns-Albert. 1979. The European Background. In Maier and Weatherhead 1979, 87–122.

Steiner-Khamsi, Gita. 2000. Transferring Education, Displacing Reforms. In *Discourse Formation in Comparative Education,* ed. Jürgen Schriewer, 155–88. Frankfurt: Peter Lang.

Stepan, Nancy. 1976. *Beginnings of Brazilian Science: Osvaldo Cruz, Medical Research, and Policy, 1890–1920.* New York: Science History Publications.

Stifel, Laurence Davis, Ralph Kirby Davidson, and James Samuel Coleman. 1982. Agencies of Diffusion: A Case Study of the Rockefeller Foundation. In *Social Sciences and Public Policy in the Developing World,* ed. Laurence Davis Stifel, Ralph Kirby Davidson, and James Samuel Coleman, 57–82. Lexington, Mass: Lexington Books.

Storrs, K. Larry. 1987. *Kissinger Commission Implementation.* Washington, D.C.: Congressional Research Service, Library of Congress.

Sutton, Francis. 1972. Interviews with Overseas Staff in Latin America. Memo to the Self-Study Committee of the Ford Foundation.

———. 1984. Foundations and Cultural Development of the Third World. In McCarthy 1984b, 137–55.

———. 1986. *Foundations and Higher Education at Home and Abroad: A Tale of Heroic Efforts Abandoned.* New York: Center for the Study of Philanthropy, City University of New York.

Taquini, Alberto (hijo). 1972. *Nuevas universidades para un nuevo país.* Buenos Aires: Angel Estrada y Cía.

Task Force on Higher Education and Society. 2000. *Higher Education in Developing Countries: Peril and Promise.* Washington, D.C.: World Bank.

Tedesco, Juan Carlos, and Hans Blumenthal. 1986. Desafíos y problemas de la educación superior en América Latina. In *La juventud universitaria en América Latina,* ed. Juan Carlos Tedesco and Hans Blumenthal, 9–30. Caracas: CRESALC: Instituto Latinoamericano de Investigaciones Sociales.

Tendler, Judith. 1975. *Inside Foreign Aid.* Baltimore: Johns Hopkins University Press.

Theberge, James D., and Roger W. Fontaine. 1977. *Latin America: Struggle for Progress.* Lexington, Mass.: Lexington Books.

Thompson, Kenneth W. 1972. *Foreign Assistance: A View from the Private Sector.* Notre Dame, Ind.: University of Notre Dame Press.

Thompson, Kenneth W., et al. 1974. Higher Education and National Development: One Model for Technical Assistance. In Ward 1974, 195–203.

Thompson, Kenneth W., and Barbara R. Fogel, eds. 1977. *Higher Education and Social Change. Promising Experiments in Developing Countries. Case Studies.* 2 vols. Vol. 2. New York: Praeger.

Thorp, Willard Long. 1971. *The Reality of Foreign Aid.* New York: Praeger (published for the Council on Foreign Relations).

Tilak, Jandhyala. 1988. Foreign Aid for Education. *International Review of Education* 34: 313–35.

Tiller, Frank. 1973. The United States Government and Latin American Universities. In Renner 1973b, 79–95.

Tisch, Sarah, and Michael B. Wallace. 1994. *Dilemmas of Development Assistance.* Boulder: Westview.

Trías, Vivian. 1978. Las transnacionales y la influencia de la "escuela de Chicago" en América Latina. *Nueva Sociedad* 38 (1): 5–19.

Trow, Martin. 2001. From Mass Higher Education to Universal Access: The American Advantage. In *In Defense of American Higher Education*, ed. Philip G. Altbach, Patricia J. Gumport, and D. Bruce Johnstone, 110–43. Baltimore: Johns Hopkins University Press.

Tunnerman, Carlos. 1965. *Problems and Strategies of International Planning: Lessons from Latin America.* Ed. Raymond F. Lyons, International Institute for Educational Planning series. Paris: UNESCO.

Tussie, Diana. 1995. *The Inter-American Development Bank.* Boulder: Lynne Rienner.

UNAM, ed. 1984. *Diagnóstico del personal académico de la UNAM.* Mexico City: UNAM, Dirección General de Asuntos del Personal Académico.

UNDP. 1991. *Human Development Report.* New York: Oxford University Press.

UNESCO. 1972. *Statistical Yearbook.* Paris: UNESCO.

———. 1975. *Statistical Yearbook.* Paris: UNESCO.

———. 1981. *Statistical Yearbook.* Paris: UNESCO.

———. 1988. *Statistical Yearbook.* Paris: UNESCO.

———. 1990. *Statistical Yearbook.* Paris: UNESCO.

———. 1991. *Statistical Yearbook.* Paris: UNESCO.

———. 1992. *Statistical Yearbook.* Paris: UNESCO.

———. 1995. *Policy Paper for Change and Development in Higher Education.* Paris: United Nations Educational, Scientific, and Cultural Organization.

Universidad de Chile. www.uchile.cl [Web site] 2002 [Accessed 06/26/2002].

Universidad de Costa Rica. 1987. *Ciudad Universitaria 1987: Documentos para ser conocidos por las asambleas.* San José: UCR.

University of Chile/University of California. 1979. *Convenio: Comprehensive Report, 1965–1978.* New York: Ford Foundation.

Urrutia, Miguel. 1994. Institutional Development of Economics. In *Laying the Foundation: The Institutions of Knowledge in Developing Countries*, ed. Benjamín Alvarez and Hernando Gómez. Ottawa: IDRC.

Urzúa, Raúl. 1973. Fundaciones y universidad: El punto de vista. In Renner 1973b, 35–55.

Useem, Michael. 1987. Corporate Philanthropy. In Powell 1987, 340–59.

Valdés, Juan Gabriel. 1995. *Pinochet's Economists: The Chicago School in Chile.* New York: Cambridge University Press.

Valenzuela, Arturo, and Samuel J. Valenzuela. 1981. Modernization and Dependency: Alternative Perspectives in the Study of Latin America Underdevelopment. In *From Dependency to Development: Strategies to Overcome Underdevelopment and Inequality,* ed. Heraldo Muñoz, 15–41. Boulder, Colo.: Westview Press.

Valverde, Gilbert A. 1999. Democracy, Human Rights, and Development Assistance for Education: The USAID and World Bank in Latin America and the Caribbean. *Economic Development and Cultural Change* 47 (2): 401–19.

Van de Graaff, John. 1982. Can Department Structures Replace a Chair System? *Compare* 12 (1): 29–40.

Van Horn, Carl E. 1979. *Policy Implementation in the Federal System: National Goals and Local Implementors.* Lexington, Mass.: Lexington Books.

Van Maanen, John, ed. 1983. *Qualitative Methodology.* London: Sage.

Van Til, Jon, et al., eds. 1990. *Critical Issues in American Philanthropy.* San Francisco: Jossey-Bass.

Van Vught, Frans. 1993. *Patterns of Governance in Higher Education: Concepts and Trends.* New Papers on Higher Education: Studies and Research 9. Paris: UNESCO.

Verspoor, Adriaan. 1991. *Lending for Learning: Twenty Years of World Bank Support for Basic Education.* Washington, D.C.: World Bank. Population and Human Resources Department.

———. 1993. Improvement and Innovation in Higher Education. In *Improving Higher Education in Developing Countries,* ed. Angela Ransom, Siew-Mun Khoo, and Viswanathan Selvaratnam, 57–64. Washington, D.C.: World Bank.

Vessuri, Hebe. 1984. El papel cambiante de la investigación científica académica en un país periférico. In *La ciencia periférica: Ciencia y sociedad en Venezuela,* ed. Elena B. Díaz, Yolanda Texera, and Hebe M. C. Vessuri, 37–72. Caracas: Monte Avila Editores.

———. 1986. The Universities, Scientific Research, and the National Interest in Latin America. *Minerva* 14 (1): 1–38.

Vicerectoría de Docencia. 1985. *Universidad de Costa Rica.* San José: UCR.

———. 1987. *Universidad de Costa Rica.* San José: UCR.

Waggoner, Barbara A. 1965. The Latin American University in Transition. In Association for Latin American Studies 1965, 5–22.

Waggoner, George. 1967. Latin American Universities. *Journal of Higher Education* 38 (1): 45–48.

———. 1972. La autonomía universitaria y la planificación nacional. In *Autonomia, planificación, coordinación innovaciones: Perspectivas latinoamericanas,* ed. Ana Herzfeld, Barbara Ashton Waggoner, and George Waggoner, 183–99. Lawrence: University of Kansas Press.

———. 1973. Analysis and Conclusions by a U.S. Educator. In Renner 1973b, 143–47.

Ward, F. Champion, ed. 1974. *Education and Development Reconsidered: The Bellagio. Conference Papers.* New York: Praeger.

Weiler, Hans N, ed. 1980. *Educational Planning and Social Change.* Paris: UNESCO International Institute for Educational Planning.

Weiler, Hans N. 1983. *Aid for Education: The Political Economy of International Cooperation in Educational Development.* Mimeo. Stanford, Calif.

Weinberg, Vicki. 1996. Intricate Details of Intimate Matters: Public Health, Women, National and International Politics in Chile, 1910–1989. Ph.D. diss., University of Arizona.

Weiner, Myron, and Samuel P. Huntington, eds. 1987. *Understanding Political Development.* Boston: Little, Brown.

Weisbrod, Burton. 1988. *The Nonprofit Economy.* Cambridge: Harvard University Press.

Weissberg, Miriam. 1980. Los programas de cooperación científica y tecnológica internacional en México. *Ciencia y Desarrollo* 33: 76–94.

Weissman, Steve, ed. 1975. *The Trojan Horse: A Radical Look at Foreign Aid.* Palo Alto, Calif.: Ramparto Press.

Westney, D. Eleanor. 1987. *Imitation and Innovation: The Transfer of Western Organizational Patterns to Meiji Japan.* Cambridge: Harvard University Press.

White, John. 1970. *Regional Development Banks: A Study of Institutional Style.* London: Overseas Development Institute.

———. 1974. *The Politics of Foreign Aid.* London: Bodley.

Wiarda, Howard J. 1981. *Corporatism and National Development in Latin America.* Boulder, Colo.: Westview Press.

Wickham, R. S. 1973. University Reform in Latin America: A Case Study of the University of Valle (Cali, Colombia). Ph.D. diss., University of California at Berkeley.

Wilkie, James Wallace, ed. 1977. *Statistical Abstract of Latin America.* Los Angeles: University of California Latin American Center Publications.

Williams, Walter. 1980. *The Implementation Perspective.* Berkeley: University of California Press.

———. 1982. *Studying Implementation: Methodological and Administrative Issues.* Chatham House Series on Change in American Politics. Chatham, N.J.: Chatham House.

Winkler, Donald R. 1990. *Higher Education in Latin America: Issues of Efficiency and Equity.* World Bank Discussion Papers, 77. Washington, D.C.: World Bank.

Wood, R. W. 1968. *U.S. Universities: Their Role in AID-Financed Technical Assistance Overseas.* Washington, D.C.: Educational and World Affairs.

Woods, Lawrence. 1993. *Asia-Pacific Diplomacy: Nongovernmental Organizations and International Relations.* Vancouver: University of British Colombia Press.

World Bank. 1980. *Education Sector Policy Paper.* Washington, D.C.: World Bank.

———. 1990. *World Development Report.* New York: Oxford University Press.

———. 1994. *Higher Education: The Lessons of Experience.* Washington, D.C.: World Bank.

———. 1995. *Priorities and Strategies for Education: A World Bank Review—Development in Practice.* Washington, D.C.: World Bank.

———. 1998. *Assessing Aid: What Works, What Doesn't, and Why.* Washington, D.C.: World Bank.

———. 1999. *Education Sector Strategy.* Washington, D.C.: Human Development Network.

———. 2002. *Constructing Knowledge Societies: New Challenges for Tertiary Education.* Washington, D.C.: Education Group, Human Development Network.

Wright, Deil, and Harvey L. White, eds. 1984. *Federalism and Intergovernmental Relations.* Washington, D.C.: American Society for Public Administration.

Ylvisaker, Paul. 1987. Foundations and Nonprofit Organizations. In Powell 1987, 360–79.

Index

academic work, 174, 191–192, 216–219; fields of study, 204–215; graduate education, 198–204; professionalism and, 174–191; research, 192–197

accountability, 77, 241

ACLS (American Council of Learned Societies), 43

Adams, Richard, 270

admissions process, 106, 154

Africa, 184, 303n31; aid amounts to, 46, 47; Carnegie Foundation aid to, 42; Ford Foundation assistance to, 36; universities, 15, 357n16

agriculture, 62, 195, 297; AID grants for, 50, 270, 271–272; brain drain in, 214; enrollment in, 298; Ford grants for, 263; partnerships and, 205; research centers and, 212; Rockefeller grants for, 42, 206

agronomy, 91, 148, 168, 208, 212

Aguascalientes, University of (Mexico), 166, 331n56

AID (Agency for International Development), 1, 15, 37–39, 102, 227; academic centralization and, 154–155, 159, 167–168; amounts of aid, 48, 283–284, 294, 313n8; archives of, 18; Brazil project, 94; cluster giving and, 121, 122, 123; expenditure underestimation, 267–273; facilities centralization and, 144; faculty development and, 179, 180; fields of study and, 206, 207, 209, 212, 214, 297; graduate education and, 198–200; linkage programs, 44, 74; management and, 135, 136; national targeting patterns and, 63–68; national universities and, 82, 85–86, 87; overreach and, 53, 54; partnerships and, 58, 61, 62; performance evaluations and, 229, 234; prior partnerships, 93; private universities and, 92, 99–100, 105; project evaluations, 306n54; public alternative universities and, 112; retreat from assistance and, 50, 51; sources for data on, 264–267; student

payments and, 137; two-year colleges and, 119–120; unpopularity of foreign assistance and, 23

AID Project History (PAICHIST), 264

Aldana, Eduardo, 96

Alliance for Progress, 2, 10, 38, 300n6; democracy and, 301n13, 304n33; overreach and, 52, 53

altruism, 4, 5, 21, 301n14

Americanization, 53, 88; academic work and, 177; California system as model, 117; campuses as, 148; cluster giving and, 122, 124; denunciation of, 106; donor goals and, 134; general studies and, 153, 157; support for, 99

Américas, University of the (Mexico), 43, 91

Anderson, Charles, 30

Andes, University of the (Colombia), 55, 62, 95–98, 111, 333n66; academic centralization at, 165, 169; access for underrepresented, 115; facilities, 145; Faculty of Arts and Sciences, 97; fields of study at, 210, 211; general studies and, 156; management and, 136

Antioquia, University of (Colombia), 59, 95, 112, 333n67; administrative centralization, 140; Arts and Sciences unit, 168; fund-raising, 139; graduate education at, 203; library, 146

architecture, 204, 208, 297

area studies, 18

Argentina, 9, 18, 51, 267; academic centralization in, 157, 165–166; AID and, 270, 283, 294; alternative public universities, 61; campuses in, 149; cluster assistance to, 121; enrollment in higher education, 280–281; fields of study in, 204; Ford Foundation and, 100, 261, 287, 293, 323n90; full-time professors in, 181; graduate education in, 198; growth in, 125; IDB and, 39–40, 274, 275, 285, 295; institutional development, 64, 67; LASPAU scholarships, 287; loan amounts to, 58; military rule

DANIEL C. LEVY is Distinguished Professor of the State University of New York. At the University at Albany, SUNY, he holds his main appointment in Educational Administration and Policy Studies, a joint appointment in Latin American Studies, and affiliated appointments with Political Science and the Public Policy Program. Levy is the founder and director of PROPHE, the Program for Research on Private Higher Education, a global scholarly network funded by the Ford Foundation. He is author of seven books and more than 100 articles on higher education policy worldwide, related nonprofit sectors, and Latin American politics. His *Building the Third Sector* won the 1997 ARNOVA prize for best book.